THE COMING OF THE KINGDOM

THE COMING
OF THE KINGDOM

By

HERMAN RIDDERBOS

Translated by H. de Jongste
Edited by Raymond O. Zorn

THE PRESBYTERIAN AND REFORMED PUBLISHING COMPANY

Library of Congress Catalog Card Number 62-15429

Printed in the United States of America

PUBLISHER'S NOTE

The Presbyterian and Reformed Publishing Company is highly privileged to make available in English this monumental contribution to the study of the kingdom of God by the illustrious professor of New Testament in the Theological Seminary of Kampen, the Netherlands.

The translation was prepared by H. de Jongste, under the direction of Dr. David H. Freeman. The Rev. Raymond O. Zorn is the English editor. George C. Fuller prepared the indices.

CONTENTS

FOREWORD

It is with a deep sense of privilege that this monumental work by Dr. Herman Ridderbos, Professor of New Testament since 1942 in The Theological Seminary, Kampen, The Netherlands, is presented to the English-reading world. Dr. Ridderbos, a scholar of international reputation, has written many books in his native Dutch language, but it has only been in recent years that a number are now beginning to make their appearance in English translation for the enrichment of the English-reading public. This book, also first published in the Dutch language approximately a decade ago, has remained a solid contribution of permanent significance to the fascinating subject of the kingdom of God. Its appearance now for the first time in English is therefore to be welcomed.

At a time when much that is taught and written about the kingdom of God is of a speculative nature based upon concessions that have been made to the naturalism of modern science or the "demythologizing" approach of higher criticism and that have been conditioned by shifting and often faulty presuppositions, it is refreshing to find a theologian of Dr. Ridderbos' stature who accepts the Scripture's claim of full integrity and permits the Bible's message to speak for itself. And, as Dr. Ridderbos ably proves, the message of Scripture is capable of defense and worthy of a hearing. Rather than coming to the Scriptures with inadequate speculative, or even philosophical, presuppositions; Dr. Ridderbos governs his exegesis by a thoroughly biblical-theological approach, i.e., the Scriptures must be understood as they furnish their own interpretation in the light of the grammatico-historical circumstances of their impartation to man by the sovereign God of the universe who is at the same time the covenanting Redeemer of his people.

The basis for an understanding of the coming of the kingdom of God, therefore, centers in Jesus Christ. It is he, as

God's promised Messiah, who gives answer to the questions and problems about the nature of the kingdom, the manner of its coming, the way in which it is now present in history, and its future, final realization beyond history. It is to him, hence, that we must turn if we would learn of the full significance and meaning of God's dominion as defined by this biblical concept, "the kingdom of God." Consequently, Dr. Ridderbos concentrates attention upon the coming of the kingdom as proclaimed by Jesus himself, according to the witness of the three synoptic gospels. From Christ's word and works, we learn of the full scope and significance of the kingdom. In short, we find that the kingdom has come in Christ's accomplished redemption, the reality and saving power of which, as announced in the gospel, being experienced through faith by union with Christ. But the full and final realization of the kingdom yet awaits the triumphal return of Christ in power and glory upon the clouds of heaven.

Dr. Ridderbos' presentation of the kingdom is thorough and comprehensive, and takes into account a broad range of influential, though varying views, including those of critical scholarship. Moreover, his exegesis is masterly and satisfying as he repeatedly marshals powerful and irrefutable arguments to disprove erroneous viewpoints while establishing the validity of his conclusions.

All readers alike will profit from the study of this book's contents, and are sure to gain a better understanding of the kingdom's nature, its fulfilled aspects and presence in the world as the result of Christ's first advent, along with its yet future final consummation to be accomplished at his second coming.

RAYMOND O. ZORN
Fawn Grove, Pa.

INTRODUCTION

The central theme of Jesus' message, as it has come down to us in the synoptic gospels, is the coming of the kingdom of God or, as it is usually expressed in Matthew, of the kingdom of heaven. This is not only borne out by the frequent occurrence of that formula, in the first three gospels, which marks them off from John's tradition, as regards their form and manner of expression; it also appears from the recapitulatory characterization of Jesus' preaching that they give in more than one passage.

Jesus entered upon his ministry with the preaching of the gospel of God, and saying: "The time is fulfilled and the kingdom of God is at hand: repent ye and believe the gospel." Thus Mark 1:14,15 introduces the description of Jesus' coming and his activity in Galilee. Matthew and Luke have the same message in different words: Matt. 4:17,23; 9:35; Luke 9:11. In Luke 4:43 we are told in Jesus' own words that the purpose of his mission was the preaching of the kingdom of God. The word of God he preached (Luke 8:11) is therefore also called, "the word of the kingdom" (Matt. 13:19); and the gospel by which the entire New Testament *kerygma* is summarized (Luke 4:43; 8:1; 16:16) has the kingdom of God and its coming for its content. It may be rightly said that the whole of the preaching of Jesus Christ and his apostles is concerned with the kingdom of God,[1] and that in Jesus Christ's proclamation of the kingdom we are face to face with the specific form of expression of the whole of his revelation of God.[2] These preliminary remarks may show that for insight into the meaning and the character of the New Testament revelation of God, it is hardly possible to mention any other theme equal in importance to that of the kingdom of heaven. And we must also add that hardly any subject in the whole field of New Testament research has provoked greater diversity of opinion

or given rise to fiercer controversy. The latter is especially true
of the last fifty years. The study of the clash of opinions entails the great danger of getting involved in all kinds of problems which later on appear to have been introduced into the
gospel from the modern world of thought and which are not
conducive to a correct understanding of the purport of Jesus'
preaching. This controversy is on the other hand also a rich
source of instruction to the attentive observer. It is above all
the confirmation that the power of divine truth which finds
its sublime and most variegated expression in the gospel of
the kingdom of heaven again and again triumphs over all
human limitations and commitments. As an introduction to
the subject proper of our study we first wish to get acquainted
with the chief points of view that have been recently adopted
by various interpreters of the gospel, with respect to the general
character of the kingdom proclaimed by Jesus.

For more than fifty years the study of the general purport
of the kingdom of heaven has been dominated by the problems
posited by the so-called eschatological school.[3] Johannes Weiss
may be mentioned as the "father" of this movement. In 1892
he published *Die Predigt Jesu vom Reiche Gottes,* which has
retained its significance to the present day. In this work
Weiss attacked the use made of the concept "kingdom of God"
by the influential theologian Albrecht Ritschl. Ritschl thought
he could appeal to the preaching of Jesus in support of his
own conception. He conceived of the kingdom of God as the
ethical-religious community founded by Jesus and composed
of all who wish to practice the evangelical law of love. It is
this community which must be promoted by the church. The
character of this kingdom of God is entirely immanent, because it belongs to this world, and is strongly determined by
the idea of development and human activity. The basic law
of this kingdom is found in Jesus' commandments, and lends
a predominantly ethical character to the entire process of its
coming and its revelation.[4]

According to Weiss, however, Ritschl's conception of the

kingdom of God can in no way make an appeal to the gospel. Its origins are rather to be sought in Kant's view of the kingdom of virtue, and in the theology of the Enlightenment. As a representative of the history of religions school, Weiss argued that Jesus' preaching of the kingdom of God can only be understood in the light of and against the background of the world of thought of his time, especially of the late Jewish apocalyptic writings. On this view, every conception of the kingdom of God as an immanent community in course of development or as an ethical ideal is consequently to be rejected; for it becomes clear that the kingdom of God is a purely future and eschatological event, presupposing the end of this world; and, therefore, cannot possibly reveal itself already in this world. For the kingdom of God, which Jesus proclaimed to be near at hand, is nothing but the commencement of the new world, expected in the apocalyptical literature, and which will reveal itself after the catastrophic upheaval of the present era.

It is true that there are passages in the gospel representing this kingdom as having come, and consequently, as being present. According to Weiss, our first concern should be to investigate their authenticity and the extent they are derived from a later spiritualizing conception of the kingdom. To such a conception Weiss also wants to ascribe the preaching of the kingdom found in the gospel according to John, in which the eschatological viewpoint is far less dominant. Still, there remain passages in the synoptic gospels in which Jesus speaks of the kingdom as being present (the so-called *Gegenwartstellen*, "present" references, such as Matthew 12:28, and others). But according to Weiss, Jesus is here in a kind of spiritual ecstasy, in which he sees the first beginnings of the great break-through, and speaks of the coming of the kingdom in a proleptic sense. However, Jesus had not always lived in the spell of this high tension. Rather, at first, Jesus expected the coming of the kingdom before his death. Only later, under the impact of disappointing experiences, did he postpone the time of its coming. There is, however, no question of a gradual revelation and development of this coming. The kingdom will come suddenly, owing to God's irresistible intervention, and it will bring the present dispensation to a close.

The echo to this eschatological keynote is heard by Weiss especially in Jesus' commandments. They do not denote the standard of the kingdom of God in its development in this world, but are intended as conditions for the entry into the future kingdom. They not only function as conditions, but are also thoroughly eschatological in character. The radicalism of Jesus' ethics is the radicalism of those who know that the end is near, and who have therefore on principle taken leave of all earthly possessions and interests. Now that the end of the world may come at any moment, there is no point in quarrelling about right or wrong. Such was the sense of crisis that gave birth to Jesus' commandments. They cannot be understood as rules of conduct given for all time, and acceptable at any period, but as a kind of "exceptional legislation." Just as in times of war the normal order of things is temporarily suspended and everything is made subservient to the great cause, so in the same way Jesus' radical commandments are to be understood only from the eschatological expectation of the coming kingdom of God.[5]

The man who has advocated this new interpretation of the gospel with the greatest energy, and who may therefore be called the most typical propagandist of the eschatological conception, is Albert Schweitzer. Weiss's writings were especially devoted to Jesus' preaching, but Schweitzer in addition tries to prove that Weiss's insight is also the long-sought-for key for the understanding of Jesus' life. Schweitzer speaks of "consistent eschatology." If Jesus lived in the expectation that the end was near at hand, the history of his life must have been dominated by such an expectation. Thus Schweitzer arrives at an entirely new and partly fantastic description of the life of Jesus. In his book *Das Messianitäts–und Leidensgeheimnis*,[6] and especially in his large volume *Von Reimarus zu Wrede*[7] (published later under the title *Die Geschichte der*

Leben-Jesu-Forschung[8]), Schweitzer gives a brilliant survey of the efforts made by theology since the Enlightenment to arrive at a consistent view of the life of Jesus.

Schweitzer clearly shows how much the whole history of exegesis has been determined, not by historical objectivity, but rather by subjective theological prejudice. He especially criticizes the liberal picture of Jesus, so long accepted by a large number of theologians of the modern school. Schweitzer's teacher, H. J. Holtzmann, the great representative of the liberal school, was one of the authors of this liberal portrait. Schweitzer sympathizes most with such figures in the history of New Testament research as Reimarus, Strauss, and Bruno Bauer who, in his opinion, have described Jesus' life in a way that is free from all dogmatic premises. He shows that it was especially these radicals who realized that Jesus lived in the eschatological tension which, according to Schweitzer, Weiss's book on Jesus' preaching of the kingdom had indicated. Therefore, in the tradition of these predecessors, Schweitzer tries to describe Jesus' life as a life which was wholly dominated by the eschatological dogma.[9]

Schweitzer's consistently eschatological reconstruction of the life of Jesus has not found much support. Nevertheless, this view has remained very characteristic of the general theological position of the eschatological tendency. On the one hand, it was intended as a protest against the humanizing and ethicizing of the gospel, and against the consequent distortion of the picture of Jesus found in the gospels. On the other hand, this movement fought for what it considered a purely *historical* rectification. By exclusively viewing the coming of the kingdom mentioned in the gospel as the beginning of the great final catastrophe, these writers could only assert that Jesus' preaching of the nearness of the kingdom was the effect of a delusion. They were thus compelled to base the ethical imitation of Jesus—which especially fascinated Schweitzer who qualified it as "the heroic surrender of life"— on something different from this eschatological expectation.

This is why both Weiss and Schweitzer have recourse to the modern idealistic outlook for their own theology and view of the world.[10] Thus their work did not result in a new theology founded on the gospel. It only frustrated the efforts previously made to establish a bond between the gospel and the current theological conception.

This failure is one of the reasons why the first great representatives of the eschatological interpretation at first had so little influence. They were unable to give theological expression to the eschatological character of Jesus' preaching which they had re-discovered. The result of their activities was only that, for the time being, the eschatological character of the kingdom of God, preached by Jesus, was more and more being recognized. But this character was considered to be merely the mythical or contemporary expression of the spiritual change which takes place in man and in the world when people begin to listen to Jesus' commandments and to regulate their lives by them.

Characteristic for this (eschatological) form (spiritual-moral) content schema was, for example, that which another well-known representative of the history of religions school, W. Bousset, adduced to refute Johannes Weiss's book. Bousset admitted that Jesus' preaching was entirely based on the eschatological conception. But in his opinion a sharp distinction should be made between the "phenomenological" and the "intelligible" character of Jesus' personality and message. The apocalyptic element in Jesus' preaching, his expectation of the kingdom of God, his words about the "Son of Man" were supposed to be only the forms of a metaphysical conviction, according to which an eternal, invisible world of a higher order surrounded our little world. "This dualism was the husk of the tremendous moral seriousness and the religious depth of the gospel. But the kernel has everywhere burst the husk."[11] The result is that according to Bousset, Jesus did not live in a mood ruled by the sense of a crisis, nor did he give exceptional commandments to his disciples who would then no longer have had any future. But, contrary to what Weiss had said, Jesus preached a positive kind of ethics in which this world was accepted, and through his faith in God the Father he really freed himself from the eschatological frame of mind. As an historian of religion, Bousset tried in this way to do justice to the historical view of Jesus' preaching and to leave room for the ideal Jesus as conceived by the liberal Ritschlian theology.

There were other influential representatives of the older school, such as Harnack and Wellhausen, who made use of the form-content schema in order to be able to appeal to the gospel for their liberal theology, and to put aside the hypothesis of the eschatological tension in Jesus' preaching. For this eschatological tension did not at all fit in with their ethical evolutionistic conception of the kingdom of God. Thus in his *Das Wesen des Christentums* Harnack relegated the eschatological aspect of Jesus' preaching entirely to the background. In fact, he admitted that the Kingdom of Heaven preached by Jesus must be understood as a future and external dominion, as a kingdom that will manifest itself on the new earth. But, in Harnack's opinion, this structure of Jesus' preaching must be explained by referring to the conditions of the time in which Jesus lived. Jesus' interest did not lie in these elements of his message. As Jesus' own spiritual possession we must consider the conception of the internal kingdom of God which is present in the souls of men. We must, therefore, lift this "essential" element from its contemporary framework, and remember that the kingdom of God is not concerned with "thrones and principalities, nor with devils and angels, but with God and the soul, with the soul and its God."[12] In this way Harnack reconstructed the eschatological traits in Jesus' preaching, and continued to appeal to the gospel for his rational-moral theology. It is true, he did not lay as much stress on the social element as did Ritschl in his conception of the kingdom of God, but he found the dominant element in Jesus' preaching in the value of the individual human soul.

In this and in similar ways, liberal theology, before the First World War, tried to maintain as the proper and lasting element that which is considered to be the spiritual purport of Jesus' preaching, notwithstanding its historical recognition of the "eschatology of the gospel." And on the other hand, it put aside as much as possible the cosmic and eschatological *endgeschichtliche* traits of the gospel as unessential.[13] The liberal theology took up a very strong position especially with respect to the eschatological interpretation of Jesus' commandments. In consequence of the heavy criticism thus brought to bear on the eschatological explanation of the kingdom of God, even Weiss was obliged to state in the second edition of his work that not all of Jesus' preaching was ruled by his eschatological expectation, and that not all his commandments could be interpreted as "crisis commandments." He admitted, for example, that the double commandment of love does not only hold for the exceptional times before the coming of the kingdom, but that it is a commandment for all time and was intended as such. In this manner Weiss detached large parts of Jesus' religious and ethical preaching from the conception of the kingdom of God, giving rise to a dualism in the content of the gospel which is difficult to explain. On the one hand, it contains the preaching of the kingdom, i.e., of the crisis, and on the other, there is supposed to be found in it a perfectly un-eschatological faith, which has nothing to do with the preaching of the kingdom. This dualistic view of the gospel[14] has been emphatically rejected by the advocates of the consistent eschatological interpretation,[15] but has not failed to find adherents, as appears from the well-known writings of H. Windisch, for example, on the Sermon on the Mount. Windisch distinguishes between two main streams in the synoptic preaching of Jesus, viz., the prophetic-eschatological proclamation of salvation and judgment, and a purified radicalized teaching of wisdom.[16] All such views have contributed to diminishing the authority of the eschatological interpretation of the preaching of Jesus, and have made it increasingly clear that the so-called crisis-motive could not be the dominant viewpoint leading to the right conception of the purport of the original gospel. It has become more and more manifest that Jesus' commandments especially form an insurmountable obstacle to any consistent eschatological interpretation of the preaching of the kingdom of heaven. On the other hand if the kingdom of heaven has a primary eschatological meaning, it must more and more become clear that this meaning could hardly serve as a "framework" or a "shell" for the liberal ethical conception of the gospel. It is remarkable how this truth suddenly seemed to dawn upon a wide circle of people, and how then the "eschatology of the kingdom of God" became the focal point of interest. This time it was discussed as a reality, which was willingly faced not only in an historical-exegetical respect, but in a thoroughly theological sense.[17] Only then did the structure of the liberal theology suddenly collapse. In spite of all the historical-exegetical researches of its own adherents, it had been able to maintain its optimistic and ethical conception of the kingdom of God. But now it had to give way to the theology of crisis, which could seemingly start directly from the gospel. Had not historical research established that Jesus' preaching of the kingdom also submitted all human data to the radical judgment of God's intervention which was so near at hand?

Yet it is clear that this new development in eschatological thought also was bound to meet with a serious obstacle in the gospel. For Weiss and Schweitzer had tried to show that all of Jesus' preaching was based on the conviction of an approaching final catastrophe, from which its fundamental sense of crisis was derived. But then it follows that any one who wishes to orientate his theology to this conception of the kingdom of God is confronted with the inevitable task of accounting for what, with an inexorable sense of reality, Schweitzer has again and again called "the delay of the *parousia*." No wonder that in order to maintain the eschatological interpretation not merely—like Weiss and Schweitzer—as an historical but as a theological principle, a conception of eschatology different than that of the fathers of the eschatological movement appeared to be necessary.[18] Thus arose what might be called the change of the final-historical (*endgeschichtliche*) into the supra-historical (*übergeschichtliche*) eschatology. This means that eschatology is no longer concerned with that which lies at the end of the horizontal line of history—this is final history (*Endgeschichte*) but it is concerned with the supra-temporal, the divine, which from moment to moment determines the existence of the world and man. The category of time is eliminated in this eschatological picture. The preaching of the approach of the kingdom of heaven should no longer be understood in the sense of the end of the world being at hand, and of the shrinking away of the time of its advent. But this message should be taken to denote the immediate relation of every moment of time to eternity. The "last things," therefore, assume a different meaning. The temporal indication of "post" is replaced by that of "trans." There is no question of an approach in a temporal sense. Every time may be the last, and at every hour the call is valid: "The kingdom is at hand."

This new interpretation of the eschatological character of Jesus' preaching is clearly based on dogmatic premises, and has had no less influence on New Testament science than the ideology of the liberal theology. As a typical transition from the old ethical-immanent conception of the kingdom of God to the new existential-eschatological interpretation we may mention M. Dibelius' *Evangelium und Welt*.[19] In this book the belief in the approaching end of the world, which is supposed to be the foundation of Jesus' preaching, is called the historical garb of the supra-historical and the permanent in Christianity. For not only have Jesus' words thereby been given an increased actuality, an inevitable seriousness, but this eschatological perspective lends to Jesus' preaching an unconditional absoluteness,[20] no longer dependent on any historical situation or chance. All this imparts to man a new ground of life,[21] elevated above any temporal contingency, and enables him to be in communion with what is eternal and imperishable, in that which Jesus called the kingdom of God.

But in this view the eschatology of the New Testament has not yet been taken quite seriously, because the immanence conception of the kingdom of God has still been maintained, although freed from any historical determination. In this respect Dibelius followed Harnack and the liberal theology. Not Dibelius, but very definitely Bultmann, is the typical representative of the new (in its turn "consistent") eschatological view of the gospel. He, too, is of the opinion that we should distinguish in the gospel between the revelational content proper and the "contemporary mythology" expressing this essential content. According to him this mythology includes the preaching of the approaching end of the world. This direction to the absolute end constitutes the permanent and essential element of the concept, kingdom of heaven. "The dominion of God is something miraculous, and the miraculous as such, that is the absolutely different, opposed to all of the here and the now."[22] The preaching of the *basileia* is the precipitation of the conviction that "even in the 'now' man is confronted with the necessity of deciding because the 'now' is the last hour for him."[23] The *basileia*, therefore, is not a condition or an entity that is realized on earth. It does not interest Jesus as an eschatological condition, but as "the miraculous event, meaning the great either-or, inducing man to come to a decision."[24] The dominion of God does not enter the world but calls to man to make a choice against the world.

K. L. Schmidt is also representative of the new eschatological view in Kittel's *Wörterbuch zum N.T.*[25] According to him, too, the kingdom of God in Jesus' preaching is purely future. In a negative sense this means—and here Schmidt literally agrees with Bultmann and R. Otto's formula—that "it is opposed to all that is present and earthly, to all that is here and now." In a positive sense this kingdom of God is a catastrophe realized in certain events described as the eschatological drama found in the Jewish apocalypses. However, that Jesus took over the conceptions of his contemporaries is not conclusive, but the important thing is that he consciously did not go as far as they did. He gives up depicting the final state and the calculations of the signs. In contradistinction to Judaism he emphasizes the fact that its coming cannot be calculated, that nobody can dispose of it one way or another, that it is an entirely divine cause. The negative statement that God's kingdom is nothing but a miracle must be maintained rigorously. This negative truth that God's kingdom is the entirely different, the absolutely "supra-cosmic and anti-cosmic" is the most positive thing that can be said about it, generally speaking. "The realization of God's dominion is future. And this future determines man's present."[26]

No wonder that in the long run this new eschatological interpretation of Jesus' preaching has also met with serious opposition. The interpretation of the biblical future as a permanent tension between time and eternity, and the explanation of the near approach of the kingdom in terms of the existential situation of decision, in which man finds himself placed from moment to moment before God, all too clearly bear the stamp of philosophical re-interpretation of the gospel. It is here almost easier to speak of an allegorical explanation than of an acceptable exegesis of the gospel. It is true that vigorous attempts have been made to vindicate the identity of the New Testament and this "suprahistorical eschatology." For example, Karl Barth for a while thought he could appeal to the New Testament and silence every protest against this conception. "For in the New Testament the end is not a temporal event, not a fabulous downfall of the world; it is entirely without any relation to any historical, terrestrial, or cosmic catastrophe, but it is the real *end*; so much the end that the nineteen hundred years (of Church history) do not only mean little, but nothing at all with respect to the nearness or the remoteness of the end. . . . "[27] But it has become more and more evident[28] that such an elimination of the time-category, and such a change of the realistic and cosmic view of the New Testament into the purely existential conception of the recent eschatology, at bottom only means relinquishing the New Testament expectation of the future (an *Enteschatologisierung*). This is why this newer eschatology stands condemned, however much it tries to make the essential element of the New Testament message about the kingdom the dominant viewpoint of theology. It is open to the same criticism as the older school which tried to distinguish between the "phenomenological" and the "intelligible" elements, the "form" and the "essence" in Jesus' preaching.[29] In opposition to this, others have argued that at bottom all such reasoning is an idealistic abstraction of the truth (revelation) and of history.[30] The temporal character of New Testament eschatology has been maintained with great emphasis. Thus, for example, joining Robert Winkler's opposition to the consistent eschatology,[31] Wendland asserts that every theology which removes the element of what is final (*endzeitlich*) and future from the notion of eschatology, estranges itself from the knowledge of faith of the New Testament.[32] Of late years this insight has been expressed in ever greater clarity, e.g., by Kümmel, who declares that there is no changing of the fact that to Jesus the prediction of the future occurrence of the eschatological consummation has a real prospective sense.[33] Especially Cullmann in his *Christus und die Zeit* has shown that the linear concept of time is characteristic of the biblical eschatology and soteriology. The *history* of salvation is the heart of the New Testament *kerygma*, and any one who tries to find an Archimedean point of orientation above it should know that he opposes the Christian message as such. That is why Cullmann rejects any attempt on the part of Schweitzer and his followers to arrive at a "theological" interpretation of the gospel while ignoring the expectation of the approaching end, which, historically speaking, they hold to be a delusion. He also points out to Bultmann that it is impossible to look upon this "mythological" conception of the end of this era as the setting to this form of the central content of the gospel. In opposition to this, Cullmann shows that the salvation preached in the gospel is bound up with a progressive course of time encompassing the past, the present and the future. It is essential for us to be keenly alive to the rigorously rectilinear conception of time in the New Testament, in contra-distinction to the Greek idea of cyclic time, and to maintain the former in opposition to every kind of metaphysics in which salvation is always restricted to the opposite side of the line between God and man (*Jenseits*).[34]

Acknowledging the real meaning of the category of time in Jesus' preaching, it is no longer possible for us to ignore the final act of the drama of history described in the *endgeschicht-liche* parts of the gospel. Nor can we pass by in silence the meaning of history and the cosmic meaning of the kingdom of heaven, if our aim is to accomplish a really theological exegesis of the gospels. Obviously, in this context renewed actuality and a new (now *theological*) importance will be attached to the questions connected with the historical nearness of the end, in general with the *Naherwartung* (the imminent advent) of Jesus, so emphatically posited by Weiss and Schweitzer. Nor is it accidental that with the decline of the supra-historical (*uebergeschichtliche*) phase of the eschato-logical interpretation it is necessary again to defend one's own position against the original theses posited by Weiss and Schweitzer, especially against the one about the *Naherwartung*. Moreover others, such as Buri and Werner, are making fresh and energetic attempts to establish the fact that Schweitzer's historical reconstruction of the original evangelical history is irrefutable. We shall have to revert to these things when elaborat-ing the theme of the future perspective of Jesus' preaching of the kingdom.[35]

Meanwhile the controversy about the purport of Jesus' preaching has not only been concentrated on the *meaning* of the evangelical eschatology, but also on its *limits*. We have already made mention of the impossibility of explaining the whole of Jesus' preaching and in particular his commandments, from the expectation of the end. Weiss also admits that this is impossible. It is true that Bultmann thought he could main-tain the unity of Jesus' eschatological and ethical message by conceiving of Jesus' commandments merely as exhortations to come to a decision, i.e., as a purely eschatological message.[36] But apart from the denaturing of the New Testament idea of eschatology evidenced in this effort, such a conception is only possible if the unity of the synoptic kerygma is dissolved after the manner of the exponents of form criticism. The kerygma is split up by them into a multitude of very small units of tradition each one of which is supposed to be capable of investigation as to its originality.

And this does not only hold for Jesus' commandments, but for the whole of the preaching of the kingdom of heaven that has come down to us. It has become increasingly clear that a large number of very important utterances and elements of the gospel will have to be denied to Jesus, if his preaching is to be considered from the viewpoint of the crisis, the approaching end, the idea of "decision." For the synoptic preaching of the kingdom is not exclusively concerned with the approaching or the expected kingdom of the future, neither in its ethical ele-ments, nor in its statements concerning the history of salvation. But in many respects the evangelical message bears the char-acter of fulfillment. In order to prove the truth of this assertion on evident grounds, an unwarranted restriction has been made in the appeal to the so-called "presence pronouncements" (i.e., to those passages explicitly stating the presence of the king-dom). But it has been seen with ever greater clearness that this is not a matter of a few scattered pronouncements but of the character of the whole gospel as the gospel of the fulfill-ment, and that in this case everything depends on the view taken of *the person of Jesus*. In other words, the question of the meaning of the kingdom in Jesus' preaching is at bottom the question of the Christological quality of the gospel.

Schweitzer has seen the importance of this fact and has

always acknowledged that where Christ is there is the kingdom. The revelation of the kingdom is the revelation of Christ. The kingdom of God and the Messiah are correlates. In perfect agreement with his consistent eschatological conceptions Schweitzer has, however, also represented Jesus' Messiahship as something that had not yet begun but was simply an honor to be conferred at a future time. Jesus was not the Messiah, but the Messiah-designate. Undoubtedly here, too, the radical wing of criticism has tried to detach the purport of Jesus' preaching from his person. So long as the preaching of the kingdom is conceived of as a purely ethical message—as was done, e.g., by Harnack—such a separation can hardly be objected to from a purely factual standpoint (i.e., apart from historico-exegetic considerations). And in the same way, if with Bultmann the preaching of the kingdom is looked upon only as a call to a "decision" (*Entscheidung*) with a view to the "approaching end," the question whether Jesus really took himself to be the coming Messiah may be declared to be of secondary importance (*nebensächlich*).[37] As soon, however, as one views the gospel with an open mind, and takes account of the central position which the gospels assign to Jesus as the Christ, it will no longer be possible to ascribe a purely future meaning to the kingdom of heaven. It is, therefore, the emphatic recognition of the Christological content of the synoptic kerygma which has revealed the limits of the eschatological purport of the gospel of the kingdom to a wide circle of people, without any relapse into the hypotheses of the liberal theology. Characteristic of the reaction to the one-sidedly eschatological conception after the first world-war are, e.g., the works of G. Gloege, *Reich Gottes und Kirche im N. T.*,[38] and of H. D. Wendland, *Die Eschatologie des Reiches Gottes bei Jesus.*[39]

These writings are typical of the new interpretation of the gospel. They start from the eschatological qualification of the concept, kingdom of God. On the one hand they reject the notion that the kingdom is developing in this world as an immanent entity, and on the other hand, they reject the basic tenet of radical eschatology, according to which the kingdom is supposed to have a merely future character.

Thus Gloege lays great emphasis on the dynamic meaning of the concept "kingdom of God," by which he understands the eschatological, redeeming and judging *activity* of God. This kingly activity cannot be merely limited to the future, says Gloege. In Jesus' action as the Messiah, God's dominion—which is his, too—has actually started.[40] Present and future have been merged into a living organic unity of action (*lebendig-organische Wirkungseinheit*) in Jesus' Messianic activity, As the Messiah Jesus introduces God's kingdom as a working power into the present. However, he will not hear of the kingdom of God as a permanent datum, not even in the person of Jesus as such, but in his action, i.e., in his action as God's Christ.[41]

Equally important and influential are Wendland's expositions. He fully recognizes the merits of the radical-eschatological movement in opposition to the earlier conception of the kingdom of God as immanent and present. "We cannot go back beyond the eschatological conception."[42] This is not saying that "eschatological" coalesces with "future." The kingdom of God is not only concerned (*endzeitlich*) with the end of time but also supra-temporal (*ueberzeitlich*), pre-existent, eternal. This eternity is not to be conceived of as timelessness, however. The eternal kingdom may break through in time and does so indeed, namely, in Christ. The pronouncements about its presence must not be understood solely in a subjective sense as psychological anticipations, as Weiss believed. Nor is it permissible to take one's stand on Bultmann's opinion according to which the transcendent kingdom of God places man before a "decision" at every moment. But the kingdom comes *into* this world in the divine miracle wrought in Christ. This presence, however, is not to be thought of in an exclusively dynamic sense, as Gloege conceives it. It also consists in Christ as a divine gift, as the creation of the new life, the being adopted as a child of God. In all these relations of the kingdom to the world this presence is connected with the person of the messenger of the kingdom. "The ultimate answer to the question about the presence of God's reign will always be of a Christological character. Any one who denies the impersonation of the kingdom in the Bearer of the kingdom deprives the reality of the presence of the kingdom of its power."[43] This Christological foundation of the presence of the kingdom and of the character of the gospel as fulfillment has found expression in all kinds of ways in the recent literature. It may be said that in Kittel's *Theologisches Wörterbuch* the majority of the articles discussing the "theological" content of the synoptic gospels are dominated by it, and, in their turn, have greatly contributed to its recognition. All kinds of monographs relating to parts of Jesus' preaching (e.g., the parables, the Church, the Last Supper, redemption, parousia) are based on this thought and thus they arrive at quite different results.[44] In what follows we shall be confronted with them in all kinds of ways.

As has been indicated, this integral Christological view of the synoptic preaching of the kingdom of heaven in the recent literature is accompanied by a definite emphasis on the redemptive historical significance of the coming of the kingdom. That which Jesus preaches is not a timeless truth, and what he brings is not only a new spirituality, a new disposition. No more is it a new form of society (in the sense of the social gospel) or an action carried on by men and slowly developing to its consummation.

The coming of the kingdom of God is most certainly to be looked upon as the realization of the great drama of the history of salvation in the sense of the Old Testament and of the Jewish apocalypses. This realization is not merely a matter of the future, however. It has started. The great change of the aeons has taken place. The center of history is in Christ's coming, in his victory over the demons, in his death and resurrection. In this sense, e.g., authors like Jeremias,[45] Stauffer,[46] Matter,[47] Cullmann,[48] Kümmel,[49] and others try to do justice to both the eschatological and the present character of the Kingdom. Stauffer, e.g., states that present day theology still considers time, more or less in the manner of Kant, as a human form of intuition (*Anschauungsform*). The New Testament, however, considers time as the form of the divine action.[50] This starting-point also enables Stauffer to speak of the presence of the kingdom. It has come with the Son of Man. He discusses this coming especially as Christ's attack on the demonical powers. The kingdom concept in Jesus' words has a pronounced polemical accent. Jesus penetrates from the heavenly world into the earthly kingdom of the powerful one. The power of the great adversary is assailed. The *Civitas Dei* must have come and will one day be victorious.[51]

Matter's picture is a little different. He, too, is very critical of the thought of the realization of the kingdom within the limitations of this world, especially when the talk is about a human share in the "building up" or the "expansion" of the kingdom of God. However, Matter will not hear of an actualistic-dynamic conception of the kingdom in the sense of Gloege and others. He views the kingdom rather as the permanent, static omnipotence of God. In virtue of his divine nature Christ participates in this power and it is intermittently revealed in the world. The coming of the kingdom is therefore, according to Matter, not to be seen in a horizontal line but, it is always vertical. The "nearness" is not temporal, but spatial. The relations between Jesus' first and last coming are not, or not in the first place, of a religious and moral nature. "These relations are cosmic. This *world* was once the scene of the *revelations of God's power*; one day it will be so in the full sense of the word in the 'future' of Jesus Christ. The interim may therefore also be called '*basileia.*' Jesus Christ is now in control of the course of things even in their natural aspect. He manifests his power in this world in its rise as well as in its decline and fall." For the character of this relation Matter refers to the Apocalypse of John whose principal theme is the *basileia* as an interim.[52]

The views advanced by Stauffer, Matter and others, are

the extreme opposites to the old immanence theology which sought the kernel of Jesus' message in the infinite value of the individual human soul, or in the spiritualization of human society. This old trend omitted every doctrine about angels, devils, thrones, and powers as a contemporary (*zeitgeschichtlich*) scaffolding. The difference of the eschatological conception, however, is that in these expositions the presence of the kingdom is taught unhesitatingly. The supra-human and cosmic character of the kingdom is again put in the center. Especially in Stauffer the dramatic history of salvation comes to the fore. Christ's coming is the decisive act in the great struggle between the kingdom of God and that of the devil.

To Cullmann, also, this great moment of the consummation of the history of salvation is the essence of the coming of the kingdom proclaimed by Christ. Where Christ acts and operates, the future is already decided upon. The time after Christ's first coming and before his second coming is the time between the decisive battle and "Victory Day."[53] The temporal tension between presence and future already exists for Jesus insofar as in his person the future may be considered to have been fulfilled and is still to be expected.[54] For this presence and future of the kingdom Cullmann can also appeal to Kümmel, whose book: *"Verheiszung und Erfüllung,"* published in 1946, again subjected the whole question of the presence and the future of the kingdom to investigation. He, too, is of the opinion that in principle the presence of the kingdom as well as the fulfillment of the promises have been given in the great history-of-salvation fact, the coming of Jesus Christ. It is true, Kümmel does so with greater reserve, and after eliminating from the gospel all kinds of pronouncements and motives that he supposes are "not to be attributed to Jesus." This author also recognizes the great importance of the eschatological interpretation of the gospel of the kingdom without, however, denying the predominating element of the fulfillment. However, this presence of the kingdom should not be conceived as an entity developing on earth or in the hearts of men, for it only consists in the person of Christ, his preaching, and his action. In all these the coming kingdom of God becomes visible and present.[55]

Lastly it must be mentioned that the exclusive view of the presence of the kingdom as well as the consistent eschatology still find powerful and able defenders. As proponents of the consistent eschatological view we have already mentioned the names of F. Buri and M. Werner. The view that Jesus considered the kingdom to have definitely arrived with his own coming has of late been defended by C. H. Dodd, in his influential work: *The Parables of the Kingdom.* His standpoint is that of the so-called *realized eschatology.* Jesus' pronouncements on the presence of the kingdom are beyond cavil. But this also means that the whole eschatological scheme has of necessity been broken through. The eschaton has become present instead of future, from the sphere of expectation it has passed into that of experience. What the apocalypse meant by the "kingdom of God" could only be expressed "in terms of fantasy." Jesus spoke about it as about an object of experience.[56] Though the gospel in its present form also contains all kinds of pronouncements about the future, Dodd thinks that there is nowhere a question of the future *of the kingdom.* This view is closely connected with Dodd's special conception of what Jesus meant by *basileia.* In his opinion the *basileia* belongs entirely to the spiritual sphere. Dodd considers the gospel from the standpoint of the history of salvation (in particular the parables), but he thinks that the whole of this eschatological expectation has been fulfilled in the spiritual world to which Jesus testified. He thus arrives at an explanation of all the parables of the kingdom of God based on the exclusive view of its presence.

Dodd's exegesis, which has met with a favorable response in the Anglo-Saxon world,[57] is at bottom a reversion to the old liberal conception of the kingdom of God in a modern scientific sense. It proves that in theology also there is nothing new under the sun. This may induce us to keep as far away as possible from any ideological presuppositions about the kingdom, and to devote all our efforts instead to the study of what the *text of the gospels* teaches us about Jesus' preaching of the kingdom of heaven.

Notes to the Introduction

[1] K. L. Schmidt, in: G. Kittel, *Theologisches Wörterbuch zum Neuen Testament* (to be referred to as T.W.B.), I. p. 584, the article on *"basileia."*

[2] H. D. Wendland, *Die Eschatologie des Reiches Gottes bei Jesus,* 1931, pp. 15, 19.

[3] For what follows compare also: H. M. Matter: *Nieuwere Opvattingen omtrent het Koninkrijk Gods in Jezus' prediking naar de Synoptici,* 1942.

[4] Cf. F. Holmström, *Das Eschatologische Denken der Gegenwart,* 1936, pp. 6ff.; E. Masselink, *Eschatologische motieven in de nieuwe theologie,* 1946, pp. 19ff.

[5] Cf. also my *De strekking van de bergrede naar Mattheüs,* 1936, pp. 76ff.

[6] 1901, 2nd edition, 1929.

[7] 1906.

[8] 1913. Since this date it has remained unchanged, (1926, 1933).

[9] Cf. his *Gesch.d.L.-J.-F.4,* 1933, pp. 368ff.; for a survey cf. my *Zelfopenbaring en Zelfverberging,* 1946, pp. 8ff.

[10] Cf. also Holmström, *op. cit.,* pp. 89ff.

[11] *Der Dualismus war die Hülle für den gewaltigen sittlichen Ernst und die religiös Tiefe des Evangeliums. Aber der Keim hat überall die Hülle gesprengt.* W. Bousset, *Die Jüdische Apokalyptik, ihre religionsgeschichtliche Herkunft und ihre Bedeutung für das N.T.,* 1903, p. 62. Cf. also Schweitzer on Bousset, *Gesch.d.L.-J.-F.,* pp. 236ff.; Holmström, *op. cit.,* p. 42.

[12] *Das Wesen des Christentums,* 1905, pp. 34-36.

[13] We refer to the well-known expositions given by E. von Dob Schütz in his *The Eschatology of the Gospels, The Expositor,* 1910; and especially to H. J. Holtzmann: *Lehrbuch der neutestamentlichen Theologie* I2, 1911 (published by A. Jülicher and W. Bauer), pp. 248ff.

[14] For this construction of Weiss's cf. H. M. Matter, *op. cit.,* pp. 70ff.

[15] Cf. my: *De Strekking der Bergrede,* p. 78.

[16] H. Windisch, *Der Sinn der Bergpredigt,* 1929, p. 20.

[17] Cf. also: G. C. Berkouwer, *Wereldoorlog en Theologie,* 1945, pp. 11ff.

[18] Cf. on this, e.g., F. Buri, *Die Bedeutung der neutestamentlichen Eschatologie für die neuere protestantische Theologie,* 1934.

[19] 1929, second edition of the work published in 1925: *Geschichtliche und uebergeschichtliche Religion im Christentum;* cf. my *De Strekking der Bergrede,* pp. 81ff., and especially N. B. Stonehouse, "Martin Dibelius and the Relation of History and Faith," in: *The Westminster Theological Journal,* 1940, pp. 105-139.

[20] *Op. cit.,* p. 41.

[21] *Op. cit.,* p. 60.

[22] R. Bultmann, *Jesus,* 1929, p. 36.

[23] *Op. cit.,* p. 53.

[24] *Op. cit.,* p. 40.

[25] Cf. article, "Basileia," 1, p. 573.

[26] *Op. cit.,* p. 588.

[27] K. Barth, *Der Römerbrief,* 1926, p. 484.

[28] Also Barth, cf. *Kirchliche Dogmatik,* II, 1, pp. 715, 716.

[29] Cf. also Holmström, *op. cit.,* p. 21; F. Buri, *Das Problem der ausgebliebenen Parusie,* in: *Vox Theologica,* April, 1948, pp. 111-115; E. Masselink, *op. cit.,* pp. 105ff.

[30] Ph. Bachmann, for example, calls the common root of the liberal and "supra-historical" interpretation of eschatology "the idealistic separation of time and eternity," cf. Holmström, *op. cit.*, p. 373.

[31] R. Winkler, "Eschatologie und Mystik," *Zeitschr. für Theologie und Kirche*, 1931, pp. 147ff.

[32] H. D. Wendland, *Die Eschatologie des Reiches Gottes bei Jesus*, 1931, p. 253.

[33] *Verheiszung und Erfüllung*, 1945, p. 88.

[34] *Christus und die Zeit*, 1946, pp. 25ff.; cf. also his: *Le Retour du Christ²*, 1945, pp. 14,15.

[35] Cf. § 43 and the literature mentioned there.

[36] Cf below § 32.

[37] As to the struggle concerning the Christology in the modern criticism of the gospels, cf. my: *Zelfopenbaring en Zelfverberging*, pp. 5-20.

[38] 1929.

[39] 1931.

[40] *Op. cit.*, p. 110.

[41] *Op. cit.*, p. 112.

[42] *Op. cit.*, p. 29.

[43] *Op. cit.*, pp. 50-53.

[44] This especially applies to the view of the Church, cf. below § 35ff.

[45] *Jesus, der Weltvollender im N.T.*, 1929.

[46] *Die Theologie des N.T.*, 1941, and the following years.

[47] *Nieuwere opvattingen omtrent het Koninkrijk Gods*, 1942.

[48] *Christus und die Zeit*, 1946, and other publications.

[49] *Verheiszung und Erfüllung*, 1945.

[50] *Op. cit.*, p. 59.

[51] *Op. cit.*, pp. 103-106.

[52] H. M. Matter, *Nieuwere opvattingen omtrent het Koninkrijk Gods*, 1942, pp. 180ff.

[53] *Christus und die Zeit*, p. 127.

[54] *Op. cit.*, p. 62.

[55] Cf. also Kümmel, *Die Eschatologie der Evangelien, Ihre Geschichte und Ihr Sinn*, 1936, pp. 12, 17.

[56] *Op. cit.*, p. 50.

[57] Cf., e.g., A. T. Cadoux, *The Theology of Jesus*, 1940; F. C. Grant, *The Gospel of the Kingdom*, 1940, who arrives at conclusions similar to Dodd's, although he has some criticism, pp. 145, 146ff.; and can only understand the purport of Jesus' preaching for the present time in the sense of the "social gospel": "In our days . . . the principles of Jesus' teaching can be applied only in terms of the social gospel," p. 134.

THE COMING OF THE KINGDOM

Chapter I

THE GENERAL CHARACTER
OF THE KINGDOM OF HEAVEN

1. The Background

1. *The Old Testament*

When pursuant to John the Baptist's message Jesus came forward in Israel with the proclamation: "Repent: for the kingdom of heaven is at hand" (Matt. 4:17, cf. 3:2), he did not give any further explanation or description of the coming event, at least according to the tradition that has come down to us. This is an indication that the expression: "the kingdom of heaven" was not unknown to those to whom this message was addressed, but was rather calculated to find an immediate response with them. The exceptional and spectacular part of John the Baptist's and Jesus' appearance was not that they spoke of "the kingdom of heaven," but that they announced to Israel that this kingdom was near at hand.

This circumstance induces us to seek the origin and explore the background of the expression "kingdom of heaven" used by Jesus and John with such emphasis. What thoughts did the people associate with this summons to repent? To find an answer to this question one cannot refer simply to the Old Testament, for the expression "kingdom of heaven" does not occur in it. Only in the writings of the later Jews do we find it, and it is fairly certain that not until this later (pre-Christian) period did it become a standard phrase from which Jesus and John the Baptist could start their teaching. And yet the roots of this linguistic usage, especially of the idea connoted by it, lie hidden deep in the divine revelation of the Old Testament and in the expectation of faith. Without this Old Testament background neither the later Jewish faith in the kingdom of heaven, nor its New Testament proclamation can be understood. That is why we must first consider its background.

As has been said, the Old Testament does not mention "the kingdom of heaven." And the phrase "kingdom of God" is not nearly such a standard expression in it as in the New Testament. There are only a few passages containing the equivalent of *basileia* in the sense of the kingship or the royal dominion of God.[1] Often, indeed, Jahwe is indicated personally as king, especially in the Psalms and the prophets,[2] and the Lord is said to be a king.[3] This application of the idea of a king to Jahwe is also found in the older parts of the Old Testament,[4] so that we must reject the assertion that the idea of Jahwe being a king only arose in post-exilian times in imitation of the so-called Deutero-Isaiah.[5] This will become even clearer when we enter a little more deeply into this thought. A twofold distinction should be made. In the first place the Old Testament speaks of a general and a particular kind of kingship of the Lord. The former concerns the universal power and dominion of God over the whole world and all the nations, and is founded in the creation of heaven and earth.[6] The latter denotes the special relation between the Lord and Israel.[7] This was later called *theocracy* in a special sense, and coincides in many respects with God's covenant in the Old Testament.

In addition a distinction can be made between those passages in which Jahwe's kingship equally encompasses the past and the future, or, as Von Rad puts it: "which lay stress on the almost timeless character of Jahwe's kingship"[8] and the places in which the dominant element is one of expectation, of Jahwe revealing and maintaining himself as king in full glory. This latter idea of the coming kingship of God is especially found in the later books of the Old Testament, particularly in those of the prophets. Its origin is closely connected with Israel's national life. During the period in which Israel's national existence was more and more in decline and the world powers threatened to crush Israel, a strong tension arose between God's kingship revealed to Israel (viz., his power over the whole world and his particular relation to Israel whose king he was) and the actual development of history. This tension was relieved by that which the prophets revealed about the coming manifestation of God's kingship. This expectation of the future has such a prominent importance in the scope of the prophetic divine revelation that it may be called the center of the whole Old Testament promise of salvation.[9] The most prominent of these prophecies is found in Isaiah 40-55, cf., e.g., 40:9-11; 52:7; and certainly not less strikingly in Isaiah 24-27. Also in the books of the other prophets this prophecy of the coming kingdom of God is an essential element, cf., e.g., Obadiah 21; Micah 4:3; Zeph. 3:15; Zech. 14:16,17.

The contents of this great expectation of salvation are many-sided. An essential feature of the prophecy is its description of the coming kingdom of God in the form of Israel's nationality. Israel will be restored as a nation; the Lord will have his throne in Jerusalem; her enemies will be subjugated. Yet again and again these ideas appear to refer to a higher, spiritual and imperishable reality. The coming kingdom of God will be inaugurated by the great day of the Lord, the day of judgment for the apostate part of Israel, as well as for the nations in general, and at the same time, however, by the day of deliverance and salvation for the oppressed people of the Lord. In the description of the one as well as in that of the other we find traits that break through temporal reality[10] and refer to an entirely new dispensation, thus, as to the last judgment, e.g., Hosea 4:3; Isaiah 2:10ff. and other places; and as to the coming salvation, e.g., Hosea 2:17; Micah 4:1ff.; Isaiah 9:1-6; 11:1-10ff. The coming salvation is imperishable (Isaiah 51:6); a supermundane reality will begin (Isaiah 60:1ff); a new heaven and a new earth will come into existence (Isaiah 60:19; 65:17; 66:22); death will be annihilated (Isaiah 25:7ff.); the dead will be raised (Isaiah 26:19). In opposition to the eternal woe of the wicked there will come the eternal bliss of the redeemed (Isaiah 66:24). At the culmination points of the prophecies this blissful future reveals its universality; basically it consists in the ruin and downfall of the power of the world (Isaiah 26:21; 27:1), and in the heathen sharing in Israel's happiness (Isaiah 25:6; 45:22; 51:4-6); the Lord being king of the whole world in that day (Micah 4:1ff.). As has been said, this picture of the supernatural reality of the divine kingdom breaking through all the boundaries of the temporal-earthly dispensation is not the usual character of the prophecies. As a rule its description remains within the boundaries of this earthly life. And yet, at bottom, this entire prophecy is focused on this eternal and indestructible salvation: "all temporal judgments announced by the prophets, are types of the great judgment of the world; every kind of bliss that has been foretold refers to the perfect happiness of the great future."[11]

As to the relation between the Old Testament thought of the kingdom of God and the messianic expectation of salvation, it has been emphatically stated that these two should be sharply distinguished from each other. And, no doubt, it is true, that the thought of the coming state of bliss in which Jahwe will assume his kingship in the full sense of the word, is often unaccompanied by any mention of the Messiah-King. But the one cannot be separated from the other, because what is said about the coming reign of God has no other reach than that of the prophecies about the messianic kingdom of peace (cf., e.g., Isaiah 9:11; 32). He is the coming ruler of the world (Isaiah 11:9,10); at least according to some of the prophecies, his kingship also bears a supernatural character (cf., e.g., Micah 5:1); in short, all that which holds for the coming divine manifestation of the king, also holds for the rule of the Messiah-King. This is to say that it is the Lord, who will again assert his rule over Israel and maintain his kingship over the whole world in and through the coming Messiah-King; whereas, conversely, also in those places where only the coming manifestation of God's kingship is mentioned, it must be connected with the promise of the Redeemer-King of David's house.

The prophecies of Daniel have a separate importance for

the understanding of the background to Jesus' preaching about the kingdom of God. They especially clarify the antithesis between what may be concisely formulated as the worldly empire and the kingdom of God. In opposition to the power of Nebuchadnezzar who usurps divine royal rights, it is in the first place maintained that God's *malkuth* is eternal and infinite (Daniel 3:33), and that, therefore, he is free to give royal dominion to whom he likes. But this general thought is given further concreteness by saying that God will at last actually deprive the worldly empires of their dominion; and that he will give dominion to the figure of one who, in the night visions of the prophet, as "a Son of Man" approached the Ancient of days on his flaming throne; "And there was given him dominion and glory, and a kingdom that all people, nations, and languages, should serve him: his dominion was an everlasting dominion, which shall not pass away, and his kingdom that which shall not be destroyed" (Daniel 7:9ff.). In the explanation of the dream to Daniel it is said that it is "the saints of the Most High who shall take the kingdom and possess it for ever" (Dan. 7:18). This should not be taken to mean that the Son of Man and the saints are identical, either because the former acts as the representative of the latter, or because in the expression "the saints of the Most High" the Son of Man is further defined. But the figure of the Son of Man is the one in whose reign the saints of the Most High will one day share. Here, too, the future kingdom of God is mentioned in which the figure of a Son of Man will make his people share in the blessings of God's dominion.[12] Though the Messiah-King of David's house is not spoken of here, and in general the earthly-national features have been replaced by transcendent-apocalyptic traits, it is clear that the one in the form of the "Son of Man" of the glorious future will receive world dominion out of the hands of God, and that this will constitute the bliss of the great future.

Finally, apart from the prophecies in the narrower sense, we must mention the so-called "psalms of the accession to the throne" as the Old Testament testimony of the coming divine rule, such as Psalms 47; 93; 96; 97; and 99. They, too, speak of God's becoming king and of the revelation of his power to all the nations. Though in the first instance they will have to be explained as referring to some historical event (e.g., Psalm 47, the bringing up of the ark?), yet, at bottom, these psalms also give expression to the expectation of a final and definite revelation of Jahwe's kingship, in which every manifestation of his power in the history of salvation already displays a beginning. The interpretation of this enthronement only in a cultic sense (i.e., as the annual accession to the throne by Jahwe which is supposed to be celebrated in the cult with a solemn procession), according to the conception advocated by Mowinckel,[13] is only based on analogies in the pagan world; in Israel nothing is known of such a New Year's festival.

To summarize what we have found, we can say that in the Old Testament the expression kingdom of God does not yet occur in the same invariable sense as in the New Testament. But the thought of a coming kingdom of God, consisting in the universal divine kingship over the whole world, for the good of his people and for the overthrow of any power that opposes his rule, has from olden times been one of the central motives of Israel's expectation of salvation. Founded on the confession that God is king (present kingship), the expectation arises that he will become king in an intensified and an eschatological sense (future kingship).

2. The Later Jews

In contradistinction to the verbal and personal pronouncements about the kingship of Jahwe in the Old Testament, we almost invariably find the abstract expression *malkuth shamaim* in later Jewish literature. Of this expression the phrase "kingdom or kingship of the heavens" (*basileia toon ouranoon*) is the literal translation.[14] In connection with the Jewish tendency to avoid wherever possible the use of the name of God, the word *shamaim* (heavens) is simply to be considered as a circumlocution of the word "God." That is why it invariably occurs without an article in this word group.[15] Although with the rabbis *malkuth shamaim* is a standard phrase, it occurs only rarely, in comparison with its linguistic usage in the gospels[16] and it has not nearly such a central significance as *basileia toon ouranoon* (*tou theou*) in the gospels. This also appears from the fact that *malkuth* in the sense of *malkuth shamaim* is nowhere used independently in pseudepigraphic and rabbinical literature in the way *basileia* occurs in the gospels. Wherever *malkuth* is used absolutely in Jewish literature, it always denotes earthly, pagan (Roman) dominion.[17] The expression *malkuth shamaim* has a twofold meaning in the later Jewish literature.

In the first place it denotes the moral dominion of God over all men, implied in the creation of man by God, a dominion which mankind renounced, until, however, in Abraham's race it was again acknowledged and maintained over Israel, especially in the Torah. The nature of this dominion is especially characterized by the expressions "to undertake and to throw off the yoke of *malkuth shamaim*." By this "yoke"[18] is understood the confession of monotheism and obedience to the Torah. This yoke is shouldered when, like the proselytes, people join the Jewish religion, but also whenever they again subject themselves to its commandments, as is done, e.g., when the summary of monotheism and of the Torah, the so-called Shema (Deut. 6:4-8) is read and recited every day.[19] This specialization goes so far that the expression: "to shoulder the yoke of the *malkuth shamaim*" becomes the technical expression for: to recite the so-called Shema. Generally, however, *malkuth shamaim* in this sense has a spiritual meaning.

Along with this—and this is the second point—*malkuth shamaim* has a much wider application, viz., as the indication of God's coming world-dominion which will liberate Israel from the power of the heathen and subject the whole world of nations to God. In this sense *malkuth shamaim* means: "the kingship of God over all mankind fully realized through its recognition by the whole world."[20] The manifestation of this *malkuth shamaim* is repeatedly the object of Jewish prayers. Thus, e.g., the *Qaddisch* opens with the words: "Glorified and sanctified be his great name in the world he has created according to his own pleasure. May he establish his royal dominion and start his deliverance of his people, and may be bring his Messiah and redeem his people in the time of your life, and in your days, and in the time of the life of the whole House of Israel, with haste and in a short time; and thou shalt say Amen."

As to the contents of the future expectation thus indicated, there was a great diversity of conceptions.[21] For a knowledge of what was actually believed in some circles prior to and at the time of the birth of Christ, the pseudepigraphic and apocryphal writings of the period are especially important. But they are far from unanimous in their eschatological outlook. It is, consequently, very difficult to state accurately what the future outlook of the Jews actually was at the beginning of the Christian era. Alongside of utterances that start from the prophecies of the restoration of the people of Israel and of the house of David, other writings lay more emphasis on the supernatural-transcendent character of the great time of salvation.

Characteristic of the former view is the pseudepigraphic writing: *The Psalms of Solomon*. The future expectations occurring in it are of an earthly and national nature. The (messianic) kingdom of the future remains within the limits of earthly life, and there is nowhere any mention of a future world, of a different, supernatural dispensation. Great emphasis is laid on Israel's deliverance from its enemies and on the resulting state of bliss. In a writing such as *The Testaments of the Twelve Patriarchs*, however, the expectation regarding the future of the nation is also accompanied by some elements that clearly bear a supernatural character: the coming messianic kingdom will entail the redemption of the whole cosmos, the resurrection of the dead, the universal judgment of the whole world and eternal life in God's paradise.

Some parts of the book of *Enoch* and the so-called *Assumption of Moses* even go further in this direction. In them there is no question at all of an earthly messianic reign, but the future kingdom is placed instead in the coming heavenly world. And, at least in the book of *Enoch*, the Messiah appears in the supernatural figure of the Son of Man (probably an analogy of Daniel 7). Here the coming world is dualistically related to the present world. Not the earth, but heaven is the domain where God's kingdom will be revealed.

In other books, such as the Syrian *Apocalypse of Baruch* and in *4 Esdras* there is a synthesis of the two conceptions. The earthly messianic dominion of the final era, after the resurrection of the dead and the judgment of the world, will be followed by the coming heavenly world in which the Messiah will also appear, but now for an everlasting, heavenly dominion. The national eschatological picture is here merely the transition to a transcendent, heavenly eschatology. In *4 Esdras*, however, the earth, renewed and reborn this time, will again be the place of the new aeon of the world, after the judgment of the world.

As regards the conceptions found in rabbinical literature, there is very little available data from the oldest rabbinical period (until 70 A.D.). The rabbinical material of this period is very scarce. Not before 70 A.D. do we have any richer sources at our disposal. From the latter it appears that, generally speaking, the rabbinical scholars entertained the views that we have found in *4 Esdras*. The miserable state of this world will be followed by the days of the Messiah which will culminate in the establishment of the *malkuth shamaim* on earth. This is the future world that will begin after the resurrection and judgment day.

From these data it appears that there are no fixed conceptions of the future state of bliss of the *malkuth shamaim*, and that those that did exist only gradually adopted a fixed form. This also holds for the position that the Messiah occupied in the expectation of the future. As far as we can ascertain, the pre-Christian Jewish writings and the later rabbinic literature do not purposely treat this subject. Nowhere, writes

Kuhn, is the thought found that the kingdom of the Messiah is the *malkuth shamaim,* or that the Messiah will bring the *malkuth shamaim* through his works.[22]   And yet in the broader context of Jewish eschatology there is a close connection between the expectation of the coming Messiah-King and that of the revelation of the *malkuth shamaim.* It should be taken into account, however, that often a clear delimitation of the various notions is lacking, and that in the multitude of writings all kinds of conceptions get mixed and also undergo a certain development and modification.   In the oldest, pre-Christian pseudepigrapha like *The Psalms of Solomon, The Testaments of the Twelve Patriarchs,* the expectation of future bliss is equated with the kingdom of the Messiah, either in a national sense, as in *The Psalms of Solomon,* or in the scheme of a dualistic view of the world, as in *The Testaments of the Twelve Patriarchs.* In this trend of thought, which is entirely based on the Old Testament, as far as the absolute meaning of the messianic dominion is concerned, the expectation of the final dominion of God as king is fulfilled in and through the coming of the Messiah. He will cause God's kingly prerogatives to be recognized again in the everlasting glory of the messianic kingdom.   His kingdom is identical with the *malkuth shamaim.*

In the later pre-Christian Apocrypha, but especially in the writings after the beginning of the Christian era, the idea crops up that the coming of Messiah does not coincide with the great epoch of salvation. The latter will only come at the end of the present world (*olam ha-zeh*), but before the coming of the future world (*olam ha-ba*); it will precede the resurrection of the dead, and will bring only a provisional deliverance of Israel.

It is clear that according to this latter opinion the *malkuth shamaim* does not coincide with the messianic kingdom, but encompasses a great deal more.   It will find its culminating point only in the realm of justice and peace on the new earth to which, in accordance with this later conception, the messianic dominion will only be the transition.

Summarizing we can say that in Jewish eschatological literature the *malkuth shamaim* is understood to be the coming universal revelation of the kingship of God with which the appearance of the Messiah is intimately connected. As the expression *malkuth shamaim* has a very general sense, it is not possible to delimit its meaning sharply with respect to *olam ha-zeh* and *olam ha-ba*. It comprises the self-vindication of God revealed in the final epoch in opposition to the apostate world, as well as his resign in the everlasting kingdom of peace.

3. No Eschatological a priori

Against the background of this short summary both of the Old Testament prophecies and those of the so-called late-Jewish expectation of the future there cannot be any doubt about the meaning of John the Baptist's and, after him, of Jesus' proclamation: "Repent, for the kingdom of heaven is at hand." It was the announcement of an all-inclusive reality in the history of salvation. The descriptions of the future manifestation of Jahwe's kingship, current in Israel in the course of history before Jesus' appearance, may have been very varied; however, one thing is clear, viz., that these words summarized all that had been the object of Old Testament prophecy and of Israel's expectation of the future from the oldest times. This was not merely the subjective opinion of the first spectators coming to John and later to Jesus from Judea and Jerusalem, even from the whole of the Jewish country, when they heard the rumor of this proclamation. It was also intended by the preachers of this extraordinary and sensational message themselves. This appears clearly enough from the words that Mark adds to the commencement of the New Testament *kerygma: the time is fulfilled.* "The time," i.e., the great turning-point of history, promised by God himself for the full revelation of his kingly glory; the time for the liberation of his people and the punishment of his enemies. It was this time that would bring the consummation and which had reached its "fullness."[23] Thus the general character of

Jesus' preaching of the kingdom has from the outset been qualified as the preaching of fulfillment in the prophetic, historical-soteriological sense of the word. And the whole interpretation of this preaching can have no other task than to set the meaning of the fulfillment thus announced in the clearest possible light.

Yet this fact does not relieve us of the duty—and this is the second point to which we must presently give our attention—to investigate the meaning of the central theme of Jesus' preaching. This theme is the idea of the kingdom of heaven that is repeatedly mentioned by Jesus. Within the limits of his own proclamation we shall have to study this idea closely. It would be a very unhistorical and therefore unreal procedure to detach the conception of the "kingdom of heaven" from its historical background. But on the other hand, the short historical exposition given above may teach us that this conception is very complicated. It has been interwoven with all kinds of divergent motives in a process of many centuries' duration. Therefore it is not possible in the face of this state of affairs to consider Jesus' preaching of the kingdom of heaven from the point of view of the late-Jewish apocalypses, as is often done. It is true, there are supposed to be two main streams distinguishable in the future expectations of the Jews at the beginning of the Christian era, viz., the nationalistic-Messianic and the prophetic-apocalyptic tendency, the *latter* being supposed to represent the matrix of Jesus' world of thought. But already our short survey proves that it is very much an open question whether such a distinction is not much too schematic. Also the apocalyptic expectation of the future occurs, as we have seen, in a great variety of forms, so that it is certainly not possible to speak simply of the "eschatological dogma" of the later Jews. And besides, we must bear in mind that in dealing with his contemporaries Jesus nowhere appeals to these Jewish apocalypses, but always to the whole of the Old Testament.

Consequently, the question as to what Jesus meant by the coming of the kingdom, or what he *cannot* have meant by it, can certainly not be answered from the apocalyptic *sector* of the late Jewish expectation of the future, as is done by Weiss and his followers. The answer is only possible in the light of the synoptic kerygma itself, with a continuous consultation of the references to the Old Testament. All these considerations compel us not to start from a certain eschatological *a priori* in order to judge the historical reliability of the synoptic tradition concerning Jesus' preaching, as if such an *a priori* were a suitable criterion of what Jesus "can" or "cannot" have said in this respect. But quite the other way round, we should investigate the evangelical tradition as the only source of the knowledge of Jesus' preaching as an independent datum.[24] Only in this way do we travel the road of "history." For it may be quite true that Jesus' preaching and the whole course of Christianity started by it cannot be understood as a timeless phenomenon, but only against the background of all kinds of historical "data." But on the other hand, the secret and the miracle implied in the preaching of the kingdom of heaven from the outset do not lie in this relation as such, but *in the entirely new way* in which this preaching was done. That is why every attempt to explain this secret and to find an approach to this miracle will have to concentrate on the peculiar and specific character of this preaching.

Notes to Chapter I

[1] Viz. Ps. 103:19; 145:11,13; Dan. 3:33; these four texts speak of the מַלְכוּת of Jahwe or of the Most High. In Ps. 22:29 and in Ob. 21 the same dominion is indicated as מְלוּכָה, while in 1 Chron. 29:11 there is question of Jahwe's מַמְלָכָה, also in the sense of kingly power and dignity. Except for these seven texts the Old Testament does not apply the abstractum "royal dominion" to Jahwe.

[2] E.g., Ps. 10:16; 24:7-10; 44:5; 47:3; Is. 6:5; 33:22; 43:15; Jer. 10:7.

[3] E.g., 1 Sam. 8:7; Ps. 93:1; 96:10; 97:1; Is. 24:23.

[4] E.g., Ex. 15:18; Deut. 33:5; Num. 23:21; 1 Kings 22:19.

[5] Thus A. Freiherr von Gall: *Basileia tou theou*, 1926, according to this writer this entire thought derives from Parseeism, from which Deutero—Isaiah took it over. But cf. G. Gloege, *Reich Gottes und Kirche im N.T.*, 1929, pp. 5ff.

[6] Cf., e.g., Ex. 15:18; (cf. vss. 11,14); 1 Kings 22:19; Is. 6:5; (cf. vs. 3); Ps. 47:3; 103:19.

[7] Cf., e.g., Num. 23:21; Judges 8:23; 1 Sam. 8:7; 12:12; Ps. 48:3; Is. 41:21; Jer. 8:19; Micah 2:13; cf. also Ex. 19:6.

[8] *TWB* I, p. 567, "basileus"; cf., e.g., Ps. 103:19; 145:11-13ff.

[9] Cf., e.g., J. Ridderbos: *Het Godswoord der profeten*, I, 1930, p. 84; cf. also pp. 76ff.; 252; II, 1932, pp. 331ff.; 352; III, 1938, p. 41; IV, 1941, pp. 193, 293; and Th. C. Vriezen, *Hoofdlijnen van de Theologie van het Oude Testament*, 1949, pp. 139, 173, 174, 176, 291ff.

[10] This is also admitted by R. Otto, *Reich Gottes und Menschensohn*, 1934, p. 28: "When depicting the Day of the Lord and the time of salvation and peace, Israel's prophets already conceive of it as a definite final state, and at the same time they ascribe to it paradisial traits of the miraculous," cf. also Vriezen, *op. cit.*, p. 173.

[11] J. Ridderbos, *op. cit.*, III, p. 21. Cf. also A. H. Edelkoort, *De Christus-verwachting in het Oude Testament*, 1941, p. 157; P. A. Verhoef, *Die vraagstuk van die onvervulde voorsegginge in verband met Jesaja 1-39*, 1950, p. 305.

[12] Thus, e.g., G. Ch. Aalders, *Daniel*, (K.V.), 1928, p. 18.

[13] Cf. also: Von Rad, *op. cit.*, p. 567.

[14] Hence the plural: *toon ouranoon*.

[15] Cf. G. Dalman, *Die Worte Jesu*, I², 1930, pp. 75, 76.

[16] Dalman, *op. cit.*, p. 77; Strack-Billerbeck, *Kommentar zum Neuen Testament aus Talmud und Midrasch*, I, 1922, p. 172; K. G. Kuhn, *TWB*, I, p. 570.

[17] Strack-Billerbeck, *op. cit.*, I, p. 183; Kuhn, *op. cit.*, I, pp. 570, 571.

[18] Cf. also Matt. 11:30.

[19] Thus Gamliel II, (c. 110 A.D.) answered those who gave him as the Bridegroom permission to omit reading the *Shema* in the bridal night: I do not obey you in this matter; I shall not take off the *Malkuth shamaim*, not even for an hour. Cf. Dalman, *op. cit.*, p. 80.

[20] Cf. Strack-Billerbeck, *op. cit.*, I. p. 178.

[21] For what follows see, e.g., E. Schürer, *Geschichte des jüdischen Volkes*, II⁴, 1907, pp. 579ff. R. H. Charles, *A Critical History of the Doctrine of a Future Life in Israel, in Judaism, and in Christianity*², 1913, pp. 167ff.; Strack-Billerbeck, *op. cit.*, IV, 2, 1928, pp. 799ff.; W. O. E. Oesterley, *The Doctrine of the Last Things, Jewish and Christian*, 1908, pp. 65ff. For the texts we refer

16

to e.g. E. Kautzsch, *Die Apokryphen und Pseudepigraphen des Alten Testaments,* 1921.

[22] *Op. cit.,* I, p. 573.

[23] Cf. also, e.g., Delling, *TWB,* III, p. 461, the article on "kairos."

[24] For this see also F. Busch, *Zum Verständnis der synoptischen Eschatologie,* 1938, pp. 29-37.

Chapter II

THE GENERAL CHARACTER
OF THE KINGDOM OF HEAVEN

2. John the Baptist and Jesus

4. *Theocentric*

Before discussing the contents of Jesus' preaching as the proclamation of the great consummation of the history of salvation, it is important to study more closely the general thought, we might perhaps say the general *idea*, lying at the basis of the concept "kingdom of God" or "kingdom of heaven," against the background indicated in the preceding chapter. This expression, it is true, had in a certain sense become a standard phrase. The later Jews used it to denote their expectation of the coming period of salvation. But this fact does not imply that the expression was in itself only interesting as a *terminus technicus*. It rather implied certain thoughts that are extremely important for our understanding of the general character of Jesus' preaching.

This statement holds all the more emphatically, since the concept "kingdom of heaven" occupies such a central position in Jesus' preaching. As a consequence this concept has acquired a very complicated content in Jesus' preaching[1] so that, as we shall see, it is not possible to circumscribe its contents everywhere in the same way. This does not detract from the fact, however, that this comprehensive reality has been described exactly as the "coming of the kingdom." Therefore the idea at the foundation of this concept may be called the prerequisite for the understanding of the whole of Jesus' preaching.

The first thing to do is to establish that there is no material difference between the terms "kingdom of heaven" and "king-

dom of God." Mark alone makes use of the latter combination.
Luke almost invariably uses "the kingdom of God," also in the
absolute sense of "the kingdom," cf. 12:32; 22:29. Matthew,
on the other hand, uses the phrase "the kingdom of God" only
a few times, viz., 12:28; 19:24; 21:31,43. Almost everywhere
else (according to Feine 32 times[2]) he uses "the kingdom of
heaven." There is, however, no reason to attach a different
meaning to these terms. The combination "kingdom of heaven"
is the literal translation of the Hebrew *malkuth shamaim.*
Matthew's almost invariable use of the term "kingdom of
heaven" is connected with the fixed Jewish linguistic usage
in which the name of God was usually avoided. Probably
Jesus (just like John the Baptist) made use of this current combination. On the other hand, it is understandable that Mark
and Luke, who addressed the Christians that were originally
pagan, avoided the specifically Jewish expression, and spoke
in a direct way of the "kingdom of God." It is therefore more
likely that the latter expression is secondary to the former.[3]
At the same time from what has been said, it may be inferred
with a high degree of probability that the repeated efforts to
detect a theological difference in this duality of expression are
due to a misconception. This duality of expression ought to be
understood as identical in meaning, as is being more and more
recognized.[4]

If this view is accepted as established, it is clear that the
great future announced by Jesus is considered entirely from
the standpoint of the divine kingship. And then it is not a
question of a general timeless statement concerning God's
power and reign, but especially of its redemptive-historical
effectuation which will one day be witnessed. That is why
the idea of the coming of the kingdom is pre-eminently the
idea of the kingly self-assertion of God, of his coming to the
world in order to reveal his royal majesty, power and right.
This absolutely theocentric idea of the kingdom of heaven
should always be borne in mind, if we want to have a correct
insight into the general purport of Jesus' preaching. It is the

basic motive of all his preaching. It explains why from the outset the announcement of the fullness of time had a two-fold content both with Jesus and with John the Baptist, namely that of redemption and that of judgment. The one as well as the other is the direct consequence of the plan of God. The kingdom means redemption, because God maintains his royal justice towards those who put their trust in him as his people. And it means judgment because God maintains his royal will in opposition to all who resist his will. This excludes any nationalistic element. It is not in the first place the heathen who are called to repent, but it is Israel. It is the glory of God, not the pre-eminence of the people, which is placed in the center both at the beginning and during the progress of the preaching of the kingdom.

In John the Baptist's preaching this is immediately evident. The announcement of the judgment here is predominant. But it is of an entirely ethical character. Within sight of God's coming the first requirement is conversion. In it nobody can make an appeal to his descent from Abraham. No doubt God will fulfill his promise to Abraham, but any one who wishes to flee from the divine judgment must bring forth fruits meet for repentance. Everything in the announcement of the kingdom is concentrated on the divine "quant a moi" (his own glory), on his self-justification and self-assertion against anything that opposes his kingship.

This theocentric viewpoint is also decisive for Jesus' preaching of the kingdom. It appears very clearly, e.g., from the first three petitions in the Lord's Prayer. The petition for the coming of the kingdom is placed between the other two, i.e., between the one for the hallowing of God's name and the one for the obedience to his will (Matt. 6:9,10). In the first petition the meaning of the coming of the kingdom is described as the effectual inducement of man to do homage to God's virtues ("hallowing his name"). And in accordance with this is the carrying out of his revealed will on earth as it is now done in heaven. The coming of the kingdom is first of all the display of the divine glory, the re-assertion and maintenance of God's rights on earth in their full sense. That is why any anthropocentric and humanistic interpretation of Jesus' preaching, which, e.g., plays such an important part in the so-called liberal theology, has to be rejected. Typical of the latter at the beginning of this century is the influential writing of Harnack, *Das Wesen des Christentums*. In it the kernel and the prevailing motive of Jesus' preaching is sought in the idea of man's being a child of God and the foundational recognition of the infinite value of the individual human soul.[5] It has rightly been observed, also on the part of liberal theology that this thought of the indestructible nobility of man, or that of the essential affinity of the soul with God may be the basis of all soteriological religions outside of Christianity, but that it would be a falsification of Jesus' preaching to seek the fundamental character of his announcement of the kingdom in such a thesis.[6] It is emphatically maintained with good reason that Jesus' preaching is much rather dominated by the conviction that man has *lost* his value and that, notwithstanding, God is willing to accept him, or, as Wendland puts it paradoxically: "It is not the value, but the unworthiness of man in God's eyes . . . which brings man into relation with God."[7] That is why in the thought of God granting remission of sins and being willing to save sinners and not the righteous, Wendland sees the center of Jesus' conception of God.[8]

And yet, however much more profound and more "evangelical" this view may be than the humanistic interpretations of the Gospel, it does not adequately express the "essence" of the idea of the kingdom. An author such as Billerbeck also makes central this soteriological view in his valuable characterization of the idea of the kingdom of heaven. Among other things, he writes as follows: "the emphasis does not lie on the divine dominion trying to accomplish something for God, but on his purpose to save man."[9] Though such a description may be typical of the orthodox Lutheran conception of the gospel, it is not quite in accordance with the theocentric basic motive of the "kingdom of heaven." Also such things as redemption, the remission of sins, the bliss of the kingdom, however much they are in the center of Jesus' preaching, can be understood aright only from the theocentric viewpoint, because they are blessings bestowed by *the kingdom*. In the coming of the kingdom God first and foremost reveals *himself* as the creator and king who does not, abandon the world to perdition but is his people's saviour and promiser. He has solemnly pledged himself to redeem them. This profound, consistently theocentric vision finds the ground of redemption and no less that of judgment in the divine sovereignty, in the maintenance of his own work and word. It is not only the basic motive of the divine revelation appearing again and again in the Old Testament, but it also remains the foundation of the gospel of the kingdom of God on which everything rests in Jesus' evangelical message. All this is not only implied in the original idea of the kingdom of God, but also determines the whole structure and form of Jesus' preaching. Such will be demonstrated in more detail in a separate chapter dealing with the contents of this preaching.[10]

What has been said so far naturally indicates what a wide, or even infinite perspective is opened by the idea of the kingdom of God, precisely because of its being dominated entirely by a theocentric point of view. The idea of the kingdom of God undoubtedly represents a special conception of the dramatic history of salvation within the totality of divine revelation. Other parts of Scripture contain different principles of integration, different dominating conceptions. We should therefore guard against absolutizing one conception at the expense of another. Yet it cannot be denied that the idea of the kingdom *in se* is wider and more universal than, e.g., that of the divine covenant, or that of justification of the sinner through faith, which elsewhere (Deut., Rom., Gal.) summarize and establish the great work of God's redemption. In the conception of the covenant everything is concentrated on the special bond between the Lord and his people and on the virtues of God revealing themselves in it. The thought of the justification of the sinner by faith is an equally important viewpoint for the whole history of revelation, as appears from the way in which Paul writes about it. All these things are also most closely connected with the coming of the kingdom, for the latter is concerned with the effectuation of God's promises to his people. We shall see later on how closely related are the thought of the covenant and that of the kingdom of God, and also, how completely God carries through his plan of salvation in the revelation of his kingdom, notwithstanding human sin and disloyalty. Yet, neither the idea of the covenant, nor that of justification—to mention only these two prominent conceptions—can represent the entire thought of the kingdom of God, at least so long as they are taken in their specific meanings.[11] The idea of the kingdom of God is more comprehensive exactly because it is not only oriented to the redemption of God's people, but to the self-assertion of God in *all* his works. Not only does it place Israel, but also the heathen nations, the world, and even the whole creation, in the wide perspective of the realization of all God's rights and promises.[12]

Here, too, the great importance of Jesus' preaching of the coming kingdom as the beginning, the overture of the New Testament may be found. It at once points out the level at which the decisive stage of the history of salvation, which has now started, is realized. And this theocentric proclamation of the beginning will also remain in force when later on in the New Testament all kinds of different facets of the same process of fulfillment come to the fore. At the end, therefore, we see everything return to the beginning, when the book of Revelation, describing the great final stage of God's work, brings to ever sublimer expression the same theme dominating the overture.

This absolutely theocentric character of the kingdom of God in Jesus' preaching also implies that its coming consists entirely in God's own action and is perfectly dependent on his activity. The kingdom of God is not a state or condition, not a society created and promoted by men (the doctrine of the "social gospel"). It will not come through an immanent earthly evolution, nor through human moral action; it is not men who prepare it for God. All such thoughts mean a hopelessly superficial interpretation of the tremendous thought of the fulness and finality of God's coming as king to redeem and to judge. Viewed from the human standpoint, therefore, the kingdom of heaven is in the first place something to keep praying and waiting for with perseverance. Its coming is nothing less than the great divine break-through, the "rending of the heavens" (Isaiah 64:1), the commencement of the operation of the divine *dunamis* (Mark 9:1). The kingdom of heaven is, therefore, absolutely transcendent in its origin, it is the revelation of God's glory (Matt. 16:27; 24:30; Mark 8:38; 13:26, etc.). That is why the doxology at the end of the Lord's Prayer in many manuscripts ("for *thine* is the kingdom . . . "), although not originally there, is still the most appropriate formula conceivable to conclude the "prayer of the kingdom." The kingdom is not only concerned with God, it also originates with him. Its coming is only to be understood on the basis of his miraculous and all-powerful action.

5. *Dynamical*

Closely connected with the above exposition is the fact that the idea of the kingdom of God has a strongly dynamic connotation. We have seen that the Old Testament most often speaks of its coming as the coming of a person. The same observation holds for Jesus' use of the word *basileia*. Until now we have translated it as *kingdom* (in accordance with current linguistic usage), but in Greek it may mean both king*ship*, kingly *dominion*, and king*dom*. There is no doubt that the former sense, especially that of *dominion* as the exercise of royal dignity, is the most prominent usage of the word in various central pronouncements about the "kingdom of heaven" in the gospels. The spatial meaning of kingdom is then a secondary one. When the text says that the *basileia toon ouranoon* "is at hand" (Matt. 3:2; 4:17, etc.); "is nigh at hand" (Luke 21:31); "cometh" or "is coming" (Luke 17:20; Mark 11:10); "should appear," (Luke 19:11); or "may come," (Matt. 6:10), we should not in the first place think of a spatial or a static entity, which is descending from heaven; but rather of the divine kingly rule actually and effectively starting its operation; therefore, we should think of the Divine *action* of the king. The well-known passage of Matthew 11:12 and of parallel texts very characteristially speak of the arrival of the *basileia* as "a powerful breaking-through and a pushing its way,"[13] and Mark 9:1 speaks of the kingdom "coming with power."

On the basis of this meaning of the word *basileia* it has rightly been said that there is a *personal* connotation in the expression "the kingdom of heaven."[14] The manifestation of the kingdom of heaven cannot be conceived as an impersonal metaphysical event, but as the coming of God himself as king. This conception is borne out by a whole series of parables about the kingdom of God. A definite person always stands in the center in these parables, and his action demonstrates the meaning of the kingdom. This person is often no other than God or the Son acting in his name and according to his instruction. Thus, e.g., in the parable of the man who had sowed good seed in his field (Matt. 13:24ff); of the king who would take account of his servants (Matt. 18:23ff); of the man who hired laborers in his vineyard (Matt. 20:1ff); of a certain householder who planted a vineyard (Matt. 21:33ff); of a certain king who made a marriage feast for his son (Matt. 22:1ff); of a man travelling into a far country, who called his own servants and delivered unto them his goods, and later returned (Matt. 25:14ff). In all these parables the *tertium comparationis* is again and again to be found in that which the chief character in the parable has done, resolved, ordained, while the purport of all this is that God will *act* likewise at the coming of the kingdom.

But this viewpoint should not be absolutized, however important and essential it may be for the understanding of the general idea of the kingdom of heaven. It is true, some authors have refused to assign to the expression *basileia* in this combination any other sense than that of *dominion,* and have rejected translating it by means of the word "kingdom."[15] In our opinion this position is untenable, for the reason that in the nature of the case a dominion to be effective must create or maintain a territory where it can operate. So the absence of any idea of a spatial kingdom would be very strange. Moreover in John's and in Jesus' preaching there are clearly some other facets beside that of the irresistible motive power of the coming kingdom. There is also the question of the consummation of the kingdom as *a state* of peace and happiness in which the blessed shall "sit down with Abraham, Isaac and Jacob" (Matt. 8:11); "eat bread" (Luke 14:15); "drink of the fruit of the vine" (Matt. 26:29, cf. 22:1ff). The kingdom is represented as *an order of things* in which there will be "superiors and inferiors" (Matt. 5:19; 11:11; 18:1,4); as an imperial *order* in which the king sits on his throne and his ministers to his right and left (Matt. 20:21); in which the righteous shall shine, and from which the wicked shall be cast away (Matt. 13:43). In another passage the conception seems to be rather that of a certain *spiritual atmosphere* which is internally alien to one, or for which one may be fit (Luke 9:62; Mark 12:34). The kingdom is occasionally denoted as a certain *good* that ought to be "sought," on account of the salvation it implies (Matt. 6:33; cf. 7:7; 13:14); a *gift* from the Heavenly Father (Luke 12:32), allotted to some (Matt. 5:3,10; 19:14), and "taken away" from others (Matt. 21:43); a gift that can be "inherited," "taken possession of," "taken by force" (Matt. 25:34; 11:12); and that is being "prepared" by God for his chosen people (Matt. 20:23; 25:34, etc.). All these passages prove the great variety of conceptions and also the fact that the meaning of the kingdom should not be forcibly narrowed down by absolutizing a certain sense or facet of the kingdom at the expense of others.

This does not detract from the fact that the kingdom of heaven preached by John and Jesus is first of all a process of a dynamic character; in the first place, because it cannot for a moment be thought of apart from the divine power manifested by it in redemption and judgment; secondly, because in John's and Jesus' preaching the coming and the break-through of the kingdom are put in the foreground, and not the state of things at the time of fulfillment. This tremendous dynamic of the divine coming which sets the world of the angels in motion (Matt. 1; Luke 2); fills the devil's empire with alarm (Matt. 4:3ff; Mark 1:24; Matt. 12:29); yes, even causes Satan to fall from heaven (Luke 10:18), permeates and transmits itself in everything and in all who are touched by it. For the coming of the kingdom is the initial stage of the great drama of the history of the end. It throws man and the world into a crisis. It is this fact which lends such an insistent and also ominous power to the call: "Repent, for the kingdom of heaven is at hand." Especially the Baptist's preaching gives expression to it in such an unmistakable way: "the axe is laid at the root of the trees," "he that cometh after me . . . his fan is in his hand" (Matt. 3:10-12). That is why Jesus is able to say that he has not come to bring peace on earth, but a sword (Matt. 10:34); he even says that he has come to send fire on the earth (Luke 12:49ff). In all this and at the back of it is always the thought that the coming of the kingdom will be full of power and energy. It confronts man with the necessity of making all-important decisions that will rule his whole existence. Its coming should rouse everybody from their false rest and complacency.

6. Messianic

The Old Testament tradition of the coming manifestation of God as king and that of the Jews in Jesus' days prove the close connection between the idea of the coming kingdom of God and that of a future personality which in a general way may be indicated as the Messiah. No doubt, he is announced and described in all kinds of ways and only rarely explicitly called by the name "Messiah." Nevertheless, the expectation of the Messiah may be said to be one of the most essential associations evoked by the concept of the kingdom of heaven.

As soon as we have crossed the threshold of the New Testament, this thought is confirmed. For the introduction to the gospel according to Luke contains the thought of the kingdom of God and the restoration of Israel in the form of the announcement of the Messiah-King (Luke 1:32,33—the angel's message to Mary). Also, Mary's hymn points to the divine grace shown to her (of the privilege of being the Messiah's mother) as evidence of God's pity on his people (the thought of the kingdom of God), Luke 1:50ff. And Zacharias also praises the Lord who has visited and redeemed his people that they should be saved from their enemies (the kingdom of God) by raising up an horn of salvation for them in the house of David (Messiah), Luke 1:68ff. The thoughts of Messiah and that of the kingdom are merged here. Also the angel's announcement of Christ's birth in the city of David and the angels' song (Luke 2:9-14), are clearly determined by this context. It is true the angels' hymn does not mention the coming of the kingdom of God explicitly. But the proclamation of "glory (*doxa*) to God in the highest," and that of the eschatological "peace on earth" are nothing but a summary of the future bliss that will be realized in and by the coming of the kingdom.

It should be noted that in all these utterances both the idea of the kingdom and the announcement of the Messiah have assumed a *national* form in many respects. Messiah's kingly reign over the house of Jacob, however, will be eternal, his kingdom will never end. He will be begotten by the Holy spirit (Luke 1:33-35). All these traits—and also the events of the Christmas night—are indications of the supernatural character of the Messiah and of his kingship.

John the Baptist's preaching confirms this coincidence of the kingdom of God and the Messiah. For John announces the kingdom of heaven by pointing to the person of him whom he describes as: "He that cometh after me" who "is mightier than I, whose shoes I am not worthy to bear." In itself this announcement of "him that cometh after me" is rather vague. Also later John speaks of "the Coming One" (Matt. 11:3; Luke 7:19). It has been suggested that John had clearly spoken of the Messiah before[16] so that he could suffice with a general indication now. In our opinion this is much to be doubted. This vague indication will much rather have to be considered as characteristic of John's messianic preaching and expectation. It is in accordance with the supernatural and divine character of the person and the work of "him that cometh." Who and what he is, is so exalted and mysterious that it is only possible to speak of his person in a general way.[17] It may not for a moment be doubted that John saw the Messiah in him.[18] Nor is there any doubt possible that John's description of the Messiah's importance passes far beyond the nationalistic Messiah-ideal, and is entirely dominated by the thought of the transcendent and universal judgment which will attend the appearance of the coming king. John calls it "the wrath to come" (Matt. 3:7), which indicates the last judgment.[19] The same thought is expressed by the words: "the axe is laid unto the root of the trees" (Matt. 3:10, Luke 3:9), and that he whose herald and way-maker John is, has his fan in his hand and will thoroughly purge his floor; he will gather his wheat into the garner, but he will burn up the chaff with unquenchable fire (Matt. 3:12; Luke 3:17). All this points to the final, world-wide judgment entrusted to him who is coming, a judgment to which not only the heathen will be subjected, but also all Israel. John's conception of the Messiah's coming may also appear from his announcement of the baptism with the Spirit and with fire (Matt. 3:11; Luke 3:26)[20], with which he that was to come after John, would baptize, in contradistinction to John's baptizing with water. By baptism with the Holy Spirit and with fire we are not to understand the same thing, i.e., that the fire would refer to the sanctifying burning away done by the Spirit in a sinner's heart.[21] In these two metaphors we are confronted with a two-fold meaning of the coming of the kingdom: those that are to be saved will be given an over-powering measure of the Spirit's operation, and those that will be lost will be abandoned to the fire, i.e., to perdition (cf. also Matt. 3:10,12).[22] Salvation and perdition are the two stages into which the tremendous future will diverge according to the prophecies: first the descent of the Holy Spirit, and then the day of judgment (cf. Joel 2:28-32; Ezek. 36:26ff; Zech. 12:9,10).[23] In a modified sense the same thing is found in the pre-Christian pseudepigraphic apocalypses, which explicitly describe the coming of the Messiah from this twofold view-point.[24]

All this proves, first, that John the Baptist's preaching con-cerning the coming of the kingdom is accompanied by the announcement of the Messiah; and in the second place that this messianic thought is not clothed in a national garb (as in Luke's introduction), but must be taken in a transcendent-eschatological sense. It does not seem to have been oriented to those prophecies and expectations that restricted their per-spective of the future to the restoration of Israel and to its deliverance from its enemies, but rather described the great future in prophetic-apocalyptic colors as a universal cosmic event, as the end of this world and the beginning of a future world. That is why "he that cometh" described by John is set in this light.

Moreover, Jesus' preaching of the kingdom is a revelation concerning the Messiah. This connection can only be estab-lished completely if the whole of Jesus' messianic self-revelation is traced in the gospels. However, such a demonstration falls outside of the scope of the present chapter, which is only in-tended as a discussion of the general character of the kingdom of heaven preached by John and Jesus. We restrict ourselves to those pronouncements in Jesus' preaching that connect the coming and the significance of the Messiah with that of the kingdom.

First, then, it is remarkable that in the synoptic gospels

Jesus himself speaks of the Christ only sporadically. The passage which is especially important in this connection is Matthew 24:5 (cf. vs. 23ff; Mark 13:21). Here Jesus warns his disciples against people who will pass themselves off as the Christ. He does so in answer to a question about what is the sign of his *parousia* and of "the consummation of the world." Here, too, we find the thought of the coming of the kingdom correlated with that of the appearance of the Christ. In most cases, however, Jesus does not speak of the Christ, but of the Son of Man. It may be said, therefore, that the messianic character of the kingdom of heaven preached by Jesus is determined by the central place occupied by the "Son of Man" in the coming of the kingdom.

It is hardly necessary to adduce proof for the latter statement. "Kingdom of God" and "the Son of Man" are correlates in Jesus' preaching. The "coming of the Son of Man" (Matt. 10:23) is synonymous with the "coming of the kingdom of God," as appears from a comparison of Matthew 16:18 and Mark 9:1. This explains texts speaking of "the kingdom of the Son of Man" (Matt. 13:41; 16:28); of the "Son of Man" "sitting in the throne of his glory in the regeneration" (Matt. 19:28); of "the coming" (parousia) Matt. 24:27ff; "the days" (Luke 17:22); "the day" (Luke 17:24); "the sign of the Son of Man" (Matt. 24:30); "when the Son of Man shall come in his glory" (Matt. 25:31), and also of "the sitting of the Son of Man on the right hand of power and coming in the clouds of heaven" (Matt. 26:64). His glory is that of the Father and of the holy angels (Luke 9:26). All these indications only describe the coalescence of the coming of the kingdom and that of the Son of Man. It is he who has to accomplish the coming of the kingdom and to carry out the divine judgment, and in whose hands, therefore, all authority has been placed.

The correlation between the concepts "kingdom of heaven" and "Son of Man" is especially important for the definition of the general character of the kingdom of heaven. It proves that to a great extent Jesus' preaching is oriented to the prophecy in Daniel 7:13ff.[25]   In this prophecy there appears the figure of the "Son of Man" as coming in the clouds of heaven to the "Ancient of days," and as he to whom was given dominion, and glory, and the kingship that was to comprise all the nations and was to have an eternal and imperishable significance.   In this prophecy, as indeed in all Daniel's visions, the universality and transcendent character of the coming kingdom are very prominent.   The "Son of Man" is, consequently, not simply an ordinary man invested with temporal and earthly dominion.   But in the great eschatological drama he is the man who has been given unlimited divine authority, and to whom God's universal royal dominion has been entrusted.   The figure of the "Son of Man" does not only occur in this sense in Daniel's prophecy (Chapter 7), but also in the book of Enoch and in the apocalypse of Ezra.   In all these places the figure of the great future in whom God's kingdom will be realized appears to have an importance far transcending that of a national Israelite king or of a human offshoot of the house of David.   He has been invested with a supernatural and divine dignity.   It is this dignity and authority of which Jesus speaks before the Sanhedrin when he warns them of the coming of the Son of Man.   This dignity, described in similar words as in Daniel 7, is that of which Jesus speaks after his resurrection: "All power is given unto me in heaven and in earth" (Matt. 28:18).

It is clear that this supernatural and universal significance of the "Son of Man" to a great extent determines the character of the kingdom of heaven preached by Jesus.   It is beyond cavil that all this is also implied in the *messianic* character of the kingdom of heaven.   In other words, within the scope of the gospel and that of the Jewish expectation of the future it appears that this "Son of Man" is the Messiah.   It is true that some authors want to distinguish between two rival figures in the later Jewish expectation of the future, viz., between the Messiah and the Son of Man.   The former is supposed to represent the prophetic-national ideal of a king, the latter that of the transcendent-apocalyptic judge of the world. And going back into the time before the gospels, some writers have applied the above-mentioned distinction to the preaching of John the Baptist and that of Jesus. According to Von Gall both Jesus and John rejected the prophetic expectations of the Messiah, and in its place they adhered to the belief in the apocalyptic figure of the Son of Man described in Daniel and Enoch. After Jesus' death his followers are then supposed to have ascribed to him both the dignity of the Messiah and that of the Son of Man. And this is the reason why in the gospels—the product of the later Church—there is a confused mixture of these two different characters.[26] This whole construction is based on the gratuitous hypothesis of two mutually exclusive and competitive forms of the Jewish expectation of the future. But even if they had really existed among the people, any indication of John the Baptist and Jesus accepting this antithesis is lacking. For the two types of the expectation of the future which are placed side by side, or with Von Gall, opposite to each other, is not only found in the late Jewish literature, but it has its background in the Old Testament itself. In the Old Testament there is the figure of the Messiah, the king, of the house of David, and of the Son of Man. If we are to accept Von Gall's hypothesis, Jesus and John the Baptist would really have rejected the far greater part of the Old Testament prophetic expectation of the future. They would have to be judged as radical spiritual revolutionaries, not only in the forum of some of their contemporaries, but also in that of the entire divine historical revelation. This construction is not only in conflict with everything we know from the gospels—the only source of our knowledge of the life of Jesus—but it also renders the whole history of Christianity unintelligible. In opposition to the most characteristic trait of Jesus' doctrine and expectation of the future, his followers would then have applied to him the Messiah-ideal which he himself had rejected, not only in its nationalistic sense but also as the *Messiah-ideal* in general.

In contrast with this, however, the testimony of the gospels that Jesus' preaching of the kingdom was dominated by the identity of the Messiah and the Son of Man is a great deal more plausible even on the basis of these general historical considerations.   Later on we shall see that in Jesus' self-revelation not only these two motives flow together but also others, such as that of the suffering servant of Isaiah 53.   In this respect, too, his preaching of the kingdom is the fulfillment of the Scriptures in the full sense of the word.   In this light we must see the undoubted prominence of the term "the Son of Man" in Jesus' preaching of the kingdom.   This does not imply the supersession of the old "prophetic Messianism," but is rather an indication of the supernatural and divine importance to be ascribed to the promised Son of David in the light of the entire prophecy.

That Jesus did not exclusively base his message on Daniel's vision but on the whole of the Old Testament Word of God, is very clear from the remarkable conversation between Jesus and the Pharisees about the Son of David, handed down to us by all three synoptic gospels (Matt. 22:41-46; Mark 12:35-37ª; Luke 20:41-44).   Here the Pharisees are officially and openly confronted with the question: "What do you think of the Christ? Whose son is he"? (Matt. 22:42).   And in reply to the answer of the Pharisees, "the Son of David," Jesus quotes what David, inspired by the Holy Spirit said about the Messiah: "The Lord said unto my Lord, Sit thou on my right hand, till I make thine enemies thy footstool."   And he concludes with the question: "If David then calls him Lord, how is he his son?"   This passage is often quoted to prove that Jesus (or the later Church) wanted to deny the Davidic descent of the Messiah.   But this opinion is undoubtedly wrong.[27]   Jesus does not reject the Old Testament testimony of the Messiah being the son of David. He wants to bring out the meaning of this Davidic kingship of the Messiah in the light of the entire Old Testament.   He apparently opposes *that* interpretation of the Davidic sonship of the Messiah according to which the latter was invested with a human-national kingship for the liberation of the Jewish nation. Jesus opposes this view by insisting on David's own prophetic testimony concerning the divine and entirely super-human kingship of the Messiah. The Messiah will receive the divine dominion and be invested with superhuman honor and power, so that even David, his father, speaks of him as his "Lord." This passage is not concerned with (the refutation of) the Davidic kingship of the Messiah, but with its importance and character. It is clear that the words about it in Psalm 110:1 are entirely in accordance with the picture Daniel 7 draws of the authority of the Son of Man. That is why Jesus quotes Psalm 110:1. This is not saying that wherever in the Old Testament the Messiah, as the Son of David, is mentioned, this divine, superhuman and universal character of his king-ship is expressed in clear words. Jesus' preaching, however, is intended to make the prophecies concerning the Davidic Messiah-King and those concerning the Son of Man from Daniel 7 understood in their deeper unity. It is not to be denied that he thus came into conflict with the nationalistic Messiah-ideal. Again and again we see that Jesus' messianic preaching was foreign to the people and their leaders and came into conflict with them. In this sense we shall have to understand Jesus' warning against the false messianic rumors: "Behold he is in the desert"; "behold, he is in the secret chambers" (Matt. 24:26; cf. Luke 17:23).

In contrast to this, Jesus makes the coming, the *parousia* of the Son of Man "like lightning shining out of one part of heaven unto the other part," i.e., revealing his divine glory, un-mistakably to those who shall see him.[28] Here, too, is the connection of the expectation of the Messiah with that of the great eschatological manifestation of his glory. But it is the Messiah-King, promised by God to Israel, of whom Jesus here speaks. For the special bond between Israel and the figure of the future that has thus been outlined is always maintained. This appears very clearly in Matthew 19:28, e.g., where Jesus promises his disciples that in *the palingenesis* when the *Son of Man* shall sit on the throne of his glory, they, too, shall sit on thrones in order to judge the twelve tribes of Israel (cf. Luke 22:30). Here the references to the *palingenesis* (the regeneration of all things) and to the Son of Man on his throne indicate the universal and superhuman character of the Messianic kingship, whereas in the "judgment of the twelve tribes of Israel" the bond with Israel has been maintained.[29] This makes it clear that both the so-called "prophetic" and the "apocalyptic" expectations of the Messiah go together in Jesus' preaching. The Son of Man is none other than the Messiah, the Son of David.[30] But, conversely, the Son of David is the Son of Man, he who has been invested with divine and universal authority. And the relation between Israel and the Messiah must be judged and understood in this light.

We can therefore draw the conclusion that Jesus' preaching of the kingdom of heaven is at the same time the preaching of the Messiah. And also that this Messiahship is especially defined by the term "the son of Man," according to Daniel 7. It is in this light that we must understand the general character of the kingdom of heaven preached by Jesus.

7. *Future*

What has been said in the preceding section about the messianic character of the kingdom of heaven preached by Jesus clearly reveals the eschatological determination of Jesus' preaching. It is true that this expression is, terminologically speaking, far from irreproachable, for it derives from dogmatics, and in this sense (viz., as eschato-*logy*) it is not applicable to the undogmatic and unsystematic preaching of Jesus. However, this word has in a way become current as a qualification of the factual contents of Jesus' preaching. It may be used insofar as it expresses that the coming of the kingdom preached by Jesus was in its fulfillment nothing less than the beginning of the great *eschaton* of history. In this respect there can be no doubt that Jesus' announcement of the future was not in the stream of the Jewish nationalistic expectations found, e.g., in the *Psalms of Solomon*. It must much rather be viewed as the continuation of the transcendent and apocalyptic predictions of the future in the prophecies of the Old Testament and the expectations based on the latter.

No further argument is needed after what has been said about the meaning of "the coming wrath" and of the appearance of "him who cometh," to show that Jesus, in this respect, could start from the preaching of his predecessor John the Baptist. In Jesus' own preaching the description of this future is elaborated from many points of view. It is not restricted to the last judgment as is true of John's preaching as recorded, nor to the *parousia* of the Son of Man. But it speaks in various ways of what will happen as a consequence of the beginning of the kingdom itself. This is the sense in which, for example, the future tenses of the Beatitudes are to be understood (Matt. 5:3ff). In them Jesus describes the bliss of the kingdom of heaven as the inheritance of the [new[31]] earth, as being filled with the divine righteousness,[32] as the seeing of God,[33] as the manifestation of the children of God, all of these expressions pointing beyond the order of this world to the state of bliss and perfection that shall be revealed in the future world.[34] This eschatological (referring to the end of time) character of the kingdom of God preached by Jesus is one of the chief presuppositions of the whole of his *kerygma,* and the references to it are like a golden thread interwoven with the whole texture of the Gospel. In this sense we must conceive of the state of moral perfection for which Jesus teaches his disciples to pray, and which is now only found in heaven (Matt. 6:10). Jesus refers to this glorious future in places like Matthew 7:21, when speaking of the entry into the kingdom of heaven; of sitting down with Abraham, Isaac and Jacob in the kingdom of heaven (Matt. 8:11, cf. Luke 13:28,29); of the righteous as shining forth as the sun in the kingdom of their Father (Matt. 13:43); of the coming of the Son of Man in his kingdom (Matt. 16.28); of the coming of the kingdom with power (Mark 9:1); of the sitting on his right hand in his kingdom (Matt. 20:21, cf. Mark 10:37); of those on his right hand inheriting the kingdom on the day of judgment (Matt. 25:34); of the drinking of new wine by Christ in his Father's kingdom (Matt. 26:29, cf. Mark 14:25, Luke 22:18). It is difficult to deny that these passages, and many others, speak of another reality—an "eschatological" reality. This is confirmed by those pronouncements in which Jesus speaks about the future reality as of "the end of the world" (*sunteleia tou aioonos*) (Matt. 13:49), "regeneration" (*paligenesia*) (Matt. 19:28), "eternal life" (*zooè aioonios*) (Matt. 19:29). Of this latter He says that it will be given "in the future world" (*en tooi aiooni tooi erchomenooi*). The same contrast of this world and that of the future is also meant when Jesus speaks of "the children of this world" (*oi huioi tou aioonos toutou*), and "the children of the resurrection" (*tès anastaseoos huioi*) (Luke 20:36), because the entry into the kingdom and the sharing the salvation of the great future are preceded by the resurrection. Such utterances are scattered throughout the Gospel. They show that the future eschatological vision does not form a mere setting or enclosure of Jesus' preaching. No more is it to be chiefly restricted to the so-called synoptic apocalypse (Matt. 24:4-36; Mark 13:5-37; Luke 21:8-36). But it is an essential element in his preaching of the kingdom of heaven. In this respect there can be no doubt that the eschatological interpretation of the gospel is justified insofar as it opposes the immanence-thought of the ethical and the liberal theology. It emphatically defends the transcendent and future character of the kingdom of heaven preached by Jesus.

Taken in this sense, the kingdom preached by Jesus bears the character of a consummation, although many attempts have been made to relegate this character to the background as much as possible and thus to deprive it of its power. The older liberal theology, as we have seen, used the form-content scheme for this purpose. Jesus' eschatological pronouncements were supposed to be merely the formal setting of the real essence of his preaching: the kingdom of heaven as a religious-ethical entity. Partly no doubt as a reaction to the exaggeration of the eschatological interpretation Dodd has recently modified the liberal view in the sense of a so-called *realized eschatology*. In it Jesus is nowhere supposed to have spoken of the future of the kingdom, and to have made the entire eschatology of the kingdom of God into a matter of spiritual and present experience.[35]

Of course, Dodd cannot deny that according to the gospels Jesus did speak about the future. Dodd considers such pronouncements partly to be predictions of coming *historical* events, such as, e.g., Jesus' passion and death, the persecution of his disciples, the sufferings and the fall of the Jewish nation. Insofar as these predictions are really attributable to Jesus himself (and not to the later Church as predictions after the event, i.e., *vaticinia ex eventu*), according to Dodd they prove nothing against the basic thesis that Jesus only preached the presence of the kingdom. They only prove that the break-through of salvation could only take place in the way of a crisis in which Jesus had to sacrifice his own life and the Jewish people had to undergo their punishment. All this, however, has its place within the realized kingdom and does not in any way presuppose a future kingdom.[36] In these prophecies there is no "eschatology of salvation" in the sense of a further revelation of the kingdom of God on earth. By their side we also find the expectation of an apocalyptic, extra-historical future in the gospel, according to Dodd. But this future is not supposed to relate to the coming of the kingdom, but only to that of "the day of the Son of Man" as a future apocalyptic event. Dodd also feels that such prophecies are only for a very small part to be ascribed to Jesus' preaching, and are derived from other sources. Nevertheless, Jesus seems to have spoken of such apocalyptic events at times. These pronouncements are difficult to connect with the historical references. Apparently there are two tendencies in Jesus' preaching which defy harmonization: the ethical tendency, which takes no account of the end, and the eschatological-apocalyptic. The latter will have to be explained as *symbolical* utterances if they are to be harmonized with the rest. The eternal order of the kingdom has come, a future kingdom is not to be expected, but its meaning is so absolute that temporal experience cannot exhaust it. This idea is expressed in a symbolic way by the eschatological pronouncements.[37]

The above shows that notwithstanding the restrictions he applies to Jesus' eschatological-future utterances, Dodd's critical adaptations of the gospel cannot disprove that such pronouncements play a more or less important role in Jesus' preaching. And, in our opinion, this circumstance invalidates Dodd's entire construction of Jesus' having only spoken of a realized eschatology of the kingdom of heaven. For it is impossible to separate the passages concerning "the day of the Lord" and "the future of the Son of Man" from those concerning the "kingdom of heaven." Even if one were willing to agree with the hypercritical operations that Dodd applies to the gospel, the separation of what he is ready to recognize as Jesus' apocalyptic pronouncements from those about the coming of *the kingdom* remains unacceptable.[38] For there can be no doubt that all the future apocalyptic events mentioned in the gospel are only to be conceived as attendant circumstances within the framework of the advent of the *kingdom*.

But apart from this insurmountable objection, Dodd's main thesis to the effect that the gospel does not speak of the future of the kingdom but only of its presence is untenable. For demonstration of this it is important to indicate accurately the pronouncements explicitly mentioning this future aspect.

First of all, we would refer to the initial proclamation both on the part of John the Baptist and that of Jesus, which we have already quoted a number of times: "the kingdom is at hand" (*èggiken*). Dodd has very ably defended the thesis that this "is at hand" should be rendered by "has come." He wants to translate *èggiken* in Mark 1:15 and Matthew 4:17 in the same way as *ephthasen* in Matthew 12:28 and Luke 11:20. He appeals to the Septuagint which sometimes has *eggizein* for the Hebrew *naga^c* and the Aramaic *mĕta*, both of which mean "reach," "arrive." These two verbs, however, are also rendered by *phthanein*. From this it would follow that there is no difference in meaning intended between *ephthasen* (has come) in Matthew 12:28 and *"èggiken"* in Mark 1:15 and Matthew 4:17.[39] A closer investigation has proved, however, that *eggizein* in the usage of the Septuagint nearly always means "to approach" and not "to come," and can have the wider sense of "to arrive" only now and then, while secular Greek lacks any example of this. In addition, it would be very strange for the same evangelist to use first one verb, then another for such a central concept, and to have placed the very unusual *èggiken* in the foreground. Finally, we should have to assume that in his initial proclamation already (cf. Matt. 3:2), John the Baptist has spoken of the presence of the kingdom, which, however, is in conflict with the entire purport of this proclamation as well as with John's conception of the kingdom.[40] That is why Matthew 4:17 should undoubtedly be translated in the same way as Matthew 3:2, by "is at hand." In both places then the coming of the kingdom is meant as a future event.

No less clearly is the future of the kingdom spoken of in the well-known passage of Mark 9:1, where Jesus says: "Verily I say unto you, that there be some of them that stand here, which shall not taste of death, till they have seen the kingdom of God come with power." The parallel text in Luke (9:27) simply has "till they see the Kingdom of God," whereas Matthew says "till they see the Son of Man come in his kingdom" (i.e., kingly majesty) (16:28). Though Mark 9:1 offers some difficulties with reference to the indication of time, it cannot be denied that it refers to the kingdom that is still to be expected, as appears from the *en dunamei* and from the parallel text in Matthew. The kingdom is spoken of here as a future reality. In order to escape such a conclusion Dodd translates: "until they have seen that the kingdom of God has come with power," and explains this "seen" as "awake to the fact" that the kingdom of God has come. It is beyond dispute, however, that *idein* in this text does not denote something that has already come, but rather the awareness of what is still to come, as very clearly appears from Matthew's version which uses the present participle (*erchomenon*).[41]

This passage is not an isolated one. In other places, as well, the kingdom of heaven is spoken of as an entirely future reality. We only mention, e.g., Matthew 8:11: "many shall come from the east and west, and shall sit down with Abraham, Isaac and Jacob in the kingdom of heaven." The same thing applies to Matthew 26:29 (cf. Mark 14:25; Luke 22:18) where Jesus declares that he "will not drink henceforth of this fruit of the vine, until that day when (he) drink(s) it new with you in (his) Father's kingdom," or, in Luke's slightly different version: "until the kingdom of God shall have come." Dodd thinks that these passages (except Luke's version which he calls secondary) are no answer to the question as to whether Jesus expected, or did not expect, a further or nearer "coming" of the kingdom apart from what had already happened during his own ministry. In the passages mentioned, one should not suppose that there is talk of any further "coming" of the kingdom in this world, but rather, of a transcendent order of things outside space and time.[42]

However, it is this transcendent order in Luke 22:18— whether as a secondary source or not does not matter; the evangelist's interpretation is in any case more authentic than that of modern science—that has been indicated as the coming of the kingdom. Nor can it mean an eternally present heavenly state, but exactly the anticipated break-through of the kingdom of God on earth. It is no doubt correct to say that this order is not of a temporal-earthly character, but is the order of the new heaven and the new earth. But this coming manifestation of the kingdom cannot be eliminated from Jesus' preaching on the ground of his "presence pronouncements." On the contrary, it is the great presupposition and the lasting perspective of his entire preaching.

There can be no doubt that in Jesus' preaching the great future perspective has been maintained. So every conception that the kingdom of heaven is an exclusively religious-ethical good, a spiritual community or a social order within the limits of this world is in open conflict with the gospel. To this we must add that this expectation of the future bears a universal and realistic character, and that it is not permissible somehow to sublimate this "eschatology of the kingdom of God." Here we have to oppose especially those who, while they lay great emphasis on the eschatological character of the kingdom of God preached by Jesus, nevertheless by their "theological exegesis" deprive the evident meaning of the pronouncements concerning its future of their power. This is done by the above-mentioned interpretations[43] which assert that the nearness or the future of the kingdom should not be conceived in a linear-temporal sense but as the expression of the fact that human existence is related to God's reality from moment to moment. It is by no means rare for such views to speak of the "mythological" character of the New Testament conceptions, supposedly derived from the late Jewish apocalypse. Insofar as they refer to the great cosmic upheaval, the collapse of the world, the struggle between God and Satan, they owe their existence to the influence of the dualistic Persian religion. But for modern man they only have value insofar as they are forms of expression of certain religious thoughts.

In like manner the fathers of the eschatological movement, Weiss and Schweitzer, tried to connect the eschatological character of the Gospel with their modern world-outlook. In recent times it is especially Bultmann who has demanded the *Entmythologisierung* (de-mythologization) of the New Testament.[44] Thus Bultmann speaks of Jesus' eschatological preaching as meaning that human existence is placed in the crisis of decision (*Entscheidung*). Dibelius formulates it as the "actualization" and the "elevation to what is unconditional" imparted to Jesus' words under the impression of his eschatological expectation. Otto mentions the idea of "sanctity" as the secret motive power in the formation of eschatological conceptions.

In opposition to this we must point out two things. In the first place the insight, repeatedly expressed of late, that the conception of time cannot be eliminated from the eschatological preaching of the kingdom of heaven without impairing the latter must be recognized.[45] The coming of the kingdom is the consummation of history, not in the sense of the end of the natural development, but in that of the fulfillment of the time appointed for it by God (Mark 1:15); and of what *must* happen before it. This latter formula is characteristic of the eschatological preaching (cf. Rev. 1:1), also of that of Jesus' (cf. Matt. 17:10; 24:6; Mark 13:10; Luke 24:44). The coming events are not only represented as an irresistible fate, but as the course of the history of salvation ordained according to God's counsel.[46] This proves that the coming of the kingdom must not only be conceived in a spatial-vertical sense (cf. Rev. 1:10) but also in a temporal-horizontal sense. This is why the sublimation of the concept eschatology (i.e., the substitution of the *übergeschichtliche* conception for that of the *endgeschichtliche*) is a misrepresentation of the central fact that history has been included in God's great work of salvation. This fact is evident in the whole of the biblical eschatology as well as in Jesus' preaching. Any efforts to eliminate Jesus' pronouncements on the expected end of this world from the gospel are in conflict with the undeniable testimony of synoptic tradition, for in various ways the latter speaks of the future that will follow *after the expiration of time*. But it is also in conflict with the factual prophetic-eschatological character of Jesus' preaching. The future of the kingdom is not only concerned with the individual "decision" of man in the face of the Divine reality, but with the consummation of the divine work in history as well as with respect to history. This is why the practical-existential meaning of the preaching of the coming kingdom is not only expressed by the categories of "conversion," "decision," *Entscheidung*, but no less also in those of "patience," "perseverance," "vigilance" and "faithfulness." This is expressed in various ways in the parables of the kingdom that we shall discuss later on.[47] All this holds not only in opposition to the conceptions advanced by Bultmann,

Dodd, and others, who consider the whole eschatological concept of the future merely as a mythological or symbolical indication of man's immediate relatedness to the divine reality which has no "posterior" or "anterior."[48] But *mutatis mutandis* it is also opposed to Delling's expositions according to which all other *temporal* perspectives have been relativized by the consummation brought about by the coming of Christ. In this context Delling only speaks of the "after-effect" of the eschatological consciousness,[49] and of the victory[50] and even the cancellation[51] of time by eternity which has penetrated into time with Christ. It is true, the motive of consummation is extremely important for the entire preaching of Jesus as well as for the expectation of the future. But the *pleroma* that has come with Christ in no way cancels the future-eschatological character of the kingdom preached by Jesus and of the salvation to be expected by the faithful. Also from the standpoint of the "fulfillment in Christ" the kingdom is conceived as being future, and the state of a Christian as that of an heir of future goods. Therefore the category of time is maintained as subject and subservient to the divine plan of salvation. It is not the victory over time but over that which opposes the consummation of the divine work in time which is the fruit of the *pleroma* which started with Christ. Therefore Cullmann can rightly say: "It is, therefore, characteristic of the New Testament conception that the calendar also continues for the history of salvation *after* Christ. It is not a *new time* that has been created with Christ, but *a new division of time*."[52]

In the second place it must be posited that neither its *temporal-future* character, nor its *universal-cosmic* importance can be given up as a mythical representation without impairing the kernel and the idea of the kingdom of heaven preached by Jesus. This is not a question of all the realistic traits of the picture of the expected cosmic upheaval found in the late-Jewish apocalypses. For one thing[53] there is a striking difference between Jesus' preaching of the great future and that of the Jewish apocalypses. The latter contain a fantastic and muggy picture of the *Endgeschichte* and of the coming world, which is entirely lacking in the gospel. There is great sobriety and restraint in the description of the collapse and the consummation of the world, the victory over Satan, and the resurrection of the body. But even so it is a sound hermeneutic principle that the prophetic description of the actions of divine judgment and *re*-creation cannot be explained by way of an eye-witness account. For these actions transcend any human experience and understanding.

But this circumstance does not detract from the fact that the idea of the kingdom of heaven implies the participation of all created life in the coming of the kingdom, to which especially resurrection and *re*-creation also belong in the most essential sense of the word. And such not only because the entire human existence is determined by the reality which the Scriptures call "the kingdom of God." The preaching of the kingdom is not a certain mold conditioned by the times to the biblical doctrine about the human situation or existence. It does not consist in a theological anthropology, but in revelation concerning God. This predominating, theocentric character of the idea of the kingdom of God is most closely connected with the universal importance of the coming of the kingdom. The whole of the revelation of God in the Old Testament and in Jesus' preaching is based on the fundamental fact of the creation of heaven and earth by God. The earth is the Lord's. The Bible knows nothing of any original dualism between God and the world (as is found in the Persian religions), between spirit and matter but it does mention the fall and the world's abandonment to a power hostile to God. This is why the coming of the kingdom, as the re-assertion of God's right and glory, also consists in the redemption and the restoration of life, in a material as well as in a spiritual sense. Because God is God, i.e., the God of the revelation, the creator of heaven and earth, the Holy One who has committed himself to Israel in his promise and covenant, the "proportions" of the kingdom are universal. So long as the world does not answer its purpose and is subject to death, God's glory will be veiled, his name will not be hallowed, and the prayer for the coming of the kingdom will not be answered.

Generally neither the prophecies, nor Jesus argue about these things. They simply state this universality of the kingdom of God with perfect certainty and as "a matter of course." Their preaching is not based on cosmological speculation, but on the revelation concerning God. It is, therefore, most intimately connected and, as it were, given with the idea of the kingdom of God. Such may appear from the "proof" Jesus gives to the Sadducees of the resurrection of the dead. Because *God* has bound himself to Abraham, Isaac and Jacob, there is also a resurrection of the dead. "For God is not the God of the dead but of the living" (Matt. 22:31,32).[54] That is why it is not possible to separate the "revelational content" from the universal "mold" of the preaching of the kingdom. The theocentric character of the kingdom of God, as taught by special divine revelation, imparts a universal content to the idea of the kingdom of God without which it is inconceivable. It is not primarily the "cosmological" but the "theological" content of the gospel which is at issue, especially in its relation to the reality of creation, the fall, and history. The attempt to "de-mythologize" the evangelical eschatology is, therefore, at bottom a neo-idealistic sublimation of the gospel. It does not only affect the "shell" but also the "kernel," because it is in flagrant and irreconcilable conflict with the most profound motives determining the idea of the kingdom of God.[55]

8. *Present*

The future consummative character of the kingdom of heaven is unmistakably in accordance with the entire basic thought of Jesus' preaching, as appears from his numerous pronouncements. By the side of these Jesus also speaks of the coming of the kingdom as a reality that is being fulfilled already during the time of his preaching, and so before the *endgeschichtliche* upheaval and consummation of all things.

This fact is predominant in the New Testament revelation of salvation. This brings us to the point at which Jesus' preaching displays a fundamentally different modality from all that had been prophesied and expected of the kingdom of heaven before him. This difference is also to be found between Jesus' preaching and that of John the Baptist's. It is true, Jesus repeats John's words: "the kingdom of heaven is at hand," which, as we have seen, does not yet mean that the kingdom is present. But there are also descriptions of Jesus' initial preaching which appear to express more than the announcement of what is *near*, and consequently imply more than the Baptist's preaching can be said to contain.

At the outset we can point to the words in which Mark describes Jesus' initial proclamation: "The time is fulfilled and the kingdom of God is at hand: repent ye, and believe the gospel" (Mk. 1:15). Especially the opening words "the time is fulfilled" speak of something that has found its completion, its final stage in the present. Therefore, *kairos* means the great moment of the commencement of the great future appointed by God in his counsel, and announced by the prophets.[56] By the side of the "is at hand" there is already the "is fulfilled." No doubt the two expressions should be understood in connection with each other. "At hand" in the expression "is at hand" does not mean the same thing as "has come," "is present," as clearly appears from the purport of John's preaching. The expression "the time is fulfilled" will thus have to be understood as the indication that the threshold of the great future has been reached, that the door has been opened, and that the prerequisites of the realization of the divine work of consummation are present; so that now the concluding divine drama can start. Owing to this, Jesus' initial proclamation of the nearness of the kingdom seems to speak of a more advanced point of time than that of John who had not yet mentioned the beginning of the fulfillment.

It is easy to prove that this distinction between the redemptive-historical moment represented by Jesus and that represented by the Baptist is based on a not too subtle exegesis of Mark 1:15, but becomes clearer and clearer in the gospel. In the first place we refer to Jesus' initial proclamation, according to the Gospel by Luke, in the synagogue of Nazareth. There Jesus first proclaimed the well-known prophecy of salvation of Isaiah 61 (Luke 4:18,19), and then he continued: "This day is this Scripture fulfilled in your ears." Here once again he uses the perfect: "has come to fulfillment." The subject of this fulfillment is not the *kairos* but "the Scriptures" and more precisely: the Scriptural place of Isaiah 61, announcing "the acceptable year of the Lord." This can only mean what is elsewhere called the coming of the kingdom or the messianic era[57] which may appear from the words following in Isaiah 61:2 "and the day of vengeance of our God" which is the "day of the Lord" preceding the revelation of salvation.

This passage is extremely important for the understanding of the coming of the kingdom according to Jesus' preaching. For it is clear that here the time of the great fulfillment is represented as having definitively started. This appears from the emphatic "this day" and from the words "in your ears" (which we shall have to understand as an analogy of the more usual "before your eyes"). On the ground of this repeated "it is fulfilled" with which Jesus starts his preaching there can be no doubt in our opinion that the salvation summarized in the expression "the coming of the kingdom" is not solely something to come in the future, but also finds fulfillment in the present. In this we are confronted with a fundamental redemptive-historical difference between the Baptist's and Jesus' proclamation. The Baptist announced as something of the future that which Jesus began to indicate as a present and actual reality. This is to say that John's summarizing vision of the one great event of the future becomes differentiated in Jesus' preaching insofar as this one great event is described as both an already fulfilled "present" and a future expectation.

In accordance with all this the general character of Jesus' preaching and action differs from that of John's. Also in accordance with this difference are the explicit and very significant pronouncements made by Jesus himself on the difference between himself and John which are found in more than one passage of the Gospel.

As to the first statement we would point to the undeniable fact that in comparison with John's preaching that of Jesus introduces a certain relaxation of severity. Jesus' preaching is not dominated, as is John's, by the certainty of the coming judgment, but is rather a proclamation of salvation.[58] This salvation is of immediate and actual significance and so does not first become effective after the judgment and the consequent cosmic upheaval. This relaxation is founded in the initial stage of the fulfillment of the "time" and of the "Scriptures" and so of the redemptive coming of the kingdom. It not only characterizes Jesus' preaching but also all his actions, in contradistinction to those of the Baptist. John is the preacher of penitence denying himself any luxury or comfort and living as an ascetic in the wilderness. Jesus, on the other hand, takes part in everyday life. He is more than once a guest at weddings and feasts (Matt. 9:10; John 2:1ff). In contradistinction to John he comes "eating and drinking" and is called "a man gluttonous, and a wine-bibber" by his enemies (Matt. 11:19; Luke 7:34), "the friend of publicans and sinners."[59] From the well-known conversation about fasting (Matt. 9:14-17; Mark 2:18-22; Luke 5:33-39), it appears that this difference is really characteristic of Jesus' position in comparison with John's with respect to the kingdom of heaven. The disciples asked Jesus why they did not fast,[60] whereas John's disciples (like the Pharisees) often did (Luke 5:33). Jesus' answer was: "Can the children of the bridegroom mourn as long as the bridegroom is with them?" These words clearly mean that Jesus' disciples were in a fundamentally different position from those of John the Baptist. Especially important is the reason that Jesus gives: "as long as the bridegroom is with them." Although Jesus here uses the language of an illustration, the meaning of this pronouncement cannot be misunderstood. It is the presence of the person of Jesus himself which is the cause of the great change. In addition, the example has been chosen in such a way that this person is not only the announcer, but he himself is the center and the cause of the joy, the bliss, which has started with his coming. Such may also appear from the fact that this condition will not remain undisturbed and uninterrupted. "But the days will come, when the bridegroom shall be taken from them . . . " (Matt. 9:15), which evidently refers to what will happen to the person of Jesus. Although within the scope of the whole gospel the *messianic* meaning of these pronouncements is undeniable, it cannot be said that the term "bridegroom" in this context is an explicitly messianic title. Here Jesus speaks of himself in an implicit, veiled way, as we shall see again and again. One thing is clear, however. John the Baptist's way of life and that of his disciples is still entirely directed to the preparation for the coming of the kingdom, especially to that of judgment (fasting and prayers), whereas Jesus' disciples may live in the joyful certainty of the break-through of the great time of salvation and may behave accordingly, *because of their belonging to him.*[61] If they were to stick to John's teaching, they would be like the people "who put a piece of new cloth upon an old garment, or new wine into old bottles." Although Jesus does not disapprove of John's actions, it is nevertheless clear that now something "new" has appeared which does not agree with the "old" forms of life. These conceptions also represent the two stages of the dispensation of salvation separated from each other by the element of fulfillment.

The difference between the redemptive-historical moments, yes even in the dispensation of salvation, from which John and Jesus speak and act is most explicitly and distinctly indicated in the well-known passage of Matthew 11:7-19, and Luke 7:24-35. The starting-point is John's question put to Jesus through some of the Baptist's disciples: "Art thou he that should come, or do we look for another?" Here, too, the criterion of the redemptive-historical moment is the significance

of Jesus' person.[62] In his announcement of the kingdom John
had spoken of "him that cometh after me" and had looked
upon him as the inaugurator of the kingdom. Now he applies
the name of "he that cometh" to Jesus in the form of a question.[63] John's question gives evidence of uncertainty and confusion, seen also in connection with Jesus' answer. Without
a doubt he had considered Jesus as "he that cometh" in the
beginning (cf. Matt. 3:13-17), but the manner of Jesus' manifestation did not correspond to John's own conception and
preaching of it.

Jesus' answer to John's question does not directly deal
with the significance of his person, but very clearly vindicates
the consummative character of his activity and thereby of the
coming of the kingdom. For Jesus refers John's messengers
to his miracles and to the preaching of the gospel to the poor.
The way he speaks of them clearly reminds us of his initial
proclamation in the synagogue of Nazareth. Jesus also refers
to the prophecies about the great time of salvation which find
their fulfillment in these miracles and in this preaching, and
shed light on the meaning and the importance of his activities
(cf. Isaiah 35:5; 29:18; 61:1). Although Jesus does not give
a direct answer to John's question and here avoids giving a
public declaration of his Messiahship, the purport of his words
can be no other than a pointing out of the fulfillment of the
prophecies, and thus of the presence of the kingdom of God.
It is true, he clearly shows that all this cannot be experimentally
established: "And blessed is he whosoever shall not be offended
in me," i.e., whosoever shall not find a reason for unbelief in the
way in which I act, and in the form in which the kingdom of
God reveals itself. Yet, the connection of "blessed" with "in
me" also implies that Jesus' present appearance and action
already contain the secret of the revelation of the kingdom
of heaven.

Very characteristic of what we are discussing here, and
also very important, is the sequel to this passage, both in Matthew and Luke (as well as the words about John the Baptist,

which occur in another context, viz., Luke 16:16). For Jesus now goes further into the significance of John in the history of revelation. In contrast to the low estimate that the people had of him later on (cf. Matt. 11:7,8; Luke 7:24,25,33), John was a prophet, even more than a prophet. For he also belonged to the *object* of the prophecies concerning the coming salvation, he had a place in the realization of the promise of the great future, namely, that of being the way-preparer of the king (cf. Mal. 3:1; Matt. 11:10; Luke 7:27): "This is he of whom it is written: behold, I send my messenger before thy face, which shall prepare the way before me." Then follow the much disputed words: "Among them that are born of women there hath not risen a greater than John the Baptist" (Matt. 11:11); (according to Luke 7:28: "Among those that are born of women there is none greater[64] than John"), "notwithstanding he that is least in the kingdom of heaven is greater than he."

If the two parts of this text are to be understood in their mutual connection,[65] the first must be taken as the indication of John's place and significance in the period before Jesus' coming, the dispensation of the prophecies. In this period John is the greatest of all, i.e., as the prophet sent by God and as the eschatological pioneer of the Lord predicted by the prophecies.[66] But his significance remains restricted to the time of the expectation; in the fulfillment of the promise, in the coming of the kingdom of heaven, he plays no part. That is why the one who is the least in the kingdom (God's office-bearer, servant, laborer) is greater than he. There exist quite a long series of views as to the meaning of this pronouncement. To my mind[67] the best of them is the one that considers John as the King's pioneer and consequently still belonging to the time before the kingdom of heaven (i.e., before the time of the fulfillment had started with Jesus' coming and his work). We should bear in mind John's place in the history of revelation, which is to be sought in the dispensation of the promise and expectation. Opposed to it is "the least in the kingdom of heaven," i.e., anyone who lives and works consciously in the light of the dispensation of the fulfillment. He is "greater" than John because, and to the extent[68] that the latter has not risen to the level of the present and the fulfillment of salvation. Here the question is not as to whether or not John will participate in the bliss of the kingdom, but we are concerned with the understanding and the proclamation of what is happening now. Here the kingdom is spoken of as a present entity.[69]

All this is corroborated by what follows in Matthew 11:12: "From the days of John the Baptist until now the kingdom of heaven is pushing its way with force, and the violent take it as a booty." There is no certainty about the way to translate this text[70] but it cannot be denied that the kingdom of heaven is here represented as a present entity. According to our translation it is pushing its way, is asserting itself with force, using violence in this world. And this has been going on (the process is being continued) "since the days of John the Baptist." We shall have to understand the word "since" in an exclusive and not in an inclusive sense. John is on the threshold, he leads on from the old to the new dispensation; he himself still belongs to the old period. With Jesus the new era has come, that of the kingdom of heaven pushing its way with force into the world. Conversely it is also a question of "appropriating," "taking" the kingdom "as a booty." This means striving for the redemption offered by the kingdom without being deterred by anything and by using all one's endeavors and staking everything for its sake.[71] The expression: "the violent take it as a booty" has been formed from the analogy of "pushing its way with force." The one corresponds to the other.

Finally, the same thought is also found in the parallel text in Luke 16:16: "The law and the prophets were until John: since that time the kingdom of God is preached, and every man presseth into it." Here, too, John is indicated as the *heilsgeschichtliche Grenzscheide*[72] (the line of demarcation in the history of salvation, cf. Acts 10:37). Since his mission the new dispensation of the gospel and of the kingdom of God has started and from all sides people rush to get in. It takes a lot of struggle and exertion, but in such a way they enter. This has been possible "from that moment," i.e., *after* John had come and had done his work. Also here Jesus points out clearly his own significance and work in contradistinction to that of John. That which was still a future matter in John's preaching, though close at hand, has become reality with Jesus' coming. In him the *future* of the prophecies has passed into the present fulfillment.

By way of summary, we can conclude that whatever of the above pronouncements may be open to more than one explanation, Jesus has nevertheless spoken of the coming of the kingdom as a present reality. This does not mean—and this also is an established fact—that there is no room for the future of the kingdom, or that it is necessary to distinguish between two kinds of kingdom, viz., one of the present and one of the future, but it means that the one great kingdom of the future has become present. Its fundamentally eschatological character is maintained as a matter of course. It is *the* great kingdom, *the* coming of God into the world for redemption and judgment. The future, as it were, penetrates into the present. The world of God's redemption, the great whole of his concluding and consummative works pushes its way into the present time of the world. This means the entirely new fact, in many respects incomprehensible and unacceptable to Jesus' contemporaries, that Jesus is to call "the mystery of the kingdom."[73] The kingdom will start before the time of the great judgment, the time is fulfilled before "the end of the world." Our further investigations will be concerned with the way this "fulfillment" has to be considered in connection with the final consummation, and what is the meaning and content of such a fulfillment without a consummation. In these things we are confronted with the most specific and characteristic part of Jesus' preaching of the coming of the kingdom. For the present we shall refrain from further qualifications of this twofold aspect, viz., that of the present and that of the future, inherent in the announcement of the coming of the kingdom by Jesus. We shall continue to hold fast to the terminology of the gospel which on the one hand speaks of the *fulfillment* of the time and the fulfillment of the Scriptures as a new dispensation of salvation that has started with the coming of Christ Jesus and with his work. On the other hand Jesus preaches the coming of the kingdom also as a future revelation, which the gospel denotes as the *consummation* of all things. We might also use other terms derived from the language of the gospels, but these two: fulfillment and consummation have the advantage of qualifying the presence of Jesus' coming and his work as well as the beginning of the great era of salvation, and, besides, they hold out the prospect of the definitive, final significance of the kingdom as something of the future.

Notes to Chapter II.

[1] This is emphatically pointed out by R. Otto, *Reich Gottes und Menschensohn*, 1934, pp. 34ff.

[2] P. Feine, *Theologie des Neuen Testaments[7]*, 1936, p. 73.

[3] Cf. also G. Dalman, *Die Worte Jesu*, I[2], 1930, pp. 76, 77.

[4] Cf. G. Gloege, *Reich Gottes und Kirche im Neuen Testament*, 1929, pp. 40, 50; and H. D. Wendland, *op. cit.*, p. 15. But in opposition to this see T. Zahn, *Grundriss der neutestamentlichen Theologie*, 1928, pp. 6, 7.

[5] *Das Wesen des Christentums*, 1905, pp. 34-45.

[6] Cf. K. Holl, *Urchristentum und Religionsgeschichte[2]*, 1927, p. 19; on this subject see also below, § 27.

[7] *Die Eschatologie des Reiches Gottes bei Jesus*, 1931, p. 14.

[8] *Op. cit.*, p. 13.

[9] *Op. cit.*, I, pp. 180, 181.

[10] See below, Chapter V.

[11] For the specific meaning of the idea of the covenant see, e.g., *Het Dogma der Kerk*, edited by G. C. Berkouwer, and G. Toornvliet, 1949, pp. 292ff.

[12] Cf. also my article in *Gereformeerd Theologisch Tijdschrift*, 1943, pp. 97ff., entitled: "Verbond en Koninkrijk Gods."

[13] For this text and its translation see below, pp. 66ff.

[14] Cf. Wendland, *op. cit.*, p. 17.

[15] In the footsteps of A. Schlatter G. Gloege has defended this view very emphatically and in great detail in his book: *Reich Gottes und Kirche im Neuen Testament*, 1929.

[16] Cf., e.g., S. Greijdanus, *Het heilig Evangelie naar de beschrijving van Lukas*, I, 1940, p. 168.

[17] It will have been formed in accordance with the Old Testament texts that speak of the eschatological "coming" of God and of the Messiah. The word *erchomai* belongs to the world of thought of the divine epiphany, Schneider, *TWB*, II, p. 664; cf. also Kümmel, *op. cit.*, p. 67; F. Hauck, *Das Evangelium des Lukas*, 1934, pp. 97, 98.

[18] See also below, pp. 48ff.

[19] Cf. Strack-Billerbeck, *op. cit.*, I, p. 115, "The future wrath means the judgment of Gehinnom."

[20] At least according to the most probable version, Mark only has: "He shall baptize you with the Holy Ghost."

[21] Thus, e.g., S. Greijdanus, *op. cit.*, I, pp. 170, 171.

[22] This view recommends itself because the subject in this case is not the Holy Spirit but the Stronger One whose activity has a twofold character: saving and punishing. Also the relative clause connected with this, viz., "whose fan is in his hand," etc., would at least sound very unexpected, if it contained, not a continuation, but a contrast of thoughts.

[23] Cf. also J. Ridderbos, *Het Godswoord der profeten*, I, 1930, p. 93.

[24] E.g., in: *The Testaments of the Twelve Patriarchs:* "In those days Messiah will appear; over Him the heavens will open to pour out the blessings of the Spirit of the Holy Father, while He himself pours out the Spirit of grace on Israel so that all may become children of God and walk in his commandments. Israel's enemies are destroyed . . . the end of the wicked is the eternal fire. . . ." Cf. Strack-Billerbeck, *op. cit.*, IV, p. 803. The idea that John the Baptist's importance is to be sought in his re-introducing the element of the

pouring out of the Holy Spirit into the totality of the Jewish expectation of the future and thus saving it from oblivion, as W. Michaelis thinks in his *Täufer, Jesus, Urgemeinde*, 1928, p. 36 does not give a reliable account of the real state of affairs.

[25] This is quite generally recognized at present; see, e.g., G. Sevenster, *De Christologie van het Nieuwe Testament*, 1946, pp. 78ff.

[26] A. Freiherr von Gall, *Basileia tou theou*, 1926, pp. 430ff.

[27] Cf. also my: *Zelfopenbaring en Zelfverberging*, 1946, pp. 36ff.

[28] As to the exegesis of these texts see § 46.

[29] For further details we refer to what follows in § 25.

[30] For the messianic interpretation of Daniel 7:13 in the Old Synagogue see Strack-Billerbeck, *op. cit.*, I, pp. 485, 957.

[31] Cf., e.g., Strack-Billerbeck, *op. cit.*, I, p. 199.

[32] See below, § 24.

[33] To be understood as the eschatological seeing of "face to face," cf., e.g., E. Klostermann, *Das Matthäusevangelium*[2], 1927, p. 37; Strack-Billerbeck, *op. cit.*, I, p. 207.

[34] For this whole passage see the detailed account in my *De strekking der bergrede naar Mattheüs*, 1936, pp. 88ff.

[35] Cf. above, p. 23.

[36] *Op. cit.*, pp. 56-80.

[37] *Op. cit.*, pp. 81-110.

[38] For an elaborate argument against Dodd's interpretation of these passages see also W. G. Kümmel, *Verheiszung und Erfüllung*, 1945, pp. 19ff.

[39] With an eye on the presumed Aramaic original we should translate both by: "The kingdom of God has come," *The Parables of the Kingdom*[6], p. 44; cf. also H. M. Matter, *Nieuwere opvattingen omtrent het Koninkrijk Gods in Jezus' prediking naar de Synoptici*, 1942, pp. 30ff. See also the opinion of R. H. Lightfoot, J. Leipoldt, and A. T. Cadoux, in Kümmel, *op cit.*, p. 12.

[40] Dodd also supposes that here in 3:2 Matthew did not exactly know how to keep separate the words of Jesus from those of John, and Dodd assumes he can show this with regard to other passages as well, *op. cit.*, p. 48. It is clear, however, that this assumption greatly affects the credibility of Dodd's view.

[41] Cf. also Kümmel, *op. cit.*, p. 14.

[42] *Op. cit.*, pp. 55, 56.

[43] Cf. pp. 13ff.

[44] Bultmann explicitly dissociates himself from the attempts made by the liberal and the comparative religion theology to purify the New Testament of any "mythical" content, cf. his: *Neues Testament und Mythologie*, 1942.

[45] Cf. above p. 16.

[46] This is also recognized by Delling, *Das Zeitverständnis des Neuen Testaments*, 1940, p. 99; cf. also Grundmann, *TWB*, II, pp. 21ff., the article on "dei."

[47] Cf. below, § 49.

[48] For this see also Kümmel, *Verheiszung und Erfüllung*, p. 88.

[49] Delling, *Das Zeitverständnis des N.T.*, 1940, p. 118.

[50] *Op. cit.*, p. 106.

[51] *Op. cit.*, p. 119.

[52] *Christus und die Zeit*, p. 80. Cf. also the objections made by Schniewind against Bultmann in *Kerugma und Mythos*, edited by Hans Werner Bartsch, 1948, pp. 114, 116ff., 122ff.

[53] See also below § 47.

[54] See below § 31.

[55] For this universal meaning of the coming of the kingdom compare also the important expositions of Wendland, *op. cit.*, pp. 21-27.

[56] Cf. G. Delling, *TWB*, III, p. 461; E. Lohmeyer, *Das Evangelium des Markus*, 1937, p. 30; E. Klostermann, *Das Markusevangelium³*, 1936, p. 12; O. Cullmann, *Christus und die Zeit*, 1946, p. 35.

[57] See, e.g., also Klostermann, *Das Lukasevangelium²*, 1929, p. 63.

[58] Thus, e.g., also E. Klostermann, on Mark 1:14: "Compared with John's well-known threat, this summary gives much greater prominence to what is new in Jesus' preaching, viz., the fulfillment of the promise"; *Das Markusevangelium³*, 1936, p. 11; and F. Hauck, "At bottom Jesus gives up the method of the Baptist and introduces to the people the open and free announcement of the message of peace saying that it has pleased God to let the time of salvation begin now"; *Das Evangelium des Markus*, 1931, p. 19.

[59] Cf. also R. Otto, *Reich Gottes und Menschensohn*, 1934, pp. 58-63.

[60] To this Luke adds *kai deēseis poiountai* ("and saying prayers") by which is probably meant the keeping of days of prayer, and the holding of prayer meetings, cf. also Luke 11:1; cf. Hauck, *op. cit.*, p. 76.

[61] Cf. also Kümmel, *op. cit.*, p. 43: "On the one hand this word also clearly refers to the present as the eschatological time of fulfilment characterized by the presence of the bridegroom, and on the other it takes account of a longer or shorter time of separation from Jesus."

[62] It is characteristic that this is one of the very rare cases in which Matthew calls Jesus "the Christ" ("having heard of the works of Christ"). It looks as if the evangelist first of all wants to safeguard his readers from the uncertainty apparent in John's question.

[63] Cf. above pp. 44ff.; at the same time this indication is strong evidence of the fact that John's question was historically determined; i.e., it cannot be considered as a later "Christian" formula, as in the later Church Christ was never referred to in this way, as far as we know. Cf. also Kümmel, *op. cit.*, p. 67; Hauck, *op. cit.*, pp. 97, 98.

[64] Some manuscripts have: "a greater prophet."

[65] If the two parts of this text are not explained (as Bultmann does) as the result of two different tendencies in the tradition of which one represents John as "the ally of the Christian cause," and the other puts his inferiority to Christ in the foreground, *Die Geschichte der synoptischen Tradition²*, 1931, p. 177.

[66] Cf. Th. H. Robinson, *The Gospel of Matthew* (in *The Moffatt N.T. Comm.*), 1945, p. 101: "John was more than a prophet, not in nature or in inspiration, but in function."

[67] Cf. my *De strekking der bergrede naar Mattheüs*, 1936, pp. 107ff; *Het evangelie naar Mattheüs*, I, 1941, pp. 215, 216.

[68] Cf. W. Manson, *The Gospel of Luke⁵*, (in *The Moffat New Testament Commentary*), 1945, p. 81: "This pronouncement, which implies that John still declines the revelation preached by Jesus, agrees with the situation revealed in the Baptist's question"; see also Greijdanus, *Luke*, I, p. 340.

[69] Cf., e.g., also N. B. Stonehouse, *The Witness of Matthew and Mark to Christ*, 1944, pp. 133, 245; C. H. Dodd, *op. cit.*, p. 47; Th. Robinson, *op. cit.*, pp. 101, 102; S. Greijdanus, *op. cit.*, I, p. 340; F. W. Grosheide, *Het heilig Evangelie volgens Mattheüs*, 1922, p. 134, and others. Again others wish to think of the future revelation of the Kingdom. Thus, e.g., already Chrysos-

tomus and other Church fathers, who connected with it the view that *ho mikroteros* is Jesus himself. In the footsteps of F. Dibelius (ZNTWXI, 190) this view is also taken by F. Hauck, *op. cit.*, pp. 99, 100: "In his relation to the Baptist Jesus is still the younger of the two, and in the eyes of many others He is even inferior. In the new order of things He will be the greatest." It is, however, difficult to understand why Jesus should be less esteemed than John, cf. also J. Schniewind, *Das Evangelium nach Matthäus*, 1937, p. 139, and Greijdanus, *op. cit.* But apart from the application of *ho mikroteros* to Jesus, there are writers who think of the future eschatological revelation of the kingdom in this case. But then the text seems to say that John will remain outside of the kingdom, and this is a conception which, to my mind, is unacceptable; cf. also Klostermann, *op. cit.*, p. 98.

70 For an account given of this translation, see my *Het Evangelie naar Mattheüs*, 1, 1941, pp. 216, 217 (note). On the other hand compare G. Schrenk, in *TWB*, I, pp. 608ff., the article on "biazomai" and Kümmel, *op. cit.*, p. 71. According to these writers the translation should be: "the kingdom is suffering violence, and the violent are plundering it." They then understand it *in malam partem*. The latter part is taken to mean that the *biastai* try to steal the kingdom from men. Some commentators explain "the violent" as the world of the evil spirits (thus, e.g., M. Dibelius, *Die urchristliche Ueberlieferung von Johannes dem Täufer*, 1911, pp. 26ff, in Kümmel, p. 72); others refer to the Jewish opponents (thus, e.g., Schrenk, *op. cit.*, Wendland, *op. cit.*, p. 48); others leave this question open (Kümmel, e.g., *op. cit.*, p. 72). The objections against this view are: (a) that there is no mention at all of such a violent opposition to the kingdom in the whole context. That is why Kümmel, like Schrenk, detaches this saying from the context both in Matthew and in Luke; (b) that Luke's version very decidedly speaks of a beneficial coming of the *basileia* (*evaggelizetai*); (c) that the stealing of the *basileia* by a third party is a hardly acceptable thought; G. Sevenster, *De Christologie van het N.T.*, 1946, quotes this passage as a proof of the presence of the *basileia*, without making a choice between the two conceptions, pp. 19, 20.

71 Albert Schweitzer's view that *arpazousin* means something like "forcing," i.e., bringing the coming of the kingdom nearer with force (by special moral achievements, Matt. 5-7, by the disciples taking on themselves the messianic afflictions, Matt. 10, by Jesus' self-sacrifice, Matt. 20:28) is very amenable to Schweitzer's consistently eschatological explanation of the life of Jesus, but does not find any support either in linguistic usage or in the context; cf. also Schniewind, *Matthew*, p. 140.

72 Hauck, *op. cit.*, p. 207; see also E. Klostermann, *Das Lukasevangelium²*, 1929, p. 167; Greijdanus, *op. cit.*, II, p. 786.

73 See below, § 17.

Chapter III

THE KINGDOM HAS COME

1. Fulfillment

9. *The Wicked One Overcome*

The question as to what constitutes the great change, viz., the coming of the kingdom which has begun with Jesus' activity, finds its fundamental and unmistakable answer in the statement made in Matthew 12:28, Luke 11:20. Here Jesus speaks very emphatically of the presence of the kingdom: "If I cast out devils by the Spirit of God (Luke has: 'with the finger of God'), then the kingdom of God has come unto you." That the last words of this text must be rendered by the perfect "has come" is pretty well certain, in spite of the criticism of some writers. Apart from the linguistic question,[1] it may be seen from the whole context, especially from what follows in Matthew. Jesus here answers the slander of the Pharisees who had said that he cast out devils by Beelzebub, the prince of the devils. He shows the absurdity of the accusation by comparing the power of the devil with that of a kingdom or a town or a house, i.e., with an organically coherent unity. If one devil should cast out another, the kingdom of the devils would not stand but would fall asunder. But this does not happen. That is why there is only one explanation for Jesus' power over the demons, viz., that by the Spirit (or the finger of God) he was able to cast them out. The opposite to Satan and his kingdom is God and the dominion that is at his disposal, viz., the kingdom of God. Its power and so[2] its presence is the explanation of Jesus' dominion over the demons. All this is further confirmed in Matthew 12:29 (cf. Mark 3:27) by what is said of the strong man[3] whose house can only be looted after he himself has first been bound. In the same way the casting out of the devils proves the victory over the devil gained by Jesus[4] and thus the break-through by the kingdom of heaven. Therefore the exclusively eschatological movement can hardly deny that the gospel speaks of the presence of the kingdom. Weiss explains this passage by saying that Jesus had spoken in a kind of prophetic ecstasy. He was occasionally in such an ecstatic condition and at such times he saw the signs that the kingdom had already come. Consequently in this passage he only spoke of the presence of the kingdom in a proleptic sense.[5] But this interpretation is in conflict with the reality of the casting out of the devils.[6]

This passage is not an isolated one. The whole struggle of Jesus against the devils is determined by the antithesis between the kingdom of heaven and the rule of Satan, and time and again Jesus' superior power over Satan and Satan's dominion proves the break-through on the part of the kingdom of God. This is already proved at the start by the temptation in the wilderness. There can be no doubt that in it the issue is Jesus' messianic kingship. Three times in succession it is Satan's point of departure, referring back to the divine words about Jesus at his baptism (Matt. 3:17; Mark 1:11; Luke 3:22; Matt. 4:3,6; Luke 4:3,9). Especially the temptation with respect to "all the kingdoms of the world" (Matt. 4:8ff; Luke 4:5ff) shows what is at issue in the struggle between Jesus and Satan. Here Satan appears as "the prince of the world" (cf. John 12:31; 14:30; 16:11); who opposes God's kingdom, and who knows that Jesus will dispute that power with him in the name of God. Here, then, together with the Messiahship, the kingdom of God is at issue. At the same time it appears that the victory over Satan to be gained by the kingdom of God is not only a matter of *power,* but first and foremost one of *obedience* on the part of the Messiah[7]. The Messiah must not make an arbitrary use of the authority entrusted to him. He will have to acquire the power that Satan offers him only in the way ordained by God. That is why Jesus' rejection of the temptation is already the beginning of his victory and of the coming of the kingdom, although this victory will have to be renewed again and again during his life on earth (cf. Luke 4:13; Matt. 16:23, and parallels; 26:38, and parallels; 27:40-43, and parallels). From the beginning of his public activity Jesus' power over Satan had already asserted itself. This is not only proved by the casting out of devils in itself, but also by *the manner in which those possessed by the devil behave in his presence* (cf. Mark 1:24; Luke 4:34; Mark 5:7; Matt. 8:29; Luke 8:28,31). When Jesus approaches they raise a cry, obviously in fear. They show that they have a supernatural knowledge[8] of his person and of the significance of his coming (cf. Mark 1:34; 3:11). They call him "the Holy One of God," "the Son of God," "Son of the most high God." By this they recognize his messianic dignity (cf. Luke 4:41). They consider his coming as their own destruction (Mark 1:24; Luke 4:34); their torment (Matt. 8:29; Mark 5:7; Luke 8:28). They feel powerless and try only to lengthen their existence on earth (Matt. 8:29; Mark 5:10), and implore him not to send them into "the deep," that is to say, the place of their eternal woe (Luke 8:31, cf. Rev. 20:3ff).[9] All this shows that in Jesus' person and coming the kingdom has become a present reality. For the exercise of God's power over the devil and his rule has the coming of the kingdom for its foundation.

And finally we must refer in this context to Luke 10:18,19. Jesus has sent out the seventy (or seventy-two), who come back to him and joyfully tell him of the success of their mission. And then Jesus says: "I beheld Satan as lightning fall from heaven." Thus he accepts the joy of those he had sent out and shows them the background of their power over the devils.[10] The general meaning of this is clear: Satan himself has fallen with great force from his

position of power.[11] This is what Jesus had seen with his own
eyes. Satan's supporters cannot maintain themselves. It is
more difficult to decide whether Jesus has a particular concrete event in view with his expression "I saw." If he had,
which one? Some authors suggest that it was the temptation
in the wilderness.[12] Others think of some experience[13] Jesus
had during the time when his messengers were busy executing
their task.[14] Some writers think of the fall of Satan in the
future, which Jesus saw with the eye of the spirit; this fall
was due to the destruction of Satan's power by Jesus' work on
earth, especially by his death on the cross.[15] It is difficult to
decide. In our opinion the most obvious explanation must be
sought in Jesus' sympathy with his disciples during their
mission. Jesus' "I saw" is then the expression of Jesus' certainty of victory over Satan which he accomplished during the
absence of his disciples. For our argument, however, the
decision about the exegesis of this passage is only of secondary
importance. The thing that counts in this connection is that
what is said here is essentially the same thing as in Matthew
12:28 and Luke 11:21, i.e., the great moment of the breaking
down of Satan's rule has come and at the same time that of
the coming of the kingdom of heaven. The redemption is
no longer only future but has become *present*. In this struggle
it is Jesus himself who has broken Satan's power and who continues to do so. Such appears from what follows when he
discusses the power of the disciples which they have received
from him to tread on serpents and scorpions and over all the
power of the enemy, so that, in the future also, nothing will be
impossible to them. By this *enemy* Satan is again meant.
Serpents and *scorpions* are mentioned here as his instruments
(Ps. 91:13) by which he treacherously tries to ruin man. But
any power Satan has at his disposal to bring death and destruction on earth (cf., e.g., Heb. 2:14) has been subjected to the
disciples. All this implies and confirms that the great moment
of salvation, the fulfillment of the promise, the kingdom of
heaven, has come. "The all-embracing power of the *Civitas
Diaboli* has been shattered, the *Civitas Dei* has broken in."[16]

10. Jesus' Power to Work Miracles

Connected with the above is the fact that in the *whole* of Jesus' power to work miracles the coming of the kingdom is realized and is evidence of its presence.[17] This is not so clearly expressed here as it is in the casting out of devils, it is true, but it is implied in the fact that Jesus' preaching of the kingdom and his miracles are repeatedly mentioned in the same breath (cf., e.g., Matt. 4:23; 9:35). Jesus preached the kingdom with words and deeds. Furthermore, in Jesus' answer to John the Baptist there is a clear indication that the coming of the kingdom was manifested in Jesus' miraculous curing of disease.[18] Moreover, the expression "the kingdom of heaven has been taken by force" in Matthew 11:12, should not merely be taken to refer to the power of the preaching of the gospel, as some authors do in their too close adherence to the *euaggelizetai* of Luke 16:16, for it also relates to Jesus' miracles. In this connection we mention Matthew 13:16 and Luke 10:23: "Blessed are your eyes, for they see; and your ears, for they hear." This "seeing" and "hearing" refer to their seeing of the miracles and their hearing of the preaching of the gospel (cf. Matt. 11:5). They make visible and audible the fulfillment of the promises, the coming of the great era of salvation, things that many prophets and many righteous people in vain desired to see and to hear. Jesus' miracles reveal the coming of the kingdom of God.

The factual connection between the realization of the kingdom and Jesus' miracles that is to be found everywhere is no less important than these isolated deliberate indications. Jesus' miracles occupy a place that is in every respect organic and "natural" in the idea of the coming of the kingdom, insofar as it renders visible the restoration of the creation, and so the all-embracing and redemptive significance of the kingdom. It is true that the redemptive-historical meaning of these miracles has been challenged. They have been interpreted as evidence of a certain charismatic talent on the part of Jesus. As a consequence they have been compared and partly put on the same level with those of the "miracle working" prophets and charismatics of the Hellenistic and Jewish world of those days.[19] Thus, e.g., Rudolf Otto's well-known conception according to which Jesus is described in the gospels—which Otto designates as "hagiological" reports—as the typical "saint" whose charismatic gifts are characteristic. Then Otto characterizes Jesus further as a type which is generally known in the history of religion (e.g., by referring to Paul, the prophets of Israel, the Mohammedan Sufis, Blumhardt, and others).[20] He maintains that this type is clearly mentioned in the gospel, viz., when Jesus is addressed as "the Holy One of God," which he supposes to be an equivalent of the Old Testament "man of God."[21] Otto indicates the charismatic gifts of the redemptive-historical type as myterious "excesses of dispositions and faculties" which have at least their analogies in psychic life in general[22] and which he tries to elucidate with the help of modern psycho-therapeutic phenomena and observations.[23]

It has rightly been proved in more than one quarter that there is no room for such an explanation within the scope of the synoptic gospels.[24] Granted that here and there a certain outward and partly very natural[25] similarity can be found between the phenomenal aspects of Jesus' miracles and those occurring in all kinds of ancient stories, e.g., the use of spittal in cures (Mark 7:33; 8:23).[26] But this does not detract from the fact that the background and the explanation of the New Testament miracles bear an exclusive character. They do not rest on some personalistic-charismatic talent or miraculous power, but on the break-through of the transcendent kingdom of heaven (Luke 10:7-9). This may be seen from the remarkable fact that on more than one occasion Jesus delegates his miraculous power to his disciples (Matt. 10:1; Mark 6:12,13,30; Luke 9:2, cf. also Mark 9:28,29). Jesus' miracles are messianic deeds of salvation, they bear an eschatological character.[27]

This factual relation between the coming of the kingdom and Jesus' miracles is also brought out not only by the casting out of devils but also by Jesus' other miracles, for they all prove that Satan's power has been broken and that, therefore, the kingdom has come. At the same time it appears that disease is considered to be generally a consequence of Satan's rule and that Jesus' struggle against the Evil One is not fought solely in the field of ethics, but in the whole of the physical domain.[28] Thus, e.g., in several cases demonic possession is mentioned as the cause of bodily disorders (e.g., Matt. 9:32ff; 12:22ff; Mark 9:25); or such possession is mentioned as first in the series of bodily diseases (Matt. 4:24). At the same time Satan is also called the cause of all kinds of physical suffering without any mention of demonic possession. Thus, e.g., in Luke 13:11,16, where the text speaks of a woman who had "a spirit of infirmity . . . and was bowed together." In the 16th verse it says that "Satan had bound this woman."[29] Apparently there is no thought of demonic possession here,[30] but Satan is mentioned in a more general sense as the cause of suffering. Not only serpents and scorpions, but also disease and death belong to the enemy's power (*dunamis*) (Luke 10:19).

In this connection we should not omit pointing out the peculiar use of the word "rebuke" on the occasion of physical cures and other miracles. The demons are said to have been rebuked by Jesus, not only when he charged them not to make him known (cf. Mark 3:17ff): but also when he ordered them to go away (Mark 9:25). The same expression is also used in Luke 4:39 with reference to Peter's mother-in-law's fever.[31] It may be asked whether this word has been chosen in view of the demonic influence.[32] The same question arises with respect to Jesus' rebuking the wind, e.g., Luke 8:24.[33] Although it is assumed that in such a case there is no direct connection between the power of the devil and the raging elements crossing Jesus' path, the word "rebuke" indicates Jesus' absolute authority in the natural kingdom over all destructive influences operating in it as a result of sin and of the curse on the world. This is, however, also a manifestation of the coming of the kingdom of God. Christ penetrates into the province of the prince of this world and vanquishes the hostile powers which devastate the creation.[34] "He is again the Ruler, the Lord and the King of nature."[35] He not only opposes the power of the enemy in the natural kingdom, but as the Son of God he also has disposal of all the riches of his Father, as appears, e.g., from the repeated multiplication of the loaves.

The connection between the coming of the kingdom and Jesus' miraculous power is most clearly visible in those miracles that have been most often denied and whose place in the gospel has been most openly ascribed to the so-called formation of legends at later times, viz., the raising of the dead (Matt. 9:18ff, and parallels; Luke 7:11ff). The gospels themselves do not reflect on the significance of death and of the raising of the dead. But in the light of the entire preaching of the kingdom it is clear that it is exactly in the delivery from death that the salvation of the kingdom reaches its climax. "Dead persons are raised, because in Jesus' action that Kingdom is beginning to be realized in which there will no more be any death" (Rev. 21:4 and 20:14).[36] It has, therefore, rightly been said that anybody who wishes to understand Jesus' work of salvation from the idea of the kingdom of God, and from Jesus' Messianic office, cannot draw a rational line of demarcation among the miracles between the so-called possible or impossible.[37] For the kingdom of God revealed in miracles signifies the redemption from all evil and the restoration of the whole of life.

It is remarkable, moreover, that the judgment for the unbelieving and impenitent nation which is entailed by the coming of the kingdom of heaven is even demonstrated by a miracle, viz., by the withering away of the fig tree (Matt. 21:18-22; Mark 11:12-14; 20-24). Although the meaning of the curse on the fig tree has given rise to a great diversity of opinions and to all kinds of arbitrary explanations about the "origin" of this miracle-story,[38] the withering of the fig tree certainly has, in our opinion, a symbolical meaning, viz., it is a prophecy of the judgment that would overtake Israel on account of its barrenness.[39] Viewed in this light this miracle is the counterpart to the saving miracles, and occupies an organic place in the scope of the preaching of the kingdom and in the totality of Jesus' miracles.

The name by which Jesus' power to work miracles is indicated and which, therefore, may be considered more or less as a *terminus technicus,* is *dunamis.* Thus Mark 6:14 says: miraculous powers are active in him; Mark 5:30: virtue had gone out of him; the power of the Lord[40] was upon Jesus to cure them (Luke 5:17); he gives commands to the foul spirits with a marvellous authority (Luke 4:36). The miracles themselves are more than once called *dunameis* (Matt. 7:22; 11:20; 13:54), or simply *dunamis* (Mark 6:5). On account of the above-mentioned significance of Jesus' miraculous works this *dunamis,* therefore, entirely assumes the meaning of the divine power of consummation, making Jesus' birth into a miracle already at the outset (Luke 1:35), determining the whole of his action and course of life (Luke 4:14, cf. Acts 10:38). He is the One in whom the glory of God, also indicated as *dunamis* (cf. Matt. 26:64), and the definitive coming of God to the world (cf. Mark 9:1; 13:26) attended by the divine *dunamis,* is now realized. "This eschatological power is historical power leading the world and history to their goal."[41]

From all kinds of characteristic traits it follows that the miracles can only be viewed within the scope of the coming of the kingdom.[42] Thus, e.g., they are repeatedly indicated as the fulfillment of the prophecies (cf. Matt. 11:5, and 8:17); or as evidence of God's "visiting" his people with the blessings of salvation (Luke 7:16). This "visiting" is to be understood as the long promised delivery of God's people which had been looked forward to for such a long time (cf. Luke 1:68,78).[43] Jesus' miracles again and again suggest to the people, who do not know him as the Messiah, the thought that he might be the Son of David (Matt. 12:23). Some of them desiring to be cured by him incidentally address him as such (Matt. 9:27; 15:22; 20:30, and parallels); just as the disciples worship him as the Son of God because of his power over the wind and the sea (Matt. 14:33). This is why Israel's recalcitrance will be laid to their charge more heavily than to any other nation, exactly because of these manifestations of Jesus' power (Matt. 11:21ff, and parallels). On the other hand the belief in Jesus as the heaven-sent sovereign Ruler will entitle the Gentiles to sit down with Abraham, Isaac and Jacob in the kingdom of heaven (Matt. 8:8-11, and parallels). Moreover, the real issue with miracles is the glorification of God (Matt. 9:8; Luke 5:26; 17:17-18ff), by those also who do not belong to the people of Israel in the narrow sense of the word (Matt. 15:31, "They glorified the God of Israel"). A miracle, as much as preaching, in its sense of being a revelation of the kingdom of God, is a confrontation which necessitates a decision: for or against Jesus as the victor of the Evil one and the Bearer of the Spirit of God (Matt. 12:30,31, and parallels; Mark 9:39,40); of faith (Matt. 8:10; 9:28; 15:28); or disbelief (Matt. 13:58), and hardness of heart (Mark 3:5); and of the sin against the Holy Spirit because of the opposition to the clear manifestation of the kingdom of God (Matt. 12:31, and parallels). For this reason the miracle in itself is not the most important thing, nor even the sharing in Jesus' miraculous power, but much rather, the participation in the redemption of the kingdom which is thereby revealed (Luke 10:20, cf. also Mark 1:38 where Jesus interrupts the miracles in order to go elsewhere to preach the kingdom of God with the words "for therefore I am sent," cf. Luke 4:42-44).

11. Preaching the Gospel

In answer to John the Baptist's question: "Are you he that cometh?" Jesus not only refers to his miracles, but also to the preaching of the gospel to the poor: "the poor have the gospel preached to them." Fundamentally these words imply that the fulfillment of the promise, the coming of the Messiah and of the kingdom are not only manifested in Jesus' miracles but also in his preaching. The same thought is found with different wording in Luke 16:16: "The law and the prophets were until John: since that time (the Good News of) the kingdom of God is preached." Here the dispensation of the law and the prophets is opposed to the preaching of the gospel of the kingdom of God. In other words, in the preaching of the gospel has been realized that which was only an expectation in the law and the prophets. This is why Jesus can call the disciples blessed not only for what they *see,* but also for what they *hear.* In this respect they were favored above the Old Testament believers even in their most important representatives (Matt. 13:16,17; Luke 10:23,24).[44] *The preaching of the gospel is no less a proof than the miracles that the kingdom of heaven has come.*

For a correct insight into these general statements it is of special importance to consider the qualification *gospel* more closely. Jesus' preaching is repeatedly summarized by it (e.g., Matt. 4:23; 9:35; 24:14; 26:13; Mark 1:14,15; 8:35; 13:10).[45] Although this word is used for the whole of the preaching of the kingdom of heaven (so not exclusively to indicate the salvation, but also the judgment brought with the kingdom, cf., e.g., Luke 3:18) the word means: good or joyful news, and characterizes the contents of Jesus' preaching as the promulgation of salvation.[46]

All this stands out against the Old Testament background of the word "gospel" which is especially to be sought in the second part of the prophecies of Isaiah.[47] There the messenger of good news is mentioned, the *mĕbassēr,* who preaches the kingly dominion of Jahwe, the dawn of the new era (Is. 52:7), bringing salvation and peace to Zion. In Isaiah 61 the messenger of salvation is himself introduced as the speaker, as he who has been anointed with the Spirit of the Lord and sent to bring good news to the meek (*lĕbassēr*). Although this kingship of Jahwe also implies strife and wrath (cf. Is. 52:10; 61:2), it is announced as a message of joy. For this royal manifestation of Jahwe is made for the benefit of his oppressed people, also and precisely then, when He bears "his holy arm" against his enemies. This is why the good news, because it is addressed to his people, can be preached as news of salvation and joy.[48]

Among the Jews living at the time of Jesus, the picture of the messenger of peace in Isaiah had remained alive. The *mĕbassēr* will come, the messianic time will start. It is not always said who this messenger is. But with his coming the *malkuth shamaim* (the kingdom of heaven) will begin.[49]

Thus the roots of Jesus' use of the word "gospel" are discovered. Even if the rabinnical places were to be eliminated, it would still be evident that Jesus identifies himself with the messenger of joy of Isaiah. For the above mentioned words: *the poor have the good news preached to them* are not only a quotation from Isaiah 61:1, but also in his initial proclamation of the gospel, according to Luke, Jesus explicitly states that the prophecy of the messenger of joy of Isaiah 61 is fulfilled now while he is addressing his hearers. This messenger has been anointed with the Holy Spirit, and has been sent to preach the gospel to the poor (Luke 4:21). Against this Old Testament background we should interpret the original meaning of the expression "the gospel of the kingdom of heaven." And it follows that in this preaching of the gospel, as it echoes in the ears of Jesus' audience, the kingdom of heaven has become a present reality: the *mĕbassēr*, the bringer of the good news to the poor, has appeared; the great moment of salvation has begun.

Furthermore the beatitudes, both in the tradition of Matthew 5:3ff and in Luke 6:20ff, must be considered in connection with the Old Testament background. They may be viewed as the classical example of Jesus' preaching of the kingdom of heaven, both on account of their place in the gospel and because of the especially solemn and emphatic form of Jesus' words.[50] But these beatitudes are in the first place addressed to the poor (in spirit), and therefore they are the most authentic illustration of the preaching of the kingdom of heaven qualified in Luke 4 and 7 (Matt. 11) as the *gospel*.

Therefore the gospel preached here is not merely a promise; nor does it consist solely in the fact that salvation has come *nearer*. Though still future as regards its perfect consummation, it has fundamentally become a fact at the present moment. It is true, Jesus does not use the terms "fundamentally" and "perfect consummation." He always speaks of the *basileia* as a unity. But by the side of pronouncements concerning the future we find those concerning the present. *The preaching is not only characterized as prophecy and announcement, but also as proclamation and promulgation.*[51]

This is explained in the first place by the authority or power with which Jesus preaches the gospel of the kingdom. His word is not only a sign, it is charged with power; it has the disposal of the matter, the salvation which it defines: it is not merely a word, but "it shall accomplish that which he pleases" who speaks it. That is why at bottom there is no difference between the word with which Jesus casts out devils and his preaching of the gospel. In both cases the word and what it indicates go together. Nowhere does this connection come to light more clearly than in the story of the healing of a palsied man (Mark 2:1-12, and parallels). Here the preaching of the gospel comes first: "Son, thy sins be forgiven thee." When the scribes consider this as blasphemy, Jesus asks: "Whether is it easier to say to the sick of the palsy, thy sins be forgiven thee; or to say: arise, and take up thy bed and walk?" The power of the word is at issue here, i.e., the preaching of the gospel: "who can (*dunatai*) forgive sins but God only?". Is the man who speaks like this entitled and able to make good the purport of his words? In an affirmative form this thought is expressed thus: "but that you may know that the Son of Man hath power on earth to forgive sins" (*exousian echei . . . aphienai . . . epi tès gès*). It is not the *preaching* of the forgiveness of sins or the *promise* that God shall forgive them (cf. 2 Sam. 12:13), but *the remission of sins itself* which is the issue here, as appears from the present tense of the verb at verse 5 ("your sins *are* forgiven"), and from the words: *on earth.* For the new and unprecedented thing here is not that forgiveness is being *announced,* but that it is being *accomplished on earth.*[52] This is Jesus' power (*exousia*) as the Son of Man, i.e., as he who has been given all kingly power, according to Daniel 7:14; and in this is manifested the presence of the kingdom of heaven. In this sense Jesus' preaching of the *basileia* is at the same time its revelation. The multitude, too, notices this authority with which Jesus preaches the gospel, although they remain outsiders with respect to its real secret. For the most part they are offended by it, because they feel it as blasphemy for a human being to speak with such authority which belongs only to God (Mark 2:7, parallels).

That is why Jesus' adversaries were able to attempt to entangle him "in his words" (*en logooi*) (Matt. 22:15; Mark 12:13; Luke 20:20,26); for in his word they sensed his claim to absolute authority and thereby his dangerous character.[53] Others, however, responded in a more positive way. Thus, e.g., on the occasion of the miracle of the healing of the palsied man, the multitude was filled with fear and praise for God "who had given such authority to men" (Matt. 9:8). Although they do not know Jesus in his true significance (they conceive that which Jesus maintains as the authority of the Son of Man, as an *exousia* given by God "to men,")[54] they recognize Jesus' authority to forgive sins when they witness the miracle. We also point to the many expressions of "fear," "amazement," "astonishment," "bewilderment," "confusion," "being beyond themselves,"[55] describing the frame of mind of the multitude upon seeing his miracles and hearing his preaching. Again and again these and similar reactions are recorded (cf., e.g., Mark 1:27; Luke 4:36; Mark 10:24; Mark 5:20; Luke 11:14; Matt. 12:23, and other places). They are not intended, however, only as historical-psychological descriptions of the impression that Jesus made on the multitude. The evangelists want to indicate that Jesus' word and work revealed the absolute, the supernatural, and the divine in such a way that even the multitude could not but be aware of it.[56] As has been said, this amazement is not only caused by their witnessing of his miracles, but also by their listening to his preaching (cf. Luke 4:22; Matt. 22:22). They are not merely amazed at Jesus' knowledge or wisdom or ability in speaking, but at bottom they respond to the powers and the authority revealed in his word. In this respect there is no difference between Jesus' preaching and his miracles. Both bring to the light the same sovereign disposal of that which only belongs to God. He has only to say "a word," he has only to command, just as a centurion commands his men (Matt. 8:8; Luke 7:7, *eipe logooi*, cf. also Matt. 8:16). This is also clear in the amazed reaction of the multitude in Mark 1:27, when they see Jesus' power over the devils and call out full of "amazement": "What thing is this? A new doctrine with authority![57] He also commands the unclean spirits and they obey him." The miracles make it clear to them that the "new doctrine" Jesus brings (that of the kingdom) is effective and therefore preached with authority.[58] This doctrine is at the same time power. The promulgation of the kingdom is also the revelation of the kingdom.

Repeatedly *exousia* is mentioned as the element in Jesus' preaching and doctrine that created the amazement of the multitude. "He taught them as one that had authority" (*hoos exousian echoon*), Mark 1:22; Matthew 7:28,29, cf. also Luke 4:32: "for his word was with power" (*en exousiai*). And this was not only true with respect to the preaching of the gospel as the proclamation of redemption, but also with regard to Jesus' commandments. In Mark 1:22 and Matthew 7:29 Jesus' preaching is thus spoken of in opposition to that of the scribes. It is true that Israel's teachers also speak with authority (cf., e.g., Matt. 23:3,4); their commandments, too, claim validity. They, however, derive their authority from another source, they "sit in Moses' seat" (Matt. 23:3); they appeal to the precepts of the ancestors (Matt. 5:21ff). Jesus' doctrine, however, owes everything to his own authority (cf. his repeated: "But I say unto you" in the Sermon on the Mount). His commands are given by an absolute authority and have unlimited· validity. Even though heaven and earth shall pass away, his words shall not pass away (Mark 13:31ff).

It is clear that all this can only be explained by the significance of Jesus' person and mission. It is this which the astonished multitude senses on seeing his miracles (Matt. 12:23), and on hearing his preaching: "Who is this that forgiveth sins also?" (Luke 7:49). The presence of the kingdom, both in Jesus' action and in his preaching of the gospel, the salvation he proclaims, the possession of bliss that he assigns to the poor in spirit, rest in the secret of Jesus' person. The only satisfactory exegesis of the gospel of the kingdom in all its facets is the Christological. In the end everything must concentrate on Jesus' self-revelation. The fulfillment, the new tidings that Jesus has brought can not in any way be separated from his own person, as, e.g., a doctrine promulgated by him and spread by the apostles, but it is present in his person, "in the historical event" which is given with him, *which he is.*[59]

12. *The Possession of Salvation*

There is one more facet of the fulfillment proclaimed by Jesus' preaching of the kingdom of heaven. A closer study of the gospel teaches us that in Jesus' coming the kingdom of heaven not only reveals itself as a *power* that brings the rule of the evil one to ruin, and restores life up to now liable to disease and death, or as a *message* of salvation and bliss preached to the poor in spirit. It is also a *gift* in which those who receive it from God may delight as in an already present possession of a future salvation one day fully to be given them. This aspect of the coming of the kingdom comes to the fore already in the terms that Jesus uses in his preaching:[60] "It is your Father's good pleasure to *give* you the kingdom" (Luke 12:32). It shall be taken from the unrepentant Jews and given to others (Matt. 21:43). Christ *appoints* (*diatithemai*) the kingdom to his disciples, just as his Father has *appointed* the kingdom to him (Luke 22:29). Conversely, men should *receive* the kingdom of God as a little child (Mark 10:15); they must *seek it* (Matt. 6:33); they will *inherit* it (Matt. 25:34); etc. But quite apart from such terminology, this significance of the kingdom of heaven is also implied in its very nature. Exactly because the preaching of the kingdom is done with absolute authority by Jesus, not only in words and promises but also by the establishment of that which is proclaimed, the coming of the kingdom necessarily consists not only in its proclamation but carries the gift of salvation with it. Thus it may be said that in this gift we receive and possess the kingdom itself. Related with this is the thought that we *enter* the kingdom of heaven, an expression of very frequent occurrence in the gospels (Matt. 5:20; 7:21; 18:3; 19:23; 23:13; Mark 9:47; Luke 11:52ff); that we *are* in the kingdom (great, least, far away from, etc., cf. Matt. 5:19; 11:11; Mark 12:34, etc.). Such phrases also make it clear that the kingdom of heaven can be shared in some way or other, that it changes the lives of those who receive it, that by virtue of God's act it becomes a *gift, a possession, a vital domain* of those to whom this privilege is granted.

For our purpose it is particularly important to ascertain to what extent this gift, this possession of salvation, already appears in Jesus' preaching in the light of fulfillment (i.e., of the kingdom *having* come). In several of the texts given above, this gift is exclusively represented as something of the great future (cf., e.g., Luke 12:32; Matt. 25:34ff). And in most cases where the text speaks of *entering* the kingdom we shall have to think of men being given a share in eternal bliss (Matt. 7:21,22; 19:23; cf. vs. 27ff). However, it does not seem strange to us, after all that has been discussed in the preceding pages, that the kingdom of heaven is spoken of also as a gift and a possession received and enjoyed already in the present. Now, it is certainly true that among those who maintain the presence of the *basileia* in opposition to the exclusive eschatology, there are several authors who will not hear of this, due mostly as a reaction against the application of an idealistic doctrine of values to Jesus' preaching of the kingdom. Yet it cannot be denied that the terminology of the gospel speaks of the kingdom as a soteriological *good* and it cannot be maintained that receiving it is only something that pertains to the future. The proclamation of the salvation of the *basileia* is from the outset also concerned with the gift implied in it which is given to the faithful already in the present.

In a certain sense, the latter idea is the essence of the gospel of the kingdom. Here, too, we should point to the Beatitudes (Matt. 5:3ff; Luke 6:20ff), in which Jesus very specially proclaims the kingdom of heaven as the blessedness, the salvation of the poor. It is true that the special character of these Beatitudes lies in the fact that the salvation that is preached is announced as a good which will be revealed to the full only in the future. Nevertheless, it is also in the present possession of the poor in spirit. For when they are here told that they are blessed because the kingdom of heaven is theirs (*estin*), we must do full justice to this present tense. Attempts have been made to understand the salvation assigned to the poor in spirit in a purely future-eschatological sense (in view of the future pronouncements in Matt. 5:4ff, and Luke 6:21ff).[61] Though the full realization of the salvation promised to the poor in spirit may be something of the future according to the rest of the Beatitudes, this nevertheless does not mean that its blessing must be conceived as something that cannot be given and received in the present.[62]

Moreover, when in other places in the Scriptures the kingdom is represented as a *treasure*, this also should not be considered as something only belonging to the future. It is true that in more than one passage the kingdom is spoken of as a "treasure in heaven" which must now be gathered together and upon which we must set our hearts (Matt. 6:19-21, cf. vs. 33). This is also the meaning of the parallel text in Luke 12:33: "provide yourselves bags which wax not old, a treasure in the heavens that faileth not." And to the rich young ruler Jesus said: "Go and sell that thou hast, and give to the

poor, and thou shalt have treasure in heaven" (Matt. 19:21).
Another image is that of the "reward in heaven" and of the
"reward of your Father which is in heaven" (Matt. 5:12; 6:1ff).
It is clear that all these images denote something that transcends
present earthly reality because it is in heaven, and which is
preserved in heaven for the faithful until its revelation in the
coming kingdom of God (cf. I Peter 1:4; Col. 1:5).

Yet it should not be conceived of as exclusively future.
Again and again it appears that the salvation of the kingdom
is assigned to the disciples and the faithful in general as a
present reality. Thus in Matthew 13:16,17 (cf. Luke 10:23,24)
the disciples are called blessed because of what they see and
hear even now. It will not do to think of this blessedness
only in a prophetic sense, no more than we can deprive Jesus'
words to the palsied man (see above) of its immediate significance for the present. To Zacchaeus of Jericho Jesus says with
great emphasis: "*This day* is salvation come to this house"
(Luke 19:9); to the disciples he says that they must rejoice
because their names are written (perfect tense) in heaven
(Luke 10:20); to the woman who praises Jesus' mother as
blessed he says, "Those are blessed who hear the word of
God and keep it" (Luke 11:27,28). In the same way we can
point to Mark 10:15 (Luke 18:17): "Verily I say unto you,
whosoever shall not *receive* the kingdom of God as a little
child, he *shall* not *enter* therein." Even if entering the kingdom
is taken in a future-eschatological sense, which in this passage
is apparently the obvious thing to do, the "receiving" of the
kingdom must needs be understood as something that precedes
the "entry" into it. The meaning is not obscure. It is certainly
the reception of the gospel, the faith in Jesus, which is meant
here. But as Jesus' words are not only language and signs but
also power and reality, the *word* of the kingdom may also be
referred to as the kingdom itself. In the preaching the salvation has already been *given*.

That is why it is often difficult to draw a line between
the present and the future of salvation, and in many cases it is

wrong to *wish* to draw such a line of demarcation. Too often all kinds of passages are sifted in an atomistic way into pronouncements concerning the "presence" and those about the "future," as if such a selection were final. Even if by means of a certain method of reduction we should retain only a limited number of passages teaching the presence of salvation and the soteriological possession of bliss assigned to the faithful *expressis verbis,* it would signify but little. For in its present and future revelation the kingdom of heaven is a unity, and the Person of Jesus on whom the promulgation of salvation is based, is the same for the present and the future. This is why the salvation, the treasure, the possession which represents the kingdom of heaven to the faithful embrace both present and future. This is not to say that every indication of salvation has a present significance. When in the synoptic gospels Jesus speaks of the kingdom as "the regeneration" (Matt. 19:28), or of "everlasting life" (Matt. 19:29), he means that which will happen and be given "in the world to come" (Mark 10:30; Luke 18:30). Thus we may wonder whether the expression "enter into the kingdom of heaven" is not exclusively used of the entry into eternal life. In our opinion this is very doubtful, to say the least, in view of passages such as Matthew 23:13 and 7:13; Luke 13:24, where the entry into the kingdom clearly means more than an eschatological moment. In any case Matthew 11:11 speaks of *being* more or less in the kingdom in a present sense. Yet, however important all this may be, it is not decisive for what we wish to argue here. Decisive is the fact that the presence and unity of the kingdom of heaven and of the person who has been invested with divine authority, are also the ground of the presence of salvation, and that already for this reason the kingdom can be spoken of as a present *possession* of salvation.

To our mind this is the sense in which we must take the parable of the treasure hidden in a field, and that of the pearl of great price (Matt. 13:44-46). It is true that opinions differ as to the *tertium comparationis* in these parables; one author points to the infinite value[63] of the kingdom, another to the sacrifice[64] this pearl demands.[65] In our view both meanings are valid, although that of the infinite value has priority. The kingdom represents a treasure which is to be desired above everything else and which is really coveted by all who have been endowed with an eye for it.

These parables, too, are the subject of all kinds of discussions about the possession of salvation, viz., as to whether or not it belongs to the present. Kümmel thinks that Jesus knows nothing of the kingdom being "present on earth" and declares that these parables cannot be adduced as a proof for it.[66] Michaelis maintains that the treasure in Matthew 13:44-46 only refers to the future kingdom.[67] In my opinion he is wrong. In the first place, considered by itself, the parable seems to speak of something present rather than of something that is exclusively future. The "treasure-digger" as well as the "merchant" take possession of the treasure they wish to have and do not merely acquire the right to it or the prospect of it. However, the whole manner of positing the problem is improper. The issue is not the presence or the future of the kingdom within the scope of these parables alone, but is connected with the whole character of the kingdom preached by Jesus.[68]

In a separate chapter we shall have to examine that which constitutes the salvation of the kingdom which Jesus assigns to his followers as a gift and as a treasure already in the life of today.[69] Here it is enough to conclude that the kingdom of heaven also signifies a possession of salvation for believers, and is also present as such, and that the explanation and the secret of *this* form of the fulfillment lies in the person of him who assigns this blessing to his people by virtue of his authority and power. In his fellowship the gift of what he proclaims is unconditionally guaranteed and granted to them.

13. *Jesus is the Christ*

In the preceding expositions it has appeared again and again that the real and most profound explanation of the presence of the kingdom is to be sought in the person of Jesus himself. The secret of the presence of the kingdom of heaven lies in Jesus' victory over Satan, in his unlimited miraculous power, his unrestricted authority to preach the gospel, in his pronouncements of blessedness and the bestowal of salvation upon his people. There can be no doubt that we are confronted here with the *messianic, Christological* character of the kingdom of heaven and that *the entire fulfillment which Jesus proclaims as a present reality is based on the fact that he himself, Jesus, is the Christ.*

It is true that, on the part of modern criticism, attempts have been made to deny this essential and indissoluble relationship between person and matter, messianic office and gospel. It is well-known that at one time Harnack thought he could detach the gospel of the kingdom from the person of Jesus as the Christ, the Son of God.[70]   And in recent times Bultmann, e.g., expressed as his opinion that the question as to whether or not Jesus considered himself to be the Messiah is of "secondary importance" with respect to the interpretation of the gospel.[71]   But such statements can only be maintained if the gospel as it has been handed down to us is deprived of its clear and unmistakable meaning. Even the great liberal theologian H. J. Holtzmann acknowledged very reluctantly that it is impossible to remove the whole chapter of Jesus' messianic self-consciousness as a *corpus alienum* from the gospel of the kingdom because without Jesus' messiahship the evangelical history loses its backbone.[72]   Later critics, including those of the "form-criticism" school, made similar pronouncements. Thus, e.g., Dibelius writes that the gospel is concentrated on Jesus' person: *"nicht vom Reich hat er ihnen etwas mitzuteilen, sondern unter dem Zwange des Reiches teilt er sich mit"* (i.e., it is not that he has something of the kingdom to share with them, but rather that, by virtue of the compulsion of the kingdom, he communicates himself with it). Not only with his word, but also with his person he is responsible for the coming of the kingdom. He is not only the mouthpiece of God, but the source of energy of the new being[73] in which, according to Dibelius, the real essence of the kingdom of heaven consists (divested of its "mythological" mold).

In a previous section[74] we have proved that the whole idea of the kingdom of heaven is of a messianic determination. This is true not only of the Old Testament and of the later Jewish expectation of the future, but also in Jesus' preaching the kingdom of God and the Messiah (especially as the Son of Man) are correlate concepts. We have considered this relation only in an objective sense, i.e., without paying attention to Jesus' messianic *self*-revelation. Our discussion dealt chiefly with those pronouncements that speak of the coincidence of the coming of the kingdom and the coming (*parousia*) of the Son of Man. Now, however, we must lay full emphasis on the subjective aspect in such a way that the whole of Jesus' proclamation of the fulfillment, i.e., of the coming of the kingdom as a present, actual reality, runs parallel with Jesus' self-revelation as the Messiah who has been sent into this world by God, a self-revelation on which his proclamation is based. In this connection—that of the fulfillment!—it is especially the present accomplished significance of Jesus' messiahship which is at issue. For here we also encounter the assertion of the exclusively eschatological school which recognizes the intrinsic connection between the kingdom of God and the Messiah, but ascribes a purely future meaning to both. In the same way that Jesus is supposed to have spoken of the kingdom as an exclusively future entity, he is also said to have spoken of the Messiah (the Son of Man) as the great figure of the future. Schweitzer gave pregnant expression to this thought in his phrase *Messias designatus*. As such Jesus is supposed to have considered himself, i.e., as the one who was appointed and destined by God as the Messiah in the great cosmic revolution. This radically-eschatological interpretation of Jesus' messianic self-consciousness is still energetically defended by such authors as M. Werner and F. Buri.[75] And another writer, viz., Michaelis, adopts the term *Messias designatus*, but he means by it that Jesus' messiahship only began with the events of

Easter and Pentecost. Thus it would follow that Jesus did not lay claim to the messianic dignity during his earthly life, but only held out the prospect of messiahship for the future.[76]

As we shall show in more detail, this thesis contains an important element of truth insofar as Jesus, for a not inconsiderable part, refers the exercise of his messianic office to the future, and in such cases not infrequently speaks of himself as the coming Messiah. Vos rightly pointed out that, often when Jesus speaks of the *parousia* of the Son of Man, this must not be translated as the *second* coming, but simply as the *coming* of the Messiah (cf. Matt. 24:27,37,39). In the same way Jesus speaks elsewhere of his future revelation as of his coming (Mark 13:26; Matt. 24:30,42; Luke 12:40; 17:30; 18:8ff).[77] From all this we might superficially infer that the Son of Man has not yet come. And the consistently eschatological view, therefore, wants to understand all the texts where Jesus calls himself the Son of Man, in an anticipatory, proleptic sense.

But on closer examination it is apparent that this conception is wholly untenable. Not only does it result in very awkward explanations of certain "Son-of-Man" statements, e.g., of Mark 8:31, which is paraphrased as follows: "as the one who is to be the Son of Man I have to suffer greatly."[78] But this view is compelled to treat as secondary other passages which undeniably speak of the presence of the Son of Man, e.g., Matt. 8:20; 11:19; 12:32; 12:40; 13:37,41; 16:13. In these a later tradition is supposed to have inserted into non-messianic "I-pronouncements" the indication of the Son of Man's self-disclosure.[79]

In itself it is not impossible for the tradition to have changed traditional "I-pronouncements" into "Son of Man"-pronouncements (cf., e.g., Mark 8:27 and Matt. 16:13). But not a single reason can be derived from the sources for the assumption that such a change was caused by some later "messianic adaptation" of Jesus' pre-messianic or un-messianic activity and self-revelation. For, not only is the whole evangelical kerygma based on the certainty that Jesus was the Messiah so that, consequently, any one who is only prepared to attach a merely future-messianic sense to the "Son of Man pronouncements" is obliged to subject the entire gospel to such a reduction. But the gospel will be deprived of its real essence and its most fundamental basis if to Jesus' pronouncements concerning his own self we refuse to assign their present-messianic significance, or if we should be inclined to take them as the fruit of a later tradition. Although we cannot here be exhaustive, the following summary may give an impression of the impossibility of positing, from the sources at our disposal, a pre-messianic conception and picture of Jesus' coming and his work.

A. Jesus' action among the people is preceded by the divine indication of Jesus' messiahship on the occasion of his baptism in the Jordan by John (Matt. 3:17; Mark 1:11; Luke 3:22). This indication is repeated during the transfiguration of Jesus on the mountain, i.e., on the eve of Jesus' passion and death (Matt. 17:5; Mark 9:7; Luke 9:35). We may pass by the question as to whether the pronouncement: "This is (Thou art) my (beloved, chosen) Son," only applies to Jesus' messianic office, or also denotes the ontological relationship between God the Father and the Son, as, e.g., is assumed by Stonehouse[80] and Sevenster.[81] In any case, Jesus is proclaimed the Messiah both at baptism and at the transfiguration on the mountain. Such appears clearly from the messianic predicates: the Beloved, the Chosen One, and from the words: "In whom I am well pleased" (cf. e.g., Isaiah 42:1-4; Matt. 12:18), and from the version of the divine words in Luke 3:22, which indicate Jesus as the messianic king in the words of Psalm 2:7. Such an indication cannot possibly be explained in a proleptic sense.[82] It explicitly sets Jesus' coming and his work in the light of the present (cf. also the words "hear ye him" during the transfiguration). Jesus' entire work following is qualified by it from the outset (cf. also Matt. 4:3 and parallels).

B. Very closely connected with this is the descent of the

Holy Spirit upon Jesus accompanied by a heavenly voice (Matt. 3:16; Mark 1:10; Luke 3:22). This, too, has a clearly messianic significance. It does not have the meaning ascribed to it in a psychological[83] or an adoptionist Christology[84], but rather, that of a divine preparation of Jesus for the task that had been entrusted by the Father to him as the Messiah (cf., e.g., Isaiah 11:2; 61:1ff).[85] In the same way we must understand Luke 4:18, where Jesus applies the words from Isaiah 61:1 to himself: "The Spirit of the Lord is upon me, because he has anointed me to preach the Gospel to the poor." Even if in Isaiah 61:1 the concepts: "anoint" and "Holy Spirit" are carefully kept apart,[86] because the anointing refers to the appointment to the office, this does not detract from the fact that the gift of the Spirit has its purpose in the exercise of the office. It is true that in another passage Michaelis refers to these facts as the "Ausrüstung für sein (Jesu) Auftreten als Messias designatus" (his investiture, i.e., Jesus', for his appearance as the Messiah designate).[87] But this restriction to a future messiahship is not founded in an exegesis of these words, but on Michaelis' general pre-suppositions. Again and again there is evidence of Jesus' being endued with this Spirit already during his earthly activity, and of his having the Holy Spirit at his disposal because of his messiahship. Thus, e.g., in Matthew 12:28, where Jesus says explicitly that he casts out devils by the Spirit of God, and that, therefore, the kingdom has come. This passage shows that his being invested with the Holy Spirit (the messianic aspect) coalesces with the coming of the kingdom. In the same context—not only in Matthew but also in Mark 3:29—the slander of the scribes is considered as blasphemy[88] or *speaking against*[89] *the Holy Spirit*. The power which turns Jesus' word into deed, the authority with which he speaks, is the Holy Spirit with whom he has been empowered, and whom, as the Messiah, he has at his disposal.

All these things are not merely based on a few utterances, but form the pre-supposition of Jesus' action. As the Messiah, sent by God, Jesus is guided and prompted by the Holy Spirit in everything. After his baptism in the Jordan "the Spirit drove him into the wilderness" (Mark 1:12); he was "led up of the Spirit into the wilderness" (Luke 4:1). Thus the temptation is not merely described as an event that took place under the leading of God's providence, but as an encounter of the divinely appointed Messiah equipped by the Holy Spirit with the great adversary. Jesus' being driven by and being filled with the Spirit also explains that the tempter's assault was fore-doomed to failure. It is also the secret of Jesus' word of power after the third temptation: "Get thee hence, Satan!" (Matt. 4:10). For it is the powerful word by which the Messiah rebukes Satan and from the outset compels him to recognize the Messiah's superiority and authority.[90]

This investiture with the Holy Spirit as Jesus' messianic privilege is one of the basic motives of the gospel, although it is not explicitly mentioned every time. In Luke 4:14 it says once more that "Jesus returned in the power of the Spirit" into Galilee. This pronouncement, too, must be understood in close connection with Luke 3:22 and Luke 4:1. His being endued with the Spirit is the principle and the power of Jesus' entire activity and from beginning to end it stamps his action as the discharge of his messianic duty. In the same way we must conceive of Jesus' power to *bestow* the Holy Spirit on men. We remind the reader of John the Baptist's word saying that he who was to come after him would baptize not only with water (like John) but with the Holy Spirit as the great messianic and eschatological gift of salvation. It is true, this baptism with the Spirit would not immediately be realized when Jesus began his activities: it was promised to the disciples after his resurrection as a revelation of God's presence (Acts 1:5). This is not saying, however, that now Jesus was only the Messiah designate. It only shows that Jesus' messiahship was not at once fully developed. This thought will receive our attention in greater detail later on.

In his *Reich Gottes und Geist Gottes nach dem Neuen Testament* Michaelis tries to show that the synoptic gospels

speak with great restraint of Jesus' possession of the Holy
Spirit. Luke represents this thought more emphatically than
Matthew and Mark, but Michaelis suggests that in this case
we have to deal with a "purposive adaptation of the evangelical tradition."[91] Thus he is willing to accept Luke 4:14
and 4:18 only with some reserve; and he is of the opinion further that in the story of the temptation Jesus was not led into
the wilderness by the Spirit he had received at his baptism, but
by an "alien power."[92] At any rate, this passage is supposed
to be the only one in the older tradition according to which
Jesus was led away under the irresistible impulse of the Spirit.
Michaelis looks upon Matt. 12:28 ("by the Spirit of God") as
secondary, in view of Luke 11:20 ("by the finger of God").
Properly speaking only the account of his receiving the Spirit
at baptism is left us in this view, and, to a certain extent, also
the saying about blasphemy against the Spirit. And yet
Michaelis thinks that these few passages are sufficient for the
assertion that tradition views Jesus as the bearer of the Holy
Spirit, and that he also looked upon himself as such. However,
this view is rarely put in the foreground, and Michaelis explains
this fact by pointing out that in his actions on earth Jesus
was only the Messiah designate. The relation of the kingdom
of God and the Spirit of God is only mentioned insofar as
Jesus was the bearer of the Spirit in his quality as Messiah
designate.[93]

We cannot help thinking that Michaelis arbitrarily restricts the position that the Holy Spirit occupies in the synoptic
gospels in favor of his view of the future character of Jesus'
messiahship. But on the other hand the number of passages in
which the Holy Spirit is spoken of is comparatively small. It
is also true that during his activity on earth Jesus did not come
forward as the one who baptized with the Holy Spirit. In this
respect, therefore, in the synoptic tradition the kingdom of
heaven is still a matter of the future. In my opinion Michaelis'
great error is that he apparently overlooks the fact of Jesus'
action *as such*. All his miracles and his words, were ruled by

an absolute consciousness of authority, and were actually borne by the gift and the power of the Holy Spirit, though this fact is not always explicitly mentioned in every case. The small number of texts assigning the Holy Spirit to Jesus cannot be explained by saying that Jesus was only the Messiah of the future. Much rather it is due to Jesus' messiahship being so much the very cornerstone of the tradition that his having the Spirit did not need repeated mention. Its infrequent occurrence does not signify any "limitation" of Jesus' messiahship, but rather an abundant amount of certainty that his authority was that of the Messiah. For it is not the possession of the Holy Spirit but the coming of Messiah that is the foundation of the gospel and the proof of the kingdom having come.

C. It may be called a very remarkable fact that in the synoptic tradition Jesus nowhere explicitly called himself the Messiah and more than once imposed silence on those who addressed him, called after him, or confessed him as such. This phenomenon will claim our attention in a later context. It has been referred to in all kinds of ways to prove the unmessianic or pre-messianic character of Jesus' action. But this can only be properly evaluated after one has seen that the whole gospel is full of all kinds of pronouncements on the part of Jesus testifying to the absolute authority he claimed. Such pronouncements are only to be explained by his unique relation to the Father and from his messianic self-consciousness. It is true that here also criticism has ever busied itself with distinguishing between what might be "historical" and what is the result of the "Christology of the church." But this effort to distinguish between what Jesus "can have said" and what he "cannot have said" of himself must be called internally contradictory. On the ground of certain pro-scientific convictions the critic feels bound to call unauthentic and secondary *every* one of Jesus' pronouncements handed down to us which testifies to this supernatural and exclusive self-consciousness. But this is not a matter of only a few outstanding pronouncements but concerns the whole character of Jesus' self-revelation. In

the latter his messiahship is only exceptionally revealed in a
direct and open way. But on closer investigation it appears
that *every* word which Jesus speaks about himself, though often
indirect and in many cases implicit, is borne by a self-consciousness which exceeds all natural boundaries and cannot be
understood in any other way than in connection with his messianic mission. We will therefore seek to bring to light the
indissoluble unity in all that has been handed down to us
concerning Jesus' messianic self-revelation rather than discuss
the criticism of all kinds of separate pronouncements.

The climax of the synoptic tradition in this respect is
found in the words of Matthew 11:27 and Luke 10:22. Here
Jesus praises the Father because he "has hidden these things
from the wise and prudent, and has revealed them unto babes."
And then Jesus goes on to say: "All things are delivered unto
me of my Father: and no man knoweth the Son, but the Father,
neither knoweth any man the Father, save the Son, and he
to whomsoever the Son will reveal him." These words are as
much about the (messianic) mission and authority as they are
about what may be called the equality and the identity of
essence[94] of the Father and the Son. For the mystery of the
Son is placed on an equal basis with that of the Father, and
the communication of the revelation concerning Father and
Son is the exclusive privilege of both. The one as well as the
other is of the greatest importance in this context, not only for
the purpose of setting the supernatural significance of Jesus'
messiahship in the light, but also to maintain its present character. For in whatever respect the significance of Jesus' person
may be related to the future, the ontological relationship between the Father and the Son, indicated here, *cannot* be
referred to the future. It presupposes the pre-existence of
Jesus' person. But from this fact it follows that it would be
absurd to entertain the thought of a purely future messiahship
in connection with Jesus' life on earth. For if in the above sense
Jesus was the Son of God, his earthly existence cannot be
deprived of its messianic character without making the mean-

ing of his incarnation and his human existence before the *parousia* altogether problematical. The idea of the Messiah designate really means a "total destruction of the Christological dogma."[95]

This holds with all the more emphasis as Jesus himself—although not without some restraint and, as it were, only in hints—repeatedly spoke of his messianic mission *in the past tense*, i.e., as of something that he had already been charged with, and that he was carrying out now. Thus, in Matthew 11:27[a] and Luke 10:22[a], the wording of which is closely related to Jesus' proclamation of his power and authority after his resurrection (Matt. 28:18). From the context it appears that these words relate to Jesus' miracles, i.e., to the present, and not merely to the future. The same past tense is found in passages about Jesus' *coming*, or about the coming of the Son of Man, in the so-called *elthon*-sayings. In a study of these sayings Harnack tried to establish that they have no messianic meaning.[96] But his view was entirely based on naturalistic presuppositions, as, e.g., Sevenster has proved.[97] It is now being more and more generally recognized that these sayings have a special Christological significance and pre-suppose Jesus' pre-existence. The "coming" mentioned here must be conceived as a "coming out of heaven." The word belongs to the world of thought of the Divine epiphany."[98] Present-day radical criticism starts from the same premises as the old liberal theologians did, but assigns a deeper meaning to the synoptic tradition. Nevertheless, it denies the authenticity of these sayings and feels entitled to characterize nearly all of them as the product of later times.[99] It is undeniable that these *elthon*-sayings, such as they are, bear witness to a special consciousness of having a call. The contents of this call appear on closer examination to be nothing else than a messianic call. Jesus has come to call "sinners to repentance" (Mark 2:17ff); "to throw fire on the earth" (Luke 12:49); "to bring the sword and not peace" (Matt. 10:34ff, cf. Luke 12:51ff); he has not come to destroy the law or the prophets, but "to fulfill them"

(Matt. 5:17); "to proclaim the kingdom of God" (Mark 1:38). We may add sayings introduced by such phrases as: "I have been sent" (cf. Matt. 10:40). Furthermore, Jesus refers to himself as the Son of Man who has come "to seek and to save that which was lost" (Luke 19:10, in some manuscripts Luke 9:56; Matt. 18:11 also); he came not to be ministered unto but to minister, and to give his life a ransom for many (Mark 10:45; Matt. 20:28; cf. also Matt. 11:18,19; Luke 7:33,34). In such pronouncements there is more implied than some prophetic self-consciousness, although such self-consciousness also belongs to Jesus' messianic self-revelation.

Some writers look upon the *elthon*-sayings, *as such*, as messianic formulas, and they appeal to Luke 7:20[100] (cf. Matt. 11:2, where *ho erchomenos* clearly points to the Messiah). Though this argument is perhaps a little too far-fetched (in other texts there is also the question of the "coming" of John the Baptist, Matt. 11:18), what is said of the character and the purpose of Jesus' coming goes to show that these *elthon*-sayings actually have a preponderant messianic significance. Thus, e.g., "the throwing of fire on the earth" (Luke 12:49), will have to be understood as the discord brought about by Jesus' word and work, but from the 50th verse it appears that for this reaction his suffering and death are also required.[101] All this is connected with the great division caused by the coming of the kingdom into the world.[102] This fire does not start on earth, but is thrown into the world out of heaven— *Ignis ille non est nativus terrae* (Bengel). In all this there is more than a prophetic mission; it speaks of a messianic task and messianic authority. The same thing applies to the discord within the family brought about by Jesus (Matt. 10:34-36; Luke 12:51-53). In it is fulfilled the well-known eschatological prophecy of Micah 7:6 which speaks of the great confusion of the end-time. In this passage Jesus says that he has come to fulfill that prophecy. So he is not only the subject, he is also the object of the prophecy from the moment he appeared on earth.

That the purpose of Jesus' having come is nothing else but a fulfilling of the messianic mission can also be clearly inferred from *the elthon-sayings concerning the Son of Man.* They unmistakably show that Jesus does not merely call himself the Son of Man in a proleptic sense but emphasizes the fact that the Son of Man *has* come. The *parousia* prophesied elsewhere does not exclude the Son of Man's having come. It is especially significant that Jesus' pronouncements about the earthly mission of the Son of Man is not only an indication of his majesty and authority in accordance with Daniel 7:13ff (cf., e.g., Luke 19:10 and Mark 2:10), but no less of his being the one in whom the prophecy of the suffering servant of the Lord is fulfilled (Mark 10:45). Although Jesus speaks in a veiled way of everything that he predicates about himself, including the *elthon*-sayings, it cannot be denied that these sayings have messianic meaning in connection with the whole of Jesus' self-revelation, and therefore speak of Jesus' messiahship during his earthly life.

There is also a close connection between these *elthon*-sayings and the so-called *ego*-pronouncements, in which Jesus emphatically manifests his consciousness of absolute authority and power. Thus, e.g., in his repeated *ego de lego humin* (Matt. 5), where, in contrast to that which the ancients had said, he speaks his authoritative word.[103]

Of special importance are those words in which Jesus posits the belonging to him and the communion with his person (*ego*) as the criterion of salvation and rejection. These utterances are not exclusively related to the future, as e.g., in the judgment-sayings in Matthew 7:23 "depart from me" (cf. also 25:41). In them we hear the future judge of the world speak. He denies that there has ever existed any personal relation between him and the workers of iniquity: "I never knew you." He drives them away from him, and thus implies their judgment. On the other hand he even now invites "all that labor and are heavily laden," saying: "Come unto me" (Matt. 11:28). This is more than the call to fulfill his commands; it is no less than the Messianic call of the Saviour. For "those that labor and are heavily laden" there is salvation in him, he will give them rest. Coming to him and having communion with him is the great prerequisite of salvation. This is the way to understand those pronouncements which show the criterion for entry into the kingdom to lie in the attitude that is adopted with respect to Jesus' own person (*ego*). This consciousness of absoluteness finds very pregnant expression, e.g., in a saying like Matthew 12:30, "He that is not with me is against me" (cf. also Mark 9:40). The conclusion of the speech on the occasion of the disciples' mission in Matthew 10 is entirely ruled by Jesus' consciousness of absolute authority (vss. 32-42). Here Jesus speaks of "confessing me" (*homologein en emoi*) and of "denying me" (*arneomai me*); of "loving father or mother, son or daughter more than me" (*huper eme*) and of being "not worthy of me" (*ouk estin mou axios*); of "following him" (*akolouthein hopiso mou*), of "losing one's life for my sake" (*heneken emou*), and of "receiving me" (*dechesthai eme*) which on the one hand is equal to receiving his disciple, and on the other to receiving him who has sent him (vs. 40). In all these expressions, which have their parallels in the other gospels and can be multiplied by many similar passages (cf., e.g., Matt. 16:24,25; 18:5; 19:29), Jesus speaks as the Christ in whose person and work lies the last and the greatest decision for the world and for man; in whom God comes to the world with his grace and justice, with his salvation and curse. This is why in Jesus' preaching the messianic *ego* alternates with the idea of *basileia toon ouranoon*, or *tou theou*. And this does not only hold for the future (cf., e.g., Mark 9:1 and Matt. 16:28), but also for the present. What is called "leaving house, or brethren, etc., for my sake and the gospel's," in Mark 10:29; and in Matt. 19:29, "for my name's sake"; is called "for the kingdom of God's sake," in Luke 18:29. "Jesus Christ's name and message, Jesus Christ himself, are identified with the kingdom of God."[104] On the ground of all these data there can be no doubt at all about the present-messianic character of Jesus' coming and work. And thus also the meaning of the fulfillment proclaimed by Jesus is revealed as to its real essence. The kingdom of heaven has come because Christ has come. He is the *auto-basileia* (Origenes). Therefore what he works and speaks and gives is the manifestation of the fulfillment of time, the revelation of the salvation God has promised to give. For this reason also the modality of the revelation of the kingdom is dependent on the revelation of the Christ. This has far-reaching consequences for a correct insight into the presence as well as into the provisional character of the coming of the kingdom. In our next chapter we shall have to go further into this.

By way of an appendix we mention O. Cullmann's opinion with regard to the relationship between Jesus' messiahship and the coming of the kingdom of God.[105] He thinks that the endless discussions of the question as to whether the kingdom of God in the New Testament is present or future might have turned in another direction if the obvious *temporal* difference had been kept in view between the *basileia tou huiou* (the reign of Christ) and the *basileia tou theou* (the kingdom of God). For such a distinction he refers to I Corinthians 15:23ff. According to Cullmann the *Regnum Christi* is based on Jesus' resurrection and it effectively starts with the ascension. For the present this *Regnum Christi* temporarily coalesces with this aeon, which is also to say that the definitive annihilation of the powers hostile to God is still delayed. The final stage of this reign of Christ will occur at his second coming. Then the final struggle will begin. In this manner the *Regnum Christi* with its final act reaches into the first act of the coming aeon, the *aioon melloon* of the new creation. Insofar as this final act already partly overlaps the coming aeon, Cullmann identifies it with the millennium of Revelation 20:4ff. After this Christ "shall deliver up the kingdom of God" and then the kingdom of God will begin.

As Christ's deed is decisive for the entire history of the world, both in the past and in the future, there is, according to Cullmann, the possibility of all the characteristic proleptic pronouncements about the kingdom in the New Testament. As such he also mentions Jesus' pronouncements that the kingdom of God has come.

"Now that Jesus lives on earth, who has come to gain the victory through his death, such proleptic sayings are only natural." Thus it is to be explained why in New Testament linguistic usage in general the distinction between the *basileia* of the Father and that of the Son has not been carried through consistently. This kingdom of Christ, it is true, cannot be separated from the kingdom of the Father, as far as their contents are concerned, as can neither the Son be separated from the Father. But Christ's kingdom represents a separate entity in a temporal sense, beginning with the ascension, continuing now, and finding its final stage in the beginnig of the future aeon.[106]

There are two important questions implied in all this. First of all the question as to whether or not the pronouncements about the coming of the kingdom before Christ's death and resurrection bear a proleptic character. In the second place, whether it is permissible to consider the *Regnum Christi* as in a temporal sense preceding the purely future eschatological kingdom of God.

The former thesis, as we have seen, is also defended by Michaelis. In our opinion it does not do justice to the significance of Christ's person and work before his death and resurrection. For though it may be that Christ's death and resurrection are of fundamental importance for the realization of his kingdom, the assumption of such realization does not start with them. The beginning of the kingdom does not lie in Christ's death and resurrection, but in his coming (cf. above), i.e., in the incarnation. Just as it is not possible to maintain, on the ground of the often quoted text of Acts 2:36, that God has made him Christ only by raising him up from death so that the synoptic Christology can be called proleptic (Christ designate); no more does the presence of the kingdom start with Christ's death and resurrection. The one thing is indissolubly connected with the other, and a proleptic conception of the pronouncements on the kingdom in the gospels would naturally entail the thought of the Messiah-designate for the time previous to his resurrection. What has been said up to now has proved that both of these views are untenable. Christ's kingship, and the coming of the *basileia* attendant upon it, are not merely based on his exaltation, but, as we saw (Matt. 11:27; 3:17, etc.), on the eternal good pleasure of the Father which was already proclaimed at the beginning of his career, and which finds its deepest ground in the unity of the Son and the Father.

Cullmann's second thesis is connected with this. No doubt, on the basis of I Corinthians 15:23 we can speak of "delivering up the *basileia* of Christ to the Father." But in our opinion it would be too schematic to lay this temporal distinction at the base of the whole of the New Testament, and to speak of "inconsistent usage" with reference to the texts in which the distinction is not to be found. It certainly can not be said that this distinction is an "absolute requirement" as Cullmann does in opposition to K. L. Schmidt. In Kittel's *Wörterbuch* the latter wrote: "the *basileia Christi* cannot be spoken of without that of God."[107] The gospel, however, does not know of Cullmann's distinction, either in word, or in matter. And the great objection against this view is that in this way the notion *basileia tou theou* assumes a purely future eschatological character. This is not based on the gospel, but is in conflict with it in every way. Much rather the *basileia tou theou* is in the foreground in the gospel. And, in and through the coming and the work of Christ, it is from that hour beginning to be realized.

Notes to Chapter III

1 See e.g. Kümmel, *op. cit.,* p. 64, who clearly shows that the word *ephthasen* used here can no more have the meaning of *ēggiken,* than in Matt. 3:2,17 *ēggiken* can have the meaning of *ephthasen.*

2 According to R. Otto, *op. cit.,* p. 79, this reference to the presence of the *basileia* is a proof of what Jesus had for a long time been teaching, but had always been doubted. The *ara* then would mean something like "really," "actually," and refer back to Jesus' former pronouncements that the kingdom had come. But this view can only be considered as a supposition.

3 This is an allusion to Isaiah 49:24ff. "Shall the prey be taken from the mighty? . . . Even the captives of the mighty shall be taken away, . . . for I will contend with him that contendeth with thee, and I will save thy children." Cf. also Bultmann, *Geschichte²,* p. 103; R. Otto, *op. cit.,* p. 77.

4 Cf. E. Stauffer, *Die Theologie des N.T.,* 1945, pp. 103-105.

5 Johannes Weiss, *Die Predigt Jesu vom Reiche Gottes,* 1892, pp. 88ff.; cf. also W. Michaelis, *Täufer, Jesus, Urgemeinde,* 1928, p. 74; R. Bultmann speaks of the "glorious feeling of the eschatological mood," and of the "eschatological feeling of power," *Geschichte,* pp. 110, 174.

6 Cf. H. D. Wendland, *Die Eschatologie des Reiches Gottes bei Jesus,* 1931, p. 48; cf. also Kümmel, *op. cit.,* p. 65.

7 Cf. Schniewind, *op. cit.,* p. 30; E. Stauffer, *op. cit.,* p. 104; see further below, § 22.

8 Cf. also my *Zelfopenbaring en Zelfverberging,* 1946, p. 51, 52; G. Sevenster, *De Christologie van het N.T.,* 1946, p. 108.

9 Cf., e.g., Klostermann, *Das Lukasevangelium²,* 1929, p. 101.

10 Cf. Greijdanus, *op. cit.,* I, p. 477; Klostermann, *op. cit.,* p. 17; Manson, *op. cit.,* p. 125; F. Hauck, *Das Evangelium des Lukas,* 1934, p. 142.

11 *ek toū ouranoū:* according to some writers this phrase denotes the sky, where Satan occupies his place as the master of the spirits (Eph. 2:2; 6:12), thus Manson, *op. cit.* According to others it indicates in a symbolical way, his position of power thus Greijdanus, *op. cit.,* I, p. 479. Others again think that it is heaven as the place where God lives and where Satan stands before God (as prosecutor) (cf. Rev. 12:7-12), thus Hauck, *op. cit.;* Sevenster, *op. cit.,* p. 17.

12 Thus Zahn, *Das Evangelium des Lukas³, ⁴,* 1920, p. 420; Greijdanus, *op. cit.,* I, p. 478, although the latter acknowledges that in this way the imperfect *etheooroun* remains unexplained.

13 This is usually thought of as a visionary scene. Bultman, *op. cit.,* p. 113; Manson, Hauck, Klostermann, *op. cit.;* cf. also Kümmel, *op. cit.,* pp. 69-70.

14 Thus also Matter, *op. cit.,* p. 36.

15 Cf. also J. Ridderbos, *Predikende het evangelie des koninkrijks,* 1911, p. 62.

16 Stauffer, *op. cit.,* p. 105; cf. also Wendland, *op. cit.,* p. 232.

17 Cf. W. Grundmann, *TWB,* II, 1935, p. 303, the article on "dunamai, dunamis": "Jesus' miracles are part of the dominion of God forcing its way into the world, and are by Jesus brought with his person in preaching and action; they are the divine dominion which conquer and push back the demoniacal satanic dominion. Jesus' miracles, like his entire history, are eschatological events."

18 Cf., e.g., Kümmel, *op. cit.,* pp. 66ff. "So Jesus' answer to the Baptist's

question requires Jesus' actions and his preaching to be considered as the proof of the commencement of God's dominion."

[19] For the literature see, e.g., Grundmann, *op. cit.,* p. 302; G. Sevenster, *op. cit.,* p. 31.

[20] *Op. cit.,* pp. 285-289.

[21] *Op. cit.,* p. 297.

[22] *Op. cit.,* p. 292.

[23] *Op. cit.,* p. 298ff., where, for instance, he refers to Fr. Fenner, *Die Krankheit im N.T.,* 1930 (who makes an elaborate attempt to explain Jesus' miracles in the light of modern psychopathology), and especially to the reports about Blumhardt.

[24] Cf., e.g., Grundmann, *op. cit.,* pp. 303ff; Sevenster, *op. cit.,* pp. 32ff, and Oepke, *TWB,* III, pp. 213, the article on "iaomai."

[25] See, e.g., the survey of the "characteristic traits" in the stories of the miracles, in Bultmann, *Gesch. d. Syn. Trad.*[2], 1931, pp. 236, 237.

[26] Cf. Klostermann· *Markusevangelium,* p. 73.

[27] R. Otto cannot deny this, but (entirely in conflict with his justified attack on the treatment of Jesus' miracles as legends according to the form—critical conception, pp. 289-292, 301), he holds that this characterization of Jesus' miracles is the work of a later tradition. According to Christ's own intention his miracles are not at all to be considered as an "epiphany of the Messiah." Apart from the fact that this thesis can in no way be proved, it must be clear to anybody that Otto's naturalistic explanation of the gospel is entirely in conflict with the purport of Jesus' preaching. And phenomenologically it is deficient, for it adduces redemptive-historical parallels for only a small number of Jesus' miracles (passing by in silence, e.g., the "miracles of nature" and the raising of dead people); and even this restricted number of cases must be understood in a very arbitrary way (e.g., as "cures" of illnesses based on nervous disorders, psychical complexes, and the like, cf. *op. cit.,* pp. 298).

[28] Cf. H. D. Wendland, *op. cit.,* pp. 224, 225, 230, 231. "God's dominion has three enemies: Satan, sin, disease. Sin and disease are consequences of Satan's rule of men. Jesus does not reflect on their metaphysical coherence but from the outset he posits these associates in *one* kingdom of demons and sin, and opposes to them God's dominion and God's Spirit.

[29] *Hēn edēsen ho satanās.*

[30] A. Plummer, *A Critical and Exegetical Commentary on the Gospel acc. to St. Luke,*[5] 1942, p. 164; speaks of "a demon" and refers to Luke 11:14; Mark 9:17, 25, and prefers to think of this as demon possession, pp. 341, 342; so also W. Manson, *The Gospel of Luke*[5], 1945, p. 164, but in this connection he speaks of a "secondary feature," because the ordinary symptoms of the state of being possessed are lacking, and also Jesus' action in this case is not in accordance with his action with respect to those possessed. Greijdanus does not regard this as a case of being possessed, but he writes: "this was bodily suffering caused by Satan's activity," *op. cit.,* II, p. 652. E. Klostermann, *Markusevangelium,* pp. 14, 15, writes that although generally the cure of illness and the state of being possessed are distinguished, here and there also a more primitive conception becomes manifest, according to which all diseases are caused by a demon.

[31] *epetimēsen tōoi puretōoi.*

[32] Cf. Greijdanus, *Luk.* I, pp. 225, 226.

[33] Greijdanus writes: "The Lord treats storm and waves and fever, as if they

were rational creatures. This is all the better understood when in this case the power of the devils was at work in this storm," *op. cit.*, I, p. 381.

34 Cf. Stauffer, *Die Theologie des N.T.*, 1945, p. 104.

35 Stauffer in *TWB*, the article on "epitimãn," II, p. 623.

36 Sevenster, *op. cit.*, p. 32; cf. also Oepke, *TWB·* II, p. 334, the article on "egeiro."

37 Cf. Wendland, *op. cit.*, p. 238: "If Jesus stands in contrast to sin, disease, and the demons as the bearer of the living, purifying, and renewing power of God, he can be no other in opposition to death."

38 Cf., e.g., Klostermann, *Markusev.*, pp. 116, 117.

39 Cf. my *Mattheüs*, II, 1946, p. 85.

40 *Kai dunamis kuriou ēn to iāsthai auton*. According to some writers the word *kuriou* means the power of God working in Jesus; it is, however, more probable that the name *kurios* is used here of Jesus himself, just as in other places in Luke.

41 Cf. Grundmann, *op. cit.*, p. 308.

42 Cf. also Sevenster, *op. cit.*, pp. 35ff; Matter, *op. cit.*, p. 91.

43 Cf. H. W. Beyer, *TWB*, II, p. 601, the article on *"episkeptomai."*

44 Cf. also Kümmel, *op. cit.*, p. 69.

45 It is remarkable that the noun is not found in Luke, but the verb *euaggelizesthai* is used all the more frequently (e.g., 4:18,43; 8:1; 16:16; 20:1). Cf. J. Schniewind, *Euangelion*, I, 1927, p. 13.

46 A different view in: J. de Zwaan, *Inleiding tot het N.T.*, I, 1941, pp. 21ff.; cf. alo Schniewind, *op. cit.*, p. 4.

47 This has been clearly established in Schniewind's book on the basis of former investigations by Johannes Müller, A. Schlatter, (in his *Neutest. Theologie*, I, 1909) and M. Burrows ("The Origin of the Term 'Gospel,' " *Journal of Biblical Literature*, 1925, pp. 21-33) and in opposition to the view that the expression *Euangelion* (gospel) was introduced by the later Church and stems from Hellenism (thus Wellhausen, *Einleitung in die drei ersten Evangelien*, 1905, pp. 108ff). For the history of this investigation see Schniewind, *Euangelion*, 1927, pp. 5-18, and the literature in *TWB*, II, p. 705.

48 In addition to Isaiah 52 and 61 the figure of the messenger of peace announcing the saving intercession of Jahwe (as King) is also found in Isaiah 40:9; 41:27 (cf. also Nah. 2:1; Ps. 68:12). See the discussion of these passages in Schniewind, *op. cit.*, I, pp. 34-51; also J. Ridderbos, *De profeet Jesaja*, II², 1934, p. 126.

49 Cf. also Friedrich, *TWB*, II, pp. 712-714, the article on "euaggelizomai" and the material in Strack-Billerbeck, III, 1926, pp. 4-11.

50 See further my: *De strekking van de bergrede naar Mattheüs*, 1936, p. 27.

51 Cf. also Friedrich, *TWB*, II, p. 715, the article on "euaggelizomai": "The message creates the new age, it makes the sign of the messianic fulfilment possible. The Word brings God's dominion nearer." So also especially Schniewind, *Euangelion*, I, pp. 1ff, and the pronouncements made by other authors (although in very different senses) quoted here.

52 Cf., e.g., also W. Foerster, *TWB*, II, p. 566, the article on *"exousia."*

53 Thus Kittel, *TWB*, IV, p. 106, the article on *"lego."*

54 Cf. also Schniewind, *Das Evangelium nach Markus*,⁵ 1949, pp. 59ff.

55 *phobeisthai, thambeīn, thaumazein, ekplēttesthai, thorubeīsthai, existasthai.*

56 "The expressions of fear and astonishment, therefore, serve to emphasize the revelational content and thus the Christological meaning of numerous

synoptic scenes of Jesus." G. Bertram. *TWB*, III, p. 6, the article on *"thambos"*; see also pp. 36ff., the article on *"thauma."*

[57] *Didachē kainē kat' exousian.*

[58] Cf., e.g., Klostermann and Hauck on Mark 1:27; also G. Sevenster, *op. cit.*, pp. 41ff., and Bertram, *op. cit.*, p. 6.

[59] Thus Kittel, *op. cit.*, p. 128. And he adds: "But this is not the 'theology of the church,' but according to the numerous testimonies of the collected tradition it is Jesus' knowledge about his mission." Cf. also Friedrich, *TWB*, II, p. 725, the article on *"euaggelion"*: "That which has been given with his person constitutes the contents of the gospel. Jesus brings the *basileia*, in his Word, it is realized," p. 726.

[60] Cf. also K. L. Schmidt, *TWB*, I, pp. 588, 589, the article on *"basileia."*

[61] Thus, e.g., H. D. Wendland, *op. cit.*, p. 41, in accordance with Michaelis. He does not think that the present tense *estin* is in conflict with this, because in Aramaic—the language that Jesus spoke—it has no equivalent. Also Kümmel, *op. cit.*, p. 26, cf. p. 74, regards the meaning of the Beatitudes as being "future-eschatological," as Klostermann who refers to Matt. 5:4-9; Mark 10:14, *Das Matthäusevangelium*, p. 35. He characterizes the possession of salvation as a promise; *Das Lukasevangelium*, p. 79. Zahn calls *estin* a timeless present, which might have been rendered by *estai*. That *estin* must be regarded as future is implied in the connection of verses 3a and 10a with 3b and 10b: "The poor and the persecuted cannot simultaneously be in this condition and in the actual possession of the *basileia*," *Das Ev. d. Matth.*[4], 1922, pp. 194, 195; cf. also Schniewind, *Matth.*, p. 39. But A. Schlatter, *Der Ev. Matthäus*, 1933, p. 134 says: "With this *esti* the future penetrates into the present. The poor are said to have a share in the kingly work of God as a present possession"; cf. also Grosheide, *Matth.*, p. 46, and A. Plummer: " 'is . . .' not 'will be.' It is not a promise, as in the next Beatitudes, but the statement of a fact." *A Critical and Exegetical Commentary on the Gospel according to St. Luke*[5], 1942, p. 180.

[62] It is also, therefore, not clear why the kingdom of heaven cannot be spoken of as "the possession" of the poor in spirit, as, e.g., is H. D. Wendland's opinion, *op. cit.*, p. 41. The important point is what is understood by this concept. The qualification "possession" need not at all imply an immanent idea of the kingdom detached from the eschatological and theocentric character of the kingdom. It is not the idea of the immanence of the kingdom as such that is objectionable, but the manner in which it has often been defined; cf. also Michaelis, *Es ging ein Sämann aus*, 1938, pp. 113-116.

[63] Thus, e.g., J. Jeremias, *Die Gleichnisse Jesu*, 1947, pp. 100, 101.

[64] Thus C. H. Dodd, *The Parables of the Kingdom*[6], pp. 112, 113.

[65] It is very doubtful whether the circumstances, namely, that the treasure was found by accident the first time and by a very diligent search for it the second time, belong to the symbolism of the parables.

[66] *Verheiszung und Erfüllung*, 1946, p. 73, A. 193.

[67] Michaelis wonders whether the treasure might represent Jesus himself or the word of the kingdom (as if the kingdom could be something different than Jesus and the gospel preached by him, compare Mark 10:29 with Luke 18:29!). Though the parable seems to point to something present, Michaelis thinks it most probable that here the kingdom itself is spoken of and then he draws the conclusion that the treasure which has been acquired is "to have a share in

God's kingdom or to be entitled to the kingdom," *op. cit.*, pp. 108-112. A different opinion is in, e.g., A. M. Brouwer, *De Gelijkenissen*, 1946, p. 152.

[68] Thus Dodd, rightly so, *op. cit.*, p. 113.

[69] See below, ch. VI.

[70] *Lehrbuch der Dogmen geschichte*, I⁴, 1909, p. 81.

[71] *Jesus*, 1929, p. 13; cf. also my: *Zelfopenbaring*, p. 15.

[72] *Neutest. Theol.* I, pp. 308, 309.

[73] *Evangelium und Welt*, 1929, p. 44; cf. also pp. 77, 78.

[74] § 6.

[75] For the conception of Jesus' messiahship formed by Schweitzer and his adherents cf. my: *Zelfopenbaring en Zelfverberging*, pp. 8ff., 17ff.

[76] This thought is found in his book *Täufer, Jesus, Urgemeninde*, 1928, and also in the smaller book: *Reich Gottes und Geist Gottes nach dem N.T.*, 1931, p. 9.

[77] G. Vos: *The Self-Disclosure of Jesus*, 1926, p. 83.

[78] A. Schweitzer, *Das Messianitäts- und Leidensgeheimnis*², 1929, p. 67.

[79] *Op. cit.*, pp. 68ff.; cf. also R. Otto, *Reich Gottes und Menschensohn*, 1934, pp. 190ff., although he does not conceive of Jesus' messiahship as purely future (among others, he applies the pronouncements on the passion to the present Son of Man, cf. p. 195).

[80] N. B. Stonehouse, *The Witness of Matthew and Mark to Christ*, 1944, pp. 16ff.

[81] G. Sevenster, *op. cit.*, pp. 101ff.

[82] Cf. also G. Vos, *op. cit.*, p. 85: "It is simply excluded that Jesus could have counted the appointment to the office itself as belonging to the futurities."

[83] Cf., e.g., H. J. Holzmann, *Das messianische Bewusstsein Jesu*, 1907, pp. 45ff., and the literature cited there.

[84] Of the more recent writers, e.g., Bultmann, *Geschichte*, p. 264 A.

[85] Cf., e.g., Hauck on Mark 1:10, *op. cit.*, p. 15: "The filling with the Spirit is the equipment for the office of the Messiah."

[86] Thus W. Michaelis, *Reich Gottes und Geist Gottes nach dem N.T.*, p. 4. See, however, J. Ridderbos, *De profeet Jesaja*, II,² p. 205. Elsewhere, in Acts 10:38, Jesus of Nazareth is explicitly spoken of as "anointed with the Holy Ghost and with power."

[87] Michaelis, *op. cit.*, pp. 13, 17.

[88] *Hē toū pneumatos blasphēmia*, Matt. 12:31; *blasphēmeĩn eis to pneũma to hagion*, Mark 3:29, cf. Luke 12:10.

[89] *Eipeĩn kata toū pneumatos toū hagiou*.

[90] In opposition to Michaelis, *op. cit.*, p. 15.

[91] *Op. cit.*, p. 11.

[92] *Op. cit.*, p. 15.

[93] P. 17.

[94] Cf. also Sevenster, *op. cit.*, p. 101.

[95] Thus A. A. van Ruler, *De vervulling der wet*, 1947, p. 83; cf. also R. Otto, *op. cit.*, pp. 131ff.; 167.

[96] A. Harnack, "Ich bin gekommen," *Zeitschr. f. Theol. und Kirche* 22, 1912, pp. 1ff.

[97] *Op. cit.*, p. 105.

[98] J. Schneider, *TWB*, II, p. 664, the article on *"erchomai";* cf. also Bultmann, *Geschichte*, p. 168.

[99] Thus Bultmann, *op. cit.*, pp. 163-174.

[100] Cf. E. Stauffer, *TWB*, II, p. 345, the article on "ego."

[101] Cf. Greijdanus, *op. cit.*, "It is true that the Lord had started to kindle this fire with his coming to earth, but it was fully lighted only with the completion of his work of redemption, his resurrection and ascension to heaven, and with the descent of the Holy Spirit."

[102] Cf. also Manson, *op. cit.*, p. 160; Klostermann, *op. cit.*, p. 141.

[103] Stauffer rightly says about this: "What Jesus says here is not a new insight into an old truth; what he demands is not merely a new advance on the endless road to the eternally valid ideal. The validity of his demand is entirely bound to the competence of his person, and to the legitimacy of his mission. The Messiah has come and, empowered by God's authority, he issues a summons to his people. Only from his *ego* do his words derive their validity." *Op. cit.;* cf. also H. Windisch, *Der Sinn der Bergpredigt*, 1929, pp. 93ff.

[104] K. L. Schmidt, *TWB*, I, pp. 590, 591, the article on *basileia*.

[105] Elaborated especially in his: *"Königsherrschaft Christi und Kirche im Neuen Testament²*, 1946.

[106] *Op. cit.*, pp. 11-19.

[107] Cullmann, *op. cit.*, p. 19, note 24. Schmidt, *op. cit.*, p. 582.

Chapter IV

THE KINGDOM HAS COME

2. The Provisional Character

14. *Presence and Future*

The argument advanced in the previous chapter on the coming of the kingdom of heaven as preached by Jesus firmly establishes that Jesus did not hold that the coming of the kingdom was only a reality to be expected in the more or less near future. Moreover he also proclaimed it as the present fulfillment of the Old Testament prophecy of salvation, manifested in his person and in his work. All this prevents us from following the "consistent" eschatological school, either in its original, historical conception, which considers Jesus as the preacher of an exclusively future, illusory kingdom of God, or in its later idealistic or existentialistic interpretation of this eschatological "thought" or "event." This eschatological school had its merits, for it stripped the New Testament concept of the kingdom of God of the modern ideas of the Enlightenment, which had been the model for the concept "kingdom of God," as conceived by the liberal theology. The eschatological school attempted to fit the idea of the kingdom of God into its own historical mold, viz., in that of the Old Testament prophecy and eschatology. Yet the eschatological interpretation, in its exclusive and consistent form, is absolutely untenable, because it is the denial of Jesus' self-revelation as the Messiah in whom prophecy has been fulfilled and salvation has come. And for this reason the exclusively eschatological interpretation leaves no room for the kingdom in its real and beneficent presence.

All this does not mean that the statement: "the kingdom of heaven has come" exhausts all that can be said. In a previous chapter we have seen—in opposition to, e.g., C. H. Dodd's conception—that Jesus again and again speaks of the future of the kingdom of God, and that this future bears the character of the consummation and fulfillment of all things. This constitutes the startling part of Jesus' pronouncements concerning the presence of the kingdom and his messianic self-revelation. They claim the presence of the kingdom and of the Messiah, whereas the great moment of the consummation has not yet arrived. The coming of the kingdom as proclaimed by Jesus, therefore, bears an incomplete and provisional character.

Meanwhile we should guard against a too schematic representation. It is remarkable that the gospel does not itself explicitly distinguish between the kingdom now and the kingdom later. It only says in one place that *the* kingdom of heaven *has* come, and in another passage that *the* kingdom *will* come. And it is often very difficult to ascertain whether the kingdom is spoken of in the present or in the future.

This phenomenon is not merely due to the lack of distinctive and systematic terminology, which in many respects is characteristic of the gospel. It also certainly has a factual significance which should not be overlooked on account of distinctions that are too superficial such as, first and second coming, provisional and definitive revelation of the kingdom (although such distinctions may be defended on factual grounds). It is based on the unity of the kingdom of heaven and on the unity of the person to whom this kingdom has been given. It implies that at bottom there is only the question of one coming, one fulfillment, one concluding work of God, as appears clearly from Luke 4:18ff. There the realized fulfillment of the Scriptures is spoken of in terms describing the great renewal of the final period. For this reason any attempt should be rejected which tries to divide the coming of the kingdom into separate parts. The kingdom of heaven appearing in the world with the coming of Christ, signifies no less than the end of prophecy (Matt. 11:13; Luke 16:16), the binding of Satan (Matt. 12:28), the wonderful and all-embracing redemption of life (Matt. 11:5; Luke 4:18,19), the authority and power of the Son of Man (Mark 2:10), and the bliss of the poor in spirit (Matt. 5:3). Any attempt to detract from this character either by the application of an ethicizing or a symbolizing reduction, or by detaching the present from the future, is a dissolution of the contents of the gospel of the kingdom. We should rather consider the characteristic and peculiar nature of Jesus' preaching to be his proclamation of the kingdom in its consummative, eschatological significance both as a present and as a future reality. The fulfillment is there, and yet the kingdom is still to come. The kingdom has come, and yet the fulfillment is in abeyance. Keeping this unity in view is one of the fundamental presuppositions for the understanding of the gospel.

And at the same time this unity is a problem in many respects. It is a problem that cannot be solved by the human intellect because it concerns the unity and the extent of the divine work of salvation in Jesus Christ. It was especially urgent to those who—after the preaching of John the Baptist— saw Jesus come to the fore with the message that the time had been fulfilled and the kingdom had come. His hearers simply supposed that the coming of the kingdom would bring the Day of the Lord, the judgment of the world, and the end of earthly reality. It is this problem which found expression in the question of the great herald and testified to his uncertainty and doubt: "Art thou he that should come, or do we look for another?" We shall have to investigate this problem of the *modality* of the coming of the kingdom which had already started in Jesus' words and works, and the relation between this presence of the kingdom and its future. Not only shall we have to trace and to compare the direct pronouncements on this point, but we shall have to discuss the question in the light of the whole gospel.

15. *The Time of the Evil One*

There is great tension between the Lord's pronouncements concerning the coming of the kingdom (present and future!).

This fact can perhaps be best demonstrated by examining what Jesus says in the gospel with respect to the continued power of the Evil One. In a previous chapter we quoted the statement in which Jesus vindicates his victory over the Evil One (the "binding of the strong one," §9). This is one of the clearest proofs in the gospel for the presence of the kingdom of heaven. By its side, however, we find in the gospel the unambiguous evidence that Satan's power has in no way been ended, but both for Jesus and especially for the disciples this power is a continual and never ceasing menace. That this is very clear is seen from the Lord's Prayer as handed down to us by Matthew, in which Jesus teaches his disciples to pray: "Lead us not into temptation but deliver us from (the) evil (one)." The very first part refers to the devil's power. "Temptation" is not only a situation which entails the danger of falling into sin,[1] but includes the active influence of the Evil One on a man to effect his fall. Our prayer, therefore, says: "Do not deliver us into the hands of the tempter."[2] The second part should not be explained as: Deliver us from *evil,* but to our mind as: Deliver us from *the Evil One.* In defence of the neuter word an appeal is made to 2 Timothy 4:18 and *the Didache* 10:5.[3] But for the *personal* expression "the Evil One" there is as strong a reason, if not stronger, to appeal to Matthew 12:28,29; 13:19,39; Mark 8:33; Luke 10:19; 22:31. In any case it is not possible to leave out the Evil One in this context. The Lord's Prayer has been entirely inspired by the coming of the kingdom, as appears most clearly from the first three petitions; it even refers to the perfect revelation of the kingdom (Matt. 6:10c!). And of this coming the victory over the Evil One is one of the main points of the contents of the prayer. This latter petition can, therefore, hardly be conceived in any other way than in connection with the Evil One himself.

According to Schweitzer this prayer must be understood in a strictly eschatological sense. The "temptation" is the great affliction in the impending messianic drama in which the hostile world is roused to action for the last time before

the coming of the kingdom. The disciples should then pray
to be kept from this misery by God's omnipotence.[4] Schweitzer
relates this thought to Jesus' own struggle and prayer in Gethsemane, and to Jesus' warning of his disciples there not to enter
into "temptation" (Matt. 26:41). There are others, too, who
conceive of the "temptation" of which Jesus speaks in Gethsemane as the eschatological affliction the messianic "woes"
(cf. Matt. 24:9).[5]

But this latter opinion is untenable within the scope of
the gospels, especially within that of the so-called synoptic
apocalyptic speeches. They speak of a more distant future
than that of Jesus' suffering and death.[6] It is also an arbitrary
and constructive narrowing down of the sixth petition if the
temptation mentioned in it is only applied to the coming "affliction" of the final period.[7] This, however, does not alter the fact
that in this case as well as in the history of the passion (especially the scene in Gethsemane) we should be aware of the
close connection between the temptation and the menace on
the part of the Evil One and the idea of the kingdom. Just as
from the beginning of Jesus' action the devil has directed his
special attacks at Jesus in order to make him fall (the temptation in the wilderness), in the same way Jesus' disciples are
the special aim of Satan's enmity and evil purpose. This
appears from the Lord's Prayer in which the deliverance from
the Evil One is the conclusion of the prayer for the coming
of the kingdom. It also appears from a passage like Luke
22:31, in which especially with a view to his suffering and
death Jesus says that Satan has claimed to have them that
he may sift them as wheat, but that he has prayed for them
that their faith fail not. In this text the word "claimed"
(exētēsato), "desired to have" is striking. The representation
corresponds to that of Job 1:9ff (cf. Rev. 12:10; Zech. 3:1ff).[8]
Satan appears as the one who claims the trial of the disciples.
He wants them to be exposed as those who side with God and
share in his salvation without being entitled to it. Perhaps this
"sifting as wheat" means the work also ascribed to the coming

Messiah in the last judgment (Matt. 3:12), and so Satan is represented here as the Antichrist,[9] who in the fire of trial will try to take away all that seems to belong to God. In any case he acts here as Christ's great adversary who wants to rob him of his booty.[10] In opposition to this Jesus raises his prayer. There is a striking contrast between *praying* and *claiming*. In praying there is an element of subjection. Here, too, the *ego de* cannot be ignored (cf. above, §13). It is the messianic *ego*.[11] Christ protects his disciples in their trial. He cannot keep the trial way from them, since, for a time he has to give them into the hands of the tempter (cf. Matt. 26:31). For this is "the hour" of his enemies and of "the power of darkness" (Luke 22:53). Only later on can Satan's claim be rejected (cf. Rev. 12:10). At the moment, i.e., the moment in which Jesus himself has to surrender, his prayer alone stands in opposition to Satan's claim. But as the prayer of the Mediator it suffices to maintain the faith of the disciples in the trial.

All this shows both that in Jesus' coming and in his work the struggle with Satan has reached a crisis, and that this struggle is not over but has to be continued with the greatest energy. The victory won by Jesus as the Christ is not yet definitive. This is applicable to himself; after the temptation in the wilderness the devil leaves him "for a season" (Luke 4:13), which, in whatever way the phrase is translated,[12] means in any case that Satan was to come back. It also applies to the life redeemed by Jesus from the power of the Evil One. Jesus warns against it emphatically in Matthew 12:43-45 (cf. Luke 11:24-26). This passage in Matthew first speaks of the unclean spirit having *gone out of* a man, which phrase is typical of the going out of the demons from those possessed because of a superior power. It is very remarkable that the warning against a relapse into the old evil is found both in Matthew and in Luke in close connection with the so-called Beëlzebub speech in which Jesus has testified most clearly to his superior power over the devil and to the coming of the kingdom thus manifested by that superiority (cf. above, §9). This "going out of the unclean spirit" must therefore be conceived of as caused by Jesus. And as appears from Matthew 12 :15 ("Even so shall it be also unto this wicked generation"), it not only reminds us of a concrete case, but illustrates the whole of Jesus' act of salvation manifested in Israel. This act implied the victory over Satan and was evidence (to faith) of the coming of the kingdom. All this, however, is accompanied by the warning: the unclean spirit will return to his prey. He has not yet been banished from the earth, but has been put outside the habitation of man only for a time, as one temporarily driven away. He yearns to come back, and he will come back to "the house" from which he had gone. And finding it "empty, swept, and tidy," i.e., not occupied by a new inhabitant (the Holy Spirit!) he will return accompanied by a whole army of demons, and again take possession of the old house, so that "the last state of that man (will be) worse than the first."

This clearly shows that with Jesus' coming and afterwards the power of the Evil One has not been ended. Only in communion with Christ is there any safety from the hosts of the devil. The old house must change its inhabitant; it is not sufficient for it to be temporarily empty and to seem to be a model of order and tidiness. Exactly on account of the decisive stage in the struggle, the danger of a counter-attack and of succumbing entirely to the Evil One is greater than ever.

This reality of the continuing and ever fiercer attacks of Satan is an element in the contents of the parables of the kingdom. Jesus especially portrays this reality in the parable of the tares among the wheat (Matt. 13:25, cf. also vs. 19). The question has often been asked whether the action of the enemy in sowing tares is imaginable in reality. There are parallels in other popular stories showing that such an elaboration of a parable is very well possible from a formal point of view in the scope of Jesus' teaching, and need not be due to a later coarsening of the original image.[13] And yet there is no denying that the image is determined by the explicit purpose to point to the enemy. If the concern were only with the tares, the mention of them would have been sufficient, just as with the thorns in the first parable of the sower. So it is clear that the enemy does not merely function as a part of the "setting" of the parable but is an essential element of the reality represented, as appears also from the explanation in the 39th verse: "the enemy that soweth them is the devil." The extreme enmity of the adversary who proceeds to the hardly conceivable act of sowing tares is an image of the devil's worst opposition to Jesus' coming and work. It is not the usual, current image of the devil's display of power, but his grim determination to maintain himself against Jesus' coming and work. Its foundation is the crisis which the kingdom of heaven has caused in the Evil One's dominion.

This again shows that the continuation of the Evil One's enmity and power must not for a moment shake the faith in the coming of the kingdom and of the Messiah. It only indicates the special modality of the coming of the kingdom. A remarkable confirmation and elucidation of what has been said is found in the story of the cure of those possessed at Gadara (Matt. 8:28ff; Mark 5:11ff; Luke 8:26ff). Here, too, above all, Jesus' power over the devil becomes manifest. Here, too (cf. §9), we read about the cry of terror with which the demons come to meet Jesus, acknowledge him as the Son of God, and throw themselves at his feet. This shows their knowledge of "the mystery of the kingdom" and of Christ.[14] They also entreat and adjure him not to "torment" them before the time. Although this word occurs in various meanings, in this context it can mean nothing less than the eternal woes of hell to which the demons fear to be delivered now already[15] (cf. Rev. 20:10,14.)[16] In the part of the story that follows in Luke 8:31, it says that they besought him not to command them to go out into the abyss (*eis tēn abusson apelthein*). According to Greijdanus the word *abusson* denotes the abode of the devils during this earthly dispensation, to be distinguished from the "lake of fire" into which they will be thrown after the last judgment.[17] However this may be, at any rate the "going out into the abyss" will have to be conceived of in accordance with the "tormenting" of the 28th verse, hence as a forced banishment of the demons to the place of their punishment[18] where they will no longer be in possession of their normal freedom of movement.[19] This is also indicated by the expression "before the time" (*pro kairou*) in the version of Matthew 8:29, i.e., before the point of time fixed by God when they will be deprived of their power and be delivered to the torture of their eternal punishment. This *kairos* is therefore the moment when Satan's power will end while, at the same time, that of his great opponent, the Messiah, will begin.[20] For the demons have recognized him. That is why his coming fills them with terror. But at the same time they protest against being delivered up by him now already to final torment. This point of time, this *kairos*, is not yet supposed to have come. In accordance with this situation—i.e., on the one hand they know they are entirely subjected to Jesus' power, and on the other they know they still have a period of time left on earth before the last judgment day—they beseech Jesus, since he wishes to exorcise them, to suffer them to enter into the herd of swine. And Jesus complies with their request. They are forced to leave the unfortunate possessed man but are then left free to enter into the herd of swine.

All this is an important indication of the character of Jesus' power over the devil and of the nature of the kingdom that began with his coming. The permission Jesus gives the demons to enter into the swine should not be considered as a kind of concession to the evil spirits. Jesus does not negotiate with the demons. Nor is their entry into the swine their undoing, but rather, the (provisional) self-maintenance of the demons. For their purpose and work is the destruction of God's creation. Jesus' compliance with their request is due to the fact, we think, that also in Jesus' opinion "the time" of the torment of the demons has indeed not yet come. For by allowing them to enter into the swine Jesus again gives them liberty (though only in such a place as he points out to them) to continue their destructive work. This explains the meaning of the exorcism of the devils in general: it does not yet put an end to Satan's power, but is the guarantee and the symbol of the definitive victory. In this sense Jesus' pronouncements on the fall of Satan from heaven[21] will have to be understood. The victory is a fact, but it only manifests itself as a sign. It cannot yet be fully realized and carried through. This realization has to await "the time" (*kairos*) appointed for it by God.

The above exegesis of the entry of the demons into the herd of swine has been obtained from J. Ridderbos, *Predikende het Evangelie des Koninkrijks*, 1911, p. 60ff, and partly from F. W. Grosheide, *Het heilig Evangelie volgens Matth.*[2], 1954, p. 142, 143; cf. also my *Het Evangelie naar Mattheüs*[2], 1952, p. 177. In support of this view we may point to Revelation 12:12, which also shows that the devil still has a time and a place on earth assigned to him by God even after Jesus' coming.

Otherwise, this passage has been subjected to a great diversity of explanations. I have found the following seven to be the principal ones:

a) Jesus' permission to the demons to enter into the swine which thereupon throw themselves into the sea, contains the "motif of the cheated devil." Thus, e.g., Bultmann,[22] Klostermann,[23] Lohmeyer,[24] in the footsteps of Wellhausen. So here the demons are the cheated ones. Wohlenberg's,[25] and Lagrange's[26] explanations tend in this direction, too, although they do not start from a mere literary motif like Bultmann's, but from the reality of what has been related in the gospel. Wohlenberg even thinks that in this way the demons left "the country." Perhaps, says Wohlenberg, we must think of them as having been banished "into the abyss." To our mind the drowning of the swine in the sea is not an unforeseen defeat of the demons, but the express purpose of their destructive attempts.

b) Not the demons, but Jesus is the cheated one. Because the demons are guilty of the destruction of the herd, Jesus has to leave the country.[27] This explanation, which has found few adherents, is incompatible with the testimony of Jesus' superiority to the demons found everywhere in the gospel and particularly in this

story. It really turns the evangelistic testimony into its very opposite.

c) The drowning of the herd in the sea is supposed to serve
as a proof of the miracle (according to the evangelist). Thus
Klostermann,[28] appealing to Jerome. According to others the
destruction of the swine gave the possessed man certainty about
his deliverance. Thus Zahn,[29] Schlatter,[30] Manson.[31] This explanation is far-fetched. In none of the stories about demons
do such "proofs" occur. And as to the man possessed, the demons'
entry into the swine was not necessary for him to be certain of his
deliverance, nor was it sufficient to convince him that they would
not come back.

d) Jesus' permission to the demons to enter into the swine is
perhaps an indication that the owners were Jews, who were thus
punished for the fact that they kept swine Thus Greijdanus.[32]
Apart from the question as to whether it is plausible for Jesus to
allow two thousand pigs to perish in the sea as a punishment to
Jews who had infringed upon the laws of purification, everything
(including the herd of swine) indicates that this occurred in a
gentile country.[33] That the owners were Jews is a pure speculative hypothesis.

e) According to Calvin the request of the demons was an attempt by them to arouse the inhabitants of that country against
Jesus, and Jesus' permission was a test of the Gerasenes. It is also
possible—thinks Calvin—to consider this permission as a punishment.
He continues: *Caeterum ut nulla nobis constet certa ratio occultum
tamen Dei iudicium reverenter respicere ea pia humilitate adorare
convenit.*[34] So Calvin hesitates. In our opinion his explanation
may indicate an additional motif, but it can hardly be the chief
reason for Jesus' permission. There is certainly evidence here of
the superstition of the heathen who were afraid of Jesus' continued
presence. But it is very doubtful whether from Jesus' permission
to the demons it may be inferred that he put the disposition of the
heathen to the test, for he had not yet worked among them.

f) The cure of the possessed man and the panic among the
swine were at a later time related to each other, though historically
they form an accidental coincidence. Thus, e.g., Robinson[35] and
Major.[36] We think this explanation purely rationalistic.[37]

g) The fright among the swine cannot be explained from the entry of the evil spirits but was caused by a last act of paroxism on the part of the lunatic before his cure. Thus, e.g., Gould.[38] This explanation, too, tries to get rid of the supernatural character and cannot serve as an exegesis of the text.

16. The Miracle as a Sign

The above mentioned respite granted to the Evil One and his power on earth is closely connected with the significance both of all Jesus' miracles and of the general character of the dispensation of salvation inaugurated by his coming. In our exposition we came to the conclusion[39] that Jesus' miracles have an eschatological character as messianic deeds of salvation. This follows from the connection that the gospel points out between the activity of the devil and the diseases, maladies, and disasters that threaten man. It also appears from the fact that the cure of diseased persons, the raising of the dead, etc., are to be considered as the renewal and the re-creation of all things, manifesting the coming of the kingdom of heaven. These miracles, however, are only incidental and are therefore not to be looked upon as a beginning from which the whole will gradually develop, but as signs of the coming kingdom of God. For the cures and the raisings of the dead done by Jesus only have a temporary significance. Those cured or revived might again fall ill and would eventually die. In connection with this, Jesus' miracles nowhere serve as a purpose but always as a means in his activities, and always remain subservient to the preaching of the gospel.

The following points must be indicated:

a) Already on the occasion of the temptation of the Lord by the devil in the wilderness, it appears that Jesus' miraculous power is entirely directed to the task given him by the Father. This holds for the temptation to make bread of stones as well as for Satan's suggestion to Jesus to cast himself down from the pinnacle of the temple and thus to rely upon the protective power of the angels. The issue in this case is not the choice between two different kinds of messianic idea, one of which is held out to Jesus by the devil: a Messiah who works miracles, desires popularity, receives world-dominion; whereas the contrary ideal is supposed to be represented by Jesus. For Jesus does work miracles, is indeed given world-dominion and will be recognized by all. But he will receive all these things only in the way of God's appointment. When the Father allows him to suffer hunger in the wilderness, he is not to withdraw from it, but must rely upon the omnipotent word of God which can keep him alive even without bread. And similarly he is not to win the favor of men by miracles and signs. Rather, he is to exercise his miraculous power in subjection to the Father and in subservience to his mission. The opposite course would be "tempting the Lord," also in his case (Matt. 4:7). All this does not in the least detract from his dignity as the Messiah and the renewer of life. Already in the wilderness—after the temptation—the angels come to serve him (Matt. 4:11). This reveals that he is the Christ, the Son of God, who is much greater than all the angels (Hebrews 1). In this the kingdom of heaven is revealed, the renewal of the earth, man delivered from the curse, i.e., according to Mark 1:13: "and (he) was with the wild beasts," indicating the paradisaical state of things (and also of the messianic dominion) in which wild animals serve man and do not injure him (cf. Job 5:23; Isaiah 11:6ff; 65:25). But this picture, too, is proleptic; revealing paradise *in the wilderness.* Jesus' miraculous power and God's kingdom revealed in it is still provisionally bound to other laws. He himself will obtain the power in heaven and on earth only through humiliation, suffering and death (Matt. 28:18). This course of the Messiah also determines the manifestation of the kingdom of heaven. The two are correlates not only in their manifestation but also in their veiled character. That is why the veiling of the Messiah also means the veiling of the wonder, as will appear more clearly in our discussion of Christ's self-revelation as the Servant of the Lord.

b) Apart from the special modality of Christ's self-revelation and from the nature of his own messianic task, we see that Jesus' miracles again and again recede into the background in comparison with his preaching. They have no purpose in themselves, they only serve as evidence of his power.[40] This is immediately apparent at the beginning of the gospel of Mark 1:36-38. When Jesus' miraculous power revealed at Capernaum causes crowds to flock together, he withdraws into solitude. And to the request of his disciples to come back because all the people are looking for him, he answers: "Let us go into the next towns that I may preach there also: for therefore came I forth." Jesus clearly states the purpose of his messianic mission (cf. Luke 4:43: *epi touto apestalēn*). However, the words "for therefore came I forth" or "was I sent" should not be taken to refer exclusively to his preaching,[41] cf. Mark 1:39 (the context shows the emphasis to be on his preaching in *all* places). But in opposition to the desire of the disciples to lead Jesus back to Capernaum, where the crowds had become quite excited by his cures, Jesus explicitly refuses to be detained by such a commotion. His first and highest aim is not the cure of as many people as possible in order to manifest the kingdom of God on earth, but his real task is preaching.[42] Although essentially connected with the nature and the significance of preaching, the miracles are only secondary phenomena, viz., they are signs of the truth of his proclamation that the kingdom of heaven has come.

c) That is why there is a close connection between a miracle wrought by Jesus and *the faith* of the people. They are mutually dependent. On the one hand a miracle serves to strengthen faith in Jesus' mission and authority (cf., e.g., Mark 2:1-12). On the other hand there is no room for a miracle if it is not expected by faith. The most striking example of this fact is the expression in Mark that Jesus "could do no mighty work there (in Nazareth) save that he laid his hands upon a few sick folk and healed them" (Mark 6:5). The cause was unbelief. This fact has been explained as Jesus' psychic dependence on the disposition of those whom he healed.[43] But in another context it is recorded that Jesus also worked miracles at a distance (cf. Matt. 8:13; John 4:50). And as to the inhabitants of Nazareth, from Luke 4:23 (cf. also Mark 6:2) it appears that they apparently did expect and desire miracles from Jesus. When, however, he works no (or only very few) miracles, this is explained by the fact that the inhabitants of Nazareth did not believe in Him (Luke 4:22), and even took offence at his action as not befitting him (Mark 6:3,4). Here the question is not whether Jesus possessed the power to work miracles, but whether he was free to exercise this power in all circumstances. Where there is no faith, there is no room for a miracle. There he could work no miracle because in such circumstances it would only have the character of a deed of power and would lack the background from which miracles derive their signifiance and against which they can only be understood. The expression "he could not" in Mark 6:5 must, therefore, be understood as an impossibility within the scope of Jesus' task and activity.[44] In this sense also it is apparently to be understood in Matthew who simply says that Jesus did not do many mighty works there because of their unbelief (Matt. 13:58).

The above also explains why on more than one occasion Jesus refuses to give a sign when challenged by his opponents. This does not only hold for himself for the reason mentioned under (a) above (cf. Matt. 4:1-7; 27:39ff and parallel places, viz., the challenge at the foot of the cross), but also in general (Matt. 12:38ff; 16:1ff, viz., the request for a sign, cf. John 7:3ff; I Cor. 1:22). The word "sign" (*sēmeion*) here apparently means the unambiguous divine proof ("from heaven") that Jesus really acted with divine and messianic powers. As such Jesus' adversaries deemed the miracles he worked to be insufficient. This shows that not only in the eyes of his explicit opponents but also in those of the crowd in general Jesus' miracles were not the concrete proof of his mission and of the coming of the kingdom. The crowds might sometimes be doubtful (cf. Matt. 12:22,23); for the true significance of miracles was discerned only where faith was present. Consequently, though Jesus did not generally withhold his miracles from the people, the proper and deepest meaning remained a secret to most. The decision with respect to Jesus was not found in miracles as such, but in the secret of his person and of his preaching.

The challenge of those who openly opposed him, he rejected with very strong, adjuring words (cf. Mark 8:12: "verily I tell you! *if ever*[45] a sign be given to this generation!"). In Matthew 16:2,3 (at least according to very old manuscripts) Jesus reproaches them for having no eye for the "signs of the times" (cf. Luke 12:54-56). This shows that there are indeed signs indicating that the time in which they live is a special, qualified time, a turning-point in the course of history. But— as a wicked and adulterous generation—they are unable to discern the decisive significance of the signs. For faith is needed to understand them. This is why Jesus will not give them any other sign than that of the prophet Jonah. This enigmatic saying has been given to us in a more elaborate form in Matthew 12:40. There Jesus predicts the Son of Man's stay in the earth just as Jonah had been in the sea-monster's belly for three days and three nights.[46] And this is the sign that is given to "this generation."

Of this saying also it is true that it can be understood only by those who have ears to hear. Its meaning, however, is unmistakable in the light of the fulfillment. In this case, too, it appears that the revelation of the kingdom is bound to that of the Messiah. But first of all he is the one who has to suffer death and rise from it before he comes to his glory as the Son of Man and the judge of the world. Hence, for this reason he himself, the coming of the kingdom and the miracles, are only to be discerned by faith.

d) All this clearly shows the meaning of the miracles wrought by Jesus. They indicate the coming of the kingdom and point to the cosmic palingenesis mentioned in Matthew 19:28. But they are not the beginning of this palingenesis, as if the latter were the completion of the miracles. For this palingenesis is something of the future world aeon; because it embodies the resurrection of the dead and the renewal of the world, it does not belong to the present dispensation. It even presupposes the precedence of the cosmic catastrophe (cf. Matt. 24:29,35,39; II Peter 3:7,10,12,13; Hebr. 12:26-29). That is why the miracles only have an incidental signifiance. This is the sense of the authority given by Jesus to the disciples to cure the sick, to raise the dead, cleanse lepers, drive out demons (Matt. 10:1, etc.). Moreover, this must also mean that they do not get the promise to put an end to Satan's dominion "before the time" and to usher in a state of salvation and bliss on earth. But they are instructed to show the signs of Christ's absolute competence and power and thus to spread and to confirm the faith in the coming of the kingdom in Jesus Christ. This they must do within the scope of Christ's messianic work of salvation, and in subjection to the way in which this work manifests itself in the present world aeon. This means that a miracle is both a demonstration of Jesus' power over the Evil One and a sign of the future palingenesis. But it has importance only in connection with the preaching of the gospel and in subservience to the latter. Nowhere in the gospels do we see that a miracle has an independent or transcendent function detached from the preaching of the gospel. In the gospel any other attempt to reveal Christ's miraculous power originates from the devil and from those who tempt Christ (*peirazontes*) (Matt. 16:1; Mark 8:11; Luke 11:16),[47] and is very energetically and sternly rejected by him (cf. also Luke 9:54,55). To him such an attempt means a deviation from the way determined by the Father, an anticipation of the time that has not yet come. This is why a miracle in itself is no safeguard against the last judgment; nor does it necessarily give a share in the kingdom of heaven to those to whom it happens (cf. Luke 17:17-19: the nine lepers who did not give honor ot God); nor to those by whom it is wrought (cf. Matt. 7:22: "Have we not cast out devils in thy name, and in thy name done many

wonderful works?"). Therefore Jesus answers those who have
returned to him from their missionary journey and reported
on their miraculous works in his name: "Notwithstanding in
this rejoice not that the spirits are subject unto you; but rather
rejoice because your name is written in heaven" (Luke 10:20).
It is true, the absolute formula used here to express the contrast
must be understood in a relative sense (cf. for this Semitic
stylistic form, e.g., John 6:27); for there is also reason to rejoice
at Christ's power over Satan. But the effectuation of this
power is no guarantee to anybody of citizenship in the kingdom of heaven. The latter depends on something else, namely,
on faith in the gospel proclamation, and in Jesus as the Christ
(cf. verse 21 and ff).

17. Speaking in Parables

That which could be inferred indirectly from the gospel
in what has been discussed above about the modality of the
kingdom of heaven which had begun with Jesus' coming, is
elucidated explicitly and in a many-sided way by *Jesus' parables
concerning the kingdom of heaven*. We shall start with the
*redemptive-historical meaning and explanation of the parables
concerned*.

Of late the conception of the parables as the forms used to
express universally valid thoughts and moral lessons has been given
up. In its turn this interpretation, advanced especially in the famous
work, *Die Gleichnisreden Jesu*, by Ad. Jülicher,[48] was a reaction to
an unrestrained allegorical explanation assigning a symbolical meaning to all the images and traits in the parables which often led to
the most fantastic results. In opposition to this tendency Jülicher
rejected any allegorical exegesis, even if it was given in the gospel
itself as in the explanation of the parable of the Sower, of the tares
among the wheat; and that of the net, etc. He wants to interpret
the parables as the pictures of a universally observable reality of life
from which also a general lesson could be derived for our moral and
spiritual life. This conception was in accordance with the liberal
view of the kingdom of heaven preached by Jesus and consequently

led to a very superficial ethical explanation of the parables (the parable of the master and his servants: an exhortation to do one's duty faithfully; the parable of "Dives": an image of man's dependence; the parable of the talents: no wages without effort, etc.).

The consistently eschatological view gave the parables an entirely eschatological interpretation. It tried to make clear that Jesus speaks of the certainty of the future kingdom, especially in the well-known chapter of the parables in Mark 4 and parallel places.[49] This view was conducive to the growing insight that the generalizing and timeless explanation e.g., of Jülicher, does not do justice to the gospel. Since then the interest has been focused on the question about the actual meaning of the parables within the scope of Jesus' activity and preaching. Special mention must be made here of C. H. Dodd's *The Parables of the Kingdom* already cited by us.[50] Although he himself has a predominantly ethical conception of the kingdom, he does not consider the parables as standards of a definite morality, but much rather as a more detailed explanation of the modality of the dispensation of the salvation that started with the coming of Christ. Also in Joachim Jeremias we find a new attempt "to place the parables in the situation of Jesus' life," as he puts it in his description of Dodd's interpretation. He has followed Dodd in this, although his own view of the kingdom of heaven is quite different from Dodd's.[51] It is true that both Dodd and Jeremias hold the opinion that several parables that have come down to us can only be explained from the situation of the later Christian Church; but in all the parables there is more or less an echo of the historical situation of Jesus' life.

Although, on the one hand, we cannot always indicate the details of the situation in which the parables were told; it is clear, on the other hand, that we must judge their meaning in accordance with the general contents of Jesus' preaching, i.e., as illustrations of the kingdom of heaven proclaimed by him. As such the parables are often explicity introduced by the formula: "the kingdom of heaven, or of God, is like . . ." etc. Thus, Mark 4:26 (the seed growing spontaneously); 4:31 (the grain of mustard seed, cf. Luke 13:18) and Luke 13:20 (the leaven a woman took); in Matthew 13:44 (the treasure hid in the field); in 13:45 (a pearl of great price); 13:47 (a net); in 18:23 (remission of sins); in 20:1 (laborers in the vineyard); in 22:2 (the great wedding feast); in 25:1 (the wise and the foolish virgins), cf. also 25:14 (the talents). But even if this formula does not occur, the parables cannot be considered as an independent part of Jesus' preaching to propagate general moral or dogmatic principles. Rather, they are very closely connected with the special redemptive-historical character of Jesus' mission and preaching. The parables illustrate the different facets of this preaching. They may serve to elucidate Jesus' commandments, or they may point his opponents to their deficiency, or they may urge the disciples to watchfulness and expectancy. They also form an important element in the promulgation of the kingdom as a present reality, giving us further revelational-historical information about it.[52]

This is applicable especially to the parables in Mark 4 and Matthew 13, and the relevant places in Luke. Here again the motive, as such, of the parables is not mentioned. Nevertheless it is undeniable that in these parables Jesus enters further into *the modality of the coming of the kingdom of God.* We have already pointed out that there is a problem with respect to the peculiar dialectics of Jesus' words about the kingdom as having come and as something to be expected, as a present and as a future reality. This was also an emphatic problem to the disciples. In these parables this problem is dealt with; it becomes the basic occasion for them. So we shall have to consider these parables from the point of view of the history of salvation.

This is what Schweitzer and Dodd also do—to restrict ourselves to these two diametric opposites, each of whom has his own basic presupposition as to the coming of the kingdom. According to Schweitzer and many others, Jesus wants to explain in these parables how the kingdom *will* come; according to Dodd, how the kingdom *has* come. In our opinion a closer examination of the parables will show that neither the former nor the latter interpretation can do justice to the contents of the parables, but that it is exactly the complex character of the revelation of the kingdom—present *and* future —which is the real subject of the parables.

It is particularly important for the understanding of this specific meaning of the parables to note what, according to the three synoptic gospels, Jesus says about the purpose of his speaking in parables in answer to a question put by the disciples: "Why speaketh thou unto them in parables?" (Matt. 13:10). According to Luke they asked after the meaning of the parable of the sower, whereas in Mark 4:10 it says that they inquired in a general way "after the parables." This question can hardly mean that the parable as a form of teaching was as such an unknown or a strange phenomenon in the eyes of the disciples or the crowd. For Jesus adopts a method of teaching which was in great favor among the rabbis[53] as an illustration and an explanation to sharpen the mind of the hearer. The latter was supposed to possess the required fundamental insight into the teacher's meaning (cf. "Who hath ears to hear, let him hear," Matt. 13:9; Mark 4:9; Luke 8:8ff).[54] The disciples are not occupied by the form of the parable as such, but by the question as to why he did not express his thoughts to the crowd in a direct way without making use of allegory. On this occasion the disciples themselves also prove to be in doubt about the purport of the parable of the sower (Luke 8:9; cf. Mark 4:13: "Do you not know this parable?").

To their question Jesus answers: "Unto you it is given to know the mysteries of the kingdom of God (Mark: "Unto you it is given to know the mystery of the kingdom of God") but to them it is not given . . . ; that is why I speak to them (Luke: to "the others") in parables (Mark: "but unto them that are without, all these things are done in parables") because (Mark and Luke: "in order that . . . ") seeing they may see and not perceive."

Most commentators, for predisposed reasons and not on account of critical considerations with respect to the text, do not regard these words as original in this context.[55] This passage is supposed to disturb the coherence of thought. To our mind these words contain the key for the understanding of the special intent Jesus has with these parables. For these words state that the meaning of the parables can only be understood by those to whom the mystery (or the mysteries) of the kingdom has (have) been given (to know). This cannot mean that the kingdom of heaven, as the object of the prophetic promise and expectation, is a mystery unknown to those "that are without." By the term "mystery" or "the knowledge of the mysteries" of the kingdom given (*perfectum*) to the disciples in contradistinction to the crowd, the special, actual knowledge of the kingdom is meant as it was revealed in Jesus' coming. It is the knowledge that in other passages also is indicated by Jesus as a special gift of God to the disciples as a result of Divine revelation (Matt. 11:25: "I thank thee, O Father, Lord of heaven and earth, because thou hast hid these things from the wise and prudent, and hast revealed them unto babes," and 16:17: "Flesh and blood hath not revealed it unto you, but my Father which is in heaven"). Above all it is the knowledge of the salvation present in Christ, the knowledge that the kingdom has come in Jesus as the Christ.[56] All this is expressed and confirmed even more clearly in Matthew 13:16, where in opposition to the crowd the disciples are called blessed because they *see* and *hear*, which according to the 17th verse refers to the beginning of the salvation that many prophets and righteous men have in vain desired to see.[57] This knowledge of the mystery of the kingdom, i.e., this insight into the fulfillment begun with Christ, is the great prerequisite for being able and being allowed to understand the parables. Without this knowledge a parable remains a verbal garb for thoughts that can be associated with many things instructive in themselves, but whose specific, redemptive-historical purport (i.e., that which is concerned with the coming of the kingdom) cannot be understood.

Jesus' speaking in parables has a two-fold effect: on the one hand it is a revelation, on the other it veils something. This is in accordance with the entire character and the modality of the revelation of the kingdom given in Jesus' coming. This speaking in parables is in a particular sense even indicated as the fulfillment of the prophecy[58], viz., of Psalm 78:2, which is explained in Matthew 13:35 in this way: "I will open my mouth in parables, I will utter things which have been kept secret from the foundation of the world."

Psalm 78:2 also mentions "parables" (Hebr. *māshāl; LXX parabolai*) but in the more general sense of: proverb, saying, poetical pronouncement. For in this psalm the poet relates the history of old Israel in short, concise pronouncements. This history contains "secrets," i.e., it has a secret spiritual background and purport. These "secrets" must be revealed by his "sayings" in their *actual* meaning; i.e., revealed to those who have the spiritual capacity to understand them.

In this sense Jesus' words are the fulfillment of the prophecies. In his parables he expresses (i.e., puts into words) the secrets of the beginning. He reveals the actuality, the realization of what had been preached long ago. This is the significance of his word, also of his parables: they aim at bringing home to the listeners that the past has been brought to fulfillment in the present and the way in which this has come about; or to put it in a messianic way, the manner in which the salvation of the kingdom has become an actual reality.[59]

The same redemptive-historical character of that which Jesus teaches in the parables can also be inferred from the conclusion of the discourse on the parables in Matthew 13, viz., verses 51, 52. Here Jesus first asks his disciples if they have understood "all this." And when they have answered in the affirmative Jesus speaks of the scribe instructed[60] in the kingdom of heaven (*mathēteutheis tēi basileiai toon ouranaan*) who is like a householder "who brings forth out of his treasure things new and old." Very important in this text are the "new things" which are even mentioned first. This does not merely refer to the form of the instruction but especially to its contents.[61] Although the old things have not been discarded, the new things have priority now. They are the new things that have come with Jesus,[62] the new things of the divine economy of salvation.[63] They again consist in the realization of what had been promised and awaited from olden times. That is why the scribe who has been well instructed in the kingdom has to preach both the old and the new things, both prophecy and fulfillment. In the treasure from which he draws he has at his disposal a new theme; the coming of the kingdom in the Messiah. This constitutes the great difference between him and the scribes who up to now have instructed the people about the kingdom but could only speak of it in terms of the future.

All this shows what great emphasis especially the parables lay on the presence of the kingdom of heaven. In Jesus' instruction of the disciples, he gives them a deeper insight into the reality of the fulfillment that has begun with him. They are themselves fitted for the task of being preachers of this fulfillment.

On the other hand the parables indicate the special veiled way in which the kingdom has come. The wisdom offered in it, the mysteries revealed in it, are only knowable to those who have been privileged to understand the fundamental secret, viz., the coming of the kingdom in Christ. To those who are outsiders and do not know what it is basically about, this way of speaking about the kingdom is bound to leave the secret undisclosed. Both Mark and Luke express this thought very sharply: to outsiders all these things are told in parables in order that seeing they may not see, etc. This is a quotation from Isaiah 6:10, where the sentence of the hardening of their hearts is pronounced against the unbelieving people, and this hardening is also called the purpose of the preaching. The same judgment passes upon those who do not believe in Christ and his preaching. They are prevented from gaining the deeper insight implied in the parables. This blindness is a *purpose* because it is not only based on unbelief but caused by it. (Matthew has *because* instead of *in order that*.) This passage does not mean that outsiders are denied any possibility of believing (cf., e.g., Luke 19:42). They only do not get an opportunity to be further instructed in the secret of the kingdom. When Matthew in 13:34 again confirms that Jesus did not say anything to the multitude except in parables, he does not mean that Jesus had shut himself up completely from them, or had spiritually withdrawn himself from them. All the time that Jesus was among the people his whole action, his person, his miracles and his continued call to them to repent and be converted were a preaching to them until the end (cf., e.g., Luke 23:28,41-43). But where a fundamental change was not brought about and the heart remained untouched, Jesus' word was bound to remain enigmatical in many respects; and neither about himself, nor about the kingdom he proclaimed did he give any but an indirect, veiled answer which therefore remained enigmatical in the light of their continuing unbelief. This not only characterizes the parables but also the enigmatical sayings, e.g., Matt. 16:4: the saying about Jonah; cf. also 21:16: "Have you never read: Out of the mouth of babes and sucklings thou hast perfected praise?", the evasive answer, e.g., 21:23-27 (the question about Jesus' authority); the unclear dispute, e.g., 22:41-46 (David's Son and David's Lord); and others. In all this there is no doubt about the divine judgment of the hardening of their hearts and of the veiling of the truth, whereas, conversely, faith also goes back to God's gift of grace and to his sovereign good pleasure alone (cf. 11:25,26, where Jesus thanks the father "because he has hidden these things from the wise and prudent and has revealed them unto babes." Christ adds: "Even so, Father; for so it seemed good in thy sight," see also Matt. 22:14). But neither divine predestination nor the miracle of faith as a gift (Matt. 11:25; 13:11; 16:17) remove the riddle and the responsibility of unbelief (cf., e.g., Matt. 11:20-24; 23:37).

All this, especially the speaking in parables and what can be equated with them indicate the specific modality of the revelation of the kingdom of heaven that has started with the coming of Jesus. The kingdom has come, the Messiah has been revealed; but this can only be discerned by faith, that is to say, by the grace of God. This will one day be changed. Then even the enemies will see the kingdom and will have to recognize the Son of Man (Matt. 23:39; 26:64). The method of preaching the gospel is in accordance with this special modality, though in a different sense before and after Jesus' death and resurrection (cf. Matt. 10:27; 16:20; 17:9 and other places),[64] but always in such a way that the preaching of the kingdom has a double effect, viz., that of revelation and of veiling, of grace and of judgment (cf. also Matt. 10:12-15).

18. *The Sower*

The contents of the parables, even more clearly than their form, clarify the meaning and the special character of the kingdom that has begun with the coming of Christ. For, as parables, it is their nature to serve as explanations and as arguments,[65] for those who have ears to hear.[66] Especially in the well-known chapters containing parables (viz., Matt. 13, Mark 4), and the corresponding passages in Luke, they have been given to eclucidate the relationship between Jesus' proclamation of the presence of the kingdom, on the one hand, and of the delay of the last judgment, on the other. This relationship was far from transparent to the disciples.

The parable of the sower has priority over the others, not only as the first of a series, but also on account of its purport. In many respects it is the starting-point and the basis for the understanding of the following parables.[67] This also appears from the question Jesus asked of his disciples: "Know ye not this parable? and how then will ye know all parables?" (Mark 4:13).[68] In the following parables we find the figures of the husbandman, the field, the seed, etc., again and again. They are in many respects elaborations of the first parable. From Jesus' question it appears (just as from Luke 8:9) that the disciples did not understand this parable. This fact brings out all the more clearly that its purport is not a general pedagogical, psychological, or even homiletical, instruction about preachers and listeners and the risks that occur during the process of listening. If the parable had no further aim than to convey this general meaning, the lack of comprehension by the disciples with respect to such simple symbolism would not only set us to wondering, but the parable could hardly serve as a vehicle keeping its significance a secret from "outsiders."

One single word might "betray" its meaning! The point of the parable, however, is something very special; the issue is the redemptive-historical element, i.e., the relationship between the events depicted in the parable and the revelation of the kingdom of heaven.[69] This relationship remains obscure to the disciples though they had been privileged to understand the mystery of the kingdom (viz., that of the presence of the kingdom). And, therefore, the revelation of this fact is the most essential part of the explanation added to the parable by Jesus. It has not unjustly been observed that the mystery of the parable does not lie in its obscurity or complexity, but in its very simplicity.[70] And this holds not only for the parable proper but also for its explanation. The only spectacular fact is that in this parable (i.e., in the sower's sowing of the seed, in the loss of part of the seed, in the fruitfulness of another part, etc.) the real issue is the revelation of the kingdom of heaven, so that the parable is actually about the mystery of the kingdom.[71]

As a matter of fact this is already confirmed in the simple statement: "The sower soweth the word" (Mark 4:14), or, according to Luke's account: "The seed is the word of God" (8:11). For it is this *word* which contains the mystery of the kingdom. This is why Matthew here says: "The word of the kingdom." By this expression the word of God is meant in the actual sense it has in Jesus' preaching of the kingdom. It is "the word," the "word of God," "the word of the kingdom," the decisive, messianic word of power that Christ, as the Son of Man, has to say on earth and in which *eo ipso* the kingdom of heaven is revealed and has come.[72] And the fact that this word can be compared to seed, and he who speaks the word to a sower, is the instruction about the modality of the kingdom of heaven that has come with and in Christ.[73] This is the redemptive-historical purport of the parable. Its spectacular aspect is its simplicity which is the confirmation of the incomprehensible supposition: this is the way of the kingdom of God, "A sower went out to sow—and nothing further; and this means the new world of God."[74]

What this implies with regard to the meaning and the manifestation of the kingdom of heaven proclaimed by Jesus can be inferred from the elaboration of the parable. Closer examination shows that it emphasizes two things, viz., its fruitlessness and the fruits of the sower's work. The former is demonstrated by the loss of the seed sown along the road, on the rocks, and amid the thorns. These are the obstructions traced back to Satan in the explanation (Matt. 13:19; Mark 4:15; Luke 8:12); they are due to the superficial condition of the human heart (rocky soil) and to its worldly-mindedness (thorns). They cannot be ascribed to carelessness on the part of the sower[75] but indicate the reality of "the way of the world." Thus things will be when the seed is sown (they cannot be avoided), this is what the people are like to whom the word comes.

However, the parable does not only shed light on the obstructions and thus on the veiled modality of the revelation of the kingdom. It not only speaks of seed falling along the road, on the rocks and amid the thorns thus to remain fruitless, but also of seed falling on the good earth and giving fruit according to the law of a great and wonderful multiplication. It has been said that, after the elaborate three-fold description of the loss of the seed, the good field more or less seems to be an exception. The picture of three-fourths of the seed being lost is supposed to be a little grotesque, but perhaps this is what Jesus really meant, because the usual result of the word of God is no result.[76] In our opinion this interpretation is far-fetched. The parable does not say that three-fourths of the seed remains without fruit. No proportions are given. By the side of the many possibilities of no crop, or a bad crop, we find the wonderful: thirtyfold, and sixtyfold and a hundredfold. It may actually be true that the preaching of the gospel is often fruitless (Matt. 7:13ff; 22:14), but the parable of the sower is not pessimistic. It points to the wonderful germinal force of the seed together with the failures. In the parable Jesus certainly does not want to draw our attention exclusively to the hidden manifestation of the kingdom threatened and handicapped by all kinds of powers; he also points out its miraculous operations and fruits. The letter may be hidden even from the disciples, but they are sure to come—in overwhelming abundance! This is why the parable is intended, not only to temper expectations and to open the eyes of the disciples to the provisional character of the dispensation of salvation started with Christ, but also to revive their hopes and to direct their attention to what is coming. It contains a rich promise for the future, also for the future work of the disciples.

Summarizing, we may say that in the basic instruction of this parable Jesus gives a very fundamental insight into the kingdom that has begun with his coming. Here is made plain the specific character of Jesus' preaching of the kingdom. It consists in the revelation that the eschatological all-conquering coming of God into the world goes the way of the seed. And, moreover, that the Messiah who has been given all authority and power by God assumes the figure of the sower.[77] In such a way will come the time of harvesting, i.e., the consummation. Whoever understands this, not only knows the mystery (that salvation has come), but also the meaning of the hidden revelation. In spite of Satan's power, of the hardness of hearts, of the cares of the world and the delusion of riches, the crop is prepared by God's powerful word and the work of Christ.

This interpretation of the parable emphasizes its redemptive-historical meaning. It differs from the more recent explanations that also stress this specific meaning, but are based on either an exclusively present or a one-sided future conception of the kingdom of heaven. A closer examination, however, shows that precisely in the light of this parable neither the former nor the latter view is tenable and that the interpretation given in §14 of the kingdom being both present and future is very clearly confirmed in these parables.

The former view is found in Dodd, according to whom in the parable of the sower and in that of the seed that grew up spontaneously (Mark 4:26ff.), Jesus wants to teach his listeners that with his coming *the time of the harvest* has come. There are all kinds of obstacles, it is true, but Jesus is here supposed to indicate that no farmer delays the harvest because of some bare patches in the field. The meaning is, then, that there is an abundant crop and that he is especially concerned with reaping.[78] In opposition to this view the other interpretation holds that in these parables there is question only of the future kingdom of God. Thus Michaelis, e.g., thinks that by the seed (the word) Jesus does not mean the presence of the kingdom but only the announcement of the coming kingdom. And the purport of the whole is supposed to be an exhortation to the disciples to exert themselves and to persevere because, in spite of any and all obstructions, the kingdom is sure to come in due time.[79]

But on account of their one-sidedness the two interpretations fail to do justice to the parable. This is most clearly seen in Dodd's interpretation. His description of "the situation" is correct: the disciples are further enlightened about the presence of the kingdom. *But this presence is not to be sought in the harvest, but in the sowing of the seed.* It is not the parable of the harvester but of the sower. Here Dodd obviously must take recourse in a shifting and distorting of the meaning of the parable. It is true that the harvest is held out as a prospect, but this does not refer to the present, but to the future. The harvest is the standing image of the final manifestation of the kingdom (cf. Matt. 13:39). Here the liberal rejection of the eschatology of Jesus' preaching wreaks its vengeance upon Dodd. Thus the way to a correct exegesis is blocked in spite of Dodd's correct view of the "situation" in which the parable was told—which he calls *"der Sitz im Leben."* The result is that Dodd must resort to far-fetched additions (the call for more laborers).

The one-sidedly eschatological conception starts from the correct view of the harvest as the future manifestation of the kingdom. But it cannot get any further, and so it fails to discover the point of the parable. For the purport of the parable cannot lie in the general truth ("supplemented" or not in the sense of Michaelis) that in spite of everything the kingdom is sure to come. This was not the real problem that needed to remain hidden from the multitude. It was rather the common supposition shared by both the disciples and the multitude, viz., that the kingdom of God meant harvest, judgment, end. What Jesus wanted to teach the disciples was the relationship between what they had accepted in faith as the "mystery of the kingdom" (viz., that Jesus Christ and the kingdom had come) and the delay of the end, the harvest, the consummation. This tension is the occasion, the "situation" of the parable. And it is exactly this tension which is ignored by the one-sidedly eschatological interpretation of the parable. The disciples, however, had understood that the kingdom and that the Christ *had* come—which is denied by the one-sidedly eschatological view. That situation, viz., of the kingdom as a present reality, required a different answer from that of the "consistent eschatology"! If this "situation" is not clearly understood and set forth, this parable in Jesus' preaching remains unintelligible and its exegesis gets mired in generalities.[80]

The above finds its provisional conclusion and confirmation in the very important aphorisms concluding the entire complex of the tradition of the parable of the sower in Mark and Luke, viz., that of the light which is not kindled to keep it hidden but to be put on a candlestick, followed by the general statement: "For there is nothing hid which shall not be manifested," etc., and the warning: "Take heed what you hear, for with what measure you mete, it shall be measured to you: and unto you that hear shall more be given. For he that hath, to him shall be given: and he that hath not, from him shall be taken even that which he hath" (Mark 4:21-25; Luke 8:16-18, cf. Matt. 13:21).

According to the context these aphorisms can only be applied to the character of the instruction given here.[81] Jesus says that the kindling of a light is always done for the purpose of spreading light, and that what has been hidden for a long time is nevertheless bound to come to light. This holds in the first place for the form of preaching. There will be a time when the disciples will make public that which is still veiled in the form of a parable (cf. also Matt. 10:26,27, where the words— "for there is nothing covered, that shall not be revealed"—are followed by: "What I tell you in darkness that speak ye in light; and what ye hear in the ear, that preach ye upon the housetops"). So even in the *proclamation* of the gospel there is a climax from mystery to revelation. One day the mystery of the sower will be revealed, and the outsiders also will hear the word about the kingdom and Jesus as the Christ without any special setting or veiling. This task given by Jesus to his disciples is concerned with their future preaching and is closely connected with Jesus' present self-veiling as the Christ (cf. below, §22). The resurrection will occasion a break (caesura) by which a great change will be brought about in the manner in which the kingdom will be preached.

Yet these aphorisms refer not only to the form and the proclamation of the kingdom, but also to *that kingdom as such.* One day it will lose its hidden modality and come to the fore fully revealed. This is pointed out not only by the general purport of the saying: "There is nothing covered that shall not be revealed" (in connection with Mark 4:11), but also by the final sayings concerning the true way of hearing. Since the mystery is to become public, *hearing* is very important now. For what will ultimately be received in the kingdom of God depends upon what a man *possesses* of it now. For "he that hath to him shall be given: and he that hath not shall lose everything." And what a man "has" of it, depends upon hearing, i.e., upon the way in which he bears the responsibility with respect to the word of the kingdom that has been scattered like seed. This hearing is now "the measure with which a man metes" (Mark 4:24). If this measure is rich and great, i.e., if the kingdom, as it is preached, is accepted with great eagerness and receptivity, a rich share will be received in like measure in the coming revelation of the kingdom, and "even more shall be given." The revelation will bring a much richer salvation and bliss than a man now dares to hope for even by faithful hearing.[82]

Here, too, everything concentrates on the unity of the kingdom in the present and in the future. What one receives from the Sower will also be received from the Judge in double measure. Only those who know the mystery in the present will share in the revelation of the future. For the seed is the word of the kingdom of God by which he comes into the world in Christ.

19. *The Delay of the Judgment*

Very closely related to the parable of the sower is that of the tares among the wheat with its explanation (Matt. 13:24-30; 36-43). As to its contents it is nothing but an elaboration and specification of the parable of the sower. It also starts by describing the figure of the sower (vs. 24) and in the added explanation, vs. 37, it is now explicitly stated that the sower of the good seed is the Son of Man (which we have already indicated in the parable of the sower as fundamental for the right understanding of this entire section of Jesus' preaching).

This parable, too, starts from the insight into the mystery of the kingdom. The kingdom has come. Jesus is the Christ; *this* is the great presupposition. The parable again brings to light the modality of this reality of fulfillment. It continues the previous instruction, i.e., the kingdom will come in the way of the word which goes out like a seed; and the Messiah comes in the form of a sower.

This parable also speaks of the obstacles which the seed encounters after it has been sown. This time they are not represented by the figure of the barren soil but by that of the enemy who sows tares among the wheat (but compare Matthew 13:19). Up to this point the two parables show a factual similarity and we may refer to the first parable for the purport of the second.[83] The new element in the second parable is the question asked by the servants of the husbandman whether they had not better remove the tares from among the wheat at once, and the answer of the husbandman that this removal will not be done now but at the time of harvesting. The opinion has been expressed that this passage is concerned with the *church* and that in it Jesus wants to warn against an excess of zeal, as if it were possible to accomplish on earth the separation which is the privilege of the Son of Man at the last judgment.[84]   This exegesis completely shifts the point at issue and deprives us of the right view of the parable. For, apart from other insurmountable objections[85], what the servants suggest to the landlord is not something provisional, a separation until further notice, which can only be applied to human beings by their fellow-men (in the church). But it is the final *extermination* of the tares from the wheat, or to put it in its real form, the definitive separation in the divine judgment. The issue between the servants and the landlord is not the question *who* is to execute the separation, nor *what* kind of separation it is to be, but *when* it will happen. Though the servants desire to carry out an immediate separation, the landlord determines that it shall be postponed till the day of the harvest, for—thus he tells his servants—you might pull out the wheat in gathering the tares.

This parable again sheds light on the relationship between the presence and the future of the kingdom. It deals with the problem raised by the pronouncements on the presence of the kingdom; i.e., the postponement of the last judgment, and the continuation of the mingling of the evil and the good even after the kingdom has come. The answer is a direct continuation of what appeared from the parable of the sower. Since the kingdom comes like the seed, and since the Son of Man is first the sower (vs. 37) before being the reaper (vs. 41) the last judgment is postponed. The delay is implied in this difference. Whoever sows cannot immediately reap. The postponement of the judgment is determined by the modality of the kingdom of God that has already come with Christ.

Ignoring this viewpoint leads to unmistakable superficiality in the conception of the meaning of the parable. This happens when the presence of the kingdom is not taken into account and the kingdom is represented exclusively as a future reality. Then the explanation given is that Jesus wanted to admonish his disciples to have patience because the separation that they hoped for will be accomplished only at the last judgment. (Thus, e.g., R. Bultmann, *Gesch. d. synopt. Tradition,*[2] 1931, pp. 202, 203; W. Michaelis, *Sämann,* pp.

74, 75). But of this fact the disciples were already convinced. What had to be explained to them was the postponement of the judgment *even after Jesus the Christ had come.* The problem was not in the fact that the Messiah's kingdom had not yet come, but rather, in the presence both of his kingdom and himself. This, however, is denied by Bultmann and Michaelis. Other writers are of the opinion that Jesus teaches his disciples that the separation between the wicked and the good is the privilege of the Son of Man with which men should not meddle (thus H. D. Wendland, *op. cit.*, p. 35; W. G. Kümmel, *op. cit.*, p. 82). But if this be true, then the point of the parable is not discovered. For, that the separation was to be made by the Son of Man (and not by human beings) did not need be told to the disciples in order to enable them to restrain their impatience. Much rather, this conviction was the cause of their impatience. For the very reason that they had been given to understand the mystery of the kingdom and had learned to recognize Jesus as the Son of Man, did the postponement of the day of judgment become a problem to them. How was it possible for the kingdom to have come without at the same time making a separation between the wicked and the good? This was the cause of their impatience, and to this the parable gives an answer.

In this respect Dodd's starting-point is much more commendable although he is only willing to accept the presence of the kingdom. According to him Jesus' aim here is to instruct those that find it difficult to accept the coming of the kingdom because there are still so many sinners in Israel. Dodd's interpretation of the parable, however, is very typical. He thinks that Jesus gives the following answer to the doubters: Just as a landlord would not delay harvesting because during harvest time there are tares among the wheat, the coming of the kingdom is not retarded because there are sinners in Israel (Dodd, *op. cit.*, p. 185). If we wish to follow Dodd we must not only eliminate "as completely as possible" the explanation of the parable in the verses 36 to 42 where the harvest is fixed "at the end of this world," but we must even reverse the meaning of the parable itself. It speaks of the harvest as the moment when the separation can no longer be postponed but must be accomplished, in other words, of the future manifestation of the kingdom; which, however, Dodd emphatically rejects. From the above it appears that both the denial of the presence and the rejection of the future of the kingdom deprive us of the possibility of getting an insight into these parables.

We may wonder to what extent the general purport of the parable can be further elaborated, especially with regard to the landlord's fear that, together with the tares, the wheat might also be pulled out. Is this a symbolic element, or does it only belong to the imagery of the parable? The difficulty of arriving at a well-founded interpretation of this detail is due to the fact that we are not certain about the cause of the landlord's fear. It is usually assumed that the tares here (Latin: *lolium temulentum*) bore such a striking resemblance to the wheat that, at least for the time being, they were difficult to distinguish.[86] Present-day authorities on Palestine, however, are of opinion that the cause is something else. For, when the tares became visible everywhere, the grain had already formed in the wheat (vs. 26). Then there was no longer any danger of mistaking the wheat for tares. But another danger had replaced the former risk since the roots of the two kinds of plants must have so much intertwined in this phase, that the tares could not be pulled out without damaging the wheat.[87]

But to our mind all these details cannot be explained in a "spiritual" sense without lapsing into illegitimate allegorizing. And the explanation in verses 36-43 does not mention anything of this kind either. It is possible to say that in the parable there is question of a twofold process of maturing, viz., that of evil and that of good, but in what sense cannot be derived from the parable. In this context, we shall have to let it go at that. It is stated that the separation, i.e., the judgment, will only take place in the future. And this is derived from the nature of the work of the sower. Further interpretation from this parable as to the why of the postponement of the judgment is, in our opinion, not possible.[88]

The parable of *the fishing net* cast into the sea (Matt. 13:47-50) has the same purport as that of the tares among the wheat, which appears from the great similarity between the two explanations (13:40-42; and 13:49,50). Here, too, the issue is not some pedagogical piece of wisdom, but very clearly the redemptive-historical element. Jesus again instructs his disciples about the manifestation of the kingdom in the present and the future.

He now uses the image of the drag-net to denote the preaching of the gospel. This preaching is again and again compared to the activity of fishing so familiar to the disciples (cf. Matt. 4:19; Luke 5:10). Especially the manner in which it is done is the center of the attention. First the net is dragged through the sea, and only after this work has been sufficiently performed, do the fishermen go to the shore to inspect the catch and make proper selection. This is an image of the way by which the kingdom comes. Preaching reveals the kingdom, for it is the Christ in whose service the "fishers of men" are employed. But the kingdom will come in a different way from what might be supposed. This mystery is the real subject of the parable. Christ (and the kingdom with him) first comes to gather together, and then afterwards, only after the gathering has been completed, does he make the definitive separation and reveal himself in his perfect glory.[89]

Here, too, the one-sidedly present conception of the kingdom as well as the exclusively future view obscure the meaning of the parable. The former is again found in Dodd. He entirely eliminates the future-eschatological trait of the selection of the fish as it is found in Matt. 13:49-50. In his opinion the selection mentioned by the parable is brought about by the different reactions of the people to the general call of the gospel.[90] Others, like, e.g., Kümmel, hold that there is here no reference whatever to a present aspect of the kingdom. The parable only points out the serious character of the summons addressed to all to be converted in view of the separation which will take place at the last judgment.[91] Michaelis goes a step further. He conceives of the catching of the fish itself as an event that will take place at the last judgment.[92] Others, again, consider that the catching of the fish does not refer to the kingdom but to the coming church.[93]

In our opinion the separation in the parable undeniably refers to the last judgment, as the catching of the fish does to the present preaching of the gospel. The 49th verse clearly shows that the analogy between the work of the fishermen and that of the angels at the end of this world is not to be sought in the gathering together but in the sorting of the fish. The real issue in this case as in that of the parable of the tares among the wheat is whether there is only a question here of a warning against the judgment of the coming kingdom or whether we are given further information about the nature of the kingdom in the present world. The opening words of the parable say that "the kingdom of heaven is like unto a net." Strictly speaking, this implies that not only the separation of the wicked from the good at the last judgment, belongs to the kingdom but also the gathering together (the work of the drag-net, in this case that of the preaching of the gospel in this dispensation). It is true that we should not draw too many conclusions from the introductory words, because they only approximately indicate the point of comparison between the kingdom and the contents of the parable. This introductory formula is often only a starting-point (cf., e.g., 13:24; 20:1; 22:2; 25:1). This is not saying that it is a foregone conclusion that here the kingdom of heaven cannot be compared to the initial work of a drag-net, and is only analogous to the final work of sorting by the fishermen. Rather, there must be weighty reasons if the former—which is also a part of the parable about the kingdom—is to be excluded from the *tertium comparationis*. And this argument is strengthened by an objective view of the parable. If its exclusive purport were an indication of the coming separation between the wicked and the good, we might wonder why Jesus needed a separate parable to illustrate a universally accepted truth. The *tertium comparationis* is much rather to be sought in the initial gathering together (*ek pantos genous*), as well as in the later separation of the wicked from the good. Here, too, the mystery (kept from outsiders) is revealed to the disciples. They have not been mistaken. Jesus is the Christ. The kingdom has come. But for the time being it will come *suo modo* (in its own way).

20. *The Effect of the Word*

The previous sections show that the dispensation of salvation that began with Jesus' coming bears a preliminary and veiled character in many respects. It presupposes an interim before the final manifestation of the kingdom.

In the parables of the sower, the tares in the field, and the drag-net, the meaning of this interim has been made clear from a certain point of view. The postponement of the last judgment is not exclusively negative, so that it simply keeps the disciples in suspense, and strengthens and purifies their faith, but it is also positive in meaning. The time of waiting is that of sowing, the mystery is an opportunity, the Son of Man scatters the seed in the field, and throws the drag-net into the sea. And this reveals the messianic character of his work in this dispensation. For his word is authoritative.

This positive meaning of the delay of the judgment is clearly taught in three other parables, viz., in that of the seed springing up spontaneously (Mark 4:26-29), that of the mustard-seed (Matt. 13:31,32, etc.), and that of the leaven (Matt. 13:33). In a sense they express the same thought as the three above-mentioned parables. Yet they deserve separate treatment because they are oriented to the idea of the growing influence and the victorious power of the salvation given in Christ's coming rather than to the thought of resistance and obstruction. As to the parable of the seed that grew spontaneously, we start from the insight gained above that here, too, "the man who cast seed into the ground" means Christ himself.[94] This also follows from verse 29; the reaper is the coming judge of the world, which is also indicated by the concluding words of verse 29 which have been derived from the eschatological prophecy of Joel 3:13. He is the same person as the sower of the seed (cf. Matt. 13:37ff).[95] In our opinion, therefore, there can be no doubt that here, too, the kingdom occurs as a present entity. The sowing of the seed is a messianic work. That this is the starting-point can only be understood by those who know the mystery (verse 10), viz., that Jesus is the Christ and that with him the salvation has come. The purpose of the parable is again to elucidate the relationship between what is now seen of the Christ and what was expected of him and, also according to the parable, what may still be expected of him (vs. 29). This elucidation is given in the nature of the work indicated as "sowing." It implies dependence upon the condition of the soil, it is up against all kinds of obstruction (cf. above) but, apart from all other factors, it also implies that the harvest will be gathered only after the lapse of a certain period of time. The interim, however, is no waste of time, for in the meanwhile something will *happen*. Things run their course. The seed springs up and reaches a certain height. This happens, "he does not know how," i.e., *unnoticed*. For the earth produces fruit *spontaneously*. This does not mean that he no longer cares for his work—no more than the sleeping and rising of the sower in verse 27—but it means that while he has to leave the seed to its fate for a while the process of ripening goes on steadily and that harvest time is approaching. And this is the great purpose, for when the fruit is ripe he *at once* sends the sickle into the grain.

The important elements are the certainty of the crop—in spite of the husbandman's temporary passivity—and also the germinal power of the seed as the cause of that certainty. For the certainty of the crop's coming is indissolubly connected with the action of the seed in the soil. The parable emphasizes this point. Those who only point to the certainty of the crop ignore the operation of the seed in the soil.[96] Thus all the parables about the harvest are explained in the same way, their individual characteristics are levelled out and removed. This is a reaction to the interpretation that applies the modern idea of evolution to the coming of the kingdom. This interpretation is certainly wrong, but we should not avoid it by amputating the purport of the parable. In this parable the future is not only guaranteed—the harvest will come as soon (*euthus*) as the time is ripe for it—but is also directly connected with the present. The word is sent out, i.e., the authoritative word of Christ. It does not fall to the earth and return empty. The preaching of the gospel is itself the guarantee of the ultimate coming of the kingdom. It brings the latter irresistibly nearer.

This interpretation again maintains the presence and the future of the kingdom and points out the internal relationship between the two. It therefore again means the rejection of the one-sidedly eschatological interpretation[97] which can here only see a consolation because of the certainty of the future, and an exhortation to patience in the present. The kingdom is sure to come without our being able to accelerate or hinder it. This is true, but it does no justice to the guarantee manifested in the present. In a certain sense we may say that the latter thought suggests a process of development in the coming of the kingdom. But this is not to be conceived of as a kingdom which operates in the soul or in human society as an independently developing principle. Neither can it be identified with a certain form of social life in the course of development (e.g., in the sense of the social gospel). But it refers to the operation of the divine word in this world. It cannot be detached from the person of Christ and for this reason it can only be considered as the coming of the kingdom. Dodd's view must be entirely rejected, for he seeks the presence of the kingdom in the harvest and quotes Matthew 9:37,38 to support his opinion. He thinks that the time of sowing and waiting was over with Christ's coming, and that Christ now sends the sickle into the corn, i.e., he reaps what had been sown before by the prophets. This idea, however, is in conflict with all of what is meant by the harvest in this world of thought. We may refer to our discussion of the parables of the sower and the tares among the wheat. The same arguments apply here as well.

This parable is very closely related to that of the mustard-seed. It has the same presuppositions: the seed, the sower, the field. Here, too, the issue is the modality of the salvation that has come and been fulfilled in Christ. The specific trait is to be sought in the mustard-seed which is one of the smallest seeds (cf. Matt. 17:20). But when it has grown up it is taller than any other seed and may even be compared to a tree in whose branches the birds of the air can build their nests. These words agree with Daniel 4:21, where the glory of Nebuchadnezzar and his empire is described. The purport of the parable is clearly the contrast between the small, insignificant beginning and the glorious fulfillment. This must be applied to the kingdom and its coming. It again deals with the confusing character of the present manifestation of the kingdom and of Christ for those who know the mystery of the kingdom. Its beginning may seem small and insignificant, we must not be mistaken about it, but remember the mustard-seed. One day the kingdom of heaven will surpass the kingdoms of the earth (Dan. 4) in glory.

Here we must also reject Dodd's view that the enormous size of the fully grown mustard-seed refers to the manifestation of the kingdom that has already come with Jesus and whose blessings have already been put at the disposal of all men. The process of the hidden development has now come to an end.[98] But this view is entirely in conflict with the tendency of the whole of Jesus' teaching in these parables. This parable, too, has an eschatological conclusion.

Nevertheless, even if Dodd's conception is rejected, there remains an irreconcilable controversy about the question as to whether in this case Jesus *exclusively* contrasts the great future of the kingdom to its presence (however conceived, e.g., as a sign)—so that here only the contrast between the beginning and the end has been pointed out—or that there is also an indication of the process of development of the kingdom that takes place in the meantime.[99] In our opinion the emphasis lies here on the glorious fulfillment by which those are comforted who are amazed at the small beginnings of the kingdom. Yet it is unnatural to have an eye only for the beginning and the end and to eliminate at all cost all that lies in between. Everything depends upon the idea that is formed of the way in which progress is made from the small beginning to the wonderful end. For the fact that the final coming of the kingdom is entirely based on God's action shows that the end is not the completion of an immanent process of development. And this is also true of the beginning. The whole of the manifestation of the kingdom is the fruit of divine action. The seed is the word of God spoken by Christ with authority. This word of power will one day make all things new.[100]   But between the beginning and the end there is a history. In this history the word has made progress and has had its effect. This progress cannot be thought of in the sense of the modern idea of evolution, but in that of the plan and the work of God. Therefore, the disciples must watch the coming deeds of God. We may consider that the tree with its branches stands for the significance of the kingdom as embracing the world and also subjecting the heathen.[101]   In any case, this progress of the power of Jesus' word is a clear illustration of the growth of the seed.[102]   We shall certainly not be allowed to eliminate this thought, although the glorious end is especially emphasized.

And finally, the parable of *the leaven*. It has been rightly observed that this parable, too, starts from the decisive character of Jesus' action.[103]   This is the great event, the mystery of the kingdom of God, that the disciples know. This situation is the starting-point of the parable. For it requires elucidation (cf. above) also to the disciples.[104]

The question is, where is the *tertium comparationis*? Is it the influence of the leaven, the great difference between the beginning and the end, or the attitude adopted by the woman, viz., that of waiting patiently? Matter defends the last view; according to him the parable has no didactic but a hortatory character; it exhorts the disciples to patient watchfulness.[105] The remarkable thing, however, is that this very element of waiting is lacking. It seems a little far-fetched to infer[106] all this from the word "until."[107]   Besides, it is doubtful whether we should identify the attitude of the disciples with what the woman does. If we are willing to suppose that there is question of a personification here, we might say that the woman does what Christ does. He is the sower; he is also the person who "puts the leaven in the meal." In our opinion the kingdom must certainly be compared with the leaven. This raises the same problem that is found in the two previous parables. Are only the beginning (the woman hides the leaven) and the end (until the *whole* is leavened) contrasted to each other in this case? Thus according to the strictly eschatological explanation: the all-embracing kingdom will come although the too small beginnings in the present seem to plead against it. The process of the leavening of the whole is not the focal point of the picture.[108]

No doubt this parable (like the preceding one) is eschatological in the sense that it leads to the *total* leavening of the meal. This indicates the certainty of the glorious future, in spite of its small beginning[109] in the present. But the grounds on which the element of the leavening in its active sense is detached from the meaning of the parable is also incomprehensible here. Is the leaven only characterized by its small beginning and its great result? Does not the idea of leaven suggest to every simple listener (i.e., one who is not under the sway of scientific problems) the thought of the continuous effect so typical of leaven? In our opinion there is no exegetical possibility of handling the contrasts: "beginning—end" so exclusively in this parable that what happens between the beginning and the end is not taken into account. Such a method is not possible here, for it was not possible in the parable of the "spontaneous growth of the seed," and it is even less possible here than in the case of the mustard-seed.

We must maintain the idea of the continuous effect,[110] but not in the sense of a "spontaneously operating" principle, as in the view of the immanent evolutionary process. It is God who uses the "effective" word. We can only inquire whether this continuous operation is further qualified here (and differently from the spontaneously growing seed). In this connection the word *kruptein* is important. Does it mean only "to put in"[111] or are we to prefer the more pregnant sense of the word "to hide"?[112] We cannot really say that the woman intentionally hides the leaven, so we cannot, therefore, infer from this that the essential characteristic of the kingdom is the circumstance that it must not be seen. Moreover, the effect of the leaven is certainly manifest (the rising of the leaven). Yet the word "hide" has its own flavor, so that it must have been chosen with an eye on the situation. It was precisely the mystery, the hidden beginning of the manifestation of the kingdom that had to be elucidated. Important is the fact that this mystery is not a sign of weakness. The leaven *operates*, and so does the word. And its operation has a totalitarian character. It leavens every part of the meal. The parable of the spontaneously growing seed sheds light upon the operation as such; that of the mustard-seed indicates the extensiveness of this operation; the parable of the leaven is concerned with the intensity of the operation. It does not only concern the totality, the extent, but also every part of the whole and all its relations. In its final manifestation the kingdom will embrace everything, both in an intensive and in an extensive sense. Even now it has this tendency owing to the power of the divine word.

21. *Seeking What Is Lost*

In the preceding sections it has been amply shown that the preaching of the gospel in the dispensation of the kingdom of heaven that began with Jesus' coming, occupies a very important place. It is this continuous preaching which is one of the reasons why the coming judgment is still delayed.

This fact leads to the viewpoint that, consequently, in Jesus' coming the possibility of conversion and salvation has become considerably greater. John the Baptist's preaching was so ominous and alarming because he said that the "axe was laid unto the root of the trees," and that he who was coming held "the fan in his hand." Now it appears that with Jesus' coming, on the one hand, the fulfillment has become a fact, but, on the other, that the time of grace has also been extended. This extension is important, but the preaching of grace is no less important. The gospel itself now operates with an entirely new force, and an intensified content; it is the preaching of the fulfillment; it is the message of the grace of God revealed in Christ which now starts its course in this world.

It is also true that the postponement of the judgment in no way signifies a weakening of the serious and urgent call to repentance, which characterized John's preaching. Nowhere does this appear more clearly than in the parable of the barren fig-tree (Luke 13:6-9), which also deals with the coming judgment. It is the sequel to Jesus' conversation with some people who told him about the massacre of the Galilaeans by Pilate. On this occasion Jesus taught his listeners to seek the deepest cause of the outrage that had not been prevented by God— as well as of all the disasters that happen to man (the tower in Siloam)—not in the special individual guilt of the victims but rather in the general impenitent nature of man.

No doubt the purpose of the parable of the fruitless fig tree is to enforce this call to repentance by pointing out that the judgment is sure to come. Yet in this parable Jesus first speaks of a year's postponement granted to the fig-tree by the landlord in response to the intercession of the vine-dresser. The question is to what extent the details are intended as symbols. In connection with what precedes, the cutting down of the fig-tree is certainly not meant to stand for the expulsion of the wicked from the church, as Michaelis has it.[113] If we do not wish wholly to abstain from any further specializing, we might say that this cutting down of the fig-tree represents the divine judgment upon Israel. This suggests the fall of Jerusalem also foretold in other passages of Luke (cf. 19:43,44; 21:20ff). But the "cutting down" in the 7th verse, together with the "bearing fruit" in verse 9, strongly remind us of John the Baptist's picture of the last judgment (Luke 3:9; Matt. 3:10, cf. 7:19).[114] Then of importance is, furthermore, the view that the vine-dresser stands for Jesus himself,[115] in connection with which Zahn even suggests that the "three years" of the 7th verse stand for the time since John the Baptist's appearance.[116] To our mind it is doubtful whether such a personification is sufficiently warranted in the context. But the meaning of the parable is not obscure. In addition to the reference to the impending judgment we find the delay of one year proposed by the vine-dresser and apparently accepted by the landlord. By this Jesus indicates that Israel no longer has a right to exist, but that God has continued the opportunity to repent, although now the extreme limit of his long-suffering has been reached. This is a clear indication that the judgment to be expected with the coming of the kingdom has again been postponed owing to God's gracious decree. Thus this parable sheds light on the character of Jesus' action. He brings judgment, but not all at once. His messianic task is also intended to save many people from the coming judgment of the world by means of his preaching the gospel.

In accordance with this is Jesus' conception of his task. Of special importance is the general characterization given in Matthew 9:35-38 (cf. also Mark 6:34), where it says that on seeing the multitude Jesus was "moved with compassion on them, because they fainted, and were scattered abroad, as sheep having no shepherd." Another image is added to this, viz., that of the harvest: "The harvest truly is plenteous, but the labourers are few. Pray ye therefore the Lord of the harvest that he will send forth labourers into his harvest" (cf. also Luke 10:2). We find the same description in Matthew 10:6; 15:24. There the text speaks of "the lost sheep of the house of Israel" (*ta probata ta apoloolata*). This concept *to apoloolos* is not only found in this general sense but also in a more individual meaning, e.g., in the story of Zacchaeus. In opposition to the muttered disapproval of the crowd in connection with his entering the house of a sinful man, Jesus says: "This day is salvation come to this house, forsomuch as he also is a son of Abraham. For the Son of Man is come to seek and to save that which was lost." Particularly characteristic of the thoughts lying at the base of these utterances is the parable of the lost sheep (Luke 15:1-7), again in contrast with the "ninety-nine just persons which need no repentance" (vs. 7). In Matthew, too, we find the parable of the lost sheep (18:12-14), but, as appears from the context, here it is applied to relationships within the Christian church.[117] In Luke 15 the parable of the lost sheep is followed by those of the lost penny and of the prodigal son (vss. 8-10, 11-32), in which the concept "what is lost" again plays a special part (vss. 8,9,24,32). Add to these the sayings that specify the purpose of Jesus' coming as the seeking and saving of sinners, e.g., Matthew 9:13: "For I am not come to call the righteous, but sinners to repentance." This theme is elaborated and explained in those stories where Jesus, in contrast to the Pharisees, mingles with notorious sinners (cf. e.g., Luke 7:37,39: Jesus anointed by a sinful woman, where the word *hamartoolos* is used twice).

Jesus' special interest in "what is lost" is so very important because of a religious antithesis within the Jewish nation of his day. They entertained the thought of a "nation within the nation," an *ecclesiola in ecclesia*. The true nation of God was represented by the party of the Pharisees and those who observed their rigorous explanations of the law, especially as regards Levitical purity and the obligations to the priests. The antithesis was formed by the mass of those who could not be supposed to observe the law so scrupulously, the so-called *am-haärets*, "the people of the land."[118] Although this term "the people of the land" does not occur in the gospels (cf., however, John 7:49) there can be no doubt that by "those that are lost," of whom Jesus speaks again and again, we must understand the large category of people upon whom the Pharisees looked with contempt and whom they had abandoned to their fate. This holds even more emphatically for the so-called "sinners," or "publicans and sinners" mentioned in the gospel in close connection with "those that are lost." They were not only the people who lived in open conflict with God's law and were, consequently, kept at a distance both by the common people and the Pharisees. Generally this category of "publicans and sinners" also comprised those who did not submit to the special

Pharisaical institutions.[119]　The same thought is implied in the term "those that are lost." They are the people who have been left to themselves, the sheep that have no shepherd who were no longer looked upon as belonging to the true people of God. These data show the great importance in the whole of Jesus' action in seeking and saving that which, humanly speaking, would have become a prey of the judgment. They also prove the necessity to pay attention to the special aspects of fulfillment, or that of the kingdom, manifested in them.

In this case, too, the general character of Jesus' coming and of his work is misrepresented in two mutually antithetical ways. On the one hand the passages in which Jesus acts as the seeker of "those who are lost" are cited to prove that the eschatological and messianic message is not the kernel of the gospel; that "the kingdom of heaven" only exists as an internal force. "Here is the complete transition to the concept of the kingdom of God as an internally operating force. Just as he calls the sick and the poor to come to him, so he also calls the sinners; this call is decisive. 'The Son of Man has come to seek and to save that which was lost.' Only now does any external and purely future trait appear to have been removed. . . . "[120] Insofar as the messianic and eschatological "framework" is still retained, it is spiritualized into the "judging" and "sifting" meaning of Jesus' *preaching*. The judgment is then no longer something future, but is to be sought in the present, in Jesus' coming and in his word. The "messianic" character of Jesus' action is thus reduced to this spiritualization.[121]

Others hold these sayings about the seeking of "that which was lost" to be evidences of the exclusively or chiefly future character of the kingdom of heaven in Jesus' preaching. They are of the opinion that in these passages there is question only of a preparation for the coming of the kingdom. For this reason little or no attention is paid by them—in contrast to the above-mentioned spiritualizing conception of the kingdom of God—to many writings of a later date upon these passages with respect to a definition of the kingdom.

In our opinion these views imply a clearly demonstrable twofold narrowing down of the idea of the kingdom lying at the base of Jesus' preaching.

Undoubtedly the pronouncements on the seeking of "those who are lost" presuppose a delay of the judgment, and they clearly prove the preliminary character of Jesus' coming and his work. Any attempt made by liberal and modern theology to spiritualize the judgment preached by Jesus and to omit the future and final character of the gospel as something accidental and unessential on the ground of this *evangelium in evangelio,* is in glaring conflict with the general character of the kingdom according to Jesus' preaching.

As serious a misrepresentation of the meaning of Jesus' preaching is the denial of the messianic character of his redemptory work for "those who are lost" and consequently also of its function as fulfillment. It is much rather an integral part of the manifestation of the kingdom. This appears from the expressions "sheep having no shepherd," elsewhere: "lost sheep," or "that which is lost." It is true that the last phrase has almost become a cliché, so that it is not always possible to ascertain whether the original metaphor is still felt (cf., e.g., Luke 19:10); moreover, the metaphor has been extended (the lost penny; the lost son, i.e., the prodigal son). This, however, does not detract from the fact that the original meaning of the concept "that which is lost" is to be sought in the expression: "lost *sheep.*" This metaphor is especially important on account of the frequent occurrence of the comparison of the people of Israel in the Old Testament to a flock of sheep, or simply to sheep who were left in the lurch by the appointed leaders or shepherds and became scattered about. As a consequence they got lost, so to speak, as the property of the Lord,[122] but then they receive the Lord's promise that he shall have pity on them, and shall find them and bring them back. The coming Messiah is then contrasted to the wicked shepherds as the true shepherd (thus especially in Ezek. 34 and in Jer. 23:1-6). The coming time of salvation will not only be that of the delivery of God's people from their enemies by the Messiah and the final separation between the sheep and the goats, but also the time when he will bring the true people of God together[123] and will unite them into one flock.

In this light we must look upon Jesus' work of salvation with respect to those who were lost. This work of gathering them together, which is mentioned by Jesus as the purpose of his coming (Matt. 12:30; Luke 11:23: "He that gathereth not with me scattereth abroad"), is not only a preparation but also a manifestation of the kingdom. In it Jesus acts as the Messiah, the seeker and the Saviour of God's people. The shepherd is the king at the same time. This is also brought out by the messianic beginning of differentiation in several of these pronouncements which are concerned with those that are lost: "I am not sent but to the lost sheep of the house of Israel" (Matt. 15:24); "for I am not come to call the righteous, but sinners to repentance" (Matt. 9:13); "for the Son of Man is come to seek and to save that which was lost" (Luke 19:10). These words testify to the messianic consciousness of authority and power that we have already pointed out.[124] This authority also includes the seeking of that which was lost. In this Jesus *is* the Messiah and in this the kingdom comes to realization.

Furthermore, the second part of Matthew 9:35-38, in which Jesus speaks of the harvest, is important in this connection. As a rule in Jesus' parables the harvest represents the last judgment, and the laborers are the angels (cf. above, §19). Here, however, the laborers are human beings, so the harvest must be understood as the scene of their labors which lies ready for them. Yet the harvest at the same time indicates the fulfillment. The seeking and the gathering of those that were lost is the beginning of the harvest. The future harvest is being accomplished where Christ proclaims the word of God with authority.[125] This does not mean, as Dodd holds, that the idea of the harvest and the last judgment may be applied to the present exclusively; it is rather an exception for the harvest to refer to the present. But it appears that in the seeking of the lost sheep something of the coming harvest is being fulfilled which in a special way realizes the dispensation of salvation of the kingdom.[126] To mention only one more point, all this is confirmed in the well-known words of our Saviour in Matthew 11:28: "Come unto me, all ye that labour and are very laden, and I will give you rest," which also applies to this context. For "those that labour" and are "laden" are troubled, not by their "cares" or their "sins," but very particularly by the "burden" of the Pharisaical prescriptions. They are to be looked upon as "sheep without a shepherd" in this particular sense.[127] It is not a timeless message of rest for their souls, but these words originate from the consciousness that the great turning-point of the times has come, and that the Divine redemption can be sought and found only in Christ.[128] In these words of the Saviour God holds out his arms to his wandering people. That is why here the kingdom is *present*, notwithstanding all its mystery and its preliminary character.

Any attempt,[129] therefore, to build up a doctrine of redemption which has not been based on the person and the work of Jesus as the Christ must be rejected. On the ground of these sayings about the seeking of those who were lost there would then be merely the message of God's fatherly love which, however, would be in glaring conflict with the redemptive-historical character of the gospel. That the lost sheep are sought, that the prodigal son can return, that salvation is preached to publicans and sinners, is only true and possible because Jesus is the Christ, and in him the kingdom of God has come. This is the great presupposition of Jesus' words as the Saviour with respect to that which was lost. If we detach these words from this presupposition we deprive the gospel of its basis. No doubt this also implies that as the Christ Jesus is not only the coming judge of the world, the Son of Man upon the clouds of heaven. But the Christological character of the entire gospel, including the "gospel to sinners," should be beyond dispute. In the following section our task will be to elucidate the "Christology" of the gospels in connection with the special modality of God's kingdom.

22. The Servant of the Lord

All the lines made visible in what precedes in this book center in one point: the person of Jesus as the Christ. In him lies the mystery of his coming, of the *fulfillment* of the kingdom of heaven (§13). In his action and self-manifestation also lies the reflection and the explanation of the *preliminary* character of this fulfillment. The latter point should now be explained in greater detail.

The "Christological" contents of the gospel have two focal points. One of them is formed by all that has been said about the Son of Man and his power. In it there already shines something of his eschatological glory. But connected with it there is also something else, which is a co-determinant, especially, of its preliminary character. It is the fact that the Son of Man can only exercise his power and glory *in a special way, pointed out to him by God.* And it is in this way that he himself has to gain the salvation he preaches to others, namely, in subjection and abandonment to his Father's will. Or, to say it at once in the words in which the Christological content of the gospel finds its most pregnant expression: *The Son of Man is at the same time the Servant of the Lord.* These are the two focal points which *together* determine the content of the gospel. Only if both are fully taken into account, can we understand what the fulfillment that started with Jesus' coming is, for it not only lies in the personal authority by which Jesus proclaimed salvation, but no less also in the way by which salvation is attained by him as the Christ. Thus it becomes quite clear that the preaching of the gospel, though scattered about as seed, surpasses everything that up till now has been revealed in Israel. It is the gospel of fulfillment, for it does not only proclaim that salvation has come but also *on what it is based.* The one as well as the other form the content of the revelation and the history of Jesus as the Christ.

Jesus' messiahship, although from the start identified by him with the Son of Man in Daniel 7, nevertheless moves in a way determined not only by glory and power, but also by other factors. This appears immediately when, after being proclaimed the well-beloved Son by God on the occasion of his baptism in the river Jordan, he was driven by the Spirit into the "wilderness." Here he was to be tempted by the devil. Already the word "temptation" brings out what should be discussed here. The meeting between Jesus and the devil does not bear the character of a trial of strength as is meant in Matthew 12:29. But it is a test to which Jesus has to submit in order to prove his perfect *obedience* to the Father and his *commitment* to the Father's mandate. The tempter's intention, accordingly, is not to deprive Jesus of his messianic *certainty*, or to make him doubt his Father's pleasure expressed on the occasion of his baptism. But, according to the account in Matthew (at least in the first two temptations), the devil tries to induce Jesus to use his messianic power in a way that is not in accordance with his mandate. In opposition to this, Jesus appeals to what "is written" as many as three times. Thus he intimates that as the Messiah and the Son of God he also is subjected to the word of God and finds his guidance in it.

The material content of the temptations shows the character of Jesus' messianic mission. For the time being it may be attended by want and hardship (his being hungry in the wilderness). It excludes any spectacular trial of strength with divine providence (the second temptation in Matthew), and does not grant Jesus the immediate command over all the kingdoms of the world (which the devil offers him). We have already established that this temptation is not concerned with the possession of honor and power over the earth but only with the manner in which Jesus was to attain them. Here, already, it appears that the bestowal of the full messianic dignity and authority upon Jesus was not only characterized from the outset as obedience and subjection to the will of the Father, but at the same time it demanded his willingness to accept even that which did not seem to be consonant with his divinely proclaimed dignity as the Son of God.

For the insight into Jesus' messianic mission and obedience

there is special importance to be attached to the frequent use in the gospel of the terms: "must" (*dei*) and "propriety" (*prepon*) which Jesus ought to observe in the carrying out of his task. This "must" is of very frequent occurrence in the New Testament (especially in Luke). In the first place it denotes God's will in general, and then it specifically refers to that which must happen to execute the divine counsel in the eschatological events (cf., e.g., Rev. 1:1; 4:1; 22:6; Matt. 24:6; Mark 13:10). The whole of Jesus' action as the Messiah is subject to this special "must" founded in the divine will to effect the consummation.[130] It already determined his conduct when as a boy of twelve he was in the temple in the midst of the teachers of the law (Luke 2:49, Did not ye know that I *must* be about my Father's business?). It accompanies him at every step in his action among the Israelites (Luke 4:43, "I *must* preach the kingdom of God to other cities also"; Luke 13:16, "And *ought* not this woman . . . be loosed from this bond on the sabbath day?"; Luke 19:5: "To-day I *must* abide in thy house.").

Especially the end of Jesus' earthly life is subjected to this "must." From the moment when Jesus told his disciples for the first time that he "must" suffer a great deal (Matt. 16:21; Mark 8:31; Luke 9:22), this word *dei* occurs again and again, especially in Luke. It may be used to denote Jerusalem as the place ordained by God's decree where Jesus will meet his death (cf. Luke 13:33, "I *must* walk today and tomorrow and the day following,[131] for it cannot be that a prophet perish out of Jerusalem"); or to confirm the necessity of suffering before the coming of the Son of Man (cf. 17:25, "but first *must* he suffer many things and be rejected of this generation"), or also to designate certain facets of his suffering as the way of the Messiah prescribed by the prophets (cf. 22:37, " . . . this that is written *must* yet be accomplished in me: and he was reckoned among the transgressors").

This last quotation shows that the contents of this *must* has not only been determined by God's hidden counsel, but has also in many respects been revealed in the Scriptures. For this reason it had not only been prescribed for the Messiah, but could thus also be understood by those to whom the Scriptures have been "opened" (cf. Luke 24:25-27; the explanation given to the two disciples on the way to Emmaus— "ought not Christ to have suffered these things, and to enter into his glory?"; cf. vss. 44,46). Such passages indicate that in obedience to the Father, Jesus as the Messiah had to fulfill a task imposed upon him by God, and that a considerable part of it consisted in his sufferings and death decreed by the divine will for the purpose of the final consummation. The attempt has been made to cancel the significance of all this by explaining such explicit pronouncements on the necessity of the sufferings as *vaticinia ex eventu* (prophecies after the events) and ascribing them to the later Christian church.[132] Others have thought that, only because of the attitude of the people, did Jesus gradually arrive at the certainty that God had destined him to suffer and to die. They try to support this opinion by all kinds of psychological considerations.[133] To this extent Jesus had a kind of psychological awareness or certainty as regards his approaching death. But it is supposed to be impossible that Jesus knew in advance the manner of his death in all its details.[134]

In opposition to such conceptions it must be maintained that the idea of the suffering and death of Christ and its necessity is one of the most essential elements of the *kerygma* of Christ in the synoptic gospels and from the outset it also determined Jesus' action in words and deeds. Anyone who wants to ascribe this to the later Christian church must consequently reject the entire historical character of the *kerygma*. Or he must reduce it to such an extent that there remains very little to say about the historical Jesus with any certainty. Such criticism, however, as it is also found in the radical group of the form criticism school, is no longer concerned with the literary character of the gospel, but only with the recorded facts themselves, as has been shown more than once and in all kinds of ways.[135]

For a careful analysis of the gospel shows that the motif

of suffering does *not* merely consist of a few explicit pronouncements made by Jesus, which, if need be, might be eliminated
without any injury to the structure of the synoptic *kerygma*.
But it shows that these explicit predictions have been prepared
in all manner of ways in the preceding history, and have been
followed by others later on.   They all have a much deeper
background than the course of history as such.

As to the history before the event, there are in the first
place a number of isolated pronouncements in the gospel which
in a more veiled way speak of the necessity of his complete
humiliation before the explicit announcement of his suffering
(cf. Mark 8:32, "And he spoke that word about his approaching suffering openly," *parrēsiai.*)[136]   Thus first of all his saying
about the bridegroom, in Matthew 9:15, and parallel places.
It is clear from a comparison of verses 15a and 15b that in this
connection the bridegroom is an allegorical indication of the
Messiah.[137]   He is said to be with the wedding guests only
temporarily, and that there will be a day when he will be
taken away from them.   This is an implicit allusion to Jesus'
death.   Many authors are immediately inclined to look upon
the second part of the pronouncement on the bridegroom as a
"secondary formation."[138]   But such a view is based on a *petitio
principii* and lacks any proof.   Nor is there any reason to
shift this saying to a time at which Jesus is supposed to have
become more and more convinced of his approaching end on
account of the increasing enmity of the people.   We shall much
rather have to understand this word as spoken at the time
when Jesus had not yet spoken openly and in detail about his
suffering and death to his disciples, although he himself was
already certain of them.   The same thing is true of the enigmatic saying in which Jesus compares the way of the Son of
Man with that of Jonah: "As Jonah was three days and three
nights in the whale's belly, so shall the Son of Man be three
days and three nights in the heart of the earth" (Matt. 12:39).[139]
It is also applicable to the pronouncement saying that "the
foxes have holes, and the birds of the air have nests; but the

Son of Man hath not where to lay his head" (Matt. 8:20). This last named statement does not mention Jesus' suffering and death, but it does denote that the Son of Man is nowhere at home on earth. He has to put up with hardships and rebuffs, in short, he is on his way to the cross. To the first audience these words may not immediately have had such pregnancy, but in the scope of the entire tradition it is clear that Jesus speaks "significantly" and that from the outset the thought of suffering has been interwoven with the whole of the historical *kerygma* of Christ. As the history told to us by the evangelists progresses, these pronouncements grow more numerous and lucid. Especially *after* the conversation in the surroundings of Caesarea—Philippi, the approaching suffering is announced in all kinds of images and parables. Thus, e.g., when Jesus speaks of "the cup that he drinks and the baptism he is baptized with" (Mark 10:38; cf. Matt. 20:22); of his "perfection" in the time after "today and tomorrow" (Luke 13:32,33); in another passage he again speaks of a "baptism" he is "to be baptized with"[140] and of his "being straitened till it be accomplished" (Luke 12:50); of his burial for which he knows he is destined beforehand (Matt. 26:18); of the killing of the son by the wicked husbandmen, and all that might be further quoted from his more and more straightforward speeches on his suffering and death especially at the time of his approaching end.[141] Already from what has been adduced here it appears that the idea of suffering permeates the gospel like a leaven, and that without these pronouncements it is impossible to derive any coherent meaning from the whole of Jesus' action and preaching.

There is another phenomenon which may be pointed out to confirm our last statement, viz., *Jesus' messianic self-conceal-ment.* Although his self-revelation was unmistakable to those who had "ears to hear," it was implicit in many respects.[142] We must add, however, that on more than one occasion Jesus rigorously *forbade* those to whom it had been given to know the mystery of the kingdom—and accordingly that of the Mes-

siah—to make him known as such. The appreciation of this
phenomenon—often indicated as the mystery of the Messiah—
has played an important part in the historical research about
the life of Jesus since the end of the eighteenth century. This
is not the place to start an elaborate discussion of all this. For
the appreciation of Jesus' preaching of the kingdom of heaven
it has been judged as only of some indirect importance—which
was an error! Insofar as Jesus' preaching of the kingdom of
heaven was conceived of as an essentially immanent religious-
ethical affair—after the manner of the old-liberal theology—his
self-concealment was looked upon as evidence of the fact that
the messianic-eschatological moment did not originally belong
to Jesus' self-consciousness. It assumed a fixed place in his
thought only gradually when his earthly mission seemed to
fail, so that every allusion to it in the time when this messianic
consciousness was still growing in him he vigorously rejected.

The very opposite view is that of the so-called consistent
eschatology. The latter holds that from the outset Jesus was
aware of his mission as Messiah designate, but imposed silence
about it on those initiated into his mystery. The reason for
such silence was the entirely future character of the kingdom
of God and of his messianic office attendant upon it. Both
of these "historical" views are opposed by the radically-sceptical
conception. Whatever signification the latter may ascribe to
the preaching of the kingdom of God, it is sceptical about Jesus'
messianic self-consciousness; at any rate it considers the elements of concealment in Jesus' self-revelation (qualified by
this school as a literary "motif") as a later adaptation of the
tradition about his life. This would imply a reminiscence of the
time when it was still known that Jesus had not posed as the
Messiah.[143]

At the moment we do not intend to enter into the historical
problems of this so-called "Messiah-mystery." Our subject
in this context is its factual meaning in connection with the
question as to whether or not from the outset the motif of his
suffering partly determined Jesus' messianic mission and self-

revelation. To find an answer we must in the first place collect the various data which are supplied especially by the gospel according to Mark.

In the first place we should point to Jesus' repeated prohibition against making his miracles known (cf. Mark 1:43-45; 5:43, and 7:36). Related to these passages are the statements that he tried to hide from the multitude (Mark 1:35-38,45; 4:35; 5:1; 6:32; 7:24; 9:30) and that with those who wanted to be cured by him he secluded himself (Mark 5:40; 7:33; 8:23, cf. vs. 26). It is true that these data are only concerned with indirect indications, but there are passages in which he emphatically prevents and forbids the demons to make him known as the Messiah when they loudly address him as such (Mark 1:25,34; 3:12). We find the same phenomenon often expressed and described in the same or in nearly related words after Peter's confession in the surroundings of Caesarea-Philippi (Mark 8:30), and also after the transfiguration on the mountain (Mark 9:9). There the three disciples are ordered not to relate to anybody what they had seen before the Son of Man had risen from the dead (cf. also parallel passages in Matthew and Luke).

No doubt, these incidental commands to secrecy should not be given a general and absolute meaning, for Jesus accepts Messianic honor at the end of his life, and makes himself known to the Sanhedrim as the coming Son of Man. Nor can all the above mentioned phenomena be treated in the same way, for Jesus' restraint in his self-revelation must be partly explained from motives determined by the different occasions. Yet the peculiar and deepest motives have not been exhausted in this manner. For it is a misrepresentation of the obvious meaning of the gospel if[144] Jesus' self-concealment is reduced to something that depends on the occasion, and thus is denied a deeper and more general tendency and signification.

The first direct explanation of this veiling and self-concealment is found in Matthew 12:15ff. Here Jesus' prohibition against making him known is looked upon as the fulfillment of Isaiah's prophecy about the appearance of the Servant of the Lord who does not try to curry favor with the people by ostentation or publicity. This connection between Jesus' appearance and that of the Servant of the Lord in Isaiah is very important. For this Servant of the Lord had to atone for the guilt of many and to submit to suffering and death before being exalted. In other passages, therefore, Jesus motivates the prohibition to make him generally known by referring to his suffering and death. He does so especially after Peter's confession in the neighborhood of Caesarea-Philippi. In all three gospels this is followed by the emphatic command to secrecy, motivated by the suffering and death to which the Son of Man has to submit, as appears in particular from the context in Luke 9:21,22. As a matter of fact, the same thing is found in Mark 9:30,31, where Jesus retires and does not want anybody to know about it. In explanation also of this conduct we read: "for he taught his disciples: the Son of Man will be delivered into the hands of men." In the same way, this motif is also the basis of the command to secrecy after the transfiguration on the mountain. The three initiated disciples are not allowed to publish the messianic glory they have seen "until the Son of Man has risen from the dead" (Matt. 17:9; Mark 9:9, cf. Luke 9:36).

It is clear that this motif of Jesus' messianic self-concealment is an important datum for us in finding an answer to the question about the place of the idea of suffering in the whole of Jesus' activity. It implies that the motif of suffering has a much deeper foundation in the gospel than can be established on the ground of the pronouncements that mention it explicitly. The messianic salvation revealed in Christ's coming is not exclusively founded in his authority and supernatural glory, but also in his humiliation and rejection. The whole of the gospel of the kingdom must also be qualified as *the gospel of the cross*, not only on account of Jesus' deliberate pronouncements about his suffering, but also because of the modality of the whole of his messianic self-revelation (*casu quo:* self-concealment).

The proper and profound import of all this can only be understood if we try to keep in mind the *meaning* of the task of suffering undertaken and performed by Jesus from the outset. We have already seen that the divine necessity of suffering to which Jesus was subjected as the Christ can be known from the Old Testament prophecy. This is clear from Jesus' own words (cf. Luke 22:37; 24:26,44-46) and no less from the frequently repeated formulas of the evangelists in the description of Jesus' suffering and death: "in order that it would be fulfilled," "as has been written," and others (cf. e.g., Mark 14:21; 14:27, cf. Zech. 13:7; Mark 14:34, cf. Ps. 42:6,12; Mark 15:34, cf. Ps. 22:2; Luke 24:46, cf. Ps. 31:6). Jesus' suffering and death was not by fate's decree, nor was it merely according to a divine decree about him which might be inferred from providence. It was the carrying out of God's will to save us which had been determined beforehand and made known by the prophets.

Especially noteworthy is the agreement between Jesus' *via dolorosa* and the prophecy of the suffering Servant of the Lord in Isaiah 53. Even before this suffering started, this agreement became visible. In the discussion given above we have already pointed out Jesus' modest and humble conduct as the fulfillment of that which is said in Isaiah 42:1-4 about the character of the work of the Servant of the Lord. It is also important that in Matthew 8:16-17 Jesus' manifold cures are called the fulfillment of the prophecy in Isaiah 53:4: "he hath borne our griefs and carried our sorrows." Here we find the thought that in his messianic work Jesus takes over the burden of disease and suffering from men. It is true that in this passage Jesus does not appear as the one who takes this burden on himself in his suffering (as does the Servant of the Lord in Isaiah 53:4). But the thought of such a transfer is clearly present and is explained in the light of the prophecy of Isaiah 53.

In this connection we should also discuss the words that Jesus said to John the Baptist when the latter did not wish to baptize him: "Suffer it to be so now: for thus it becometh us to fulfill all righteousness" (Matt. 3:15). It is true here also that there is no direct connection with the prophecies about the Servant of the Lord.[145] Both in John's refusal and in Jesus' answer ("Suffer it to be so *now*") it is implied that in a certain sense the baptism of Jesus is an absurdity. The order that Jesus now observes is of a preliminary and temporary character. There will be a time which will be in accordance with John's views. The "now" is the present of the concealment of Jesus' glory.[146] And this entails the task of having himself baptized as any other sinner, and of following the policy required from him by God, and John also in this matter (the fulfillment of all righteousness). This implies that in his official duties Jesus must be united with sinners and take their sins upon himself.[147] "He associates himself with sinners and ranges himself in the ranks of the guilty, not to find salvation for himself, not on account of his own guilt in his flight from the approaching wrath, but because he is at one with the Church and the bearer of divine grace and of divine mercy."[148]

All this acquires its most profound meaning in Christ's suffering and death. The dominant thought in them is again that of the taking of sin upon himself and his solidarity with sinners. And the prophecy of the suffering Servant of the Lord is continually in the background. It is true that only one pronouncement has come down to us in which Jesus himself explicitly calls his suffering the fulfillment of Isaiah 53 (viz., Luke 22:37, "For I say unto you that this that is written must yet be accomplished in me: and he was reckoned among the transgressors," cf. Mark 15:28). But in Mark 9:12 we find a clear allusion to Isaiah 53 when Jesus asks: "And how is it written of the Son of Man that he must suffer many things, and be set at nought?" In itself the phrase "it is written" need not refer to a particular Scripture passage. Nor has the Messiah's suffering been foretold only in Isaiah 53.[149] But the expression "be set at nought" (literally: "considered as nothing"—*exouthenēthēi*) can hardly be explained in any other way than as the translation of the corresponding term in

Isaiah 53:3.[150] And similarly the expression "suffer many things" (cf. 8:31) is a very appropriate summary of all that is written in Isaiah 53 about the Servant of the Lord. Finally we must point to Mark 10:45; 14:24, and similar passages with the frequently recurring phrase: "for many." These "many" are no others than the many mentioned in Isaiah 53:11,12a,12b, cf. 52:15, a fact that is being more and more recognized.[151] Here, too, there is a verbal agreement between Jesus' words about his suffering and those of the prophet about the suffering Servant of the Lord.[152]

This brings us to those pronouncements which give an explicit explanation of Jesus' suffering and death, viz., that about the ransom (Mark 10:45; Matt. 20:28) and what Jesus said about the meaning of his death on the occasion of the last supper (Mark 14:24; Matt. 26:28; Luke 22:19,20). The first text describes Jesus messianic mission ("the Son of Man has come . . .") as service. This service is meant in a very totalitarian sense, i.e., not only as the summarizing phrase for all the activity of his helping love, but also for the offer of his life which leads to his death.[153] Thus he "serves" for the salvation of others, and sacrifices himself for others. This fact is further characterized thus: the Son of Man has come "to give his life (*psyche*) a ransom for many." The last two words refer to "ransom," as appears from the word-order and not to "to give," i.e., Jesus' self-sacrifice has a unique significance. Through it "many" are redeemed. They could not pay that price themselves. He intercedes for them, producing in their place that which is needed for their liberation. The word used here for "life" (*psyche*) denotes the all-comprising character of this "price." It does not merely denote a particular aspect of human existence, but its meaning is something like "himself,"[154] i.e., the whole of the existence granted to man by God in all its possibilities and connections (also with regard to God himself).

This substitution bears the character of supplying a ransom (*lutron*). Apart from the special connection with Isaiah 53[155] this word must certainly be understood against the background of the Old Testament world of thought[156] in which "ransom" (*kōfer*) denotes a payment made for a forfeited life (cf. Ex. 21:30; Numbers 35:31). The possibility of such payment rests on the willingness of the person to whom such payment is offered.[157] The giving of a ransom means the liberation from a state of guilt. This only refers to the relation of guilt on the part of man with respect to God.[158] That is why there can be no doubt as to the party to *whom* this price is due. It is true, this is not mentioned *expressis verbis* in the text, but the question cannot be eliminated.[159] As a matter of fact, the answer is implied in the context, even if the idea of the giving of a ransom were to be conceived of in the general and colorless sense of "liberation," "redemption." For it is the state of guilt towards *God* from which man must be liberated. Besides, in the whole of his suffering and death Jesus serves *God.* God desires his Son to suffer. It is God to whom, of course, the price must be paid, whose rights have been violated and must be restored. The possibility of such restoration is a proof of grace. But the terrible nature of sin must be exposed, and God's rights must be asserted in opposition to sin. The meaning of sin as well as that of forgiveness can only be understood in the death of the Son of Man sent by God himself for this purpose.[160] This is why the Son has to pay the ransom in his immeasurable service of love and substitution. It will be all the more clear that this is the meaning when the whole of this passage is considered in the light of Isaiah 53.[161] Here the price paid by the Servant of the Lord is explicitly called an offering for sin in Isaiah 53:10. For it is in the offering for sin that the idea of satisfaction of the violated divine right comes to the fore.[162]

No other meaning can be attached to Jesus' pronouncement on the occasion of the last supper when he says of his body that "it is given" for those that are his, viz., given in death, and of his blood that it is the blood of the covenant that is shed for many to obtain forgiveness of their sins. We shall return to this passage again when discussing the meaning of the Lord's Supper.[163] In the present context, however, we can already state that by qualifying his blood as the blood of the covenant he gives it the meaning of an offering made for the expiation of the sins of those who are his. This offering is the possibility as well as the basis of the fulfillment of the promise of the new covenant (Jer. 31:33).

23. *The Kingdom and the Cross*

There can be no doubt that all these facts, both as to the manner of Jesus' self-sacrifice, his life and death, and *the meaning* of the latter, are of great importance for a true insight into the history of salvation with respect to the manifestation of the kingdom of heaven preached by Jesus. It may even be said that the motif of suffering is one of the most constitutive factors determining the sense of Jesus' preaching of the kingdom.[164] The Son of Man had been invested by God with all power and authority for the revelation of his dominion, and was at the same time the one who "had to" suffer and die. He had come to give himself as a ransom for many. All this is the most characteristic and "revolutionary" part of Jesus' messianic self-revelation—on account of the correlation existing between the Messiah and the kingdom of heaven—and consequently also of the revelation of the kingdom. The denial of this connection, or the failure to do sufficient justice to it is, therefore, one of the most important causes of all kinds of one-sided interpretations and errors in the explanation of Jesus' preaching of the kingdom.

And, conversely, the end of the gospel (the *kerygma* of the suffering, death, and resurrection) brings to light in a surprising way the profound sense of all kinds of pronouncements and parables. The ignoring of the motif of suffering in Jesus' preaching of the kingdom is especially manifest in the interpretation which is still influenced by the so-called liberal picture of Jesus.[165]

The insight has since gained ground that the failure to do sufficient justice to the idea of suffering deprives the whole of the gospel of its power. Here, too, the consistent eschatology, on the front of a radical criticism, has launched vehement attacks on the liberal conception. The attempt has been made to establish an organic and insoluble unity between the idea of suffering in the gospel and the eschatological concept of the kingdom of God. Schweitzer's well-known theory served the same purpose. He held that after vainly waiting for the break-through of the kingdom, Jesus began more and more to be convinced that only his own death could effectuate the kingdom. This death bore a substitutive character, for in his suffering and death Jesus took upon himself the distress which, according to the Jewish dogma, would have to be borne by the world before the coming of the Messiah and the kingdom. According to Schweitzer Jesus really died for the sins of men, though in a different sense from that of Anselm's theory.[166]

This conception may, in a way, be pointed to as an example of the perfect estrangement of modern theology from the idea of suffering and death in the gospel. But in a formal sense it does more justice to the fundamental significance which Jesus' suffering and death has for the coming of the kingdom of heaven. Others, also, have tried to assign to Jesus' suffering and death a more important place in the center of the gospel, e.g., with the aid of all kinds of religio-historical parallels.[167] Thus they aimed at establishing a closer connection between the kingdom of heaven and the "motif of suffering." But at the same time there are many authors who continue to ignore the correlation of these two central data in the gospel. In the footsteps of the liberal theologians of Jesus, they ascribe only a secondary significance to the idea of suffering, and deprive this idea of its substitutive and most profound meaning. Or they consider the significance of Jesus' preaching of the kingdom in itself (i.e., apart from the idea of suffering of the gospels).

In our opinion the significance of Jesus' suffering and death for the coming of the kingdom must be examined as closely as possible.

To summarize, the following points should be investigated:

a) So long as Jesus' suffering, death, and resurrection has not become a fact, the kingdom of heaven can only very partially be realized. Closely connected with this is all that has hitherto been said about the preliminary character of the manifestation of the kingdom, the remainder of the power of the Evil One, and the mystery of the kingdom of heaven. It has been erroneously inferred from these facts that so long as Jesus had not yet fulfilled his mission to suffer and die, he was not yet the Messiah in the proper sense of the word, and the kingdom was only something to be expected in the future. This view is wrong, because all that Jesus did and suffered in obeying God's commands was part and parcel of his messianic office in the full sense of the term. And in all this the kingdom had come. The world of God's redemption was not only revealed in Jesus' power over the Evil One, in his miracles, in his authoritative preaching of salvation. It was no less revealed and present in the perfect obedience of the Servant of the Lord to the will of the Father, in his taking upon himself the infirmities of his people, in his substitutionary self-sacrifice as a ransom for many. This is the thought of the mediator who fulfills the law, offers the sacrifice, expiates the guilt; and representing the people in this, thus redeems them. This, too, is the kingdom of heaven. Here the theocentric motif[168] of the kingdom comes to the fore in an incomparable way. In Christ God maintains his royal rights and accomplishes his royal redemption. But this happens not only in Christ as the Son of Man invested with all authority, but also in Christ as the obedient Servant, and in Christ who suffers and dies for the many. The judgment and the redemption of the kingdom of heaven are not only brought about *through* him, but also *by* him and *in* him. This is why the history of his suffering is full of hints, which unmistakably indicate the judgment brought upon the Son of Man (Gethsemane, Pilate, the cross). This is why his resurrection is the final stage of all that God reveals on earth about his kingdom. Essentially and in an anticipatory way the great eschatological drama inaugurating the coming of the kingdom is realized in him as the Mediator. All this

also implies that with the coming of Jesus the kingdom cannot at once be fully revealed.   The Son of Man cannot come in
the clouds of heaven *before* suffering many things and before
being rejected by "this generation" (Luke 17:25).   And thus
also the manner is determined in which the kingdom of heaven
was to manifest itself for the present.

b) This raises the question whether, and to what extent,
Jesus' suffering, death and resurrection signify a postponement
of the judgment and lengthening of the world's time; in other
words, whether this very self-sacrifice of the Son of Man in his
death did not imply the possibility and the necessity of a
renewed delay in the definitive revelation of the kingdom of
God and the consummation of the world.   This question is
very closely related to questions that will be discussed later on
with regard to the so-called *Naherwartung* (the imminent
advent).   Its provisional solution will be found if attention
is paid to the following points:

In the first place Jesus' suffering and death show something of the divine judgment, even of the great day of the
Lord.   The ransom that Christ had to pay for "the many"
was nothing less than his being delivered up to God's judgment
in the place of "the many."   In this sacrifice Jesus suffered
in anticipation, as it were, all that those who are his would
have had to endure according to the law on account of their
sins.   But in it he also gave them the guarantee of their perfect
redemption.   He opened the gates of paradise (Luke 23:43),
gave them assurance of the kingdom (Luke 22:29,30); in
short, he laid the judicial foundation of the entire preaching
of the gospel.   Herein also lies the possibility of his people
continuing to live in this world.   However much they may long
for the perfection of God's kingdom (cf. eg., Luke 18:7),
their life has nevertheless been founded on the fulfillment, the
acquittal, the redemption accomplished by Jesus' death and
resurrection.   Jesus' body and blood may henceforth be their
meat and drink.   The new-covenant God had promised to
make with his people when he would forgive their sins and

write his law in their hearts (Jer. 31:33,34), has been inaugurated by his blood[169] and has thus become possible and legally valid (Luke 22:29). This means that for the participants in this propitiation the great line of demarcation not only lies in the future, but also in the past: in the acquittal and renewal of life he acquired and accomplished for all of them by giving himself as a ransom. In this sense we can no doubt say that in Jesus' suffering, death and resurrection the preliminary character of the kingdom of heaven is confirmed. Since the whole of life has been based on acquittal and renewal, the consummation of all things can be delayed, as it were. A new level has been reached so that all that is old is past. But the road leading to the top yet goes on.

In the second place *the preaching of the gospel* could only fully develop after Jesus' death and resurrection. Only then was it allowed to speak freely of the Christ in his glory (cf. Mark 9:9). Only then could the veil be lifted that had been laid over his suffering and death, and the preaching of the gospel of the kingdom could become the preaching of the cross in the profoundest sense of the word. Exactly because Jesus laid so great a stress on the necessity of continuing the preaching of the gospel—the real and most profound grounds on which the gospel rests being Jesus' suffering, death and resurrection—does this imply a continuation of the "day of grace" and of the time of conversion.

Closely connected with this is, thirdly, that Jesus, especially in relation to his suffering and death, speaks about "the many" for whom he pays the ransom and sheds his blood. In whatever way this expression is understood,[170] it is clear that by "the many" a great many are to be understood, a greater number than that of those whom Jesus had attached to himself during his earthly life. Here it is especially the "many of the future" that are thus indicated, just as in another passage there is question of the *many* fruits produced by the seed of the gospel. This multitude will be the fruit of the gospel in which Jesus' saving death will be preached. In this light the parables of the sower and of the seed assume a deepened sense from the standpoint of Jesus' suffering and death. That which is sown is the word, but at its base lies the deed which includes his messianic work accomplished in his death. And since it is *this* word, it bears "many" fruits, it must also grow and "become lengthened," i.e., develop its strength in the times ahead. Jesus' suffering and death open up a new future, grant a delay, and create new possibilities for the continuance of earthly life. For their residual power for the many must expand and be communicated, just like the leaven in the flour, like the small and insignificant mustard seed which becomes an imposing and luxurious growth. The kingdom could not reach its consummation as long as Jesus' suffering and death still belonged to the future. But even after this great redemptive process has reached its end, the kingdom again needs time to gain its purpose and to bear the fruit for many implied in it.

c) Accordingly we see that, because of the resurrection of Christ, the great stimulus for the promulgation of the gospel is communicated to the apostles. The risen Christ himself calls them to this task after first showing them through the Scriptures that the suffering and death of the Christ were necessary (Luke 24:25ff, 44ff). And the royal authority of the Son of Man given him by the Father, a power and authority embracing heaven and earth (Matt. 28:18), is then first of all put to the service of this preaching of the gospel. This infinite power calls the disciples to a continuing task whose execution is possible because of the unending community that Christ promises them—*all* authority, *all* nations, *all* the days (Matt. 28:19,20; Mark 16:20). Of *these* things, viz., Christ's suffering, death, and resurrection, the missionaries must be witnesses (Luke 24:46-48). Because of the gospel of the cross a new future has been opened, and the progress of this preaching may be made the measure of the progress of the time of salvation and of the expectation of the consummation of all things (cf. Matt. 24:14).[171]

Notes to Chapter IV

[1] Thus Zahn, *op. cit.*

[2] Schniewind, *Matth.* p. 85.

[3] E. Klostermann, *Das Matev.*, p. 59; cf. also M. Dibelius, *Evangelium und Welt*, 1929, who wants to interpret "the evil" as "the evil world," p. 72.

[4] *Op. cit.*, p. 85: "That is why men may pray God to put an end to those difficult hours of trial."

[5] Cf., e.g., Dodd, *op. cit.*, who explains these afflictions as present, viz., as the "hour of the crisis" of Jesus' sufferings and death.

[6] See further below, § 47.

[7] Cf. also Schniewind, *op. cit.*, p. 85.

[8] Cf., e.g., Klostermann, *Das Lukasev.*[2], 1929, p. 212; Greijdanus, *op. cit.*, II, p. 1070.

[9] Thus Stählin, *TWB*, I, 1933, p. 194, the article on "exaiteo."

[10] Greijdanus also thinks especially of Satan's temptation of Jesus through his disciples: "The issue was between God and Satan. Could Satan cause the fall of our Lord Jesus who had been given by God as a Mediator and Redeemer? Hence, Satan demanded of God to allow him to do his utmost for this purpose; moreover, to let him attack the Lord through his disciples in the narrower sense, in order to . . . combat him thus and, if possible, to conquer him. . . ." However, though it is possible to think that this thought is also implied in this context, the issue is primarily concerned with the trial of the disciples.

[11] Cf. Stauffer, *TWB*, II, p. 346.

[12] (For Satan) "opportunity," "suitable time," thus, apparently Greijdanus, *op. cit.*, I, p. 203; also Plummer, *op. cit.*, p. 114, appealing to John 14:30; Luke 22:53, etc. Others translate the word by: "the time to be appointed by God," e.g., Delling, *TWB*, III, p. 463, the article on "kairos," cf. also Klostermann, *op. cit.*, p. 61.

[13] Cf., e.g., G. Dalman, *Orte und Wege Jesu*[3], 1924, p. 201.

[14] Cf. my: *Zelfopenbaring, etc.*, pp. 51ff.

[15] Entirely insufficient is Schneider's explanation, *TWB*, I, p. 561, the article on *"basanos"*: "Meeting Jesus is felt to be a painful occurrence on the part of those possessed by demons." In opposition to this see Klostermann, *Das Mattäus evang.*, p. 79: "torture of hell" (*Höllenqual*).

[16] Cf. also Mark 1:24, where *apolesai* is used in the same sense: "to cast away into the place of eternal punishment," F. Hauck, *Das Ev. d. Mark*, 1931, p. 23.

[17] Thus Greijdanus, *op. cit.*, I, p. 387.

[18] Cf. also Plummer, *op. cit.*, pp. 230, 231; Klostermann, *op. cit.*, p. 101: "The demons were afraid they would now be sent by Jesus to the place of their punishment"; Joachim Jeremias, *TWB*, I, p. 9.

[19] The much weaker expression in Mark 5:10: "to be sent out of the country," also points to this loss of their freedom of movement.

[20] Cf. Delling in *TWB*, III, p. 402, the article on *"kairos"*: "the beginning of the messianic power over the demons." Zahn's explanation that by "the time" the demons meant the time during which Jesus could also command in a heathen country, *op. cit.*, p. 367, is too far fetched, in my opinion. There is no support for it whatever in the context.

[21] Cf. above, § 9.

175

[22] *Gesch. d. syn. Trad.,* p. 224.

[23] *Das Mrkev.,* p. 47.

[24] *Das Ev. d. Mark.,* pp. 96, 97.

[25] *Das Ev. d. Mark.,* pp. 153, 154.

[26] *Evangelie selon S. Marc.,* 1947, pp. 129, 130.

[27] O. Bauernfeind, *Die Worte der Dämonischen in Mr.,* 1927, pp. 42-45.

[28] *Op. cit.*

[29] *Das Ev. d. Lk.,* p. 335.

[30] *Der Ev. Matth.,* p. 294.

[31] *The Gospel of Luke*[5] (in *The Moffat N.T. Commentary*), 1945, p. 96.

[32] *Op. cit.,* I, p. 388.

[33] Cf., e.g., Zahn, *op. cit.,* p. 350; see also *The Westminster Historical Atlas of the Bible,* 1946, pp. 83, 84.

[34] Calvin, *In Harmonium, etc.,* ed. Tholuck, 1833, p. 233.

[35] Th. H. Robinson, *The Gospel of Matthew*[6] (in *The Moffat N.T. Commentary*), 1945, p. 77.

[36] *The Mission and Message of Jesus,* 1946, p. 76.

[37] It reminds us of the explanation of the miracles by H. E. G. Paulus, 1828. Cf. A. Schweitzer, *Gesch. d. L-J-F.,*[5] 1933, pp. 49ff.

[38] E. P. Gould, *A Critic. and Exeg. Comm. on the Gospel acc. to St. Mark,*[6] 1921, p. 92.

[39] § 10.

[40] Cf., e.g., Schniewind, *Matth.,* pp. 29, 30; M. Albertz, *Die Botschaft des N.T.,* I, 1, 1947, pp. 134ff.

[41] See also Klostermann on Mark 1:38, *op. cit.,* p. 19.

[42] Cf. Schniewind, *Markus,* pp. 52, 53; Hauck, *Markus,* p. 28.

[43] In the same sense also Klostermann apparently, who denies that Mark would mean "a moral impossibility," *op. cit.,* p. 56.

[44] Greijdanus wants to explain this by saying that the inhabitants of Nazareth did not bring their sick people, "so he did not get an opportunity to cure them," *Lukas,* I, p. 215. But it does not say this in the text and in view of Mark 6:2, Luke 4:23, it cannot be inferred from the text. At Nazareth people did indeed expect and desire miracles. But precisely by refusing them here Jesus made the signification of the miracles stand out all the more clearly.

[45] Cf. Hauck, *op. cit.,* p. 98: "*ei,* complete this by 'May God do so and more to me,' a Semitic self-imprecation intended as a very strong affirmation." Schniewind translates: "never more," *op. cit.,* p. 105.

[46] On the phrase "three days and three nights" see my *Mattheüs,* I, pp. 244, 245; *TWB,* I, p. 148, the article on *"haides";* Schniewind, Matth., p. 157.

[47] Even if this word is not taken primarily in the sense of a (develish) temptation, but rather in the neutral sense of "putting to the test," its factual meaning is that of a temptation in the sense of Matt. 4:8 (cf. also *peirazein* in Matt. 4:1; Mark 1:12; Luke 4:2 and *ho peirazoon* in Matt. 4:3).

[48] Ad. Jülicher, *Die Gleichnisreden Jesu,*[2] I and II, 1910.

[49] Cf., e.g., Schweitzer, *Gesch. d. L-J-F.,* pp. 402ff.

[50] *The Parables of the Kingdom,*[6] 1943.

[51] J. Jeremias, *Die Gleichnisse Jesu,* 1947, p. 13.

[52] Cf. also, e.g., M. Albertz: "The dominant object of wisdom (proverbs, parables, allegories) is the eschatological kingdom of God. And just because it is the kingly dominion of God that is dealt with, the wisdom about it has been withdrawn from the grasp of man. . . . This wisdom is, therefore, at

bottom the revelation of a secret, or secrets, from whose source all wisdom comes"; *Botschaft*, I, 1. p. 101; see also pp. 82, 85, 94.

[53] Cf., e.g., P. Fiebig, *Die Gleichnisreden Jesu,* 1912.

[54] Cf. my *Mattheüs,* I, p. 253.

[55] Thus also Jeremias, *op. cit.,* p. 8; see, however, Albertz: "Against all liberal and rationalistic criticism the authenticity of this word of the Lord will have to be defended," *op. cit.,* p. 102.

[56] Thus also G. Bornkamm, *TWB,* IV, p. 824: the article on *"mustērion"*: "The mystery cannot be related to a general meaning content of the *basileia,* but only to the fact of its beginning"; cf. J. Schniewind, *Markus,* pp. 72ff and *Matthäus,* p. 162; also Jeremias, *op. cit.,* p. 8: "By the mystery of God's kingly dominion no knowledge of any kind is meant about the coming kingdom of God but the knowledge about its present beginning"; see also my: *Zelfopenbaring en Zelfverberging,* pp. 49, 50.

[57] See above, § 11.

[58] Cf. my *Mattheüs,* I, p. 262.

[59] The strong term *ereuxomai,* which we have translated by "express," is important. Its proper meaning is "to pour out" and points to an abundance of content, cf. also M. J. Lagrange: "En mettant *kekrummena* après un verbe qui signifiait diretrès haut, Mt. a insisté sur le caractère révélateur des choses cachées qu' avaient les paraboles pour qui les comprenait. . . . Jésu exposait les mystères du règne de Dieu, cachés jusqu' à présent, révélés aux seuls disciples. . . ." ("By placing *kekrummena* after a verb which meant 'to speak very loud,' Matthew has insisted on the revelational character of the things hidden in the parables for those who understood them." And further: " . . . Jesus laid bare the mysteries of God's dominion that had up till then been hidden, and were revealed to the disciples alone. . . .") *Evangile selon S. Matthieu,*[5] 1941, p. 272.

[60] The translation is uncertain; it is also possible to translate: "who has become a pupil for the kingdom of heaven," i.e., who has suffered himself to be made a pupil for the sake of the kingdom, cf. Schniewind, *op. cit.*

[61] Lagrange, *op. cit.,* pp. 282, 283.

[62] See also Schniewind, *op. cit.,* p. 169.

[63] On the meaning of new-old see also Behm, *TWB,* III, p. 451, the article on *"kainos."*

[64] For further details, see below, § 23.

[65] Cf., e.g., Dodd, *op. cit.,* p. 23.

[66] See also Albertz, *op. cit.,* p. 101.

[67] Bengel writes in his *Gnomen: Parabola de semine prima ac fundamentalis:* (the parable of the seed is primary and fundamental); cf. also G. Wohlenberg, *Das Ev. des Markus,*[3] 1930, p. 129.

[68] *Pasas tas parabolas: pas* may approach the meaning of: "any one, whatever; thus Mk. 4:13," Blass-Debrunner, *Grammatik des neutestamentischen Griechisch,*[7] 1943, p. 275.

[69] Thus Schweitzer, and also writers like Dodd, Schniewind, Jeremias, and others.

[70] Bornkamm, *TWB,* IV, p. 825, the article on *"musterion."*

[71] Cf. also R. Otto, *Reich Gottes und Menschensohn,* 1934, pp. 56, 57.

[72] Cf. G. Kittel, *TWB,* IV, p. 127, the article on *"lego"*: "The explanation of the parable of the seed, whether to be traced back to Jesus or not, derives its meaning and point from the conviction that the 'seed' which is explained

as the 'word,' is the event of Christ (*'das Christus-Geschehen'*) which has come to pass in Jesus." And on page 124 he writes: "What the explanation of the parable of the seed with its application of the term 'the word' tries to assert about Jesus, is nothing but that which constitutes the ultimate background to the entire tradition about Jesus: in his: *ego de lego humin* (Mt. 5:22ff), in the judgment of the cities (Mt. 11:20ff), in the power of the word and the deed with reference to the palsied man" (Mt. 9:5ff).

73 Cf. also J. Ridderbos, *Predikende het Evangelie des Koninkrijks,* 1911, pp. 64-74.

74 Schniewind, *Markus,* p. 73; Bornkamm, *op. cit.*

75 This becomes even clearer if with Jeremias we may suppose that the parable is based on the custom to sow the seed before ploughing the land: "Now it becomes understandable why he sows on the road: he purposely sows on the road that the villagers have made by crossing the stubble-field because it will be ploughed under with the rest. He purposely sows amid the thorns standing withered on the fallow land, because they, too, will be ploughed under. And it need no longer be surprising that there are grains of corn which fall on the rocky ground, for the rocks are covered with a thin layer of fertile soil and are hardly to be distinguished from the stubble-field before the plough-share bumps against them with a grating noise. So, what seems to be inappropriate to a Westerner proves to be the rule in Palestinian conditions"; *op. cit.,* p. 6. Cf. also G. Dalman, *Arbeit und Sitte in Palästina,* II, 1932, p. 194, who, however, does not come to a decision.

76 Schniewind, *Markus,* p. 71.

77 All this receives a deeper "dimension" with the later announcements of Jesus' sufferings and death. This will be seen below, § 23.

78 Dodd, *op. cit.,* pp. 180-183.

79 W. Michaelis, *Es ging ein Sämann aus, zu säen,* 1938, pp. 34-39. Compare also pp. 44, 45, however, where Michaelis admits that this tendency does not appear in Jesus' explanation of the parable, and where Michaelis suggests that in the synoptics we only have a fragment of Jesus' explanation. Cf. also J. Jeremias, *Die Gleichnisse Jesu,* 1947, p. 112, who reasserts Michaelis' interpretation of the parable thus: "In spite of any failure God's kingly dominion will be revealed." (*"Allem Miszerfolg zum Trotz kommt die Offenbarung der Königsherrschaft Gottes"*).

80 It is very remarkable that in the valuable expositions by Kümmel, and also in those of H. D. Wendland, there is no exhaustive discussion of the parable of the sower to be found. The result is that for the determination of the nature and the presence of the *basileia* a very fundamental datum is being ignored, which has had bad effects upon their interpretation of the other parables. Here, too, the "situation" lying at the basis of the parable and entirely dominating it, seems to be ignored.

81 Cf. also Fr. Hauck, *op. cit.,* p. 57, and A. Oepke in *TWB* on Matt. 10:26, the article on *"kalupto,"* III, 1938, p. 559 and the article on *"krupto,"* III, p. 974.

82 *In this context* this exegesis seems to be more obvious than the one according to which the "meting out" does not mean the meting out to oneself, i.e., the appropriation (of the salvation implied in the word), but refers to the meting out to others, i.e., in the preaching of the gospel (thus Hauck, *op. cit.,* p. 57: "If they mete the gospel out richly to the people waiting for the message of salvation, the disciples will receive a rich reward.") But then we would expect the beginning to be: "Take care how (or what) you preach"

instead of: "Take care of what you listen to"! Cf. also Schniewind, *op. cit.*, p. 77.

[83] Cf. also above, § 15.

[84] Cf., e.g., A. M. Brouwer, *De gelijkenissen*, 1946, p. 143, and Zahn, *D. Ev. d. Matth.*,[4] 1922, pp. 493, 494; A. Schlatter, *Der Evangelist Matthäus*,[2] 1933, p. 442.

[85] This view is in the first place in conflict with the 38th verse which explicitly says that the field in which wheat and tares grow together is (not the church but) *the world*. The mixing of wheat and tares refers to the intercourse of believers and unbelievers in the whole of the world-order. And further, the above mentioned view would mean a prohibition of church discipline emphatically commanded by Jesus elsewhere. The attempt is made to found this view on the 41st verse, which says that the angels "shall gather out of his kingdom (ek tēs basileias) all things that offend and those who do iniquity." Although we admit that here *basileia* is not meant in a future-eschatological sense (thus, e.g., Bultmann: "out of the kingdom then appearing," *op. cit.*, p. 203[1]) because the tares will be removed from the good crop that has previously sprung up; and also because the preventive *apo* has not been used but the elective *ek; basileia*, however, cannot be conceived of here as a "visible community," "the church," (thus Zahn, *op. cit.*, p. 123). *Basileia* is meant in a general sense as that which has been produced by the good seed sown in the world (cf. also Schlatter, *op. cit.*, p. 455). The church as the community that has been sanctified and set apart according to the law of Christ does not come into view here; cf. § 36.

[86] Thus, e.g., already Jerome, see Klostermann, *op. cit.*, p. 121.

[87] Cf. Dalman, *Arbeit und Sitte*, II, 1932, p. 325 and the literature cited there.

[88] So the conclusion is not: the judgment is postponed because the good and the evil must first manifest themselves clearly. For in the parable the tares are yet not exterminated even after having become quite manifest. Nor can we say: the full ripeness of the evil and the good still requires a delay of the judgment. For the tares are not spared because they must first ripen; but they are spared because it is too risky to pull them out before the wheat. So, no allegorizing, please! This is not saying that the meaning of the delay of the judgment is not disclosed in Jesus' preaching. For this fact, see below, § 20, 21.

[89] Cf. also M. J. Lagrange, *Evangile selon Saint Matthieu*,[5] 1941, p. 278. Schlatter, also, *op. cit.*, p. 448 gives this explanation: "In the environment of Jesus everybody immediately thought of a judge when the Messiah was spoken of. Did not Jesus relinquish the messianic office by his patient kindness and forgiving grace? His answer was: At this moment the kingdom is being proclaimed without any restriction, and forgiveness and calling is offered to all. This does not cause a breach in the juridical order, however." Schlatter adds to this that the task imposed on the disciples implies mixed conditions in the church, and that even more clearly in this parable than in that of the tares among the wheat it appears that the application of the juridical order is not a matter for the disciples. In its absolute sense (i.e., with an eye on the last judgment) this is correct, but it is liable to being misunderstood. For in the church there is certainly a juridical order, and its "carrying out" (by man) has been commanded. The parables given here are not concerned with the church but speak of the general manifestation of the kingdom in the world. The purification in this parable can only refer to a Divine purification in the final judgment. There is even less question of a warning against any premature

action than in the parable of the tares among the wheat, "because it is wholly impossible to think of extracting the bad fish from the net during the fishing"; Lagrange, *op. cit.* The problems about the church remain outside of the discussion, and it is misleading to draw them in. This remark also holds for Zahn's exegesis, *op. cit.*, 501.

90 C. H. Dodd, *op. cit.*, pp. 187-189. He writes: "The Kingdom of God . . . is like the work of fishing with a drag-net, for the appeal is made to all indiscriminately, and yet in the nature of things it is selective; and, let us recall, this selection is the divine judgment, though men pass it upon themselves by their ultimate attitude"; p. 189.

91 Kümmel, *op. cit.*, pp. 83, 84.

92 Michaelis, *op. cit.*, p. 122.

93 Schniewind, *op. cit.*, p. 168; cf. also Brouwer, *op. cit.*, p. 155.

94 Cf. also Michel *TWB*, III, the article on *"kokkos,"* p. 811, in explanation of Matt. 13:31-32, and parallel texts: "The man who scatters the seed, the field that receives it, are customary material for parables; in them is hidden the mysterious reference to Jesus himself and his preaching in the world."

95 See also the elaborate and accurate exegesis by H. M. Matter, *op. cit.*, pp. 51-60.

96 Thus, e.g., Kümmel, *op. cit.*, p. 76.

97 Like, e.g., Weiss, Schweitzer, Dibelius, Bultmann, Hauck, Gloege, Wendland, Kümmel, cf. in Kümmel, *op. cit.*, p. 76.

98 *Op. cit.*, pp. 190, 191. Moreover, Dodd wants to eliminate the idea of the extreme smallness of the mustard-seed, *op. cit.*

99 Here, too, Kümmel defends the former view and can appeal to many others, *op. cit.*, p. 78. He writes that the emphasis is only laid on the contrast between the small beginning and the great final stage. "That is why this parable also can only emphasize that the glorious final stage of God's dominion is perfectly certain in spite of the small beginnings. There is no thought of evolution. . . . At any rate, this parable also does not want to elucidate the rise of the divine dominion, but it wants to exhort us to have faith in the certain coming of God's rule." Opposite to this, is, e.g., E. Klostermann, "The miraculous expansion of the area disclosed to salvation is visualized," *Markusev.*, p. 94.

100 Cf. also Michel, *TWB*, III, p. 811: "With the grain-seed of the word of God the heavenly dominion itself has been given, embracing all nations and all men; the seemingly insignificant occurrence of Jesus' preaching implies the mystery of the comprehensive all-embracing action of God."

101 Thus, e.g., Schniewind, *Markus*, p. 78.

102 See also my: *Mattheüs*, I, pp. 260, 261.

103 Matter, *op. cit.*, p. 64.

104 Cf. also Matter, "The eschatological great tension, which later induces them as true-born Jews to inquire so passionately after the time "when" of the kingdom, might easily reduce them to a state of impatience and despair on seeing the great distance between what the *basileia* was yet to be and what it was in the works of Jesus"; *op. cit.*

105 *Op. cit.*, p. 64.

106 *Op. cit.*, pp. 61, 62.

107 The woman is not so passive here as she is supposed to be. She does not simply put the leaven in the meal, but mixes it with the meal until the latter is leavened in every part, although it is true that the dough, thus, prepared

still has to stand for quite a long-time (at least according to the method of present day housewives).

[108] Thus again Kümmel, *op. cit.*, pp. 78, 79 with an appeal to many other recent writers.

[109] From the circumstance that the leaven was put in three measures of meal and from the final clause, "till the whole was leavened," it appears that the emphasis is laid on the smallness of the beginning, cf. Gal. 5:9; cf. also Windisch *TWB*, II, p. 907, the article on "zumē."

[110] Cf. Windisch, *op. cit.*, referring to Matt. 5:13.

[111] Thus Matter, appealing to Bauer's dictionary, which translates it by *hineintun, hineinmischen* (putting it in, mixing it in), but adds, *ohne die Absicht, jedoch mit dem Ergebnis, dasz man das Betreffende dem Anblick entzieht.* (without the purpose, but with the result that the thing concerned is hidden from sight), p. 718.

[112] Thus Oepke in *TWB*, III, pp. 973, 974.

[113] *Op. cit.*, p. 186. Influenced by his view that the coming of the kingdom occurs with and after Christ's resurrection; the phrase "the coming of the Lord," verse 2, he (wrongly) takes to refer to the time after Jesus' death, *op. cit.*, p. 182.

[114] Cf. also K. H. Rengstorf, *Das Evangelium nach Lukas*, 1937, p. 153.

[115] Thus, e.g., Greijdanus, *op. cit.*, II, p. 651, cf. also Rengstorf, *op. cit.*

[116] Zahn, *op. cit.*, pp. 526ff.

[117] Cf. *Matt.* vol. II (K.V.), p. 44.

[118] Cf. E. Schürer, *Geschichte des jüdischen Volkes*, II⁴, 1907, pp. 465, 469.

[119] For further details cf. Rengstorf, *TWB*, I, p. 331, the article on *"hamartoolos."*

[120] Thus A. Harnack, *Das Wesen des Christentums*, 1905, p. 39.

[121] Thus, e.g., Dodd, *The Parables of the Kingdom.* He writes, "So Jesus went about the towns and villages of Galilee, seeking the lost; and that was how the Kingdom of God came." (*op. cit.*, p. 199). "Yet the Kingdom of God does come with judgment. The religious leaders, who censured Jesus for His work and teaching, were at that very moment pronouncing judgment upon themselves." . . . (p. 200). "Thus the coming of the Kingdom of God displayed its character as judgment, that is to say, as the testing and sifting of men." (p. 201). "It is the business of the Church, to which is committed the Gospel of the Kingdom of God, to interpret the crisis by the light of that supreme crisis of the past." (p. 205). Cf. also H. Windisch, *Der Sinn der Bergpredigt*, 1929, "We only transfer the decision from the future into our present, and consider as the religious meaning of the eschatology thus made present the fact that in it we are directly placed before God." (p. 158). (*"Wir übertragen die Entscheidung nur aus der Zukunft in unsere Gegenwart und sehen die religiöse Bedeutung der vergegenwärtigten Eschatologie darin, dasz wir in ihr unmittelbar vor Gott . . . gestellt werden."*)

[122] Cf. also A. Noordtzij, *De profeet Ezechiël*, 1932, p. 348; also Oepke, *TWB*, I, p. 395, the article on *"apollumi."*

[123] For further information about this see below, § 25.

[124] Above, § 13.

[125] Cf. Schniewind, *Das Evangelium nach Matt.*, 1937, p. 122.

[126] . . . "das Bild der Ernte ist deshalb möglich, weil unter dem Verkünder des Wortes sich schon die Entscheidungen des Jüngsten Tages vollziehen. Im Wort wird die künftige Königsherrschaft Gottes schon gegenwärtig." . . . Schniewind, *op. cit.* ("the image of the harvest is possible because in the

preaching of the word the decisions of the day of judgment are realized.   In the word of future royal dominion of God is already present." . . .)

[127] Cf. my *Matth.*, I, p. 226.

[128] Cf. § 27.

[129] See further below, § 27.

[130] Cf. Grundmann, *"Christus ist also nicht nur Verkünder der Eschatologie, sondern seine Geschichte ist Eschatologie. Dieses "dei," unter dem Leiden, Tod, Auferstehung und (bei Lk) Himmelfahrt stehen, gehört zum geheimnisvoll richtenden und heilenden Handeln Gottes in der Endzeit."* ("Christ, therefore, is not merely the preacher of eschatology, but his history is eschatology.   This 'dei' (to have to) to which his suffering belongs as well as his death, resurrection and (in Luke) ascension, is part of the mysterious judging and saving action of God at the end of time."), *TWB*, II, p. 24, the article on *"dei."*

[131] This word corresponds with the answer Jesus has the Pharisees bring to Herod, . . . "I cast out devils, and I do cures today and tomorrow, and the third day I shall be perfected" *(teleioumai)*.   Here, too, Jesus states the certainty of his death indicated as his perfection, the way by which he will be brought to his destination.   The "today" and "tomorrow" of the 32nd verse mean the continuation of his saving activity for some time, with the coming of the end after it.   The 33rd verse adds that for this purpose he cannot stay where he is, but will have to start the journey.   On his way there he will have to finish his work of today and tomorrow, in order to arrive at Jerusalem and be killed there.

[132] Cf., e.g., Heitmüller in *R.G.G.*, III, 1912, p. 387, the article on *"Jesus Christus"*: *"Er (Jesus) zog nach Jerusalem durch Peräa, Mrk. 10. Warum bleibt für uns dunkel. Jedenfalls nicht, um zu leiden und zu sterben — die Leidenweissagungen entstammen, so wie sie vorliegen, der Gemeinde, die die Entwicklung von rückwärts betrachtete."* ("He travelled to Jerusalem through Perea, Mrk. 10.   We are left in the dark about the reason.   In any case he did not do so to suffer and die—the prophecies of his suffering as we have them originated in the church, which considered the development of things in retrospect.")   Cf. recent authors, e.g., Klostermann, *Markusev.*, pp. 78, 79; Bultmann, *Geschichte*, p. 163.

[133] Cf., e.g., H. J. Holtzmann, *Lehrb. der Neutest. Theologie*, I², 1911, p. 353ff and the older literature cited there.

[134] Cf. also Ed. Meyer, *Ursprung und Anfänge des Christentums*, I, p. 117, *"Dasz ihm dasselbe Schicksal bevorstehe, wie so vielen Propheten, mochte er ahnen und aussprechen, die Einzelgestaltung konnte niemand im voraus wissen."* ("He might suspect and express in words that the same fate as that of so many prophets was in store for him, but its particular shape could not be known in advance by anybody.")

[135] Cf., e.g., F. Büchsel, *Die Hauptfragen der Synoptikerkritik*, 1939; Vincent Taylor, *Jesus and His Sacrifice*, 1948, *passim*.

[136] Cf. Hauck, *Markus*, p. 103, *"Im Gegensatz zu blosz verhüllt andeutender Rede wird diese Vorhersage und Belehrung als unverhüllt, frei . . . bezeichnet."* ("In contradistinction to a merely veiled communication, this prediction and teaching were unveiled and free.")

[137] Cf. Jeremias, *TWB*, IV, p. 1096, the article on *"numphē,"* although (to our mind on insufficient grounds) he is of the opinion that this allegorical sense is originally alien to this proverbial saying.

[138] E.g. Bultmann, *op. cit.*, p. 17; Jeremias, *op. cit.*

[139] For details cf. also Schniewind, *op. cit.*, p. 157.

[140] Cf. Klostermann, *Lukasev.*, p. 141, "Gethsemanestimmung" (the mood of Gethsemane).

[141] Cf., e.g., Sevenster, *Christologie*, pp. 109, 110; and especially the elaborate and valuable discussion of all the sayings of the passion by Vincent Taylor, *Jesus and His Sacrifice*, 1948, pp. 82-200.

[142] Cf. above, § 18.

[143] Cf. for details, my *Zelfopenbaring en Zelfverberging*, 1946, pp. 5-20.

[144] As Greijdanus wants to maintain emphatically, *Bizondere Canoniek*, 1947, pp. 226, 227.

[145] Although the voice from heaven following Jesus' baptism is a clear reflex of Isaiah 42:1 (indicating the Servant of the Lord).

[146] Cf. my *Matth.*, I, p. 60.

[147] Thus also Sevenster, *Christologie*, p. 111.

[148] A. Schlatter, *Matth.*, p. 89. Cullmann's view *Die Tauflehre des Neuen Testaments*, 1948, p. 14, that "all righteousness" here means something like "righteousness for all," is in my opinion difficult to maintain.

[149] Cf., e.g., G. Ch. Aalders in *Christus de Heiland*, 1948, pp. 23ff.

[150] Cf. R. Otto, *Reich Gottes und Menschensohn*, 1934, pp. 209ff; cf. also my *Matth.*, II, p. 17, note.

[151] Cf. G. Dalman, *Jesus Jeschua*, 1929, p. 110.

[152] In his very valuable article on *"lutron," TWB*, IV, pp. 341ff. Büchsel's remark seems to take too little account of this fact when he says that the words on the ransom (Mark 10:45) do not clearly refer to Isaiah 53, p. 344; cf. also the arguments advanced by Sevenster in his *Christologie*, p. 112.

[153] Cf. also Beyer, *TWB*, II, p. 85, the article on *"diakoneo."*

[154] Cf. Blass-Debrunner, pp. 283, 4, *"Das Semitische umschreibt das Reflexivverhältnis durch näfas 'Seele'; daher in der Uebersetzung aus dem Semit. bisweilen tēn psuchēn autou";* ("the Semitic circumscribes the reflexive relation by means of '*nefas*'—soul—hence in the translation from Semitic we sometimes find *ten psuchen autou*.")

[155] See above.

[156] In opposition to such criticism as by Bultmann and Klostermann, who consider these words to be of a secondary nature because they presume they must be thought of in the sense of the Hellenistic-Christian doctrine of satisfaction. But see Procksch's discussion of the Old Testament equivalents of *lutron* for the elucidation of the meaning of Mark 10:45, Matt. 20:28, *TWB*, IV, pp. 330ff, the article on *"lutron,"* and Taylor's *op cit.*, pp. 100ff.

[157] Cf. also Dalman, *Jesus Jeschua*, p. 110, and Porcksch, *op. cit.*

[158] Cf., e.g., Büchsel, *op. cit.*, p. 344. Sevenster, *op. cit.*, p. 115.

[159] As Sevenster thinks, who (wrongly I think) denies that here and elsewhere God is both the subject and the object of the satisfaction.

[160] Cf. also the elaborate explanation by Büchsel, *op. cit.*, pp. 345-348.

[161] The connection with Is. 53 has been clearly demonstrated by Sevenster.

[162] Cf. also my article "De Christologie van het N.T.," *Geref. Theol. Tijdschrift*, 47th year, 1947, p. 60.

[163] Below, ch. IX.

[164] Cf. also Taylor, *op. cit.*, pp. 258ff, pp. 278ff.

[165] Cf., e.g., A. Schweitzer, *Gesch. d. Leben Jesu Forschung,*[5] 1933, pp. 193ff; a summary in his *Das Messianitäts- und Leidens-Geheimnis,*[2] 1929, pp. 1-3.

[166] *Das Messianitäts- und Leidens-Geheimnis,* p. 89.

[167] Cf. R. Otto, *Reich Gottes und Menschensohn.*

[168] Cf. above, § 4.

[169] "His outpoured life would be the medium of a renewed fellowship with God," Vincent Taylor, *The Atonement in New Testament Teaching,*[2] 1945, p. 14.

[170] In our opinion *polloi* in this text is not an equivalent of *pantes,* cf. below, § 25; cf. also Büchsel, *TWB,* IV, p. 344.

[171] See further below, § 47.

Chapter V

THE GOSPEL OF THE KINGDOM

1. The Basic Motif

24. *The Gospel of the Poor*

In the two preceding chapters we have above all paid attention to the redemptive-historical aspect of Jesus' preaching of the kingdom of heaven. It has been established that in more than one sense Jesus spoke of the presence of the kingdom, i.e., of the consummation of the times and the fulfillment of the Scriptures; and also, that this fulfillment only bears a preliminary character as yet, and points to a more distant future.

We repeatedly came across the significance of the preaching of the gospel. On the one hand—as we have seen—this preaching is evidence that the kingdom has come, since that which is preached by this proclamation of the gospel is not only a word, but a deed, not only a sound, but reality, because it is supported by the person of Christ and is founded on his work, especially on his suffering and death. On the other hand it has also been seen that it is exactly this continuation of the preaching of the gospel which constitutes the preliminary character of the coming of the kingdom. This is especially implied in the parables dealing with the redemptive-historical meaning of the preaching of the gospel.

All this induces us to consider the *content* of the preaching of the gospel described in this way. No doubt in what has been said above we have touched upon this content in various ways. Yet we were concerned only with general and formal points of view. It will now be our task to enter into details with respect to the material content of this preaching, as well as to its internal structure by which it is ruled, and its importance for the present.

At first sight the gospel of the kingdom of heaven consists of two parts which together form an unbreakable unity. The first part is related to the *gift*, the *salvation*, given in the gospel[1]; the other part is related to the *demand*, the *command* in which it is expressed. We are aware of the fact that such a division is a kind of schema, or pattern, which, as such, does not occur in Jesus' preaching. We shall also become more and more aware of the fact that the gift of salvation preached thus also contains a command, and that, conversely, the command, the demand of the kingdom also belongs to the salvation proclaimed by Jesus. But in the nature of the case there is reason to distinguish between these two parts. Just as in that great and glorious example of Jesus' preaching of the kingdom, viz., the Sermon on the Mount, we first find the beatitudes and afterwards the commandments. For it is in accordance with this example that we apply such a division and regulate the course of our investigation by it.

On closer examination, however, it appears that something else should precede this treatment. For so soon as the attempt is made to circumscribe the gospel preached by Jesus, we are confronted with certain presuppositions imparting a very peculiar expression and structure to this preaching of salvation. The gospel of the kingdom is not something entirely new, but it is much rather the fulfillment of what is old. This applies to the commandments, as we shall see and equally for the salvation preached by Jesus. The whole of the promulgation of salvation is terminologically and factually determined by the history of the revelation preceding it, and cannot be understood apart from it. Before going into the content proper of the salvation promulgated by Jesus, it is therefore necessary to lay bare the factual foundations determining the entire pattern and structure of Jesus' preaching. Thus we shall try to gain a more accurate insight into the specific significance of Jesus' preaching of salvation as well as of his commandments.

The importance of such consideration may at once become manifest when we pay attention to the remarkable fact that in the first part of Jesus' preaching of the kingdom of heaven he repeatedly qualifies *the gospel* as that *of the poor*. This phrase is found in Jesus' first preaching in the synagogue at Nazareth (Luke 4:18) in connection with the prophecy of Isaiah 61. It also occurs in Jesus' answer to John the Baptist giving further details about the meaning of Jesus' coming and activity (Matt. 11:5, Luke 7:22). And the Beatitudes, so characteristic an example of Jesus' preaching[2] both in Matthew and in Luke, begin with the mention of the poor (in spirit) who are emphatically denoted (*autoi*) as those for whom the salvation of the kingdom is destined. It is therefore in the nature of the case that we must trying to get a better insight into the significance of the gospel by taking account of this close connection between "the kingdom of heaven" and "the poor (in spirit)." It is well-known that, e.g., Harnack based his entire ethical-religious conception of the kingdom of heaven upon the beatitudes because, in his opinion, the beatitude on the poor in spirit indicates the root of the whole of the new righteousness, viz., humility.[3] In contrast to this is the view of those who start from an entirely different conception of the kingdom of heaven and consequently impart a quite different sense to the programmatic expression "the gospel of the poor." Thus, e.g., Bultmann understands the "poor in spirit" as "the sinners" and looks upon this indication as the confirmation of the absolutely objective, transcendent character of the kingdom. By addressing "the poor" in the first place Jesus is supposed to preach the kingdom as God's sovereign act, as a purely eschatological gift, of which man can in no way be the disposer.[4] Generally speaking, it may be said that in the recent literature on the subject the view prevails that the contents of the gospel do not have an immanent-ethical meaning, but are intended in a transcendent-soteriological sense. In accordance with this the "poor in spirit" are conceived of as "sinners," or at least as those who are troubled by suffering and distress. Because they look to God for redemption they are destined for the kingdom of God.[5]

There is no doubt that the name "poor in spirit" cannot be taken to mean a new religious-ethical ideal of "being" preached or imparted by Jesus and embodying the proper meaning of the kingdom of heaven. But neither can it be said to signify a general need and susceptibility to the divine redemption according to which the salvation of the kingdom of God is supposed to be implied in a timeless, universal sense. We should rather realize the specific, historically determined meaning of the qualification "poor in spirit," and from this standpoint study the character and the contents of the gospel of the kingdom.

This will become clear when we consider the Old Testament background both to the notion "poor" (*ptoochos*) and "poor in spirit" (*ptoochos tooi pneumati*). The former agrees with the Hebrew *āni*, the latter rather approaches the meaning of *ānāw*. Both words mention an external kind of distress or oppression. The latter (*ānāw*, poor in spirit) refers in particular to the humility of the sufferer in his distress. Its meaning is approximately the same as that of the word: "meek" (in suffering), the "*praüs*" of Matthew 5:5, which is used also there as a synonym of "poor in spirit." Meanwhile we shall also have to understand the single word "poor" (Luke 4:18; 6:20; 7:22) in this sense as the equivalent of "poor in spirit." Moreover, the Hebrew *āni* has this connotation (cf. Ps. 18:28; 72:2; 74:19). We also point to Luke 4:18; 7:22 (agreeing with the Septuagint) which renders the Hebrew *ānāwîn* of Isaiah 61:1 "the meek." And in Matthew "poor" and "poor in spirit" evidently have the same meaning (cf. 5:5 with 11:5).

These "poor" or "poor in spirit" (meek) occur again and again in the Old Testament, particularly in the Psalms and in the prophets. They represent the socially oppressed, those who suffer from the power of injustice and are harassed by those who only consider their own advantage and influence. They are, however, at the same time those who remain faithful to God and expect their salvation from his kingdom alone.

They do not answer evil with evil, nor oppose injustice with injustice. That is why in the midst of the ungodliness and worldlimindedness of others, they form *the true people of God*. As such they are again and again comforted with the promise of the coming salvation of the Lord and the manifestation of his kingly redemption (cf. Ps.22:27; 25:9; 34:3; 37:11; 72:12,13; 147:6; Isaiah 11:4; 29:19, etc.).

The concept "poor" occurs more than once in this sense also in the later, pre-Christian scriptures of the Jews. At the moment—this is the thought that is entertained there, too—God's people are scattered amid the heathen; the pious and the wicked are intermingled in what had from olden times been God's people. But one day the true Israel will be assembled by God and become manifest. This *nucleus of God's people* is then called the *ptoochoi*, the *penētes*, in imitation of Old Testament texts, especially in the *Psalms of Solomon*. To these, all was related that had been promised by the prophets and that was eagerly awaited in the circles of those whose hopes were on God as regards the salvation of Israel as God's people.[6]

Against this background we shall have to consider "the poor" to whom the gospel is preached, as well as "the poor in spirit" and "the meek" of the beatitudes. We are not concerned here with a new ethical ideal, nor merely with the indication of some social injustice that will be redressed. Neither are we confronted with some general religious notion of the knowledge of personal imperfections and sin as if such knowledge could make one fit for the kingdom of God. It may be said that the concept "poor" is determined both socially and in a religious-ethical sense. But above all, this word derives its meaning from the fact that such "poor" and "meek persons" have been the bearers of the promise of salvation from olden times in a special sense, because they are the true people of God. And, in contrast to those who have fastened their hope upon this world, they expect the salvation God has held out to his people as "the consolation of Israel" (Luke 2:35, cf. 6:24; 16:25; Matt. 5:4).

All this is confirmed by the further qualifications of these "poor in spirit" that Jesus gives in the beatitudes, especially in the words: "they that mourn" and "they which hunger and thirst after righteousness" (Matt. 5:4,6, cf. Luke 6:21). It is true that many writers think of such righteousness as a subjective agreement with God's demand, and explain "hunger" and "mourn" as sorrow about moral imperfection.[7] To our mind such a view must be decisively rejected. For, in the first place, Luke 6:21 does not mention "righteousness" at all, but only speaks of "ye that weep" and "ye that hunger." In the following text in Luke, "But woe unto you," the opposite to "those that weep and hunger" is "those that are full" and "that laugh now." In our opinion it is clear that these words refer to the *social position* of "the laughers" etc. in the world (cf. John 16:22,20) and to their overboldness based on their position (and not on their moral qualities). In contrast to them are the "poor" that "hunger now" and "that weep now," i.e., who look forward to God's redemption of his people from the power of oppression and injustice that is continued for the present.[8] And it is this longing for deliverance which is indicated as "hunger and thirst after *righteousness*" in the beatitudes in Matthew.

This is also in agreement with what is said elsewhere about "righteousness" in connection with the poor and the meek. The Greek definite article already suggests that the expression refers to something supra-personal, to righteousness "in the full sense of the word," divine righteousness. And it is precisely this divine righteousness which is again and again represented in the Old Testament as the hope and the consolation of the poor and the oppressed.[9] It must not be understood in the Pauline sense of imputed forensic righteousness, but as the kingly justice[10] which will be brought to light one day for the salvation of the oppressed and the outcasts, and which will be executed especially by the Messiah (for this complex of thoughts cf., e.g., 2 Sam 14:5ff; 2 Kings 6:26ff; Jer. 23:6; 33:6, etc.). It is to *this* justice to which "the poor in spirit" and "the meek" look forward in the Sermon on the Mount. And to them it is promised. It follows in every way from the idea of the kingdom of God. When God starts his kingly dominion his oppressed people who look to him for everything will be filled with his justice, and those who are full now will have reason to weep.

Jesus' own teaching also contains a very clear confirmation and illustration of this thought, viz., in the parable of the unjust judge (Luke 18:1-8). This parable is dominated by the thought of the rights of the poor. In this light the figure of the widow must be viewed when she prays for justice against her adversary (vs. 3) in words that remind of Psalm 43:1.

Here, too, the metaphor is one of a life hungering for justice. But not only in the parable itself, but also in its application the thought of redeeming justice recurs twice: "Shall not God avenge his own elect[11] which cry day and night unto him?" And again "I tell you that he will avenge them speedily" (Luke 18:7,8).

The justice mentioned here is nothing but the deliverance (from oppression) to which God's people (his elect) may lay claim as the salvation promised them by their king. And it is this salvation which is proclaimed as "the gospel of the poor" in Jesus' preaching of the kingdom.

Nowhere is the nature and the specific significance of the connection between the "kingdom of God" and "the poor" brought home to us in a clearer way than in Mary's hymn (Luke 1:46-55). It is dominated by the same thought of "the gospel of the poor" and its contents are very closely related to those of the Beatitudes.[12] Here, too, is the contrast between the "mighty" and "the humble," of "those that hunger" and "the rich," and the mention of the redemptive intercession of "the Mighty One," and of the "strength he has shown with his arm." Here also is the beatitude, because of the salvation, that God's handmaiden receives in her "low estate."

The ground of all this is explicitly mentioned in this hymn. It is the fact that the Lord "hath holpen his servant Israel"[13] "in remembrance of his mercy;[14] as he spoke to our fathers, to Abraham and to his seed for ever." It is this relationship which also forms the basis of the salvation of the poor that is proclaimed in the Beatitudes, and which sets forth the first definition of the gospel of the kingdom of heaven.

It is clear that from the outset the salvation of the kingdom of heaven proclaimed by Jesus must be viewed against this background of its own historical determination. Above all Jesus addresses "the poor" or "the poor in spirit," and the whole gospel of the kingdom of heaven can be characterized as "the gospel of the poor." But this does not mean, as is often assumed, that the gospel is thereby universalized, thus to exceed the bounds of its particularistic scope. The message of salvation is not placed on a common level of humanity in general. On the contrary, this message is purposely adapted to the special relationship which God has established from olden times between himself and his people. No doubt the spiritual character of this relationship is very strongly emphasized, as also appears from the announcements of disaster that follow the beatitudes in Luke. Nevertheless, it is clear that the assignment of salvation to the poor is above all founded upon the special redemptive-historical relationship between God and his people.

It is the reality of God's covenant and of his theocratic relationship to Israel as his people which is the basis of the description of the gospel as the gospel of the poor. It is this true people of God which is addressed in the beatitudes and to whom the salvation of the kingdom is granted as their lawful right. And it is this special relationship which from the outset co-determines the contents and the structure of the gospel of the kingdom of heaven.

This fact induces us to examine more closely the entire preaching of Jesus, and not to be satisfied with a merely general characterization of the gospel of the kingdom.

25. *The New Covenant*

Behm has made the remark[15] that the word covenant (*diathēkē*) has come down to us as a term only used once by

Jesus himself, and that it does not occur in the rest of the gospel. But this fact, Behm says, does not diminish the central importance of the content of this notion in the gospels. We shall see that this opinion is doubtless correct. Only, it will be necessary to deduce an accurate definition from the gospel itself as to the content of this concept in Jesus' preaching.

Already at the outset, in the stories of the nativity, we are confronted with the aspect of the covenant. Thus, e.g., in the angel's announcement of Jesus' birth to Mary (Luke 1:32ff). Here Jesus is introduced as the king from the house of David. Other passages are Mary's hymn (Luke 1:54ff), and especially that of Zacharias (Luke 1:68-79) where the coming salvation is characterized as "the redemption of God's people, the raising up of an horn of salvation in the house of David, deliverance from our enemies, mercy promised to our fathers, a remembering of his holy covenant," etc. A further important indication is found in the angel's message to Joseph that Jesus "shall save his people from their sins" (Matt. 1:21), which is certainly intended to refer to Israel.[16] The same thing is seen in the message to the shepherds in which there is the question of "good tidings of great joy which shall be to all people,"[17] and which indicates Bethlehem as "the city of David" (Luke 2:10,11). This is a clear allusion to the fact that Christ's nativity is the fulfillment of the promise of the covenant to Israel. Simeon, too, speaks in the same way when he says that the salvation given with Christ's nativity is the glory of the people of Israel (Luke 2:32). In all these passages the idea of the covenant and the people of God come to the fore in an undifferentiated sense. They speak of "the house of David," "the people of the Lord," "Israel," and of "the whole of the people" or of "thy people Israel." There is no question yet of any separation within the people of Israel. It is true that in Mary's hymn "the mighty" and "the proud" are contrasted with "those of low degree"; and "the hungry" with "the rich." But immediately the hymn continues with, "He hath holpen his servant Israel" (Luke 1:54). In the song of the angels peace on earth is promised to "men of his good pleasure," but apparently this must be taken in the same sense as the preceding words mentioning the great joy "which shall be to all people" (Luke 2:10,14).[18]

Moreover, at the outset there are also utterances which ascribe a universal significance to salvation, in accordance with the prophets, thus, e.g., Luke 2:14 (peace on earth) and 2:32 (. . . "thy salvation which thou hast prepared before the face of all peoples: a light to lighten the Gentiles"). But this does not detract from the fact that the whole of the initial part of the gospel speaks of the coming of the salvation promised to *Israel* and therefore views the gospel of the kingdom from the standpoint of the Old Testament theocracy and from that of the covenant between God and Israel. It would, however, certainly be incorrect to infer from this that the opening of the gospel is dominated by a particularism which ascribes the salvation of the Lord exclusively to the empirical people of Israel. Much rather are we to understand these pronouncements in the sense that at the dawn of the Lord's salvation the idea of Israel as God's people comes strongly to the fore in its ideal and spiritual meaning, which can also be known from the Psalms and the prophecies of the Old Testament. From this point of view and without further differentiation the gospel speaks of "Israel" and of the Lord's people, etc. We cannot say, however, that now already the true, spiritual Israel is contrasted with the carnal people. The Lord's salvation is applied to God's people as a whole in virtue of the idea of the covenant. The totality of Israel is viewed from its nucleus and is called fortunate.

At first sight John the Baptist's preaching seems to contradict this view of Israel as the Lord's people. The thought of totality is replaced here by the call to repentance, which bears a strongly personal character and makes salvation at the coming of God's dominion dependent on this personal conversion. In his penitential preaching John rejects with great sharpness any confidence in descent from Abraham (Matt. 3:9). All this may bear the semblance of religious individualism which does not take account of Israel's election as God's own people. But this is no more than a semblance. For, even apart from a text like Luke 1:77, which mentions the preparation of "God's people" as John's special task, it appears from his own preaching that the Baptist keeps connecting the fulfillment of the promise with Abraham's children. Only in this passage there is the germ thought of an entirely new determination of the concept "children of Abraham." It is implied in the well-known words: "God is able of these stones to raise up (*egeirai*) children to Abraham" (Matt. 3:9).

Here, in the first place, the concept "children of Abraham" has been further defined. It does not mean all who have been born of Abraham, but the *real* children of Abraham,[19] the children "to whom the promises were made," as Paul says in Galatians 3:16. Here it is thus seen that the promise is fulfilled and the people of God is formed in spite of Israel's disbelief and aversion. Here also appears the real constitutive factor of the seed of Abraham and the real ground of belonging to it. It is found neither in biological descent, nor in human activity, but in the vivifying power of God (*egeirai*).[20] All carnal reliance on descent from Abraham is rejected, but the redemptive-historical significance and determination of the idea of God's people (the promise to Abraham!) is not given up. On the contrary, it is revealed in its proper and most profound sense, as it is entirely returned to God's free-re-creating grace.[21]

In Jesus' action and preaching we find the above-mentioned idea of the totality of Israel as God's people and also, in fact, the idea of the new Israel replacing the old one. *Both* these conceptions are expressed from the outset, and they continue to exist side by side, even when the line of demarcation in the historical Israel is becoming more and more marked. But the general aspect of Israel as God's people without any narrower differentiation comes to the fore. From the start Jesus addresses the whole of Israel as God's people to whom the deliverance of the kingdom of heaven has been promised. As the "children of the kingdom" they find themselves in a special relation to what has been given and revealed in Christ's coming. They may, therefore, be said to have been given the kingdom as a privilege that is especially meant for them (otherwise it could not be "taken away" from them and "given to" others, as is expressed in Matt. 21:43). They are "the children" that have a claim to the bread that must not be given to "the dogs" (Mark 7:27; Matt. 15:26). In these and in other texts it is clear to what degree the starting-point of Jesus' action lies in the historical and particular relationship between God and Israel. This relationship concerns not only "the people within the people" but all who belong to the people. There is no mention of a universalistic kind of evangelization which would break through the idea of election and that of God's people.[22]

In this context we would recall[23] Jesus' words about the Saviour in which he indicates as the purpose of his coming the search for "*what was lost.*" These words are not only important because they clearly reveal the saving character of Jesus' action, but they also strongly emphasize his bond with the people of Israel.

The "state of being lost" mentioned here must not be taken to mean a general religious decline; but it is the condition of a sheep that has wandered away from the *flock,* and so has gotten lost with respect to *the Lord of the flock,* i.e., to God. It is true that these pronouncements on "what was lost" (the one sheep, the prodigal son, etc.!) have been quoted to prove that Jesus broke through the particularistic idea of Israel's election as God's people. He is then supposed to have insisted on a kind of religious individualism and on the infinite value of the separate and single human soul (the *one* sheep, etc.). But this is incorrect. The "lost state" of the publicans and sinners that Jesus sought to save consisted just in their complete estrangement from the totality of the flock, i.e., of God's people. And this is why they run the risk of losing the salvation promised to this people of God. The special interest manifested in Jesus' whole messianic activity in behalf of what is lost, his pity, are clearly founded on the fact of *their belonging to God's people*. It is the lost sheep of the house of Israel that he seeks, and he seeks and saves the despised and lost publican "as he, too, is a son of Abraham" (Luke 19:9). The entire people, even in its least elegant members, is God's flock and as such the object of Jesus' mercy and love.

By the side of this there is another feature in Jesus' preaching, viz., that of *reprobation* both in a collective and in an individual sense. No less than John the Baptist did Jesus draw the line of separation within the Jewish nation. The beatitudes are the classical example of the fulfillment of God's promise to his people, but to those that lack the spiritual characteristics of this people of God Jesus preaches his "woe unto thee" with its ominous emphasis. His announcement of the kingdom is the preaching of the gospel, but no less is it the proclamation of the judgment within Israel. It is not the fact of belonging to the people of Israel that can save them, but repentance. "Dives" in hell makes an appeal to his relationship to Abraham and is called "child" by the latter (Luke 16:24-30), but neither he, nor his "five brothers" can possibly be saved if they do not obey "Moses and the prophets." Although Jesus restricts his action within the boundaries of the Jewish country (Matt. 10:5,6), he declares that the children of the kingdom shall be cast out whereas many shall come from the east and west and sit down with Isaac and Jacob in the kingdom of heaven (Matt. 8:10-12, cf. Luke 4:25-27). The unbelieving towns of Israel will be punished more severely at the judgment day than the heathen (Matt. 11:20-24; 12:41ff). At the end of his preaching, when it becomes obvious that the people as a whole do not accept Jesus, he then announces explicitly that Israel as the people of the Lord will be rejected and its privilege given to another "people" (Matt. 21:40-41,43; 22:8ff; 23:38,39ff).

But none of the above detracts from the thing of special importance for the entire structure of Jesus' preaching of the kingdom, viz., that the coming of Christ, the salvation given by him, and the community of those who believe in him, *remain qualified* by God's covenant and the relationship to Israel established therein. However, in accordance with what we noted about John the Baptist's meaning of "Abraham's children," we also see that in Jesus' preaching the character of the special relationship between God and Israel has been deepened and has become more definite. The same concepts which had been applied to the empirical, historical circle of Israel from olden times in an inclusive sense, and by Jesus as well, are also used in an exclusive sense to denote the community of those who accept the gospel in faith and will therefore inherit the kingdom. The term "the children of the kingdom" indicating Israel "according to the flesh" (Matt. 8:12), is now used in the new sense of the "good seed" (Matt. 13:38). The special relation to God that was first applied to the totality of Israel, is now restricted (and extended) to those who respond to the preaching of the kingdom with faith and repentance and have been elected by God to this end.

This change, noticeable in the gospel, finds its basis already in the Old Testament (Jer. 31). And it is very characteristic of Paul's view that inclusion with God's people (i.e., in the relationship of the covenant) is not constituted by the outward bond established by birth, but that all these categories are applicable in the proper and original sense of the word only to the true, faithful people of God whom he has elected. It is true that in the synoptic gospels these things are not explicitly mentioned in these terms, but it is not difficult to adduce factual—and to some extent—also terminological evidence of the matter as such. Such evidence is already forthcoming at the outset from the fact that Jesus gathered together a circle of *twelve* disciples or apostles (Mark 3:14; Matt. 10:1,2; Luke 22:14, etc.). This is not an arbitrary or merely a symmetrical number, but has a redemptive-historical significance. It must without doubt be related to the number of the twelve tribes of Israel. And this not merely because in this number Jesus summons the whole of Israel, despite its unfaithfulness and unbelief, unto the kingdom of heaven and thereby exhorts it to repent;[24] but much rather because these twelve disciples represent the new people of God.[25] A comparison of Matthew 19:28 and Luke 22:30 very much favors this exegesis. Jesus promises his disciples in these texts that "in the regeneration (they) shall sit upon twelve thrones, judging the twelve tribes of Israel." Here, too, the number twelve is specified, and with explicit reference to the twelve tribes of Israel. In our opinion the expression "in the regeneration" proves that the twelve tribes refer to the eschatological people of God, which can only mean the community of those who will inherit the salvation of the kingdom of heaven.[26] This community is named "the twelve tribes of Israel" because God's plan of salvation is continued in it and his covenant with Israel reaches its purpose and destination in it. Although the old Israel rejects the fulfillment of God's promises in Christ and is in its turn rejected by him, the covenant as such remains in force. The whole of the soteriological dispensation which began with Christ's coming not only displays the inner structure of the covenant but the group of the twelve disciples is also its out-ward symbolical image. This is the connection with the idea of the *ekklēsia* found elsewhere in Jesus' preaching and instruc-tion, as we shall have occasion to demonstrate in greater detail.[27]

Special significance must also be ascribed to the parables of the wedding-feast (Matt. 22:2-10), and of the great supper (Luke 14:16-24). These parables are rightly cited for the universal (embracing the heathen also) significance of the kingdom of heaven.[28] But the thought of the covenant is also maintained in them. Those who were invited in the first place (the Jewish nation) did not listen to the invitation. They stayed away under all kinds of pretexts. But the host neverthe-less carries out his plans of the wedding-feast in spite of their unwillingness. He sees to it himself that the feast is held, however strange and unprecedented the means that he employs may be. This is parallel to the Baptist's words that God is able of "these stones" to raise up children unto Abraham. In these parables the idea of God's people and that of the covenant are in the center, as appears from the images used to indicate salvation: supper, wedding-feast, which are standing phrases for the eschatological salvation[29] promised to Israel, together with the remarkable words of the host in Luke 14:23: "Compel them to come in, that my house may be filled." This "house" is the community of God's people, and the compulsion exercised by the servants at the command of the host is not in the first place intended to point out *who* the fellow-guests at the feast are, but rather, to establish *that* God's plan of salvation is carried out in spite of Israel's unwillingness.[30] Although those who were invited refused to come, the feast is nevertheless held. This is entirely in accordance with what we have found above: the idea of the covenant remains in force and is maintained notwithstanding the unwillingness of the historical people of God. Only, now there are others who replace those that had been originally called, and they become the guests at the wedding-feast of the Lord.

The whole structure of the gospel preached by Jesus is determined by the idea of the covenant. The clearest evidence of this fact, finally, is found in the only statement that has been preserved as spoken by Jesus himself and which explicitly mentions the covenant. It is his statement spoken on the occasion of the last Supper. In it Jesus refers to his forthcoming death and says: "For this is my blood of the new testament (covenant) which is shed for many for the remission of sins" (Matt. 26:28, cf. Mark 14:24; Luke 22:20). These words are important because they place the whole of Jesus' messianic action in the light of the covenant.[31] His death is its seal and provisional conclusion. But they are above all important because they reveal in an incomparable manner the foundation, the character and the scope of this relation in the covenant. It is not unimportant to note that the words spoken at the last Supper in its different versions[32] very clearly recall the prophecy of Jeremiah 31:31-34, in which the *new* covenant is mentioned. This is already seen in the tradition of Matthew and Mark. The words "for the remission of sins" must be understood in connection with Jeremiah 31:34. This connection with Jeremiah 31 is even more clearly stated in Luke 22:20[33], which speaks of "the new testament in my blood" and in which there appears to be an immediate reference to the promise of "the new covenant" in Jeremiah 31.[34] This reference to Jeremiah 31 is so important because according to this prophecy the Lord God himself will accomplish the fulfillment of the condition for the maintenance of the new covenant. For he will write his law in the hearts of his people. To this end he will forgive their former iniquity and will no longer remember their sins (Jer. 31:33,34). According to these words at the last Supper, this fellowship of grace between God and his people is guaranteed by God himself and is consequently unbreakable, and finds its foundation and strength in Christ's substitutive suffering and death. For it is his blood which, as the blood of the covenant, is shed for many for the remission of sins and thus makes the new and eternal covenant possible. He is the Mediator of this covenant and of the mercy for the renewal of the heart promised in it. It is clear that in this statement the whole of the salvation given in Christ and preached by him is concentrated in the idea of the covenant.

Thus are revealed the deepest ground and the real significance of the message of the angels before and immediately *after* Jesus' nativity, and that of the hymns of Mary and Zacharias about the salvation of God's people, in which are said that he "shall save his people from their sins" (Matt. 1:21), that "great joy shall be to the whole of the people," for "this day the Saviour is born, namely Christ the Lord" (Luke 2:11); and when they spoke of "the salvation of *God's people* by the remission of their sins" (Luke 1:77). Here is revealed the mystery of all the summarizing pronouncements giving expression to the salvation of the kingdom as the *gospel of the poor*, the *saving of those who were lost*, etc. The entire gospel of the kingdom can be explained in the categories of the covenant promised by God.

At the same time it becomes perfectly clear that the words "Israel," "his people," "God's people," occurring in many respects in an undifferentiated sense in the beginning of the gospel, assume a new sense. On the one hand their meaning becomes more restricted, and on the other it is extended in connection with Israel as the historical and empirical people of God. God's people are those for whom Christ sheds his blood of the covenant. They share in the remission of sins brought about by him and in the unbreakable communion with God in the new covenant that he has made possible. In his speech at the last Supper Jesus himself calls them *the many* for whom his blood is shed. This designation also occurs in the well-known statement about the ransom (Matt. 20:28; Mark 10:45).[35] This word has sometimes been equated with the word "all" and is thus interpreted in a universalistic sense. But the context contradicts such an explanation in every way. The "many" are those who receive remission of their sins in and through Christ and who are thus enabled to partake of the salvation of the new covenant according to the prophecy in Jeremiah 31. In the light of the whole gospel they are the people who have accepted the preaching of the gospel in faith and conversion. It is they, and no one else, who receive the salvation of the kingdom. They are "Israel," "God's people," and it is to them that all the promises of the covenant apply. The rejection of Israel as God's people does not annihilate the idea of the covenant, but imparts to it a new, or at least a more definite content. The particular character of grace and of communion with God is fully maintained. But the circle in which it is granted and where God's people are found, is no longer that of the empirical Israel, but it is that of those who are given remission of sins in Christ's death, and whose hearts have been renewed by the Holy Spirit.

26. The Good Pleasure of the Lord

Only in the light of what has been said above can those pronouncements be understood that assign the salvation given in Christ's coming to those in particular who have been *elected*. In a certain respect the gospel of the kingdom might be characterized as "the gospel of the elect" as much as that "of the poor," as we have done in the relevant paragraphs given above.

It is true that in contradistinction to the latter designation the former does not occur anywhere in the gospel (for which reason we do not wish to introduce it), but this does not detract from the fact that those who inherit the salvation of the kingdom of heaven are again and again designated as the objects of God's good pleasure or of his election. Closer examination, however, shows that these places are very closely related to those in which the idea of God's people predominates in the sense as qualified above.

Already at the outset this relation is manifested at the birth of Christ when the angels praise the salvation that has come as "peace on earth among men in whom he finds good pleasure" (Luke 2:14).[36] In *eudokia* (good pleasure) God's free and saving grace is expressed[37] which is the ground of the salvation proclaimed here. In it the element of love in the divine election comes strongly to the fore. The question is, who are those men in whom God finds good pleasure? In the tenth verse we find "the great joy" mentioned "which shall be to all people," and more than once the two pronouncements have been considered to be contradictory. But the phrase, "men in whom he finds good pleasure" does not in the first place *restrict* the group in which there will be messianic, eschatological peace, but it rather contains a further, positive *qualification*. It is not a definite sector within the circle of "the people," for the "great joy shall be to *all* people." So we shall have to explain the former phrase in close relationship with the latter and reject an individualistic exegesis of the words, "the men of his good pleasure." These words are a further definition of the people to whom great joy has been promised. And, conversely, "all the people" of the tenth verse cannot denote the empirical people of Israel, but God's people in the true, ideal sense. It does not mean Israel in its obstinate unbelief, but Israel as it has been privileged to be given God's promise, upon which it fixes its hopes, and by which it is redeemed.[38]   This again shows that from the outset the gospel of the kingdom has been determined by the particular relationship between God and his people, and that this relationship is founded upon the divine good pleasure.

Elsewhere, too, the gospel of the kingdom is derived from the divine good pleasure.   This is, e.g., very obvious in Luke 12:32: "Fear not, little flock, for it is your Father's good pleasure to give you the kingdom."   The idea of God's people as the heirs of the kingdom of heaven is implied in the address, "Fear not, little *flock*."   The emphasis on the smallness of the flock— "little flock"—implies that the "people of God" intended here are only a remnant, a seemingly vanishing remainder of what they used to be and of what one might expect them to be. That is why there was reason to fear that this small remnant might also perish.   And yet this remnant of the *flock* has been preserved and its deliverance is certain on the part of God.   For it rests on the Father's *eudokia,* the "divine counsel, free and independent of any human influence.   This counsel not only has the redemption of the church in the *basileia* for its purpose, but carries it out as well."[39]   The three concepts: God's people, kingdom of heaven, and election, are not only coördinate but also determinate of each other.   The gift of the *basileia* is intended for the people which God has elected from olden times and which comes to light in its proper and profoundest sense in their faithful acceptance of Jesus as the Christ, the Bearer of the salvation of the Lord.   Here, too, election is not conceived of in an individualistic sense, but as the election of God's people.   And, conversely, the magnitude of this people is not determined by historical and biological factors, but by the free and saving divine decree.

In accordance with this we must also understand Jesus' well-known pronouncement in Matthew 11:25,26 (cf. Luke 10:21ff): "I thank thee, O Father, Lord of heaven and earth, because thou hast hid these things from the wise and prudent, and hast revealed them unto babes. Even so, Father: for so it seemed good in thy sight" (*houtoos eudokia egeneto emprosthen sou*). Here, too, the separation made among Israel by Jesus' coming is traced back to God's sovereign good pleasure. The words *emprosthen sou* are difficult to translate but are a particularly telling characterization of God's decree. This decree is, so to speak, something that God has pictured to himself and has striven after as his purpose.[40] The saving character of this good pleasure of the Lord consists in the manifestation of the kingdom ("these things") to "babes" (*nēpioi*). This does not merely denote a particular mentality, but refers to the poor and destitute people of the Lord who are despised by "the wise and prudent," but who have fixed their hopes on God's redemptive action on their behalf. The concept *nēpioi*, babes, is a very near approach to that of *praeis*, the meek, and to *ptoochoi*, the poor[41] (cf. Matt. 11:28ff). And the pronouncement that they are the object of God's good pleasure again shows that the gospel of the kingdom is deeply rooted in God's special revelation to Israel and must be understood above all as the proclamation of salvation to the true people of the Lord.

This is nowhere clearer than in the parable of the unjust judge. There the coming and the salvation of the kingdom, which ought to be the object of the incessant prayers of the faithful (Luke 18:1, cf. the 8th verse), are called "the justice of God's elect" (*tēn ekdikēsin toon eklektoon autou*, vs. 7, cf. vs. 8).

We have already shown above that this "justice" or this "compensation" is the same thing as that which has been promised to the poor in spirit and to those who hunger after righteousness. So our observation at the beginning of this section is confirmed, viz., that the expressions the "elect" and "the poor in spirit" mean the same persons.

The expression "the justice of his elect" is very illustrative of what we would establish in this connection. On the one hand, the designation of "the justice" of the poor, implies that there is a firm basis for their faith in the Lord's salvation, and for their incessant prayer that it be realized. Their deliverance is their "*ekdikēsis*," their "right" or "justice," their satisfaction,[42] upon which they may base their claim. In a sense this lends to their prayer the character of a lawsuit, however paradoxical this term may seem to be. It implies that election is not an unpredictable divine decree unknowable to men, but a reason for the elect "to cry day and night to him." It presupposes that this election creates *a relation* in which the elect have been given God's promise of their satisfaction and redemption. On this ground they may pray for the coming of the kingdom as a right granted them by God. This relation is also at the basis of the beatitudes. It is the same basis as that of the covenant in which God has guaranteed the deliverance of his people from their oppression.

On the other hand, the phrase: "the justice of his elect" also implies that the special relationship between God and his oppressed people is based solely on the free and saving divine grace with respect to the people that will be saved.[43] This is the deepest ground of their participation in God's dominion and, therefore, of their obedience to the call directed to them (Matt. 22:14). In a negative sense this expression points to the fact that neither biological connection with Israel, nor a claim founded on human activity entitles them to the salvation of the kingdom, but only God's sovereign grace. But at the same time it implies that this election is not to be identified with fatalism or quietism. For the idea of election is so strongly emphasized just because it must urge us to a never ceasing activity of prayer in faith.

Finally it should be said in addition that this idea of election which is so obvious in the gospel of the kingdom is *Christologically* determined. Just as Christ in his meekness (Matt. 11:29), represents the true people of God, and his blood seals the new covenant and opens the way to the reception of the salvation contained therein (cf. Luke 22:20; Matt. 26:28), so in the same way Christ is the center and the realization of the divine good pleasure. This is seen in the first place in those passages in which Jesus is announced emphatically as the object of God's good pleasure, viz., on the occasion of his baptism in Jordan, and on that of his transfiguration on the mountain (Matt. 3:17; Mark 1:11; Matt. 17:5, cf. 12:18). There, too, "good pleasure" means the divine decree.[44] In virtue of this "good pleasure" Christ was elected by the Father for his messianic task (cf. Luke 9:35: *ho ekleleg-menos*). Thus the election of those who will receive the kingdom of heaven is concentrated upon the election of the Christ in whom they are saved.

God's good pleasure in his people is called into being in and through Christ. This appears from what follows in Christ's words of thanks in Matthew 11:25-26 with respect to his Father's good pleasure. There this good pleasure is further explained by pointing out that the Father has delivered all things to Christ by virtue of the same decree, and that nobody knows the Son but the Father, and nobody knows the Father but the Son, and any one to whom the Son will reveal him. The mystery of the knowledge of the Father, i.e., this revelation to the children of God, on the ground of God's good pleasure, is entirely in the hands of the Son. In him this good pleasure is realized of which he is also its object. It is the Son who is elected by the Father to be the bearer of the messianic office. And it is in him, too, that God's pleasure toward his people is founded and realized.

In summary we can say that the proclamation of the gospel of the kingdom as the gospel of the poor rests upon the covenant relationship between God and his people which has its deepest origin in the divine good pleasure.

The confirmation and renewal of this covenant receive their basis and character from Christ's word and work, especially from his expiatory death. They form the great presupposition and consummation of the blessedness of the kingdom of heaven as the latter has been preached by Jesus in all kinds of ways and which can now be considered by us in its various aspects.

Notes to Chapter V

[1] Cf. § 12 on the possession of salvation.

[2] Cf. my *De strekking der bergrede naar Mattheüs*, 1936, p. 27.

[3] A. Harnack, *Das Wesen des Christentums*, pp. 45-47.

[4] *Jesus*, p. 186.

[5] Cf., e.g., Wendland, *op. cit.*, p. 58.

[6] *Ps.* 5:2,13; 10:6ff; 15:2, etc. Cf. also R. Bultmann, *"Die Frage nach der Echtheit von Mt.* 16,17-19," *Theol. Blätter*, 1941, p. 269.

[7] See *De strekking der bergrede*, p. 91 and the literature cited in, e.g., Schrenk, *TWB*, II, p. 200, *"die Rechtsbeschaffenheit vor Gott,"* the article on *"dikaiosunē"*; E. Stauffer, *Theol. d. N.T.*, who explains the hunger and thirst mentioned here as the result of listening to the torah, p. 73; however, cf. also p. 205; H. M. Matter, *op. cit.*, p. 80.

[8] Cf. Stählin, *TWB*, IV, p. 1109, the article on *"nun."*

[9] On this subject see also Th. C. Vriezen, *Hoofdlijnen der Theologie van het Oude Testament*, 1949, pp. 109ff; and Schniewind on Matt. 5:6, *op. cit.*, pp. 43ff.

[10] Cf. Vriezen, *op. cit.*, p. 270.

[11] Here *ekdikēsis* in the sense of "compensation."

[12] This is also pointed out by Rengstorf, *op. cit.*, p. 23.

[13] According to Is. 41:8,9 (*LXX*), which passage is also entirely dominated by the thought of God's saving justice by virtue of his covenant.

[14] Bultmann points out that *eleos* occurs here in the original Old Testament sense of God's faithfulness, *TWB*, II, p. 480, the article on *"eleos."*

[15] *TWB*, II, p. 137, the article on *"diathēkē."* Cf. also N. A. Dahl, *Das Volk Gottes*, 1941, pp. 144ff.

[16] Cf. Schlatter, *Der Ev. Matth.*, p. 19, "That Israel is his people should not be said in the first place. For the name of Christ is not empty to Matthew. Because the latter assigns the royal office to Jesus, Israel is 'his people' independently of the result of his works, . . . even before he has been born."

[17] Cf. Strathmann, *TWB*, IV, 52,[99] the article on *"laos."*

[18] Cf. below, § 26.

[19] Greijdanus, *Lukds*, I, p. 162, "John does not belittle the importance of Abraham, nor that of being a child of Abraham, nor of God's promise to Abraham. He only says that the carnal descent from Abraham is no guarantee of being a real child of Abraham in the full sense of the word, and that God can give Abraham children apart from any carnal descent."

[20] Thus also Schniewind on Matt. 3:9, *op. cit.*, p. 22: "God's promise to Abraham is not cancelled. But God can fulfil it in such a way that there arise children out of stones, a new creation, in the way that God formed Adam out of the earth. Paul reasons in a similar fashion about being Abraham's child, Rom. 9:7ff, Gal. 3:7; 4:22ff."

[21] Cf. also A. Oepke, *Jesus und der Gottesvolkgedanke, Luthertum*, 1942, p. 43, "Here (i.e., in Matt. 3:9, etc.) being a child of God is traced back to a divine act of creation or election and in a more spiritual sense again connected with being a child of Abraham."

[22] Thus the older, liberal thought, by the side of all kinds of newer literature dominated by the national-socialistic ideology, explained the contrast between Jesus and the Pharisees as racial, especially from antithesis to the Jewish race! Then Jesus is supposed to have originated in Galilee with a more syncretistic population and view of the world, and to have joined issue with the Jewish

208

pretension of being God's people. On these fantastic speculations, see in Oepke, *Jesus und der Gottesvolkgedanke,* the literature cited and also his cautious (!) but conclusive refutation, *Luthertum,* 1942, pp. 33-53.

[23] Above, § 21.

[24] Thus apparently Oepke, *op. cit.,* p. 45; cf. also Hauck on Mark 3:14, *op. cit.,* p. 45, and others.

[25] Schniewind, "The number of the disciples represents in a newer form the people of the twelve tribes, the new flock of God," *Matth.* pp. 123, 124. And with respect to the remarkable *epoiēsen doodeka* in Mark 3:14 he writes, "He 'makes,' he 'creates' the twelve . . . , this means that Jesus creates the new people of the twelve tribes, cf. Matt. 19:28ff; the new Israel, the new church of God"; *Markus,* p. 65.

[26] The exegesis of this passage differs widely among writers. Some of them look upon it as the indication of the restoration of the people of Israel, thus, e.g., Zahn, *Matth.,* p. 605; in his commentary on Luke this view is a little weakened, because there he allows the possibility that there may also be non-Israelites among the people of the twelve tribes. In this connection he refers to Luke 3:8; 13:29, *Lucas,* p. 681.[60] Schlatter mentions the Jewish expectation of the union of the twelve tribes, e.g., in Josephus. However, he does not find such a picture in Matthew or anywhere else in the New Testament. In his opinion this passage only speaks of the judgment upon the whole of Israel to be executed by Jesus in which the disciples will cooperate, *Der Ev. Matth.,* p. 584. In the same strain apparently also Gutbrod, *TWB,* III, p. 387, the article on *"Israël."* In his opinion the name of Israel is not anywhere applied in the synoptics to the members of the new church. Greijdanus' opinion also is that the phrase "the twelve tribes of Israel" refers to the "people of God with its many ancient privileges," and that the glory of the twelve will be the fact that, however much despised now, they will one day pass judgment on those who reject him and them, *Lucas,* II, p. 1067. In the same strain also Plummer, *St. Luke,* 1942, *(I.C.C.);* p. 502, 503, and Allen, *St. Matthew,* 1947, *(I.C.C.),* p. 212, and apparently also Rengstorf, *Lukas,* p. 228. To our mind this view is untenable. Quite apart from Zahn's arguments against it, *Matth.,* p. 604, the apostles on their twelve thrones are clearly to be thought of in their unity with "the twelve tribes of Israel" (viz. as representatives and rulers) and not as Israel's punishing judges. Here the translation should not be "judging," but "governing." The metaphor refers to the future glory of the twelve tribes under the rule of the twelve apostles and, therefore, can only be understood as indicating the glorified church. The expression "the twelve tribes of Israel" denotes the coming Church by the name of the old people of God. It is the continuation of the latter and its fulfillment; cf. for this view also Grosheide, *Mattheüs,* p. 232; Schniewind, *Matth.,* p. 201; T. W. Manson, in *The Mission and Message of Jesus,* 1946, p. 509.

[27] See below, § 36.

[28] Cf. below, § 38.

[29] Cf. also Behm, *TWB,* II, p. 34, the article on *"deipnon."*

[30] For this viewpoint see also B. Sundkler, *Jésus et les paiens,* in *Revue d'Histoire et de Philosophie religieuses,* 1936, pp. 462-499.

[31] See also the important argument by D. Plooy, *Novum Testamentum regnum aeternum,* 1932, who subjects the word on the covenant in the account of the last supper to an elaborate linguistic analysis, and who advances the thesis that the new covenant inaugurated by Jesus' death is nothing else but

what is invariably denoted by the category of the kingdom, and who also refers to the remarkable connection mentioned in Luke 22:29, "And I appoint (*diatithemai*) unto you a kingdom," which expression in his opinion, and in view of the entire context, has been formed on the analogy of *diatithemai, diathēkēn;* p. 20.

[32] Cf. Schniewind, "Jeremiah 31:31-34 is noticeable in all the forms of the giving of the cup"; D. Plooy, *op. cit.,* pp. 9, 10.

[33] For the textual-critical problem of the "authenticity" of this verse see, e.g., the elaborate discussion in Greijdanus, *Lucas,* II, pp. 1045-1053.

[34] Cf. also Behm, *TWB,* II, p. 136, the article on *"diathēkē"* and IV, p. 452, the article on *"kainos."*

[35] Cf. above, § 22.

[36] As is well-known, the text is not certain. Some of the mss. have *kai* instead of *en;* then the verse has three parts. Other mss. even lack *en;* and finally the question arises whether we ought to read *eudokia* or *eudokias.* We prefer to read the text *without kai* (which may have been added on analogy of what precedes) and *with en* (a reading that seems to be more difficult than that without *en*). And further, we choose *eudokias* (a better textual witness and a more difficult reading); cf. also M. J. Lagrange, *Evangile selon Saint Luc.*[5], 1941, p. 77, and Schrenk, *TWB,* II, pp. 745-747, the article on *"eudokeo."*

[37] Some writers want to apply *eudokia* to the human good will towards God and his revelation: people of good will (*bonae voluntatis*). Thus, e.g., Lagrange, *op. cit.,* following the Vulgate; but also Zahn, *op. cit.,* p. 145; however, in our opinion this is an error. In the first place *eudokia* is not found anywhere in Luke in this sense, and only rarely in the rest of the New Testament (in Paul, Rom. 10:1; Phil. 1:15). In any case such usage in this context would be very remarkable. Human good would then really determine the extent of divine salvation. On the other hand, in this song of the angels in which everything speaks of God's glory, God's grace, and God's salvation, it is far more obvious that God's good will should be mentioned, cf. Rengstorf, *op. cit.,* p. 31; W. Manson, *The Gospel of Luke,* 1945, p. 18; Plummer, *op. cit.,* p. 58; Klostermann, *op. cit.,* pp. 38, 39; Greijdanus, *op. cit.,* I, pp. 115, 116, and especially Schrenk, *op. cit.,* pp. 748, 749.

[38] "What has been said is neither particularistically Jewish nor universalistic without any redemptive-historical roots. It is meant in an eschatological sense about the chosen people of God." Schrenk, *TWB,* II, p. 748.

[39] Cf. Schrenk, *op. cit.,* p. 739.

[40] A little different, Schlatter, *Matth.,* p. 383, who suggests a celestial consultation before God in which his will is determined. But is this deducible from the single word *emprosthen?* Cf. also Preuschen-Bauer, *op. cit.,* the article on *"emprosthen,"* sub d.

[41] Bertram, *TWB,* IV, pp. 922ff, the article on *"nēpios."*

[42] Cf. also Schrenk, *TWB,* II, p. 44, the article on *"ekdikēsis."*

[43] Cf. Schrenk, *TWB,* IV, p. 192, the article on *"eklektos,"* and Michaelis, *Das hochzeitliche Kleid,* 1939, p. 257.

[44] This is indicated both by the aorist tense, *eudokēsa,* and by the meaning of the verb, cf. Schrenk, *TWB,* II, p. 738, the article on *"eudokeo";* Zahn, *Matth.,* p. 147. Differently Greijdanus on Luke 3:22, who explains *eudokēsa* only as God's pleasure in Christ on account of Christ's obedience in baptism. In our opinion this is wrong.

Chapter VI

THE GOSPEL OF THE KINGDOM

2. Salvation

27. Remission of Sins

It has been rightly said that it is characteristic of the entire New Testament *kerygma* that in it the redemption is first and foremost conceived of as the victory over guilt and sin, and not, as, e.g., in the (nature- and) mystery religions, as the deliverance from the transitoriness to which man is subjected through his earthly life.[1] In other conceptions of redemption the faith in deliverance is based upon the conviction of the irradicable nobility of man, or upon a certain metaphysical equality of the soul with God which ultimately will be given its due. But the gospel starts from the idea of the cleft existing between God and man,[2] and of the great *moral* distress in which man finds himself before God. This distress goes so deep and is so all-overpowering because of man's guilt before God owing to which man with his entire existence runs the risk of being delivered to the divine judgment.[3] Conversely, redemption consists in the remission of sins, of guilt, in the communion between God and man who is sinful in himself. Here, also, the gospel contradicts all the ideas of deliverance found outside of Christianity.

A closer view of Jesus' preaching of the kingdom of heaven and of the *kerygma* of his redemptive coming into the world will convincingly prove the truth of this statement. When Jesus' birth is announced, the name given him at the command of God and summarizing the whole of his significance, is interpreted as follows: "For he shall save his people from their sins" (Matt. 1:21). The word rendered by "save" has a very

211

general and all-inclusive meaning, just like the Hebrew word on which the name Jesus is based. It denotes Jesus as saviour, redeemer. It not only has a negative and preventive sense, but a very positive content. The central and most profound meaning implied in this work of the saviour is the fact that Jesus delivers his people from their *sins*. The same thought is expressed in Zecharias' hymn which says of the Baptist that the latter "will go before the face of the Lord to prepare his ways; to give knowledge of salvation unto his people *by the remission of their sins*" (Luke 1:76ff). This knowledge is not merely knowledge about an objective and as yet unrealized promise, but much rather, the knowledge of what will be given and communicated now, hence as a knowledge of experience that has never before been granted in this sense.[4] The remission of sins is represented here as the gift of the fulfillment that began with Christ as an "eschatological" possession of salvation.[5] That is why the knowledge of it is described as the coming and the gift of the long-expected salvation of the Lord, as God's visiting of his people.

The preaching of John the Baptist announcing the kingdom of heaven, is concentrated on the remission of sins. His call of the people unto repentance resulted in the people coming to him "confessing their sins" (Matt. 3:6). His baptism itself is indicated as "the baptism of repentance for the remission of sins" (Mark 1:4; Luke 3:3). This "remission of sins" does not mean an assertion by John to those who had themselves been baptized by him that their sins had been forgiven. Nor did it denote some washing away of sins realized by John's baptism, but, as appears from the whole context of John's preaching, their acquittal in the judgment to come: "their escape from the wrath to come" (Matt. 3:7; Luke 3:7). John exhorts them to repent, to turn away from, to do away with sins, so that those who obey may forthwith hear the definitively exonerating sentence of acquittal out of the mouth of the coming One who is mightier than John. The remission of sins, consequently, is here the "salvation of the Lord" that would be seen at the Lord's coming (Luke 3:6).

There is no doubt that in Jesus' own preaching the concept of the remission of sins is not so central as in that of John.[6] Nevertheless, in the initial proclamation by Jesus in the synagogue of Nazareth, in which he announces the fulfillment of the prophecies and the commencement of the great time of salvation, the idea of *aphesis* at once plays an important part. Although this word must be translated by *deliverance* (of prisoners, Luke 4:18) and by *freedom* (for the broken hearted), and not by *remission,* the context also clearly implies the idea of the remission of sins. For this deliverance is based on remission and acquittal. For the whole of the salvation that began with Jesus' coming is concisely characterized as "the acceptable year of the Lord." These words originally denoted "the year of jubilee" or "the year of the ram's horn" in which, e.g., the debts of the Israelite who had become poor and a slave was to be remitted and he himself was to be delivered from his bondage and to have his property restored to him (cf. Lev. 25:39ff; Ezek. 46:17). All this is an image of the messianic time of salvation announced by the prophets and beginning with the coming of Christ. In it the bound and bruised life was redeemed and delivered because—and this is the basic idea—the guilt which caused the misery is remitted by God (cf. Isaiah 40:2). Again and again we find the remission of sins mentioned in the gospel as the proper and central purpose of Jesus' coming. Thus, e.g., when to the palsied man who had come to him to be cured, he says: "Son, thy sins are forgiven thee" (in Luke: "Man, thy sins have been forgiven thee"), he makes clear by these words to all the people present, as well as to the palsied man, that the real and deepest distress of man is not that particular lot in life which happens to be his, but the fact that he is a sinner, and that Jesus has been authorized by God to deliver men from their sins (on earth)[7] at this very moment. Jesus' statement here should not be explained merely from an exceptionally penitential mood of the palsied man that must have to be assumed in this case. Nor should it be supposed that his palsy was occasioned by certain verifiable sins for which he was being punished. Rather, it is the messianic proclamation, the announcement of the coming of the kingdom, the commencement of the great time of salvation whose heart and sum is the *remission of sins*. This is, therefore, the greatest blessing confronting those who have faith (cf. Mark 2:5), i.e., those who have understood something of Jesus' divine authority: the remission of their sins is here!

The significance of this remission of sins is above all the doing away with the *guilt* of sin. In this respect the purpose and meaning of the gospel is unmistakable. Again and again it represents the relation of man to God as that of a debtor to his creditor. Thus, e.g., in the Lord's Prayer (Matt. 6:12, cf. also Luke 11:4b), "and forgive us our debts, as we forgive our debtors." The idea of sin as debt and of deliverance as remission also dominates the parable of Matthew 18:22-35 (on the duty to forgive one's neighbor). Sin places man in the position of one who must pay, give satisfaction (*apodounai*). At the banquet in the house of Simon the Pharisee, Jesus speaks in a similar way of a certain creditor who had two debtors neither of whom could pay (Luke 7:41,42). Thus Jesus indicates the relationship to God of both of them, the "righteous" as well as the "sinners." The parables, too, about the character of stewards belong to the same sphere, especially that of the dishonest steward of Luke 16:1ff. In its application this parable shows that Jesus looks upon man as one who at the hour of the divine settlement will not be able to account for what he has done with the goods of his Master whose steward he was, and will have to remain God's debtor (Luke 16:9ff). Moreover, the passage on repentance in Luke 13 speaks in a general way of guilty people who will perish if they do not repent (Luke 13:4).

And finally the remission of sins is indicated in a still more juridical way in the parable of the Pharisee and the publican. The publican is said to have gone "down to his house justified rather than the other" (*dedikaioomenos*). This is the only passage in the synoptics where the remission of sins is represented as a forensic justification: an acquittal, a judicial justification by God.[8] No doubt this use of the word is co-determined by the contrast between the publican and the Pharisee. For the latter represents those who try to justify themselves before God according to the doctrine of meritoriousness (cf. Luke 16:15). In opposition to this, Jesus makes it clear that God accepts the sinner out of his sovereign grace. But he maintains the idea of justification, of confrontation with the divine judgment. And this is one of the basic thoughts of the gospel.

This fundamental conception of redemption as remission of sins not only distinguishes the gospel from all non-Christian religions, but also from all humanistic and modern-dualistic interpretations of the gospel. The latter hold that the starting-point of Jesus' preaching lay in the infinite *value* of the human *soul*, or in the antithesis between nature and spirit. Often an appeal is made to Mark 8:36ff: "For what shall it profit a man, if he shall gain the whole world, and lose his own soul?" This entire view, however, which was advocated by Ritschl's theology and given its classical expression in Harnack's *Das Wesen des Christentums*, contradicts the gospel in its very essence.[9] The starting point of the gospel is not the value, but the guilt of man; and redemption is not the preservation of the soul, as in itself the imperishable and higher part of man, but the saving of the whole of human existence in the last judgment. Neither is difference from this indicated in the words: "to lose one's soul." The word "soul" means the whole of human life and not merely the inner part or the spirituality of man. We remind the reader of Jesus' related statement: "And fear not them which kill the body, but are not able to kill the soul: but rather fear him which is able to destroy both soul and body in hell" (Matt. 10:28, cf. Luke 12:4,5). Here we do not find a contrast of soul and body, the spirit to the flesh, and Jesus does not want to point to the superior of the former over the latter. But here we are warned against the divine judgment, in which every man who has rejected God's will with respect to his life will perish with body and soul.[10] So it is not the spiritual value of man, but his moral distress that prompts Jesus' warning, and which is the foundation of his entire preaching about the remission of sins.[11]

All this is very important for an insight into the salvation proclaimed by Jesus. But there can be no doubt that the idea of sin as guilt, and that of redemption as the remission of sins, are not *in themselves* the new and specific characteristic of Jesus' preaching. Jesus did not speak in concepts that were strange but rather in ones familiar to his contemporaries.[12] Again and again he declared that the remission of sins he proclaimed and gave was nothing else than the fulfillment of the future salvation promised by the prophets. Already the Old Testament sought the essence of redemption in the grace of the Lord who, like a father, shows his mercy upon his people by forgiving them their sins (Ps. 103:8-10). And the salvation of the future was sought in the fact that God would redeem Israel of all its iniquities (Ps. 130:8).[13]

The frequent modern assertion that in comparison with the Old Testament Jesus came with a new idea about God, especially in his promulgation of the remission of sins, is therefore entirely contrary to the gospel itself.[14] According to Jesus' own emphatic pronouncement, the gospel of the poor, the prophecy of the acceptable year of the Lord, the Lord's new covenant with his people, find their fulfillment and realization in the remission of sins proclaimed by him (Luke 4:16ff; Matt. 26:28; Luke 22:20).[15]

This fundamental agreement with the historical revelation of God in the Old Testament is the great presupposition of Jesus' preaching of the remission of sins. To gain a correct insight in the purport of Jesus' preaching of salvation we must first establish that the new and striking feature in it is not found in the qualitative view of sin and forgiveness, but in the great moment of fulfillment, i.e., in the fact that in Jesus' coming and messianic activity the blessing of God's merciful remission of guilt promised from of old has passed from the promissory stage into that of actual realization. Or, to describe it in the words of the mission that the apostles received later on, the new feature is that from henceforth this gospel must be preached *"in his name"* for repentance and remission of sins (Luke 24:47, cf. John 20:23).[16]

But this is not all. In addition to its great redemptive-historical motif, even a superficial examination of the gospel of the kingdom will show that Jesus' preaching is also determined by an *antithetical motif* directed against the teaching of the scribes. It may even be said that this latter motif comes very strongly to the fore after the first proclamation of the fulfillment. It dominates the whole aspect of Jesus' preaching and is considered as the specific trait in Jesus' proclamation of the remission of sins (not infrequently while ignoring the great moment of fulfillment!). This antithesis not only refers to Jesus' messianic pretention of forgiving sins upon earth, but also to the content and the possibility of the remission of sins, especially in view of the aspect of absolute grace in Jesus' preaching.

We see this antithesis in action on the part of the Jewish leaders when Jesus eats and drinks "with publicans and sinner" (Mark 2:16 and related texts); when at the Pharisee's banquet he has dealings with repentant sinners (Luke 7:36-50); in the story of the adulterous woman (John 8:1-11); in that of Jesus' entry into Zacchaeus' house (Luke 19:1-10). Conversely it is Jesus who opposes the attitude adopted by the scribes and Pharisees in his preaching of the remission of sins. Thus in the parable of the prodigal son as he depicts the figure of the elder son who disapproves of the father's doings (Luke 15:25-32, cf. vss. 1 and 2); and in the parable of the Pharisee and the publican where he gives the most impressive picture of this antithesis (Luke 18:9-14).

For a real insight into the nature of this antithesis between Jesus and the scribes, it is very illuminating to examine what the rabbinical and pseudo-epigraphic writings of the so-called late Judaism teach us about *the Jewish schema of redemption* which formed the scope of Jewish soteriology at the time of Jesus' stay on earth.

Its basic motif is the idea of reward—and correlated with it—that of the meritoriousness of the fulfillment of the law. It is true that the torah as a means of deliverance has been given by God as a special favor to Israel. But the purpose of this gift is for Israel to earn *a reward* from God by fulfilling this torah. That is why it was assumed that in himself man has the moral strength to fulfil the torah. For man has received a pure and holy soul from the hand of his Maker, and whatever evil instincts he may find in himself because of his sensuous body, he not only has the moral power to suppress, but above all he has the torah as a means by which to subdue them. This scheme of redemption starts from a perfectionist idea of man. And as to sin, it was not denied, of course, but it was conceived of in a quantitative way. The important thing in the fulfillment of the law is that the *number* of infringements of the law should be inferior to the *number* of the fulfillments of the law. In other words, the credit side of man's account with God must be greater than its debit side. This view also determines the concepts "righteous man" and "sinner." There is, however, no certainty of salvation for the righteous. That is why they are advised always to live in a way as if the scales are balanced and as if their salvation is every time dependent on a new act of fulfillment of the law. Such fulfillment is always attainable, for it consists in conforming to the literal text of the commandments. The Jewish soteriology, therefore, had a legalistic and quantitative meaning. It was a religion of self-redemption starting from a shallow view of the nature of sin and a perfectionist conception of man.[17]

By the side of this doctrine of consistent reward there was, no doubt, among the Jews a continuation of the Old Testament thought of God's goodness and his willingness to remit the sins of those who turn to him in repentance. This thought cannot be subsumed under the Jewish theology of reward without further ado. Here this theory breaks down, for here reward is only possible because of God's mercy.[18] It is often said that the remission of sins in the Jewish doctrine is based on the meritoriousness of repentance and thus leaves the schema of reward intact. But such a view does not do sufficient justice to the Jewish theory of redemption.[19] On the other hand the remission of sins and God's mercy is also connected in all kinds of ways with the all-important doctrine of reward. The aim of repentance and remission is to restore the sinner to a relationship with God in which the godly are already found because of their merits, and in which, therefore, restored sinners, too, may again build for their eternal future.[20]   The idea of reward is and remains the great dominant element of the Jewish doctrine of redemption.

Against such a background the antithesis between Jesus and the Jewish doctors of the law that comes to light again and again in the gospel assumes very sharp contours.   Jesus' preaching of the remission of sins is nothing less than a fundamental break with the entire Jewish schema of redemption.   This is apparent in the first place from Jesus' pronouncements on *the universality of sin* and the *necessity of repentance* which are at the basis of the whole of his preaching.

Entirely unlike the Jewish doctrine of redemption, Jesus' preaching is dominated by the thought of the universal necessity of repentance.   This repentance not only means sorrow or penitence on account of certain infringements of God's commandments, but is connected with the general relationship in which empirical man finds himself towards God, and signifies the radical turning from it on the part of man.[21]   Man has turned away from God.   He is on the road that leads away from God.   This is why the notion "conversion" is a *totalitarian* concept both in a negative and positive sense.   It does not denote an incidental act of penitence but an all-embracing attitude of life.   It consists in turning away from sin and in doing the works of righteousness producing fruit worthy of repentance or conversion (Matt. 3:8).

This also holds for the preaching of the Baptist.   Even before his birth he was announced as the one who was to turn many of the children of Israel to the Lord, their God, to make ready a people prepared for the Lord (Luke 1:15ff).   Not merely a few individuals but the nation as a whole had to be called to repent.   The same thing is seen in Jesus.   His action among Israel also starts with the general preaching, "Repent, for the kingdom of heaven is at hand."   The necessity of conversion is the presupposition at the basis of the entire promulgation of the gospel.   It is addressed to everyone individually.

The demand to repent is addressed to the disciples as well as to the cities of Galilee (cf. Matt. 18:3,[22] 11:20ff); to the chief priests and the Pharisees as well as to the publicans and sinners (Matt. 21:31ff; Luke 15:1ff). It appears from these few but very general pronouncements that Jesus' preaching of salvation, especially that of the remission of sins, begins from the standpoint of man's universal sinfulness, of his being turned away from God.

It is true that some writers have tried to deny this fact on more than one ground. In the first place they point to those passages in which Jesus himself distinguished between "the righteous" and the "sinners," and which say that he has come to call, not the former, but the latter to repentance (Mark 2:17; Luke 5:32). Similarly Jesus speaks elsewhere of the one sinner who repents over whom there is more joy in Heaven than over ninety-nine just persons who need no repentance" (Luke 15:7). On the basis of such texts, it is alleged that the existence of "just persons" should be conceded because it would not be possible to compare a non-existent class of people with another group. According to Jesus there are good and bad people (Matt. 7:17,18; 12:33); just as there are good and bad trees (cf. Matt. 5:45: "the wicked and the good," "the righteous and the unrighteous").[23]

The saying, however, that Jesus has not come to call the righteous but sinners to repentance is not simply to be interpreted as an ironical utterance[24] but as an existing distinction made by the Jews and now adopted by Jesus[25] who, no doubt, recognized its relative value. On the other hand it is not to be supposed that by "the righteous" Jesus means those who ought to be acknowledged as such on principle and before God, and that Jesus honored their righteousness by calling those who had fallen and not the righteous people.[26]   For here, and in Luke 15:7 (cf. v. 2), Jesus obviously refers to the righteousness imputed by the scribes and the Pharisees to *themselves* (cf. Luke 18:11,14). And within the scope of the whole of the gospel it is indisputable that Jesus did not recognize this righteousness as sufficient, but judged it to be a strange kind of righteousness based on self-deceit and therefore "hypo-critical" (cf. Matt. 5:20ff; 6:1ff; 23; Luke 18:14). He rejects such righteousness as a dangerous delusion, as appears from Luke 14:8ff. Seated at table with the Pharisees he seems to lay down a mere rule of politeness and good manners about the right behavior of a guest at a banquet. But he does so by way of a parable, and thus in reality warns the guests not to be mistaken about the banquet in God's kingdom with respect to God's judgment of their excellence.[27] That is why the pronouncement in Mark 2:17 must be understood as an indication that, in Jesus' coming as God's curing (physician!), guilt-remitting grace goes out to fallen men. But this grace is only extended to those who are made to realize that they are in need of it. Taken in this sense this pronouncement in-directly implied a call to those who pretended to righteousness to search their own hearts and to ascertain whether they had reliable reasons for thinking that this kind of righteousness was sufficient.[28] In the same sense we shall have to interpret the expression "the ninety-nine righteous people who were not in need of repentance." Jesus cannot mean that the relationship between the righteous and the sinners is as one to a hundred. The pronouncement much rather means that (as a manner of speaking, for the word has the typical char-acter of a riddle) the repentance of one sinner is held to be more important in heaven, i.e., before God, than the "righteous-ness" of the ninety-nine. The phrase "who are not in need of repentance" is only an expression of human judgment.[29] By these words Jesus wants to induce those who are righteous in their own eyes (verse 2) to see the error of their ways.[30]

As to the texts in which Jesus speaks of "evil and good," "righteous and unrighteous," the above discussion sufficiently shows that Jesus by no means wants to deny the necessity of repentance for some people. He rather speaks of a relative distinction which obtains among men and is recognized by him as such (cf. Rom. 5:7; 13:3). In the scope of the gospel it is perfectly wrong to suppose that here Jesus wished to state or to vindicate the "natural" righteousness before God which is true in the case of some people.[31] This is not only apparent in those passages in which Jesus opposes the pharisaical delusion of righteousness, but also in those texts in which he says to his disciples—apparently as something that is neither doubted by him or them—"If ye then, being evil, know how to give good gifts unto your children, how much more" . . . etc. (Matt. 7:11, and Luke 11:13).[32]

Elsewhere he speaks of "the human heart" as the place from which proceed evil thoughts and all kinds of crimes.[33] He teaches his disciples to pray for forgiveness of their debts as well as for their daily bread (Matt. 6:12). In the parable of the debtor and his creditor he gives as the motive of the duty to forgive repeatedly one's brother his trespasses the infinite debt that the heavenly Father has to forgive his children (Matt. 18:23-35). And, to mention only one more example[34]—to the rich young ruler with his moral optimism and self-complacency he says: "One (only) is good" (Matt. 19:17); "there is none good but one, that is God" (Mark 10:18; Luke 18:20). All these pronouncements unmistakably show that Jesus' preaching is based on a view which denies to the man principally the attribute of "good" and characterizes him rather as "evil," as a sinner, a debtor before God.[35]

Such more or less incidental pronouncements on the universality of sin and the consequent necessity of repentance are no isolated phenomena. For the gospel also clearly shows the cause and gives the explanation of this view. It is to be found in *Jesus' judgment of the extent, the depth and the serious nature of sin.* This judgment is pregnantly expressed, and antithetically represented in the well-known triplet of Matt. 5:21,22: "Ye have heard that it was said by them of old time:[36] Thou shalt not kill; and whosoever shall kill shall be in danger of the judgment.

"But I say unto you, that whosoever is angry with his brother shall have to answer to the judgment; and whosoever shall say to his brother, Raca, shall have to answer to the Sanhedrin; and whosoever shall say. Thou fool, shall have to answer to hell-fire."

Here Jesus points to the meaning of the commandment, "Thou shalt not kill" (not only manslaughter, but also anger, and abuse are infringements of the commandment) and also the measure of punishment for the slightest offense in the scale: it can only be punished with hell-fire. This view on principle cancels any quantitative view of sin and replaces it by a qualitative conception: any sin, even the "slightest," makes a contract-relationship with God impossible. It urges man to rely entirely on God's gracious remission of guilt.

And this passage is not an isolated one. It characterizes the whole of the Sermon on the Mount, especially in Matthew's form, which is one long judicial summation against the Pharisaical conception of justice. It contrasts to the latter the most radical, "perfect" obedience as the meaning and fulfillment of the law. We reject the view that the Sermon on the Mount is intended to show exclusively the great moral misery of empirical man.[37] But a serious listener cannot escape from the fact that if Jesus' commandments had been given to show man the way to redemption by his own merits, they must deprive him of any hope. In fact, such a reaction has indeed been recorded in the answer of the disciples to Jesus' pronouncement concerning the entry of a rich man into the kingdom: "Who then can be saved?" (Matt. 19:25). The disciples have understood that the way in which Jesus speaks of the rich in fact blocks the road to the kingdom for *any* human being. They are frightened by Jesus' radical demand. For this reason Jesus' answer saying: "With men this is impossible; but with God all things are possible," is a key to understanding his entire preaching and all his commandments.[38] Salvation is an utter impossibility so long as man is obliged to obtain or merit it for himself on his own; with God, however, there are unlimited possibilities, so also with regards to man's salvation.

The parable of the debtor and his creditor is based upon the same presupposition (Matt. 18:23-35). Man's debt to God is so infinitely great (ten thousand talents) that he can only pay it by being delivered up to the terrors of hell, unless God acquits him by the remission of his sins (18:34). Jesus is far from starting from the Jewish schema of meritoriousness and substituting for it a much more profound conception of sin and righteousness.[39] Much rather it is exactly this new proclamation of God's demand and this taking perfectly serious God's punitive justice which reduces the soteriology of the Jews *ad absurdum* and places the redemption of man on an entirely new basis.

In this light we can understand the depth of the antithesis between Jesus and the Jewish system as regards *the remission of sins.* It is perfectly true that *in itself* the idea of the remission of sins is nothing new with respect to the Jews. But anyone who appeals to this fact to argue that on principle Jesus' doctrine of redemption is a *"Leistungs-religion"* (i.e., a religion of human achievement) and not "a religion of sinners,"[40] misinterprets the fundamental difference in the conception of sin and in the conception of remission. It is true in Judaism there was sometimes a deeper tone audible with respect to the fulfillment of God's demand, as appears from the gospel (cf. Mark 12:32-34) and from other sources.[41] But there remains this fundamental difference that Jesus' preaching of God's demand and the insufficiency of human righteousness renders entirely impossible any relationship between God and man that might be based on the moral achievement of man. That is why the remission of sins in Jesus' preaching is not an incidental corrective of the imperfection of human righteousness. On the contrary, it is the necessary, basic condition for man in order to live before God, and in general, to make room for the idea of "righteousness." In other words, in Jesus' preaching the concept "remission of sins" lies on a principally deeper level than in Judaism. It does not only occur at the "reckoning," nor does it lie only in the moral sphere, but it forms the real and most profound criterion of man's relation to God. Nowhere is this fact so clear as in the pronouncements (often quoted to prove the opposite view) in Luke 15:7: "I say unto you, that likewise joy shall be in heaven over one sinner that repeneth more than over ninety and nine just persons, which need no repentance." Here the repentance of the one sinner is valued higher than all the righteousness of the "righteous." The same thing is found in the parable of the Pharisee and the publican. However much the former had of "righteousness" whose acts he enumerates, and for which he thought he was thanking God, Jesus points us to the repentant publican who could only say: "God be merciful to me a sinner," but whom Jesus nevertheless declared that he went down to his home justified, rather than the other (Luke 18:10-14).[42]

This thought is incomprehensible within the scope of the Jewish soteriology. It is not that in the Jewish view God has no mercy upon a repentant sinner. But in it the repentant sinner is placed at a disadvantage in comparison with a righteous man. For, from God's love for a sinner, it is again and again inferred that his love for a righteous man will be even greater. It has been established that nearly all rabbinical pronouncements on God's goodness are accompanied by the conclusion: "If such is his love for sinners, how much greater will it be for the righteous."[43] That is why the inversion of this relationship in the statement that "the publican went down to his house justified rather than the Pharisee" is so significant. That there is more joy in heaven over one sinner that repents than over ninety-nine righteous means a fundamental break with Jewish soteriology because it removes the latter's foundation. And this is the point that the Jewish leaders did not tolerate of Jesus and where their opposition was most fundamental. For Jesus preaches the remission of sins as the only way of escape for anyone from God's wrath and bases man's deliverance from God's judgment exclusively on God's grace and not on any human merit.

It is true that in the gospel Jesus often speaks without

restraint of the *reward* that may be looked forward to by those who behave according to God's will.[44] And such not only in a negative or hypothetical sense, but not infrequently he holds this reward out to his disciples as something upon which they can rely. Thus, e.g., when he calls those people blessed who are reviled and persecuted for his sake, because "their reward will be great in heaven" (Matt. 5:11,12). He speaks of the reward that the heavenly Father will give those who do not perform their works of righteousness (alms, prayers, fasting) to be seen by men (Matt. 6:4,6,15). To those who do good without hoping for a reward or recompense he says, "Your reward will be great" (Luke 6:35). Whoever receives a prophet as a prophet and a righteous man as a righteous man, or shall give to drink unto one of these little ones a cup of cold water because he is a disciple, shall in no wise lose his reward (Matt. 10:40-42). Such passages might be multiplied. They explicitly speak of a reward and recompense. Moreover, it appears especially in the description of the divine judgment that there is an unbreakable correlation between that which man has done and what he will one day receive, though the word reward is not mentioned (cf. e.g., Matt. 24:45ff; 25:14-30; 25:31-46; 12:36,37). Consequently man should be aware of the eternal consequences of his words and actions from moment to moment (Matt. 7:13-27).[45]

This idea of recompense is very important in the gospel, and it would be destructive to the whole plan of Jesus' preaching if it were thought to be incompatible with the remission of sins, or if it should be deprived of its power for the sake of such remission.[46] But on the other hand it is perfectly clear that in Jesus' preaching salvation is not based on human merit and right, but on divine remission of sins and grace. This is not only apparent from the way in which Jesus judges sin, it is also clear from the idea of reward in the gospel itself.

There are two parables which are particularly significant in this connection, viz., that of Luke 17:7-10 (the reward of a slave), and that of Matthew 20:1-16 (the laborers in the vineyard). The former denies any claim to a reward, even to those who may have done everything they were in duty bound to do before God. Even they are mere *douloi achreioi*, i.e., useless, "miserable"[47] slaves. They are not called useless in every way, but as slaves of their lord they never could have a claim to gratitude or reward. Such is the formula of the thought, as crassly put as possible, that God is under no obligation whatever to man who is his creature. All good that is given by God to man is evidence of God's kindness, and is undeserved by man.

No less illustrative is the parable of the laborers in the vineyard. Its purpose is to reveal God's sovereignty in the granting of a reward. It is not concerned with the right of those who have worked the whole day, but, quite the other way, it rejects the delusion that a man would be entitled to God's particular acknowledgment if he had only done what had been demanded of him. Those who think of the relation to God in terms of a labor contract and on this basis raise objections to God's undeserved grace, are warned that "the last shall be first, and the first last" (Matt. 20:16, cf. 19:30). The parable vividly reminds us of the picture of the elder son in the parable of Luke 15:25ff.[48] In contrast to this God's loving kindness ("Is thine eye evil, because I am good?"—vs. 15) is set in the clearest light. On the great day of reckoning he is willing to grant his salvation also to those who would have no claim to it according to the standard of merit. The fact that, notwithstanding this, they get a reward proves that the Judaistic idea of reward has been broken down and that reward in this case can only be upon the basis of God's forgiving love. The idea of a reward as such has not thereby been eliminated. Still less is the threat of divine retribution cancelled or made relative. The reward, however, is seen only after there has first been remission of sins. Sharing in the salvation of the kingdom (to which all claims to a reward refer) is entirely a matter of God's gracious action and not of human claims. So, also with respect to the idea of a reward, the gospel of the kingdom means a complete break with the Judaistic schema of redemption.

In summary it can be stated that the preaching of God's gracious remission of guilt is the center and the basis of the gospel of the kingdom, especially because it is constantly contrasted by Jesus to the Jewish soteriology. The parables and stories in which this gospel of forgiveness finds its sublimest expression have often been rightly considered as the culmination-points of the whole gospel. Such parables and stories are, e.g., that of the prodigal son (Luke 15:11-32); the Pharisee and the publican (Luke 18:9-14); the story of the repentant sinner (Luke 7:36-50); the adulterous woman (John 8:1-11); and Zacchaeus (Luke 19:1-10).

Nowhere have the concepts of sin, repentance and divine grace been depicted more vividly and impressively than in the parable of the prodigal son: sin—as leaving the fellowship of the father, in living far away from the father, in the wasting of the father's goods; repentance—in the discovery of his own distress, in his consciousness of having sinned against the father and having lost all the rights of a child, in his return to the father; grace—in the father's awaiting of the son, in his pity for him, and in the joyful reception of the lost son into the father's house. And in the background is the elder son who is no less alienated from fellowship with the Father because of his own self-complacency and self-righteousness, but who has understood nothing of repentance, nor of mercy and remission of guilt. In an incomparable way this parable depicts what Paul is later to call: "the Spirit of bondage again to fear" and "the Spirit of adoption whereby we cry, abba, Father" (Romans 8:15).

And, also in agreement with Paul, it should not be lost sight of for a moment that this impressive preaching of the remission of sins and of divine grace do not contain timeless truths apart from any situation. But in accordance with the nature of Jesus' parables[49] and of the whole of the synoptic *kerygma, it bears the character of the preaching of the kingdom of heaven.* In other words, the antithetical motif in all of these parables and stories comes strongly to the fore and should not for a moment be separated from the predominant motif of fulfillment already mentioned previously. The decisive fact at the basis of the whole of Jesus' proclamation of salvation is the integrally Christological significance of such fulfillment, i.e., it is founded in Jesus' person and work as God's Christ. There is not a more serious misconception of Jesus' preaching than detaching its most central part, viz., the remission of sins, from the evangelical motif of fulfillment. This constitutes the unbridgeable chasm between the synoptic *kerygma* and the liberal and other modern interpretations of the gospel. They recognize in Jesus the proclaimer of the remission of sins and of God's Fatherhood, but they do not consider this communication of salvation to be based in the person and the work of Christ. Such a view can be expressed in various ways. Harnack maintains that the Father, and not the Son, belong to the content of the gospel.[50] K. Holl (although doing more justice to the redeeming character of the gospel than did the old liberal theology) is of the opinion that the parable of the prodigal son shows that Jesus thought of the will to forgive to be founded in God's being as such, entirely independent of "any time-situation."[51] And, finally, there are those who agree with the well-known formula that Jesus preached the remission of sins solely on the ground of repentance.[52] All the above pronouncements conceive of the remission of sins as a timeless reality, not connected with the coming of God's kingdom and with the person of Christ.

It is true that with this view there is the recognition of "another" soteriology occurring elsewhere in the gospel, namely, one which connects the remission of sins with Jesus' death. But, after all, there are only two passages which suggest this (viz., one on the ransom, Mark 10:45, and one about the Lord's Supper, Mark 14:22-25). They are said merely to prove the existence of more than one kind of soteriology within the gospel.[53] It is clear, however, that this view entirely dismisses not only the unity but also the character of the gospel as the preaching of the coming of the messianic kingdom of God. In this case the issue is not only the meaning of Jesus' expiatory death, but the Christological character of fulfillment of the whole of the gospel of the kingdom of heaven. If, however, this motif were the dominant basis of the gospel, the parable of the prodigal son, or the fifth petition in the Lord's Prayer would much rather have to be removed as a *corpus alienum* from the gospel, than considering the *Christological* character of the remission of sins as secondary and "foreign to the essence" of the original gospel.

In our opinion the one view as well as the other is based upon a fundamental misunderstanding of the gospel of the remission of sins. As the proclamation of salvation of the kingdom, this remission *eo ipso* bears the Christological character of fulfillment. This is very obvious in Jesus' first preaching in the synagogue of Capernaum, and in the story of the cure of a palsied man. Elsewhere Jesus especially maintains the character of the remission of sins as an act of divine grace without explicitly mentioning the soteriological situation dependent upon his own person. But it would be a very arbitrary conclusion to infer from this fact that here we are face to face with a gospel without Christ.

Rather, we must go even a step further. Because of the antithetical motif in Jesus' preaching of the remission of sins, he opposes the doctrine of meritoriousness advanced by the scribes and Pharisees, and derives redemption exclusively from divine grace. This motif should not be detached from the motif of fulfillment which is its deepest explanation. It is true that this preaching of the remission of sins is not in itself something new but the continuation of what is revealed about remission and satisfaction in the Old Testament. But there is something in Jesus' preaching and action with respect to sin and remission that is far ahead of the Old Testament proclamation of salvation. The measure of grace and the assurance of salvation are preached in a matchless way. This again applies to the parable of the prodigal son in particular, and to that of the Pharisee and the publican; it also applies to the emphasis with which the beatitudes proclaim salvation and to that which is said to Zacchaeus: "This day is salvation come to this house." All these passages are not (what is called) "explicitly-Christological." And yet the exuberance of Jesus' first proclamation of salvation, and the incomparable depiction of the absolutely gratuitous character of the remission of sins are direct consequences of the break-through of the new world *aeon* that has started. In other words, Jesus is able to proclaim the remission of sins in such a matchless way because he is not only the prophet, but also the king of the kingdom. He not only proclaims salvation, but is its bearer, and acquirer, and sharer of it with his followers.

That is why there is an intrinsic connection between Jesus' preaching of the remission of sins as an act of pure divine grace and all that in his self-revelation Jesus tells about his messianic authority and mission. That which Jesus preaches about remission of sins and redemption he proclaims by virtue of his divine mission as the Son of Man to whom all power and authority has been given. And at the same time he does so as one who has to carry out all that with which he has been commissioned and that which has been written concerning him as "the Servant of the Lord." Salvation, including the remission of sins, is vested in his person, in the carrying out of his mission, in his obedience to the divine will. That is why the two pronouncements, according to which redemption and remission of sins are dependent upon the ransom that Christ has to pay and upon the shedding of his blood, do not represent a different and later soteriology. But in an organic way they connect the significance of Christ's death with that of his life, and they reveal the deepest mystery of the assurance of salvation and of the remission of sins as the only basis of redemption. All this is founded in the sacrifice that Christ offers for those who are his, in his substitutive obedience as the ransom for many, in the shedding of his blood as the condition and basis of the new covenant.

The authenticity of the Christian *kerygma* depends upon

this unity in the proclamation of salvation in the synoptic gospels. The parable of the prodigal son, the petition for forgiveness of sins in the Lord's Prayer, the preaching of salvation in the Sermon on the Mount, and all that may be said to be equal to it, cannot be deprived of their meaning as the proclamation of the *kingdom* and of the Christological character coalescent with this. For then the root of the Christian *kerygma* would be cut through, and the gospel would be detached from the *history* of salvation thus to hang in the air and assume an idealistic content. But in the synoptic *kerygma* everything rests in the certainty of the fulfillment, in the messianic character of Jesus' preaching and miraculous power, and of his life and death. Remission of sins is remission *in Christ*. This is the heart of the original unadulterated gospel.

28. *The Fatherhood of God*

The idea of God's fatherhood is immediately connected with the thought of the remission of sins. These two are tied together so closely that the one cannot really be discussed apart from the other. The parable of the prodigal son with its two "focal points" of the remission of sins and the (divine) fatherhood proves this. Moreover, elsewhere these two are each other's complement (Matt. 6:14,15). It may be said that the remission of sins is the presupposition of[54] the Father-child relationship as applied in Jesus' preaching to God and his people. Conversely, God's fatherhood and the sonship (*hiothesia*) of the faithful are the realization of the communion in which the remission of sins is brought about. Especially in Matthew do we find a long series of pronouncements in which Jesus speaks to the disciples about God as "your Father," "your heavenly Father," "your Father who is in heaven" (cf. 5:16,45, 48; 6:1ff; 6:9; 6:14,15; 6:26,32; 7:11; 10:20; 10:29; 13:43; 18:14; 23:9). The word "your" usually denotes the plural, but sometimes also the singular (Matt. 6:4,6,18). In Luke the addition "heavenly," or "in heaven" is lacking (cf. 6:36; 11:2; 12:30,32, except in 11:13).[55] The address in the Lord's Prayer in Luke is simply "Father." In Mark we find God's name as "your Father who is in heaven" only in 11:25 (26).

In accordance with this, but far less frequently, we find the term "children" or "sons" (*huioi*) of God, either to denote the future state of bliss (Matt. 5:9; Luke 20:36), or a present relationship (Matt. 5:45; Luke 6:35). To this may be added what some parables say about the father and his children or sons, with reference to God and those who are his (Matt. 7:9; Luke 11:11; 15:11ff). So the number of passages in the synoptic gospels which speak of God's children or sons is rather small.

Just as in the case of the proclamation of the remission of sins, we must distinguish accurately what is new in such an indication of God as "your Father" (who is in heaven), or, in other words, what is the gospel of the kingdom in it. In itself the idea of God's fatherhood is not a matter that is found for the first time in Jesus' preaching. We will pass by in silence what might be quoted from non-Christian religions. For here also,[56] with respect to man's sonship to God, the real issue in non-Christian religions is always at bottom the deification of man ànd the deliverance of the divine in his essential being from his material and temporary life.[57]

Things are entirely different, however, with the Old Testament and later Judaism. In the Old Testament the nation of Israel repeatedly called "God's son" and the Israelites are accordingly called "God's sons" or "children" (cf., e.g., Ex. 4:22; Deut. 14:1; 32:6,18; Isaiah 1:2; 63:8ff,16; Jer. 3:19,31; 9:20; 31:20; Hos. 11:3ff; Mal. 2:10, etc.). In general this denotes the theocratic relation of the covenant in which Israel is related to Jahwe *as a people*. Nowhere in the Old Testament do we find an example in which the individual believer approaches God as his Father. But from passages as Psalm 73:15 and especially Psalm 103:13 it may be inferred that the peculiar privilege of Israel as a nation was also conceived of in a more personal sense.

In the later Jewish literature this individualization of sonship to God becomes very clear. The expression is no longer used exclusively with reference to the people or the king, but to the godly as individuals. This holds for the Pseudepigrapha and the Apocrypha, although here such a usage is comparatively rare. In rabbinical literature the name of Father to denote God is frequent, especially from the end of the first century onwards, mostly with the addition "who is in heaven." The address of the prayers, "our Father," also "my Father," can be pointed to in old Jewish prayers.[58] This does not detract from the fact that the spirit permeating all these writings is not one of certainty of salvation and religious confidence, but rather one of timidity and uncertainty (cf. Romans 8:15), and that for the manifestation of the divine fatherhood they looked forward to the great future.

Comparison between Judaistic usage and that of the synoptic gospels shows that in the latter the name of Father has a much more central and intimate meaning[59] and is entirely dominated by the thought of the certainty of salvation which is alien to Judaism (cf. Luke 12:32, etc.). Yet it would be a mistake to consider the specific character of Jesus' preaching of God's fatherhood as nothing but a deepening of the late Judaistic idea. That which imparts a unique significance to Jesus' preaching of the relation of Father-child is the *dimension of fulfillment* which is totally absent in Judaism.

No doubt the origin of the use of the name Father, in the gospel too, is to be found in the special covenant relationship between the Lord and his people Israel.[60] In the parable of the two sons (Matt. 21:28ff), not only the obedient son but also the disobedient is the Father's son, and in the parable of Luke 15, the issue is clearly the antithesis between the "sinners," "those who are lost," and the "righteous" *within* Israel. In both cases the Father-son relationship remains. This therefore shows[61] that, with respect to hostile and apostate Israel, Jesus in his preaching of salvation starts from the theocratic relationship of the covenant and derives one of his most powerful motives from it for Israel to repent.

Yet this use is not the rule. It is applied only rarely and then by way of a parable. Wherever Jesus speaks of "your Father in heaven," and the "heavenly Father," or of "children of the heavenly Father," he has in view the exclusive relationship between the Lord and those who will share in the bliss of the kingdom of heaven, and share in it now already. Here, too, it appears that the new covenant has begun with the kingdom of God, and that those to whom salvation is promised are the new people of God. But full stress, however, must be laid on this idea of *a community*. The salvation Jesus proclaims is the salvation of the people of the Lord, as we have discussed in great detail in the preceding chapter. And this also applies to God's Fatherhood. The whole gospel proves that this relation must not be thought of in an individualistic sense, i.e., it does not in the first place denote a relationship between God and individual human beings, but between the Lord and his people. This fact is not at all affected by the circumstance that membership with this people in the fullness of time is not due to natural descent from Israel but to personal conversion and faith in Jesus as the Christ. Sonship to God must be understood in a redemptive-historical sense. It is the realization of the promise of the new covenant, the continuation and fulfillment of the bond between the Lord and Israel.

This is the reason for the fact that Jesus nearly always speaks in the plural of "your (plural genitive pronoun) Father who is in heaven." No doubt this phrase does not exclude but rather includes a personal relationship between the Father and his children. This appears from those passages in which Jesus refers especially to the personal piety of the disciples (Matt. 6:4,6,18). Yet this singular form of reference occurs only sporadically. Nearly always sonship to God is indicated as the relationship between the people of the Lord as a whole and their God. The most characteristic instance is found in the Lord's Prayer which begins with "Our Father." This does not mean that it is forbidden for each believer to call upon

God as *his* Father when he turns to him after having shut the door of his closet (Matt. 6:6). Nevertheless, the prayer that Jesus teaches his disciples suggests in its tone a plurality, and is determined by its form of address "Our Father." This is entirely in agreement with the fact that Jesus *as the Christ* empowers his disciples to pray like this. They are restored to communion with God as the new church, the redeemed *people of the Messiah.*[62] Jesus himself indicates the nature of this communion by calling those who do God's will his brother and sister and mother (Mark 3:35) and, especially from the idea of God's fatherhood, does he very emphatically hold his disciples responsible for the communion of God's children (Matt. 18:10-14).[63]

The specific and new trait in this Father-child relationship preached by Jesus is therefore not to be sought in its formal indication or its individualization, and only partly in the deepening of this relationship. It is above all to be sought in the redemptive-historical situation in which he proclaims it as an actual reality. In the Old Testament this relationship had only a provisional significance (cf. Hos. 1:10; 2 Cor. 6:18), but with the coming of the kingdom it has been fulfilled.[64] This is explicitly proclaimed in the beatitudes, in which the content of the salvation of the kingdom is described in the words about the peace-makers who "will be called children of God." In this connection sonship has a purely eschatological meaning. The "being called" is not the same thing as "being." It indicates *publicity,* recognition by all (cf. Romans 8:23). The same thing is meant in Luke 20:36, which says of the blessed "for they are the children of God, being the children of the resurrection." It is true that the phrase "sons of God" has an absolute sense ("are," not "are called") but it is pregnant with meaning. The full glory of the children of God (cf. Matt. 13:43) is meant here, as also appears from the causative clause, "being the children of the resurrection," i.e., in the whole manner of their existence as determined by the resurrection.[65]

For the rest, it is clear that the privilege of sonship to God is not merely a matter of the future.[66] Even now Jesus calls those who accept his words the children of the heavenly Father (Matt. 5:45), and he again and again calls God their Father (Matt. 5:16,45,48, etc.). In sonship to God, the present and the future of salvation are one, they only differ modally. The real and deepest explanation of this relationship between God and those to whom the kingdom of heaven is promised lies in the person of Jesus himself; or to put it more accurately, *in Jesus' own relationship with the Father*. These two kinds of relationships, viz., that of Jesus and that of the believers to the Father, must not be identified. The former is not an absolutization of the latter, as liberal theology tried to maintain for a long time.[67] This needs no further demonstration, since a better insight to the super-natural character of the Christological *kerygma* of the synoptics has steadily been gaining ground.[68] Jesus never speaks of "our Father," so as to identify himself with his disciples, but distinguishes between "my Father" and "your Father." The former expresses the exclusiveness of his Sonship which had been proclaimed when he entered upon his duties (Matt. 3:17 and parallel passages), later confirmed (Matt. 17:5) and therefore always maintained by him as a special privilege (cf., e.g., Matt. 17:24-27; the payment of the *didrachmas*).

On the other hand Jesus is *the Mediator* with respect to the sonship of believers (Matt. 11:27), "No man knoweth the Son, but the Father, neither knoweth any man the Father, save the Son, and he to whomsoever the Son will reveal him." Knowledge of the Father, therefore, depends upon the Son. From the character of the gospel it follows that such knowledge is not merely intellectual, but creates a personal relationship[69] (cf. Matt. 7:23). This revelation of the Father by the Son is, therefore, based on the whole of Jesus' work. It is indissolubly connected with all that he accomplishes for the remission of sins of all those who are his.[70] This clearly shows that the whole of the salvation of the kingdom, and also sonship to

God, can be a reality only if Jesus is the Son of God, the One who has been given authority, and who is the Servant of the Lord. It is entirely determined by the Christological character of the gospel as fulfillment. So sonship is a sheer impossibility outside of faith in Jesus as the Christ sent by God. According to the modern interpretation of the gospel, Jesus meant God's fatherhood to be a natural relationship,[71] needing only man's awareness by "reflection upon" the fact. But such a view is a radical misconception of the meaning of the gospel.

The above exposition makes clear that *fatherhood* and *kingship* in Jesus' preaching are not two different trends; nor can the conception of God as king and judge be considered as less important than that of God as Father. It is certainly improper to assign a lower rank to the former view.[72] To see this point it is hardly necessary to recall all that Jesus has proclaimed in all kinds of pronouncements and parables about God as king and Lord, to whom we are accountable, whose slaves we are, whose "house" must be kept, etc.[73] For this fatherhood itself, in the way Jesus speaks of it in the gospel, is entirely determined also by the idea of God's kingship (and vice versa). With respect to God's fatherly care for the temporal life of his children, we shall show this in a separate section.[74] Here we wish only to indicate the general basic relationship between these two conceptions.

The fact that from the outset God's fatherhood denotes a relation which coalesces with the theocratic relation of the covenant, indicates the close connection between the two. God's fatherhood over Israel consisted in the fact that he was Israel's king. And this connection is again and again found in Jesus' preaching. Jesus teaches his disciples to pray to the *Father* that his name be hallowed and that his *kingdom* may come. The salvation of God's people lay in the fact that he would fully reveal and sanctify himself as king. The good pleasure of the Father towards his children is his giving them the kingdom (Luke 12:32). In their Father's kingdom the righteous will shine like the sun (Matt. 13:43). This is the relationship between the theocentric and the soteriological aspect of Jesus' preaching of the kingdom. Instead of depreciating God's kingship as less essential or less "evangelical" than his fatherhood, we must say that the latter has been entirely included in the dynamics of the former for the present as well as the future. God's fatherhood is not a general, immobile thought, a timeless idea, but it is the fatherhood of him who manifested himself as king. The idea of fatherhood is everywhere surrounded by the forces issuing from the consummation of all things; it is not at rest but is full of eschatological movement. It is involved in the tensions ruling the world and history, and originating from the fulfilling divine action; in a word, it is the fatherhood which is proclaimed to the people of the Lord as the long-expected bliss and deliverance of the kingdom. This imparts to the words "who is in heaven" an especial accent and a particular pregnancy in the gospel, although they are not new in themselves. These words denote—as also, e.g., in some Jewish prayers—the sublimity and the transcendence of God's fatherhood which excludes any thought of familiarity and any earthly thought of his heavenly majesty. In the light of the coming of the kingdom all emphasis is laid on heaven as the abode from which the Father comes and works, and from which also Jesus Christ has been "sent" and has "come." There God's will is being done now already as it will one day be done on earth (Matt. 6:10). There salvation is kept and guarded as a "reward" and "treasure" (Matt. 6:1,20), and the names of the children of God have been "registered" there (Luke 10:20). Because of the coming of the kingdom, heaven is not only the place of the divine transcendence and inaccessibility, it is also the center of the Father's divine work of salvation which has been set in motion and is being continued and directed to the consummation of all things. This shows that God's fatherhood is, as it were, full of and laden with the power of his kingship. The two do not represent timeless ideas (the former the idea of nearness, the latter that of transcendence), but their indissoluble

unity implies that God's fatherhood derives its special significance from the great fulfilling events of the salvation identified
by Jesus in his preaching with the coming of the *kingdom.*

On the other hand God's kingship is determined by his
fatherhood. This fact, too, sheds a clearer light on the purport
of the gospel. As to the future, amidst all the apocalyptic
events and phenomena announcing themselves on the horizon
of the coming kingdom, God will view his people as *his children,* he will comfort them, show them his face and have mercy
upon them (Matt. 5:4,7,8,9). And for the present, too, the
same fatherhood imparts to the gospel of the kingdom a tender,
trustworthy and winning tone. For God's fatherhood is depicted in human fatherhood and is repeatedly represented by
Jesus in the image of an earthly father (Matt. 7:9-11; Luke
11:11-13; 15:11ff). And this is done in a way that expresses
the communion and the loving care of God for his children.
God stoops down to his children and speaks to them intimately.

Whoever comes to God need not approach him in a cring-
ing way and with the servile fear of a heathen calling to his
god. For the Father "knows" everything before we pray to
him (Matt. 6:7,8). He "knows" the needs of the simple
earthly life of his children (Matt. 6:32), for he also takes care
of the flowers and the birds. He will not fail them in what
he gives to them on the table of life, just as an earthly father
will not give his child a stone for a loaf, or a snake for a fish
(Matt. 7:9ff; Luke 11:11ff). It is he apart from whose will
not even a sparrow falls to the ground (Matt. 10:29), and
who, as a true father, is especially concerned about "the little
ones" (Matt. 18:14). In all this the world and history embracing
preaching of the kingdom assumes a form which does not keep
aloof from the most trivial and commonplace things of life,
but reveals itself as a preaching of God's fatherly mercy capable of fathoming the hidden distress of every human being.
This unity of God's fatherhood and kingship in Jesus' preaching constitutes the inexhaustible richness of the gospel. We
shall discuss its different facets in what follows.

29. The Fulfillment of the Father's Will

The proclamation of the salvation of the kingdom of heaven, the remission of sins, and God's fatherhood are indissolubly bound up with the duty of doing the Father's will. The Sermon on the Mount is the great example of this. The beatitudes are followed by the commandments. The Sermon on the Mount also shows the importance of the commandments in Jesus' preaching. Starting from Matthew 5:13, the whole Sermon on the Mount is one impressive exhortation to do "good works" (Matt. 5:16), to do "justice" (5:20; 6:1; 6:33), to fulfill "the law and the prophets" (5:17-48; 7:12), to go through "the narrow gate" and upon "the narrow path" (7:13,14), to bear "fruit" (7:16-20), to do the Father's will (7:21), and to "hear and do" Jesus' words (7:24-27, cf. also Luke 6:27-49). We are confronted here with the positive aspect of repentance as it was also preached by John the Baptist when he spoke of "bringing forth fruits meet for repentance" (Matt. 3:8 and parallel passages), and as it is required and indicated in all manner of ways in Jesus' preaching, again and again summarized in the commandment of radical love and self-sacrifice (Matt. 10:37-39; Luke 14:26-27), of taking Jesus' "yoke" upon us (Matt. 11:29), of self-denial (Matt. 16:24ff, and parallel texts; 18:1-5, and parallels), of doing the great commandment (Matt. 22:34-40, parallels), and of love of one's neighbor (Luke 10:29-37, etc.).

This is not yet the place to enter into the content of Jesus' commandments in a detailed way. Our present goal is to ascertain their position within the scope of Jesus' preaching, and to determine in what relation the promulgation of God's demand stands with respect to the remission of sins and God's fatherhood. In other words, our present subject is to determine the relationship between the indicatives preaching God's work of salvation and the imperatives calling man to action.[75]

In evaluating this extremely important subject we are confronted with different conceptions: a) According to some, Jesus' entire preaching of the kingdom is essentially ethical and the salvation he preaches is an ethical renewal. The indicatives of salvation are identical with the imperatives. The new "righteousness" is the center of Jesus' preaching. This view, advanced especially by Ritschl's theology, finds its most pregnant expression, as far as the New Testament "theology" is concerned, in Harnack's statement: "The whole gospel may be represented as an ethical message without depriving it of its value." ("*Man kann es (das ganze Evangelium) als eine ethische Botschaft darstellen, ohne es zu entwerten*").[76] b) According to others Jesus' promises of salvation should be sharply distinguished from his commandments. The imperative ranks first. The fulfillment of Jesus' commandments is the prerequisite of the entry into the kingdom, and in the scope of his preaching it has no other function. According to these authors the whole of Jesus' preaching operates within the Jewish schema of redemption with its "do this and thou shalt live." Such a view is especially found with those who conceive of the *basileia**, (i.e., kingdom), exclusively in a future-eschatological sense, e.g., J. Weiss, Albert Schweitzer, E. Peterson, H. Windisch, and others.[77] There are others again who start from an entirely different soteriology in the gospel, but also deny the presence of the kingdom in man's ethical conduct. They consider the obedience demanded by Jesus exclusively as a preparation for entry into the kingdom.[78]

A formally related view but with a radically different purport is that of those authors who also give priority to the imperative of Jesus' commandments, but deny to them any other meaning than that of convincing man of his moral powerlessness and of teaching him to seek another kind of righteousness than his own. These writers assume that, especially in the Sermon on the Mount, Jesus wants to bring home to his hearers the *impossibility* of fulfilling God's will. In particular they refer to Matthew 5:20: "For I say unto you, that except your righteousness shall exceed the righteousness of the scribes and Pharisees, ye shall in no case enter into the kingdom of heaven," and to 5:48, "Be ye therefore perfect, even as your Father which is in heaven is perfect." These passages are supposed to be a particularly clear evidence of the impossibility of Jesus' demands. This view has been defended especially by Lutheran theologians.[79] d) Bultmann's conception deserves separate mention. He, too, calls the fulfillment of God's will the prerequisite of participating in the salvation of the kingdom. However, he wants to vindicate the unity of the ethical and the eschatological preaching. The kingdom of heaven is an actual reality now insofar as it calls man to repent, and confronts him with the great "decision" (*Entscheidung*). The commandments serve no other purpose. At bottom they are supra-ethical. Just like the preaching of the kingdom, the commandments show man his "present" as the hour of decision before God. So in a sense exactly opposite to that of (*a*) above, the imperatives coalesce with the indicatives.[80]

There is no denying that those who qualify Jesus' commandments as the proclamation of the *conditions* for entering into the coming kingdom can, regardless of what presuppositions they assume, appeal to important and numerous data in the gospel. This comes to the fore especially in the Sermon on the Mount. That is why Windisch characterizes the Sermon on the Mount as the "conditions of admission" (*Einlassbedingungen*), or, by way of analogy, what had to be done to be admitted into the sanctuary (*thoroth-d'entrée*).[81] The whole of Jesus' call to repentance, so forceful already from the very beginning, as a matter of fact bears the very obvious character of an exhortation *to be prepared* for what is coming. And though the Sermon on the Mount may, in a primary sense be addressed to those who have already repented,[82] thus to unfold further in a positive way the demand of repentance, it is none the less true that in the Sermon on the Mount the concept of conditionality also occupies a very important place. Thus in Matthew 5:20, "Except your righteousness shall exceed the righteousness of the scribes and Pharisees, ye shall in no case enter into the kingdom of heaven." It is clear that the carrying out of the commandments cannot be identified with the coming of the kingdom. The same thing is found in all those passages that exhort us to obey in view of the coming judgment (5:22,25,29), or in which there is a reference to the reward given by the Father (6:4ff). Especially in the epilogue to the Sermon on the Mount, the entry into the kingdom is again and again made dependent upon the doing of Jesus' words (7:13,14,19,21,24-27).

This concept of conditionality is not only characteristic of the Sermon on the Mount. We come upon it repeatedly in Jesus' preaching. There are separate pronouncements, such as Matthew 18:3: "Except ye be converted and become as little children, ye shall not enter into the kingdom of heaven" (cf. 19:14). Moreover, this is seen especially in the story of the rich young ruler (Matt. 19:16-26, and parallel passages), in which Jesus makes entry into life dependent upon keeping the commandments (verse 17), points out the treasure in heaven that the young man will receive if he sells his earthly possessions (verse 21), and finally speaks of the difficulty for a rich man to enter into heaven (vss. 23,24). All these pronouncements are clearly concerned with the fulfillment of certain conditions. Equally impressive in the parable of the dishonest steward is the emphasis on the significance of good works for entry into the kingdom (Luke 16:1-9), and in the words added to it about the management of earthly goods. On the one hand they contain the warning that at the great settlement of the accounts on judgment day, "the books will not tally," as was true in the case of the steward. Then the friends that have been made with the help of the mammon of unrighteousness at the time previous to the settlement will be all-important (Luke 16:9). This is the meaning of the "wise forethought" that Jesus praises[83] in the dishonest steward's conduct and which he recommends to his disciples (vs. 8). The "friends" thus made are those to whom we have done good with our earthly possessions. This will be very important in the last judgment, for the text continues as follows, "that they may receive you into everlasting habitations." The "they" mentioned here may either be the friends thus made who are represented as having already died and being in possession of an "everlasting habitation" in which they welcome their former benefactors,[84] or the word *dexoontai* may be rendered by "One will receive you" and refer to God himself.[85] In both cases the issue is the decisive significance of our moral conduct on earth for our entry into the kingdom. The same thought is expressed in a very pregnant way by the *māshāl* (or enigmatical saying) added to the parable (16:10-12): "He that is faithful in that which is least is faithful also in much. If therefore ye have not been faithful in the unrighteous mammon, who will commit to your trust the true riches? If therefore ye have not been faithful in that which is another man's, who shall give you that which is your own?" By "that which is least" and "another man's," as well as "the unrighteous mammon" is meant that which is temporarily at the disposal of man on earth. It is in contrast to "the much," "the true riches" and "your own" as an indication of what we hope to receive from God for all eternity. Again we find the thought that future gifts are dependent upon the way in which we have used our earthly goods. The dependence of entry into the kingdom upon fulfillment of certain conditions is nowhere so impressively stated as in the description of the judgment of the nations which the Son of Man will pronounce at his coming in glory (Matt. 25:31-46). The basis of separation between the sheep and the goats is that of "the King's" identifying himself with "the least of his brethren," and of his judgment in accordance with the sympathy shown him in this respect. The almost literal repetition in a negative form of the words "For I was an hungered, and ye gave me meat," etc., is intended, as it were, to imprint upon the mind that which will be essential on the day of judgment: it is not saying "Lord, Lord," or having acted in Jesus' name and done many wonderful works by his power (cf. Matt. 7:22; Luke 13:26); but it is simple obedience to his commandments. And again and again Jesus shows that the sentence pronounced at the last judgment will be different from what might have been expected on the basis of human relationships and privileges (cf. Luke 13:30; 14:11; 16:15, etc.).

So there can be little doubt that Jesus considered the carrying out of God's will as the condition and the preparation for entry into the kingdom of heaven. But *in what sense* is this to be taken? There can be no question here of a Jewish belief in meritoriousness, for this already follows from what has been said above about the position of the remission of sins in Jesus' proclamation of salvation. It is now necessary to discuss the opinion mentioned above under (c), namely, that Jesus did not mean such conditions in a positive but in a hypothetical sense. He wished to lead his disciples indirectly to the recognition that in the way of the fulfillment of the law they could never enter into the kingdom, and to open their eyes to a "better" kind of righteousness.

This conception is much nearer in agreement with the gospel than that of Windisch and others insofar as it takes seriously Jesus' profound view of sin. It is far from basing Jesus' moral demand on a perfectionist conception of man and lays great emphasis on the remission of sins as the most indispensable and central element of his preaching. At the same time it sets forth the evangelical thought (cf. Matt. 19:25,26) that anyone who takes Jesus' commandments sufficiently serious must arrive at the conclusion that nobody on earth has accomplished them or is able to do so. But the question is not whether Jesus' commandments do not or should not also induce man to be humbly repentant and feel his guilt. The real question is whether or not the demand explained by Jesus for doing God's will also has *a positive* significance, and if the obedience demanded by him is not really the condition for entering into the kingdom of heaven. In our opinion this question can only be answered in the affirmative. For, apart from other considerations which make unacceptable the taking of an exclusively negative attitude toward Jesus' commandments,[86] the most decisive argument against this view is the fact that Jesus not only posits the doing of God's will as a condition and a preparation for entry into the kingdom, but also preaches it as *a gift* belonging to the salvation of the kingdom proclaimed by him. And besides, he speaks of this gift, neither hypothetically nor as something irrational, but in a very positive sense.

The truth that obedience to God's commandments is a

gift belonging to the salvation of the kingdom is already clearly implied in *the first three petitions of the Lord's Prayer.* The last of them explicitly mentions the doing of God's will (Matt. 6:10) as a gift that must be asked for of God. This petition does not merely express agreement with God's *decree* or resignation to his will, but much rather the longing that what God *requires* from man may be done on earth as it is in heaven. At present God's will as expressed in his commandments is not yet being done on account of all that opposes God on earth. Both redemption and ethics are implied in this "will of God" (*thelēma*).[87] The same thing is found in the first and second petitions with respect to the hallowing of God's name and the coming of his kingdom. All emphasis is laid on what *God* is doing. May he sanctify himself, i.e., prove himself to be God before the world and to his people (cf. Lev. 10:3; Deut. 20:13). The factual content of this petition is nothing else than the coming of God's kingdom. This does not detract from the fact that this all-embracing statement also has an ethical meaning. For God also sanctifies himself in the life of his people. That is why these petitions are closely connected with Jesus' commandments. They are intended for the realization of the sanctification of God and the coming of his kingdom in the obedience of his children.[88] This obedience is at the same time qualified as something that must be given by God and prayed for by us. The doing of God's will is also one of the permanent elements in the Old Testament prophecy of salvation (cf. Ezek. 36:23,27; Jer. 24:7; 31:33; 32:39) and, naturally, belongs to the perfection of God's kingdom. *It is the salvation of the Lord for his people that he makes them different human beings and writes his commandments in their hearts, and, because of this, obedience to God's will can be effectively asked.*

This viewpoint is no less central in the Sermon on the Mount than the above-mentioned motif of conditions. It is the starting-point of all the commandments in Matthew 5:13-16. For in close connection with the beatitudes we find here the *ethical indicative of salvation:* "Ye are the salt of the earth, . . .

Ye are the light of the world." The reason is clear, for they belong to the kingdom of heaven. This is their advantage over "men" (verse 16), and in this they have a preserving (salt) and a redeeming (light) significance for mankind and the world. Their advantage is not a gift of an exclusively objective nature consisting in the promise, but is a new station in life into which they have been transposed, in which they have become different human beings, have had their hearts, their being, changed. That is why they are capable of doing good works by virtue of the gift granted them. These indicatives are connected with the imperatives that follow: those who are the light of the world and the salt should effectuate the working of salt and light in their "good works," i.e., in their ethical fulfillment of God's will. That is why the characterization of the commandments of the Sermon on the Mount as "conditions of entry" (*Einlaszbedingungen*) or "*thoroth-d'entrée*" (Windisch) is one-sided, to say the least. Exactly because of the dominant position of Matthew 5:13-16 in the Sermon on the Mount,[89] the good works Jesus demands from his disciples must in the first place be viewed as the result and as the manifestation of the salvation of the kingdom in which they participate in Christ. So, too, Bultmann's conception of the commandments, as of the preaching of salvation itself, as having no other significance than to place man in the position of decision (*Entscheidung*), appears to be insufficient.[90] Jesus' commandments not only place man *in* the crisis but also *beyond* it. The Sermon on the Mount especially, mentions, not only a continually repeated decisive moment of conversion, but even more, a continuous and persevering life proceeding from such a decision, of the "shining light," the "doing of God's works," the "doing of justice," the "being perfect," the "showing of one's sonship," the "doing of the Father's will." "The new man of the Sermon on the Mount is not just a beautiful dream nor merely a divine promise. . . . The new man of the Sermon on the Mount . . . is present reality." ("*Der neue Mensch der Bergpredigt ist also kein schöner Traum und auch nicht ein bloszes göttliches Versprechen. . . . Der neue Mensch der Berg-predigt . . . ist gegenwärtige Wirklichkeit."*)[91]

In perfect agreement with this, the doing of God's will is repeatedly described as the *counterpart* of the salvation of the kingdom. The structure of the Sermon on the Mount already proves this: first the beatitudes, then the command-ments. And it can also be pointed out with respect to the separate blessings of the kingdom. The first example is the remission of sins. On the basis of the blessing given in the remission of sins, God demands from the man thus blessed with this grace his readiness also to forgive. Moreover, this willingness is also represented as the fruit of the grace of God that has been given him. The clearest case is that of the story of the penitent woman and the parable of the two debtors in connection with it (Luke 7:36-50). The teaching of both is that only *those* people have true *love* who also know the bliss of *forgiveness*. "Jesus brings the remission of sins, and in a man who has experienced such remission there will be released an entirely new abundance of overflowing love." (*"Jesus bringt die Vergebung der Sünden, und wer diese Vergebung erfahren hat, in dem wird eine ganz neue, über-quellende Liebe entbunden."*)[92] This is why Jesus says of the woman who was a sinner (vs. 47): "Her sins which are many, are forgiven; for she loved much." "For" does not indicate the *ground* of the remission of sins,[93] but its *proof*. This also appears from the preceding parable of the two debtors and from what follows: "but to whom little is forgiven, the same loveth little."[94] The absolute use of the verb "to love," which does not occur elsewhere in the synoptic gospels, emphasizes the character, the qualification of this love all the more strongly: it is the love that proceeds from forgiveness and is entirely dominated by it. In other passages, too, Jesus very clearly points to this connection. Thus, e.g., in the parable of the debtor and his creditor (Matt. 18), in the statement about forgiving (Matt. 6:14,15), and in the fifth petition of the Lord's Prayer. These passages especially emphasize the indispensability of human readiness to forgive if there is to be any participation in the divine forgiveness. This is again an instance of the idea of condition. Yet this is not saying that human action precedes God's work of salvation. The parable of Matthew 18 derives the former from the latter. And also the words of the fifth petition "as we forgive our debtors" do not point to human forgiveness as the ground but as the necessary accompaniment of divine forgiveness.

So the remission of sins as a divine act of salvation in the coming of the kingdom is of *primary* importance, and human readiness to forgive our debtors is its result. This truth can hardly be expressed more correctly than in the *Heidelberg Catechism's* explanation of the fifth petition: "even as we feel this evidence of thy grace in us, that it is our firm resolution from the heart to forgive our neighbor."[95]

The nature of the relationship between the salvation of the kingdom of heaven proclaimed by Christ and doing God's will is even more clearly revealed *with respect to sonship to God*. Very emphatically good works are spoken of as *the manifestation of the sonship of believers*. This is done especially in Matthew 5:45,48 (cf. Luke 6:35,36). There the disciples are exhorted to love their enemies, with the motivation being "that ye may be the children of your Father who is in heaven." It is clear, especially in the verses that follow in which the disciples are exhorted to do as their Father does (to be perfect[96] as he is perfect) that sonship is not to be considered here as a future goal[97] but as a present state. So, loving the enemy is *evidence* of the communion in which the disciples live with their heavenly Father. Sonship to God (a gift of the kingdom) thus appears also to have a moral meaning. From this side also "the priority of the divine work"[98] is expressed in the obedience of the disciples to do God's will. Sonship to God is a gift of the fulfillment accomplished in Christ, and is not only a new redeemed relationship but also "a communion of will" with God.[99]

From the above we may infer that the great imperative

of the gospel and what belongs to it, as well as the indicative proclaiming the salvation of the kingdom, is granted as a gift of God and is again and again ascribed to God's redemptive action. Even the ethical message itself occurs in the gospel in the form of the proclamation of salvation (Matt. 5:13). This is and remains the great element of truth in Harnack's conception mentioned above (sub *a*). Thus it now becomes clear to us how we may consider the relationship between the two dominant viewpoints of Jesus' ethical preaching, viz., that of condition and that of gift. For the very reason that the salvation of the Lord embraces not only divine but also human action, the human aspect may be subsumed under all the categories of salvation (viz., that of fulfillment, the remission of sins, sonship to God), and conversely, the divine salvation may be subsumed under all ethical categories (as a reward, as dependent upon ethical conditions, as the destination of "the narrow path," etc.). They are both inseparable, the one always fits into the other and forms its counterpart, as it were. They do not nullify each other, however, nor is the character of the one sacrificed to that of the other. The fact that nobody will enter into the kingdom of heaven unless he does the will of the Father does not mean that the gift of the kingdom is not solely dependent upon God's gracious action. And conversely, God's gift of grace does not render fictitious human responsibility with respect to God's will, nor does it deprive the commandment of its character of a condition. Here we are confronted with a relationship which is not fathomable by human understanding, namely, the relationship between the all-embracing (including human action) divine work of salvation and human responsibility with respect to salvation. Jesus' preaching leaves both aspects of this relationship intact and does not formulate a reflective observation about it. Yet it is clear that there is here no question of a correlation in a sense of two equivalent entities that correspond with each other, nor of what might be called a "dialectical paradoxical synthesis of two antinomous theses: man must do something although God has already done everything." (*"Eine dialektisch-paradoxe Zusammenschau der beiden antinomischen Thesen: Der Mensch soll etwas tun, obgleich Gott schon alles getan hat."*)[100] As the preaching of *the kingdom, as the proclamation of Father's will, all the imperatives of the gospel are always founded in the great indicative that the time has been fulfilled and the salvation has come.*

In Jesus' commandments, also, it is God himself who sanctifies his name and saves his people. Good works issue from his sovereign fatherly decree and from his powerfully effective fatherly communion. The radical demand, the positing of conditions, the promise of a reward, proceed from the Father's will of salvation and are borne by it. In the form in which these things are included in the gospel they belong to the new covenant that has begun with the coming of Christ, to the gift of sonship in the kingdom of heaven (cf. Jer. 31:33).

Nonetheless, the imperative has an extremely *critical function* in the gospel, not infrequently for the disciples, too, for it is often accompanied by the threats of judgment and reprobation and thus seems to cast a doubt on the certainty of the indicative of salvation. Thus, e.g., in the parable of Matthew 18:23ff (on the remission of sins) which ends in the master's anger with the slave so that the latter is delivered to the tormentors till he should pay all that was due to the master. Jesus draws the following conclusion from the parable: "So likewise shall my heavenly Father do also unto you, if ye from your hearts forgive not every one his brother their trespasses" (Matt. 18:34,35).

To this pronouncement many others might be added (cf. Matt. 5:13ff; 7:22; 24:42).[101] Still, this motif cannot detract anything from the soteriological character of Jesus' preaching and the fulfillment of God's will as a gift of the kingdom. It is rather an impressive exhortation of love not to be mistaken but to put oneself to the test of sonship by the doing of God's will. The latter is the criterion of the former. In this sense the following words are also applicable: "For by thy words thou shalt be justified, and by thy words thou shalt be condemned" (Matt. 12:37).

These words and others denote without doubt the fulfillment of God's will as the norm and standard of sonship to God and of entry into the bliss of the coming kingdom. But for the carrying out of the divine will man is by Jesus' imperatives referred to the grace of God and not to his human self. This is the difference between Jesus and the Pharisees, between the gospel and "the spirit of bondage again to fear" (Rom. 8:15; Gal. 4:24). This is also the new element, namely, that of fulfillment in doing God's will. It is not this will which is new (although given its most radical meaning in Jesus' commandments);[102] nor is it the law as the order of grace and as God's gift to his people. But the new feature is God's inauguration of the new covenant, his writing his law in the hearts of his people. He himself undertakes the fulfillment of the conditions of the covenant (Jer. 31:33).[103] This is why repentance and doing of righteousness, as well as withstanding the temptation of Satan (Luke 22:32), are acts of *faith* (Matt. 21:32; Mark 11:31, cf. Mark 1:15). For, indeed, the principal part of the law consists of justice, mercy, and faith[104] (Matt. 23:23), i.e., in the certainty of God's help and salvation.

Everything is concentrated in our relation to Christ in whom God remits our sins and in whom he is a Father to his people. This already follows from the fact that the fulfillment of the law is the fruit of these gifts of grace. In more than one passage this thought is expressed in a direct way. The first instance of this is in Christ's word of judgment (Matt. 7:23): And then I will profess unto them, I never knew you: depart from me, ye that work iniquity." This, "I never knew you," is all-important.[105] It does not denote an intellectual kind of knowledge, but "recognition," "accepting as his own," "election."[106] It is not in a man's appeal to Jesus (Lord, Lord) on his own authority, but in Christ's taking him into his fellowship, that we must find the explanation and the criterion of doing righteousness. Outside of this fellowship there is no obedience, however strong a claim for a reward may be made because of works supposed to have been done "in his name." Only those who are known by him in the sense of this fellowship will receive the grace of the doing of the Father's will (cf. Matt. 13:50).

There is no passage in which this truth is revealed in a more central and glorious way than in the well-known words of the Saviour in Matthew 11:28-30: "Come unto me all ye that labour and are heavy laden, and I will give you rest. Take my yoke upon you and learn of me; for I am meek and lowly in heart: and ye shall find rest unto your souls. For my yoke is easy, and my burden is light."

The "weary" and the "heavy laden" are not those who are bent down by the weight of life or by the burden of their sins, but, as appears from the words "my yoke" and "my burden," they are those who are oppressed by the heavy demands of the Pharisaical conception of the law (cf. Matt. 23:4).[107] They do not know any rest or relief, i.e., they are haunted by uncertainty and fear. For they cannot bear this yoke, this burden (Acts 15:10), and so they lack peace (Jer. 6:16). In contrast to this state of things, Jesus mentions his "yoke" and his "burden." These words are the standing phrases for what one must *do*, i.e., for Jesus' commandments. This yoke is easy and this burden is light, not because these commandments are no heavy demands to man's self-love and self-assertion (cf. Matt. 7:13ff), but because it is *Jesus* who teaches them. For he is "meek and lowly in heart." He himself is one of the "poor in spirit," "the meek," to whom he preaches the gospel. He is the Lawmaker, but he is also entirely dependent upon God, rejected by men, on his way to the cross.[108] Those who learn God's will from him and accept it, are, consequently, not only dependent upon his word as a *command*, but are also called to fellowship with his person for its fulfillment. He it is who gives those who live in his fellowship the rest, the assurance of salvation. For he teaches them how to bear this burden in their new relation to God as children of their heavenly

Father, because he himself bears this burden as the one that has been sent by the Father. Therefore, all the commandments, as well as the warning not to be mistaken, and the threat of the last judgment, at bottom only point to Jesus himself. In his fellowship the salvation of the kingdom is received and the "yoke of the kingdom"[109] becomes easy. For through his lowliness and meekness he has laid the foundation of the new covenant in which God writes his law in the hearts of his own.[110] What is true of the remission of sins and of sonship to God also holds for the carrying out of the Father's will. The new element of fulfillment is not to be sought in the thing as such, but in fellowship with the person of him who demands it. Together the indicative and the imperative denote the salvation that has begun with Christ's coming and work for his people.

Finally the question arises whether or not the gospel of the kingdom contains any further details about the subjective, or if you will, *the anthropological presuppositions* of the fulfillment of God's will. This question is not easy to answer. There is no denying that there are such presuppositions. Again and again Jesus teaches his disciples and the multitude that doing God's will is not only an actual deed or decision, but is founded in man's *being*, in his state. Thus, e.g., in the frequent mention of a tree and its fruit (Matt. 7:16-20; Luke 6:43-45; Matt. 12:33-35, cf. also Matt. 21:43): " . . . every good tree bringeth forth good fruit. A good tree cannot bring forth evil fruit, neither can a corrupt tree bring forth good fruit" (Matt. 7:17ff). " . . . a good man out of the good treasure of his heart bringeth forth that which is good; and an evil man out of the evil treasure of his heart bringeth forth that which is evil; for of the abundance of the heart his mouth speaketh" (Luke 6:45). " . . . O generations of vipers, how can ye, being evil, speak good things? For out of the abundance of the heart the mouth speaketh. A good man out of the good treasure of the heart bringeth forth good things: and an evil man out of the evil treasure bringeth forth evil things" (Matt. 12:34,35).

Elsewhere these fruits are called the evidence of conversion (Matt. 3:8, and parallel passages). In the above they are considered as characteristic of the inner state of man[111] and are called its necessary ("cannot do otherwise") products. Jesus also speaks of "the good man" and of "the heart" as the explanation of a man's way of life. Again and again we find the heart (*kardia*) mentioned. Thus, e.g., in addition to the above quotations, in Luke 1:17 (the conversion of the heart); 8:12 (the heart as the place where the word of God must take root); Matthew 15:18,19 (the heart as the place from which issue unclean things); Matthew 13:15; 15:8; Mark 3:5; 6:52 (the hardening of heart, its callousness), etc. In all these places the heart means the inner existence of man which determines his outward behavior, which is the center of his being, which must be converted, to which God's word is addressed and which is determinative of the question whether a man is good or evil. Here we are confronted with a totalitarian view of man, a criticism of his actions from one central point of view. The same thought is intended when the gospel speaks of a "dead" and a "living" man. This is found sporadically though. Thus, e.g., in Jesus' answer to one of the disciples who requests of him permission to go and bury his father: "Follow me; and let the dead bury their dead" (Matt. 8:22; Luke 9:60). And, further, in the well-known words of the father of the prodigal son: "For this my son was dead, and is alive again; he was lost, and is found."

The "dead" in Matthew 8:22 and Luke 9:60 can only be the spiritually dead.[112] And Luke 15:24,32 will have to be taken in the same sense, and not merely as "lost to the father,"[113] or "supposed to be bodily dead."[114] For the expression not only denotes what the son in a foreign country was to the father, but also what he was in himself. This is why the words "is alive again" must also be understood to indicate the inner change of the prodigal.

In this indication of the unconverted man as "a dead man" and of conversion as "being alive again," we have to do with a conception of the spiritual and moral state of man as a unity of being in which a radical and totalitarian change must be made if he is to be capable of doing God's will. It is clear that this thought is a near approach to that of regeneration (John 3:5), or that of "a new creature" (II Cor. 5:17; Gal. 6:15). As a matter of fact the whole thought of sonship to God is related to that of regeneration (or the "being born from above," (John 3:3).[115] Those to whom the salvation of the kingdom is promised (viz., the remission of sins, sonship to God) are also enabled to do God's will. But there is no denying that in Jesus' preaching as recorded in the synoptic gospels, there is no explicit indication or explanation of the manner by which they are put in such a position. The *fact* is beyond any possible doubt. The receivers of salvation do not only have *treasures in heaven*, but speak and act "out of the good treasure of their hearts" (cf. also II Cor. 4:7), just as "an evil man out of the evil treasure of his heart bringeth forth that which is evil." The gift of the kingdom does not only consist of what is objective, but of that which a man receives and possesses as an inward blessing. Yet there is lacking here anything that might be designated as fixed concepts. The deeper thoughts rise to the surface in flashes of imagery only incidentally and for a moment. Moreover, we should always bear in mind that this *kerygma* is *historically determined*, i.e., it is not the theology of the church after Christ's resurrection and after the descent of the Holy Spirit, but it is Jesus' proclamation of the gospel before these events. This will explain the infrequency of the mention of the Holy Spirit, whose work is the true and deepest explanation of the renewal of "the heart," of "being made alive," of the evidence of sonship, and of the fulfillment of God's will.

It is true that John the Baptist mentions Christ's "baptizing with the Holy Spirit." He thereby expresses both what the prophets had promised with respect to the great messianic time of salvation and what expectations survived in the Jewish people. Of John himself it was said that he would be filled with the Holy Spirit and would turn many of the children of Israel to the Lord their God (Luke 1:15ff). There is no doubt that this promise of the Holy Spirit refers to a great spiritual change that would take place at the coming of the Messiah. But the "baptism with the Holy Spirit" in John's preaching does not refer to conversion and the fulfillment of God's will that is demanded by the gospel. As appears from Acts 1:5 it refers to the special gifts that would be given to the disciples (the apostles) on Pentecost after Jesus' resurrection and ascension, and which would enable them to execute their important mission (cf. also Matt. 10:20, etc.). Finally, it seems to us that the pronouncement in the gospel on the gift of the Holy Spirit in Luke 11:13 is of a more general significance. Here the Holy Spirit is called the gift that God is willing to grant his children in answer to their prayer (the parallel passage in Matthew only has "good gifts," Matt. 7:11). The context proves that the gift of the Holy Spirit has a more general meaning than, e.g., in Matthew 10:20 and parallel texts. It occurs here in answer to the asking, seeking, and knocking of God's children. They may count on God's Spirit as much as they may expect the necessary food from their earthly father (vss. 9-12). This proves that the life of God's children is based upon the gift of the Holy Spirit, who is not only the secret of their moral strength but of their entire spiritual existence, of their search for the kingdom of heaven, of their trust in the Father's love, of their discernment of his will and their expectation of the coming salvation, in short, of all that they need in order to live as children of the Father.

It must be observed that the Holy Spirit is called the most important gift of all that God grants to his children in answer to their prayer.[116] He is eminently *the* good gift. This promise is immediately connected with the Lord's Prayer[117] in Luke 11. We need not assume that in the second verse of the current version, "thy kingdom come" should be replaced by that of Gregory of Nyssa: "Thy Holy Spirit come to us and cleanse us," as the more original version.[118] In any case the gift of the

Spirit is the sum total of all that for which Jesus teaches his disciples to pray in the Lord's Prayer. The Holy Spirit is the author of the whole of the renewing and re-creating work of God which will become manifest with the coming of the kingdom. But apart from this fact, in the dispensation of fulfillment that began with Christ's coming, the Spirit distributes the gifts of the salvation of the kingdom of heaven among the children of God. He creates and maintains the communion between the Father and his children (*our* Father). He, too, is the agent of the sanctifying of God's name and the doing of God's will on earth. He relieves the believers of care for their daily bread, gives them the certainty of the remission of their sins and protects them from the power of the Evil One. Though all these things are not explicitly and literally mentioned in the gospel, there is no doubt that this thought is the basis of the pronouncement in Luke 11:13.

This promised gift of the Holy Spirit is the result of the coming of the kingdom of heaven and belongs to the salvation proclaimed by Jesus. Its deepest ground and explanation lies in the fact that Jesus himself is the Messiah[119] who has been equipped by God with the Holy Spirit. Though the synoptic gospels contain only a few explicit passages on the gift of the Spirit as the treasure of salvation of believers, it nevertheless cannot be denied that the concurrence of the kingdom of God and the Holy Spirit is one of the great presuppositions of the entire gospel.

30. *God's Fatherhood and Temporal Life*

Among the words of Jesus about God's fatherhood there are utterances that occupy a special place. They relate this fatherhood to God's fatherly care for the temporal and natural life of his children. Special mention must be made of the well-known paragraph on "taking thought," i.e., worrying, in Matthew 6:25-34 (Luke 12:22-31); Matthew 10:29-31 (Luke 12:6,7): "Are not two sparrows sold for a farthing? and not one of them shall fall on the ground without your Father. But the very hairs of your head are all numbered. Fear ye not, therefore, ye are of more value than many sparrows." We also mention the words in the Lord's Prayer on "our daily bread" in this connection.[120]

The question is, in what way are these words related to the preaching of the kingdom; or, to put it more accurately, what position is to be assigned to Jesus' idea of providence expressed with such emphasis in these texts in the context of his Christological preaching of fulfillment. For the latter is the real central theme of Jesus' preaching.

Such a relationship has more than once been denied. Windisch, e.g., thinks that the paragraph on "not worrying" (i.e., not taking thought) is based on a view of life and the world entirely opposite to eschatology, (apart from the eschatological saying in Matt. 6:33, "but seek ye first the kingdom of God," etc.). He supposes that this paragraph is founded upon the observation of religious wisdom. Here the world is considered as a cosmos in which every being has its divinely appointed place and is taken care of daily and bountifully. Since the order of cosmos has been thought out harmoniously and logically, it can therefore be logically grasped. "It is a view of the world"—he writes—"permeated by optimism and the warmth of pious rationalism, a piety like that of the Enlightenment, but a genuine, and rigorous piety which condemns doubt as heathenish. It is self-contained, so that the arguments for the folly of worrying inferred from it are really sufficient. Hence, the last, eschatological 'argument' (6:33), almost seems to be a foreign element (*corpus alienum*). In any case it is a jump into another sphere of religious faith." (*"Es ist eine Weltanschauung die von starkem religiösen Optimismus und frommen Rationalismus durchwärmt und durchdrungen ist, Aufklärungsfrommigkeit, aber wirkliche, strenge Frömmigkeit, die den Zweifel als heidnisch verdammt. Sie erscheint in sich geschlossen, daher die aus ihr geholten Beweisgründe für die Torheit des Sorgens eigentlich hinreichend sind. Das letzte, eschatologische "Argument," 6:33, erscheint dann demgegenüber fast wie ein Fremdkörper, es ist jedenfalls ein Sprung in eine andere Sphäre des religiösen Glaubens"*).[121] Bultmann, also, has discussed this question in great detail in his well-known book

Jesus.[122] He also speaks of a childlike faith in providence and naive optimism manifested in these sayings. He is of the opinion that in themselves they contain nothing that is characteristic of Jesus' preaching. On the other hand, he rejects the idea that they express such a rational view of nature as was the case with, e.g., the Stoics and the philosophy of the Enlightenment. The faith in providence expressed in these words of Jesus bears a different character because it does not start from the theology of a pantheistic faith in nature, but from the personal and sovereign work of God. It is true that this faith in God is remarkably optimistic in this case and does not yet take account of the problem of suffering and that of the theodicy. On the other hand, Jesus' eschatological preaching contains words in which the human situation is described with a different serious-ness. But this is no reason to consider the absence of the problem of suffering and of the theodicy as an immature kind of childlike optimism. Much rather, this absence will have to be thought of in the scope of Jesus' preaching as a fundamental denial of man's sup-posed right or possibility of submitting his questions to God. On account of Jesus' eschatological preaching, every human situation is that of "decision" (*Entscheidung*), including that of suffering. The view of the "wisdom" expressed, e.g., in the words on "taking thought," is supposed to be of secondary importance (*nebensäch-lich*) and only occasional (*gelegentlich*).[123] Neither Windisch's view of a dualism between eschatology and optimistic faith in providence in the paragraph on "taking thought," nor that of Bult-mann, who thinks the latter only incidental and not essential within the scope of Jesus' preaching, is able to do justice to the relationship between the kingdom of heaven and providence in the gospel. In our opinion this is due to the fact that the ground on which Jesus bases his exhortation to the disciples "not to take thought" is insuffi-ciently brought to light by them. This ground is not some general faith in providence, but is to be found in the gospel of the kingdom of heaven. A closer study of the passage in Matthew 6:19-34 will show this.

No doubt in Jesus' preaching there are also pronouncements which testify to a divine goodness of a universal character that makes no special distinction between human beings.[124] In the Sermon on the Mount Jesus says that God "maketh his sun to rise on the evil and on the good, and sendeth rain on the just and the unjust." It is evident that here Jesus indicates God's gracious and *merciful disposition towards all men*. For this pronouncement occurs in a context which speaks of love of one's enemy and in which God's conduct is held up as an example to all of God's children. At the end it is repeated that (by doing so) they must be perfect, consistent, not half-hearted (in love), "even as your Father which is in heaven is perfect." The correctness of this exegesis also follows clearly from the version in Luke where, in the same context, and thus to promote such love for all men including the enemy, it says, "Be ye therefore merciful, as your Father also is merciful" (i.e., merciful–*oiktirmoon*–in the same sense of including both evil and good, Luke 6:36). Moreover, the preceding verse speaks of God's mercy (*chrēstos*) upon evil and good. It is true that this text does not speak of a universal *fatherly* love (cf. the repetition of the words "*your* Father" in this context). But it cannot be denied that Jesus holds up God's universal, merciful, and kind disposition as an example to his disciples.[125]

Doubtless this is only one aspect of this matter. In the same way Jesus discovers in natural phenomena the threat of God's judgment on those who do not repent. Therefore is it not correct to say with Bultmann that, at any rate, in Jesus' pronouncements those words are lacking which are concerned with the problem of suffering, and that he did not know the question of the theodicy.[126] In Luke 13:1-5 the relationship between guilt and human destiny and the meaning of suffering are very explicitly discussed by Jesus (they had been implicitly submitted to him by those who told him about Pilate's massacre). And then Jesus extends the problem from the secondary to the primary, i.e., the divine cause, when he does not restrict himself to Pilate's outrage, but also includes in the discussion the "accident" at the tower of Siloam. In all these disasters befalling man Jesus sees a manifestation of the divine judgment, as clearly appears from the repetition of the saying, "except ye repent, ye shall all likewise perish" (viz., in the final judgment).[127]

Although it may be clear that we should not too hastily speak of the naive optimistic faith in providence in those passages in which Jesus discovers God's generous hand in natural phenomena, there is no denying that in the natural order he finds the evidence of God's universal care for and mercy upon all men. So also in cases where Jesus speaks of God's *fatherly* care for *his children,* he derives his argument from nature. The flowers in the field and the birds in the air should keep the disciples from any idle worry. This is in fact not only true with respect to the sayings about "taking thought." All of Jesus' parables have a tendency to illustrate the truth about the kingdom by means of universal human relationships and observations. This does not prove that Jesus considered nature an independent source of revelation. But he does clearly start from nature and what is manifest in it to everybody, and from it ascends to God as he points out to man God's work and guidance in nature.[128] This is in no way some self-contained piety after the style of the Enlightenment finding its ground of religious confidence and faith in God the Father for the order and course of natural life. Bultmann is perfectly right when he emphatically points out the difference between the non-Christian wisdom resting in man and nature and the wisdom of the Old Testament from which Jesus spoke and to which he attached himself. This is why Windisch misinterprets this passage when he says that the fatherhood Jesus taught his disciples in the passage on "taking thought" is the "wisdom" inferred from the nature of things. God's fatherhood and his fatherly care for his children are not here based upon the contemplation of nature, or of the beauty of the flowers in the fields and the adventurous life of the birds. It originates from a totally different world of thought, namely, from the special, historical revelation of God. It is not the "book of creation" but that of the law and the prophets which lies at its base. Therefore in this passage the heathen can be held up as a warning example. They, too, know the birds in the air and the flowers of the field, but they do not know God as the one who has revealed himself in his mercy.

That is why in their unceasing restlessness they are always in search of "these things" (vs. 32). They cannot learn from nature to be carefree. Only where the God of the revelation of salvation is known can the "arguments" derived from nature be conclusive.

This is not all, however. For this passage not only represents—though it would be important enough in itself—the faith in providence which had already been demanded by the Old Testament revelation in general and by the "religious wisdom" it contained, in particular. Its significance is not secondary or incidental in the scope of Jesus' preaching of the kingdom, but adheres to it at its very heart. And at bottom the real issue here is the relationship between "eschatology" and "providence," between the preaching of the kingdom and natural life. This relation is not merely established in an exterior and secondary way by the "eschatological" saying in Matthew 6:33 ("But seek ye first the kingdom of God") which is to be seen in this context as a jump into another sphere, as a foreign element (*Fremdkörper, corpus alienum*) according to Windisch. But it is implied in the whole of the outer and inner structure of this passage.

This fact can already be inferred from the way in which the exhortation against "taking thought" is introduced by Matthew and by Luke. In Matthew 6:19-24, the sayings about "taking thought" are preceded by those about laying up treasures, the "single eye," and serving two masters. All these sayings are placed squarely under the full weight of the dispensation of salvation that began with Jesus' coming. The present issue, therefore, is "the treasures in heaven," the salvation of the kingdom. This must be sought with the utmost energy and with an undivided heart. In the closest connection with this Jesus adds, "Therefore (*dia touto*) I say unto you, take no thought for your life." This is not the preaching of some general religious wisdom, nor a word of consolation and encouragement to the disciples who are oppressed by earthly cares. Much rather, this is a protest against any form of an earthly mindedness (the concern for riches as well as the anxiety about poverty) which has its point of origin in the coming of the kingdom and the time of fulfillment. Jesus' "therefore" derives its power from *the choice* that must be made in view of the kingdom of God, the heavenly treasure, and the Lord of heaven. The same "therefore" (*dia touto*) is found in Luke 12:22. It is true that there its background is different, namely, that of the parable of the rich fool (vss. 12-21). But the issue here is true riches (the "laying up treasures" and "being rich toward God," (vs. 21) and opposite to this the loss of everything in God's judgment. In both cases the introductory formula confronts us with the great question as to where salvation and peace are to be sought. What should be our concern? What is of the earth only, or riches with respect to God, the treasure in heaven as it is included in the kingdom of heaven and is given with it?

Only from this viewpoint can the inner structure of Matthew 6:25-34 be understood. Its proper theme is *how to find security*. This is especially apparent from the beginning and from the end of this passage. For it does not say that we need not and must not take thought at all "for our life" or "for our body" as if such thought were unnecessary. The utterance is much more to the point and special. Its meaning may best be translated by saying, "take no thought *with reference to* your means of subsistence, no thought about the question of what to eat, nor *with reference to* your body,[129] about the question of how to clothe yourself. It is not that we should be without any care with respect to our bodies and lives as such, but that we should be free of care with respect to their *maintenance* by means of food and clothes. This is more than clear from the motivation in what follows (Matt. 6:25; Luke 12:23): "Is not the life more than meat and the body than raiment?" In other words, the commandment "not to take thought" is not motivated by saying that life and body do not require any care (or not so much care), but by the consideration that *their existence is not safeguarded by food and clothes* which, of themselves, are no guarantee for the maintenance of life. What does preserve life and body is not specified, but we cannot misunderstand. For the thought expresssed in the words, "Is not the life more than meat, and the body than raiment," is very general and finds its sharpest formulation in the well-known pronouncement, "For what is a man profited if he shall gain the whole world, and lose his own soul? or what shall a man give in exchange for his soul?"[130] Thus in Matthew 16:26 and Mark 8:36. Luke 9:25 has, "and lose himself or be cast away?"[131] The issue is the saving of *life*. The concept *psuche* not only denotes man's *inner* life in contradistinction to his outer gain (thus Luther), but denotes man's *entire* existence, as appears from the parallel text in Luke, "At the cost of his *psuche*." This phrase refers to the loss that must be borne in eternal life: the being lost and destroyed in hell. This is why Matthew and Mark continue by saying, "what shall a man give in exchange (*antallagma*) for his soul?" The concern here is not merely with inner life, but with the salvation of the whole of human existence in God's judgment.

All this proves that what is called life (*psuche*) by Jesus has an eternal significance surpassing everything else. The same thing holds true for the body. That is why it is foolish to think that the temporal death of the body is the worst thing that can happen. We must rather fear him who can destroy both *psuche* and body in hell (Matt. 10:28). The significance of the body extends as far as that of the soul.

The eternal destination of life and body is therefore the reason for life's being "something more" than food and the body's being something more than clothes. Food and clothes cannot guarantee their salvation (cf. Luke 12:15). Salvation demands more, namely, the salvation of the soul and body in *God's kingdom*. This kingdom should be man's first concern. We must start from the beginning.

Taken in this sense, the "faith in providence" expressed in such a special way in the passage about "taking thought" does not fall outside of the "eschatological sphere" and is not a leap into a different realm of thought (Matt. 6:33, Luke 12:31, "but seek ye first the kingdom of God"). The whole passage can only be understood against the background of the eschatological perspective. Exclusively on account of the certainties implied in the kingdom for the disciples of Christ, they may be carefree and optimistic with respect to the means of their earthly existence, as well as being able also to understand the "language" of flowers and birds. For God's work in nature is not the basis of their freedom of care, but proves that everything is at the disposal of God who provides his creatures bountifully with all that they need as long as it pleases him to keep them alive. All this, however, as a motive for being free of care, is true only in the case of God's children, i.e., from the standpoint of the kingdom of God. The heathen will not understand this motive. That is why to the promise of the necessary means of subsistence it is specified, "all these things shall be added unto you." "Added" (*pros-tethēsetai*), means that the *original gift* consists in something else, viz., in the eternal bliss God gives his children in the kingdom which embraces the whole of their human existence, with the means needed for this life being on the second plane and subordinate to the eternal gift. But the two are inseparable. God the consummator is also God the preserver, and from the certainty of the consummation (the kingdom, the fulfillment in Christ, above all on the cross) the book of creation becomes readable, namely, as the comforting revelation of God's omnipotence and wealth. This is no dualism or spiritualism, but rather, the description of the different degrees of existential security ("first the kingdom"). Then what is less follows from what is "more." For God's fatherhood embraces the present and the future, and at the cross we also learn to confess God's providence for this earthly life of his children. Here Paul's words in Romans 8:32 are to the point, "He that spared not his own Son, but delivered him up for us all, how shall he not with him also freely give us all things?" However, temporal life is preliminary and subordinate to what is eternal. It does not have its goal and destination in itself, but derives them from what is eternal.

The relationship between God's kingdom and his providence also finds expression in the fact that Jesus teaches his disciples to pray for the preservation and needs of their earthly existence. The fourth petition in the Lord's Prayer is the clearest example, "Give us this day our daily bread" (Matt. 6:11; Luke 11:3). This petition is entirely included in the expectation of faith with respect to the kingdom of heaven. In the first three petitions, the structure of the Lord's Prayer points, above everything, to the great future. The latter three are determined by the provisional nature of the present situation. Nevertheless, both the petition for remission of sins and that for deliverance from evil are entirely conceived of from the standpoint of the salvation of the kingdom. And this is also true of the petition for our daily bread. It is made with an appeal to God's fatherhood. Although in itself this petition might just as well fit into a quite different world of thought, in its present context it can unmistakably be understood only from the new relation to God given with Christ's coming. Just like the exhortation not "to take thought," it is as Christologically determined as the petition for the remission of sins. In both cases the basis of the petition and its answer is found in God's fatherhood as realized in the coming of Christ.

The same thing holds true of all "good gifts" for which the disciples make prayer unto God. Their whole life of prayer must be ruled by their faith in God's fatherhood (Matt. 7:7-12; Luke 11:9-13). Moreover, in those sayings which hold up human fatherhood as an example, there is no question of a certain natural knowledge of God as Father which is inferable from this earthly relationship. Neither are we confronted with a kind of naive optimism of faith which has not yet discerned the problem of history and the riddle of suffering. But everything becomes intelligible only against the background of God's fatherhood in Christ.

This is why "asking," "seeking," and "knocking" do not remain restricted to the desire for the supply of earthly needs. Nor to the "good gifts" that, according to Jesus' promise, the heavenly Father will give to those who pray to him for them. Prayer to God is all-embracing, it may start from all the promises of the kingdom, it may extend both to what is temporal and to what is eternal. But always, even with respect to the needs of the temporal life, it is dominated and supported by the gospel of the kingdom. Providence and the kingdom of God are not two separate worlds or spheres of life. The one does not originate in creation and the other from the "consummation of all things." Therefore, God's providence, which embraces the whole of God's creating and preserving power and wisdom, is invoked over themselves by God's children because they have been adopted as God's children in the kingdom in Christ. And, conversely, the kingdom is the guarantee that they will not be disappointed by God when they pray like this.

31. God's Fatherhood and Eternal Life

The previous sections have proved that the salvation of the kingdom of heaven has already been proclaimed as a present reality, but in its perfection and consummation it is always preached as something of the future. Our discussion of the salvation of the kingdom will, therefore, now focus its attention on the character and the contents of this future gift.

In a sense this future salvation of the kingdom may be said to be already present, namely, *in heaven*. Jesus more than once speaks of "treasures" of "the treasure" in heaven which can now already be laid up. Thus in the well-known antithetical saying of Matthew 16:19,20: "Lay not up for yourselves treasures upon earth, where moth and rust doth corrupt, and where thieves break through and steal: But lay up for yourselves treasures in heaven, where neither moth nor rust doth corrupt, and where thieves do not break through nor steal." The same thought, but in other words, is found in Luke 12:33, "Sell that ye have, and give alms; provide yourselves bags which wax not old, a treasure in the heavens that faileth not, where no thief approacheth, neither moth corrupteth."

To the rich young ruler Jesus says, "If thou wilt be perfect, go and sell that thou hast, and give to the poor, and thou shalt have treasure in heaven. . . . " Jesus here accommodates himself to the manner of speech and the ideas that were current in Judaism.[132] By this treasure is meant a kind of heavenly capital which will be paid on the great day of settlement at the time of God's judgment. Although any notion of meritoriousness is absent from Jesus' preaching, he uses this idea of the heavenly treasure in order to urge his disciples to do their utmost with respect to their future salvation. For this treasure is the future revelation of salvation of the kingdom. This fact cannot be denied within the scope of Jesus' preaching. Thus the parable of the treasure in the field and of the pearl of great price are dominated by the same thought although they include the present salvation.[133]

In speaking of the *heavenly* treasures Jesus indicates the place where the future salvation of the kingdom is being kept (cf. I Peter 1:4,5), and also the supra-mundane and eternal character of this treasure which is being kept for his disciples. It has been rightly observed,[134] that the proclamation of salvation appears to be different from that of the Old Testament. In the Old Testament the promise of the future has, in the main, earthly features. Yet it cannot be said that the heavenly character of the prospect of salvation held out by Jesus constitutes the new and spectacular aspect of Jesus' preaching. And the difference between the Old and the New Testament proclamations of salvation cannot be characterized by the words "earthly" versus "heavenly." For *in the first place,* the Old Testament also shows traits that do not find a satisfactory explanation within the limits of the earthly dispensation.[135] *In the second place,* the transcendent representation of the future salvation is especially dominant in some apocalyptic writings of the contemporary Judaism.[136] And *in the third place,*

Jesus also visualizes the ultimate revelation of the kingdom *upon earth* (cf. Matt. 5:5).

All this, however, does not detract in the least from the significance of Jesus' words about heavenly treasures. For it not only implies that the salvation of the kingdom is a gift descending from God—this is true of the remission of sins, sonship to God, etc., as well—but also, that its contents are not fully realizable within the plan of this earthly dispensation. The revelation of this heavenly bliss is no less than the great cosmic revolution which is indicated in the gospel in different ways. In Matthew 13:39 it is called "the end of the world" (*sunteleia aioonos*, cf. vs. 49; 24:3; 28:20). *Aioon* means something like "world-time," which implies that the future salvation can only manifest itself after the time that God has allotted to this world has come to an end.[137] In a positive sense, the cosmic revolution in conjunction with the consummation of the world-time is indicated as the *regeneration* (*paliggenesia*, Matt. 19:28). In the parallel text in Luke we find the simple phrase, "in my kingdom" (Luke 22:30). Elsewhere the dispensation that will start then is called "the world to come," in which Jesus' followers will receive "life everlasting" (Mark 10:30; Luke 18:30).

This salvation which will be revealed as the gift of the kingdom at the end of the world, in the regeneration (of all things), in the coming *aioon*, and is summarized in the term "life" or "life everlasting," is indicated in various ways. It begins with the "resurrection of the dead." The most elaborate mention of it is recorded in the dispute between the Sadducees and Jesus (Matt. 22:23-33, and parallel places). Elsewhere, in Luke 14:14, we find the expression, "the resurrection of the just," at which time any charity towards those who cannot repay will be rewarded. Here the word "resurrection" apparently does not mean the act of rising from the dead but the state of bliss which begins with it.

The Sadducees denied the resurrection of the dead. This denial was contrary to the general opinion of Judaism in Jesus' time, at least insofar as this can be inferred from the apocalyptic, pseudepigraphic and rabbinical literature.[138] Jesus' answer to the catch question of the Sadducees implies two things. First, his rejection of the presupposition that the present functions and relations of earthly life will be restored in the resurrection. At that time there will be no marrying nor giving in marriage, but men will "be equal unto the angels." In Luke 20:36, this equality is not only mentioned in relation to marriage, but Jesus also explicitly states that "neither can the just die any more." From this it does not follow that those who will rise from the dead will be equal to the angels in everything, nor does Jesus say that the angels have a heavenly kind of body.[139] This text deals only with a comparison of a concrete point, namely, that of marriage. And, for the rest, Jesus contradicts the current conception of the Jews who expected that the earthly relations and the bodily organs of man would be restored at the great resurrection.[140] In opposition to this he lays full emphasis upon communion with God as the great purpose and center of the resurrection life . . . "and they shall be the children of God, being the children of the resursection" (Luke 20:36).

Besides maintaining the *character* of this resurrection life, Jesus also—in the second place—maintains the *fact* of the resurrection. He does so by appealing to the Scriptures and to God's power. Jesus' quotation from the Scriptures only indirectly speaks of the resurrection, "I am the God of Abraham, the God of Isaac, and the God of Jacob" (Ex. 3:6). Jesus connects this with his pronouncement, "For he is not a God of the dead, but of the living." Here, faith in the resurrection is based upon faith in God. Hence the appeal to "God's power," which is not meant as a static, timeless quality, but as a power in the service of the kingdom, working towards the consummation of all things (cf. Matt. 6:13b). Jesus here speaks of God who has revealed himself in the history of salvation (Abraham, Isaac, Jacob). This God is the creator of the world who sanctifies himself in his people, and maintains himself as the God of heaven and earth. This naturally implies the resurrection of the dead. For it is not only inferred from a definitive text here, nor "demonstrated" in a subtle way after the manner of the rabbis; but is pointed out as a postulate of God's work of salvation which from the origin of Israel's existence has been directed to the consummation of the kingdom of heaven. It is based on the whole revelation of creation and redemption.

Finally, from the fact that God is not a God of the dead but of the living, it follows that there will be a resurrection of the dead (i.e., a restoration of the *body*). This is an irrefutable conclusion which needs no further proof of demonstration. For it is entirely implied in the New Testament view of man, according to which the body together with the soul belong to the essence of man's existence, the body not being the soul's temporary and inferior covering.[141]

When we try to discover what constitutes the bliss of the life of the resurrection according to Jesus' preaching, we nowhere find an elaborate or explicit "description." But, just as in the case of the whole of the proclamation of salvation, we find only the affirmative promise in all kinds of widely scattered pronouncements. The gospel is without any apocalyptic revelations about the great events of the future. Again and again salvation is represented as the gracious communion of God with his people, as the deliverance from life's distresses, as the fulfillment of the promise, as a compensation for temporary oppression. The beatitudes call the life of the resurrection "consolation," "being filled" with righteousness, "mercy," "revelation of the children of God," "seeing God." Elsewhere we find "sitting down with Abraham, Isaac, and Jacob" (Matt. 8:11, and parallel places); "being saved" (Matt. 10:22, etc.); "the righteousness shall shine as the sun" (Matt. 13:43); "finding his life" (Matt. 16:25, etc.); "sitting on twelve thrones" (said of the disciples, Matt. 19:28); "sitting down to the wedding feast" (Matt. 22:1-14); "entering into the joy of thy Lord" (Matt. 25:14-30); "inheriting the kingdom" (Matt.

25:34); "drinking new wine" (Matt. 26:29, and parallel texts, etc.). It is especially significant that in Matthew 5:5 Jesus also points to *the earth* as the place where the kingdom will reveal its glory. This "inheriting the earth" (cf. Ps. 37:11; Isaiah 60:21), does not refer to the gradual conquest of the world by the gospel,[142] but to living upon the new earth,[143] to which the kingdom of heaven will one day descend at the end of the world.[144] "God's work done to the earth not only consists in cleansing all violence and wickedness away from the church, but also in giving the earth into the possession of those to whom Jesus gives his promise."[145] In this respect, too, the gospel is free from any dualism. The earth is not "nature" in the sense of a philosophical concept of nature, but "creature" in the sense of having been created. It owes its origin to almighty God's creating will and word.[146] This is why, again and again, Jesus expresses the divine right to earth and the divine power over it, when, e.g., he addresses God as "the Lord of heaven and earth" (Matt. 11:25; Luke 10:21). He calls the earth God's "footstool" (Matt. 5:35). Thus the deliverance of the kingdom consists in the subjection of the whole earth to God's perfect dominion. The beginning of this is seen in Jesus remitting sins "upon earth" (Matt. 9:6, and parallel texts). After his resurrection "all power is given to him in heaven and in earth" (Matt. 28:18). It is also manifested in Jesus' claim to "all the kingdoms of the world and the glory of them" (Matt. 4:8 and parallel texts), in the prayer that God's will "be done in earth as it is in heaven" (Matt. 6:10). The future revelation of the kingdom will also be the commencement of the perfect bliss for the earth in accordance with the prophecies of the renewal of the cosmos (Is. 65:17; 66:12), as well as of the unlimited capabilities of the Son of Man (Daniel 7:14). The earth is involved in the divine deliverance. Thus it can be understood that the future bliss is repeatedly described not only as a spiritual enjoyment or elevation, but as a kind of joy embracing the whole of human life. It is entirely in agreement with the biblical idea of creation that the deliverance of the whole of life, including its bodily and material aspects, also belongs to the contents of the preaching of the gospel,[147] though it is clear that such deliverance must pass through the catastrophe, the "passing away" of this world, so that it thus bears the character of renewal, re-creation, in the full sense of the term. The whole of the future bliss is concisely summarized in the word "life" (Matt. 7:14; 18:8ff; Mark 9:43,45); or sometimes "everlasting life" (Matt. 19:16,29; Mark 10:17); that can be "inherited" (Matt. 19:29; Mark 10:17; Luke 10:25); "received" (Mark 10:30; Luke 18:30), that into which we can "enter" (Matt. 18:8; 19:17; Mark 9:43). By the term "life" Jesus means authentic, imperishable life. It is not a certain element of "immortality" carried by man within himself. This is clear from the above examples of Jesus' use of language. But this immortality is a gift of God given to the elect in the resurrection from the dead, whereas eternal "destruction" is prepared for the wicked (Matt. 10:28, etc.).

Meanwhile, it is clear that the reception of eternal life is closely connected with earthly life, i.e., with the way in which man has acted with respect to God's will. This is why the fulfillment of the commandments can be called "the way leading to life" (Matt. 7:14). As a gift of the kingdom of God, this "life" is prepared for and begun with the sonship brought about by God's Spirit, and by God's fatherly care for his children (Matt. 19:29, etc.). Even now a distinction is made between the "living" and the "dead" among human beings living at present. Though the synoptic gospels always speak of "life" as a gift of salvation granted by God in a future-eschatological sense, it is nevertheless unmistakable that there is an unbreakable connection and unity between this future gift and the salvation now already given, viz., that of the remission of sins, sonship to God, the gift of the Holy Spirit. Both are gifts of one and the same kingdom, and so are founded in the great saving act of the revelation of Jesus Christ.[148] In the preaching of the kingdom recorded in the first three gospels, the proclamation of the resurrection and life only have an implicit Christological character. For that preaching cannot yet look back on the death and resurrection of Christ as "events determining the present" (*"die Gegenwart bestimmende Ereignisse"*). But this does not detract from the fact that these future gifts of salvation as the salvation of the kingdom *eo ipso* find their ground and fulfillment in Christ. This is expressed in all kinds of ways in the continuation of the New Testament proclamation of salvation. In the synoptic gospels, however, it is only Jesus' "miracles" of resurrection from the dead (Matt. 9:18ff; 11:5; Luke 7:11-17, cf. also Matt. 27:52,53), that proclaim eternal life as a gift of Christ. But presently, everlasting life as the fruit and outcome *of Jesus' resurrection from the dead* will be proclaimed as the heart and core of the Christian *kerygma.*[149]

Finally, special mention must be made of the words which Jesus spoke to the malefactor on the cross in answer to his request, "Jesus, remember me when thou cometh into thy kingdom." Jesus replied, "Verily, I say unto thee, Today shalt thou be with me in paradise" (Luke 23:42,43). The special importance of these words in this context is the fact that whereas the malefactor's mention of the kingdom apparently refers to the great messianic future when Jesus will "come into his kingdom," Jesus promises to him the bliss of paradise already for the "present" (*sēmeron*).[150] This can only mean that, already before the resurrection of the dead and the coming of the kingdom in conjunction with it, there is an intermediate state of bliss for those who have been deemed worthy.[151] Such a conception also occurs in the Jewish world of Jesus' day[152] and lies at the basis of the parable of Dives and Lazarus (Luke 16:19-31, where the state of bliss is described as being "in Abraham's bosom").

That which is striking about Jesus' pronouncement is, in the first place, the absolute power and authority with which he bestows the partaking of the heavenly glory, and in the second place, the expression, "with me." It is the communion with Jesus, whom the malefactor confessed openly as the Christ, which guarantees salvation to him immediately after death. Although the conception of provisional bliss before the resurrection does not occur elsewhere in the synoptic gospels, the purport of this expression is nevertheless clear enough. In Christ, the king of the kingdom, is perfect bliss. He is the salvation of his disciples already when they have to leave this life, even though the great dawn of his coming and of the resurrection of the dead have not yet arrived. Nothing, not even death, can separate them from his love (Rom. 8:38,39, cf. also Phil. 1:23; 2 Cor. 5:1-8).

Notes to Chapter VI

[1] J. N. Sevenster, *De boodschap van het Nieuwe Testament*, I, 1939, p. 111.

[2] Cf. K. Holl, *Urchristentum und Religionsgeschichte*, 1927, p. 19.

[3] Cf. also Bultmann, *TWB*, I, p. 509, the article on *"aphiēmi."*

[4] Cf. Greijdanus, *op. cit.*, I, p. 86, "For such *gnoosis* is meant here, namely, knowledge from our own experience, enjoyment, possession."

[5] Bultmann, *TWB*, I, p. 509, the article on *"aphiēmi"*: Grundmann, *TWB*, I, p. 307, the article on *"hamartano,"* and many others.

[6] Cf. also Grundmann, *op. cit.*

[7] See above, § 11.

[8] Cf. also Schrenk, *TWB*, II, p. 219, the article on *"dikaioō."*

[9] The same thing applies to Bultmann's interpretation of the New Testament *kerygma*, it seems to me, (after his "de-mythologizing" application to it). Using the categories of the modern existence-philosophy (esp. that of Heidegger) he explains God's gracious remission of sins as the liberation of man from his past in which he is imprisoned. This is further described as being liberated from "the sphere of the visual, the given, what is at hand, the measurable," (*die Sphäre des Sichtbaren des Vorhandenen Verfügbaren, Messbaren*) which is at the same time "the sphere of the perishable" (*die Sphäre des Verganglichen*). Freedom of all this is found in the faith "that the invisible, the unknown, the non-available meets men as love . . . and does not mean death to him, but life" (*das gerade das Unsichtbare, Unbekannte, Unverfügbare dem Menschen als Liebe begegnet . . . nichl Tod, sondern Leben für ihn bedeutet*), *Neues Testament und Mythologie*, included in H. W. Bartsch, *Kerugma und Mythos*, pp. 29, 30. In another passage this grace is called "the detachment from anything that is available in the world, consequently the attitude of de-secularization, of freedom," p. 31. (*die Gelöstheit von allem weltlich Verfügbaren, also die Haltung der Entweltlichung, der Freiheit*).

[10] For these texts, see also below, pp. 238ff.

[11] Cf. W. G. Kümmel, *Das Bild des Menschen im N.T.*, 1948, pp. 11ff, against Harnack and the related conceptions of the basic motive of the gospel.

[12] Cf., e.g., Bultmann, *TWB*, I, p. 508, the article on *"aphiēmi."*

[13] According to Schniewind the phrase "for he shall save his people from their sins," Matt. 1:21, has been borrowed from Ps. 130:8; *Das Ev. nach Matth.*, p. 13.

[14] Thus also, e.g., K. Holl, *Urchristentum und Religionsgeschichte,*[2] 1927, pp. 19ff.

[15] See also above, chap. V.

[16] This is expressed by Bultmann from his viewpoint (that of "the theology of the church") thus, "the new and specifically Christian feature (is) this, that the church is aware of having received remission of sins from God which has been offered to man by means of the act of salvation that was manifested in Jesus Christ," *TWB*, I, pp. 508-509.

[17] Cf., e.g., Strack-Billerbeck, *op. cit.*, IV, I, pp. 4-15.

[18] See the elaborate account in E. Sjöberg, *Gott und die Sünder im palästinischen Judentum*, 1939, pp. 148ff.

[19] At least not so far as rabbinical literature is concerned; in the apocryphal pseudepigraphical literature there prevails a much more rigorous doctrine of meritoriousness and retribution, Sjöberg, *op. cit.*, pp. 261ff.

[20] Sjöberg, *op. cit.*, p. 168.

278

[21] Cf. Behm in *TWB*, IV, pp. 994ff, the article on "*metanoeo*," and the literature mentioned there; and also W. G. Kümmel, *Das Bild des Menschen im N.T.*, 1948, pp. 8ff; J. Schniewind, *Das biblische Wort der Bekehrung*, 1948, pp. 7ff.

[22] Here the word *strephomai* is used in exactly the same sense as *metanoein*.

[23] Thus H. J. Holtzmann, *Lehrbuch der neutest. Theol.*, I, 1911, pp. 218, 219.

[24] Thus, e.g., H. Weinel, *Bibl. Theol. des N.T.*,[4] 1928, p. 181, who speaks of the "tone of mocking rejection in the word"; cf. also E. Klostermann, "if in opposition to these adversaries the concepts 'sinner' and 'righteous man' are not meant, *kat' eirooneian* thus Theophylakt," *Das Markusev.*, p. 27.

[25] Cf., e.g., Schrenk, *TWB*, II, p. 191, the article on "*dikaios*."

[26] Thus Schlatter, *Der Ev. Matth.*, p. 309; cf. also Rengstorf, *TWB*, I, p. 333, the article on "*hamartoolos*."

[27] For this exegesis cf. also Greijdanus, *op. cit.*, II, p. 696.

[28] Cf. also my *Mattheüs*, (K.V.), p. 184.

[29] Greijdanus interprets "repentance" differently, viz. as a repentance similar to that of the *hamartooloi* mentioned. In our opinion the point of the paradox is not found in the word "repentance," but in "not being in need of."

[30] Cf. also Kümmel, *Das Bild des Menschen im N.T.*, 1948, p. 10.

[31] Cf. also the conlusive discussion of this question by G. Sevenster, *Christologie*, pp. 54ff.

[32] For these passages as well as for this entire question see also my *De strekking de bergrede*, 1936, pp. 126ff.

[33] "The heart is wicked; this phrase alone is developed in V. 19-23," Schniewind on Mark 7:19, *op. cit.*, p. 100.

[34] Cf. also, e.g., Sevenster, *op. cit.*, pp. 50-56, and my *De strekking der bergrede*, pp. 126-128.

[35] Cf. also Grundmann, *TWB*, I, p. 15, the article on "*agathos*."

[36] For this translation see below, § 33.

[37] Cf. below, § 29.

[38] Cf. Schniewind on Mark 10:23-27, *op. cit.*, pp. 131, 132.

[39] Thus, e.g., H. Windisch, *Der Sinn der Bergpredigt*, 1929, pp. 95ff.

[40] Cf. Windisch, *op. cit.*, pp. 130, 141.

[41] Cf. the arguments of Jewish authors like J. Klausner, C. Montefiore, and others, like Strack-Billerbeck, *op. cit.*, IV, I, p. 15; and Windisch, *op. cit.*, pp. 102ff.

[42] The text (*mallon*)? *par' ekeinon* is uncertain, but the meaning has been established, cf. Bl. Debr. § 185,[3]*.

[43] E. Sjöberg, *Gott und die Sünder im palästinischen Judentum*, 1939; cf. also W. G. Kümmel, *Die Gottesverkündigung Jesu und der Gottesgedanke des Spätjudentums*, in: *Judaica*, 1st Year, 1945, pp. 57ff.

[44] Cf. also G. C. Berkouwer, *Geloof en Rechtvaardiging*, 1949, pp. 111ff.

[45] On the idea of reward in the gospels and on its relation to the Jewish doctrine of meritoriousness, cf. the articles by Preisker and Büchsel in *TWB*, IV, pp. 699ff, the article on "*misthos*," and I, pp. 170ff, the article on "*apodidoomi*," especially F. K. Karner, *Der Vergeltungsgedanke in der Ethik Jesu*, 1927 and O. Michel, *Der Lohngedanke in der Verkündigung Jesu*, in: *Zeitschrift für systematische Theologie*, 1932, pp. 47ff; G. Bornkamm, *Der Lohngedanke im N.T.*, 1947.

[46] This has been rightly pointed out by Büchsel, *op cit*.

[47] The word *achreios* seems to have been a current qualification of the social

class of the slaves, in the sense of "poor," "miserable," expressing that a slave never had anything to say and could not rise above his status of being a slave, cf. Preuschen-Bauer, *op. cit.*, p. 202, and also A. Jülicher, *Die Gleichnisreden Jesu,* II,[2] p. 21, who, among other things, refers to Deissmann.

[48] Cf. my *Matth.*, II, p. 73; cf. also Preisker, *op. cit.*, p. 723.

[49] Cf. above, § 17.

[50] *Lehrbuch der Dogmengeschichte,* I,[4] 1909, p. 81.

[51] *Op. cit.*, p. 18.

[52] In the Netherlands this heritage of liberal theology has been defended especially in Windisch' writings; but also by G. J. Heering, and others; on this see the elaborate fundamental criticism in G. Sevenster, *Christologie,* pp. 47ff; also M. H. Bolkestein, *De verzoening,* 1945, pp. 52ff.

[53] Thus, e.g., Windisch, Der Sinn der Bergpredigt, p. 96. *Die Gotteskind-schaft der Christen nach dem Neuen Testament,* 1939, pp. 44ff.

[54] Cf. W. Twisselmann.

[55] Although there the text is uncertain.

[56] Cf. above, § 27.

[57] Cf., e.g., Twisselmann, *op. cit.*, pp. 10-25, 102-105 and the relevant literature on p. 10.

[58] For the references in the Pseudepigrapha and Apocrypha as well as in the Talmud, cf., e.g., Strack-Billerbeck, *op. cit.*, I, p. 219, pp. 392-396; also Dalman, *die Worte Jesu,* I, pp. 150ff and Twisselmann, *op. cit.*, pp. 31ff.

[59] Cf. also G. Kittel, *TWB,* I, p. 6, the article on *"abba"*; "Jewish linguistic usage shows that the earliest Christian relation to God as the relation of a father to his son far surpasses all possibilities of intimacy which existed in Judaism, and much rather puts something new in its place." This is also pointed out by Kümmel, *Die Gottesverkündigung Jesu und der Gottesgedanke des Spätjudentums,* in *Judaica,* 1st Year, 1945, pp. 53, 54.

[60] Kittel's assertion that Jesus derived the name of Father from "the every day linguistic usage of the family," *op. cit.*, p. 5 (cf. Kümmel also *op. cit.*), is certainly incorrect insofar as the relation between God and the believers is concerned. Such a derivation would only be possible if the invariable use of the opposition "which art in heaven" is ignored. And as for the address in Luke 11:2, the Jews, too, already addressed God with the appellation of "Father!" only.

[61] Cf. above, § 25.

[62] On this more is found below, § 36.

[63] Cf. also Twisselmann, *op. cit.*, pp. 47, 48.

[64] In the late-Jewish expectation also, sonship to God belonged to the salvation of the glorious future, thus, e.g., *Jubil.* 1:24ff. "Their souls (i.e. the souls of the Israelites) will follow me in the whole of my commandment (i.e. at the end of time) and they will act according to my commandments, and I shall be a Father to them and they will be children to me. And they will all be called the children of the living God, and all spirits and all angels will know them, and will know that they are my children and that I am their Father. . . ." Cf. Strack-Billerbeck, *op. cit.*, I, p. 219.

[65] Cf. Greijdanus, *Lukas,* II, pp. 962, 963.

[66] Michaelis and Kümmel wrongly say that in Jesus' pronouncements in the synoptic gospels, sonship to God only occurs as an *"endzeitliches Ziel"* (a purpose to be realized only at the end of time), cf. Kümmel, *Die Gottesver-kündigung Jesu,* pp. 55, 56; cf. also his *Das Bild des Menschen im N.T.,* 1948,

p. 19. In the face of all the texts in which Jesus speaks of "your Father," it is very arbitrary to infer from the small number of pronouncements on sonship that they only refer to a purely eschatological gift. Nor can Matt. 5:45 be forced into this schema.

[67] Cf., e.g., H. J. Holtzmann, *Neutest. Theologie,*[2] 1911, pp. 335-340.

[68] Cf. my *Zelfopenbaring en Zelfverberging,* 1946, p. 35.

[69] See, e.g., Oepke, *TWB,* IV, pp. 595, 596, the article on *"apocalupto."*

[70] Cf. above, § 27.

[71] Thus, e.g., K. Holl, *Urchristentum und Religionsgeschichte,*[2] 1927, pp. 31, 32, Bultmann, *Jesus,* 1926, p. 177; *Theologie des Neuen Testaments,* 1948, p. 23. But see also Twisselmann, *op. cit.,* pp. 40ff.

[72] As is done by W. Grundmann, *Die Gotteskindschaft in der Geschichte Jesu,* 1938.

[73] Cf. Twisselmann, *op. cit.*

[74] Cf., § 30.

[75] Thus E. Stauffer, *Die Theologie des N.T.,* 1945, p. 160.

[76] *Das Wesen des Christentums,* 1905, p. 45.

[77] For more details see my *De strekking der bergrede,* pp. 74ff, 120ff.

[78] Cf., e.g., Kümmel, *Verheissung und Erfüllung,* 1945, p. 74.

[79] E.g., by C. Stange, A. Runestam, G. Kittel, cf. my *De strekking der bergrede,* pp. 122-125.

[80] Besides Bultmann's book *Jesus,* pp. 120, 121, see also his *Theologie des N.T.,* 1948, pp. 19, 20.

[81] H. Windisch, *Der Sinn der Bergpredigt,* p. 10.

[82] This is also admitted by Windisch, *op. cit.,* p. 81.

[83] Thus at least I understood *ho kurios* in verse 8, cf., e.g., Greijdanus, *op. cit.,* II, p. 773 and Klostermann, *op. cit.,* p. 163.

[84] Thus, e.g., Greijdanus, *op. cit.;* some authors think these words imply the idea of intercession with God, a thought which also occurs, e.g., in the *Book of Enoch* (39:4ff), cf. Klostermann, *op. cit.*

[85] Thus, e.g., Klostermann himself. Cf. for such impersonal indications of God in the Jewish way, Dalman, *Die Worte Jesu,*[2] 1921.

[86] Cf. a detailed account of this in my *De strekking der bergrede,* pp. 138-144. Here the appeal to Matt. 5:20 and to 5:48 is rejected. For in 5:20 Jesus does not wish to point out something (the righteousness of the scribes and Pharisees) that was already almost unattainable in itself. But he much rather indicated this kind of Pharisaic righteousness as morally far inferior, as appears in the context which follows it. And in 5:48 *teleioi* must be taken in a formal sense, viz., as perfect, consistent, not giving up when only half finished. For the subject here is love which must not be restricted to those alone who are of the same mind. This is why in Luke 6:36 this meaning can be rendered by the words, "Be ye therefore merciful, as your Father is also merciful."

[87] Cf., e.g., Schniewind, *op. cit.,* pp. 80, 81; Schrenk, *TWB,* III, pp. 55ff, the article on *"thelēma."*

[88] Cf. E. Gaugler, *Heiligung im Zeugnis der Schrift,* 1948, p. 25 and Schniewind, *op. cit.,* p. 81.

[89] *Strekking der bergrede,* pp. 53-58.

[90] This insufficiency—very characteristic of the whole of Bultmann's theology! —of the idea of "decision" with respect to the interpretation of Jesus' preaching of the kingdom is also pointed out by Wendland, *op. cit.,* p. 52.

91 Thus Karl Barth, whose discussion of the Sermon on the Mount in his *Kirchliche Dogmatik*, II, 2,² 1946, pp. 766-782 is very important from the standpoint of the exegesis of the history of salvation.

92 Cf. Stauffer, *TWB*, I, p. 47, the article on *"agapao."*

93 Thus, e.g., the Roman-Catholic Commentary by Joseph Schmid, *Das Evangelium nach Lukas* (*Regensburger Kommentarwerk zum N.T.*), 1940, pp. 116, 117.

94 For more details, see, e.g., Klostermann, *op. cit.*, pp. 92, 94.

95 *Heidelberg Catechism*, Answer 126.

96 For the meaning of *teleioi*, cf. above, note 86.

97 As Michaelis and Kümmel have it, in virtue of their one-sidedly eschatological conception, see above, p. 229. But see also Twisselmann, *op. cit.*, p. 94.

98 Thus Schlatter, *Der Ev. Matth.*, p. 193.

99 Schlatter, *op. cit.*

100 In which, according to Stauffer, the newer theology likes to discuss the problem of "God's will and human will," *Die Theologie des N.T.*, 1945, p. 160.

101 See also my *"De strekking der bergrede,"* pp. 136ff.

102 See below, § 33.

103 Thus also Barth on the Sermon on the Mount, *op. cit.*, pp. 767ff.

104 Others translate *pistis* here by *faithfulness;* compare, however, my *Matth.*, II, pp. 135, 136. It is possible that the sayings on faith in Luke 17:5ff should be understood in connection with Jesus' demand (for willingness to forgive), as, e.g., Zahn and Greijdanus do, but on account of the different application of such sayings in Matt. 17:20, it is not probable in my opinion.

105 Cf. also Barth, *op. cit.*, p. 773.

106 See also Bultmann, *TWB*, I, p. 705, the article on *"ginoosko."*

107 Cf. Klostermann, *op. cit.*, p. 103.

108 Cf. Schniewind, *op. cit.*, p. 150.

109 Cf. above, § 2.

110 Cf. Schniewind, *op. cit.*

111 Cf. Hauck, *TWB*, III, p. 618, the article on *"karpos."*

112 Cf., e.g., Klostermann on Matt. 8:22, *op. cit.*, p. 78, and Greijdanus on Luke 9:60, *op. cit.*, I, p. 453; Bultmann, *TWB*, IV, p. 898, the article on *"nekros."*

113 Thus Bultmann, *op. cit.*

114 This possibility is considered by Klostermann, *op. cit.*, p. 160.

115 This is pointed out by H. D. Wendland, *op. cit.*, p. 67; cf. also P. Feine, *Theologie des N.T.*,⁷ 1936, p. 84.

116 Cf. Greijdanus, *op. cit.*, p. 534, and his quotation of Calvin.

117 This is also pointed out by Rengstorf, *op. cit.*, p. 131.

118 Thus, e.g., Klostermann, *op. cit.*, p. 124.

119 See above, § 13; cf. also W. Michaelis, *Reich Gottes und Geist Gottes nach dem N.T.*, 1931, pp. 10ff; E. Gaugler, *Die Heiligung im Zeugnis der Schrift*, 1948, pp. 24ff.

120 As is generally known, the translation is uncertain. The word, translated by "daily," denotes a certain measure, viz., that of *what is sufficient*, cf. *Matth.*, I, p. 132, and especially W. Foerster, *TWB*, II, pp. 587-595, the article on *"epiousios."*

121 H. Windisch, *Der Sinn der Bergpredigt*, 1929, pp. 17, 18.

122 *Jesus*, 1929, pp. 147-158.

123 Bultmann has a slightly different formula in *TWB*, IV, pp. 596, 597, the

article on *"merimnao,"* where he also discusses Matt. 6:25-34, "Man . . . is told that his concern should be God's dominion; then the anxieties with respect to his life will vanish." And he adds, "By these thoughts the exhortation in Matthew 6:25-33 is distinguished from the Stoical view . . . in which the anxious care with respect to the means of subsistence is also called foolish by referring to the animals. For in the Stoa the freedom of care is based upon the conviction of the divine *"pronoia,"* which has equipped every creature, and therefore man also, with what he needs, and especially in the dogma of the freedom of man." . . . See, however, also Bultmann's *Gesch. d. Syn. Trad.,*² p. 109.

¹²⁴ Note the chiasma in the next pronouncement!

¹²⁵ It is, consequently, contrary to the explicit words of the text when, in order to combat the doctrine of common grace, some writers say that in this case only the actual facts (*rain* on the righteous and on the unrighteous, *sun* on the evil and on the good) are spoken of, and not God's disposition.

¹²⁶ *Jesus,* p. 156.

¹²⁷ A remarkable parallel is found in John 9:3,4. There, too, the problem of suffering is posited from an individualistic conception of guilt and is rejected by Jesus as also in Luke 13:1-5. Here, however, the *meaning* of suffering is not said to be a judgment, but God's glory in grace, "so that the works of God should be made manifest in him." Suffering, calamities, etc., are not only a prelude to God's *eternal judgment;* there is also a kind of suffering in which God is through Christ glorified in his grace, and which thus becomes an example and a prelude of *eternal salvation.*

¹²⁸ Cf. also Oepke on the "rational" and the "natural" in Jesus' preaching, *TWB,* III, p. 584, the article on *"apokalupto."*

¹²⁹ The datives *psuchēi* and *soomati* are to be interpreted as datives of relationship. If this view is rejected, it will still be necessary to admit that the freedom of care demanded by Jesus is not concerned with life and body as such, but with the way they are *maintained* in their earthly existence, cf. my *Matth.,* I, pp. 140, 141.

¹³⁰ The translation of *tēn psuchēn autou zēmioothēi* is difficult. For the question is whether the element of punishment also plays a part here by the side of the element of loss, damage; cf. Schlatter, *Der Ev. Matth.,* p. 522, and Stumpff, *TWB,* II, pp. 893, 894, the article on *"zēmia."*

¹³¹ Here, too, *zēmiootheîs* is more than merely suffering damage. It refers to the price that has to be paid.

¹³² Cf., e.g., Strack-Billerbeck, *op. cit.,* I, pp. 429-431.

¹³³ Cf. above, § 12.

¹³⁴ J. Ridderbos, *Predikende het evangelie des koninkrijks,* 1911, pp. 94ff.

¹³⁵ See on this, e.g., J. Ridderbos, *Het Godswoord der profeten,* II, 1932, pp. 357ff; 468ff; IV, 1941, pp. 181ff; 204ff; cf. also above, § 1.

¹³⁶ Cf. Strack-Billerbeck, *op. cit.*

¹³⁷ Cf. on this concept *aioon* and the "linear" conception of time in the N.T. in addition to that of Sasse, *TWB,* I, pp. 202ff, especially also the important expositions of O. Cullmann, *Christus und die Zeit,* 1946, pp. 31ff.

¹³⁸ On this subject see especially Strack-Billerbeck, *op. cit.,* I, pp. 892ff; IV, 1, p. 344; IV, 2, pp. 1167ff; see also Oepke, *TWB,* I, 370, the article on *"anistēmi";* and Ph.H. Menoud, *Le sort des trépassés d'après le Nouveau Testament,* 1945, pp. 27ff. The latter, however, is of the opinion that for a long time the belief in the resurrection among the Jews had been "a more or less optional"

belief and was in no case an article of faith. Not until the third century after Christ was the anathema formulated against those who denied the resurrection, *op. cit.* Yet the view of the Sadducees seems to have been the exception to the rule.

[139] Cf. Greijdanus, *op. cit.*, II, p. 962, and my *Matth.*, II, p. 120.

[140] Strack-Billerbeck, *op. cit.*, I, pp. 888ff; cf. also Menoud, *op. cit.*, pp. 28, 29; and Hauck on Mark 12:25; *op. cit.*, p. 146.

[141] Compare for this, e.g., Menoud, *op. cit.*, pp. 11-21.

[142] Cf. Strack-Billerbeck, *op. cit.*, I, p. 200.

[143] Schniewind, *op. cit.*, p. 42.

[144] Klostermann, *op. cit.*, p. 37.

[145] Schlatter, *Der Ev. Matth.*, p. 136.

[146] Cf. Sasse, *TWB*, I, p. 678.

[147] Cf. on this also H. D. Wendland, *op. cit.*, pp. 77ff, rejecting the modern spiritualizing interpretations of the gospel.

[148] Cf. Wendland, *op. cit.*, pp. 79, 80.

[149] See also Bultmann, *TWB*, II, pp. 864-867, the article on *"zao."*

[150] See, e.g., Zahn, *op. cit.*, p. 701; Klostermann, *op. cit.*, p. 229; Greijdanus, *op. cit.*, II, pp. 1148, 1149.

[151] So the "intermediate stage has not been skipped" as, e.g., M. van Rhijn thinks, *Een blik in het onderwijs van Jezus*, 1924, p. 135. It is also admitted by P. Althaus, *Die letzten Dinge*,[5] 1949, p. 143, that in Luke 23:43 an intermediate state is spoken of. Cf. also O. Cullmann, *Christus und die Zeit*, 1946, pp. 212ff; Ph.H. Menoud, *Le sort des trépassés*, 1945, p. 45.

[152] Cf., e.g., Strack-Billerbeck, *op. cit.*, pp. 1118, 1130; E. Stauffer, *Die Theol. des N.T.*, 1945, p. 190.

Chapter VII

THE GOSPEL OF THE KINGDOM

3. The Commandments

32. *"Kingdom of God" and "Righteousness"*

We have seen what an important place the demand to do the Father's will occupies in Jesus' preaching. We have been able to form an idea of the general meaning of this moral demand within the scope of the gospel of the kingdom proclaimed by Jesus.[1] We are now confronted with the task of entering more minutely into the content and the purport of Jesus' commandments.[2] The first question, then, is in what respect the content of Jesus' commandments is determined by the idea of the kingdom of heaven or, in other words, what constitutes the specific meaning of these commandments. Even a superficial view reveals a certain unity, a specific character both as to their form and nature, which one, however, would like to define more precisely. That which Jesus demands in these commandments is also summarized by himself in general qualifications. The most important of these—occurring especially in the Sermon on the Mount as given by Matthew—is that of "righteousness" (*dikaiosunē*). The entire passage on the antitheses in Matthew 5:21-48 is nothing but the description of the "righteousness" which the disciples need in order to enter the kingdom of heaven (5:20); in 6:1, the starting-point is again the idea of "righteousness," and 6:33 summarizes what is needed above everything else in the words, "But seek ye first the kingdom of God, and his (i.e., God's) righteousness." Elsewhere (Matt. 5:10), righteousness is called the cause of persecution, and there the kingdom of heaven is promised to those who have to suffer such persecution. In all these places,[3] righteousness means the sum total of God's demand imposed upon all who would enter the kingdom.

These pronouncements also show the close connection between the concepts "kingdom of God" and "righteousness." In Matthew 6:33, the kingdom of God and righteousness are spoken of in the form of a hendiadys, and the phrase "for the sake of righteousness" in 5:10 is elsewhere replaced by that of "for the sake of the kingdom" (Luke 18:29); or by "for my sake and the gospels" (Mark 10:29), or by "for my name's sake" (Matt. 19:29). It may rightly be said, therefore, that kingdom and righteousness are synonymous concepts in Jesus' preaching.[4] The one is unthinkable without the other.

This lends all the more force to the question about the general purport of Jesus' commandments. If the righteousness demanded by Jesus is that of the kingdom, what is then its general character? Or, in other words, in what way is the content of the concept righteousness determined by that of the kingdom of God? Here we are confronted with the question about what is generally called the relationship between "eschatology and ethics" in the gospel.

Any interpretation of Jesus' commandments starting from an *idealistic* conception of the kingdom of God either in an individual sense (the kingdom is concerned with the infinite value of the human soul; accordingly, Jesus' commandments are regulated by an ideal of personality), or as a whole (the kingdom is the new ideal form of human society, and Jesus' commandments are intended to bring about its realization) must be rejected immediately. Such views are not only in conflict with what the gospel teaches us about God's kingdom, but they also give a completely distorted idea of the gist of Jesus' commandments. To give a few examples,[5] we would point out that Jesus' deepened view of manslaughter and of adultery cannot be explained from his respect for human personality and from the value he assigns to womanhood. Such an explanation does not really touch the essence of the matter. If it is permissible to draw conclusions from the result as to the motive, there are enough commandments to be quoted which would lead to the opposite conclusion as regards Jesus' appreciation of human personality. For Jesus not only forbids anger, abuse and the dismissal of one's wife with a letter of divorce, but he also commands us to suffer ourselves to be struck and robbed (Matt. 5:39ff). He also speaks of situations in which one must leave wife and children in the lurch (Matt. 19:29ff). He also speaks of people to whom one should not give that which is holy because they are "dogs," and his is also the saying, "do not cast your pearls before swine" (Matt. 7:6). In all these commandments the thing at issue is exactly this, that all kinds of "values," including one's personality, one's wife, marriage, etc., must be sacrificed if necessary for the sake of the kingdom of God. It is not these values that determine the content of Jesus' commandments, but quite the opposite, the kingdom is again and again represented as the highest good which dominates and puts into the shade all human values, interests, and ideals. The "righteousness" required from his disciples by Jesus is not the "righteousness of the kingdom" because it asserts these "values," but much rather, because it demands the absolute sacrifice of all these things for the sake of the kingdom. It is the absolutely *theocentric* character of the kingdom which determines the content of Jesus' commandments. Especially in their radical demands they are intended to govern the whole of life from this theocentric standpoint and to put everything in the balance for this single goal. The same thing holds true for the collective ideal of the kingdom of God that is supposed to be reflected in Jesus' commandments. When, by way of an example, and always only incidentally, Jesus commands his disciples to relinquish their rights, their property, their marriage (Matt. 5:38ff; Luke 12:33; Matt. 19:12), these commandments are not then meant as the foundations of a new social order. On the contrary, Jesus bases himself upon the foundation of a society in which these institutions (right, retribution, property, marriage, etc.) are *operative*. Now, however, at God's command, and for the sake of the kingdom, Jesus wants his disciples to give up their rights, interests, benefits and safeguards. He does not substitute one social order for another, but subjects everything a man possesses by virtue of his capacities, environment, social order, etc., or to which a man may lay claim, to the great proviso of God's kingdom. He contrasts right with self-denial, possession of property with readiness to sacrifice it, marriage with continence. This is not saying that the kingdom of God consists in having no property, or in the absence of rights, or in celibacy. But it means that God's kingdom represents something higher than a hierarchy of human values and interests, and that the "righteousness of the kingdom" teaches us to subject everything to this.

Although interpretations of the relationship between the kingdom preached by Jesus and the content of his commandments which are mostly based on humanistic presuppositions, such as above, may be rejected immediately. No less objectionable is the consistently eschatological conception of Jesus' commandments. It also establishes a close connection between "kingdom of God" and "righteousness," but in such a way that God's kingdom means the *end* of all things. For it means an absolute devaluation of all earthly rights, interests, pleasures, etc., and in many respects imparts a negative sense to the righteousness oriented to the kingdom of God. It is in this sense that both Jesus' demand for self-denial, etc. for the sake of the kingdom and the general content of his radical commandments are explained. Johannes Weiss, the father of this eschatological view, in this connection spoke of "exceptional legislation" and compared to a state of war the situation in which Jesus supposed that he was. In a time of war, the course of normal life is suspended—if only temporarily. What is abnormal becomes "normal," and everything that is important and desirable in a time of peace must be made serviceable to the one great interest: the winning of the war.[6] Schweitzer formulated this conception by saying that Jesus' commandments represent an "interim-ethic," i.e., they are to be oriented to the short interval which he considered possible before the coming of the end of all things.[7]

There is nothing in the consistent eschatological interpretation of the gospel that has proven to be more questionable than this very interpretation of Jesus' commandments. For nowhere is the content of these commandments motivated by an appeal to the speedy end of the world.[8] This is especially true with regard to those commandments that are held to be the most "radical," and the most characteristic examples of the "eschatological ethics," viz., the commandments to love one's enemy and not to resist evil (Matt. 5:43ff). Here the motive of crisis is entirely absent. Jesus demands love of one's enemy on the basis of the motive that his disciples shall be manifest as children of the heavenly Father, "for he maketh his sun to rise on the evil and on the good, and sendeth rain on the just and on the unjust." It is not the approaching end of the world that must "free" the disciples from revenge, and self-love, but it is the action of their heavenly Father with respect to sinners. This motive has not been derived from the eschatological situation, but has existed from the time of the world's fall into sin.

The same thing holds true for the great summary of the will of God which Jesus gives in more than one passage, viz., in the commandment of love (Matt. 7:12; 22:34-40; Mark 12:28-31, cf. Luke 10:27,28; Mark 12:32-34). This commandment of love obviously cannot be explained from a fundamentally eschatological mental attitude, but is pointed out by Jesus as the gist and content of God's will which is valid, not only in an eschatological situation, but for all time[9] as the great commandment for human life. But in this way the whole construction of Jesus' commandments as being characteristically an ethics of the interim, or an exceptional legislation, proves to be untenable on the most essential point. And it is understandable that those who consider Jesus' preaching to have originated in the expectation of the imminent advent of the kingdom are increasingly rejecting the connection established *in this way* between "eschatology" and "ethics."[10]

No doubt we can say that more than once Jesus motivates his rigorous demands by an appeal to the relativity of temporal and earthly things as compared with the heavenly treasure or the woes of hell (cf., e.g., Matt. 5:29,30; 5:25,26; 19:12,21). Moreover, it is undeniable that the expectation of the coming kingdom is a powerful stimulus to obey Jesus' commandments and to withhold oneself from abandonment to the treasures of earthly life. Yet it would be a serious misconception of the profundity of Jesus' commandments if we tried to explain them merely by an appeal to the relative value of earthly, temporal life. A text like Matthew 5:13, "Ye are the salt of the earth, ye are the light of the world," shows that not only the relativity of earthly life but also its preservation and its furtherance are held out to the disciples as motives. And lastly—and this is really the main point—this "eschatological conception" ignores what we have established in more than one way up to now, viz., that the good works required by Jesus are not only a preparation for the coming kingdom of God, but themselves already demonstrate its presence. It is "God's will" that is being done in these "good works" and in this "righteousness." In this "hallowing of God's name" is manifested the coming of his kingdom.[11]

The norms of the righteousness demanded by Jesus are not founded in an earthly ideal of God's kingdom, nor in the future and transcendent character of the kingdom. God's will expressed in Jesus' commandments is not subordinated to certain creaturely values, nor is it to be derived from the latter, nor does it consist in their negation. It rests solely in God's own communication. Jesus' "ethics" does not consist in some doctrine concerning "goods," nor in asceticism. It is the "ethics" of *obedience* in the full sense of the word. That which is "righteousness," and may be taught as such, is always to be traced back to God's own words. This fundamental notion is the great presupposition of the remarkable fact that again and again Jesus speaks of "God's will" without any further explanation (Matt. 7:21; 12:50; 18:14; 21:31; Luke 12:47,48), the "commandment" or "God's commandments" (Matt. 15:3; Mark 7:8,9; Matt. 19:17; Mark 10:19; Luke 18:20), "God's word" (Matt. 15:6; Luke 11:28), as that which man has to "fulfill," to "do," to "keep," and which as such is known, or at least can be known. If, therefore, the question is asked by what Jesus' commandments are regulated, the ultimate answer is only this: *by God's will as it is revealed in his law*. This is the meaning of the great program of the Sermon on the Mount, "Think not that I am come to destroy the law, or the prophets: I am not come to destroy, but to fulfill" (Matt. 5:17). What is implied in this "fulfillment" of the law we shall have to investigate in a later chapter. But it must be emphatically stated at the outset that Jesus' ethical preaching does not have a deeper ground than the law as the revelation of God's will to Israel, the people of the covenant. And this not only appears from Matthew 5:17, but as we shall see, from the whole of Jesus' teaching that has come down to us. Again and again it is the law, and only the law, the meaning and purpose of which is also the meaning and purpose of Jesus' commandments.

That is why the connection between the "kingdom of God" and "righteousness" does not mean that God's kingdom represents a new ethical norm expressed in the righteousness preached by Jesus. But this connection is to be sought in the preaching of the kingdom as that of God's coming in Jesus Christ, and it takes the revelation of God's will seriously as the great criterion for the coming of the kingdom. This revelation is again and again referred to by Jesus as set down in the law and the prophets. Therefore, one may not only speak of the *theocentric* character of Jesus commandments (in contrast to all humanistic ideals of the kingdom of God), but also of the *theonomy* of the righteousness preached by him. The will of God finds expression in the revelation of the law. This is why the preaching of the kingdom is also that of the law. So we should not be surprised that Jesus as the Christ not only proclaims the coming of the kingdom as the *fulfillment* of the great *time* of salvation and as the *fulfillment of Scripture* (Mark 1:15; Luke 4:21), but that he also gives supreme emphasis to the *fulfillment of the law* as the purpose of his messianic coming and as the content of the gospel of the kingdom.

33. *The Fulfillment of the Law*

For a correct insight into the meaning of the righteousness demanded by Jesus, we must first determine more closely the character of his commandments as the fulfillment of the law. Then we have to deal with those texts in which Jesus' relation to the law set down in the Old Testament is explicitly mentioned. We have already quoted Matthew 5:17ff which may be considered of paramount importance in this connection. But this pronouncement is not an independent and isolated one.

For one thing, we should point out a whole series of references in support of the programmatic words of Matthew 5:17.[12] Jesus' own life had been subjected to the law from his earliest youth. The data found in Luke's gospel about it are undeniably meant in this sense (Luke 2:22ff). Moreover, Jesus behaves in accordance with the precepts of the law when he goes to the temple, keeps the festivals, the Sabbath, pays the temple-tax (Matt. 17:24ff), wears the clothes prescribed by the law (Matt. 9:20; 14:36), refers to the priest the lepers he had cured (Matt. 8:4), defends the sacred character of the temple against those who use this building as an object of gain (Matt. 21:12ff[13]; Mark 11:16). In connection with this, we might also refer to the well-known words spoken to John at his baptism, "for thus it becometh us to fulfill all righteousness" (Matt. 3:15). It is true that the law is not mentioned here *expressis verbis,* but the phrase "to fulfill all righteousness" certainly suggests the divine demand revealed in the law and the prophets before Jesus' (and John's) entering upon his public career. Thus this phrase also implies a very important indication of the fact that Jesus' messianic and substitutionary work, including his suffering and death, are to be considered as the fulfillment of God's law. But this meaning is no more than indicated within the scope of the synoptic *kerygma*.[14]

No less clear are the numerous data in which Jesus' teaching also binds *others* to the revealed law of God. In addition to Matthew 7:12, where Jesus gives a summary of the law and the prophets as the content of his commandments, his conversation with the rich young ruler is especially important. To the young man's question, "Good Master, what good thing shall I do that I may have eternal life?" Jesus answers, "Keep the commandments" (Matt. 19:17). Thou knowest the commandments (Mark 10:19; Luke 18:20). And then he repeats several of the ten commandments separately, together with the demand for love of one's neighbor (Lev. 19:18). So in these passages we are told what is needed to enter the kingdom of heaven, viz., the fulfillment of the law. Even when in the continuing conversation, the young man is told by Jesus to sell all that he has and to give it to the poor, this demand does not exceed that which the law requires us to do.[15] It is its actual application. Here, too, the issue is that of being perfect, i.e., doing good consistently;[16] though it is nothing but the keeping of the law that Jesus requires, and is that which is needed to enter the kingdom of heaven (cf. Matt. 19:24).[17]

Moreover, the commandment to love God and one's neighbor which is repeatedly given by Jesus as the summary of all his commandments, is nothing else but the summary of the law (Matt. 7:12; 22:40, cf. also Mark 12:34; Matt. 24:12). So Jesus' most radical commandments, which are always the particluarizations of this love (cf., e.g., Matt. 5:38ff, 43ff), do not represent a new kind of righteousness (e.g., that of love in contrast to that of right), but only give expression to what Jesus proclaims as the demand of the law and the prophets. Obedience to these commandments is the fulfillment of the law. In this light, consequently, we must view Jesus' extremely severe criticism of the scribes and Pharisees' doctrine and practice of the law. For it is clear that, with respect to the fulfillment of the law, Jesus' preaching is also dominated by an antithetical motive no less than with respect to the remission of sins.[18]

The question now is, what is the meaning of this continuous appeal to the law, and what is the sense of Jesus' emphatic pronouncement in his introduction to the great antithetical passage of the Sermon on the Mount when he says that he has come to fulfill the law and the prophets (*plēroosai*), Matthew 5:17? This question can only be fully answered (if such an answer is possible) after a survey of the whole of Jesus' ethical preaching. Nevertheless the words quoted from Matthew 5:17-19 are of great importance, because this general pronouncement is not obscure in itself, nor incompatible with the rest of the context, for which reason we reject as an arbitrary judgment any verdict of its being inauthentic.[19]

The first thing to be observed about the fulfillment (*plēroosai*) in Matthew 5:17 is that here the category "law" in its sense of an external authority is fully maintained—which follows logically especially from verse 17 (cf. Luke 16:17). Hence there can be no question here of a replacing of the law as the source of our knowledge of God's will by "the new disposition," "conscience," etc. Moreover, any exegesis which explains the text as if it meant a quantitative supplement of the law does not do justice to the meaning of the words. In this sense, e.g., Jeremias wishes to take Matthew 5:17. He thinks that Jesus, as the bearer of "the complementary and final will of God," contrasts himself here to Moses, the bearer of "the provisional divine will."[20] But "fulfillment" does not mean "completion of the law as the source of our knowledge of the divine will," but the effectual assertion of the demands of the law. The word suggests a vessel that is being filled. The "vessel" of the law is given its rightful measure. For this purpose Jesus has come. And this measure, naturally, consists in the demands of the law being accomplished.

In this connection there arise a few important questions.

In the first place, the question as to whether the phrase "the law and the prophets" means not only the demand but also the promise, especially that about the Messiah in its entire multiform extent, which Jesus would then claim to fulfill. The words "the law and the prophets" in themselves do not decide this point, as they may denote the promise (Matt. 11:13; Luke 24:44) as well as the source alone of the knowledge of the divine will (Matt. 7:12). In our opinion the context clearly shows that both "the law" and "the prophets" refer to the divine demand. The seventeenth verse explains the sixteenth, which deals with "good works." And the whole paragraph of Matthew 5:21-48, to which 5:17-20 forms an introduction, deals with the divine demand. We therefore think that we must conceive of "the law and the prophets" in the same sense as in the rest of the Sermon on the Mount (7:12 and also Matt. 22:40). (On these two *commandments* hang all the law and the prophets.) It also appears from the sole mention of the law in verses 18 and 19.

A second question is whether or not by the "fulfillment" of the law Jesus also, or even primarily, means his own messianic carrying out of the law and thus his own obedience to the law, or whether he only refers to his *doctrine* concerning the true content and purpose of the law.

This question has found various formulations and answers. Calvin distinguishes between Jesus' "doctrine" and his "life," and writes that, although Christ on account of his perfection of life was entitled to say that he had come to fulfill the law, he speaks of his "doctrine" here, not of his "life."[21] Klostermann speaks of a practical and a theoretical fulfillment, and thinks that the first interpretation fits in better with reference to the 19th verse (contrasting the "*doing* and teaching" to "*breaking* and teaching"), but that in the sequel (vss.21-48), there is only a *theoretical* fulfillment of the law.[22] Van Ruler observes that, according to Matthew 5:17, the fulfillment of the law is an action "which takes place not only in the world of meaning, but also in the world of fact."[23] And a little later he adds (apparently again on the basis of Matthew 5:17 in particular) that the real meaning of the word "fulfillment" is not to be found in the "ideological sphere, but in that of eschatological history." The reference is not primarily to its "noetic and rational content," but to something that "occurs." Fulfillment is a "messianic category," and the fulfillment of the law was accomplished in Jesus' coming and in his work, "to speak dogmatically: in his passive and active obedience, in the work of atonement and sanctification."[24]

In our opinion it is best to observe Calvin's restraint. In this part of the Sermon on the Mount Jesus speaks especially with the authority of the Messiah who *promulgates* God's will (cf. 7:28,29). This is clear from the whole of the Sermon, but especially from the antithetical part in which he combats what the old rabbis had taught. That is why this passage is concerned primarily with his "doctrine" and not with his "life." Yet this does not mean that there is a contrast or that one should exclusively think of a "theory of fulfillment." Just as Jesus opposes in verses 19 and 20 (cf. 23:3) not only the teaching of the Jewish rabbis of the law but also their way of life, so also his own doctrine and manner of life are a unity. Thus his life as the fulfillment of the law is at the same time a doctrine for his disciples (cf. Matt. 11:29). The substitutive element, however ("passive" and "active" obedience), is absent here in Matthew 5:17. But in the second place, it must be borne in mind that Jesus' fulfillment of the law, also in relation to the life of his disciples (which is the subject of the discussion here), is never merely "word," "prescription," but also action, gift. His preaching of the gospel (and so also his fulfillment of the law) is an effective word. It brings his disciples into communion with the Father. It creates the relationship of Father-child, and enables them to live as children of the heavenly Father.[25] Therefore, it is entirely in agreement with the whole character of Jesus' preaching when this word about the fulfillment of the law and the prophets is taken to refer to the promise of the new covenant[26], according to which God will write his law in the hearts of his people and thus himself answers for its fulfillment (Jer. 31:31ff).

All this, however, does not detract from the fact that in the exegesis of Matthew 5:17 we are primarily concerned with the prophetic-messianic *interpretation* of the law and, consonant with this, that for which the disciples are held to be responsible. And we must particularly concentrate all our attention on what this means.[27]

However, it has often been asserted that Jesus' definitive exegesis of the law and its attendant criticism of the Jewish scribes distinctly contains a criticism of the law itself, if not literally, at least implicitly. That is why Jesus' positive pronouncements with respect to the law are thought to be hardly compatible with the actual content of his commandments. This view is especially based on what is called the incompatibility of Matthew 5:17-20 (the explicit maintenance of the law)[28] with the antithesis following it, Matthew 5:21-48. To refute this argument we restrict ourselves to the following.[29] Firstly, these antitheses are formally directed against the scribes' doctrine of the law, not against the law itself.

Connected with this is the translation of *tois archaios* (vss. 21ff). In our opinion it is almost indisputable that this should be translated, "*by* them of old time," and not, "*to* them of old time." Those of old time are then those who had explained the law in the so-called *halacha*. In Jesus' days the teaching of the scribes went back to this exegesis.

For this opinion we can adduce the following arguments:

1) Jesus does not quote what has been *written*, but what has been *said* (*errethē*, not *gegraptai*), whereas in verse 18 he speaks of the law as that which has been expressed in letters (jot and title). By what has been *said*, he refers to what the scribes taught the people orally as the tradition of the teaching of the law by "those of old time."

2) The linguistic usage followed in *hoi archaioi* distinctly points in the direction of the old rabbis or transmitters of tradition, but not in that of the old recipients. It is true that in another context *archaioi* may also denote the old prophets when there is no question of the law (Luke 9:8,19). But when "those of old" are mentioned in

connection with the law, the scribes are meant, at least in Jewish writings. In the tracts of the Talmud and in the Midrashim, there is repeated mention of the "words of them of old." There is a warning against those who place these words in opposition to the Tora (e.g., in Tanchuma 202a: A man should not say, I shall not keep the commandments of those of old because they do not belong to the Tora.). Their words and those of the prophets are placed side by side.[30] On the basis of all this, it is not to be supposed that by "them of old" Jesus meant "our ancestors"[31] who received the law. It is obviously the learned rabbis against whom he objects.

3) This is corroborated by Matthew 15:2, in which Jesus explicitly mentions the "tradition of the elders," and contrasts God's law to it (verse 3). It is true that the text here does not mention *archaioi* but *presbuteroi*, but there is no technical difference between these two words. In both cases the Jewish *zekenim* are no doubt referred to.[32]

4) Another argument—which in our opinion is conclusive—is that what Jesus quotes as "having been *said*" is for the greater part not found in the Old Testament in this form, but contains all kinds of additions and which, in at least one instance, are in obvious conflict with the Old Testament (cf. 5:43). These quotations clearly bear the character of *instruction* in the law, interpretation, *halacha*, not that of quotations from the law proper.[33]

5) In contrast to what has been said ("by them of old"), Jesus emphatically asserts his: "But *I* say unto you." The antithesis not only relates to the contents of what was said in olden times and to what is said now, but also to the persons responsible for such "sayings," i.e., Jesus and "them of old."

But it is not only from the form in which the antithesis is expressed but also from the contents of the antithetical commandments themselves, that it appears that Jesus does not combat the law but the superficial conception, the devaluation of the demand of the law.[34] This is at once obvious with respect to the commandments given in Matthew 5:22-26,27-30, 43-48. And as to the dissent from the letter of divorce, the oath, and retribution (Matt. 5:32,34-37,39-42), there is only conflict between Jesus and Moses if Jesus' commandments are judged from a purely formalistic standpoint. For, in the case of the prohibition of divorce Jesus can appeal to Moses (cf. Matt. 19:8). Moreover, the institution of the letter of divorce did not sanction this sin, but only made provision for it in the civil law, and kept it within certain limits. Jesus does not attack this civil order which has become necessary on account of sin (Matt. 19:8). But he makes it clear that this civil law did not fulfill God's commandment. The same thing applies to the *ius talionis*. The civil authority has been entrusted with the task of maintaining justice even by coercion if necessary. But this does not cancel the demand of love; nor is the subject entitled to appeal to God's retribution rather than obeying this demand. And as for the prohibition against taking an oath, this must certainly not be taken to mean that Jesus dissents from all current oaths in the Old Testament along with any explicit appeal to God's omniscience. But in opposition to a *corrupt* practice of taking an oath, he strongly emphasizes the demand to speak the truth simply and in accordance with the purport of the law and the prophets. Though in the antithetical part of the Sermon on the Mount the fulfillment of the law is certainly something different than a mere repetition, there nevertheless can be no doubt that in these commandments Jesus only wanted to do justice to the law as the normative instance. Therefore, he does not here correct or complete the law of God, but is its defender and guardian.

There are a few more passages on the same question. We have already mentioned Matthew 15:2,6; Mark 7:5ff, in which Jesus emphatically places the traditions of "them of old" and God's law in opposition to each other. He exposes the hypocrisy of the Jewish restriction to the duty of providing for indigent parents (the "Corban" case, Mark 7:11; Matt. 15:5). He also discusses the Pharisees' and the scribes' reproach that his disciples do not observe the purification rites of "the elders." The answer to this seems to abolish not only the elaborate provisions of the scribes but the entire ritual notion of pure and impure in general. This applies especially to the pronouncement "there is nothing from without a man that entering into him can defile him: but the things which come out of him," and to the further explanation of these words given there (Matt. 15:10-20; Mark 7:14-23).

The whole context, however, shows clearly that Jesus does not abolish all the ritual laws of purification in such a rather casual way.[35] If his words about pure and impure were to be taken as an attack on all that belongs to ritual purity, we should have to include not only the laws on meat in Leviticus 11 but also those on the purity of the priests. In opposition to this, however, Jesus nowhere appears to reject the temple service and its prescriptions on ritual purity. Much rather, he submitted himself to them and also required others to observe them (cf. Matt. 8:4; 23:23; Luke 2:22). The conflict therefore arises about their interpretation in the rules of "them of old." Jesus' disciples did not observe these rules and Jesus defends them in this. On the other hand, Jesus' pronouncement on the things that defile or do not defile is formulated in a very general way, so that although Jesus observed the ceremonial prescriptions of purification found in Moses' law, the consequences of this pronouncement seem to involve those prescriptions themselves no less than the elaboration of them by the "elders."[36] This seeming contradiction between Jesus' words and his actions is removed as soon as Jesus' meaning is rightly understood. He obviously does *not* want to abrogate the Mosaic laws on purification and meat, nor to declare them to be senseless, but to do away with the delusion that sinful man could attain to true purity before God in this manner. Jesus shows that here the issue is the human *heart* (but not as though the inner life of man were the only thing that matters) as that which determines man's whole action and inaction. For "meat" and "heart" have "nothing to do with each other." It is not denied that the purification of meat and body occupies a place in the whole of God's law. But this law in itself lacks the power to purify any one before God. Jesus' criticism agrees with the seemingly negative criticism of the prophets with respect to Israel's public worship (cf. Is. 1:11ff; 58:5ff; Jer. 6:20; 14:12; Am. 5:22; Mic. 6:7; Ps. 50:8ff). Their criticism, too, was certainly not meant to abolish public worship but to show its worthlessness before God so long as it was attended by an unregenerate heart and an unconverted life. The same thing is found in the Sermon on the Mount (Matt. 5:23-24: first be reconciled, then offer thy gift). This is also the meaning of Jesus' words about purity. In our opinion, there is doubtless reason for distinguishing between ritual and ethical purity, although Jesus himself does not use such abstract terms. Although the distinction is not intended as a contrast (ethical purity does not render ritual purity superfluous), it does imply difference in rank. For ritual purity cannot be detached from its religious-ethical foundation.

Another conflict between Jesus and the Pharisees confirms our opinion that the solution of the problem must be sought in this direction. The conflict arose because of *Jesus' eating with publicans* (Matt. 9:9-13). Here again the point of issue was over the validity of the Jewish rules.[37] Jesus reminds his hearers of the words of the prophet, "I will have mercy and not sacrifice" (Matt. 9:13, cf. Hos. 6:6). This quotation is very important in this connection because it raises the conflict between Jesus and the Pharisees to a general level. The words also occur in Matthew 12:7 in the debate concerning the Sabbath. They also explain Jesus' words on purity. It may be said that neither in the question of the eating with "publicans and sinners," nor in the conflict about the Sabbath is the issue one of sacrifices, i.e., the temple service. But Jesus considers in the light of Hosea's prophecy the scrupulousness and vehemence of the Pharisees with regard to these points. He lays bare a general attitude (not merely a misconception within the scope of casuistry). He, therefore, blames his opponents in the terms of a general prophetic motif (as he did in Mark 7:6,7). Here he clearly contrasts sacrifice (insofar as it can be carried to the temple with hands), to mercy, kindness, love, in which the heart is involved. This, too, does not mean a depreciation or rejection of sacrificial service as something merely external; but the condemnation of a religion of which only the external phenomena, cultus, and ritual have been retained, and in which the heart is absent. The antithesis has been formulated in an absolute form (I will have mercy . . . and not sacrifice), but it has a relative meaning. This is a form of style that occurs very frequently (cf. Joel 2:13; John 6:27). It means that the former term of the antithesis cannot exist without the latter and is only valuable through the latter. Yet "sacrifice" and "mercy" are not related to each other as action to disposition as is the case with manslaughter and hatred. There are here really two different spheres, the ethical and the ritual. Jesus' criticism is not intended to tear them apart, but rather, to reveal the unity of the law, so that the ethical sphere is shown to be the indispensable foundation of the ritual sphere.

Nowhere is this *relation* more clearly indicated than in Jesus' speech against the Pharisees in Matthew 23 (cf. Luke 11:39ff). This whole speech is important for our understanding of Jesus' attitude with reference to the scribes and their observing of the law. It opens with a very positive pronouncement in which Jesus acknowledges their authority because they "sit in Moses' seat," and their right to exercise this authority.[38] Here, too, any misconception as if Jesus were opposing Moses' law must first be repudiated. However, we are especially interested in the passage starting with the 23rd verse. The issue is again the meaning of what belongs to the cultus in its wider sense, "for ye pay tithe of mint and anise and cummin." Jesus does not even oppose as such this extremely severe explanation of Deuteronomy 14:22ff. But instead, he points to "weightier matters of the law, viz., judgment, mercy, and faith." The expression "weightier matters" (*ta barutera*) does not imply that these commandments are more difficult to fulfill and so require greater effort. But it means that they represent the weightiest and the most decisive part of the law.[39] Not everything in the law is of equal weight.

The fulfillment of the law also means that we know and practice the spiritual *distinction* taught in God's revelation itself (cf. vs. 23 with Mic. 6:8; Zech. 7:9). This does not mean that action, the outward performance, the ritual part do not matter. Jesus continues by saying, "these ought ye to have done, and not to leave the other undone." But the most important thing is that which should lie at the basis of what is external and ritual, the right disposition of the heart. Again and again it appears that Jesus does not place the ethical in antithesis to the ritual, but considers the former to be indispensable to the latter, and in this sense as the most important part of the law.

Finally we must discuss the passages relating to the keeping of *the Sabbath* and to *fasting*. We have already mentioned the important motive found in Hosea 6:6. It is not the only one, however. In another place, on the occasion of the cure of the man with a withered hand, Jesus asks those who hoped to catch him transgressing the law of the Sabbath, "Is it lawful to do good on the Sabbath days, or to do evil; to save life or to kill?" (Mark 3:5; Luke 6:9). In Luke 13:15ff he refers his accusers to their own care of the cattle, and asks them if a daughter of Abraham ought not to be loosed from the bond (of Satan!) on the Sabbath day. A similar answer is given to the scribes and Pharisees in Luke 14:1-6 on the occasion of the cure of the dropsical man on the Sabbath. In these passages the argumentation starts from the nature and the character of the day of rest given by God. This day has not been given to oppress and destroy life, but to save it (cf. also Mark 2:27). Besides, there is no question here of an infringement of the Mosaic law concerning the Sabbath. There is certainly question, however, of a deviation from the late-Judaistic views which, in spite of all their scrupulous regard for the letter, did not fulfill God's law but destroyed it (cf. also John 7:22-24).

The story of the conflict with respect to the Sabbath as it is given by all the three gospels on the occasion of the disciples' plucking of ears of corn on the Sabbath (Matt. 12:1-8 par.) shows a slight difference. In this case, also, the issue is an infringement of a typical *interpretation* of the law concerning the Sabbath and not of the Mosaic precept itself.[40]   Neverthe- less Jesus answers by way of a more comprehensive context the criticism directed against his disciples. He makes an explicit appeal to that which is written ("have you not read?", Matt. 12:3 par., v. 5), viz., to David's infringement of the prohibition to eat of the shewbread. Already in this there is a clear allusion to the messianic motive. For David, too, had done this as the Lord's anointed, because the way he took was a holy way (1 Sam. 21:5 A.V.).[41]   Similarly Jesus appeals to the priests who broke the letter of the commandment of the Sabbath, and yet were to be regarded as blameless notwith- standing. And then he adds: "But I say unto you, that in this place is one greater than the temple" (Matt. 12:6). This is a clear appeal to his own greatness and to the mission en- trusted to him by God. These exempted him from keeping formal ceremonial precepts if they conflicted with his own divinely prescribed purposes. Something similar is found in Matthew 17:24-27, where Jesus vindicates his exemption from paying taxes for his Father's house on the basis of his Sonship. With respect to the Sabbath, this is summarized in the above- mentioned paragraph in the following way, "The Son of Man is Lord ('also,' in Mark) of the Sabbath." So, when Jesus as the Son of Man, i.e., because of the authority given him by God, calls himself the Lord of the Sabbath and acts accord- ingly, he does so knowing that he is not thereby frustrating his Father's will, but fulfilling it in accordance with the Scrip- tures themselves. This messianic motif of the fulfillment of the law, finally, is found in a still more comprehensive sense in Jesus' words on fasting, "the children of the bride-chamber cannot mourn as long as the bridegroom is with them" (Matt. 9:15ff), followed by pronouncements on putting a piece of new cloth upon an old garment, and new wine into old bottles. We ought to bear in mind that the fasting prescribed by the

Pharisees was not based on Moses' law. Yet Jesus does not reject the criticism of the Pharisees on this account. In other places it appears that Jesus has not rejected every form of fasting, either for his own time (Matt. 6:16-18), or for the future (Matt. 9:15b). The importance of his words on fasting is that he wants the formal service of God, and the manner of the worship of God in general, to be viewed in the light of the historical situation of salvation and that he makes this worship dependent on the latter. At the present time, it is the stage of the fulfillment, of the presence of the Bridegroom, of the passing of the old (*palaion*) and the coming of the new (*neon; kainon*)[42] which must dominate everything, even the manner of worship. This is why maintaining what is old (fasting as the expression of sorrow and repentance with a view to the approaching judgment, the subject of John the Baptist's exhortation) means a misunderstanding and ignoring of the time of salvation that has already begun, as well as the proclamation of salvation that is being fulfilled. Here, too, it is not the law that is opposed by Jesus nor the observance of certain religious forms attendant to it, but rather, the basically unbelieving mechanical maintenance of what is old without recognizing what is new. Though these pronouncements refer primarily to fasting and characterize the time inaugurated by Jesus' coming as the (provisional) messianic time of joy, there is nevertheless no denying that especially the last saying about new wine in old bottles is of very general meaning. If anywhere, it is here that an extremely important and comprehensive criterion is given, not only for the meaning of fasting, but for the entire existence and the value of the Old Testament way of worship. This statement must, therefore, be taken to be the complement of such a pronouncement as is found in Matthew 5:18, "Till heaven and earth pass, one jot or one tittle shall in no wise pass from the law, till all be fulfilled." It is exactly with reference to this "till all be fulfilled" that the messianic viewpoint proves to be so very important. Not only the prophecies, but also the law finds its fulfillment in Jesus' coming, and must be understood in the light of such fulfillment. The pronouncement in Matthew 5:18 therefore occupies a very remarkable place in Luke. It follows the saying in Luke 16:16,17, "The law and the prophets were until John: since that time the kingdom of God is preached, and every man presseth into it." Here, too, on the one hand, the lasting validity of the law is pointed out (even after the fulfillment of salvation has commenced); and on the other, however, the fulfillment of the law is set in the light and closely connected with the fact that "what is new" has come. Neither here, nor in Matthew 9:14ff, nor anywhere else in the gospel, in the transitory importance of all kinds of Old Testament precepts, especially the entire manner of divine service, spoken of *expressis verbis* (cf., however, Matt. 27:54; 24:2, par.!). But the messianic motif of fulfillment, as it is expressed in Matthew 9:16ff., was to have far-reaching consequences for the future.[43] Here, too, "fulfillment" and "provisionality" go hand in hand.[44] This provisional fulfillment is not yet complete. Jesus is still to suffer, to die, and to rise from the dead. All this is a co-determinant of the meaning and the form of divine worship, which even in its Old Testament shape has not been done away with by Jesus but has been brought to fulfillment. Nevertheless, it now appears clearly that *the "fulfillment of the law" is subject to the norm both of the literal Old Testament wording of the law, and of the meaning of the salvation manifested in Christ.*

This is the important motif which can be derived with undeniable clarity from Jesus' pronouncements relating to the manner of divine worship.

Summarizing all that has so far been found about Jesus' attitude towards the law and about the factual meaning of the fulfillment of the law proclaimed by him, we should point to the following.

In the first place we must reject any antithesis between "the ethics of law and the ethics of disposition" as the basic scheme of Jesus' moral teaching.[45] It is true that Jesus again and again has strongly emphasized the necessity of a heart disposition to please God in contrast to an external view of the law. He makes the possibility of a good deed dependent upon a good disposition of the heart, found especially in the sayings about the tree and its fruit (Matt. 7:17ff; 12:33ff). But all this does not in the least cancel God's law as an external authority and source of knowledge, nor does it replace this law by man's good disposition. When Jesus puts the Pharisees to blame because they only teach the people the letter of the law relating to the exterior action (of manslaughter, adultery, etc.), and do not indicate the disposition of the heart as the real origin of wickedness; he does not go back to what lies behind the law, but maintains the latter in its deepest meaning and purport. The disposition of the heart (indicated in whatever way it may be) is not some attribute transcending the law, but is subjected to the law and demanded by the law. This appears nowhere more clearly than in the summary of the whole of the obedience that Jesus demands, viz., in the commandment of love. As we know, this commandment is again and again indicated as the summary of *the law and the prophets.* In a similar way the phrase "with all thine heart, and with all thy soul, and with all thy might" has been borrowed from the *law* (Deut. 6:5). All the problems posited in modern times according to which the disposition of the heart, love, etc., "cannot be commanded," and which subsume Jesus' commandments to the schema of autonomy-heteronomy, outward and inner authority, etc., are foreign to the gospel. The disposition of the heart is an indispensable condition of a good deed for the very reason that it is included in the precept of the law and is demanded by God in the revelation of his will. The theonomy of the gospel is subjection to the law, and any attempt to eliminate the category of law from the gospel is frustrated by the continuous and undeniable maintenance of the law by and in the gospel.

Consequently, as our second point, it may be said that we fail to hit the mark when we seek the fulfillment of the law in the displacement of the cultus by ethics. It is true that in more than one passage Jesus shows the absolute insufficiency of the cultus without ethics, and, moreover, he very clearly gives priority to ethics over formal cultus-activities. But in all this he knows himself to be at one with God's law which contains both cultus and ethics, and nowhere does he oppose the cultus as such. He maintains the *meaning* of the observance of certain religious forms in opposition of all kinds of legalistic exaggeration and mechanicality (e.g., of the law on the Sabbath). Yet here, too, he appeals to the clear meaning of the law prescribing such religious forms. Particularly important is the messianic motif audible in the words on the bridegroom. Here a certain form of religious practice (fasting) is declared to be rendered out of date, although provisionally, because of the fulfillment brought about by Jesus' coming. Hence the fulfillment of the law assumes the meaning of "rendering superfluous." This motif only once occurs in Jesus' words (cf., however, Matt. 27:51!) and this is the effect, not of an ethical, but of a redemptive-historical principle. Ethics and cultus are put in the places according to their own nature to which they are entitled by the whole of the revelation of the divine will. And, like the entire divine revelation, they are set in the light of the coming of the salvation and the fulfillment of the time that has started with Christ's coming.

In the third place we must reject the thesis that Jesus placed the commandment of radical love over against the juridical sphere of civil legislation. This view, too, is based upon a schema that does not apply to Jesus' ethical preaching. It may be true that Jesus does not point out God's demand by way of civil, political, and social commandments; and that he shows that those who determine their ethical attitude by what is possible and permissible by virtue of civil legislation (*ius talionis*, divorce), shirk God's radical demand with respect to their lives. But this does not at all mean that Jesus takes sides against this civil juridical order as such, nor that the point of his ethical preaching is to be sought in the contrast of the commandment (of love) with the ordinances (resulting from the creation and made necessary on account of sin)[46]. It is true that by referring back to the original will of God ("from the beginning it was not so") Jesus has restored the order of creation which does not presuppose sin as a datum.[47] But it is not true that Jesus has "cancelled" the law insofar as it presupposes man's sin.[48] Jesus does not reject these ordinances as such, for they have been given to restrain sin and not to allow it (*limes non fomes peccati,* Augustine), but he rejects that application and appeal to them which tries to escape from the real and original divine demand.

All such views consider the fulfillment of the law by Jesus as the cancellation of the category of law or of part of its contents at the expense of another part of the law. In opposition to them it must now be stated that Jesus' attitude toward the law is invariably and exclusively positive. The meaning of this is clearly seen from the antitheses of the Sermon on the Mount. Here Jesus explains the meaning of the law by means of a number of *examples* of its application. These examples must not be looked upon as a number of "new independent commandments," nor must they be divorced from the given law, but they must be viewed within the scope of the whole of the law. Jesus does not give a new description or summary of things ethical, but he gives profound insight into the depth of the revealed divine law. This is why the validity of all these separate commandments is not exclusive. They do not represent the whole will of God, nor do they embrace the complexity of the law and of life. It would not be difficult to contrast certain pronouncements of Jesus (in which he fulfills the law) to other words or actions in which he does the same thing qualitatively, viz., fulfilling the law but acting and speaking differently. Jesus forbids taking an oath because it proceeds from evil, but he himself takes an oath (Matt. 26:64). He says that a man who says to his brother "thou fool" shall be in danger of hell-fire, but he himself not only calls the Pharisees and scribes fools (and blind), but in reprimanding them for their hypocrisy, goes even further in his descriptions (Matt. 23:19 and *passim*). And similarly, Jesus commands his disciples to turn the other cheek to "whosoever shall smite thee on thy right cheek," but he himself protests (according to John 18:23) when somebody gives him a slap on the face during his trial before Caiaphas. All this clearly reflects the character of his commandments as concrete applications of the law that must be understood in connection with all of the revealed law of God and be interpreted by its light.

This is why it is incorrect to say that, in spite of his appreciation for and fulfillment of the law, Jesus adopted a critical attitude towards the law which resembled the criticism of the Old Testament prophets, and belonged to revelation as such[49] because it was the result of a new entry of the living God into the reality of existence. An appeal is made to those passages in which Jesus is supposed to abrogate the duty of obedience to certain commandments in order to make room for the real divine demand. But this is not a criticism of the law but of its application. Jesus demands mercy and not sacrifice. He contrasts the demands of justice, mercy and faith to the scrupulous and exaggerated observance of duties of the law such as paying tithes, etc. All this is not intended as a criticism of the law, nor as the putting aside of certain commandments, nor as making room for the renewed speaking of God. But Jesus introduces this demand explicitly as "the weightier matters" *of the law* (Matt. 23:23). Moreover, in the Sermon on the Mount he summarizes all the commandments in one sole commandment, "Therefore all things whatsoever ye would that men should do to you, do you even so to them" (Matt. 7:12). In this he grounds what he has previously said, e.g., about relinquishing the *ius talionis* (as regulated by the law!). But here, too, he does not rise above the law, nor does he abolish this *ius talionis* as a principle of jurisdiction, but only desires to fulfill the law, "for this is the law and the prophets." There is no question of any criticism of the law, nor of its negation, not even when Jesus rejects an appeal to the letter of the law. For such rejection is again and again paired with a renewed appeal to the law on the part of Jesus. Only on one point—although a very important one—has the law been suspended, viz., when its contents can no longer be made compatible with the meaning of the administration of salvation inaugurated by Jesus' coming. This is not due to the "mobility" of revelation, but to its *progress* in the history of salvation, in which the validity of the Old Testament law is placed under the condition of its fulfillment.[50] Here the term "critique of the law" is not to the point. Between Jesus and the Pharisees there is only the *zeitgemäsze* (up-to-date) verifiable meaning of the *given* law. Therefore Jesus' ethical preaching is specific only with respect to his specific *interpretation* of the law.[51]

This is saying, moreover, that Jesus' ethical preaching cannot be characterized as a *deuteronomium*, a repetition of the law. In Jesus' commandments there is a concretizing of the demand of the law which has no parallel in the entire Old Testament, especially in those parts in which Jesus rejects the inadequate interpretation of the Pharisees and scribes and gives expression to the meaning of the law by means of all kinds of examples. Moses speaks of killing, Jesus of calling names, Moses of the love of one's neighbor, Jesus of the love of one's enemy, etc. If the purport of Jesus' separate applications of the law is studied more closely, it will appear to be extremely difficult to give in one formula a further characterization of this fulfillment of the law. In one case that interpretation of the law which is exclusively concerned with the overt sinful action, he opposes by reference to the disposition of the heart as equally subjected to the law (Matt. 5:27,28). In another instance Jesus points out that the sin mentioned in a special commandment of the law must not only be abstained from, but that we are also held responsible for the "positive part" of the law, viz., the doing of what is righteous (Matt. 5:23-26). More than once Jesus appeals to a rule of law different from what "those of old time" and the scribes have taught the people. In opposition to the application of the *ius talionis,* provided for by the law and entrusted to the authorities, Jesus emphasizes the consequences of the commandment of love also taught by the law (Matt. 5:38ff). Similarly he opposes the casuistry based on a particular word of the Scriptures with regard to the taking of an oath by insisting on the demand of truthfulness which renders an oath superfluous (Matt. 5:33ff). The arrangements made for divorce in the Mosaic law are opposed by the demand of absolute conjugal fidelity (Matt. 5:31ff; 19:3ff). The demand to do the "weightier matter" of the law is placed over against the scrupulous observance of ritual and cultic precepts (Matt. 23:23, *passim*). Sometimes the fulfillment of the law formulated by Jesus in his commandments consists in a deepening, a refinement, a qualitative reduction of a particular sin to its root and origin; at others it contains the rejection of the atomistic conception of sin and righteousness, and sets God's demand in the light of the *original* meaning of *the whole* of all the divine commandments. It is always the law that Jesus claims to maintain and fulfill. And every time it appears that the interpretation of the law, i.e., the knowledge of the divine will from the law, must satisfy higher demands than those made by the current interpretation of the Jewish teachers of the law. The issue is not the law as such but its interpretation. And the only question is in what the interpretation demanded by Jesus and practiced by him consists.

Van Ruler here uses the remarkable formula that the special character of Jesus' interpretation of the law is the fact that man is placed by it in "the open reality," and by this he means that Christ not only binds us *to our neighbor,* in which every ethical system, even though it has been deduced from the law, falls short, but above all, that always and everywhere man *stands before God.* What this implies and what it demands of man especially, cannot be put into words, nor can it be expressed by the law. God cannot be "grasped." The encounter with God and with his demand does not take place in the law but in God's entry into human existence,[52] although the form of the law is indispensable as a particular *modality* of God's coming into human existence.

This conception contains the important truth that the divine will has not been put into words for every separate and concrete situation, and that God holds man responsible for his decisions not only with respect to the *doing* but also with respect to the *knowing* of his will. The divine law is not a textbook with sections for every situation in life, not a doctrine of cases that needs only to be consulted to know God's will. Rather, the law requires spiritual discernment and judgment from man with respect to the *knowledge* of God's will and desires to lead him to such knowledge. This does not mean that there is no question at all of a law as a permanent and universally valid instance, or only of divine commandments of a concrete character. The divine law not only gives a few applications of the divine will, a few actual examples or demonstrations, but also undoubted basic lines of conduct, summaries, general principles. In this respect, e.g., the ten commandments have a different character than that of the commandments in the Sermon on the Mount, which, at least in part, have this character of actual application (cf. above). This does not detract from the fact that, with respect to the Old Testament law also, the knowledge of the divine will is a matter of spiritual judgment and discretion, and that in the antithesis between Jesus and the Pharisees this discretion is again and again the real issue.

Although Jesus consistently rejects the appeal to particular pronouncements of the law, it would be forcing problems upon the gospel that are foreign to it if this rejection is supposed to refer to the "giveness" and "stability" of the divine revelation in the law. For Pharisaism was not put in default because it thought it could "grasp" God and his will in the law, or because it inferred consequences from particular principles or general precepts of the law. But it was blamed because it did so in such a way that the real and profound sense of the law was deprived of its force. There is not one single text to be indicated in the whole of the gospel in which Jesus blames Judaism's concentrating on the law as an impermissible shutting off of the "open reality" of God. Much rather, the whole of his teaching is dominated by the thought of the living reality of God's revealed will *in* his law. Jesus does not appeal from the law to "the open reality" of God, but points out this reality in the law. His frequently recurring reproach is not directed against commitment to the law but against their refusal to be really committed to the law (Matt. 15:6; 9:13 *passim*). No doubt the most basic cause of this refusal of Judaism's was the fact that it had divorced the law from the living God, and had made the law merely a subject for formal and scholarly learning. In contrast to this Jesus leads his disciples back to God himself for the knowledge of the divine will. They must show that they are the children of their heavenly Father. But this encounter only takes place in the law, conceived however, as the translation and wording of God's will, as the personal address by the living and holy God. The specific trait in Jesus' fulfillment of the law is not that he allows man to look beyond the limits of the law, but that within these limits he holds man responsible for the knowledge of God's will.

If the question is asked as to what is special and characteristic in Jesus' fulfillment of the law, the answer must be that it is certainly not to be found in the pointing out of the limited importance of the law as a source of knowledge about the divine will, but much rather, in Jesus' vindication of the totalitarian and all-embracing nature of the demand of the law. This, and nothing else, is the meaning of the radicalization of the law's demand in the applications given by Jesus in his commandments. This is also the starting-point of the antithesis, "Unless your righteousness shall exceed the righteousness of the scribes and Pharisees." This "excess" demanded by Jesus is not meant in a quantitative sense (reality confronts us with more situations than are provided for by the law), but in a qualitative sense (the demand of the law goes deeper and reaches further than the very elaborate interpretation of the law by the scribes would suggest). The dimension in which such fulfillment moves is not one of width but of depth. This indication of the totalitarian character of God's law is, therefore, the common tendency of all the examples of the interpretation of the law given by Jesus. Always, such an example is like a vertical section of the law revealing its all-embracing demand. Hence, the tracing back of manslaughter to hatred and quarreling, of adultery to unclean lust; hence, the radical formulation of the commandment of love, both intensively and extensively; hence, the demand imposed upon the rich young ruler (put in a general form in Luke 12:33) to sell all that he has and give to the poor (Matt. 19:21). This is the "perfection" required by Jesus, viz., the holding of nothing back, the unconditional surrender to the will of God with all that one is and has. This, and nothing else, is the meaning of the reduction of the content of the law to the duty of loving God above all and one's neighbor as oneself. Gutbrod rightly observes that this summary must not be explained from the desire for systematic perspicuity of the many kinds of commandments of the law, nor does it owe its origin to "playful constructive tendencies." Moreover, it does not tend to "weaken the divine law and make it harmless," but quite the opposite, it serves to make the law radical.[53] This is the meaning of the concept of "love" in the gospel, as also of the phrase "with all thine heart and with all thy soul and all thy understanding," including that of "thy neighbor . . . as thyself."

As for the first concept, that of love, its meaning is nowhere clearer than in the saying of Matthew 6:24 (cf. Luke 16:13), "No man can serve two masters: for either he will hate the one, and love the other; or else he will hold to the one, and despise the other. Ye cannot serve God and mammon." And also that in Matthew 10:37 (cf. Luke 14:26), "He that loveth father or mother more than me is not worthy of me; and he that loveth son or daughter more than me is not worthy of me."

From such pronouncements it appears that the "love"

which Jesus demands in the gospel is based on a radical *choice.* Properly speaking, it is another word for "conversion." It consists in the complete surrender of the will, in being at the disposal of the Lord in the same way as is a slave. This is why the battle that this love is summoned to fight is the battle against "competition," against compromise, against that which is "an obstruction" to love in its service, against all other commitments which keep love from this totalitarian service. This is also the meaning of the parable of the eye which in Matthew 6 precedes the saying about love, "The light of the body is the eye: if therefore thine eye be single, thy whole body shall be full of light. But if thine eye be evil, thy whole body shall be full of darkness. If therefore the light that is in thee be darkness, how great is that darkness" (Matt. 6:22,23, cf. Luke 11:34-36). This passage is concerned with the contrast between "sound" and "bad" (*haplous-ponēros*), which in this context means "hampered or unhampered in its functioning." As the eye cannot do its duty to man (as an illuminating organ which points the way), if the organism of the eye cannot function freely, so neither can a man who is divided in his mind, whose heart strives after two incompatible things (vs. 21). In the service of God everything depends upon integrity, perfection, the readiness to serve without any reserve. This is the love that Jesus demands, and which is also the love that is the content and summary of the law. Hence the addition "with all thine heart," etc. which expresses in a positive way what is said antithetically in the above-mentioned pronouncements.

Things are not at all different with the demand to love one's neighbor. In all manner of ways it also appears that this love consists in complete surrender to God's will. It is something different from sympathy, which is an effect engendered by the quality of its object. For the love Jesus demands is love *of one's neighbor,* that is to say, not some general love of mankind, but a love that does not pick and choose, that is unreservedly and principally committed to God's will and guidance also with respect to its *object*. For the neighbor is anyone whom God places in our way, as is described in such an unparalleled and beautiful way in the parable of the Good Samaritan (Luke 10:29-37). This conception culminates in Jesus' commandment to love our enemy, to pray for our persecutors, to do good to those who hate us, and to bless those who curse us (Matt. 5:43-48; Luke 6:27-28,32-36). This concerns people in whose doings there is nothing lovable, who extinguish any sympathy one would have for them. But thus it becomes clear what according to Jesus' words is to be understood by the love demanded by the divine law. It is only possible if the heart has been converted to God. It is the obedience that will perform any service which God demands from his children, and that presupposes the total, unhampered surrender of heart and will. And finally, the same thing is indicated by the words . . . "as thyself." This, too, is not a motivation (as if it were possible to infer love of one's neighbor from the "duty" of loving self), nor a restriction (love of one's neighbor being limited by what one owes to oneself), but it indicates that in a sense the demand of love is boundless. With the same unreasoned spontaneity with which a man seeks his own happiness and defends his own interests, so ought he to take his neighbor's interests to heart, or as it is put in the golden rule of Matthew 7:12ff (cf. Luke 6:31): "Therefore all things whatsoever ye would that men should do to you, do ye even so to them." There is no stronger way of expressing the fact that the love of one's neighbor should proceed from an "unhampered" and undivided heart, and that this love originates and is possible only from a whole-hearted readiness to serve and from our self-surrender to God.

And because *this* love both to God and to our neighbor is the great content of the law, Jesus' commandments expressing the divine will are of such a radical nature. To put it in one statement, we can therefore say that *the fulfillment of the law by Jesus consists in his setting in the light in a matchless way the character of love of the obedience demanded by the law.* In this statement love is conceived of as the totalitarian all-embracing self-surrender.

From what has been said it follows that the purport of Jesus' commandments as well as the fulfillment of the law intended by him very clearly refer to what lies behind the specifically ethical aspect, and really concentrate on the religious root of obedience to the divine will. This is the important element of truth in the conception (held by Bultmann and others) that the real issue in the commandments, as also in the other parts of Jesus' preaching, is always one of decision (*Entscheidung*). There is no doubt that Jesus' commandments are more than exhortations to come to a decision. They are genuine commandments demanding obedience, and they also include the life out of the decision. But they all make clear that *without this decision* there is no possibility of obedience and of fulfillment of the law. This is the sense of their radicalism. This is why the great antithesis between Jesus and the Pharisees regarding the fulfillment of the law cannot be expressed in a particular ethical schema. For this fulfillment lies in the great pre-ethical decision, in the way wherein a man stands before God.

This is also the meaning of Jesus' repeated qualification of official Judaism as "hypocrites" (Matt. 6:2,15,16, etc.). This expression sheds light on what we are discussing here. For we must not think of some vulgar, consciously hypocritical attitude lacking any subjective sincerity, although such an attitude is also implied in the qualification so often used by Jesus. But the discord denoted by this word lies deeper. It is the disagreement between what a man seems to be in the opinion of his fellow-men and what he is before God.[54] On the one hand he scrupulously observes all kinds of prescriptions and commandments, but on the other he does not surrender himself to God. The real issue is of a *religious* nature which is described in the gospel in all kinds of ways, e.g., in Matthew 15:8, "This people honoreth me with their lips, but their heart is far from me. But in vain they do worship me teaching for doctrines the commandments of men."

From this point of view it appears that the fulfillment of the law is *a matter of the heart*. This does not mean that our heart is elevated to the source of our knowledge of the divine will. But it does imply that the sole possibility of fulfilling the law is dependent upon our conversion to God, and any zeal in behalf of the law without such conversion (i.e., while keeping our hearts far away from God) is hypocrisy. Elsewhere Jesus speaks of the "leaven of the Pharisees and scribes," i.e., of the all-pervading principle of their "doctrine" (Matt. 16:6,12). Even though the Pharisees were the upholders of Moses' law, and should be recognized as such, the spirit ruling their teachings was pernicious. For it was the spirit of hypocrisy in the above mentioned sense. It is this great religious antithesis with regard to the fulfillment of the law which dominated the relation between Jesus and the scribes.

And finally, this love is not only the root and the prerequisite of our doing the Father's will, but also of the true spiritual *knowledge* of God's will. Without this great presupposition of love, the divine will remains a closed book, notwithstanding the learning applied to it. In view of this fact Jesus says in Luke 11:52 that the lawyers have taken away the "key of knowledge," i.e., the prerequisite for the correct insight into God's will."[55] On analogy of Jewish linguistic usage[56] the word "knowledge" (*da'at*) undoubtedly refers to the knowledge of God's will. The lawyers had taken away the key, i.e., they had concealed it. In the whole of the context this key can hardly mean anything but the right disposition of the heart, self-surrender, love. If this love were absent and no longer taught to the people as the principal thing in the whole fulfillment of the law, knowledge would be obscured, too, and the entrance into the kingdom of heaven at this point would be completely barred.

After discussing the fulfillment of the law designated by Jesus as part of the purpose of his coming and so of his messianic task, we are confronted with the question of what constitutes the new and *specifically messianic* character of such a fulfillment of the law.

A Jew has made the remark that although fundamentally Jesus' doctrine was derived from Judaism and could be characterized as Jewish ethics, it was carried to such an extreme consistency that it was no longer Jewish, but led to *Unjudentum* (i.e., to being un-Jewish). This is why the Jews could not accept this spiritual Judaism that had turned into its opposite. So we are confronted with the remarkable phenomenon that Judaism gave birth to Christianity in its original form (as the doctrine preached by Jesus), but disowned its daughter when she tried to smother her mother in a deadly embrace.[57]

Apart from the historical problem of the rejection of Jesus by the Jews, this judgment contains the truth that Jesus' commandments have no other aim than the fulfillment of the law revealed by God to Israel. On the other hand these commandments give a concrete form to these demands that will be vainly sought in the Old Testament and in the Jewish expression and rendering of the law of the Lord. To say that Jesus transcends the Old Testament is not to give a correct expression to this truth. When in Deuteronomy 6:5 it says that Israel shall love the Lord its God with all its heart and with all its soul and with all its might, and in Leviticus 19:18, "Thou shalt not avenge, nor bear any grudge against the children of thy people, but thou shalt love thy neighbor as thyself; I am the Lord," one cannot say that practically Jesus leaves the Old Testament behind him, for it is from these general pronouncements that he derives concrete, practical applications for life. All that can be said is the fact *that* he does so, and does it in such a *central* and *continual* way that his commandments are characterized by it, which formulation, moreover, has no parallel in the Old Testament.

This implies instruction more than elucidation. Here, we must be reminded of the fact that the salvation of the kingdom includes the renewal of the heart and the fulfillment of the new covenant in which God will write in the hearts of his people all that he has proclaimed as his law.

In this light, therefore, we must view the difference between the Old Testament and Jesus' preaching with respect
to the place and the formulation of the demand of love. The
grace of God revealed in Christ also carries the demand of
love to its highest consequence. Jesus' commandments are
the counter-part of salvation preached by the gospel. Here
appears the full messianic meaning of the depth, i.e., the character of the demand of love of all of Jesus' commandments.
It lies in the noetic *and* in the existential sphere, discloses not
only the law, but also the heart. It refers to the letter as much
as to the Spirit, and is at once a demand and a gift. These two
mutually determine each other. In the fulfillment of the law
as an interpretation, the heart is revealed as the place from
which come the issues of life, as the center upon which the
demand of the law is focused. Conversely, the depth of the
law is revealed only where the hearts of God's children have been
opened by the grace of Christ, for the gift of love alone bestows
the knowledge of the law. Thus the fulfillment of the law
is both word and deed, as is true in the whole of Jesus' preaching. In his mouth it is in the highest and deepest sense the
preaching of the gospel of the kingdom.

34. *The Application of the Demand of Love*

Jesus' teaching about the law is not a general theoretical
exposition but consists of very concrete incidental applications
of the law, that is to say, indications of the way by which to
consider the nature and the scope of its validity in the light
of the gospel. This point is all the more important because
these commandments reveal the radical character of the demand of love in such a matchless way, and the problem arises
as to how they may be carried into effect in human society.
It is this question that has always evoked and kept alive the
discussions about Jesus' commandments in general and about
the Sermon on the Mount in particular, and has again and
again been indicated as *the problem of their feasibility*. It is
true that in our exposition this category (of *the feasibility*)
is of little use. Here we are not concerned with the naturally sub-

jective question about the possibility, but with the necessity of the execution of Jesus' commandments posited in the gospel. Nevertheless, anyone who is willing to obey this demand in faith will be induced to try to form as accurate an idea of the concrete meaning of these commandments as possible. This concerns especially the radical commandments of the Sermon on the Mount such as the demand for leniency towards the adversary (Matt. 5:25ff, cf. Luke 12:57-59), the prohibition against taking an oath (vss. 33-37), of retribution and the concomitant demand of so-called "defenselessness," of lending without asking back (vss. 38-42, cf. Luke 6:29-30); of love of one's enemy (Matt. 5:43ff, cf. Luke 6:27ff).

The same questions occur again in the case of Jesus' demand of the rich young ruler that he sell all that he possessed and give the proceeds to the poor (Matt. 19, etc.), a demand which has a general form in Luke 12:33, "Sell that ye have, and give alms." These latter commandments refer especially to property and are further connected with other pronouncements made by Jesus about riches and the rich, such as the saying that, "it is easier for a camel to go through the eye of a needle than for a rich man to enter into the kingdom of heaven" (Matt. 19:24ff), the warning against laying up treasures upon earth (Matt. 6:19ff), the parable of the rich fool (Luke 12:16ff), the words about serving God and mammon (Matt. 6:24, cf. Luke 16:13), the parable of the rich man and Lazarus (Luke 16:19-31, *passim*). Luke's gospel, especially, is full of pronouncements which seem to be against riches and property. For this interpretation an appeal is often made to the wording of the beatitudes in Luke and the recurrent "woe unto you that . . . ," e.g., "woe unto you that are rich!" . . . "woe unto you that are full!," etc. In connection with this the question may arise whether Jesus forbids his disciples to have any possessions, or at least insists on each of them having an equal amount of possessions. In this context we cannot discuss all the questions that may arise, nor enter into details about all the texts quoted, but we wish to point out the following facts.

1. In our opinion the view that Jesus' commandments in general have only a limited sphere of validity must be rejected. According to this view, these commandments were supposed to apply only to the life of Jesus' disciples who were chosen by him to preach the gospel, or to the life of those who want to enter the kingdom of heaven by a safer and more perfect road (Jesus' commandments must then be conceived of as "evangelical advice"). Others seek the sphere of validity of Jesus' commandments in a particular *sector* of human life (the "personal" sector, in contradistinction to the sphere of an "office"), or in the mutual relations between the faithful in the fellowship within the Christian church.

To our mind such a restriction of the sphere of validity of these commandments has no support in the gospel, which consistently removes all limitation from the "sphere" of validity of the divine law. The gospel emphatically warns us against any "geographical" escape from the demand of the divine law as much as it does against the hypocrisy and the "leaven of the Pharisees." For not only few but all men must pass along this narrow way and through this strait gate. Not only personal responsibility but also that of an office falls under the righteousness of the kingdom of heaven (cf. Luke 3:10-14; 19:8); not only the relations within the church and among people of the same mind, but no less that which must be suffered at the hands of one's enemies, persecutors, etc., is subsumed under the demand of the consistent ("perfect") love of Jesus' commandments (Matt. 5:43-48).

2. On the other hand it is clear that to interpret Jesus' concrete applications of the divine law as a "new law" is to create an erroneous impression. These applications are not a number of general rules that must be followed by everybody in all kinds of circumstances. Such a conception would be in open conflict with the general picture that the gospel gives of Jesus' own life and of that of his disciples[58] and would also be a misrepresentation of the character of these commandments. Many of them (and precisely those that always give rise to the question of their "practicability") are *examples*

of the way in which particular principles of the law must be applied if this law is taken with full seriousness. This applies especially to the much debated commandments of Matthew 5:21-48. They have an illustrative value. Their validity, of course, is the same as that of the law or the principle of the law of which they are applications. The commandment of love illustrated, e.g., by the commandments of "defenselessness," of love of one's enemy, etc., in itself does not always mean that one should give in to any demand or to any pressure. But there are other commandments and principles that have been embodied in the divine law. By the side of the prohibition to kill there is the demand from the authorities to insure justice, if need be, with the sword. And by the side of the demand for truth which renders superfluous every declaration upon oath that one means what one says and shall do what one promises, there is the *sacred* oath originating, not in the faithlessness of society, but in the confession that one lives in the presence of God. This is the complexity of the revealed law of God which takes account of the complexity of human life and of the power of sin. The idea that in his application of the law Jesus has denied or annihilated this multiform complexity and has, instead, reduced the whole of righteousness to a few radical rules of life is obviously in conflict with the explicit character of these commandments. Jesus' warning is not directed against this complexity and the complicated content of the revealed divine will, but against any "hypocritical" appeal to it.

3. In all this, account must be taken of the peculiar form of Jesus' sayings which makes special demands upon our exegesis. His words are characterized by a certain amount of paradoxy and one-sidedness which throws a strong light on a particular aspect of truth without mentioning possible exceptions to the rule or another aspect of truth. This fact can be clearly demonstrated within the scope of Jesus' commandments. In Matthew 5:16, Jesus demands that our good works shall be "seen" by men. In Matthew 6:1 he warns his

disciples against doing their righteousness "before men to be seen by them." In Matthew 7:1 Jesus says, "Judge not, that ye be not judged," in 7:6 he forbids his disciples to "give that which is holy unto the dogs," or "to cast (their) pearls before swine." This last implies a very sharp distinction and judgment by the disciples with respect to their fellow men. It is obvious that we are not here beset with the problem of antinomies, but with the different aspects of the truth and of God's demand. All this, however, is not mentioned in one single saying or in one single context. Here, too, the rule holds, "He who has ears to hear, let him hear!"

However much such considerations may perhaps serve the purpose of a "hypocritical" exegesis of Jesus' commandments, without it, and without realizing the peculiar character of his doctrinal form, we shall only arrive at an absurd and one-sided interpretation. In the radical commandments everything is always focused on one thing, the character of love (in the above-mentioned sense) expressed by the righteousness demanded by the divine law. The arbitrary obstacles erected to restrict the depth and the extent of the divine will are hit with heavy blows. Jesus' word is like a flame of fire. Unparalleled are his soundings of God's law. No objections or statement of exceptions can be brought forward. But it is and remains the *law*, the revelation of the will of God, which is thus fulfilled. This determines the fundamental form of righteousness. And in its light we must judge and understand the validity of any application of the law.

4. The above is also the basis for a correct understanding of Jesus' pronouncements on property, the renunciation of one's rights, the absence of positive precepts for the organization of social and political life, and generally of what is sometimes called the negative, or again the revolutionary tendency, or even the "culture-less" character of Jesus' "ethics." All this, too, may not be detached from the Old Testament, the revealed divine law, to which Jesus appeals again and again. And in this we find a very positive appreciation of justice, of

the ordinances that have been from the beginning or that have been instituted on account of sin. Jesus does not abolish or devaluate all of this. Such appears also from incidental pronouncements in the gospel in which, e.g., Jesus speaks of marriage as instituted by God "at the beginning" as an indissoluble union (Matt. 19:6-9), or when he orders us to "render unto Caesar the things which are Caesar's" (Matt. 22:21). Therefore, every radical legalistic conception of the commandments of the Sermon on the Mount, such as that of the Mennonites, of various sects, of Tolstoi, and others, tending towards a fundamental devaluation of these ordinances or towards asceticism, is in conflict with the foundations of Jesus' doctrine, however much such radicalism may be represented as "evangelical" Christianity or as the "Christianity of the Sermon on the Mount."

Therefore, Jesus' attitude towards natural life is fundamentally a positive attitude, founded in the belief in the creation and maintenance of the world by the same God who is also the Father of those who enter into the kingdom of heaven. This is why they are not merely permitted but even ordered to take part in the promotion and the building up of natural life as long as the present dispensation lasts. They are to accept the gifts of natural life from God's hand, and the concept of "blessing" is as valid in the New Testament as it was in the Old Testament. In a word, living according to these "ordinances" by the light of God's revealed will belongs as much to "righteousness" as that which is done outside of natural life (in the church, in private life, etc.). Any sacrifice *for the sake of* this natural society made in obedience to God's will cannot be less great than the sacrifice of what is guaranteed in this society with respect to property, right, benefits, etc. Here, too, the rule holds that love, i.e., perfect willingness to serve, is the fulfillment of the law.

5. Nevertheless, it remains true that Jesus' commandments, much more than the Old Testament, emphasize the relative nature of earthly life with all its goods, and the danger of

setting one's heart on them. On the one hand this is due to the eschatological motive of the kingdom. The prospect of treasure in heaven obscures the glamour of that on earth. The New Testament, much more emphatically and clearly than the Old Testament, proclaims the reality of the kingdom as the imminent coming of the end of all things, and binds the acceptance of temporal and earthly life to much stronger conditions. There is no dualism in this, as if the expectation of the consummation of all things robs of their force and value the belief in creation and the task to be performed by the faithful. But it does bring to light the defective condition of earthly life which can only be saved by God's renewing action. We can only find life by losing it to God, and maintain it by abandoning it in this sense. This all-important reality of the coming kingdom and the previous abandonment of the present form of things in the world is one of the foundations of Jesus' appreciation of temporal life. Notwithstanding all positive valuations of the present dispensation, there is always the warning against laying up treasure on earth and refusing to be rich toward God (Luke 12:21).

6. Yet this is not the predominant viewpoint. The latter— even with respect to earthly goods—is not to be found in the eschatological but in the religious motif, i.e., not in the conviction that there will be an end of all the claims that may be made on earth and that this end is near, but in the belief that God is the Lord of life and that therefore a life which is not borne by his grace and does not consist in surrender to him is a lost life. This is made very clear in the parable of the rich man and Lazarus (Luke 16:19-31). There is no mention of any special and outstanding sins of the rich man. Yet in hell he lifts up his eyes being in torment. This is stated, without any further elucidation, as something inevitable and, as it were, as a matter of course. It is not due to his wealth as such, but to the fact that the whole course of his life could be described in the words, "There was a certain rich man, which was clothed in purple and fine linen, and fared sumptuously every day."

In contrast to this, the poor man is not only represented in his poverty, but also given the name of Lazarus, i.e., "God's help," "dependent on God's grace," "having no other refuge but God." In this integrally-*religious* antithesis lies the difference between the rich man and Lazarus. The lost state of the life of the rich man (whose life was sought in his earthly treasure) and the salvation of the other one (whose basis of life lay in God's help) are *revealed* in the light of the relations beyond the grave, where semblance and reality are forever separated. But when in his torment the rich man protests against God's decree (in the seemingly humble request to have his five brothers warned by Lazarus who was to be sent back from the dead for this purpose), he is referred to *Moses and the prophets* as the only and unsurpassable authority that can lead a man to conversion. This is to say that, *not only* and not initially is it the insight of the approching end of things which determines a right relationship to God and which is the secret of living according to his commandments, but faith in all that God has revealed and commanded from the beginning. Only the concern for the love of God and of one's neighbor required by the law lies at the base of all the seemingly negative pronouncements by Jesus on wealth, property, the assertion of one's right, etc., although this also shows that it was just such riches which Jesus considered as a permanent menace to this love.

7. Inquiring, finally, into the meaning and validity of these concrete applications of the law expressed by Jesus in various ways in his preaching, we shall discover that the radicalism of all these commandments is nothing else but the religious radicalism of love as self-surrender and perfect willingness to serve. Thus any kind of dualistic interpretation is ruled out, and at the same time it must be acknowledged that this radicalism can in no way be mitigated without affecting the great theocentric motif of the whole of the preaching of the kingdom of heaven. Jesus' commandments indicate the only level upon which the revealed law of God in its concrete demand can be understood and fulfilled. That this level is so

high is because it is the level of grace and of the redemption of the kingdom of heaven which has appeared in Christ.

On this level Jesus' commandments are meaningful and obligatory as concrete applications of the one great principle of love. This also implies that love is not a law unto itself. Love is the prerequisite and the root of the fulfillment of the law. But it is directed and guided by the divine law as the expression of God's will. And it is also guided by Jesus' commandments as applications of this revealed divine law.

Jesus' commandments, therefore, certainly contain indications of how the children of the kingdom are to act in certain concrete situations. However paradoxical their form may sometimes be, and how indispensable the light of the whole law to interpret them is, they nevertheless give rules and not exceptions! They actually demand from us a practical attitude in which we permit ourselves to be struck in the face, to lend without asking repayment, to love our enemies, even to sacrifice everything that might prevent us from following Jesus. The fact that all has not been said with this, that this is not intended to disrupt society, cannot diminish the force and the serious nature of these commandments. It is also clear that *without love* we can "bestow all (our) goods to feed the poor" and "give our body to be burned" (1 Cor. 13:3). It is not a fanatical legality, however, but love that determines the amount of "profit" of our deeds in accordance with Jesus' words. Yet Jesus' concretizing of the demand of the law is not a toying with paradoxes, but is the fulfillment of the law *according to its true nature.* Not all questions are solved here, and neither are all ethical decisions made superfluous. But here a root is laid bare, and here fruits are pointed out which are "worthy of conversion," as the demand and the grace, as the grace and the demand of the kingdom of heaven. And, finally, *within the scope of the law* we hear the call, "He who has ears to hear, let him hear," as also, "with men this is impossible, but with God all things are possible" (cf. Matt. 19:26).

Notes to Chapter VII

[1] See above, § 29.

[2] The quintessence of this subject has been discussed in my thesis, *De strekking der bergrede naar Mattheüs*, 1936. But we cannot simply refer to what is found in this thesis, because Jesus' commandments comprise more than the Sermon on the Mount, and also because the purport of the present book necessitates a brief discussion of Jesus' moral preaching.

[3] It has already been indicated that the phrase, "hunger and thirst after righteousness," has a different meaning, cf. § 24. We may also ask ourselves if 6:33 (God's) "righteousness" should not be interpreted in this sense (of the saving revelation of God in his kingdom which procures justice). It would not appear impossible, although we prefer the current view (viz., that here "righteousness" is the conduct of life demanded by God).

[4] Cf., e.g., K. L. Schmidt, *TWB*, I, p. 583, and H. D. Wendland, *op. cit.*, p. 72.

[5] For an elaborate discussion of these idealistic views (on the one hand those of Harnack, Grimm, Weinel, Baumgarten, etc., on the other, that of Tolstoi, the social picture of Jesus, the social gospel, etc.) cf. my *"De strekking der bergrede,"* pp. 192-204; 218-233.

[6] J. Weiss, *Die predigt Jesu vom Reiche Gottes,*[2] 1900, p. 139.

[7] A. Schweitzer, *Die Geschichte der Leben Jesu Forschung,*[4] 1933, pp. 594ff; 613ff; *Das Messianitäts- und Leidens-Geheimnis,*[2] 1929, p. 19.

[8] A well-known example of a non-eschatological motivation is, e.g., Matt. 6:34, "Take therefore no thought for the morrow: for the morrow shall take thought for the things of itself. Sufficient unto the day is the evil thereof." If Jesus' ethics were entirely eschatologically determined, we might certainly have expected here "for tomorrow may be the end," or "tomorrow the kingdom of God will come." About this J. H. Leckie is right when he makes the remark, (*The World to Come and Final Destiny*, p. 56), "This would have been a most powerful argument to have used if Jesus had been possessed by the conviction that the end was at hand. Yet he is content to base his appeal on a homely and familiar thought which implies that things will be in the days to come even as they have been in days gone, and that the old pathetic human experience will go on repeating itself," quoted by H. A. Guy, *The New Testament Doctrine of the "Last Things,"* 1948, p. 69. For the relationship between "kingdom of God" and "not taking thought," cf. above, § 30.

[9] The last mentioned fact was already recognized by Weiss—under the protest of some of his followers!

[10] Cf., e.g., Bultmann, *Jesus*, pp. 117-119.

[11] Cf. above, § 29.

[12] Cf. also Gutbrod, *TWB*, IV, p. 1053ff, the article on *"nomos,"* and A. A. van Ruler, *De vervulling van de wet*, 1947, pp. 327ff.

[13] Cf. my *Matth.*, II.

[14] From the standpoint of exegesis and redemptive-history, Van Ruler's exposition of the synoptic data concerning the fulfillment of the law is both important and profound; but he wrongly blames (*op. cit.*, 327-367) Gutbrod (*op. cit.*, p. 1053ff) for not bringing out more clearly Jesus' messianic expiation as the satisfaction of God's justice and thus of God's law, and his sacrificial act on Golgotha as *the* great affirmation of the divine law, p. 330. No doubt this truth is also implied in the synoptic *kerygma* (see above, § 23). But

330

exegetically it cannot be demonstrated by means of the synoptic pronouncements on "the fulfillment of the law," because these pronouncements are silent
about it. Here (and elsewhere) exegesis and *historia revelationis* should stick
to their own task, precisely for the sake of the evidence of dogma.

[15] Cf. also Gutbrod: "Beyond this (i.e., beyond the will of God revealed
in the law) there is nothing else to be fulfilled by him" (*"Darüber hinaus gibt
es keine etwa von ihm zu vertretende Güte"*), *op. cit.*

[16] Cf. also above, § 29.

[17] Cf. more details in my *Matth.*, II, pp. 61ff.

[18] Cf. above, § 27.

[19] Cf. on this, *De strekking der bergrede*, pp. 155ff.

[20] Jeremias, *TWB*, IV, p. 872, the article on *"moousēs."* He refers to the
Talmud (Schabbath 116b) quoting Jesus' word in Matthew 5:17 in Aramaic,
and where the word translated in Matthew 5:17 by *pleroosai* means: "to add
to" (*asaph*). But the Talmud can hardly be used as an arbitrator for the
establishment of the expression used by Jesus originally, and certainly not if
it is in conflict with the context in the gospel (see the text above). Besides,
the Talmud gives Jesus' pronouncement in a form which deviates entirely
from the gospel. In Billerbeck's translation it reads (*op. cit.*, I, p. 242) as
follows: "I, gospel, have not come to detract from Moses' Tora, but I have
come to add to it." But Jeremias certainly will not be prepared to interpret
"destroy" (katalusai) as "detract from"!

[21] *"Etsi Christus, qua fuit vitae perfectione, iactare merito poterat, se venisse
ad implendam Legem, hic tamen de doctrina agitur, non de vita,"* ed. Tholuck,
I, p. 143.

[22] *Das Mattheus-ev.*, p. 40.

[23] A. A. van Ruler, *De vervulling van de wet*, 1947, p. 305.

[24] *Op. cit.*, p. 320.

[25] Cf. above, § 29.

[26] In the exegesis of Matthew 5:17, this has always been rightly pointed
out; cf., e.g., Calvin, *op. cit.;* Schniewind, *Matthäus*, p. 52; Barth, *Kirchliche
Dogmatik*, II, 2,[2] 1946, pp. 766ff.

[27] That is why I think Schlatter's exegesis a misrepresentation of the specific
sense of Matthew 5:17. He understands the fulfillment of the law apparently
only as Jesus' messianic obedience. "Insofar as Jesus considers the purpose of
his coming to be the doing of the commandment of the Scriptures and the
obedience of the whole of them, he makes it clear that the congregation disobeys
Scripture and cannot obey it. His purpose passes beyond what others do and
can do. Up till now God's law has remained transgressed; now, however, he
has come who does what God has commanded." *Der Ev. Matth.*, 1933, p. 154.

[28] Cf., e.g., H. J. Holtzmann, *Handbuch der Theol. des N.T.*, I, 204; W. C.
Allen, on Matthew 5:17-20, *op. cit.*, p. 45; Klostermann, *op. cit.*, p. 40; C. G.
Montefiore, *The Synoptic Gospels*, II,[2] p. 29.

[29] For more details cf. my *De strekking der bergrede*, pp. 153-174.

[30] Cf. Strack-Billerbeck, *op. cit.*, I, p. 693; also p. 692 *passim* and p. 254.

[31] Thus, e.g., Delling, in *TWB*, I, p. 485, the article on *"archaios."*

[32] Cf. Strack-Billerbeck on Matthew 5:21 and 15:2, *op. cit.*, p. 254 and
p. 691.

[33] This argument retains its force even if one were to explain "them of old"
as the recipients of the law. For even then one must think of the *teaching* in
the *explanation* of the law that they had received, not of the law itself. Thus,
e.g., W. Geesink, *Gereformeerde Ethiek*, I, 1931, p. 457.

34 Cf. my discussion in: *De strekking der bergrede*, pp. 167-174.

35 Some authors translate Mark 7:19b by "and thus he declared all meats to be pure"; but *katharizoon* must be taken as the continuation of *ekporeuetai*. The process of digestion is at the same time the purification of the food!

36 Thus, e.g., Schniewind, *Das Ev. nach Markus*, pp. 99-101. "This verse (15) really explodes the entire O. T. legislation of the cultus." ("*In Wahrheit sprengt der Vers (15) die ganze alttestamentliche Kultusgesetzgebung.*")

37 Cf. Strack-Billerbeck, *op. cit.*, I, pp. 489ff.

38 The exegesis of the 3rd verse is very difficult, "All therefore whatsoever they bid you observe, that observe and do." This cannot mean that Jesus subscribes to all their rules, as appears, e.g., from the speech itself, viz., vss. 16-22! Cf. also my *Matth.*, II, pp. 130ff.

39 Cf. for the evidence of such linguistic usage Schlatter, *Der Ev. Matth.*, p. 679.

40 The plucking and rubbing of the corn in the hands (Luke 6:1) was explained as a form of reaping forbidden by Moses (Ex. 34:21).

41 Cf., e.g., C. F. Keil, *Die Bücher Samuels*, 1875, p. 17.

42 Cf., e.g., also Behm, *TWB*, III, pp. 451ff: "*Kainos* is the essence of what is totally different and miraculous, and what is brought by the final period." "Moreover, the parables of what is new and that does not fit in with what is old, Mark 2:21ff refer to the totally different character of Jesus' message." "*Kainos*" *ist der Inbegriff des ganz Anderen, Wunderbaren, das die Endheilszeit bringt.*" "*Auch die Gleichnisse von dem Neuen, das nicht zum Alten paszt*, Mark 2:21ff. *par weisen hin auf das totaliter aliter des Inhaltes der Botschaft Jesu*").

43 Cf. also Behm, *TWB*, IV, p. 902, 903, the article on "*neos*"; Hauck, *Das Ev. d. Mark*, 1931, pp. 38, 39.

44 Cf. also Schniewind on Mark 2:18-22, *op. cit.*, pp. 60, 61.

45 This view has had a wide circle of adherents owing to Hermann's theology, and especially in the school of H. J. Holtzmann it has been very influential in particular with respect to New Testament theology. It is opposed in my, *De strekking der bergrede*, pp. 146ff; 175ff; also Van Ruler, *op. cit.*, pp. 337ff.

46 On this conception of Brunner's and its untenability in the light of the gospel, see my *De strekking der bergrede*, pp. 210ff, 235ff.

47 Gutbrod, *op. cit.*, p. 1056.

48 Gutbrod, *op. cit.*

49 Thus Van Ruler, *op. cit.*, p. 345. In this connection he speaks of "a moment in the mobility of revelation as a self-revelation of the living God who never gives up the possession of himself . . . and maintains his law himself and in his own way."

50 The importance of this viewpoint is also clear from the civil laws of Israel whose validity cannot be rightly established without taking into account the stage reached by the revelation of salvation and the consequent special character of Israel's national existence as a result.

51 Cf. also G. C. Berkouwer, *Geloof en heiliging*, 1949, p. 185.

52 Cf. Van Ruler, *op. cit.*, pp. 348ff; he bases his views chiefly on Gutbrod's expositions, *op. cit.*, pp. 1055ff.

53 *Op. cit.*, p. 1055.

54 Cf. Cremer-Kögel, *Bibl.—theol. Wörterbuch*,[11] 1923, p. 638.

55 I look upon *gnooseoos* as a gen. objective (a key to knowledge) and not as a gen. appositive (key, i.e., knowledge); but cf. Jeremias, *TWB*, III, pp.

746, 747, the article on *"kleis."* It is true that verse 52b speaks of entry into the kingdom, but this is not saying that "the key" is the key of the kingdom and not that of knowledge. On the other hand, the absolute use of the word "key" (although defined more precisely as "knowledge") seems to be less obvious than when it is taken to mean a key *to* knowledge.

[56] Cf. Bultmann, *TWB*, I, p. 700, 701, the article on *"ginoosko."*

[57] Joseph Klausner, *Jesus von Nazareth*,[2] 1934, p. 523, cf. also pp. 529ff.

[58] Cf. my, *De strekking der bergrede*, pp. 229ff.

Chapter VIII

THE COMING OF THE KINGDOM AND THE CHURCH

35. *General Viewpoints*

As we have seen in chapters III and IV, one of the most important forms in which the kingdom appears in this world is the preaching of the gospel. Its *contents* have been discussed in Chapters V through VII. We are now confronted with the question whether there are any pronouncements made by Jesus that shed more light on the results of this preaching, and consequently, on the entry of the kingdom of heaven into this world.

In a general sense this subject has been dealt with in the parables (cf. chapter V) of the sower, of the tares among the wheat, of the fishing net, of the seed growing up spontaneously, of the mustard seed, and of the leaven. They more or less explicitly deal with the action and the fruits of the word, and of the vivifying force of the preaching of the gospel. Though they contain very important indications concerning the coming of the kingdom and the nature of its presence, the pattern revealing the progress and the effects of this preaching, however, is only vaguely outlined in general terms. From this point, therefore, we shall have to continue our investigation, broken off after the fourth chapter.

We are now confronted with the question concerning the place of the idea of the *church* in Jesus' preaching, or, to put it more accurately, with the meaning of the well-known pronouncements on the *ekklesia* in Matthew 16:18ff and Matthew 18:15ff within the scope of Jesus' preaching of the kingdom of heaven.

For a long time,[1] because of a particular interpretation of the kingdom of heaven preached by Jesus, many authors were induced summarily to deny the authenticity of the pronouncements. The general character of the kingdom of heaven was supposed to be incompatible with the idea of the *ekklesia*. Thus, e.g., the liberal theology asserted that, as a visible gathering of believers with a certain amount of organization, the church lay entirely outside the field of Jesus' vision. Jesus was only supposed to be the prophet of the "inner" religion directed to every individual apart and making its start with him. Only in a process of historical development (after Jesus' death) did his religion assume its sociological significance revealed in visible communities and organizations. It is true that from the outset Jesus' preaching was also directed to a community, but one of an ideal and invisible character, a *jenseits-Kirche* (a church in the life beyond) as an ultimate goal.[2] The church as a visible and organized unity is supposed to have been completely foreign to Jesus' world of thought and preaching. It was held to be of an absolutely secondary character, a human-sociological phenomenon. Its origin was to be sought in the local churches (*ekklēsiai*) of the first few decades after Jesus' death which were later united. This unifying process reached some sort of final stage in the third century A.D. Similarly, leadership in the church was supposed to be founded, not on any authority ordained by Christ, but partly on charismatic gifts and partly on the democratic transfer of authority to some individual members. Only later did this charismatic leadership make room for the juridical idea of an office.

It is true, these ideas have not remained unchallenged, even on the part of the liberal critique of the gospels. Thus, e.g., the Tübingen school (under the leadership of F. C. Baur) assumed that there was an antithesis between the Christian church at Jerusalem and the churches founded by Paul in pagan countries. The former was supposed to be much more juridical and authoritarian in its organization because of the presence of the apostles while the latter had an entirely charismatic basis.[3] In line with this antithesis is the thought that at Jerusalem the church was taken to be the continuation of Israel, to be Israel proper, whereas in Paul's view the idea of the spiritual "body of Christ" (*sooma tou Christou*) was considered to be the foundation of the church. In connection with this view of the church of Jerusalem, therefore, the special significance of the number twelve (the twelve disciples of Jesus) with respect to the founding of the church was again given importance. But all this does not detract from the fact that the leading scholars in the main agreed that Jesus had nothing to do with the church, and that there could be no doubt but that the pronouncement on the *ekklesia* in Matthew 16:17-19 was unauthentic.

The eschatological interpretation of the gospel has contributed even more than the liberal-spiritualistic view of the kingdom of heaven in the attempt to discredit the authenticity of Jesus' pronouncements on the church. According to this interpretation, it is quite out of the question that Jesus took account of an earthly development in which there would be room for the life of a church and for its organization.

It is true that the father of the consistently eschatological interpretation, Albert Schweitzer, has defended the authenticity of Jesus' pronouncement in Matthew 16:18 and 19, but in his opinion these sayings have nothing to do with the empirical church. The church mentioned here is the pre-existent church that will be revealed at the end of time and will coalesce with the kingdom of God.[4] Those, however, who think that in Matthew 16 the "empirical" church is doubtless referred to and who, notwithstanding, adhere to the eschatological interpretation of the kingdom, are bound to combat the authenticity of Matthew 16:18,19. Thus Bultmann writes: "There can be no doubt but that Jesus proclaimed the imminent coming of God's dominion . . . his proclamation was an eschatological preaching, his own appearance and activity were an eschatological phenomenon." And he continues, "How can he have had in view the future rise of an organized community of adherents and have instituted Peter as the holder of the doctrinal and disciplinary office!" . . . Now the coming of God's dominion announces itself in forces that are at work beforehand. And now there will first be a time in which "binding and loosing" is a necessary measure for the maintenance of the church? . . . But enough of such questions that really no longer need be asked since the time of J. Weiss![5]

Instead of assigning the church a place in Jesus' preaching of the kingdom of God, as is found in Matthew 16:17-19, it is thought, rather, that the church is the consequence of the non-fulfillment of the *parousia* of the Son of Man announced by Jesus. The church is then supposed to owe its origin to the fact that those who had been waiting for the coming of the kingdom in vain had no other alternative in the continuation of history than, as Jesus' disciples, to form an organization. This is the great discrepancy between Jesus' preaching and the reality of history, viz., that Jesus preached the kingdom, and what came was . . . the church.[6]

According to the critics, this eschatological argument against the authenticity of Matthew 16:18,19 is confirmed by the fact that nowhere else in Jesus' preaching, save in Matthew 16 and 18, is there any statement of "the church" or of "his church." And this is not only a statistical fact, but also the entity denoted by this word, in short, the whole idea of the *ekklesia* is supposed to be foreign to the synoptic tradition. "In a word, the ecclesiological language and conception is foreign to the original words of the Lord."[7] This argument is not only advanced by the exclusively eschatological view. For even Kümmel, e.g.—who acknowledges that Jesus saw in his own person and word the presence of the kingdom—is of the opinion that the sources do not offer a sufficient basis for the idea that Jesus thought of a closed circle of disciples. Nor do they warrant the thought that Jesus had wanted to form a church community in the time between his resurrection and his *parousia*. Jesus in the gospel is supposed to have spoken, not of a new church, but only of a community of men who gathered round him as the coming Messiah.[8]

In addition to these two principal arguments two others are sometimes brought forward. The first of them is of a psychological nature. The significance attached to the name,

Peter, in this connection is not supposed to be in accord with his unstable character. The second argument is that in the oldest form of Christianity Peter did not occupy the position of authority which such a distinction would have entailed had it been conferred upon him by Jesus.[9]

The latter arguments have little weight. For Peter does not get his name of honor on the basis of his character but on that of his confession.[10] And if it is thought that the authority attributed to Peter in his context is in conflict with his later position in the Christian church, this objection is based on an exegesis of Matthew 16 which, on the one hand, assigns to Peter a more exclusive place among the disciples than is acceptable on the basis of the text[11] and, on the other, is based on a view of Peter's position in later history which fails to do justice to his great importance. Besides, if the authority attributed to Peter in this passage in Matthew is not in accordance with the real state of affairs in the original form of Christianity, it would be impossible to understand in what way such a pronouncement could arise. For, if it is unauthentic, it must have been a product of the same community in which Peter would then have occupied a quite different position from the one this community itself gave him. There is no question here of a *vaticinium ex eventu,* because there is the lack of events!

And lastly, we must mention the fact that the authenticity of the *ekklesia* text in Matthew 16:18 has been combatted for a considerable time on text-critical and literary grounds. The words about Peter and the church are not supposed to occur in the original text of Matthew, having been inserted not before the second half of the second century (and consequently are taken to be an interpolation).[12] But this view has gradually been given up. The fact that the disputed words of Matthew 16:17-18 (or even only those of Matthew 16:18) occur in all the Greek manuscripts, and in all old translations, plus the fact of the strongly Semitic coloring of this paragraph in the gospel, make it impossible to assume on good grounds that these words do not belong to the original tradition of Matthew.[13]

It may therefore be said that the theory of interpolation defended on text-critical grounds has been exploded.[14]

And it is also impossible to adduce the circumstance of the sole occurrence of the pronouncement on the church in Matthew and its absence in Mark and Luke as a proof that these words do not owe their origin to Jesus himself but have been incorporated into the old Palestinian tradition in some other way. For in other cases critics do not call a tradition unauthentic simply because it occurs exclusively in one of the three synoptics.[15]

So we may conclude that of late the verdict of the unauthenticity of the pronouncements on the *ekklesia* rests only upon considerations derived from the contents of the pronouncements as such, and can be reduced to two chief arguments:

a) The idea of an *ekklesia* is foreign to the whole of the other contents of Jesus' preaching.

b) This idea is in conflict with the eschatological character of the gospel.

Meantime this minimizing of the idea of an *ekklesia* in Jesus' teaching has for some time past provoked a rather sharp reaction leading to a new consensus, but this time of a positive nature. It is not restricted to the defense of the authenticity of Matthew 16:18, but concerns itself with demonstrating that the general idea lying at the base of this passage forms an integral part of Jesus' preaching of the kingdom of heaven. This is closely connected with the acknowledgment on the part of the majority, in contrast to the exclusively eschatological conception, that Jesus saw in his own mission and activity the presence of the kingdom. This of itself gave a clearer foundation to the idea of the church as the Messiah's people already manifesting itself in the present. Kattenbusch's expositions in particular have had a great influence.[16]

Kattenbusch has strongly pleaded the cause of the authenticity of the *ekklesia* pronouncements in Matthew 16, and has sought the

origin of the idea of the church in Jesus' teaching based upon his
self-consciousness of being the Son of Man spoken of in Daniel 7.
According to Kattenbusch this figure in Jesus' self-revelation not
only has the meaning of an individual person with whom Jesus
identified himself, but also represents the "people of the saints of
the most high" mentioned in the same chapter of Daniel.

This is why Jesus not only lived in this consciousness himself,
but also tried to realize this idea of the people among the followers.[17]
And this is the origin of the idea of the church. Kattenbusch's view
of the relation between the *basileia* and God's people is that the
basileia is *given* to God's people (just as in Daniel 7 the Son of Man
is given dominion). The *basileia* consists, above all else, in love,
i.e., in service, self-sacrifice, just as the Son of Man came into the
world primarily to serve.[18] Furthermore, Kattenbusch is of the
opinion that we should not stop at this idea of "God's people," but
we must assume on the ground of Matthew 16:18ff that Jesus really
did *establish* an *ekklesia*. By this term he understands a religious,
cultic assembly called *kenischta* in Aramaic. So Jesus wanted to
organize his disciples about Peter into a "special synagogue" within
Judaism.[19] In Matthew 16 this is seen as yet future (oikodomēso).
At the time of the Last Supper this *ekklesia* was actually founded.[20]
As to the question whether Jesus reckoned with a future in which
there would be room for such an organized church, Kattenbusch
expresses as his opinion that what we know of Jesus' expectation
of the future furnishes no basis for answering this question in the
negative.[21]

Kattenbusch's ideas have found adherents in a wide circle
and have been elaborated and supplemented in all kinds of
ways by others.[22] In this the Christological motif again and
again comes to the fore. To the Messiah belong a people.
The church is not a merely sociological phenomenon originating from the will of men, but is the necessary revelation of the
messianic people. Many authors follow in the footsteps of
Kattenbusch who thought he could derive this idea of the
people of the Messiah especially from Daniel 7. But by its
side a broader foundation for the idea of God's people is
sought. According to Gloege the idea of the *ekklesia* in the

gospels must be considered as the continuation of the Old Testament datum of the "remnant" church of the future.[23]   He elaborately discusses the Old Testament concept of a *remnant* (*shar* and *sherith,* cf. Is. 10:22; 14:22, etc.).   In the identification of this "remnant," "remainder" of Israel with the New Testament "church," he is followed by others.[24]   Others, like Oepke, reject the thought that Jesus derived the idea of the *ekklesia* especially from the idea of a "remnant," or from Daniel 7.   The idea of God's people is a general and central notion in the Old Testament.   This *central* idea of God's people is the foundation of the New Testament *ekklesia,* which should be seen by Oepke's further investigations of the gospels.[25]

By the side of these Christological and redemptive-historical bases of the *ekklesia*-idea in Jesus' preaching, all kinds of arguments from the gospels have been adduced to prove that the notion of the *ekklesia* in Matthew 16 is certainly not an isolated one.   This so-called statistical argument[26] is supported, e.g., by the reference to the image of a flock which is again and again used by Jesus (Matt. 26:31; John 10:16, cf. 1 Cor. 9:7).   Jesus calls his disciples his "little flock" (Luke 12:32), or—in the gospel according to John—*his* sheep and *his* lambs (John 21:15,16) just like *his* church.[27]   Special mention is frequently made of the formation of *twelve* disciples, the representatives of the true Israel, the nucleus or germ-cell of the *ekklesia.*[28]   And finally, with reference to Matthew 16:18, the works of K. L. Schmidt in particular deserve mention.   He follows Kattenbusch and has collected very detailed and extensive lexicographical material for his conception.   According to Schmidt, Jesus used the Aramaic word *kᵉnischta,* and not *kāhāl* or *kᵉhāla.*   The latter terms are used in the Old Testament for God's people as a whole.   *Kᵉnischta* may also be used in this sense.   In addition, however, *kᵉnischta* may denote a synagogue assembly which has been specified in one way or another.   It is likely that Jesus wished to specify his adherents as a special synagogue assembly within Judaism which, however, lived in the certainty that it represented the true people of God as such.[29]   In summary we may agree with the Roman Catholic author Braun (who follows Linton) who speaks of a *new consensus* among Protestant authors.   The kingdom is not only future, it is present in the Messiah.   Therefore the *ekklesia* is not only an eschatological reality but also an empirical one given in Christ.   It is not a charismatic phenomenon. The beginning of its organization is found in Christ's calling of the disciples.   The founding of the church by Christ mentioned in Matthew 16 is to be acknowledged as genuine in the full sense of the word, in opposition to the old liberal and the recent eschatological conceptions.[30]

36. *Basileia and Ekklesia*

In our opinion one of the most important results of the recent investigations of the gospel is the fact that the organic place of the *idea* of the *ekklesia* in Jesus' preaching of the kingdom of heaven has again been recognized so that the two texts containing the *word ekklesia* have been liberated from their former isolation.   In a way, this has been due to the return to a more correct understanding of the concept *basileia.* As long as this concept was only conceived of in a spiritual sense, after the manner of the liberal theology, and as long as it was deprived of its messianic-eschatological character, the idea of *ekklesia* was robbed of any ideal foundation in the gospel.   And as long as the *basileia* was viewed as something exclusively future, after the manner of the radical eschatology, there was no room left for the *ekklesia* as a temporal messianic institution.   The one as well as the other could be met with only when the messianic and present meaning of the *basileia* was again recognized.   No doubt this is not a refutation of all of the "eschatological" argument.   For it is not an answer to the question of the future perspective of Jesus' preaching.   The fact, however, that the fulfillment began with Jesus' coming implies in principle that there is room (perhaps we might say an *a priori* necessity) for the *ekklesia* as a fact in history and not merely at the end of it.   And this is fundamental for what we are here concerned with. The question about the span of time covered by the history to be expected after the fulfillment is of secondary importance. We shall discuss it later. The acknowledgment in principle of the character of Jesus' coming and work as fulfillment in this connection has brought the gain that it is no longer possible to deny *a priori* the authenticity of the words about the *ekklesia* in Matthew 16 on the basis of the eschatological pronouncements. And this means that the tables have been turned. The *a priori* now lies on the side of the new "consensus."

We want to define accurately the position of the idea of the *ekklesia* in the scope of Jesus' preaching of the kingdom. The *ekklesia* is the name of those who have been united into one community by the preaching of the gospel. First of all we should point out that the concept *basileia* nowhere occurs in the sense of this idea of the *ekklesia*. Nor is it used in the sense that the kingdom of God in its provisional manifestation on earth would be embodied in the form and organization of the church.[31] It is true that these concepts sometimes seem to be nearly parallel, and it would be possible to speak of "borderline cases." This is in the first place due to the very complicated linguistic usage of the concept *basileia* in the gospels.

We have already observed that by the term kingdom of God we can denote not only the fulfilling and completing action of God in relation to the entire cosmos, but also various facets of this all-embracing process.[32] Thus, e.g., the territory within which this divine action occurs and in which the blessings of the kingdom are enjoyed is called the *basileia* of God or that of heaven. Well-known examples of this are e.g., the sayings about *entering into* the kingdom of heaven, *being in* the kingdom, *shutting up* the kingdom, etc. (cf., e.g., Matt. 5:20; 11:11; 23:13). Among them there are also passages in which we may assume with a great measure of certainty that Jesus speaks of the presence of the kingdom, e.g., Matthew 11:11; 18:3,4; Mark 10:15. It is not always easy to ascertain what idea is connected with such usage. It is clear that we are confronted here with a certain derivative meaning of the concept *basileia*. It may perhaps be said that on account of the central and universal meaning of this concept in the synoptic gospels, there have arisen connections that are intended to indicate a very close relation to the one great event without, however, expressing a sharply outlined idea of it. When mention is made of being the greatest or the least in the kingdom and this refers to a present or a possible present reality, as, e.g., in Matthew 11:11; 18:4, cf. also 5:19; it remains to be seen whether a sharply outlined spatial idea is intended, e.g., of the sphere of power or salvation which a man has entered into and in which he is either great or small, or whether there is also a question of a particular community of men. In our opinion the possibility must be seriously considered that the word *basileia* here has a somewhat stereotyped and blurred meaning, and that "being in the kingdom" means the participation in the fulfillment of salvation that began with Christ's coming. That such a derivative usage of the word *basileia* may sometimes refer to the church, (viz., as the sphere or the community within which the salvation of the kingdom has been received and the righteousness of the kingdom has attained validity) should not therefore on factual grounds be deemed impossible. But this would have given to the concept *basileia* such a pregnant and concrete sense as could not have failed to draw attention and would soon have led to a new kind of linguistic usage. And such is not the case. Moreover, outside of the synoptic gospels the church is nowhere in the New Testament called the *basileia*.

Although a few texts can be mentioned in which linguistic usage is not very clear, they certainly cannot be adduced as a proof of the transition of the one notion into the other. For when *the being in* the kingdom or *the entry into it* are mentioned and have to be taken in the sense of a reality that has been fulfilled, they are certainly not intended in the sense of a participation in or admittance to a particular community of men. The same thing holds for "being greater or less in the kingdom." If this should at all suggest a present reality, it cannot be taken to mean the more or less organized assembly of the faithful. But we shall no doubt have to think of the various ways in which the faithful are the objects or the organs of the saving action of God in the world. In a practical sense the idea of the totality and the community of the persons who have a part in it may be not far apart, but on the basis of this and similar pronouncements it is impossible to arrive at a clear idea or a fixed concept of such a community.

A second series of passages to be referred to here is made up of the parables mentioned above which deal with the operation of the Word and thus are strongly suggestive of the idea of the coming church. Thus, e.g., Calvin tried to apply some of them to the church, viz., that of the tares among the wheat[33] and also that of the fishing net.[34] Some present-day Protestant interpreters also identify the *basileia* in the present dispensation with the *ekklesia*-idea.[35] On the other hand, even Roman Catholic exegetes oppose this interpretation of the *basileia* in Jesus' teaching.[36]

When we were discussing these parables in a previous context, we already came across the notion that in the parable of the tares and in that of the fishing net the issue was the mingling of the wicked and the good *in the church*.[37] On the basis of the explanation of this part of Jesus' teaching given there, this application must unhesitatingly be rejected. This as a matter of fact, also appears from the explicit pronouncement that the field in which the wicked and the good are growing up together is *the world* (and therefore not the church, Matt. 13:38).[38] In this connection we must also mention the parable of the mustard seed. Lagrange, who with regard to the parables of Mark 4 makes the general statement that we are not concerned here with an *"annonce claire de L'Eglise"* (with a clear reference to the church) because it has not been indicated by any of its specific characteristics, notwithstanding writes that in the mustard seed we are necessarily led to the recognition of the Church. For this extremely small seed ultimately develops into something very large.[39]

Opinions on this parable are very much divided, as we have observed in an earlier context.[40] We have agreed with those who find the *tertium comparationis* not only in the difference between the insignificant beginning and the (eschatological) fulfillment, but also in the growth, the development from small to large. The question now however is, how must we think of this development, and what is it exactly that develops from very small to very large? The idea that we are naturally induced to think of some "institution"— and that for historical reasons this institution can only be the ecclesiastical institution—seems to be too much inspired by the Roman Catholic view of the church. Even less are we here to think of the development of an external unity than in the case of the parable of the leaven. It is true that in the parable of the mustard seed the quantitative notion is in the foreground. This suggests the question of whether the reference is to the number of people sharing in the salvation of the kingdom. In his elaborate discussion of this parable, Newton Flew is of the opinion that we are here primarily to think of the totality of the divine action in the life of Jesus.[41] The mustard seed does not refer to the few people who at the outset share in the salvation of the kingdom, but to the humble character of Jesus' action and work, his word and appearance. He also, however, points to the detail in the picture of the birds building their nests in the branches of the tree. This trait is connected with Daniel 4:12 and Ezekiel 31:3,6 (cf. vs. 12), as is well-known. There the birds stand for nations. Are we to interpret this detail in the parable in a similar way? Newton Flew thinks it probable. If the preaching of the word were to be followed by great results, what could such results be but the addition of men and women to the company of Jesus' disciples? Thus Jesus is supposed to show here that he had in view the gathering together of a community.[42]

No doubt this parable is about the continuous, world-wide importance of that which in Christ's coming began as something seemingly insignificant. The progress of the divine work of fulfillment can already be observed in this administration and will be seen in its public significance at the consummation of all things. It is obvious that this progress includes the salvation of all those who will inherit the kingdom. In our opinion it is difficult to decide whether or not this implication is expressed in the parable by means of the "birds of the air."

At any rate we think it a little far-fetched to derive from this particular aspect the idea of the new community of men that Jesus was to found. Besides, the glory of the coming kingdom consists not only in the great multitude of human beings, but in the universal work of the divine salvation. So the leading thought of this parable is too general for it to be narrowed to the idea of the community of the *ekklesia*. For this idea, Jesus' preaching contains more important points of view.

Although the gospel does not contain any passage in which the word *basileia* is used in the sense of "church,"[43] the *idea* of the *ekklesia* is a very essential element in the scope of Jesus' preaching and self-revelation. This fact has of late been rightly emphasized. Its elaboration, however, did not always—or at least not immediately—strike the correct notes; and in our opinion the required clarity for the origin of the *ekklesia* idea in the gospel has not yet been attained all along the line.

This especially applies to Kattenbusch's view which places both the origin of the *ekklesia* idea and that of the Son of Man in Daniel 7. Although in this way the *ekklesia* is again recognized as an integral part of Jesus' messianic self-revelation and thus of his preaching of the kingdom, in our opinion the connection sought here is too uncertain and too much forced to explain the *ekklesia* idea in the gospel. Already within the scope of Daniel 7 it may be seriously questioned whether the Son of Man is a symbolical representative of the "saints of the Most High."[44] And even more decisive for us is the fact that in the gospel Jesus nowhere appears to entertain such a collective view of the Son of Man. He applies this title exclusively to himself, i.e., to his own individual person.[45] Though there may be a close connection between the Son of Man and "the people of the saints of the Most High" according to Daniel 7,[46] and this chapter may contain the thought of the people of the Messiah, there can be no question, however, of identification either in an absolute or in a partial sense. And since this people of "the saints of the Most High" is never as such mentioned in the gospel, we think we are not warranted in seeking especially in Daniel 7[47] the starting-point for the idea of the *ekklesia* in Jesus' preaching of the kingdom.

The same thing holds true for the view that Gloege and others have defended, namely, that Jesus referred especially to the prophecy of "the remnant" of the people of Israel (which, according to Isaiah 10:22ff alone would be saved) for his idea of the *ekklesia*. For, notwithstanding its factual correctness, this special interpretation lacks any foundation in the gospel.[48] Precisely because this view concentrates upon this "remnant" nowhere mentioned in the gospel, it therefore does not convince those who are of opinion that in Jesus' preaching there is no room for the idea of the *ekklesia*.[49]

We agree with Oepke that, since such special explanations of the origin of the *ekklesia*-idea are not sufficiently founded in the gospel, they are really superfluous. For the idea of God's people has a much more general foundation in Jesus' messianic preaching of the *basileia* than in those few Old Testament passages, and occupies a much more central place in it than can be made plausible on the ground of such special connections.

In the first place there is the *a priori messianic* viewpoint. The concept of a Messiah without a people is unthinkable. This is admitted by all, including the radical-eschatological school.[50] The same thing is true of the fact that those who belong to God's kingdom form a community, a kingdom-of-God-community.[51] This is not merely a presupposition as the foundation of the whole of the preaching of the messianic *basileia*, but can be inferred from the gospel itself. Moreover, in the pronouncement on the *ekklesia* in Matthew 16, the pronoun "my" (church) has this meaning. It is not identical with the "my" of a teacher or a prophet who has gathered a number of pupils or adherents about himself, nor with that of the founder of a new religion who organizes his followers. But it is the "my" of the Messiah speaking of the people to whom he has given his grace and whom he rules. Such usage may be rare in the synoptic gospels (cf., however, Matt. 1:21, "his" people; 13:41, "his" kingdom, in which two cases the possessive pronoun is used twice with reference to the Messiah), but the thought that the Messiah cannot be without his people for whom he acts and for whom he is answerable, and with whom he is united, is everywhere in the background. It is they whom he says he "will confess before his Father which is in heaven" (Matt. 10:32,33). He calls them his "brothers" (Matt. 12:50; 25:40); they are the "children" of the (messianic) bridegroom (Matt. 9:15).

On the part of the eschatological school the attempt is made to maintain that this "messianic people" is a purely eschatological entity which could not appear until the *parousia* of the Son of Man awaited by Jesus. Accordingly, neither Jesus himself nor his disciples in their association with him were charged with the task of gathering already in this world such a messianic people. They only had to preach the coming of the kingdom as the approaching great decision.[52]

This theory, since it applies the eschatological principle to the whole of the gospel, is incompatible with the character of Jesus' coming as fulfillment. But apart from this, it does not in the least do justice to the clear language of the gospel with regard to Jesus' messianic work of *gathering* his people. If it is established that he acted and spoke not merely as the "Messiah designate" but as the Son of Man *who had come,* it is obvious that he had such a gathering in view.[53] For in the gospel Jesus not only speaks in an exclusively future eschatological sense of the sifting and gathering implied in his messianic task. He also certainly means the effect of his action in *this* world. Thus, e.g., when he says that he has come to bring dissension among men, even among those who are most nearly related to each other (Matt. 10:34-36, cf. Luke 12:51-53); similarly when with an eye on the inevitable choice he says, "He that is not with me is against me; and he that gathered not with me scattereth abroad" (Matt. 12:30; Luke 11:23); and when in opposition to the excessive zeal of those who forbid the mention of Jesus' name by any one that does not follow Jesus in the company of his disciples, he says, "For he that is not against us is on our part" (Mark 9:40; Luke 9:50). In both cases (i.e., sifting and gathering), the point is the *effect* of Jesus' messianic action in leading men to himself which is explicitly mentioned in the words "gather with me," and although less emphatically, also in "on our part" (note the plural form, for Jesus and his disciples represent a communal cause in the world). In this connection reference must be made to Jesus' expression "to follow after me" (Matt. 10:38; Luke 14:27 *passim*), which not only applies to the small circle of the disciples living with Jesus, but has also a metaphorical sense which holds for all who hear the word.[54]

And what is true for Jesus' own activity as the Messiah, viz., that he seeks fruit, gathers men, partly also applies to the work of the disciples.[55] We have already seen[56] that the saying about the laborers sent forth into his harvest (Matt. 9:37,38), does not refer to the future eschatological gathering of those who believe Jesus' words but to the present. These laborers, therefore, are those who assist Jesus in his work and continue this work. Some writers think it absurd that, within sight of the coming kingdom, Peter should have been given the task to organize a church and to exercise doctrinal and ruling power. But it should not be forgotten—apart from the secondary question of organization—that from the outset Jesus had promised to give his disciples some special powers with respect to the winning and gathering of men for him (something that comprises more than simply announcing the kingdom). Thus, e.g., when on the occasion of the calling of his disciples he says, "I will make you to become fishers of men" (Mark 1:17; Matt. 4:19, cf. Luke 5:10). In the same way, e.g., the miraculous feeding of the multitude (Mark 6:36-45), and Jesus' command to the disciples—"give ye them to eat" (Mark 6:36ff; 8:1-10), have a clear symbolical meaning referring to the future activities of the disciples.[57] In the future the disciples will dispose of Jesus' messianic gifts and distribute them on his behalf. Moreover, the sayings mentioning the future sufferings of the disciples (Matt. 10:16; 17-25; Luke 12:11ff; Mark 13:9-13ff), and pointing to the future gulf between them and official Jewry may show to any one who does not wish to explain them simply as *vaticinia ex eventu* that Jesus continues his messianic work in and through his disciples and is thus scattering his seed and preparing for his harvest (Matt. 13; Mark 4 *passim*); i.e., he not only announces the kingdom but is already gathering his messianic eschatological church preformatively upon earth. In view of the total picture of Jesus' activities described in the gospels, it is impossible to understand how we could admit that Jesus founded a community of disciples to whom he had promised part of the inheritance of the kingdom, but that this can*not* be considered as the beginning of the formation of the church.[58] Undoubtedly, the revelation of this community during Christ's earthly life was in accordance with his self-revelation so that it did not have the explicit character of an organized messianic church. But those who accepted his words were essentially nothing else than his people, the people of the Messiah. And it is entirely in accordance with this fundamental thought that, upon the public confession of him as the Messiah by his disciples and his own announcement of his death and resurrection, Jesus immediately speaks in a formal sense of his *ekklesia*. When, presently, Jesus is proclaimed as the Messiah by the disciples, his church will also manifest itself as such. The one is closely connected with the other and naturally proceeds from it.

In addition to this messianic viewpoint and that which already becomes visible with Jesus' coming, namely, the gathering of the messianic church; it is necessary to point to the rejection of unbelieving Israel as the people of the covenant and the concomitant *new formation of God's people.* The special relation between God and Israel as his people is one of the foundations of the gospel. For this reason Jesus directs his beatitudes to the poor, because they represent the true people of God; and also for this reason his messianic pity is extended to the lost sheep of the house of Israel. At the same time we have noticed a transition in this basic idea, in the sense that, by the side of and in the place of empirical Israel, those who believe the gospel are considered as the flock of the Lord, the seed of Abraham, and the children of the kingdom.[59]

This result is of the greatest importance for the question under discussion. For this rejection of Israel and this new formation of God's people is not simply something of the eschatological future, but has already begun to be realized with the coming of Jesus.

As for the first point, the rejection of Israel, we point especially to the parable of the wicked husbandmen (Matt. 21:43-46). The beginning of the parable runs closely parallel to Isaiah 5:2, and immediately centers upon the thought that Israel is the special vineyard of the Lord. The elaboration of this theme reveals the judgment incurred by Israel through its rejection of the Christ (the "Son" of the proprietor of the vineyard). It is noteworthy that all three evangelists quote Psalm 118 in connection with "the stone which the builders rejected but which is become the head of the corner: this is the Lord's doing." By this "building" is meant the special care taken of Israel as the people of the Lord.[60] This work is done by Israel's leaders (the "builders") at the command and under the supervision of God. The builders, however, reject the stone that has been destined by God as the crown of the work.[61] This again means the rejection of Jesus as the Messiah. God, however, will elevate him above all. In the building up of Israel as his people, his marvelous work is accomplished in the Messiah. But this cannot be done without rejecting unbelieving Israel and its leaders as God's people. In Matthew the quotation from Psalm 118 is followed by the words, "Therefore say I unto you, the kingdom of God shall be taken from you, and given to a nation bringing forth the fruits thereof" (vs. 43). By this "people" is not meant some particular "nation," but the new people of God to whom, in passing over the old Israel, he will give the salvation of the kingdom.[62] Here we find in the same context the concepts kingdom of God and God's people as the new people of God to be gathered by the Messiah. It is evident that the revelation of the kingdom is directed to the formation of a people that will replace Israel in the history of salvation. At the same time it is evident that this other, this new people of God, is spoken of not only in future-eschatological terms, but also in a future historical sense. It is about a people who yield the fruits (of the kingdom) i.e., who are converted by the preaching (of the kingdom) and thus reveal themselves already in the present as the new people of God. In this light the texts must be understood in which Jesus refers to his disciples as a flock, or as sheep (Luke 12:32; Mark 14:27). The important thing in this is not so much the sociological viewpoint (Jesus gathers his followers into a community) as that of the history of salvation (the flock means the people of God which are now gathered together by Jesus and one day, as the new twelve tribes of Israel, will be governed by the twelve apostles).[63] *Twelve,* as the number of the disciples, also has a representative meaning already for the present, not only in that they are the preachers of the salvation to the empirical people of Israel,[64] nor only in that they are an anticipation of the eschatological people of God,[65] but in that they are those in whom is embodied from the outset the church assembled by Jesus' word. They may therefore be considered in many respects as the foundation of this new church. All this proves clearly that from the start the idea of the formation of the new people of God also directed and determined Jesus' messianic activity.

No doubt this does not yet completely justify the *ekklesia* idea in the sense of a somehow organized and closed community operating in public. But the way for it has been paved in every respect, because it is in the concept *ekklesia* that from olden times onwards the organized covenant relationship between God and Israel found expression. For whatever Aramaic or Hebrew word may be recognized as the basis of the Greek word *ekklesia* used in Matthew 16—either *kāhāl* or *kᵉhāla,* as most authors do, or, with Kattenbusch, Schmidt, and others, *kᵉnischta*

—in both cases[66] its basic idea is the gathering together of the people of the divine covenant. So when Jesus speaks of *ekklesia*, he remains entirely within the sphere by which also his preaching of the gospel as directed to the people that has been elected by God to be his own is especially determined. Just as the idea of the *messianic people* naturally results from the messianic character of Jesus' appearance and activity, so in the same way the no less essential basic motif of the covenant and of the people of *God* just as naturally leads to the appearance of the *ekklesia*. The connection between the messianic aspect and that of the covenant is expressed by the words *"my ekklesia."* The people of God are the people of the Messiah. And conversely, those who confess Jesus to be the Messiah are the new Israel. Thus the *ekklesia* is the community of those who, as the true people of God, receive the gifts of the kingdom of heaven provisionally now already since the Messiah has come, and one day in the state of perfection at the *parousia* of the Son of Man. In our opinion this is the irrefutable result of further reflection upon the general tenor of Jesus' preaching of the kingdom.

On the basis of what has been said above it is possible in our opinion to summarize our view of the relation between the *basileia* and the *ekklesia*. There can be no uncertainty about either the connection or the difference between these two fundamental notions: *The basileia is the great divine work of salvation in its fulfillment and consummation in Christ; the ekklesia is the people elected and called by God and sharing in the bliss of the basileia.* Logically the *basileia* ranks first, and not the *ekklesia*. The former, therefore, has a much more comprehensive content. It represents the all-embracing perspective, it denotes the consummation of all history, brings both grace and judgment, has cosmic dimensions, fills time and eternity. The *ekklesia* in all this is the people who in this great drama have been placed on the side of God in Christ by virtue of the divine election and covenant. They have been given the divine promise, have been brought to manifestation and gathered together by the preaching of the gospel, and will inherit the redemption of the kingdom now and in the great future. This is no doubt why the kingdom is revealed *in* the *ekklesia,* viz., in its redeeming and saving significance, in all the gifts and treasures promised and granted now already in and through Christ. So there is no question of *basileia* and *ekklesia* as being identical. The former directs all our attention to God, to his consummative will, to the power with which he carries it out, to his virtues in the most comprehensive sense of the word. The latter is to a certain extent—i.e., as far as humanity is concerned—the soteriological goal of the former. To say that the *ekklesia* gradually replaced the *basileia,* that Christ came to inaugurate the kingdom but that a church arose in its stead, is an absolute misconception of the permanent eschatological perspective that encompasses the church on all sides in her expectation and service; a misconception also of the universality of the divine redemption and judgment in which the church is herself included. There is no foundation at all for the statement that the idea of the *basileia* as proclaimed by Christ is incompatible with that of the *ekklesia* because the *basileia* is either only present and spiritual or future and eschatological. For salvation bears both a messianic and a historical character. As it is messianic, it is inconceivable without a people (the new Israel, the people of the covenant); and as it is already being realized in history, the *ekklesia* is not only of an eschatological but also of an historical nature. The *ekklesia* is the fruit of the revelation of the *basileia;* and conversely, the *basileia* is inconceivable without the *ekklesia.* The one is inseparable from the other without, however, the one merging into the other.

Attempts have been made to formulate the relation between the *ekklesia* and the *basileia,*[67] but it remains doubtful if such a procedure is possible. For the *ekklesia* can be viewed in all kinds of ways from the standpoint of the *basileia.* It is a community of those who await the salvation of the *basileia.* Insofar as the *basileia* is already a present reality,

the *ekklesia* is also the place where the gifts and powers of
the *basileia* are granted and received. It is, further, the gathering of those who, as the instruments of the *basileia*, are called
upon to make profession of Jesus as the Christ, to obey his
commandments, to perform the missionary task of the preaching of the gospel throughout the world. In every respect the
church is surrounded and impelled by the revelation, the
progress, the future of the kingdom of God without, however,
itself being the *basileia*, and without ever being identified with
it.

37. *Foundation and Authority*

When it is clear that the general idea represented by the
concept *ekklesia* occupies an organic and integrating position
in the framework of Jesus' preaching of the kingdom of heaven,
it now becomes possible to discuss the contents of the specific
pronouncements on the *ekklesia* (in Matt. 16 and 18). That
in Matt. 16:17-19 is the most explicit of all, for which reason
we shall take it as our starting-point.

The first question is, what does Jesus mean when he says:
"Thou art Peter and upon this petra (rock) I will build my
church (*ekklesia*)." Does this suggest the people of God (i.e.,
the people of the Messiah) in the general sense of the word,
or are we to think of a special form of this people as is supposed
by, e.g., Kattenbusch, Schmidt, and others who speak of a
"Messiah-Jesus-Synagogue"?[68] By this they understand a separate organization of Jesus' disciples within the whole of the
Jewish community. If put in such a way, our choice is not
difficult—at least as far as Matthew 16:18 is concerned. For
in the first place it is questionable whether such "separate
synagogues" (i.e., distinct from the official ones) actually existed, so that the linguistic usage to which Schmidt makes
appeal has certainly not been established.[69] And furthermore,
the factual basis for such a specialization[70] of the word *ekklesia* = *kᵉnischta* = *"Sondersynagoge"* (special synagogue)
cannot be discovered.

It is true that the argument has been advanced that "building" the church is not an obvious metaphor if *ekklesia* is taken to mean "God's people," whereas this objection would be removed if we conceive of *ekklesia as kenischta* because the latter word may also denote the house of the synagogue.[71]   But the following objections must be made against this:

a) The metaphor "building" the church is not based on the association of the *house* of the synagogue but is already current in the Old Testament when it deals with God's special relation to Israel as his people (cf., e.g., Jer. 12:16; 18:9; 24:6; 31:4; 42:10; Amos 9:11; Eph. 2:20; Jude 20). This metaphor of Israel as God's "building," as well as that of "husbandry," "field" of God[72] is very frequent (cf. also I Cor. 3:9). The use of the notion "building" does not compel us to understand the term *ekklesia* of Matthew 16 in an especial sense, but rather, it is exactly this combination of "building" with *ekklesia* which imparts to the latter the general meaning of the gathering of those who by God or by the Messiah are united as "his people."[73]

b) The whole context of Matthew 16 contrasting *ekklesia* to the gates of "hades" points to a much wider perspective than that of the community of a synagogue. Here in the most comprehensive and ideal sense of the word the text speaks of the menace to the *ekklesia* by the powers of perdition surrounding it. Whatever may be thought of the metaphor of the *ekklesia* as built upon a rock,[74] the idea of the building of a synagogue, to our mind, is far below the level at which in this case the imagination operates.

c) And, finally, the objection to this interpretation of a "separate synagogue" is that, not only in this metaphor but in the entire world of thought of Jesus and of the later Christian church, the messianic people, (or the new Israel), do not play the part of a synagogue community establishing itself within Judaism, but are looked upon as the new people of God that must replace the old and does replace it.[75]

There is no doubt that we have to interpret *ekklesia* in Matthew 16:18 in the general sense of the word according to the analogy of the Old Testament *kahal* which the Septuagint nearly always renders by *ekklesia*. When used in a religious sense (the *kᵉhal Jahwe*), it has the meaning of the people in its unity and collectivity elected by God and set apart from other nations.[76] As such its equivalent is the Greek *laos*, people of God, people of the covenant. Here Jesus speaks of *his* church, *his* people, without referring to a particular or a general organization. The text here is about the *ekklesia* in the ideal sense of the word.

It should be noted that Jesus speaks of the building of this *ekklesia* in the future tense. This is not saying that the earliest beginnings of this church are only future. We should bear in mind that Jesus mentions the building of his church *on this petra*. In this sense the building was only future. In this connection we must also reject the opinion that here Jesus refers to the institution of the Last Supper as the commencement of the foundation of the church,[77] or to his death and resurrection[78] for then it would not be clear what meaning is to be attached to the words "on this petra." There is no doubt that the subject is the building of the Christian church on (the work of) Peter, which was to start after Jesus' death and resurrection.[79]

As is well-known, many Protestant exegetes have considered that by the words "this petra," it was not the person but the faith,[80] the confession or the office of Peter that was meant. This was very probably a reaction to the Romanist teaching of the church. Other expositors went even further and understood "this petra" to indicate Christ himself,[81] or his messiahship and his existence as the Son of God.[82] The change from *Petros to petra* has been adduced as an argument in favor of this view. The second term, "petra" (and not "petros," or simply the pronoun "you") is explained as a means by which to put Peter's confession in the foreground and his person in the background.[83]

In our opinion such explanations are far from convincing. The use of the word "petra" can be best explained by consulting the original meaning of the word. *Petra* means *rock*, whereas *petros* has the general meaning of *stone*.[84] The feminine ending in *petra,* however, was not suitable as a name for Simon, so that instead, he was called *Petros.* But when the proper name is again made a substantive, as here, *petros* must be replaced by *petra.*[85] The most natural view is that *petra* is simply a repetition of *petros.* Here, Christ certainly means Peter himself.

The question about the sense in which Peter can be the rock on which Jesus builds his church is not difficult to answer. He will be such as an apostle, i.e., as the witness of what he had seen and heard, and as the confessor of Christ's glory;[86] and not only because he would be the first stone of the new building to which later believers would have to be joined.[87] The building of the church upon Peter can hardly mean anything else than Peter's future apostolic activity. The fact that it was he and not the other disciples here mentioned is explicable, on the one hand, by pointing to the circumstance that he and not the others made profession of Christ in answer to Jesus' question. On the other hand, it is also in accord with the prominent place that Peter seems to have occupied both among the disciples in the first Christian church (cf. Matt. 10:2; 17:1; 17:24; 18:21; Acts 1:15; 2:14; Gal. 1:18; 2:7-9).

In this context Christ not only says that he will build his church on Peter, but circumscribes Peter's authority in a particular way in the well-known words about "the keys of the kingdom" and about "binding" and "loosing" on earth and in heaven. The gift of the keys indicates a particular power, in this case one connected with the kingdom of heaven, viz., the power to open and to shut it (cf., e.g., Matt. 7:23; 23:13; 25:21ff; 25:34). There is no suggestion of a gatekeeper.[88] Rather, it is that of a caretaker who gets the keys from his master (cf. Is. 22:22; Rev. 3:7), and who is now in charge of what is done inside, as well as of gaining entrance into the house.[89] The principal thing, however, is that Peter is given authority with respect to the kingdom of heaven. And this cannot be taken to refer to anything else than to admission to the kingdom and entry into it (cf. Matt. 23:13; Rev. 3:7;

1:8). This certainly does *not* mean the church, nor is a certain identification made between church and kingdom.[90] These two are clearly differentiated in these pronouncements. This is why the power of the keys cannot mean merely that to Peter was entrusted the explanation of the Scriptures,[91] nor even that "as the first theologian of the Christian church" he would come to the fore in the debate with the Jewish scribes after Jesus' death.[92] Nor does it mean that he would receive the competence to distribute the spiritual gifts of Christ to the church,[93] nor that he was commissioned simply with the task of proclaiming the gospel.[94] All such descriptions may contain certain indispensable prerequisites of the exercise of the power of the keys, but they do not express the specific character of Peter's authority. Peter is authorized by Christ to open and to shut the kingdom of heaven. This does not mean that he will replace Christ on the Day of Judgment (Matt. 7:23; 25:34); but that now on earth he is already entitled to pronounce judgment as to who will enter the kingdom and who will not.[95] What is thus here meant is a judicial authority.

This is explained at the end of the 19th verse by the words: "And whatsoever thou shalt bind on earth shall be bound in heaven: and whatsoever thou shalt loose on earth shall be loosed in heaven." The words "bind" and "loose" are rabbinical *termi technici* for ·"decide with authority." They were used with respect to the doctrinal authority of the rabbis. "Binding" thus meant something like, to declare to be unlawful; and "loosing," to declare to be lawful.[96] This is the most usual meaning. By its side another sense has been found, viz., to put under a ban ("binding") and to relieve the ban ("loosing"), by which expulsion from or reinstatement into the synagogue was meant. In this sense, however, it is rare in rabbinical literature. Finally, "binding and loosing" may also have the more general meaning of, "consigning to the divine judgment" and "acquittal" from it.[97] In the case of Matthew 16:19, the safest method will be to interpret these words in close connection with what has been said above, namely, to make pronouncements of condemnation or acquittal with respect to entry into the kingdom of heaven. And a heavenly reality will correspond with this in that he who is promised entry into heaven by Peter will ultimately go in, whereas he who is told that the kingdom is shut to him will actually find it shut. So the general point at issue here is the judicial power given to Peter with reference to admission to or exclusion from the kingdom of heaven.

However, this conclusion does not exhaust the meaning of the words if we also include in our discussion the pronouncement made in Matthew 18:18. As is well known, there is an almost literal repetition here of the instruction to bind and to loose, this time, however, in the plural ("you"). Moreover, the instruction here occurs in a more specialized context. Its words are at the end of the order that is to be carried out with respect to the brother who has misbehaved. In the event that private admonition and that with the help of others is of no avail, the rule is to be: "Tell it unto the church." It is clear that the word "church" has a more specialized sense here than in Matthew 16:18. There the church was meant in the general, ideal sense; but here it is a church with a definite "address," i.e., the church formed at a particular place which can assert itself in a particular case and which can be represented ("if he neglect to hear the church"). Anyone who also disobeys this church "shall be unto thee as an heathen man and publican." And then follows the repeated saying of "binding" and "loosing."

In this context these words apparently have a more specific meaning than in Matthew 16:19 because they are more closely connected with the activities of the local church. So "binding" and "loosing" also certainly refer to the enacting, disciplinary authority in connection with membership in the church. In connection with 18:17, they must also denote expulsion from and reinstatement into the church. To the general viewpoint of 16:18 is to be coupled the special. They are not contradictory but complementary. For the *ekklesia* is the community of those who have been given the promise of entry into the kingdom. Expulsion from the kingdom, therefore, also implies expulsion from the church, and vice versa. In both cases, the point is that of the disciplinary, judicial authority exercised on earth and confirmed in heaven. This authority certainly can not be detached from doctrinal authority; for in a certain sense it depends upon the latter. Nevertheless, because of the original usage of the terms "binding" and "loosing," we are of the opinion that these pronouncements are also concerned with disciplinary, judicial authority and that any attempt in particular to eliminate this judicial meaning when these texts are to be explained,[98] destroys the essential purport of Jesus' pronouncements.

We are now confronted with the much debated question of the applicability of Peter's authority to those who came after him, in general to the church that was to be founded by his efforts.

It is well-known that Roman Catholic theology considers itself to be entitled by this passage, especially, to speak of "the papal primacy based on the Scriptures."[99] This claim rests upon the idea of *apostolic succession* resulting from Peter and his powers, and on that of his hierarchical position both with respect to the other apostles and to the entire church. In opposition to this, Protestant exegetes have argued that Matthew 16:18 is really concerned with Peter alone and not with his successors.[100] Others extend this power to the other apostles, but emphasize its absolutely peculiar and *einmalige* (unique) character.[101]

In our discussion above we have pointed out the prominent place that Peter occupied among the disciples (and the later apostles), so that we might speak of him as the *primus inter pares* (cf. Matt. 10:2). Yet, if the single pronouncement in Matthew 16:18 is not deliberately isolated, it is impossible to maintain for a moment that he *alone*, or even only *pre-eminently*, can be called the rock or the foundation of the church; nor can it be proved that the powers of the keys of the kingdom of heaven were assigned to Peter exclusively.

A twofold idea is at stake here; namely, that of *foundation* and that of *authority*. In both cases Peter will have to be looked upon as the representative of the other disciples. As to the question of the rock-foundation, it is sufficient to refer to places like Ephesians 2:20; Revelations 21:14, in which the apostles together are called the foundation of the church. Although these passages are not a direct exegesis of Matthew 16:18, they show that, concerning this matter, there was no uncertainty in the apostolic preaching. The other apostles have *shared* his importance as the foundation of the church (cf. also Gal. 2:9). In this respect it is hardly possible to speak of primacy. It is indeed clear that Peter and the other apostles were given a unique and intransmissible position as to their importance in being the foundation. This is naturally implied in the characterization of rock (foundation). This is why the historical question of the *successio apostolica* can be disregarded. The position of a foundation is in the nature of the case intransmissible.

Things are different with respect to authority. Here, too, the statement holds that all the apostles share in it in the same way as Peter. For, apart from the fact that this authority is really and actually applied to the whole of the apostolic preaching (cf. e.g., Gal. 1:8,9; I Cor. 16:22), both John 20:21-23, and Matthew 18:18 suggest that it had not been meant for Peter alone. Matthew 18:18 is especially important, for it repeats in the plural nearly the same words of authority given to Peter.[102]

But we must go a step further. In contradistinction to what has been said about "the rock," the powers are given, not to the apostles alone, but to the entire church. The office of the twelve apostles called by Jesus may have been of a peculiar nature and "unique," but on the basis of Matthew 18:18 it will be difficult to maintain that the power of binding and loosing was exclusively theirs.[103] This holds even through the whole of the gospel shows that they had accepted their task as apostles, not only by virtue of some charismatic gift, but primarily by virtue of a mandate given them by Christ. Therefore, to refute[104] the apostolic succession taught by the Roman Catholic church, it is especially necessary to emphasize the positive aspects of the authority mentioned in Matthew 16:18,19. That is to say, there can be no question of the institution of a hierarchy here, because the task of binding and loosing has from the outset been entrusted to the church and not exclusively to Peter or to the other apostles.

To establish this statement it will be necessary to study the whole of Matthew 18 somewhat more closely. This is one of the great connected "speeches" in the gospel according to Matthew. The specific subject of Matthew 18 consists of the mutual relations among the disciples, but again and again it appears that the speech not only concerns the *twelve* disciples (although the historical annotation in the first verse, "At the same time came the disciples unto Jesus . . . , " might suggest this at first sight),[105] but also concerns that which in verse 17 is called "the church." Not unjustly has what follows been called a rule for "the church."[106]

This already follows from verse 6 where Jesus speaks of "one of these little ones which believe in me." The little ones are no longer the little children mentioned in the 5th verse, but the simple believers who in their spiritual attitude resemble these children. The same thing holds for the "despising of these little ones" mentioned in verse 10, and for the "seeking of that which is gone astray" in verses 12-14. As appears from verse 14 ("Even so it is not the will of your Father which is in heaven that one of these little ones should perish"), the parable of the shepherd and his flock here is not primarily applicable to those stray sheep among the Israelites who run the risk of perishing, as is true in Luke 15. But the reference is to the pastoral care the disciples will have to devote to the "little ones" among the believers. It is true that some authors think especially of the twelve in their quality as shepherds of the flock,[107] but in view of what follows—the instructions to be observed with regard to a brother who has misbehaved—it seems necessary to apply this whole series of sayings to believers in general, i.e., to the church. For the contents of verses 15 and following are concerned in a very general sense with the mutual relations among believers, as appears from the expression "your brother."[108]   Therefore in the 17th verse, the church is mentioned as the entity that must intervene if personal and private admonition has had no effect. From all this it is clear that Matthew 18 is again and again concerned with the life of the church.

This is why, in our opinion, there can be no doubt that the pronouncement on authority in verse 19 must be taken to refer to what the church as such has been given by Christ and what is due to the church as such.

As a matter of fact, the transitions between the twelve in verse 1, the believers, and finally the church are fluent. This would be inconceivable if the authority in Matthew 16:18 were to have an exclusive character, whether we think exclusively of Peter or also of the other apostles, however unique and unrepeatable the instruction and significance of the apostles may have been as the foundation and the founders of the church.[109]   All this is confirmed by the remarkable words following the pronouncements of Matthew 18:18 on authority, "Again I say unto you, That if two of you shall agree on earth as touching anything that they shall ask, it shall be done for them of my Father which is in heaven. For where two or three are gathered together in my name, there am I in the midst of them" (vss. 19,20). We shall have to understand these words in connection with the preceding pronouncements (cf. the expression "on earth" in vs. 18 and repeated in vs. 19). They must be applied, not only to the gathering together of the twelve or of some of them, but to the church that has come together to act, to judge, or to pray for some such purpose as is mentioned in the preceding verse. This is also suggested by the phrase "gathered together in my name"[110] in verse 20. The power of the keys is not only given to the apostles, but in a wider sense to the church and to its organs, as appears very clearly from a later passage like I Corinthians 5:2-5.[111]

Moreover, the mention of "two or three" should not be taken in an individualistic sense, as if any arbitrary small group of men were to receive full authorization even though the others were of a different opinion. For then the saying would cancel itself. The meaning is that when at a certain place or on a certain occasion there are no other believers to agree with them, those two or three as Christ's church may be certain of God's special help.[112]

Lastly, all this also implies an indication of the way in which the *nature* of these powers is to be understood, or rather, of the manner of their functioning. The latter is not automatic and unconditional. Jesus' powers are not promises of infallibility; they guarantee the *validity* of the judgment of the apostles and that of the church when in agreement with each other, and when in communion with Christ, both of them act in his name. "There am I in the midst of them" (Matt. 18:20). Here lies the mystery of the agreement between what happens on earth and what happens in heaven. The exalted Christ himself works with them, leads them to unanimous prayer, and in this way also assures them of his divine approval. Those who have gathered and act in the name of Christ have a very great responsibility to bear with respect to the Word that he has revealed to them. The divine sanction of their judgment is dependent upon agreement with his revealed will. This remains the great presupposition which is founded in the entire character of Jesus' promises of salvation. Not everything that is done in Jesus' name is accepted and sanctioned by him. By the side of the promise of Matthew 18:20 we find the warning in Matthew 7:22, in which mention is made of those who have prophesied "on earth" in Christ's name, have cast out demons in Christ's name, and have done many wonderful works (again!) in his name, and who appeal to all these at the last judgment. But "in heaven" they are told that "he never knew them." By this the point of gravitation is not shifted from the Spirit to the letter, and from divine authority to human responsibility. Christ will build his church. This is the unconditional promise. But he will do so through those whom he "knows" as his (Matt. 7:23) in their readiness to listen to his Word, to accomplish his will and to build upon the foundation laid by the apostles.

Finally, we may ask, to what extent does the organization of the church become visible in the gospel? In answer to this question we would observe that such an organization in the pregnant sense of the word, is hardly noticeable (as far as the equipment of the church with its offices and functions is concerned). To our mind Matthew 16 only means the *ekklesia* in the general, ideal sense of the word. This passage is the charter of the church, not its elaborated plan. This does not alter the fact that the general concept *ekklesia* implies the notion of a unity which manifests itself externally. The *ekklesia* is not merely an ideal, invisible entity, but also something concrete and visibly manifest. This is evident from the fact that the apostles are not only told to preach the gospel, but they also receive the power of the keys. This entitles them to draw the line of demarcation already on earth between those who will enter the kingdom and those who will not. This authority implies the visibility of the church. In Matthew 18 all this is very much clearer because there the local congregation is spoken of to which one can appeal, and which in a particular case can assert itself. According to Klostermann who follows in the steps of Wellhausen, this text refers to the church of Jerusalem.[113] This saying is then supposed to originate from the later Jerusalem church. It is difficult to see how such an assertion can be proved. The word "church" is unaccompanied here by any further indication; though apparently it presupposes a Jewish environment ("heathen and publican"). But such an environment is the presupposition of the whole of Jesus' preaching, even when he speaks of the future.[114] Moreover, the mention of "two or three" certainly does not refer primarily to Jerusalem. We are to think here of the church as it was to be formed after Jesus' death wherever the gospel would be preached. Although in this place there is no mention, either, of the further organization of the church, it is thus clear that in Matthew 18 the church is spoken of in a more definite way than in Matthew 16. That is why several exegetes who are prepared to accept the authenticity of the *ekklesia* pronouncements in Matthew 16 think they have to look upon this text of the church as a later addition (e.g., Kattenbusch). Now it is a fact that in Matthew 18 Jesus here and there speaks about himself in a way that does not occur anywhere else. Thus, e.g., the phrase, "those who believe in me," does not occur anywhere in the synoptic gospels except here and in the parallel text in Mark 9:42. The expression "there am I in the midst" (Matt. 18:20), is also very remarkable. Here Jesus speaks as the exalted Lord. These words remind us of the parting speeches in John's gospel. And further, the 18th verse without any introduction speaks of the life of the local church.

In our opinion the possibility must be considered that to a certain extent in this case, as in others, the evangelist has influenced the *formulation* of the several words of Jesus. Since he spoke for and out of the church, his words about "the" church in Matthew 18 had no need of any further explanation. Moreover, the words, "there am I in the midst," do not seem to *predict* the exaltation of Jesus, but to *presuppose* it. Such a presupposition may also have been formulated from the historical viewpoint of the later church.

On the other hand, it is possible in the first place that in reality Jesus said a great deal more about the formation of the church than has come down to us in the gospel. For it goes without saying that in the Gospel of Matthew, also, the tradition of Jesus' words is only of a partial nature. And, in the second place, it is clear that Matthew 18:19,20 only speaks of the beginnings of the formation of the church. The phrase, "two or three are gathered together in my name," points to a situation in which the church has not yet received a permanent organization or "address," but yet manifests itself only in the faith and in the gathering together of a few individual persons. All this is applicable both to the time when the church was still to be formed, and to that in which its organization had reached a stage of provisional establishment (the time at which the evangelist wrote).

The principal thing, however, is not the form in which these words have come down to us. It is whether or not Jesus himself spoke of his church and of its formation in the time following his death. And about this there can be no doubt. The idea of the *ekklesia* occupies an organic place in his words and is far from being a *corpus alienum* in the gospel of the kingdom of heaven. And it does so not only as something of the eschatological future, but also as an historical reality. It has been given in principle in the coming of Jesus and in his self-revelation as the Messiah. And as to the perspective for the time after Jesus' suffering and death, we have already seen that the redemptive significance of Christ's death and resurrection does not bring the end but, much rather, the continuation of the earthly future. The gathering together of the church was not ended by Jesus' death but in many respects was first really made possible. We shall find all this confirmed in our last chapter dealing with questions relating to Jesus' pronouncements on the future.

38. *Apostolate and Baptism*

What has gone before prepares the way for a summary view of those pronouncements in the gospel by which Jesus charged his disciples with the task of preaching the gospel of the kingdom. It is obvious that this charge was very closely connected with the idea of the *ekklesia*. The building of the church mentioned in Matthew 16 goes together with the preaching of the gospel and is its fruit. It was demonstrated that Jesus thought especially of the future activities of his disciples when we discussed the significance and the powers assigned to Peter. Here we are concerned with those passages that mention in so many words Jesus' commission of his disciples and their task to preach the gospel. The first passage in this connection is about an incident during Jesus' stay in Galilee. It is the sending of the disciples mentioned in Matthew 10, Mark 6, and Luke 9, together with the sending of the seventy(-two)[115] mentioned in Luke 10.

The first thing that strikes the attention is the notion of "sending forth" (*apostellein*) (Matt. 10:5; Mark 6:7, cf. Mk. 3:14; Luke 9:2; 10:1); and "apostle" (*apostolos*) (Matt. 10:2; Mk. 6:30; Luke 6:13; 9:10, cf. also Matt. 10:16; Luke 10:3). Recent research based especially on the knowledge about later Judaism has in every respect elucidated this *terminus technicus*. The word (especially the substantive noun *apostolos*) must first be approached from the juridical sphere. It denotes an ambassador with a special mission who acts on behalf of a person, represents him and has been given full powers and authority for this purpose.[116] Accordingly, we read that during his ministry in Galilee, Jesus empowers his twelve disciples (and later the seventy(-two)) to drive out demons, to cure diseases and to proclaim that the kingdom of heaven is at hand (Matt. 10:2,7,8 and parallel places). Entirely in accordance with the character of their charge, they *report* on their doings when they have returned (Mk. 6:30, *apaggello*, cf. Luke 9:10). There is not yet any question of a permanent office. Their apostolate—as well as that of the seventy(-two) in Luke 10—is still of a temporary nature. From this it follows that the instructions given by Jesus (just as those to the seventy(-two) later) refer to this particular charge and need not have a permanent and universally valid significance. This holds for their starting on their way without taking money or food with them (as is clear from a comparison with Luke 22:35ff). Nor is it permissible with regard to the later preaching of the gospel, to draw conclusions from the prohibition to go into the way of the Gentiles or to enter into any city of the Samaritans (Matt. 10:5). This is a question of a particular authorization within temporary and local limits.[117]

This does not detract from the fact that already in this first mission the principal characteristic becomes visible of that which Jesus later entrusted to the disciples as a permanent and continuous charge, viz., preaching the gospel in word and deed. It is true that there is here no explicit question of the initial stage of the formation of a church. But Jesus does say that the disciples must go to the lost sheep of the house of Israel (Matt. 10:6). Already at the outset the purpose of their action on Jesus' behalf is the gathering together of God's people. This work also appears to bear a selective character. On entering a town or village they are to find out which of the inhabitants is "worthy." They are to remain at his house and not to go from one house to another (Luke 10:7). Moreover, they are to say, "Peace be to this house." If that house is worthy of that peace (Matt. 10:11), if there is "a son of peace" in it (Luke 10:6); their peace shall rest upon it, which will be proved by the fact that the residents receive them and believe their words (Matt. 10:14). In the event that this is not the case, their peace will return to them again; it will have no soteriological effect. Then they must wipe off the very dust of that city from their feet, break off communication with its inhabitants, yet notwithstanding this, tell them that "the kingdom of God has come nigh unto you" (Luke 10:11). And it shall be more tolerable for Sodom and Gomorrha on the day of judgment than for that city, although its people belong to Israel (Matt. 10:15; Luke 10:12).

All this reveals the character of the first mission of the disciples as a sifting and a gathering together of the true people of God. Their coming brings peace (*eirēnē*), i.e., salvation in the most comprehensive sense of the word. For their having been "sent" by Jesus stamps their blessing, not simply as a wish, but characterizes it as a gift which is either accepted or rejected. Their mission makes manifest those who shall go free on the judgment day; it gathers together the true sheep of the house of Israel.

Viewed from an objective standpoint, it is not strange that Matthew adds to this first mission of the disciples a whole series of pronouncements made by Jesus which refer to the future task of the apostles after Jesus' resurrection, viz., verses 17 and following. For, even apart from the great commission recorded in Matthew 28, the gospel repeatedly shows that this missionary task awaits them in the future without, however, mentioning the words "being sent" or "apostles." This occurs particularly in the parables about the administration and care of goods entrusted by a master to his servants while he himself went away on a journey (Matt. 25:14ff; Luke 19:12ff). It is clear that here Jesus refers to himself and to his disciples, and that by the administration and care of his goods of which his servants are to render account on his return, he especially means the calling of his disciples in the service of the gospel.[118] In the same way the central thought of the synoptic parting speeches—which we intend to discuss in greater detail later— is that precisely because the disciples belong to Jesus and profess him as the Christ, they will be submitted to all kinds of afflictions and persecutions (both in Matt. 10:17-25; and in Mark 13:9-13; Luke 21:12-17, cf. Luke 12:11,12). With a view to this, they are exhorted by Jesus to profess his name without fear (Matt. 10:26-33; Luke 12:2-9, cf. Mark 8:38; Luke 9:26); and he also assures those who will "receive" his disciples (as those who have been sent by him) that they will be receiving him. Everybody who receives a prophet because of his being a prophet will receive the reward of a prophet (Matt. 10:40,41, cf. also Mark 9:41). Jesus counts his disciples among the prophets and the righteous. Thus he makes clear that the meaning of apostleship is the continuation of Jesus' mission in the world.[119] These words prove that a continued and permanent apostolate is the presupposition of the whole of Jesus' teaching, especially of that which is related to the time after his departure from the earth. In the same way Jesus also warns against the false prophets that will operate "in his name," and of these he says that he never "knew" them, i.e., recognized or sent them out as his authorized apostles (Matt. 7:21-23).

This does not alter the fact that this permanent task of the disciples to act as Jesus' apostles and substitutes is given them only *after the resurrection*. We do not read about such a formal commission before that time.   This is also seen from the fact that the apostles, in the later and permanent sense of the word, are repeatedly called witnesses of Jesus' resurrection (cf. Luke 24:48; Acts 1:22, etc.).   Only then does their proclamation fully assume the character of the preaching of the fulfillment according to the Scriptures, with the universal aspect of their mission coming to the fore—another proof that the fulfillment has come.

This new and permanent authorization of the disciples by their risen Lord is found in the *locus classicus* of the missionary commandment, Matthew 28:16-20, as well as in the (probably secondary) conclusion of Mark 16 (viz., in verses 15 and 16) and in Luke 24:46-49.   It is true that the word *apostolos* is not used in these accounts, but there can be no doubt that the charge imposed on the disciples here makes them permanent apostles.   In all three there is mention of the preaching of the Word; Mark denotes it as "preaching the gospel," Luke as "being witnesses of these things," Matthew as "making disciples."   In addition Mark mentions the power to work miracles, speak in foreign tongues, face dangers.   Luke makes the taking up of this charge dependent upon the gift of the Holy Spirit. The difference in terminology and in the elements of these three records cannot be reason to speak of mutual contradiction or of a difference in spiritual climate.[120]   Rather, it can be said that the three evangelists must be understood as being in mutual harmony because all that is found here is in full agreement with the whole of the preceding gospel of the kingdom of heaven, and forms its natural conclusion.

In this mandate we wish to point out the following.

In the first place, in all three records it is the eleven disciples who in the first instance receive this mission (cf. Matt. 28:16; Mark 16:14; Luke 24:33, cf. Acts 1:13).   On the basis of this authorization by their risen Lord, it is they who in a special sense are the bearers of the apostolate, although this is not saying that their charge is to be restricted to them.   Undoubtedly, the name of *apostle* was used only in a restricted sense by the first church; for the original apostles received this charge as the foundation of the church, their number of twelve signifying that they were to be the representatives of the new Israel.[121]   In this sense there can be no doubt that the task imposed by Christ upon his disciples which stamped them as apostles, is the permanent task of the church, although the latter remains dependent upon the apostles for the *contents* of its preaching. The significance of the *ekklesia* is therefore not exhausted in this dispensation merely by its listening to the divine Word and putting it into practice. Its service is also one that is rendered to the world. In a very considerable degree this service determines the redemptive-historical importance of the church in the time between Christ's resurrection and his *parousia*.[122]

In the second place, the *purpose* of this duty imposed by Christ is perfectly transparent within the scope of the whole of the preaching of the kingdom of heaven: it is the gathering together of the messianic people which as God's people have from of old been given the promise of the great future.   And this also means[123] the establishing and building of the church. The great instrument for this is the preaching of the gospel which, however, is more than merely a proclamation of salvation and judgment; for it has continuous significance, viz., making disciples (*mathēteuein*, Matt. 28:19) and teaching (*didaskein*, vs. 20) to observe (*tērein*) all that Christ has commanded *his disciples*.[124]   The latter element refers to the life of the *ekklesia* in the world. It has to observe, to maintain all Jesus' orders, which is especially related to doing his commandments (*entolē*). The purpose of the missionary preaching is not only salvation from judgment (Mark 16:16), but—and what is a matter of course, though too often neglected in practice—in conversion as a positive and all-embracing reformation of life (Matt. 5:13ff). That this is separately mentioned in Matthew 28:20 points to the permanent and continuous fruit of the preaching of the gospel in the life of the *ekklesia* and in that of the nations in which it is established (which appears from the concept *tērein,* implying a longer period of time). We are reminded here of what has been said in a previous chapter (in connection with the parable of the leaven) on the operation of the Word, and of a passage like Matthew 5:13,14, which speaks of obedience to Jesus' commandments—a gift of the kingdom—as of a permanent positive-critical principle for the life of the world.[125]

In the third place, we would point to the *universal* character of the duty the risen Lord imposed upon his apostles. This characteristic is emphasized in all three accounts of the resurrection. Matthew and Luke speak of "all nations" (*panta ta ethnē*), and Mark of "the whole of mankind" (*pasa hē ktisis*).[126] The text does not at all imply a conversion or change to Christianity on the part of a whole nation; nor does it mean that "church" and "people" are to some extent identifiable, as is sometimes asserted by some missionary theories.[127] Such would be in conflict with the entire character of the New Testament people of God; for they are so constituted through faith in Christ and not in the nation or in the national bond.[128] That the text speaks of people of all nations does not exclude the fact that "by becoming disciples, these people become important for the existence of their nations so that the latter as such thus come within the sphere of the apostolate and its message, and have their hidden center in the church that exists among them."[129]

Here, however, another question arises which requires a much more detailed answer. For there are many authors who deny that Jesus *himself* charged his disciples with their mission to the nations.

In this respect many have often written from the contradictory concepts, particularistic-universalistic. Thus Harnack, e.g., tried to show that Jesus himself did not give any definite directions for missionary work among the heathen, although his doctrine was intensively universalistic in character, since he freed religion internally from its national soil and made man, and not the Jew, its bearer. Yet, he nevertheless, wanted to limit himself to the Jews only and, consequently, in this respect did not break through the particularistic schema.[130]   Others, on the basis of the eschatological interpretation, have held a mission among the heathen to be impossible in Jesus' thoughts. Thus, e.g., Schweitzer, who makes an appeal to Matthew 10:5,6.[131] Similar conceptions are also entertained by those authors according to whom in Jesus' expectation the eschatological events (including those of salvation) were to extend from Israel as the center of the world to all nations, but of any *mission* to the heathen there was no talk.[132]

The result of all this is that the missionary commandment of the risen Lord in Matthew and Luke is considered to be unhistorical, and all the words that Jesus, already before his death, spoke with respect to the heathen world are held to be a later composition. This holds in particular for the words handed down to us in the account of the anointing at Bethany, "Verily I say unto you, Wheresoever this gospel shall be preached in the whole world, there shall also this that this woman hath done, be told for a memorial of her" (Matt. 26:13; Mark 14:9); together with the pronouncement in the so-called synoptic apocalypse, "And this gospel of the kingdom shall be preached in all the world for a witness unto all nations; and then shall the end come" (Matt. 24:14, cf. Mark 13:10, "And the gospel must—redemptive-historical necessity!—first be published among all nations."). In connection with this the following observations must be made:

a) Sundkler, e.g., has rightly emphasized the fact that the alternative between particularistic and universalistic cannot be applied to the gospel.[133] The entire central idea of the kingdom of heaven has an essentially universal significance, although at the beginning it was revealed to Israel and related to Israel. This is true, not only in a cosmical but also in an ethnical sense. For it means that God's dominion over all that has been created will yet again shine in unbroken glory. Thus Billerbeck also writes that the idea of the *basileia* as an eschatological concept naturally implies its attaining the purpose of its coming, viz., its manifestation in glory; and for this reason the idea of the kingdom brought and preached by Jesus and that of the "world-wide mission" are indissolubly connected.[134]

Even apart from the idea of a world-wide *mission,* the universal character of the coming salvation remains one of the essentials of the *basileia.* All this is based upon the Old Testament "eschatology." All through the Old Testament there is this tendency that the whole world and its nations are concerned with the salvation promised to Israel.[135] This holds in particular for those prophecies from which Jesus especially takes his starting-point, viz., those of Isaiah 40-66. Here is the origin of the figure of the proclaimer of salvation and of the concept of the gospel as a *kerygma.* And exactly in these prophecies is clearly revealed the character of the salvation of the Lord as embracing all nations. In the prophecies concerning the Servant of the Lord, all this is given special import. On the one hand, we find the thought that the Servant has been elected by God to let Israel and all the nations share in the Lord's salvation (cf. Is. 43:1ff: This prophecy has been applied to Christ's work by the gospel of Matthew, cf. 12:18ff). And, on the other hand, the Servant's suffering and death are here represented as the indispensable and substitutionary task he must perform in order to become the cause of the salvation of "many" (here the whole context of these prophecies prevent us from conceiving these "many" as an indefinite number only *within* Israel). "Nowhere in the Old Testament do we find the world vision more clearly expressed; nowhere do we find so clear a call to active missionary effort; and nowhere do we find the basis of that activity in passivity, in a suffering which by its spirits becomes the most potent and active of all forces."[136]

b) This universal tendency is, therefore, observable in the gospel from the outset and in an increasing degree.[137] It is already significant that Luke traces Jesus' geneology back to Adam (Luke 3:38), and that Matthew in his geneology purposely mentions Jesus' heathen female ancestors by name

(Tamar, Rahab, Ruth; Matt. 1:3,5). Immediately after Jesus' birth, the wise men from the land of the heathen make their appearance in Jerusalem (Matt. 2:1ff), and Simeon publicly testifies in the temple that now God has prepared the salvation revealed to him "before the face of all people," "a light to lighten the Gentiles" (Luke 2:31,32). And furthermore, Matthew more than once points out that Jesus' appearance and action is the fulfillment of the prophecy which, in the salvation promised to Israel, also included the Gentiles (thus already in Matt. 4:15, but especially in 12:18-21). As to Jesus' own preaching, we must point out the very clearly universalistic purport of his prediction (on the occasion of the heathen centurion's manifestation of faith) that many would come from the east and west and would sit down with Abraham, and Isaac, and Jacob in the kingdom of heaven (Matt. 8:11; Luke 13:28); as also the description of the judgment of the *nations* (in Matt. 25:32 and other places) in which the sheep will be separated from the goats. Moreover, Jesus' initial proclamation in the synagogue at Nazareth at once contains an implied warning, that—as in the days of Elijah and Elisha—salvation may pass Israel by and fall to the lot of the Gentiles (Luke 4:25-27). And healings of Gentiles point in the same direction, although within the borders of the territory of the Herods, viz., in the country of the Gadarenes (Matt. 8:28-34ff), in Bethsaida and the Decapolis (Mark 7:31ff; 8:22). Very significant in this respect is the cure of the ten lepers of whom only the Samaritan came back, and Jesus' words spoken on this occasion, "Were there no others to come back and give glory to God save this stranger (*allogenēs*)?" (Luke 17:11-19). All these pronouncements, in the light of which other sayings also assume a universalistic purport (e.g., Matt. 5:13,14, where the disciples are called the light of the *world* and the salt of the earth; Matt. 13:38, where the *world* is pointed out as the field of the good seed); are emphatically confirmed in the parable of the royal marriage feast in Matthew 22:1-14 and that of the great supper in Luke 14:15-24. Although these parables cannot be simply identified,[138] they have in many respects the same purport. Instead of those who had been invited to salvation but who had all kinds of excuses and who even ill-treated and killed the men who had been sent by the King, finally (according to Luke, after the poor and the maimed and the lame and the blind had been called), other people who were found in the highways and the lanes of the city are constrained to come. The latter group certainly stands for the Gentiles.[139] No doubt this first occurred after the calling of the Jewish nation had ended in failure. The shift to the Gentiles, though it is not mentioned as such, is undeniable.[140] The same thing applies to the parable of the wicked husbandmen, which we have already discussed. Here the judgment pronounced is that the kingdom of God shall be taken away "from you" (the Jewish nation represented by the husbandmen) and given to a people (*ethnos*) which will bring forth its fruit. The whole context makes it clear that a new community which is to replace the Jewish people is meant. Here, too, the transfer of salvation to the Gentiles is intended.

No doubt there is in all this not yet any explicit mention of *mission* among the Gentiles. Yet the two last named parables point this way very naturally, for in the parable of the supper (the marriage feast), the issue is that of being called by the messengers of the lord (the king). And the parable of the wicked husbandmen speaks of a people who bring forth the *fruits* of the kingdom of God. These fruits are doubtless faith and conversion, which presuppose the preaching and the promulgation of salvation.

c) The latter statement can be deduced from more than a number of isolated pronouncements, however important they may be. For, though the universality of salvation had already been revealed in the Old Testament and is confirmed in the synoptic gospels in all kinds of ways as for the time being to consist especially in the preaching of the gospel, *this fact is bound up in the character of the fulfillment inaugurated by Jesus' coming.* For in what precedes we have established that the *manner* of this fulfillment is a provisional one and consists exactly in the preaching of the gospel which has its foundation and content in Jesus' suffering and death. This is why the preaching of the gospel to the Gentiles is the natural *consequence* of such fulfillment. For the universalism of salvation is realized in fulfillment, and only thus can it be realized in consequence of the provisional character of the fulfillment. This specific modality of the fulfillment is misrepresented by such authors as Sundkler, Dahl, Kümmel, etc., and this is why they do not see the necessary connection between universalism and preaching.

In the face of this fact, the old objections[141] derived from Matthew 10:5 ("Go not into the way of the Gentiles," etc.) and Matthew 15:24 ("I am not sent but unto the lost sheep of the house of Israel") have no force at all. We have already spoken about the provisional, local, and temporary character of the "sending forth" in Matthew 10:5. And the same thing holds for Matthew 15:24. The fact that Jesus did not consider it to be his *own* task to go to the Gentiles does not prejudice anything with respect to the later duty of the disciples. Already in Isaiah 53, it appears that only the suffering and death of the Servant of the Lord opens salvation to "the many." This is just what is confirmed in Jesus' messianic self-revelation. And this is the cause of Jesus' preaching being restricted to Israel until his death; it is not to be sought in the centripetal idea of Jerusalem or the temple as the center of the world.[142] Only after Jesus' death and resurrection can the gospel be preached to the Gentiles. All this is founded both in the prophecies and in Jesus' self-revelation, and is not the unforeseen outcome of the "uneschatological situation" that arose after Jesus' death. In this complex of factors the rejection of the gospel by Israel plays an important part.[143] It is, as it were, the negative condition for preaching among the Gentiles, and for the universal content now imparted to the concept "God's people." The chief thing, however, is that in the administration started with Jesus' coming, all these factors together impel and urge the salvation to break through the barriers that had up to now contained it. This break-through became definitive after Christ's death.

d) On the basis of the above, there can be no doubt about the authenticity of the pronouncements in the gospel announcing the universal proclamation of salvation in the period after Christ's death (Matt. 26:13; Mark 13:10)[144], or those commanding such proclamation explicitly (Matt. 28:16-20; Luke 24:46ff; Mark 16:15ff). It is true that some authors have also denied the authenticity of Matthew 28:16ff on other grounds,[145] especially because they suppose that the "trinitarian formula" is "premature" here, and also because the conflict about the mission to the Gentiles described, e.g., in Acts (15), would then be unintelligible. As to the first argument, the words "in the name of the Father, and of the Son, and of the Holy Spirit" must not be conceived as a baptismal "formula," but much rather as an indication of the significance of baptism. As such, nobody can then on good grounds say that they "fall outside the scope of Jesus' preaching" and are therefore secondary.[146] And as to the second argument, a sharp distinction must be made between the mission to the Gentiles and the manner in which they would be admitted into the Christian church. The mission itself was never disputed. And Matthew 28:16-20 does not speak of the manner of admittance.

In whatever way, however, the latter question may be answered as to its details, the commandment to preach the gospel to all nations is in every respect an organic and natural conclusion of the preaching of the kingdom of heaven. In itself it is not strange that the apostles did not at once understand how to perform the task of preaching the gospel to every creature, observing the order as given: Jerusalem, Judea, Samaria and "the ends of the earth" (cf. Luke 24:47; Acts 1:8). But this does not alter the fact that this commandment itself naturally flows from the general character of Jesus' preaching. It is a redemptive-historical necessity not only in itself, but also as viewed within the scope of the entire administration of fulfillment that began with Jesus' coming and work (cf. *dei*, Mark 13:10). It gives to the coming period of the world its meaning and purpose; it is one of the most essential duties that the church has to fulfill in the world at this time.

Finally, in this connection we must call attention to the *commandment of baptism*. Both in Matthew 28 and in the conclusion of Mark it is paired with the missionary call of the disciples. These are the first and the only passages in the gospel of the kingdom of heaven mentioning baptism *as a commandment of Christ*. In the first part of our investigation we spoke of John's baptism, which the gospel calls "the baptism of repentance for the remission of sins" (Mark 1:4; Luke 3:3). This baptism like the whole of John's preaching had a clearly eschatological character. It served to assure any one who was baptized that in the way of conversion he would obtain the remission of his sins in the face of "the wrath to come" (Matt. 3:7; Luke 3:7). Recent investigations have pretty well established[147] that this baptism as a ceremony is a continuation of the baptism of the so-called proselytes. John, however, administered this baptism within the circle of the Jewish nation, so that its connection with the baptism of proselytes acquired a very pregnant meaning. Baptism thus made a separation between the sons of Abraham and such (cf. Matt. 3:9; Luke 3:8), the idea of the new and genuine people of God thereby coming to the fore.

At the same time John contrasted his baptism with that of the coming Messiah. His own baptism was one with water, i.e., John was able to wash off sin only metaphorically. He did not have at his disposal what he represented in an image, and could only promise it in God's name (cf. Matt. 21:25 and parallel passages, 32); the coming Messiah was to baptize with the Holy Spirit and with fire, which denoted both the gift and the judgment of the coming time of salvation. No doubt these words in John's preaching have a symbolic meaning, i.e., they do not refer to Christian baptism (with water!), but to the eschatological separation to be brought about by the Messiah in the manifestation of his glory. The baptism ordained by Christ cannot, therefore, be said to have been predicted by John, although the fulfillment of John's prophecy concerning baptism with the Holy Spirit was to be realized on Pentecost, i.e., in the present era (Acts 1:5). The meaning of Christian baptism, thus, cannot be derived from this word of John's.

Recently, Cullmann has closely related Christian baptism with the baptism of Jesus. He—rightly—hears in the voice from heaven on the occasion of the baptism of Jesus, an allusion to Isaiah 42:1 and then infers from it that Jesus' baptism pointed to his death. For, according to the prophecy beginning with Isaiah 42:1 about the Servant of the Lord, he had to surrender himself to this death. Jesus' words to John, "thus it becometh us to fulfil all righteousness" (Matt. 3:15), Cullmann interprets as saying that here Jesus is baptized for all men whereby his entering into death for them is thus beforehand symbolized. Cullmann speaks of a *Generaltaufe* (a universal baptism) which, first in Christ's baptism and then in his death, is brought to realization. So all men, whether they are aware of it or not, have been baptized into Christ's death and the administration of Christian baptism is nothing but a passive and causative inclusion into the body of Christ. Faith is then not a condition, but rather an effect and a result of baptism.[148] We must also mention Cullmann's opinion that the meaning of Christ's baptism as the acceptance of suffering and death also appears from the two pronouncements in which Jesus speaks of baptism before his death, viz., Mark 10:38, "Can ye be baptized with the baptism that I am baptized with?" and Luke 12:50, "But I have a baptism to be baptized with; and how am I straitened till it be accomplished!" In both cases the phrase "be baptized" as the indication of his approaching suffering must be understood in its proper sense. Jesus' suffering and death is his baptism which had already been symbolized by the baptism in Jordan, the "universal baptism" which he underwent for all men. This would also be the explanation why Jesus did not baptize himself. He baptized only in his suffering and death.[149] In our opinion this view of Cullmann is partly constructive, but also partly in open conflict with the New Testament.

No doubt Jesus' baptism also indicates his humiliation. This is expressed in Matthew 3:14,15, and may perhaps be inferred by an allusion to Isaiah 42:1, although it does not refer to his humiliation exclusively. Yet all this cannot prove that Jesus' baptism is a symbol of his free surrender to suffering and death. For in our opinion, there is not a single basis in the account of Jesus' baptism for establishing such a direct connection. The appeal to Mark 10:38; Luke 12:50 furnishes, in our view, the only semblance of support. The use of *baptizein* (to baptize) is really striking. But the inference that Jesus calls his suffering and death a "baptism" because his baptism by John already represented to him, his suffering and death, seems to be insufficiently warranted. "Baptizing" is here used in the general metaphorical sense of going down, sinking away.[150] For not only is Jesus' suffering spoken of as a "baptism," but also that of James and John (Mark 10:39).

Though it will always be difficult to state exactly to what degree this striking use of "baptizing" in Mark 10:38 and Luke 12:50 might in some way have been determined by John's baptism of Jesus; the way Cullmann uses this material to arrive at his conception of Jesus' suffering and death as a "universal" baptism can certainly *not* be accepted. Cullmann here refers to Matthew 3:15. But the "fulfillment of all righteousness" cannot be explained as a universal act taking place for the whole of mankind, for everybody. This would extend Jesus' baptism quantitatively. But the word "all" in the text has a qualitative sense; namely, all that the Father requires of Jesus and John ("us"), they must fulfill.

The characterization of Jesus' baptism (and death) as a "universal baptism" in which all men, independent of their consent, faith or insight, are once for all baptized and of which their later baptism is only the application and individualization is, in our opinion, a mere construction. Jesus' baptism in Jordan is certainly a messianic act by which he unites himself with sinners, and thus there is indeed something "universal" in it (viz., an act on the part of the Messiah for his people). But there are no sound reasons on the basis of this text for our saying that Jesus' baptism and death (which this baptism then would denote) is that by which all men have been baptized in Jordan and on Calvary. What is later said of the baptism of the Christian Church (viz., that it is a baptizing into Christ's death, Rom. 6:3); is under this view first extended to all men, and then projected back and made explicit in the account of Jesus' baptism. Neither this extension to all men, nor this interpretation of Matthew 3 with the help of Romans 6, however, are feasible without violating and straining the text of Matthew 3 and parallel places. The Pauline interpretation of the Christian baptism of the church has a legitimate connection with Christ's death (cf. below). It is based on the whole of the meaning of the gospel. But it will not do to exchange what is first in the history of revelation with what is later, and we must guard against the theologizing of history. Jesus' baptism occurs in the gospel as *his* messianic act of salvation, as that which he does for those who are his, and not as *their* baptism. The objection against such an *a priori* expansion of what the gospel says about Jesus' baptism gathers even more momentum when Cullmann speaks of a *Generaltaufe* (a universal baptism), so that all men, *alle Welt* (the whole world) are supposed to be baptized in Jesus' baptism. Such a conception not only applies Christ's satisfaction to all men in a universal way and to each of them separately, which must be judged as contrary to the purport of the whole gospel which limits salvation to the church of the Messiah, the people of the new covenant; but it also deprives baptism of its specific meaning as incorporation into the new people of God, for baptism presupposes faith and is not a call to faith subsequent to it. Already with John the Baptist, baptism was based on faith (Matt. 3:7, and parallel texts), and in our opinion this is also the meaning of baptism with Paul (although in the present context this statement cannot be further demonstrated). And it is also the meaning of the commandment to baptize which was given by the risen Christ.

Jesus' commandment to his disciples is, after all, clear enough. Its meaning is perfectly transparent if it is viewed in the light of the time for which this baptism is intended, viz., the period between Jesus' resurrection and *parousia*. On the one hand, there is an undeniable connection with John's baptism and that of the proselytes in the background of the latter. Baptism remains an image of purification, and thus it is a separation between men. It incorporates its recipients into a new community which is the church, Messiah's people, the new Israel. That is why this commandment to baptize without doubt also presupposes faith. Both in Matthew 28 and in Mark 16 the preaching of the gospel precedes baptism. In Mark 16:16 faith is explicitly mentioned, obviously as something antecedent to baptism. For the whole idea of the new people of God implies that faith and conversion are required for the incorporation of men into this new Israel. In this respect there is certainly no contradiction between Jesus and John the Baptist, for it was the latter who laid such great emphasis upon faith as a prerequisite. On the other hand, the baptism given by Jesus to his disciples is not a continuation of John's baptism, as if there had been no change except the prolongation of the time preceding the "wrath to come" announced by John. Here, too, the same difference obtains as has been mentioned in chapter II with reference to the administration of salvation between John's and Jesus' appearance, which difference can be denoted as the category of fulfillment. The remission of sins represented by the washing and purification of baptism is founded on Christ's finished work, especially his suffering and death. This is why Paul could say later that "so many of us as were baptized into Jesus Christ were baptized into his death." This does not mean that Christ's death is a *Generaltaufe* (a universal baptism) for all men, or even for all his people. Christ's death is the presupposition and foundation of Christian baptism, but not baptism itself. The same thing holds for the Lord's Supper, as we shall see.

Similarly, Christian baptism rests on Christ's self-surrender in death. This is also the explanation as to why Jesus himself did not baptize, but only ordered his disciples to do so after his death. Oepke rightly says that this is in accordance with the entire character of Jesus who directed himself to his anticipated messianic expiatory death.[151] In this respect it may thus also be said that the gathering together the church could only really begin after Christ's resurrection.

Christian baptism is not only an act related to the consummation of God's kingdom, like John's was; but much rather, represents the commencement of the fulfillment. Insofar as this fulfillment implies the eschatological gift of the Holy Spirit already announced by John, it appears to be closely connected with the baptism ordered by Christ. This does not mean that baptism makes this gift possible, but quite the reverse, because Christian baptism is the visible manifestation and sanction of the spiritual gifts of the administration of fulfillment which started with Christ's coming and was confirmed by his death. This is why in the course of history we see the gift of the Holy Spirit precede as well as follow baptism (cf. Acts 8:16ff; 10:44,47ff). From this fact it follows that baptism is not intended in a causative sense, but has a representative meaning, viz., with respect to the salvation brought about by Christ's death and resurrection.

And lastly, this character of fulfillment of the baptism commanded by Christ of his disciples is also clear from the words, "in the name of (*eis to onoma*) the Father, and of the Son, and of the Holy Spirit." The words "in the name of" offer some difficulty. They have nothing to do with our expression "in the name of" meaning "at the command and the authority of." Some authors relate these words to the linguistic usage in Hellenistic banking, in which *eis to onoma* means something like "on account," "for the credit account of."[152] Baptizing "in the name of" would then mean that the person baptized is held at the disposal, for the account of the Father, of the Son and of the Holy Spirit, and is thus sealed as God's property. On the other hand, Jeremias is of the opinion that we are here confronted with the translation of the Hebrew Aramaic *leshēm* or *leshum*, which in rabbinical literature denotes the intention of such cultic activities as sacrifice, baptismal washing, etc. He therefore simply translates the phrase by "for" or "with respect to" (*mit Rücksicht auf*).[153] However this may be, it is clear in any case that baptizing in the name of the Father, the Son and the Holy Spirit determines the character of Christian baptism. On the one hand, the person baptized is thus dedicated to God and given into his charge; and on the other, this three-fold name also includes all the salvation that was fulfilled by the coming of Christ and his work of redemption; adoption as a child of the Father in the fellowship of the Son,[154] and also the gift of the Holy Spirit as that of the messianic people of God which has become theirs through Christ's death and resurrection. All this is made applicable to the person baptized in this three-fold name of God, which is not to be characterized as a dogmatical formula, but qualifies the administration of salvation that began with Christ. And thus Christian baptism is indicated in its full redemptive-historical significance, in contradistinction to that of John, for the period between Jesus' death and *parousia*.

Notes to Chapter VIII

[1] A very instructive and interesting survey discussing the most important views of this problem between the years 1880-1930 is found in Olof Linton, *Das Problem der Urkirche in der neueren Forschung*, 1932, pp. 157-183. Of recent literature we mention especially R. Newton Flew, *Jesus and His Church*, 1945; W. G. Kümmel, *Kirchenbegriff und Geschichtsbewusstsein in der Urgemeinde und bei Jesus*. (*Symbolae Biblicae Upsaliensis*, Heft 1), 1954; Nils Alstrup Dahl, *Das Volk Gottes, Eine Untersuchung zum Kirchenbewusstsein des Urchristentums* (*Skrifter utgitt av Det Norske Videnskaps — Akademi i Oslo*), 1941; A. Oepke, *Jesus und der Gottesvolkgedanke, Luthertum*, März/April 1942, pp. 33-62; A. Oepke, *Der Herrnspruch über die Kirche Mt. 16,17-19, Studia Theologica*, 1949-50, pp. 110-165; and further, the survey of F. M. Braun, O.P., *Neues Licht auf die Kirche*, 1946.

[2] Cf., e.g., Linton, *op. cit.*, pp. 3ff; Braun, *op. cit.*, p. 40.

[3] This view is also found, e.g., in K. Holl, *Der Kirchenbegriff des Paulus in seinem Verhältnis zu dem der Urgemeinde*, 1921, and M. Goguel in "*L' Idée de l'Eglise dans le Nouveau Testament*," in: *Origine et nature de l'Eglise*, Paris, 1939; cf. also Braun, *op. cit.*, p. 44, 56-58, and A. Verheul, *De moderne exegese over apostolos, Sacris Erudiri*, I, 1948, pp. 380ff.

[4] *Gesch. der Leben-Jesu-Forschung*, p. 416.

[5] *Die Frage nach der Echtheit von Mt. 16,17-19, Theologische Blätter*, 1941, p. 273.

[6] A. Loisy, *l'Evangile et l'Eglise*, 1902, p. 111; cf. also M. Werner, *Die Entstehung des christlichen Dogmas*, 1941, pp. 74ff. Michaelis, also, in his *Reich Gottes und Geist Gottes nach dem Neuen Testament*, 1930, still seems to hold this view, cf. p. 20, although in his later book, *Der Herr verzieht nicht die Verheissung*, 1942, he sharply combats Schweitzer's and Werner's consistent eschatology.

[7] Bultmann, *op. cit.*, p. 268.

[8] *Verheissung und Erfüllung*, pp. 84, 85. In his *Kirchenbegriff und Geschichtsbewusstsein in der Urgemeinde und bei Jesus* (*Symbolae Biblicae Upsaliensis*, Heft 1), 1943, Kümmel has given a detailed defense of this view. Dahl, also, although not prepared to deny the authenticity of Matthew 16:18 altogether, opposes the thought that here Jesus speaks of the organization of God's people as the true Israel. Jesus did consider his disciples as the representatives of the true Israel, but this fact must not be interpreted in the sense that he recognized in their community a messianic people, a new Israel, or the church (*op. cit.*, p. 163). Insofar as such an idea is really demonstrable, it relates to the eschatological church of the future, and not to the empirical church of Christ in the present (*op. cit.*, 162). The only possible way to recognize Matthew 16:18 as authentic is by the exegesis that understands the building of the *ekklesia* as a symbolical indication of the community in the eschatological kingdom of God (p. 165).

[9] Cf. Linton, *op. cit.*, p. 175. He mentions four arguments, the statistical (cf. above), the eschatological, that of church history (Peter's position in the original church), and the psychological argument. K. L. Schmidt adopts this classification in *TWB*, III, p. 524, the article on "*ekklēsia*."

[10] Cf. also Linton, *op. cit.*, p. 182, and Braun, *op. cit.*, p. 83.

[11] Cf. below, § 37.

[12] For the arguments adduced for this hypothesis of Harnack, Resch, Grill, Guignebert, Schnitzer, Soltau, and others, cf. Linton, *op. cit.,* pp. 159ff.

[13] Cf., e.g., Bultmann, *Gesch. d. syn. Trad.,*[2] pp. 148ff.

[14] Cf. also, e.g., Schmidt, *TWB,* III, p. 523, the article on *"ekklēsia."*

[15] Cf. Linton, *op. cit.,* p. 158; Schmidt, *op. cit.:* also Bultmann, "It is, of course, not impossible that in the special contents of Matthew (and Luke) there are words of the Lord derived from a reliable old tradition" (*"Nun ist es natürlich nicht ausgeschlossen, dasz sich im Sondergut des Mt (und Lk) Herrenworte finden, die aus zuverlässiger alter Tradition stammen."*) He adds, "But this must be made plausible in each separate case; and the criterion must be that such words should fit in with the speech, the conceptual content, and the relatedness to the Lord's words which can be recognized as old on the basis of the tradition preserved in Mark and in the source sayings of Jesus." (*"Aber das ist doch in jedem einzeln Fall erst wahrscheinlich zu machen; und darfür musz doch als Kriterium gelten, dasz sich solche Worte in Sprache, Begrifflichkeit und Interesse zu der Spruchquelle erhalten Ueberlieferung als altes Gut gelten können,"*) *Die Frage nach der Echtheit, op. cit.,* p. 268. It is obvious that such a criterion is extremely subjective ("fit in with," and "can be recognized as").

[16] F. Kattenbusch, *Der Quellort der Kirchenidee,* in: *Festgabe A. V. Harnack,* 1921, pp. 143-172; *Der Spruch über Petrus und die Kirche bei Matthäus,* in: *Theol. Studien und Kritiken,* 1922, pp. 96-131; *Die Vorzugstellung des Petrus und der Charakter der Urgemeinde zu Jerusalem,* in: *Festgabe Karl Müller,* 1922, pp. 322-351.

[17] *Der Quellort, op. cit.,* pp. 160, 161.

[18] *Op. cit.,* pp. 162ff.

[19] *Op. cit.,* p. 166.

[20] *Op. cit.,* p. 169.

[21] *Der Spruch über Petrus, op. cit.,* pp. 117ff.

[22] Cf., e.g., G. Gloege, *Reich Gottes und Kirche im N.T.,* 1929, p. 262; H. D. Wendland, *op. cit.,* pp. 165ff; J. Schniewind, *Das Ev. nach Matth.,* 1937, p. 184; O. Cullmann, *Christus und die Zeit,* 1946, p. 132; A. J. Bronkhorst, *Schrift en Kerkorde,* 1947, pp. 20ff, and especially K. L. Schmidt (cf. below).

[23] Gloege, *op. cit.,* pp. 212ff; 241ff.

[24] In addition the literature mentioned above in which the idea of the "remnant" occurs again and again, cf. also Newton Flew, *op. cit.,* pp. 39ff.

[25] *Jesus und der Gottesvolkgedanke, op. cit.,* pp. 45ff; 58ff.

[26] Cf. above.

[27] Thus, e.g., K. L. Schmidt, *TWB,* IV, p. 524, the article on *"ekklēsia";* however, cf. also T. Zahn, *Das Ev. des Matth.,* 1922, p. 547.

[28] Schmidt, *op. cit.;* cf. also Braun, *op. cit.,* pp. 62, 69-75, 160.

[29] Cf. Schmidt, *TWB,* III, pp. 529ff, and the earlier writings of this author mentioned at the beginning of this article. Bronkhorst closely follows the argument given by Kattenbusch-Schmidt; Bronkhorst, *op. cit.,* pp. 20ff.

[30] Cf. Braun, *op. cit.,* pp. 93ff.

[31] As is well known, this idea has found many adherents as the result of the influence of Augustine's *De Civitate Dei,* cf., e.g., J. Wytzes, *Augustinus' De Staat Gods,* 1947, p. 13, "Augustine shows some inclination to consider God's kingdom apart from organized human communities. Only a small part of this kingdom is 'on a pilgrimage' on earth, and as can be inferred from several pronouncements, this part is the concrete Catholic Church of these days." Cf. also Newton Flew, *op. cit.,* p. 30.

[32] Cf. above, § 5.

[33] *"Quare hic meo iudicio* `simplex est parabolae scopus. Quam diu in hoc mundo peregrinatur Ecclesia, bonis et sinceris in ea permixtos fore malos et hypocritas"* . . . ed. Tholuck, II, 1833, p. 14.

[34] . . . *"Evangelii praedicationem scite comparat verriculo sub aquis demerso, ut sciamus praesentem Ecclesia statum confusum esse,"* op. cit., p. 21.

[35] Cf. Newton Flew, p. 20.

[36] Thus Joseph Schmidt, *Das Evangelium des Markus*, 1933, p. 64 (in connection with the parable of the mustard seed) "According to the gospel, the church is not God's kingdom on earth" (*"Die Kirche ist nach dem Evangelium nicht das Gottesreich auf Erden"*).

[37] Cf. above, § 19.

[38] In our opinion, the only expression in this connection which might cause some uncertainty is the pronouncement made in Matthew 13:41 that in the end of this world, "the Son of Man shall send forth his angels, and they shall gather *out of his kingdom* all things that offend. . . ." But here we can refer to our discussion of this text in § 19, footnote 85, where it appeared that by *basielia* is not meant the church, but more generally all that has come from the good seed that has been sown.

[39] M. J. Lagrange, *Evangile selon Saint Marc*, 1947, p. 122. He adds, "One almost feels naturally inclined to regard the dominion as an institution which is developing and will become very extensive" (*"On est presque naturellement porté à regarder le règne comme une institution, qui se developpe et qui deviendra très grande"*). On this point cf. the above quoted statement (footnote 36) made by the Roman Catholic author Joseph Schmidt.

[40] Cf. above, § 21.

[41] *Jesus and His Church*, 1945, p. 27.

[42] *Op. cit.*, p. 28.

[43] Cf. also H. A. Guy, *The New Testament Doctrine of the "Last Things,"* 1948, p. 71.

[44] Cf. also G. Ch. Aalders, *Het boek Daniël*, 1928, pp. 134ff, p. 140.

[45] In this respect Bultmann's criticism of Kattenbusch and others is in our opinion irrefutable, *op. cit.*, esp. 277. Cf. also Oepke, *Jesus und der Gottesvolkgedanke, op. cit.*, p. 59.

[46] Cf. Aalders, *op. cit.*, p. 140.

[47] Cf. also Newton Flew on Kattenbusch's appeal to Daniel 7, "It is probably truer to say that the idea of the Ecclesia is like a river issuing forth purified from a great lake into which many tributary streams have flowed," *op. cit.*, p. 36.

[48] Cf. also Oepke, *op. cit.*, p. 45.

[49] Bultmann calls Gloege's exposition a "fantastic construction," *op. cit.*, esp. 274.

[50] Cf. Bultmann, "this goes without saying," *op. cit.*, p. 277.

[51] "The concept of an eschatological church does not go back merely to Jesus' preaching of the kingdom, but is already Judaistic" (*"Der Begriff einer eschatologischen Gemeinde geht nicht erst auf Jesu Reichspredigt zurück, sondern ist schon jüdisch"*), Bultmann, *op. cit.*, esp. 275.

[52] Cf. Bultmann, *op. cit.*, esp. 275.

[53] Cf. above, § 13.

[54] Cf. also Kittel, *TWB*, I, pp. 214, 215, the article on *"akoloutheo."*

[55] Cf., e.g., R. Liechtenhan, *Die urchristliche Mission*, pp. 19ff.

[56] Cf. above, § 21.

[57] Cf. my *Matth.*, I, pp. 275ff.

[58] Dahl, *op. cit.*, pp. 158-167, Kümmel, *op. cit.*, p. 85.

[59] Cf. above, §§ 25, 26.

[60] Cf. the concept "building" in connection with God's people, P. Bonnard, *Jésus-Christ édifiant son Eglise*, 1948; the relevant point, pp. 14ff.

[61] On "corner stone," cf. Jeremias, *TWB*, IV, pp. 272ff, the article on *"lithos."*

[62] Cf. also Schniewind, *op. cit.*, p. 212.

[63] Cf. above, § 25.

[64] Thus, e.g., Bultmann, *op. cit.*, esp. 275.

[65] Cf. Dahl, *op. cit.*, p. 158, "The twelve not only refer back to the historical twelve tribes, but also forward to the eschatological people" (*"Die zwölf weisen nicht nur auf das geschichtliche Zwölfstammenvolk zurück, sondern auch auf das eschatologische voraus"*).

[66] Schmidt, too, is unwilling to give up the idea of the k^{c}hal Jahwe, but wants to impart a special shade of meaning to it from the concept of k^{c}nischta.

[67] Cf., e.g., Braun, *op. cit.*

[68] Cf. Schmidt, *TWB*, IV, p. 530.

[69] Cf. also Bultmann's criticism, *op. cit.*, p. 269, A 54.

[70] Cf. note 66.

[71] Thus Schmidt, *op. cit.*, and in his footsteps also Bronkhorst, *op. cit.*, p. 26.

[72] On these concepts cf. Bonnard, *op. cit.*, pp. 11ff.

[73] Cf. Bonnard, *op. cit.*, p. 27.

[74] This depends on the idea of the "gates of hades," cf., e.g., Schniewind on Matthew 16:18 who thinks of the temple in the sense of Ephesians 2:20-22; 1 Peter 2:4ff, *op. cit.*, p. 184. Dahl, also, speaks of the temple and, referring to Jeremiah, wants to explain *petra* as the cosmic rock which holds back the waves of the underworld, *op. cit.*, p. 165. In the same spirit Bonnard, also, *op. cit.*, pp. 26ff. This in our opinion is a very doubtful exegesis.

[75] Cf. also Oepke, *Jesus und der Gottesvolkgedanke*, *op. cit.*, pp. 45, 46.

[76] Cf. K. L. Schmidt, *TWB*, III, p. 531, the article on *"ekklēsia."* To my mind it is to be doubted that *kahal* is primarily in this sense a liturgical term, as Bultmann avers; rather, like the concept *hagios*, it refers primarily to being set apart and elected by the Lord in his covenant (cf. Deut. 9:10; 10:4); and from this its meaning as to a cultus-community is derived (Ps. 22:23,26, etc.). Cf. also my article, *De Heiligheid der gemeente volgens het Nieuwe Testament, Vox Theologica*, 1948, 18th year, No. 6, pp. 187-194.

[77] Thus Kattenbusch, *Der Quellort*, op. cit., pp. 168ff.

[78] Wendland, *op. cit.*, pp. 193ff; Bultmann, *op. cit.*, p. 272.

[79] Cf. also Cullmann, *Königsherrschaft Gottes und Kirche im N.T.*, 1941, p. 22.

[80] Thus Calvin. He argues that the name of Peter is applicable to both Simon and to other believers because they are built in holy harmony upon faith in Christ and are fashioned into a spiritual edifice. For by stating that this was to be the common foundation of the whole church, Christ wanted to gather unto Peter all godly men in the world. (*"Super hanc Petram. Hinc patet, quomodo Petri nomen tam in Simonis nomen, quam deinde in alios fideles competat: quia scilicet fundati super Christi fidem sancto consensu in spirituale aedificium aptantur, ut Deus in medio ipsorum resideat. Nam Christus hoc commune fore totius Ecclesiae fundamentum denuntians, quicquid piorum in mundo futurum erat, Petro aggregare voluit."* etc.) ed. Tholuck, II, 1833, p. 107.

[81] Thus Luther in his *Responsio ad librum Ambrosii Catharini*, 1521; cf. in K. L. Schmidt, *Die Kirche des Urchristentums*, in: *Festgabe für Adolf Deissmann*, 1927, pp. 298ff; cf. also Braun, *op. cit.*, pp. 86ff.

[82] Thus Strack-Billerbeck, *op. cit.*, I, p. 732.

[83] Cf. Grosheide, *op. cit.*, p. 200.

[84] Cf. also Preuschen-Bauer, *op. cit.*

[85] Cf. also Zahn, *Das Ev. d. Matth.*, pp. 539, 540. He also refers to the Aramaic word *kēyphah* lying at the basis of the two words and probably used in both cases by Jesus.

[86] Cf. also H. Bavinck, *Gereformeerde Dogmatiek*, IV,[4] 1930, p. 320, "The words 'this petra' can only refer to the person of Peter, but he is a rock and has proved to be so by his profession of Jesus as the Christ."

[87] Cf. the above quotation from Calvin. Zahn, *op. cit.*, p. 545, and Wendland, *op. cit.*, pp. 175, 180 also represent this view. But Peter is not here called the first stone but the rock on which the whole building rests.

[88] Thus, e.g., Kattenbusch, *Der Quellort der Kirchenidee, op. cit.*, p. 167, A 1, cf., however, also his, *Der Spruch über Petrus und die Kirche bei Matthäus, Neutestamentliche Forschungen (Sonderheft der Theol. Studien und Kritiken)*, 1922, p. 121.

[89] Cf. also Jeremias, *TWB*, III, p. 749, the article on *"kleis."*

[90] In this sense, e.g., Zahn, *op. cit.;* cf. also Jeremias, *op. cit.*, p. 750.

[91] Kattenbusch is of opinion that by "the keys of the kingdom of heaven" are meant the Scriptures which open the kingdom, *Der Quellort, op. cit.*, pp. 120ff, 126.

[92] A. J. Bronkhorst, *Schrift en Kerkorde*, 1947, pp. 36, 37.

[93] Jeremias, *op. cit.*, p. 750.

[94] Cf. E. Schweizer, *Das Leben des Herrn in der Gemeinde und ihren Diensten*, 1946, p. 92, and the literature cited there.

[95] In our opinion it is very doubtful that Matthew 16:18 should be explained according to the analogy of 23:13, as Jeremias and others insist. In Matthew 23:13, "closing the kingdom" means the setting up of a practical obstacle before people which prevents them from entering the kingdom (viz. by means of doctrine and conduct). There is here no question of any authority or authoritative attitude with respect to entry into the kingdom of heaven.

[96] Cf. Strack-Billerbeck, *op. cit.*, I, pp. 738ff; F. Büchsel, *TWB*, II, pp. 59ff, the article on *"deo";* Jeremias, *op. cit.*

[97] Following Schlatter's example, Jeremias especially points to this usage (in a certain passage of the Talmud).

[98] In our opinion this happens if by the power of the keys is understood only the separation brought about by the preaching of the gospel; thus, e.g., H. D. Wendland, *op. cit.*, p. 180, "From the attitude adopted towards the message follows either inclusion into the kingdom or exclusion from it, and hence participation in the church of the end or separation from it. . . . The apostle's authority is not based upon some law-conformity but is founded in the message of the kingdom which has been entrusted to him and which creates the new church," (*"Es ergibt sich aus der Haltung ihr (nl. der Botschaft) gegenüber entweder die Zugehörigkeit zum Reiche bezw. die Scheidung von ihm, und d. h. nun auch die Zugehörigkeit zur Endgemeinde bezw. die Scheidung von ihr. . . . Die Vollmacht des Apostels ruht nicht in einer Gesetzlichkeit, sondern in der ihm gegebenen Botschaft vom Reiche, die die neue Gemeinde schafft"*). The words of Matthew 18:18 are difficult to

harmonize with this view. Wendland thinks it likely that "the practical experiences of the earliest church have influenced its redaction," *op. cit.*, p. 183. R. Newton Flew, *Jesus and His Church,* 1945, p. 97, is also inclined to this explanation, "The binding and loosing would be the inevitable result of the apostolic preaching which was the word of judgment. The saying would then be parallel to Luke 10:16, 'He that heareth you, heareth me; And he that rejecteth you, rejecteth me.'" This view is also found in K. Barth, *De apostolische geloofsbelijdenis,* (adapted by K. H. Miskotte), 1935, p. 172, "The word (about the "keys of the kingdom of heaven") cannot be understood if it is taken to be an extension of the office and the task of the church, but it is the circumscription of the only thing that can be valid, viz. of the *ministerium verbi divini,* in the sense that the authority and its effect are stated. . . ." Cf. also in opposition to this view of Barth's, and of others, A. A. van Ruler, *Religie en Politiek,* 1945, pp. 97ff.

[99] This is how Braun expresses himself, *op. cit.*, p. 90.

[100] Thus emphatically K. L. Schmidt, *Die Kirche des Urchristentums,* in: *Festgabe für Adolf Deissmann,* 1927, p. 300.

[101] Cf. Schniewind, *Matth.,* p. 185; also Grosheide, *Matth.,* p. 202 . . . "what Jesus says to Peter here is not applicable to all the members of the church or even to all its office bearers, but very definitely to the apostles. They receive revelations for the guidance of the *ekklesia*. We are bound to their revelations as recorded in the Scriptures. The exclusion from the kingdom of heaven, as well as the declaration of what is unlawful, should be made according to the rules given by the apostles."

[102] It is true that here the keys of the kingdom of heaven are not mentioned, but the factual meaning is nonetheless implied in the "binding" and "loosing," cf. also Jeremias, *op. cit.*, p. 751.

[103] Cf. also A. J. Bronkhorst, *op. cit.*, p. 44.

[104] All the essential things are already to be found in Calvin's exegesis of Matthew 16:17-19; cf. also Bronkhorst, *op. cit.*, pp. 186-188.

[105] Thus Jeremias, *TWB,* III, pp. 751ff, the article on *"kleis."*

[106] Cf. Zahn, *Das Ev. d. Matth.,* pp. 573ff; Schniewind, *Das Ev. n. Matth.,* pp. 191ff.

[107] Jeremias, *op. cit.*

[108] Von Soden wrongly thinks that *adelphos* still occurs in the "Jewish linguistic sense" of "fellow-believer," "fellow-countryman," *TWB,* I, p. 145, the article on *"adelphos."* In our opinion the Christian use of the language is very clear.

[109] The metaphors "foundation" and "founder" alternate in the apostolic writings; compare Ephesians 2:20 with I Corinthians 3:10.

[110] Cf. Klostermann *eis to emon onoma,* "as a church," *op cit.*, p. 151.

[111] On this see esp. F. W. Grosheide, *De eerste brief van den apostel Paulus aan de Kerk te Korinthe,* 1932, pp. 175-180.

[112] Cf. my *Matth.,* II, 1946, pp. 47, 48.

[113] *Das Matthäusevang.,* p. 151.

[114] Cf. below, § 47ff.

[115] The text has not been established here.

[116] Cf. the summarizing exposition by Rengstorf concerning the late Jewish concept of justice *"shalich,"* *TWB,* I, pp. 414ff.

[117] Cf. Rengstorf, *op. cit.*, p. 427.

[118] Although there is a considerable difference between the elaborations, and

consequently, between the thoughts embodied in the parable of the pounds (Luke 12), and that of the talents (Matt. 25); cf., e.g., Greijdanus, *Lucas*, II, pp. 900.

[119] Cf. Grundmann, *TWB*, II, p. 52, the article on *"dechomai."*

[120] In his very important treatise *Auslegung von Matth.* 28:16-20, 1945, p. 21, Barth thinks, wrongly, that the pronouncement made in Mark 16 on the accompanying signs is an argument against the canonicity of this text. Apart from the question whether the working of these miracles "is declared to be obligatory," as Barth thinks, the activity of the apostles in the book of Acts proves that the end of Mark is quite in accordance with the situation after the resurrection.

[121] Cf. above, pp. 336ff.

[122] Cf. also what J. C. Hoekendijk writes on "the biblical context of the Christian mission," in his *Kerk en Volk in de Duitse Zendingswetenschap*, 1948, pp. 223ff.

[123] Cf. above, pp. 341ff.

[124] K. Barth is right in emphasizing this, *op. cit.*, p. 21, *"Sie und nur sie haben in der Gemeinde zu lehren. Denn ein anderes Objekt des tērein als das von Jesus ihnen befohlene kommt in der Gemeinde nicht in Frage. Von dem ihnen Befohlenen aber nicht weniger als alles, der ganze Umfang jener Dienstordnung. Dies ist die neutestamentliche Begründung des Schriftprinzips, mit dem wir der römische Kirche den Rücken zu kehren haben. Alles Unterrichten in der Kirche wird immer nur in einer Wiederholung des apostolischen Unterrichtens bestehen können"* ("They, and they only, are to teach in the church. For there is no question of any other object of this teaching (*tērein*) than that which Jesus has commanded *them*. But of what has been commanded them, the church has to teach nothing less than everything, the entire compass of this order of service. This is the New Testament foundation of the scriptural principle with which we must turn our backs upon the Romanist Church. Every teaching in the church can only consist in a repetition of the apostolic teaching").

[125] It is from this element in the great commission that we must regard the problem of the "comprehensive approach" which plays such a great part in the present discussions about the missionary task, cf., e.g., Hoekendijk, *op. cit.*, pp. 277ff. In this, however, we should be on our guard against the idea of the "social gospel," and against exceeding the boundaries within which the church offices are to function. On the other hand, we ought to recognize fully the all-embracing meaning of the gospel of the kingdom, and from the outset do justice to it in our missionary activities.

[126] This restriction to the human creature is supported by Col. 1:23, cf. also Bauer, *Wörterbuch*, p. 715, and Foerster, *TWB*, III, p. 1027, the article on *"ktizo."*

[127] Cf. also the masculine *autous* in the remainder of vs. 19 and in vs. 20 by which, not the nations, but ordinary believers are meant.

[128] Cf. on this theory, e.g., J. C. Hoekendijk, *Kerk en Volk in de Duitse Zendingswetenschap*, 1948, pp. 58ff, 108ff.

[129] Thus K. Barth, *op. cit.*, p. 15.

[130] A. von Harnack, *Die Mission und Ausbreitung des Christentums*, I,[3] 1915, pp. 35-37, 44. For a detailed survey of older literature on this subject, cf. M. Meinertz, *Jesus und die Heidenmission*,[2] 1925.

[131] *Die Mystik des Apostels Paulus*, 1930, pp. 176-178.

[132] Thus in detail in Bengt Sundkler, *Jésus et les païens*, in: *Revue d'Histoire et de Philosophie religieuses*, 1936, pp. 462-499, and in connection with this, N. A. Dahl, *Das Volk Gottes*, 1941, pp. 145, 149, 150; W. G. Kümmel, *Verheissung und Erfüllung*, 1946, pp. 49, 50.

[133] *Op. cit.*, p. 470.

[134] Strack-Billerbeck, *op. cit.*, I, p. 181.

[135] Cf. more about this, e.g., in H. H. Rowley, *The Missionary Message of the Old Testament*, 1944; and especially J. Blauw, *Goden en mensen*, pp. 19ff.

[136] Rowley, *op. cit.*, p. 64.

[137] Cf. also R. Liechtenhan, *Die urchristliche Mission*, 1946, pp. 31ff.

[138] Cf. my *Matth.*, II, pp. 109, 110.

[139] For the exegesis of these parables, see above, § 25.

[140] Cf. also Schniewind, *Matth.*, p. 214.

[141] Repeated by Kümmel, *op. cit.*, pp. 49, 50.

[142] Thus Sundkler, *op. cit.*, pp. 481ff. The idea in the prophets that Zion and Jerusalem are the religious center of the world is accompanied by the centrifugal thought of the Thora and of the Word of the Lord going out to all the nations of the earth. This appears clearly from a passage like Isaiah 2:2-4 which is, therefore, rightly applied to the universal New Testament preaching of the gospel, cf. G. Ch. Aalders, *Iets over exegese van profetische voorzeggingen, Geref. Theol. Tijdschrift*, 1926, p. 5; and P. A. Verhoef, *Die vraagstuk van die onvervulde voorsegginge in verband met Jesaja 1-39*, 1950, pp. 275, 332.

[143] For the various motifs, cf. H. Schlier, *Die Entscheidung für die Heidenmission in der Urchristenheit*, in: *Evangelische Missions Zeitschrift*, 1942, pp. 166ff.

[144] The objection that these pronouncements do not agree with the time ordained by Jesus for his second coming will have to be investigated in our last chapter.

[145] Cf., e.g., Liechtenhan, *op. cit.*, p. 42 (see, however, also pp. 48ff); and W. Flemington, *The New Testament Doctrine of Baptism*, 1948, pp. 105ff.

[146] Cf. below, p. 369.

[147] In addition to earlier investigations (such as those by J. Leipoldt, *Die urchristliche Taufe im Lichte der Religionsgeschichte*, 1928, and by Strack-Billerbeck, *op. cit.*, I, p. 112), see also J. Jeremias, *Hat die Urkirche die Kindertaufe geübt?* 1949, and the recent literature mentioned there.

[148] O. Cullmann, *Die Tauflehre des Neuen Testaments*, 1948, pp. 18ff.

[149] *Op. cit.*, pp. 14, 15.

[150] On this question cf. also Oepke, *TWB*, I, p. 536, the article on *"baptizo."* Although Oepke could not yet discuss Cullmann's view, he already rejects a similar interpretation of Mark 10:38; Luke 12:50 (that of Reitzenstein).

[151] *Op. cit.*, p. 536.

[152] Cf., e.g., Oepke, *op. cit.*, p. 537.

[153] J. Jeremias, *Hat die Urkirche die Kindertaufe geübt?* 1949, pp. 20, 21.

[154] Cf. above, § 28.

Chapter IX

THE COMING OF THE KINGDOM AND THE LORD'S SUPPER

39. *The Twofold Motif of the Lord's Supper*

In the previous chapter we were more than once confronted with those pronouncements in Jesus' preaching that deal with the meaning of the coming of the kingdom for the period after Jesus' death and resurrection. We shall finish our investigation by a summarizing view of the prospects offered by the gospel with regard to the period of the history of salvation which started with Christ's death and will be finished by his *parousia*. But first we must consider a matter given in the gospel which is closely connected with what precedes. Its special significance requires separate treatment. We are referring to the institution of the Lord's Supper handed down to us in all three gospels (Matt. 26:26-29; Mark 14:22-25; Luke 22:15-20).

Dogmatics, too, discusses the Lord's Supper in immediate connection with the church. And this is obvious. From the outset the Lord's Supper proves to have been one of the most important institutions in the Christian church. The evangelists, too, doubtless wanted to indicate the basis and the starting-point of the later celebration of the Lord's Supper by the Christian Church by their account of Jesus' Last Supper with his disciples, although Matthew and Mark do not mention any formal institution of the Lord's Supper. This appears clearly from the so-called remembrance commandment—"this do in remembrance of me"—in Luke (and also in Paul, I Cor. 11:25). Not only from the point of view of the historical order of events, but also from a factual standpoint this is the most suitable place to deal with this very important part of the synoptic tradition. Yet we must follow a different method from that of dogmatics when we discuss the Lord's Supper. We are especially concerned with the meaning of this institution of Christ's within the scope of the entire preaching of the kingdom of heaven. We have to pay especial attention to the redemptive-historical importance of the Lord's Supper, i.e., to the relation between the Lord's Supper and all that has come to our attention in the previous chapters with reference to the coming of the kingdom both in its fulfillment and in its provisional character.

From this point of view a very comprehensive literature has in the last few decades been devoted to the Lord's Supper. In it the issue of the great confessional conflict since the days of the Reformation has again come to the fore; namely, the meaning of the literal words of the institution insofar as they are connected with the bread and wine handed by Jesus to his disciples in relation to his body and his blood. Especially in the recent sacramental theology this relation continues to play an important part. Yet the boundaries within which the present conflict is carried on are much wider than they used to be. They are now determined by the total vision entertained with respect to Jesus' coming and his work, especially that of the kingdom of heaven preached by him. We should not be surprised, therefore, that in the treatment of the institutional words of the Lord's Supper we again meet with the same problems, though in a modified sense, as those that have claimed our attention in the previous chapters.

This will be clearer to us when we examine the institutional words more closely. Two motifs come to the fore in them. The first is that of the *expiatory death* of Jesus, which we have already encountered in another context. Jesus here points out his forthcoming death as the substitutionary sacrifice for the remission of sins. The second motif is the *eschatological* one, expressed by all the synoptic evangelists, but especially by Luke. It follows from Jesus' words, in close connection with the Lord's Supper, about the "new wine" he will drink (with his disciples) in the kingdom of God (Matt. 26:29; Mark 14:25, cf. Luke 22:18); and also the words about the "fulfillment" of the passover in God's kingdom (Luke 22:16). In the previous chapters of this book it has been seen that it is just these two motifs in Jesus' preaching which are the subjects of a ceaseless struggle. It is therefore understandable that this struggle is above all concentrated on the meaning of the Lord's Supper.

The chief questions at issue are: *in the first place,* whether or not the expiatory death motif has from the outset also determined the character of the Lord's Supper; and *secondly,* what function the Lord's Supper fulfills in the coming of the kingdom preached by Jesus.

It need surprise no one that those who still share the liberal view that the original gospel knows nothing about the expiatory power of Jesus' suffering and death, do not think that they can rely upon the synoptic institutional words for establishing the original meaning of the Lord's Supper. For these words mention the blood of the covenant, the idea of sacrifice, etc. Very often these words have been declared to be unauthentic. Liberal theology in this way removed the motifs that it considered to be objectionable in the institutional words and retained little more than the idea that the Lord's Supper was "a commemorative meal as a remembrance of an unforgettable moment in the history of the passion"[1] ordained by Jesus when he saw the hour of his death approaching. Many recent authors, however, who also reject the motif of Christ's expiatory death, now emphasize the eschatological motif occurring in all three records of the institution and derive the original meaning of the Lord's Supper from it.

Lietzmann's conception, especially, has been an important factor in this development.[2] This author distinguishes two types of Eucharist in the old liturgies of the Lord's Supper and supposes that they are also recognizable in the New Testament, viz., a "Jerusalem" and a "Pauline" type. The former is then the continuation of the meals so often shared by the disciples with Jesus before his death (the so-called *chabura* that the Jews were familiar with). It was continued after the passover in the joyful certainty of Christ's presence and did not include the use of wine (the so-called "breaking of bread" in the book of Acts). This exercise of table fellowship was especially directed to the speedy *parousia* of the Lord, and even already anticipated it. This is the Jerusalem, and at the same time eschatological, type. Its form is supposed to be recognizable in Luke's story according to the redaction of codex D (in which verses 19b and 20 are lacking). It should be entirely detached from the celebration of the passover and its thoughts of sacrifice.

By its side a second type is said to have arisen, the so-called Pauline type, determined by the idea of sacrifice, the commemoration and the *Vergegenwärtigung* (representation) of Jesus' death by bread and wine. All the emphasis is laid upon "the elements." They become the vehicles of the Holy Spirit, effecting the remission of sins and giving eternal life to their recipients. In the records given by Mark and Matthew we have to do with this Pauline type. Its connection with Jesus' expiatory death is the essential element. This type soon superseded the original, eschatological type.[3]

On the basis of these or similar considerations the attempt is made to reconstruct Jesus' *actual* words at the Lord's Supper. Thus, e.g., Klostermann writes that the record of the Eucharist that has come down to us (in Mark) if taken out of its context proves to be a cult-story. This story is to justify aetiologically the celebration of the Lord's Supper in Hellenistic circles (i.e., its purpose is to represent the Eucharist as a custom originating from Jesus himself). Klostermann contrasts with it the possibility that only Mark 14:25 (about the "new wine" in God's kingdom) is the remainder of an earlier tradition which should be supplemented by Luke 22:14-18. According to this heavily truncated tradition, Jesus is supposed to have held out the prospect of his early reunion with his disciples at the *messianic meal in God's kingdom,* because he lived in the certainty of the imminent catastrophe and of the beginning of God's dominion. But he had no thought of instituting a commemorative ceremony and did not draw a direct parallel between bread and wine in relation to his body and blood. Klostermann seeks to establish his opinion by an appeal to the statement that, at the Eucharist in the older Palestine churches, a tone of joyful hope was predominant and not the commemoration of Jesus' death (Acts 2:46,

where the word *agalliasis* is found, which is also used to express
the joy in the coming kingdom of God). He also adduces as an
argument the fact that in this older way of celebrating the Lord's
Supper, there is only mention of the "breaking of bread," and nothing
of the wine which is so closely connected with Jesus' blood.[4]

But, e.g., Plooy (agreeing with Lohmeyer) has rightly pointed
out that the whole basic motif of this argument moves in a vicious
circle. First, some sort of presupposition is made of what, according to so-called historical data, Jesus may or may not have thought
and said at the Lord's Supper; then, if the data prove to be in conflict with this presupposition, the troublesome element is eliminated
as "the theology of the church."[5]

In more recent literature, however, many authors turn
away from this prejudice with respect to the motif of the
expiatory death. There is a growing recognition of the fact
that, in accordance with the prophecy of Isaiah 53, Jesus'
substitutional suffering and death occupy an integrating place
in the gospel, and that it is impossible to eliminate this expiatory death motif from the tradition of the institution of the
Eucharist. At the same time, however, increasing emphasis
is laid upon the eschatological character of the Lord's Supper,
and the discussion again and again revolves about the question of the relation between these two motifs and in what sense
this institution of Christ's is to be viewed.[6]

Very characteristic—and influential!—of the eschatological
interpretation of the Lord's Supper are Albert Schweitzer's expositions on the subject. They are embodied in his older writings as well as in his later great work, *Die Mystik des Apostels
Paulus*. Schweitzer's view differs from that of authors like
Lietzmann, Klostermann, etc. (cf. above), in that he also takes
the motif of the expiatory death into account when determining the character of the Lord's Supper. This does not,
however, detract from the fact that he makes this element
entirely subordinate to what he considers the principal thing,
viz., the eschatological meaning of the Lord's Supper.

The motif of the expiatory death is even more emphatically

put in the foreground in Rudolf Otto's expositions about the
Lord's Supper.[7] It is true that this author, also, explains the
last meal of which Jesus partook with his disciples as an
eschatological institution not to be connected with the meal
of the passover. As a consequence of the special emphasis which
he lays upon the meaning of Isaiah 53 for Jesus' messianic
self-consciousness, Otto, however, very closely approaches the
old conception according to which Christ's imminent suffering
and death and their expiatory power were decisive for Jesus'
words and actions during the Eucharist.

Schweitzer wants to define the real character of the Lord's
Supper in close connection with other meals that Jesus shared with
his disciples. The most glorious example of these Schweitzer finds
in the story of the miraculous feeding of the crowds on the Lake of
Gennesareth (Mark 6:32ff). A later tradition wrongly sought the
special character of this meal in the miraculous satisfaction of the
appetite of so many people with the aid of such a small quantity of
bread. But, according to Schweitzer, the important thing in this
meal is the fact that to a large circle of people Jesus as the *Messias
designatus* gives a preliminary celebration of the eschatological messianic festival in the kingdom of God that is so near at hand. In this
way the participants of this meal were inaugurated in a cultic manner as partakers of the kingdom. All this was still hidden from
them. They did not yet know Jesus as the Messiah. But what
was a secret in these earlier meals was openly expressed at the Last
Supper at Jerusalem. For then the messianic secret was divulged
and the circle of the disciples was explicitly called the representation
of the new community in the kingdom of God. And, at the same
time, the motif of suffering makes its appearance, and this is also
something special. Only in the way of Jesus' suffering and death
would the kingdom be manifested. The *essence* of the Lord's Supper, however, was independent of this reference to his body and
blood, though it consisted in the cultic "preliminary festival of the
messianic meal in the circle of participants who believed in the
kingdom."[8] In accordance with this, after Jesus' death the apostles
and the faithful awaited his coming and the messianic meal in the
same room where Jesus had celebrated the Last Supper with them.

There, too, they repeated this meal with each other as a thanksgiving supper with a view to the coming kingdom and the *parousia* of Christ. Only later, when the faith of the church lost its eschatological character, did the original meaning of "breaking bread" disappear. The emphasis then shifted to the bread and wine as the means of communion with the body and blood of Christ. Instead of the eschatological conception, the Greek-sacramental meaning came to the fore.[9]

Schweitzer thus connects the motif of suffering in the Lord's Supper with the eschatological point of view. In his view the former is granted a place because the idea of suffering and death constitutes an integral part of Schweitzer's eschatology.[10]   This is why Schweitzer has no objection to considering the Last Supper as a paschal meal, and rejects as unnecessary the "artificial" distinction made by Lietzmann and others between two different types of original Christian Eucharist.[11]   The eschatological character of the Supper, however, remains predominant. The Lord's Supper is given its proper meaning from Jesus' conviction that with his death the kingdom will begin. It is the prelude to eating and drinking in the kingdom of God.

Rudolf Otto's elaborate discussion of the Lord's Supper starts from a very radical reconstruction of Luke's story of the Last Supper.[12]   He also agrees with Lietzmann in that he does not explain the Last Supper of Jesus and his disciples from the standpoint of the paschal meal, but from the more general type of a religious table-fellowship,[13] the so-called *chabu* or *chabura,* of which also Lietzmann speaks. There was no need of wine here. The religious consecration consisted in the blessing of the food (the so-called *eucharistia*). At the Last Supper, however, Jesus did pass around a cup of wine. It is the cup at the beginning of the meal, mentioned in Luke 22:17. On this occasion he pronounced the eschatological words referring to the drinking of the new wine in God's kingdom. The cup at the Last Supper bears no relation to blood or to the institution of the covenant. It is the cup of parting and the cup of reunion in the coming kingdom.[14]

In addition, however, Jesus passes out bread representing, according to R. Otto, his body broken in death. The accompanying words, "this is my body," should be connected with Luke 22:29 in which, by virtue of the promise of the covenant, Jesus gives his dis-

ciples a share in God's kingdom.[15]   By his death "effectively represented"[16] by the broken bread, Jesus bequeaths the kingdom to his
disciples.   For this idea of delegating the kingdom on the basis of
Christ's suffering and death, Otto thinks he can appeal to the
prophecy of Isaiah 53 and 54.[17]

Up to now we have been giving attention to representatives
of the more radical wing in the more recent literature about
the Lord's Supper. But there is also a long list of authors who
think this bold and often arbitrary tampering with the text
and the meaning of the gospels is unwarranted. It is remarkable that the view of the longer text in Luke as being the
original form is now being accepted by an increasing number
of authors, although for a long time it had been generally
rejected.[18]   But even in cases where this view is not defended,
the historical situation in which the synoptic gospels place the
Lord's Supper has been placed in a very clear light on the basis
of accurate investigations, and the reliability of the synoptic
tradition of the Last Supper has been maintained. This is
especially true with respect to the recognition that the meaning
of the Lord's Supper must be understood within the framework of the paschal meal, in accordance with the evangelical
record.[19]   Then, grateful use is made of the data available in
the Jewish paschal rites. From this, all kinds of details given
by the synoptic tradition about Jesus' last supper have again
been examined and explained.[20]

The most important characteristic, however, is always the
way in which, on the one hand, the eschatological idea and,
on the other, the significance of Jesus' death are combined in
order to understand the last paschal meal shared by Jesus and
his disciples with the Eucharist in the Christian church which
is its continuation. The majority of recent authors acknowledge the motif of the expiatory death as belonging to the
nucleus of the gospel and wish to do full justice to this motif
in the words about the Last Supper. But there is no denying
that the specific feature of this meal is sought by many in the
eschatological sphere. It is very remarkable that sometimes

the attempt is made to retain Schweitzer's thought about Jesus at the Last Supper expecting the break-through of the kingdom in the near future. Thus, e.g., Markus Barth, in his study of the Lord's Supper, speaks of the *brennendste Naherwartung* (the most passionate expectation of the imminence of the kingdom) that occupied Jesus' thoughts entirely during the Last Supper. He does not, as Schweitzer, conceive of this expectation as an illusion, but is of the opinion that the coming of the kingdom mentioned by Jesus became possible by his death and was realized in his resurrection.   From the standpoint of this *realized* eschatology, we must consider the Lord's Supper in the Christian church. At present, after Jesus' death, the kingdom has come, the "new wine" of which Jesus spoke has been drunk, and the "passover" has been "fulfilled."[21] Now Jesus is seated at table with his disciples in the new community of the kingdom. The time has even arrived wherein Jesus' disciples are seated on twelve thrones to judge the twelve tribes of Israel (as an indication of their royal authority).[22]

Closely connected with this is the fact that a celebration of a Lord's Supper which were to concentrate upon the cross and the death of Jesus would be entirely wrong. At the Lord's Supper, as the realized eschatological meal, joy and jubilation should be predominant, and we should avoid "thoughts of Good Friday, confession of sins, absolution, the funeral mood." They would deny the character of the Eucharist as a celebration of the resurrection and as a manifestation of the arrival of the kingdom.[23] Those who agree with this view are, therefore, of the opinion that we should strive for a new understanding of the Lord's Supper (and at the same time for a return to the original Christian idea). They assert that we are on the threshold of a new period in which the prophetic conception of the Eucharist, which was that of the Reformation, should be replaced by the royal view.[24] Even such an author as Cullmann points in this direction, although he expresses himself more guardedly. He thinks, moreover, that the messianic meal promised by Jesus at the Last Supper was partially fulfilled

in the meals Jesus celebrated with his disciples after his resurrection and before his ascension; and that the Eucharist in the
original Christian church was celebrated especially in the
light of the resurrection.[25]   In all of these more conservative
conceptions, the eschatological interpretation as "realized"
eschatology plays an important part, and the thought of the
expiatory death in the celebration of the Lord's Supper is
relegated to the background.   Others make more of an attempt
at some synthesis and give more emphasis to the connection
between the bread and wine and Jesus' body and blood surrendered to death.[26]   In a later context we will give more
attention to the details of this view.

40. The Redemptive-Historical Meaning of the Lord's Supper

By concentrating upon the synoptic tradition concerning
the institution of the Lord's Supper itself, we wish to gain an
insight into the general meaning of this Supper within the
scope of the administration of salvation inaugurated by Jesus'
coming and work.   Thus we are at once confronted with the
diversity which is to be found in this tradition.   It is impossible
to avoid the discussion of this diversity because it appears to
play an important part exactly with respect to the general
characterization of the Lord's Supper.

This does not hold for the differences in the texts on the
Eucharist in Mark and Matthew.   As a matter of fact, apart
from the question we are dealing with now, they are generally
speaking very slight and without actual significance.   The most
important difference between them is that to the so-called
words of the cup, "this is my blood of the new covenant which
is shed for many," Matthew adds, "for the remission of sins."
Thus he more clearly than Mark refers to the prophecy about
the new covenant in Jeremiah 31:31ff. Things become different,
however, when we include Luke in the discussion.   In the first
place, there is then a very important question concerning the
original text.   For in some manuscripts and old translations,
verses 19b and 20 are lacking.   The text abruptly breaks off

with, "this is my body." The words, "which is given for you; this do in remembrance of me," are missing, as are also the words about the cup in verse 20. The missing words are exactly those that refer to the connection between the Last Supper and Jesus' suffering and death. The result is that those who consider as secondary the so-called motif of the expiatory death in the words on the Lord's Supper often appeal to this shorter text in Luke. For the present, the arguments in favor of the authenticity of the disputed words seem to us to be conclusive.

In the first place, far and away the largest number of the old and important manuscripts have the longer text. The shorter one is only found in a branch of the tradition of the so-called western text.[27] In itself this is already a strong argument in favor of the authenticity of the longer text. Rightly Jeremias writes, "If the shorter text is considered as the original one, it would mean that, from the standpoint of the history of the tradition, appeal is made to the utmost improbability. For it would be assumed that an addition to the Luke-text has penetrated into *all* manuscripts except that of D and some old Latin and Syriac translations.[28] Besides, in the manuscripts with the shorter text there are mutual deviations (some have vss. 17 and 18 after vs. 19a), which may be an indication that there was an awareness of the fact that the D reading could not represent the original.

In spite of this, there are many scholars who regard the shorter text as the original one. The reason is that the shorter text, breaking off suddenly at verse 19a, is much more difficult than the long version which records the institution of the Lord's Supper in perfect agreement with I Corinthians 11:24,25, and which may thus have been derived from the latter passage. The longer text is therefore often considered as a compilation from Paul (and Mark). On the other hand, the originality of the short abrupt text is also difficult to explain, and the agreement between Luke and Paul need not be based upon the dependence of the former on the latter. It may also be explained from the stereotyped oral (cultic?) tradition which both may have reproduced almost in the same form but independent of each other. However this may be, it is a fact that the value of the textual evidence is very strongly in favor of the longer version and that it is being accepted as the original text by an increasing number of authors.[29]

In view of all that has been discussed above, we shall abide by the longer text, which means that in our opinion the motif of the expiatory death in Luke is no less clearly a co-determinant of the Lord's Supper than in Matthew and Mark. And we do so all the more wholeheartedly because, according to I Corinthians 11:24,25, the contents of these verses belong to the oldest tradition of the Lord's Supper that have come down to us.

When we compare the record of the Lord's Supper in Luke with that of Matthew and Mark, we come upon a considerable difference in structure, even when we maintain the longer text. This difference proves to be important for the determination of the general character of the Eucharist. We realize this difference best when we put down the three traditions side by side in a somewhat schematic way like this:

Matthew 26:26-29	Mark 14:22-25	Luke 22:15-20
		15. And he said unto them, with desire I have desired to eat this passover with you before I suffer:
		16. For I say unto you, I will not any more eat thereof, until it be fulfilled in the kingdom of God.
		17. And he took the cup, and gave thanks, and said, Take this, and divide it among yourselves:
cf. vs. 29	cf. vs. 25	18. For I say unto you, I will not drink of the fruit of the vine, until the kingdom of God shall come.

26. and as they were eating, Jesus took bread, and blessed it, and brake it, and said, This is my body.	cf. vs. 22	19a. And he took bread, and gave thanks, and brake it, and gave unto them, saying, This is my body
		19b. which is given for you: this do in remembrance of me.
27. And he took the cup, and gave thanks, and gave it to them, saying,	cf. vs. 23	20. Likewise also the cup after supper, saying, This cup is the new covenant in my blood, which is shed for you.
28. This is my blood of the covenant, which is shed for many for the remission of sins.	cf. vs. 24	
29. For I say unto you, I will not drink henceforth of this fruit of the vine, until that day when I drink it new with you in my Father's kingdom.	cf. vs. 25	cf. vs. 18

Apart from some smaller differences, noteworthy in themselves, between the parallel parts of the tradition in Luke (vss. 19 and 20), in Matthew (vss. 26-29), and in Mark (vss. 22-25); Luke has an introduction that is lacking in Matthew and Mark (vss. 15-18) and that is remarkable for more than one reason. In the first place because in it the "eschatological motif" comes to the fore twice and from the outset, whereas Matthew and Mark give expression to it only at the end of the text on the Lord's Supper, and then only once. Compare the italicized words in Luke 22:14-18:

"And when the hour was come, he sat down and the apostles with him. And he said unto them, With desire I have desired to eat this passover with you before I suffer. For I say unto you, *I will not any more eat thereof, until it be fulfilled in the kingdom of God.*

"And he took the cup, and gave thanks, and said, Take this and divide it among yourselves. For I say unto you, *I will henceforth not drink of the fruit of the vine, until the kingdom of God shall come.*"

As has been said, this introduction is lacking in the other two synoptics, and consequently also the emphasis on the eschatological perspective. For this reason, especially, the distinction between two types of Eucharist is defended by those who consider the eschatological type as the oldest and look upon these initial verses in Luke as the most original part of the tradition, only putting the final verse in Matthew and Mark on the same level.

Although such a separation of the eschatological motif from that of the expiatory death is in our opinion entirely arbitrary, we shall have to do full justice to the emphasis on the eschatological perspective in Luke. The more so as there are indications that Luke's tradition is a more accurate and more detailed description of the historical course of events than that of the other evangelists. This is connected with a second difference between Luke and Matthew (and Mark). Luke mentions the passing of the cup *twice.* The first time is mentioned immediately at the beginning (vs. 17) and is not connected with Jesus' blood, but with Jesus' drinking of the wine in God's kingdom (vs. 18). Later, Luke again mentions a cup (vs. 20), which he relates to Jesus' words about his blood of the new covenant, just as the other synoptics have it. In Matthew and Mark, on the other hand, only the conclusion of the narrative mentions the passing around of the cup, and they connect with it both "this is my blood of the testament," and the eschatological prospect (the drinking of the "new wine").

The basis for our assumption that Luke gives a more accurate account of the events than do Matthew and Mark is the fact that Luke mentions *two cups,* which is a more elaborate description; and also because, already at the outset in connection with the first cup, he speaks of "the fruit of the vine." This phrase was a standing expression in the Jewish paschal rites. For it was used in the father's thanksgiving at the *first* cup which was passed around, and *not* in the thanksgiving at the cup *after* the meal[30] (where Matthew and Mark mention it). If we may rightly assume that the mention of more than one cup in Luke is not based on some confusion caused by the extension of the text, but on a more detailed description of the events; and if in anticipation of the results of our further investigations we may take the phrase "fruit of the vine" to be an allusion to the paschal rites, it is obvious to suppose that the allusion to the drinking of the wine in God's kingdom (the eschatological perspective) was made immediately at the beginning of the meal, just like the saying about the fulfilled passover in God's kingdom. *So we may conclude that Jesus began his Last Supper with his disciples with this double reference to the kingdom of God.*

It is therefore evident that we must consider Jesus' Eucharistic words and, hence, the institution of the Lord's Supper for the Christian church within the general framework of his preaching. It is also clear that the eschatological viewpoint is very important for determining the character of the Lord's Supper. As a matter of fact, this does not only appear in Luke. For Mark and Matthew also have the words, "Verily, I say unto you, henceforth I will not drink of the fruit of the vine, until that day that I drink it new in the kingdom of God" (Mark 14:25). Matthew adds, "with you" (26:29). This undoubtedly brings out Mark's meaning more clearly to the effect that Jesus not only refers to his own exaltation and glorification, but also to his reunion with his disciples in the coming manifestation of the kingdom of God. In this kingdom, that which is now provisional and incomplete will be *new* (a word used again and again with reference to the state of fulfillment and consummation) or, as Luke has it with reference to the eating of the passover, "until it be *fulfilled* in the kingdom of God."

The great importance of this viewpoint is obvious. No

doubt, in the first place, with respect to Jesus himself. No-where more impressively than here does it appear that he faced death in the certainty of his future exaltation. In his leave-taking and death he triumphantly awaits the messianic time.[31] But at the same time—and this is significant for the character-ization of the Lord's Supper—the meal Jesus partakes of with his disciples assumes a prefigurative character. That which happens at this meal will be fulfilled in the kingdom of God. But also conversely, that which will be the fulness of joy in God's kingdom has its commencement and foretaste in this meal. The relation between the Eucharist and eating and drinking in the coming kingdom of God is not merely that between symbol and reality, but that between commencement and fulfillment. Another significant feature is the fact that Jesus, when taking leave of his disciples, ordains what in the coming time also takes the form of a meal, i.e., eating and drinking. For in accordance with the conceptions of the Old Testament (and those of late Judaism), the joy and bliss of the kingdom of God is represented as the sitting down to and enjoyment of a meal (Matt. 8:11; 22:1ff; 25:1ff; Luke 13:28; 22:30, and others). This is also why the meeting of the disciples *at a meal* for the time to come cannot be an acci-dental form of the bond of union which embraces them all and which is founded in their faith in Christ. But this concep-tion expresses their common participation in the joy of the coming kingdom of God, the gospel of which had been preached to them by Christ.

All this is given a special foundation in the words with which Jesus ordains this permanent table-fellowship. For whatever explanation is given to these words, their general tenor is at once clear. Jesus relates this meal to his suffering and death, and this in the sense that the soteriological meaning of his death is the starting-point and the content of the eating and drinking of the disciples, as well as of the permanent table-fellowship of the coming *ekklesia*. For in Christ's death—as has been demonstrated in great detail in our exposition—lies the basis and the secret of what Jesus proclaimed as the administration of the fulfillment and as the coming of the kingdom. This is why the meal founded in the soteriological meaning of Christ's death is actually the meal of fulfillment, of the *sharing* in the salvation of the kingdom, of the receiving of the pearl of great value, the commencement of the redemption in the life of the church and in the history of the world.[32] In a word, it is the meal in which "the powers of the world to come" have been released in Christ's coming, and in which the "heavenly gift" and the Holy Spirit have been given and "tasted."[33]

Consequently, there can be no doubt that the "eschatological perspective" disclosed by Jesus repeatedly at the Last Supper is a co-determinant of the character and the content of the gift to his disciples, and of the table-fellowship ordained by him for the church.

Yet this is only one aspect of the matter that has been brought to light. For although we fully accept the consequences of the relation established by Jesus between the Eucharist and eating and drinking in God's kingdom; Jesus during the last meal repeatedly mentions the coming kingdom of God, not merely and *even not primarily* to point out the pre-figurative and fulfilling character of the Lord's Supper, but rather to make clear the *provisional* and *temporary* significance of the latter. This is why we are convinced that the tendency in present-day literature to let the "eschatological motif" prevail over the so-called motif of the expiatory death is a misconception of the real meaning of the eschatological perspective disclosed by Jesus at the Lord's Supper. Once again, this is one of the bad effects of the one-sided eschatological interpretation of the gospel.

It is a complete misrepresentation of the meaning of Jesus' words if this reference of the Lord's Supper to the coming kingdom of God (found especially in Luke) is conceived of as evidence of a most passionate expectation of that kingdom's imminence (*Naherwartung*); or if it is taken to mean that the kingdom was expected to come within the time during which a man can do without food (as Markus Barth following in the footsteps of Schweitzer maintains). For Jesus does not say that there will be no more passover eaten and no more wine taken until the kingdom has come; but he only asserts that *he himself* will no more partake of them on earth. His very meaning is that all this will go on (without him)[34] and that Jesus and his disciples will *resume* their common celebration of the passover and their drinking of the wine in the kingdom of God. His reference to the coming kingdom in this context, thus, is predominantly of a *negative* nature. Jesus will not celebrate the festival with his disciples until God's kingdom has come. This also implies that neither will do so anymore now. Because of his approaching death, it is no longer appropriate for him to drink wine.[35] Likewise it must be assumed that Jesus himself did not eat of the bread that he apportioned to his disciples. Jesus' exhortation to his disciples to take and eat (Matt. 26:26; Mark 14:23) already points in this direction. For this was unusual and will have to be explained from the fact that Jesus himself did not eat of the bread and therefore had to invite his disciples to eat, since he could not give the signal to them to start by eating the bread himself, which was the custom of a father with his family.[36] Another argument is to be found in the words, "This is my body." It is difficult to imagine Jesus symbolically eating his own body.[37]

Whatever may be thought of this last argument, it is undeniable that the words expressing this "eschatological perspective" are to be conceived of as *parting words*. This appears also from the repetition of the phrase "no more" and is particularly evident in the opening words of Luke's account of the Last Supper. There, Jesus says that he had eagerly desired to partake of this passover with his disciples before he suffered, *because* ("for I say unto you") he would no more eat it before it was fulfilled in the kingdom of God. The cause of this eager desire lay in the coming *separation*. To our mind, this undeniably indicates that this passover and his words bear the character of a farewell pointing to the future. This is why the general character of the Lord's Supper cannot be viewed as an anticipation of the imminence of God's kingdom, neither in the sense of Schweitzer who called this anticipation Jesus' great delusion, nor in the sense of those who look upon it as being fulfilled by Christ's resurrection and in the celebration of the Eucharist by the Christian church. Jesus himself certainly did *not* mean this by his words at the Supper. When he speaks of the "fulfillment of the passover" and of "the new wine" in the kingdom of God, he has in view the great future to be inaugurated by the *parousia* of the Son of Man. Here it is not possible to call in the aid of the distinction between the messianic kingdom and the eternal kingdom of God in the sense that Jesus' words refer to the former and not to the latter.[38] For, apart from the doubtful character of such a distinction,[39] Jesus in Matthew and Mark, as well as in Luke, specifically speaks of eating and drinking in *his* FATHER's *kingdom,* and therefore in the eternal kingdom. Moreover, in our opinion, it does not do to appeal to the so-called "Easter meals" (*Oestermahlzeiten*), i.e., the meals taken by Jesus and the disciples after the resurrection, of which Luke and John speak and which are mentioned by Peter in Acts 10:41. These meals did not have the character of messianic festive meals but of the confirmation of the reality of Christ's (bodily) resurrection (cf. Luke 24:41-43); and are mentioned as such by Peter in Acts 10:41. It is also hardly possible to look upon the food taken at this meal, viz., bread and fish, as the "fulfilled passover," or as the "new wine" in the kingdom of the Father. There is no doubt that these meals after Easter are also evidence that communion between Jesus and his disciples had again been restored; but that which is said in the eschatological sayings of the Eucharist refers to something more than to these temporary incidental meals.

And the same thing holds for the celebration of the Lord's Supper in the Christian church. If this Supper may be considered as a direct continuation of the Last Supper celebrated by Jesus with his disciples,[40] it cannot be conceived of as the fulfillment of what Jesus promised at this Supper with reference to the drinking of new wine, etc. The Lord's Supper celebrated in the Christian church after Jesus' death, in spiritual communion with the risen Lord (cf. Matt. 18:20), is only the prefiguration of this "eating and drinking in the kingdom of God." That is to say, it is the continuation and celebration of the administration of salvation directed to the future,[41] which was inaugurated by Christ's coming. In this respect it does not factually transcend that which Jesus already gave his disciples to eat and to drink at the Last Supper.

It is true that with Jesus' coming the fulfillment of salvation commenced in principle and may be celebrated as such at the Lord's Supper. But the specific redemptive-historical significance of this Supper is not to be sought primarily in the eschatological perspective disclosed by Jesus, but much rather, in connection with Jesus' expiatory death, or in other words, *in the meaning that Jesus attributes to the bread and wine* which he gives to his disciples. The eschatological perspective imparts the character of a farewell to the last meal which Jesus had together with his disciples. And this fact should lead to our understanding of the permanent meaning of the Eucharist. For that which is no longer valid for Jesus on earth (eating bread and drinking wine); his disciples are allowed, and even obliged, to do henceforth. What holds for him does not yet hold for them.[42] Certainly this rule is not without its limit, since for them, also, there will be the "fulfillment of the passover" and the "drinking of new wine" in the kingdom of God. Nevertheless, they must eat the food and take the cup that Jesus now allows to pass by him. Only, they must do so realizing that what they in this way will henceforth eat and drink is *the body and the blood of the Lord.*

This is the great "revelation" which Jesus discloses. This is the spectacular part of his words. It is *not* the eating and drinking that is new, nor the reference to the coming messianic meal, nor even the institution of a communal meal as such. All this has been presupposed and already expressed in all manner of ways in the gospel. *The new feature is that from henceforth Jesus' body will be the food and his blood the drink of his disciples.*

Thus, on the one hand, there is the element of fulfillment and, on the other, that which is provisional. The element of fulfillment, for all the salvation and redemption brought about by Christ for his disciples is founded in the body and blood he gives them to eat and to drink at the Eucharist. The provisional character, for what he thus gives them yet occurs only as an anticipation of the future reunion in which he and his disciples will eat and drink in the kingdom of God. The Lord's Supper, therefore, is the meal of redemption, the cup of salvation, the bread of the church, because it is founded in Christ's death. But it is so for the time between the times, for the interim between the fulfillment that has begun and the consummation that is to be expected. Jesus gives to his disciples his body and his blood as their food for the way which is yet ahead. With this he sends them into the path of history as with the sufficiency of bread upon which they can live. But all their eating and drinking is done only *in anticipation* of the new earth and of the new wine, i.e., of the fulness of joy. The Lord's Supper, therefore, remains what Paul says, "the preaching of the Lord's death till he come" (I Cor. 11:26).[43]

In contrast to those who want to let the eschatological motif prevail over that of the expiatory death, we are of the opinion that the latter imparts to the Lord's Supper its specific meaning. This does not detract from the *perfectum* of the fulfillment. Rather, the whole of this completeness is implied in Jesus' expiatory death. But it characterizes the Eucharist as the communal meal ordained by Jesus for his disciples and for the coming church during the time following his departure from them. For this period, the Lord's Supper is the meal at which Christ indicates, as their permanent food and drink, his body and blood delivered up to death for his own. Receiving this nourishment from his hand by faith, they are to eat and to drink till he has come to drink the new wine in his Father's kingdom with all who are his.

Next, we shall have to reflect upon the way in which "the motif of the expiatory death," thus given a central position by Jesus, functions in the Eucharist in the light of the tradition.

41. *The Character of Jesus' Action at the Last Supper*

The first and most important question confronting us is that about *the way in which* Jesus gives his disciples, and in them his church, his body and blood as their food and drink in the time previous to the fulfilled communion in God's kingdom. This leads us to a further determination of the character of Jesus' action at the Last Supper in breaking the bread and in pouring out the wine and apportioning them to his disciples while saying the familiar words, "This is my body," etc.

At this point the first question that arises is how we are to judge the relation between the Last Supper and the actions related to it in connection with the Jewish paschal meal. As has been said,[44] the historicity of such a relation is denied by many. They are of opinion that what the synoptic gospels tell us about Jesus' Last Supper did not take place during the celebration of the paschal meal. It is true that there is no denying that the evangelists, Mark, Matthew, and Luke, have conceived of Jesus' last meal as a paschal meal. In Luke, Jesus himself explicitly speaks of "this passover" (22:15) and also in Matthew 26:17ff and Mark 14:12ff the preparations for the meal are implied in the words, "Where wilt thou that we go and prepare that thou mayest eat the passover?" The correctness of this description is disputed on two grounds.

In the first place, these writers appeal to John 18:28; 19:14, where it seems that the paschal meal took place on the day of Jesus' death (hence, on the day following that of the Last Supper). The 15th of Nisan, the day of the passover, then would not have begun with the evening of the Thursday when Jesus and his disciples came together in the upper room, but with the evening of the Friday after Jesus' death. And *in the second place,* it is thought that closer study of the Last Supper described by the synoptics is bound to lead to the same result, namely, that in this description there is nowhere any mention of a lamb, or of the reading of the story of the exodus which was customary at the paschal meal. Moreover, there is the simple mention of "bread," and not that of the "unleavened cakes" eaten at the paschal meal. And, in Matthew and Mark at any rate, only one cup is passed around, whereas at the paschal meal at least four cups were put on the table. *Finally,* it is objected that the events described in the synoptic gospels as having happened on Thursday evening and Friday are hardly compatible with the commandment of *a rest* on the 15th of Nisan (reference is made to the action of an armed force, of the session of the judicial court of the Sanhedrin of the condemnation of Jesus on the night of the festival, of his crucifixion on the festival day, of the purchase of spices, of Jesus' burial, etc.).[45]

Although we cannot go into the details with respect to this historical question, it must be established that little value can be attached to the objections derived from the synoptic description of the meal itself.

In the first place, it must be observed that the intention of the synoptic story is certainly not to give an accurate description of the paschal meal, but to tell us about the special things that Jesus said and did. Much rather, the knowledge of what happened at the paschal meal is presupposed or even considered as superfluous. And then, after a closer view, all kinds of individual traits in the story very clearly refer to the paschal meal.

Jeremias has pointed this out in great detail[46] and others have followed him in this and given further support by the adduction of fresh arguments.[47] The following can be pointed out. The meal took place at Jerusalem, according to John also, whereas at other times Jesus at night left the town. In view of the overcrowded condition of the town, this can only be explained from the paschal *ordinance.* It was held at a very unusual time and lasted into the night in accordance with the customs of the passover. It had a special and festive character: the participants *lay down* at table and drank *wine*. This was not an every-day practice but belonged to the paschal rites. All of this may be inferred from both the synoptic gospels and that of John. To this we must add from the synoptics that the manner in which Jesus characterizes the bread and wine reminds us of the explanation given by a father to his family of the meaning of the different elements; that the eschatological perspective revealed by Jesus is in agreement with the desire expressed at the paschal meal for the future liberation of Israel; that according to Luke a cup was passed around at least twice; that Jesus passed the cup around *after the meal* (*meta to deipnēsai*), Luke 22:20, quite in accordance with the paschal rites; that the words "the fruit of the vine" also occur in it; that in rabbinical literature, "bread" is also used for unleavened bread; that the words "do this *in remembrance of* me," as well as the singing of the Hallel at the end, are entirely in accordance with the paschal meal.

In the synoptics there can be no doubt that by Jesus' last meal we have to understand the celebration of the passover. It is true that some authors have suggested that the meal was a solemn preparatory meal before the passover, or a so-called *chabura*-meal. But apart from the question whether such meals were customary immediately before the paschal meal,[48] the above-mentioned details point especially to the passover.

Already for this reason it does not seem possible for us to dispute the historicity of the synoptic account with the argument that by virtue of the Jewish ordinances, no work was allowed on the 15th of Nisan. Had this been the case, then the bearing of arms, a session of the Sanhedrin, the participation of the people in Roman judicial activities, the purchase of a shroud for Jesus, etc., mentioned in the synoptic accounts would be incompatible with the laws. For in the first place, it is inconceivable that the evangelical tradition should have become so completely derailed as to give an account which, (although verifiable by every Jewish Christian on this point, i.e., that of the rest on the 15th of Nisan), would have been in conflict with the simplest concepts of the festive ritual of the Jews.   But in addition to this serious objection, there are scholars like Dalman[49] and Billerbeck[50] who have demonstrated that, on the basis of the rabbinical writings themselves, the Jewish ordinances with respect to the actions narrated by the synoptics as having happened on the 15th of Nisan were no insurmountable obstacles.

The historical objection must, therefore, be reduced to the description that John seems to give in 19:14 and in 18:28, to the effect that on the day of Jesus' death the paschal meal had still to be eaten.   As is well-known, we are here confronted with one of the most difficult questions about the relation between the synoptics and John.   The attempt made in the course of the investigation to establish some agreement between John and the synoptics on this point is not to be considered merely as an example of some harmonistic policy with nothing in John's gospel to support it.   We have already mentioned Jeremias' arguments according to which the meal mentioned in John 13:1 clearly had the character of a special festive gathering together.   But in our opinion, John 13:1 and 2 itself offers strong argument in favor of the view that the paschal meal is meant by this Supper.   John 13:1 opens with the words, "*before the feast of the passover*" (*pro de tēs heortēs tou pascha*). In the second verse we read, "and when the supper had come" (*kai deipnou ginomenou*).   The combination of these two data is most natural when the supper mentioned in the 2nd verse is understood to be the paschal meal.   It is true that in verse 1 it says "*before* the passover," but this time-adjunct must not be connected with the principal verb *ēgapēsen* (he loved) and with what follows in the second verse, but with *eidoos* (having known), verse 1.   The meaning is that, already before the passover, Jesus knew that his end was near and therefore acted in accordance with it during the paschal meal.   In our opinion, this time-adjunct only makes sense if what is told in the second verse and further, took place at the feast of the passover and if, therefore, *deipnon* denotes the paschal meal itself.   The paschal feast is doubtless not explicitly referred to at this meal.   But the *argumentum e silentio* does not hold here. For the institution of the Lord's Supper is not mentioned here either. Yet it is not reasonable to assume that the evangelist wants to combat this institution, or to ignore it, or that he did not know about it.

The Lord's Supper was undoubtedly celebrated at the time when this gospel was written and was also traced back to Jesus' Last Supper. We are here thus confronted with the peculiar character of the fourth gospel, which was written for those who already knew the gospel of Jesus Christ (also historically).

When, therefore, other authors try to remove the seeming contradiction between John and the synoptics on this point, and for this purpose explain the two "difficult" texts, 18:28 and 19:14, in such a way that the 15th of Nisan remains the day of Jesus' death and the paschal supper as eaten the day before, they base this view upon that which the evangelist of the fourth gospel himself suggests in 13:1ff about this meal. Consequently, 19:14 and 18:28 can only with difficulty be held to speak of the usual paschal supper. John 19:14 does not offer great difficulties, because *paraskeuē* can be conceived of as a *terminus technicus* for "Friday," just as in verse 31 (cf. vs. 42) *paraskeuē* probably means the day before the sabbath. The genetive *tou pascha* then merely means (the day before the sabbath) *during the feast of the passover*. The real crux lies in 18:28. There are different views possible here. The fact of their plurality shows, on the one hand, that the matter is not simple, but on the other, that we should not speak of an evident and insoluble chronological contradiction between John 18:28 and the synoptics. The simplest way is to understand *pascha* in John 18:28 in a wider sense than that of a meal at which the paschal lamb was eaten. Zahn, e.g., looks upon it as an indication of the paschal-*mazzoth*.[51] Older experts in Judaism, like Lightfoot and Schoettgen, appeal to the Talmud and explain the word as "eating the festive sacrifice," and have found many adherents of late. In our opinion, this view has many points in its favor. Other experts in the Talmud, such as D. Chwolson, J. Klausner and Strack-Billerbeck, say that both John and the synoptics give a correct account of the facts when they fix the celebration of passover on a different day. For it is said that there existed among the Jews a difference of opinion as to the date when the passover ought to be eaten. Jesus and his disciples are assumed to have followed the view of the Pharisees and to have celebrated the meal a day earlier than the Sadducees, to whose celebration John 18:28 is supposed to refer.[52] If this view is correct, a different light is shed on the objections derived from various activities that are supposed to have taken place on the 15th of Nisan (cf. above). Although there is no generally accepted solution to the difficulty, the latter will have to be reduced to its rightful proportions by bearing in mind: a) that the account of the synoptics undeniably refers to the Last Supper as the passover meal; b) that considered in itself, John 13:1ff may also be looked upon with full justification as a description of the passover; c) that John 18:28 does not mean an evident contradiction of this general view. From a historical point of view there is, in our opinion, no other way in the discussion of the synoptic account than to start from the assumption that the institution of the Lord's Supper took place *during the passover meal*.

The question now arises with regard to the extent that this sheds light on the meaning of these words and the character of these actions. We need not enter into details about the Jewish passover in order to compare with it the separate acts in the course of the Last Supper. Of course we are only concerned now with the position and the meaning of *the bread* and *the wine* of the paschal meal with which Jesus connected the well-known words about his body and blood.

The bread is mentioned with the adjunct "while they were eating" (*esthiontoon autoon*, Mark 14:22; Matt. 26:26). This is probably the meal proper which was taken after the first course (consisting of bitter herbs, green herbs and a kind of sauce) and the passover liturgy (at which the father gave his family an explanation of the paschal feast in answer to his son's question about it, after which the first part of the paschal hallel was sung). This meal consisted of the paschal lamb which lay roasted on the table, unleavened bread, bitter herbs, a kind of stewed fruit and wine. The bread of which Jesus said, "this is my body," must have been the unleavened bread that was taken together with the paschal lamb. The "blessing" mentioned here (*eulogēsas*, Matt. 26:26; Mark 14:22; *eucharistēsas*, Luke 22:19) is the grace said before the meal proper.

As to the *wine*, from Matthew and Mark we might get the impression that this is the wine that was passed around during the principal dish, the so-called second cup. From Luke

22:20 (cf. I Cor. 11:25) it follows that this cup was taken *after the meal* (*meta to deipnēsai*). It was *the third cup,* over which thanksgiving took place after the meal, and which, therefore, was known as "the cup of blessing," "the cup of thanksgiving (*potēsion tēs eulogias,* I Cor. 10:16).[53]

When Jesus imparts to the bread and wine the meaning of his body and blood, he certainly does so on the analogy of what a father did at the celebration of the passover, viz., relating the elements of the meal to the exodus from Egypt. The question is, however, what does Jesus here mean by the words, "this is my body." According to Dalman, Jesus said, at the breaking of the bread, *dēn hu guphi,* which latter word may mean (this is) "my body," as well as (this is) "I myself." Some authors prefer the latter meaning and hold that Jesus did not especially speak of his *body* but of his *person,* and thus wanted to guarantee to his disciples his personal presence at their common celebration of the Lord's Supper in the future.[54] To our mind this conception is erroneous. Even if Dalman's Aramaic translation is taken as a starting-point,[55] it is not necessary to translate, "this is I myself" instead of "this is my body." The Greek text with which we are concerned clearly speaks of *sooma,* "body," and therefore represents another conception. Moreover, what is said about the blood in what follows makes the rendering "my body" necessary.[56]   Body and blood undoubtedly occur here as the two components of man's material make-up which are separated at *death.*   And it is death that is meant here.   For Jesus' body is mentioned here as that which "is given for you" (Luke), and his blood as that which "is shed for many for the remission of their sins" (Matt. and Mark).   Both this "given" and this "shed" refer to Jesus' impending death.[57]

This is why Jeremias is perfectly right in connecting the words of the Last Supper with the terminology of sacrifice.[58] In the language of the cult, the flesh and blood of the sacrificial animal is repeatedly mentioned, and the expression "to shed blood" is also frequently used.   Besides, according to Matthew and Mark, Jesus refers to his blood as "my blood of the covenant," which is an obvious allusion to Exodus 24:8, where "the blood of the covenant" also denotes the sacrificial blood that had been sprinkled upon the people.

Now the question arises whether or not Jesus, by speaking of his body and blood in this way, indicates himself as the true paschal lamb. This opinion is advanced by many scholars.[59] However, it should be noted that such a direct connection between Jesus' death and the killing of the *paschal* lamb is not expressed. In the first place, it should be borne in mind that Jesus speaks of "his body" when distributing *the bread* and not when serving *the meat* of the paschal lamb. Dalman's explanation is that a ritual did not exist in connection with the serving and eating of the lamb of the passover, so that Jesus could not take this as a starting-point. Hence, already for this reason, Jesus had a better one in the bread which was divided in a special and solemn way. Moreover, that which stood ready on the table was no longer a suitable representation of "the lamb brought to the slaughter" to which Jesus could compare himself, for it was probably already a tasty roast cut up into pieces serving as a festive repast and, therefore, that with which Jesus could hardly identify his own body.[60]

One can thus undoubtedly conclude that the meat of the lamb set on the table in this form was not as appropriate to be connected with Jesus' body as the bread that was distributed. Yet it is undeniable that, by Jesus' reference to his body by means of the bread and not by the meat, the direct relation between Jesus' death and the death of the paschal lamb is absent. This is even more clearly the case with the sharing of the wine. Jesus here speaks of his blood but does not refer to the blood of the paschal lamb, but to the blood *sprinkled* at the making of the *covenant*. It is true that there were pronouncements quoted from Jewish literature which denote the blood of the passover as the blood of the covenant,[61] but they are exceptional and only found in the exegesis of the scribes.[62] And what is conclusive is that by the words "this is my blood of the covenant," Jesus clearly quotes the words of the making of the covenant on Mount Sinai[63] (cf. also Hebrews 9:20), and that any allusion to the blood of the slaughtered paschal lambs is lacking.

From all this it appears that the so-called institutional words are unduly stretched when they are interpreted like this, "Jesus says, 'my body is the true paschal flesh, my blood is the true paschal blood, I am the true paschal lamb.' "[64] Elsewhere in the New Testament, Jesus is clearly indicated and explicitly called the true paschal lamb (I Cor. 5:7; John 19:36, cf. also John 1:29,36; I Peter 1:19; Rev. 5:6; 12:11), and his words at the paschal meal certainly justify such a designation. But in spite of all such considerations, it must be stated that the words especially, "This is my blood of the covenant," set Jesus' sacrificial death in a wider perspective than that merely of the paschal offering. For this reason Jesus' death must be viewed not only as the fulfillment of the slaying of the paschal lamb, but more generally as that of the entire Old Testament sacrificial service which made the remission of the sins of the people and life with God in the covenant possible. This general character of Jesus' expiatory death also appears from his allusion to Isaiah 53 saying that his blood is shed "for many," thereby opening the way for the "new covenant" announced by Jeremiah and Ezekiel. The great and central thought is that Jesus' death is the eminently propitiatory sacrifice, the fulfillment of everything that had been symbolized as such under the old covenant. And it is the fruit of this all-embracing, all-fulfilling propitiatory sacrifice which he gives to his disciples to eat and to drink as his body and blood.

Everything in this context depends upon a true insight into the connection of the sacrifice with what is eaten and drunken at the Communion table. In this respect the meaning of the Supper is entirely determined by the character of the paschal meal. That which held for it now holds for the "fulfilled" meaning of the Lord's Supper; it is a sacrificial repast, the sacrificial repast in a pre-eminent sense, viz., that of the new covenant. That is to say, the eating and drinking, the meat and drink that are given, are based on the sacrifice made and are its fruit and result. Israel is given freedom to eat and drink as the redeemed people of God because the sacrifice has been made. Exactly the same thing happens in the Lord's Supper except for the fact that its first celebration anticipated the sacrifice that was to follow. The body had not yet been "given," and the blood had not yet been "shed." Jesus was, as it were, still busy bringing the sacrifice. Nevertheless, that which Jesus calls the bread and wine of the disciples, their life, their strength, their joy, is the fruit of the sacrifice he was going to make for them. In *this* sense the bread is his body and the cup contains his blood, i.e., *that which is received in bread and cup is the sacrificial food and drink of the new covenant, the fruits of the New Testament sacrificial blood.*

Consequently, there can be no doubt about the general meaning of the action at the Lord's Supper in the light of both the celebration of the passover and the reference to Exodus 24:8. For Jesus calls his sacrificial death the source and cause of the salvation of his followers, the founding act of the new covenant. And in the division of the meat and drink representing his body and blood, he assures his disciples of their share in the salvation brought about by his death. Here, the salvation of the kingdom of heaven proclaimed by Jesus' preaching is once again revealed in its messianic foundation and made visible and tangible to his disciples while at the same time being apportioned to them. In one supreme concentration as it were, in one turn of the hand, the Lord's Supper focuses the whole of the preaching of the gospel upon Christ's sacrifice and sets the table with it. The disciples are permitted to partake of the bread and wine of this sacrificial offering, and derive from it life and joy as the permanent fruits for the time now to come.

From this it follows that there is no foundation whatever for the idea that at the Lord's Supper the sacrificial act itself takes place and that the Lord's Supper and the sacrifice can be identified. This Supper is not the sacrifice itself, but its application, its celebration. But only a slight shift in thought is needed to lead one astray and to land one on a different (and unbiblical) track. In our opinion this happens to Van der Leeuw when, on the basis of the texts concerned with the Last Supper, he draws this conclusion, "He broke the bread as his body, he poured the wine as the blood of his new covenant. . . . He replaces the sacrificial blood of the old covenant with his own blood. Essentially, he sacrificed himself at this Last Supper, Golgotha is only the completion of what happens here."[65]   And further, "Jesus makes the sacrifice at the Supper in the form of a prophetic allegory, yet in a concrete essential sense; this is my body, i.e., this is me."[66]

We are confronted here with a very fundamental conception of the gospel of the Last Supper which forms the basis for an entire sacramental theology, but which, in our opinion, diverts the river-bed in a clear and remarkable way already at the source of the stream. The Lord's Supper is no more a sacrifice than is the paschal meal. It is, however, a sacrificial *meal*. The sacrifice is the presupposition and not the content of the meal. At the paschal repast the lamb was no more killed (though *eaten*) than did Jesus offer himself in parabolic form at the Last Supper. He only assures his disciples in the most vivid way of the fruit of the sacrifice of his life. So long as the Last Supper is viewed within the framework of the paschal meal, there can be no doubt at all about the meaning of Jesus' actions with the bread and wine. It is true that Van der Leeuw will not admit that Jesus' last supper was a paschal meal[67] in spite of the undeniable pronouncements of the gospel. But even apart from this framework (which, however, is more than a setting, but in all kinds of ways proves to be the foundation of the entire record of the Lord's Supper), an accurate exegesis of Jesus' words can never infer from them that during the Supper he was busy sacrificing himself "in the form of a prophetic allegory."

When Jesus says, "this is my body," he does not at all refer to what he is *breaking*, but to what he is *distributing*. It is not the action of breaking, but the food received out of Jesus' hands that is spoken about "in the form of a prophetic allegory." Already for the understanding of the action with respect to the bread, this has a fundamental significance. It is true that, later, the *breaking* of the bread was also incorporated into the symbolism as signifying the "breaking" of Christ's body.[68] But it is very doubtful if this extension of the symbolism is effective and meaningful. There is no point in appealing to the account in I Corinthians 11:24, "which is broken for you," because it is not an authentic interpretation, for exactly the word "broken" is obviously not original.[69] And further, the breaking of the bread in no way suggests the violent tearing asunder of a body. It was much rather the customary action of the father of a family at every meal. The bread was not cut into pieces but was broken. And besides, the idea of the "breaking" of flesh or of a body was entirely foreign to the sacrificial terminology. The sacrificial action consisted in the shedding of the sacrificial blood, not in the tearing asunder of the sacrificial flesh. And finally, elsewhere in the gospel it is emphatically stated that in Jesus' death—just as in that of the paschal lamb— "not a bone of him was broken" (John 19:36). But even if one should hold that this "breaking" can be meaningfully applied to what happened to Jesus' body, it remains undeniable that at the Last Supper this symbolism is in no way expressed in the so-called words about the bread, and that there can be no question of a sacrificial ritual.

This statement holds even more clearly for the wine than for the bread. When Jesus says "for this is my blood of the new covenant which is shed for many," it *cannot* refer to the action of pouring the wine into the cup, but only to the distributing of the wine as the blood of Christ. And this for the simple reason that the pouring of the wine into the cup cannot possibly be linguistically denoted as a "shedding" (*ekkein*).[70] When Van der Leeuw writes that Jesus "poured out" the wine as the blood of his new covenant and infers that in essence he was sacrificing himself at this meal, he only transfers his own ideas into the original text, and that in a very radical way. There is not the faintest suggestion in the text of a symbolic "pouring out" of the wine into the cup. The parallelism between pouring out of wine and shedding of blood is perfectly alien to the text and to linguistic usage. Besides, from the passover ritual it may be inferred that the wine had been standing ready when Jesus applied the figure of his blood to it.[71] What is symbolized, therefore, is not Christ's self-surrender, but its fruits for the life of his followers.[72] Not the altar, but the table characterizes the activity at the Lord's Supper. The sacrifice is the presupposition preceding this eating and drinking but does not itself pertain to this "allegory." This cannot be disputed for a moment with any semblance of justification, either from the passover meal or from an accurate exegesis of the words connected with the bread and wine.

This is also why the repeated attempt to establish a connection between the Lord's Supper and the incarnation is entirely foreign to the world of thought of the synoptic records.[73] For "body" and "blood" in no respect whatever represent the flesh as the mode of existence of the divine Word, so that those who partake of his body and blood would share in his divine-human existence. All that is imparted to the disciples here in Christ's body and blood is his self-surrender unto death. This is why we think it an error to suppose that, in the body and blood at the Lord's Supper, more is meant than "the fruits of the crucifixion, propitiation, remission, of sins." Some suppose that what is also meant is the eschatological-pneumatic reality consisting in "the flesh and blood of Christ himself," and not simply in "its fruit."[74] For, again, Christ's body and blood do not occur here *as such*, neither in their earthly-temporal condition nor in their glorified state; so that after Christ's ascension to heaven the eating and drinking of this flesh and blood cannot be supposed to be his followers reception of or entry into the eschatological reality of Christ's glorification. The point of view from which the body and blood of the Lord are regarded in this connection is that which occurs in his death. All that goes beyond this, all that the body and blood as Christ's earthly or heavenly mode of existence allegedly denotes, is a *metabasis eis allo genos,* a misrepresentation of the situation at the Lord's Supper as a sacrificial meal, as well as a misrepresentation both of the connection between this Supper and the passover and that between Supper and meal of the covenant, by which the entire exegesis of the institutional words is to be determined.[75]

From this indisputable, clear character of Jesus' action at the Last Supper is also inferred the *purpose* he wanted to achieve. He pointed out to his disciples his propitiatory death as the cause and the foundation of the salvation he had proclaimed to them as the gospel of the kingdom which consisted in the realization of the new covenant promised by the prophets. At the same time this reference was a confirmation and a seal. For he *gave* them bread and wine as his body and blood for them to eat and to drink. And all this as an ordinance they had to observe and maintain. The anamnestic commandment, "do this in remembrance of me" (Luke 22:19), is undeniable. It makes the Lord's Supper into the meal of the covenant of the new people of God, of the church that Christ gathers together for himself. This is also expressed by the words "for many," the meaning of which we have already tried to define: they are those who in their gathered totality (*Gesammtheit*) are benefited by his propitiatory death. They are the new people of God, the messianic community in its generality for which Jesus dies and for which he ordains the Supper in remembrance of him.

Consequently, the Lord's Supper has the character of a redemptive meal, a meal of joyfulness because of the Lord's expiatory death. Doubtless this is possible only because Christ returned from this death, because he is not only the crucified but also the risen Lord, and because he is and remains the host of this meal. Yet the Lord's Supper is no resurrection meal, but a sacrificial expiatory meal because of the cross. Good

Friday is certainly the focal point in our remembrance of Christ as the day on which our salvation was accomplished. It is the day on which Christ's death became his people's life, his anxiety became their delivery, his fear became their joy, his body and blood surrendered to death became their bread and wine; he, the crucified one, even became "the food and drink of eternal life for their hungry and thirsty souls." This is why the bread is the bread of salvation, the bread of life; and the cup is the "cup of redemption" and "the cup of salvation." And all this in the sense that there is here not only that which is symbolized and offered, but that which is also realized and confirmed. Christ's body and blood are eaten and drunken at the Communion table, the cross becomes an actual and living reality in the midst of the congregation. It is this combination of sign and seal, of symbol and reality, which we shall have to examine further in the light of the gospel.

42. *Symbol and Reality*

We have now come to the question of the relationship that Jesus, in the so-called institutional words, established between the bread of the Lord's Supper and his body, and between the cup (of wine) and his blood, and which are expressed in the words, "this is my body," and, "this is my blood of the covenant" ("this cup is the new covenant in my blood"). This question has been the subject of hot disputes since ancient times. It is of course impossible for us to discuss all the exegetical positions occupied in the great confessional struggle about the meaning of the words of the Lord's Supper. On *exegetical grounds,* the thesis that the words "this is my body" refer to a relation of identity between the material substance of his body and the bread of the Eucharist, involving an essential change in the bread and the wine, no longer needs any refutation.[76] The dogmatical literature with respect to the exegesis of the word *touto* shows what violence exegetes are compelled to resort to in order to demonstrate the so-called "evidence" of this conception.

This word *touto*, after all, can only mean "this bread." After Jesus had pronounced the words "(is) my body," is would then have changed its meaning. And the disciples would have thought of bread only when listening to these words up to and including "*touto*," but after the designation "my body" they would no longer have been able to think of bread.[77] It can hardly be denied that from an exegetical point of view there is here no question of evidence but of an instance of unbearable artificiality.

The same thing holds, *mutatis mutandis*, of the old Lutheran conception based as it was on the isolated, literal exegesis limited to the bare words of the institution of the Lord's Supper.[78] It is true that the change of the bread into the body, etc., was rejected here, but it was maintained that in, with, and under the bread and wine the body and blood of Christ were present in the concrete sense of the word, either conceived of as a union (*unio*) of the two substances of bread and body or, as Luther had it, applying the figure of a synecdoche to *touto*. Hence, the word *touto* (*hoc*) refers to the bread indeed, but not only to the bread but to all that Jesus here distributes which, as the predicate says, is not merely bread but specifically bread *and* body. The predicate (body) puts the invisible and valuable part of the whole in the foreground, whereas the subject first denotes the less valuable and visible bearer of the invisible good. So while *touto* is related both to the visible and the invisible part, the predicate only indicates the body (synecdoche).[79]

Nowadays, Lutheran exegetists as well as many dogmatists admit that this isolated, "literal" exegesis of the words of the Eucharist is untenable. Gollwitzer, e.g., rightly argues that within the scope of the Last Supper, no question on the part of the disciples could have arisen as to the meaning of what Jesus gave them, because the idea that it might be something different than bread that was given them could not have occurred to them. If Jesus' words were an indication of "the content" of the bread, this should then have been clearly expressed, for within the scope of this meal it was not immediately evident in the words themselves. That is why the very fact that Jesus spoke these words without any further comment does *not* require, as Luther thought, but much rather prevents a literal conception of the predicate "body" as an indication of its content (*Inhaltsangabe*).[80]

On the other hand, no real objection can be raised against the symbolical[81] conception of the institutional words. Not only is this conception quite obvious in the situation in which these words were uttered and in which the disciples would be unable to attach any other meaning to these words in Jesus' bodily presence; but it is also entirely in accordance with Jesus graphic, imaginative, symbolical manner of speaking, so that the parables have rightly been referred to in this case.[82]   Moreover, the fact that the Greek text has *estin* cannot alter anything here.   For the Greek *estin* may express the identity of subject and attribute,[83] but this does not detract from the equally undeniable fact that *estin* may just as well have a comparative or symbolical meaning (Matt. 13:38,39 and *passim*).   It is not in the least necessary for this pronouncement to be preceded by a comparison[84] (cf. Matt. 5:13).   And as to the argument that bread and wine cannot have a symbolical meaning here but only a "realistic" signification because they are not natural symbols for the flesh and blood of a man,[85] from this latter circumstance it can only be inferred that it is the point of comparison that should be primarily considered.   As to its nature, salt is not a symbol for man; but with an eye on a special point of similarity, Jesus can say to people, "Ye are the salt of the earth" (Matt. 5:13).

Yet the whole narrative of the institution of the Lord's Supper shows that Jesus does not simply draw a comparison between bread and his body and between wine and his blood. These words are accompanied by a certain meaningful *action* (viz., distributing) which is also to be incorporated into the symbolism, as well as the exhortation to take and to eat and drink.   Bread and wine are not Jesus' body and blood for the reason that, objectively and apart from this action, they show some resemblance to his body and blood within the scope of this Supper, but because of their *use* ordained by Jesus and realized by the disciples.   That is to say, they are such because Jesus *distributes* this food to the disciples in this situation and in this specific sense.   And that is why the disciples receive his body and blood in a symbolical way in this bread and wine. *So bread and wine not only depict Jesus' body and blood but also function in another way, i.e., by representing them.* Therefore, anyone who receives the one also receives the other. Undoubtedly, this can take place only in the way that his body and blood can be received, i.e., *in accordance with their nature.* For Jesus' body and blood, of course, are not food and drink that can be taken with our physical mouths.   Everything remains symbolical, although in such a way that this symbolical activity is connected with reality by virtue of the action accomplished with bread and wine as symbols of Christ's body and blood.   The Roman Catholic and the old Lutheran exegesis do not err because of the close connection they established between bread and body, wine and blood, but in that they made the symbol itself into the reality whereas they should have realized that the connection between the symbol and its intended reality is to be sought in the action of giving, on the one hand, and in that of eating and drinking, on the other.

To understand the connection between bread and body, it is constructive to read what R. Otto writes about what he terms "the special type of Christ's action with the bread."   It belongs to the general type of a parable.   The master of parables in *words* here *acts* in a parable.   This action anticipates the future, viz., the death of our Lord,[86] but at the same time it is an *Anteilgabe an dem Anticipierten* (giving a share in what is being anticipated); namely, by what Otto calls *effective representation.*   This is in accordance with the ancient conception which found adherence over a very wide area and is still found at present.   It is the view—never strictly defined, but for this reason all the more alive—that the essence, the virtue, the speciality, the curse, or the blessing inherent in some object or event (X) can be transmitted or appropriated by using a representation of X.   Such a representation becomes effective through the will of him who has X at his disposal.

It is always objects and events that in themselves show some analogy, some similarity with respect to the objects or events to be represented, that are especially suitable for effective representation. Often enough, because of this analogy, such things or events spontaneously attract the idea of an effective representation. Such a special case is the present instance. The taking of the food and drink and the strength derived from it implies an analogy with the appropriation of the virtue or the working of what it represents, viz., his body and blood. Thus Paul says that those who eat the sacrifices are partakers of the altar. For the sacrifice represents the altar. And he who is a partaker of the altar is also a partaker of the sanctifying power of the altar.[87] Elsewhere, Paul speaks of *fellow-ship* between those who eat of a certain food and the powers disposing of such food (cf. I Cor. 10:20,21). Being partakers of the Lord's table spoken of by Paul in this context, as well as partaking of the table of devils, establishes a fellowship, gives access to a reality represented by bread, wine, a table, a meal. There is no question or thought of the transition of one "substance" into the other. But the relation thus created is not only a noetical one but also something actual and real. It is entry into living contact with the reality of what is represented by the outward signs.

The expression "representation," denoting the effective and actual bond between symbol and reality in the Lord's Supper, is not only found in Otto's expositions but is used by a large circle of authors.[88]   It is, therefore, extremely important to realize that this term only expresses *the nature of the relation* between the sign and that signified, and that for a correct use of this term it is all-important to know the content, the *res* of what is represented. Here we must revert to what has been said in the previous section about Jesus' *body* and *blood*. For if it is thought that at the Lord's Supper Jesus sacrificed himself in a prefigurative and anticipatory way; it is understandable, that in the repetition of the action with bread and wine, the sacrifice of Christ *as an action* is each time considered to be represented as actual and present. This is, therefore, the view of many recent authors who begin with the idea of the Lord's Supper as a *sacrifice,* as is especially done by the more recent Romanist and Romanizing theologians.

In opposition to this, we must maintain that within the scope of the records of the institution of the Lord's Supper, the concept "representation" cannot refer to any sacrificial action by which Christ sacrificed himself. It can only be applied to that which is distributed to the believers, i.e., to the fruit, the atonement, the remission of sins brought about by Christ's sacrifice. This is the undeniable and pregnant meaning of the phrases "my body" and "my blood." It is that which can be partaken of at the sacrificial *repast*, as the food of redemption, as the cup of salvation. Moreover, that is why any conception of this representation as being based on a new divine act of creation which has its basic form in the incarnation of the Logos, and changes the elements of the bread and wine of the Eucharist into being the bearers of the real presence of Christ's work of salvation,[89] would be an intrusion into the gospel of thoughts from another world. The Lord's Supper is only concerned with an actual *assurance* of salvation, not with the rendering present or the actualization (to avoid the term "repetition") of the unique fact of salvation. *It is not the acquisition but the application of salvation that is represented.* Body and blood—and we must not go any further—only occur at the Lord's Supper as that which can be partaken of by the faithful. This is the only thing in the Lord's Supper capable of prolongation. The Lord's Supper represents salvation and distributes it by virtue of Jesus' authoritative messianic *word*, and not because in some way or other it signifies an extension *in mysterio* of the incarnation of the Logos by virtue of a divine act of creation. So it belongs to the miracle of Christ's *work* and not to that of his *person*.

Finally, this also indicates the foundation of the reality of the body and blood of Christ conceived of in the above sense and the guarantee of the relation between symbol and reality. Its explanation is not found in the quality of the elements of bread and wine either on account of their change into the body and blood or of their material connection with them. Nor is it permissible to think in a subjectivistic way that the real connection between the bread and wine and Christ's self-sacrifice is based on the faith of the recipients of the bread and wine. The disciples are exhorted to "take," "eat," and "drink," and only in this "taking" do they partake of Christ's body and blood in the Lord's Supper. They are also exhorted to continue doing so in remembrance of Christ. So they are to perpetuate this action of eating and drinking Christ's body and blood. And it is supposed that in this believing act of remembrance they will actually continue to receive the virtue of his expiatory death, or, in other words, that in this act of remembrance the linkage of bread to body, wine to blood will continue to exist. But it does not mean that the reality of this connection rests in faith and is made entirely subjective. Jesus' institutional words are not "Eat this as my body," or "Consider this as my body." *The connection between bread and body, wine and blood, rests in Christ's words, in his command, in the fact that he is the dispenser and the host.* So everything here depends on *the reliability of his promise,* on the efficacy and the authority of his words. Because Jesus has power over his "body" and "blood," i.e., over the fruits of his propitiatory sacrifice, he can make bread and wine represent his body and blood. So the reality of this "sacramental" process, i.e., the relation between symbol and reality, can never be too much emphasized if only this realism is not shifted from Christ to the elements. For the bread and wine "are" the body and blood of Christ because of the fact and to the extent that they are their representatives by virtue of Christ's promise. This is why the certainty of receiving salvation is not vested in the eating and drinking as such, nor in faith alone, but in accepting from the hands of Christ these symbols as thus qualified. The nature of the elements need not even be mentioned—the visible manner in which they are the bearers of salvation does not lie upon a different plane from the audible way in which this salvation is communicated by the divine Word—the essential and exclusive thing is the "nature" of *Christ's promise.*

This is nothing less than that which he made known to his disciples and communicated to them on the night before his death with the same authority as that with which he pronounced the poor in spirit to be blessed. And with the disciples he also included his church as partaking of the expiatory power of his death. The parabolic form in which this is done is not as such a more effective demonstration of the power of redemption embracing the whole of human existence than the assurance of their salvation by the preaching of the gospel. The main thing is for them to accept this salvation from the hands of him who sacrificed himself in his surrender to death. The essential thing is the connection between the gospel and his expiatory death, the founding of the whole of the preaching of the kingdom in Christ's death. And in this he himself acts as the dispenser of salvation in the Last Supper, and also every time the church does so "in remembrance of him." For all these things have been said on the basis of the same certainty with which he elsewhere assured his disciples of his permanent communion (Matt. 18:20; 28:20). Now also the guarantee of the church partaking of the expiatory power of Christ's death in bread and wine is not that in them the mystery of Christ's presence is transferred to the bread or embodied in the wine, but only in the fact that the living Christ still backs up his word with his authority, and that he authorizes others to speak in his name.

That is why this last word is "a word of the church." Given at the time of his departure, this word denotes the mode of existence of the church in the time before the second coming of the Son of Man in his glory; it is an existence rooted in the effective assurance of salvation given by Christ, it is receiving from his hands and eating and drinking of the fruits of his cross until he comes to drink the new wine with his followers in his Father's kingdom.

Notes to Chapter IX

[1] Thus H. J. Holtzmann, *Lehrbuch der neutest. Theologie,* I, 1911; p. 378.

[2] In his book *Messe und Herrenmahl,* 1926.

[3] *Op. cit.,* p. 249ff; cf. also K. L. Schmidt, *Abendmahl im N.T.,* R.G.G., I,[2] 1927, pp. 6-16; E. Käsemann, *Das Abendmahl im N.T.* in the anthology *Abendmahlsgemeinschaft?,* 1937, pp. 60ff.

[4] E. Klostermann, *Das Markusevangelium,*[3] 1936, pp. 146, 147. He can, for the greater part, refer to Bultmann, *Gesch. der synopt. Trad.,*[2] pp. 285-287, although the latter is still more sceptical about the possibility of penetrating to the real history of Jesus.

[5] D. Plooy, *Novum Testamentum regnum aeternum,* 1932, p. 11.

[6] Cf. for this positing of the problem also E. Schweizer, *Das Abendmahl eine Vergegenwärtigung des Todes Jesu oder ein eschatologisches Freudenmahl? Theol. Zeitschrift,* 2 Jhrg., 1946, pp. 81ff.

[7] In his *Reich Gottes und Menschensohn,* 1934, pp. 223-281.

[8] *Das Messianitäts- und Leidensgeheimnis,*[2] 1929, pp. 55-57; cf. also his *Geschichte der Leben-Jesu-Forschung,*[4] 1933, p. 421; and *Die Mystik des Apostels Paulus,* 1930, pp. 108 and 235ff.

[9] *Die Mystik des Apostels Paulus,* pp. 264-284.

[10] Cf. also my *Zelfopenbaring en Zelfverberging,* 1946, p. 10.

[11] *Op. cit.,* pp. 244, 245.

[12] *Op. cit.,* pp. 227ff.

[13] *Op. cit.,* p. 235.

[14] *Op. cit.,* pp. 244, 248.

[15] *Op. cit.,* pp. 245ff.

[16] *Op. cit.,* pp. 255ff.

[17] *Op. cit.,* pp. 249ff.

[18] Thus, e.g., E. Gaugler, *Das Abendmahl im N.T.,* 1943, pp. 18ff; G. Sevenster, *De Christologie van het N.T.,* 1946, pp. 123ff; E. Schweizer, *Das Abendmahl, op. cit.*

[19] An elaborate defence is given, e.g., by J. Jeremias, *Die Abendmahlsworte Jesu,*[2] 1946; cf. also Behm, *TWB,* III, pp. 726ff, the article on *"klao."*

[20] Cf. especially G. Dalman, *Jesus Jeschua,* 1929, pp. 80-166; Strack-Billerbeck, *op. cit.,* IV, 1, pp. 41-76; Jeremias, *op. cit.*

[21] Markus Barth, *Das Abendmahl,* 1945, pp. 43, 44.

[22] Thus J. Plooy, *Het heilig Avondmaal in het N.T.,* in: *Kerk en Eredienst,* 1947, pp. 5ff.

[23] Thus M. Barth, *op. cit.,* pp. 55, 57, 43ff.

[24] Thus Plooy, *op. cit.*

[25] O. Cullmann, *Urchristentum und Gottesdienst,* 1944, pp. 14, 15.

[26] Thus, e.g., Gaugler and E. Schweizer. Cf. also L. D. Poot, *Het Oud-Christelijk Avondmaal,* 1936, and M. H. Bolkestein, *Het heilig Avondmaal,* 1947.

[27] All the uncials, except D, have the longer text. For the material cf. A. Merx, *Die vier Kanonischen Evangelien,* II, 2, 1905, pp. 432ff; also J. Jeremias, *Die Abendmahlsworte Jesu,*[2] 1949, pp. 67ff.

[28] *Op. cit.,* p. 70; cf. also E. Gaugler, *La Sainte Cène* (par. G. Deluz, J. Ph. Ramseyer, E. Gaugler), 1945, pp. 56ff.

[29] For a survey of defenders and opponents, cf. Jeremias, *op. cit.,* pp. 75, 79, 80. This author, in his second edition, has joined the defenders of the

longer text. S. Greijdanus, *op. cit.*, II, pp. 1045-1050, also gives an elaborate discussion and defense of the authenticity of verses 19b and 20, and appeals to P. Benoit, *Le récit de la cène dans Lc. XXII*, 15-20, *Revue Biblique*, 1939, pp. 357-393. For its authenticity cf., e.g., also E. Schweizer, *Das Abendmahl*, in: *Theol. Zeitschr.*, 1946, pp. 81ff; E. Gaugler, *Das Abendmahl im N.T.*, 1943, p. 20; G. Sevenster, *Kerk en Eredienst*, 1 Jg., 1946.

[30] Cf. Strack-Billerbeck, *op. cit.*, IV, 1, p. 62 sub c.

[31] Schniewind, *Markus*, p. 173.

[32] This is the truth in the combination of "Culture" and "Sacrament."

[33] Cf. Hebrews 6:4ff.

[34] Cf. also Kümmel, *Verheissung und Erfüllung*, 1945, pp. 16, 17.

[35] Cf. Greijdanus, *op. cit.*, II, p. 144; Klostermann, *Das Lukasev.*, p. 288; Dalman, *Jesus Jeschua*, 1929, pp. 141, 142, 144.

[36] Dalman, *op. cit.*, p. 128; Jeremias, *op. cit.*, p. 103.

[37] Cf. also my *Matth.*, II, 1946, p. 188; Zahn, *Das Ev. des Matth.*,[4] 1922, p. 695.

[38] This is apparently J. Plooy's view, art. cit., *Kerk en Eredienst*, 1947, pp. 4, 6ff.

[39] Cf. above, pp. 100ff, in our discussion of Cullmann's view.

[40] Cullmann, *Urchristentum und Gottesdienst*, pp. 14ff, thinks that the earliest Eucharistic meals in the Christian church can be traced back to the Last Supper, but that in the dazzling light of the resurrection, the idea of the substitutionary suffering (the motif of the expiatory death) had entirely receded into the background, and that these meals were the direct continuation of the meals with Christ between Passover and Ascension. Later, Paul is supposed to have been compelled to lay full stress again upon the idea of the passion. To our mind this is too constructive a hypothesis.

[41] In spite of M. Barth, who thinks he may call such a continuation or repetition of the "anticipation" (*Vorwegnahme*) simply (*schlechterdings*) absurd, *op. cit.*, p. 47.

[42] Cf. also Behm, *TWB*, IV, p. 734, the article on "*klao.*"

[43] Cf. also my *Woord en Sacrament* in the collection *Het Avondmaal*, 1949, pp. 32, 33.

[44] Above, § 39.

[45] Jeremias, *Die Abendmahlsworte Jesu*,[2] 1949, pp. 7-9, mentions as many as 79 authors (beginning with Renan) who advocate this view. The above named arguments are chiefly borrowed from Lietzmann, *op. cit.*, pp. 211ff.

[46] *Op. cit.*, pp. 18ff.

[47] Cf. Behm, e.g., *op. cit.*, p. 733.

[48] This is emphatically denied, e.g., by Jeremias, *op. cit.*, pp. 23ff.

[49] G. Dalman, *Jesus Jeschua*, 1929, pp. 80-98.

[50] Strack-Billerbeck, *op. cit.*, II, pp. 815-834.

[51] Th. Zahn, *Einleitung in das N.T.*, II,[3] 1924, pp. 518-530.

[52] For these views and the criticism applied to them, cf. Jeremias, *op. cit.*, pp. 14, 15.

[53] Cf., e.g., Strack-Billerbeck, *op. cit.*; J. Jeremias, *Die Abendmahlsworte Jesu*,[2] 1949, pp. 48, 49.

[54] Thus Behm, *TWB*, III, p. 735, the article on "*klao*," with an appeal, in my opinion, to Kattenbusch and Seeberg; cf. also Schniewind, *Markus*, p. 173.

[55] Which, however is opposed by others, such as Jeremias, *op. cit.*, pp. 102ff.

[56] Thus also Dalman himself, *op. cit.*, pp. 130, 131.

⁵⁷ Cf. Mark 10:45; Gal. 1:14; I Tim. 2:6; Tit. 2:14. Cf. also Büchsel, *TWB*, II, p. 168, the article on *"didoomi";* Schlatter on Matthew 20:28, *op. cit.,* p. 602.

⁵⁸ *Op. cit.,* p. 105; cf. also V. Taylor, *Jesus and His Sacrifice,* 1948, pp. 121, 261.

⁵⁹ Thus, e.g., M. Barth, *op. cit.,* pp. 10ff; Jeremias, *op. cit.,* p. 104.

⁶⁰ *Jesus Jeschua,* pp. 113, 115; cf. Greijdanus, *Lukas,* II, p. 1056.

⁶¹ Cf. Jeremias, *op. cit.,* pp. 80ff.

⁶² Cf. E. Gaugler, *op. cit.,* p. 38.

⁶³ Cf. also Taylor, *op. cit.,* p. 139.

⁶⁴ Thus M. Barth, *op. cit.,* p. 13.

⁶⁵ G. Van der Leeuw, *Sacramentstheologie,* 1949, p. 52.

⁶⁶ *Op. cit.,* p. 54; cf. also p. 36.

⁶⁷ *Op. cit.,* p. 52; he still sides with the old view of Lietzmann, remarkably enough, without saying a word about the overwhelming mass of material advanced by the ablest judges of Judaism (like Dalman, Billerbeck, Jeremias) against such a violent reconstruction of the gospel.

⁶⁸ Thus Greijdanus, *op. cit.,* II, p. 1054; R. Otto also strongly emphasizes this "breaking of the body," *op. cit.,* p. 250. He supposes, however, that Jesus expected his death in the form of stoning (*"also von faktischer Brechung . . . seines Leibes,"* i.e., thus the literal breaking of his body), p. 256.

⁶⁹ Cf. also Grosheide on I Corinthians 11:24; *op. cit.,* p. 390, *"Het is een oude glosse om de tekst gemakkelijker verstaanbaar te maken"* (it is an old gloss to make the text more easily understandable).

⁷⁰ Greijdanus speaks of "the wine flowing out of the cup," *op. cit.,* p. 1085, apparently also to point out an analogy in the "pouring out" between wine and blood. But in the paschal ritual there is nowhere any talk of such a "pouring out" or "flowing out." And as to the word *ekcheo,* when it is used of wine, it means spilling it on the ground and thus abandoning the contents of the wine-bag or cup, (Matt. 9:17, cf. Luke 5:37; Rev. 16:1ff); cf. also Preuschen-Bauer, *op. cit.,* p. 384.

⁷¹ Cf. Jeremias, *op. cit.,* pp. 104, 105. This contains some more archaeological arguments against the view that the sacrificial action has been symbolized.

⁷² *"Der Tod Christi in seiner Heilsbedeutung,"* (the death of Christ in its soteriological significance), Behm, *TWB,* I, p. 173.

⁷³ On the so-called Eucharistic words of John 6, cf. my article *Woord en Sacrament,* in: *Het Avondmaal,* 1949, pp. 39ff.

⁷⁴ Thus G. C. van Niftrik, *Luther en Calvijn over het Avondmaal,* in: *Het Avondmaal,* 1949, p. 59. Van N. supposes he can appeal to the institutional words for his view but, in my opinion, quite wrongly so.

⁷⁵ Cf. also Behm, *TWB,* I, p. 173, the article on *"haima." "Das Interesse des N.T. haftet nicht an dem Blute Christi als Stoff, sondern an seinem vergossenen Blut, dem ihm als gewaltsam genommenen Leben; 'Blut Christi' ist wie 'Kreuz' nur ein anderer, anschaulicherer Ausdruck für den Tod Christi in seiner Heilsbedeutung."* ("The New Testament is not interested in the blood of Christ as such, but in his shed blood, in his life taken from him by violence; the 'blood of Christ,' like the 'cross,' is only another, more graphic expression for the death of Christ in its soteriological meaning"). He also explains the institutional words in this way.

⁷⁶ All the essential things are already to be found in Calvin's exegesis of the gospels. Of recent authors, see, e.g., Stauffer, *Theol. des N.T.,* pp. 281ff, who

mentions seven exegetical grounds against "pressing" the *estin* of the words of Christ at the Last Supper.

[77] Cf. G. C. Berkouwer, *De Strijd om het Rooms-Katholieke Dogma*, p. 244.

[78] Cf., e.g., H. Gollwitzer, *Coena Domini*, 1937, pp. 8ff the same in the volume *Abendmahlsgemeinschaft?* 1937, pp. 102ff, quoting Luther's words, *"Ista verba (hoc est corpus meum) me ceperunt."*

[79] Cf. Gollwitzer, *Abendmahlsgemeinschaft?* pp. 110, 111; cf. also J. Loos, *Het heilig Avondmaal bij de Lutherschen, Kerk en Eredienst*, 1st Jg., 1945, pp. 77ff.

[80] Gollwitzer, *op. cit.*, pp. 111, 112.

[81] Cf. also Calvin, *"Hoc est corpus meum. Quod his verbis panem consecratum fuisse dicunt, ut fieret carnis Christi symbolum, non improbo, modo recte hoc nomen ac dextre sumatur,"* Comment. ed. Tholuck, II, 1833, p. 312.

[82] Cf., e.g., Jeremias, *Die Gleichnisse Jesu*, 1947, p. 113.

[83] M. J. Lagrange, *Evangile selon Saint Marc*,[8] 1947, p. 113.

[84] Lagrange, *op. cit.*

[85] J. Schmid, *Das Evangelium nach Markus*, 1938, p. 168.

[86] Otto speaks of a *"drastische Voraussage"* (a drastic prophecy), because in his opinion the breaking of the bread portrays the breaking of Christ's body. To our mind this is wrong, and certainly so in the sense in which Otto takes it, viz. as the prophetic depiction of the stoning of Christ's body, cf. footnote 68 above.

[87] R. Otto, *op. cit.*, pp. 255-258.

[88] Cf. Van der Leeuw, *op. cit.*, p. 263. It seems that it is even used by many Roman Catholics (especially by the so-called mystery theologians) to replace the crass terminology of transubstantiation.

[89] Cf. Van der Leeuw, *op. cit.*, pp. 249, 268 and *passim*.

Chapter X

THE FUTURE OF
THE KINGDOM OF HEAVEN

43. *The Problem of the "Nah-erwartung" (i.e., the Imminence of the Kingdom)*

Our last chapter must be devoted to the pronouncements in the gospel concerning the future of the kingdom of heaven. In contrast to the view advanced by C. H. Dodd that the kingdom is something exclusively of the present, we have already established as one of the basic motifs of the whole gospel that, generally speaking, the kingdom really has a future also (cf. §7). The present issue is the summary of all the data in the synoptic gospels relating to the future of the kingdom.

This is a very complicated matter belonging to those problems that, in our opinion, are most difficult to elucidate and, hence, demand a modest attitude. Such will appear when we now attempt to get acquainted first with the chief interpretations given by the so-called synoptic eschatology.

Of course we are here concerned with the purport and the scope of the direct eschatological pronouncements in the preaching of Jesus which have been given to us. It is here that the so-called "struggle about the eschatology" must be decided.

The older liberal theology sought the essence of the gospel in the timeless preaching of love. It pushed Jesus' pronouncements on the great future into the background as much as possible, and declared them to pertain to the inessential "contemporaneous" (*zeitgeschichtliche*) setting of Jesus' preaching.[1] In opposition to this, the eschatological tendency has attempted to explain the whole preaching of Jesus from the

444

actuality of the *Nah-erwartung*, i.e., from the expectation attributed to Jesus of the very speedy coming of the great future in the sense of the Jewish apocalyptic. Jesus' preaching is *ruled* by the idea of the *immediately* imminent divine dominion. So it is tied together historically with the Jewish expectation of the end and future, and is obviously not determined by the picture of the national hope. Jesus, much rather, shares the cosmological expectation of Jewish eschatology.[2] It is no exaggeration to say that since Johannes Weiss, this thesis (with all emphasis on the word "immediately") has been the issue of the struggle about the meaning of the New Testament, and especially of the synoptic eschatology.[3] It may even be said that the questions connected with this *Nah-erwartung* occupy a more prominent position in the present-day exegetical discussions (especially in Switzerland) than they have for a long time. In a previous chapter we saw how the attempt has been made to eliminate the problem of the expectation of the kingdom as near at hand by the application of the so-called *übergeschichtliche* (i.e., supra-historical) interpretation, i.e., by trying to explain the "nearness" of the kingdom not in a temporal but in a transcendent sense. But it has become increasingly more evident that such a conception of the "nearness" of the kingdom is not in accordance with the gospel, because the latter undoubtedly speaks of the future in a temporal sense, and this linear idea of time cannot be eliminated without changing the meaning of the gospel. But thus the problem of the imminence of the kingdom has again become acute. If the pronouncements on its nearness (and among them, especially, those that seem to mention a *term* for the approaching end, as in Matthew 10:23; Mark 9:1 and parallel texts; 13:30, and parallels) really relate to the speedy end of the world and to the *parousia* of the Son of Man, as is supposed by a wide circle of people,[4] the question becomes inescapable as to whether or not this datum should be considered as the dominant viewpoint of the entire preaching of Jesus.

On a closer investigation of the whole of the gospel, it is

at once evident that the question of the *Nah-erwartung* is put in too simplified a way if we assume that it is incorporated only in the explanation of the pronouncements on the so-called "nearness." For these words are only a part of a very extensive and complicated text-material. In the first place, we can refer to the connection between Jesus' pronouncements on the great future, and those on his approaching passion, death and resurrection. If in the so-called imminence pronouncements, Jesus expected the eschatological kingdom of God in the immediate future, the question becomes inescapable as to what function is to be assigned to Jesus' death and resurrection in this great event, i.e., what is the mutual relation between these series of events expected by Jesus within such a short space of time.

In the second place, the picture of the eschatological future (found in the synoptic apocalypse in Mark 13; Matt. 24; Luke 21), makes it difficult to answer the question about the period of time that Jesus expected to elapse before the coming of the kingdom. For his eschatological discourses place the end of all things within the framework of a long series of future events and signs which seem to require a long time. By the side of such words as are found in Mark 13:30, there are others saying, e.g., "of that day and that hour knoweth no man, no, not the angels which are in heaven, neither the Son, but the Father" (vs. 32, and parallel places), and in another context, that "the gospel must first be published among all nations" (Mark 13:10, and parallels).

This shows that the eschatological "material" given to us in the synoptic gospels (even apart from what in the previous chapters has been said about the presence of the kingdom of heaven) has a great many aspects. It need not be surprising, therefore, that the discussion of all that is related to this eschatology of the gospels in general and to the so-called *Nah-erwartung* in particular, forms a very intricately interwoven complex. We will try to point out some main outlines within which this debate about the eschatology is carried on, rather than give a detailed survey of all kinds of various views.

1. The most radical position as to the eschatological preaching of Jesus is that held by those who think that the gospels as they are do not give us a reliable account at all either of Jesus' life or of his preaching. The complexity of the eschatological material should, therefore, be considered as the result of the activity of the later church. Only some particular parts of Jesus' pronouncements are held to be historical, viz., those concerned with the coming of the kingdom within a short time (the specific sayings of the kingdom as being near at hand). According to this view, the synoptic predictions about Jesus' death and resurrection are of a secondary nature, i.e., they are the product of the church which has projected back in Jesus' words the non-eschatological course of history. Owing to this procedure, the evangelical tradition has acquired an internally contradictory character. This view, expressed especially in Wrede's work, *Das Messiasgeheimnis in den Evangelien*,[5] is advocated, although in a slightly modified form, by authors such as Klostermann[6] and Bultmann. In this conception, the problem of the correlation between the *Nah-erwartung* and the pronouncements about Jesus' approaching death and resurrection has been eliminated by calling the latter the "theology of the church." The same thing holds, *mutatis mutandis*, for the so-called synoptic apocalypse. Bultmann's view is that in this case, we are confronted by a Jewish apocalypse in a Christian adaptation which is ascribed to Jesus.[7] He can refer to a hypothesis already posited in the last century (by Colani) which has since found many adherents.[8] The historical Jesus is supposed to have abstained from any indication of prognostic signs in nature or in the world of the nations (as described in Mark 13), as well as from a description of the last judgment, the resurrection and the coming glory. Everything is merged into the one thought that God will then rule and that this reality is immediately at hand.[9]

2. A second view tries to establish a close relation between the expectation of a speedy end and Jesus' prophecies about his death and resurrection. Here Jesus' preaching

handed down to us in the gospels is considered to be of greater historical value than in the interpretation mentioned under 1. We find this opinion in its most pregnant form in the view of the father of the consistently eschatological movement, Albert Schweitzer. In the first place, it is supposed that Jesus already expected the coming of the eschatological kingdom of God during his own life, viz., during the first sending out of his disciples. Schweitzer bases this view on Matthew 10:23. For he interprets this passage as the announcement that the kingdom would begin during the tour of the disciples. But this expectation by Jesus did not occur—the first delay. From that moment, Jesus withdrew and inclined more and more to the expectation that the kingdom would come only if forced to come, as it were, by his own passion and death (the great *Drangsal*, i.e., distress, or messianic sorrows). Thus, remarkably enough, Schweitzer connects Jesus' pronouncements about the coming of the kingdom and those about his approaching death. This is why, according to Schweitzer, Jesus' perspective of the future is restricted to his approaching passion and death. His death would be simultaneous with the *parousia* of the Son of Man. Jesus thus undertook the great task of his passion and death in order to obtain his messianic dignity. In this sense we must explain the pronouncements in which a time before the end explicitly seems to be indicated (Mark 9:1; 13:30; Matt. 23:39; 26:64). Starting from this *Naherwartung* in which, in the mind of Jesus, the coming of the kingdom would coalesce with his death and glorification, Schweitzer gives his well-known consistently eschatological interpretation of the whole life of Jesus and of all the different facets of his preaching as we have explained in the previous chapters on more than one occasion. But its starting-point is the expectation of the imminent coming of the kingdom in the sense of the late Jewish apocalyptic. This applies to the whole of the consistent eschatology and to the explanation of the development of early Christianity and of the history of dogma based on it as described in Martin Werner's great work.

It is clear that in this view no room is left for those pronouncements in the gospel which quite clearly speak of the
time *after* Jesus' death. This holds above all for the so-called
synoptic apocalypse insofar as it presupposes an interim between Jesus' death and the *parousia* of the Son of Man and
also, of course, for Jesus' words on the resurrection. The
Nah-erwartung is restricted to Jesus' death. Here, Schweitzer
seeks the criterion for the authenticity of the synoptic tradition.[10]

Although Schweitzer's great consistently eschatological
exegetical "experiment" (as he himself calls it) has, on the
whole, few adherents; it is still very influential in all kinds of
details.[11] This is also true with respect to his view that, in
Jesus' mind, his death and the *parousia* of the Son of Man were
simultaneous.[12]

It is remarkable that in this respect Dodd's expositions, which
we have already mentioned before, are a very near approach to
Schweitzer's. Although Dodd rejects the idea that in Jesus' preaching there is an expectation of the manifestation of the kingdom, so
that Dodd is Schweitzer's exact opposite in this respect, he is
obliged to admit that Jesus made some pronouncements on *his own*
future. According to Dodd, at times he calls himself the apocalyptic
Son of Man who is to act as the judge of the world, at other times
he vindicates the claim that he is to rise from the dead. Dodd thinks
it likely that he did not see an interim between these two events
expected by him in the future.[13] For *nowhere in the pronouncements about himself do we find a temporal distinction made by Jesus
between his coming in the clouds and his resurrection.* This is why
Dodd is inclined to think that by "the third day" (that of his resurrection) Jesus meant "the day of the Son of Man," and that later,
in accordance with its own experience, the church made a temporal
distinction[14] between these two events which really lay on one and
the same plane in Jesus' consciousness. So it is supposed that Jesus
expected this one great event in the near future, just as the disasters
that struck Jerusalem and Judea before that date. Hence, Dodd
here very nearly approaches Schweitzer's reconstruction of the
original meaning of the gospel insofar as Jesus' predictions regard-

ing his own future are concerned.[15]   But Dodd is of the opinion that we are here confronted with a particular trait in the pronouncements of the gospel. Jesus' further teaching, his commandments especially, are supposed to give evidence of an entirely different and non-eschatological tendency and cannot, according to Dodd be reconciled with these eschatological sayings. He himself has recourse to a symbolical interpretation of Jesus' apocalyptical pronouncements about himself.[16] According to Dodd, at any rate, it is clear that they were not realized.

Dodd's views about the *Nah-erwartung* of the gospel have been reported by Jeremias with a great deal of approval, although he does not agree with Dodd's distinction between Jesus' statements about the kingdom as a purely present reality and Jesus' expectation of his own future. But Jeremias does think that in the pronouncements on the future there is a remarkable parallelism (a *Nebeneinander*) between those that represent the end of things as very near at hand and those that refer the end to a remote future. It is, however, impossible—thus Jeremias—to call either of the two series unauthentic in favor of the other. Just as Dodd does, Jeremias points in the first place to the fact that not a single one of Jesus' pronouncements has come down to us in which his resurrection and his *parousia* are mentioned side by side and as temporally distinct from each other. Jesus always speaks either of the one or of the other. And in the second place, both Jesus' resurrection and the restoration of the temple (Mark 14:58; Matt. 26:61; Mark 15:29; Matt. 27:40; John 2:19) were expected by him after or within three days, i.e., within a short period of time determined by God. As the restoration of the temple is an apocalyptic event coincident with the day of the Son of Man, the obvious inference is—thus Jeremias—that originally the third day is the day of the Son of Man. Only later is the church supposed to have made a temporal distinction in this one great event expected by Jesus. From the above, however, it might be concluded that Jesus considered the day of the Son of Man and hence, the new aeon of divine grace, to be very near at hand.[17]

Some exegetes suggest a variation of this view with reference to Mark 14:28 (cf. 16:7). Here, immediately before his arrest Jesus says, "But after that I am risen, I will go before you into Galilee"; and the angel at the open tomb refers to these words saying, "He goeth before you into Galilee, as he said unto you." It is supposed that this "seeing him in Galilee" is meant to denote the *parousia*. The fact that this did not materialize testifies to its early date and its originality.[18] Lohmeyer, too, is of the same opinion and looks upon it as evidence of a Galilean kind of Christianity which, in distinction from the Jerusalem type, had a strongly eschatological expectation of the future and of the immediate coming of the Son of Man.[19]

3. In contrast to this radical form-giving of the *Nah-erwartung* ascribed to Jesus, there are a great many exegetes in recent literature, too, who start from an entirely different interpretation of the kingdom of heaven preached by Jesus, and approach his eschatological pronouncements accordingly. This holds in particular for those who, in contradistinction to the "orthodox" eschatological view, consider that the kingdom of heaven was present with Jesus' coming and work. This presence is then manifest in his miracles and in his preaching or, as e.g., Michaelis assumes, in his resurrection from the dead and the subsequent giving of the Holy Spirit.[20] It is clear that this view of the general purport of the gospel, rooted in a fundamentally different conception of the person of Jesus himself, entails a different view of the time preceding the *parousia* of the Son of Man and the coming of the kingdom in glory. For in this case the great break-through *has* come and, consequently, it is not primarily the future of the kingdom but its already having come that will be the standpoint from which we consider this interim. Especially in the writings of Cullmann, Kümmel, Schniewind, Michaelis, etc., this basic motif has been elaborated.

It is also obvious that in this view Jesus' death and resurrection no longer need to be considered simply in their relation to the *parousia* and the future of the kingdom, but much rather, form the (provisional) conclusion and foundation of the fulfillment that began with his coming. Similarly, the interim between Christ's death and *parousia* is no longer a "complication" of the *Nah-erwartung* that is most difficult to explain. This interim is rather to be evaluated as the almost indispensable space for the realization and continuation of the already inaugurated fulfillment. We may even go a step further on this entirely different standpoint and say that the problems of the expectation of the future have totally shifted. For now it is not that which seems to cause tension with the *Nah-erwartung* or to be in conflict with it which gives offense or rouses the suspicion of being "unauthentic," or "the theology of the church," etc. It is much rather the *fulfillment* already initiated by Jesus' coming that dominates and, therefore, those texts that seem to speak of the end of all things in the near future are the cause of the difficulty of an all-embracing view of the whole of the pronouncements about the future that have been given to us. The problem is now the delimiting of the time of the world within "this generation" (Mark 13:30), and not the church, nor the apostolate, nor baptism, nor the Lord's Supper.

There are basically two solutions to this problem.

a) The first of them does not deny that a close examination of the gospel shows that there are a small number of passages left which have to be explained in the sense of the *Nah-erwartung*. But these passages are not to be considered as essential for a correct judgment of the purport of the whole of the gospel.

b) According to the second solution, Jesus does not really speak of the ultimate coming of the kingdom or of the *parousia* of the Son of Man in those places that are appealed to for this eschatological *Nah-erwartung*. But he speaks of the time of salvation inaugurated by his resurrection. That which is called the *Nah-erwartung* by the eschatological interpretation was, therefore, not founded on a delusion or an error, but was only the announcement of what would happen immediately after Jesus' death.

We would submit a further elucidation of these two conceptions.

a. Characteristic of recent views are the expositions given by Cullmann. In opposition to the eschatological interpretation ad-

vanced by Werner, he maintains that according to the clear pronouncements of the gospel, the kingdom of Christ *has* come. The
theological importance of the preaching of the nearness of the
basileia is that, since Christ's coming, we have been in a new "epoch"
and that, consequently, the end is nearer at hand. There is no doubt
that in the New Testament the nearness of the end is limited to one
generation. But this error of perspective (*"Perspektivenirrtum"*),
which is corrected in only one place of the New Testament (2 Pet.
3:8), does not represent the theological content of the statement,
"the kingdom is at hand." For this content is to be found in the
fact that with Christ the fulfillment has come. The error is to be
explained psychologically in the same way as premature datings of
the end of a war after it has become certain that the decisive battle
has been fought. Moreover, the three somewhat ambiguous synoptic passages (Mark 9:1; Matt. 10:23; Mark 13:30), about which
there has been so much controversy, are therefore not so pre-
eminently important as is sometimes thought. The interpretation
of the evangelists who, in each instance (*"ja wohl auf jeden Fall"*),
related these words to Jesus' death, is correct in a higher sense.[21]

Kümmel has a similar view. According to him, Jesus expected
the end in the near future after his death. Kümmel refers to Mark
9:1;[22] Matthew 10:23;[23] Mark 13:30;[24] to the pronouncements on the
"nearness" of the end;[25] to the so-called "word of the cup" (Mark
14:25), which should also prove that Jesus did not locate "that day"
at too great a distance;[26] to Matthew 12:41, which speaks of the
resurrection of "this generation," again confirming the fact, it is true,
that Jesus expected the commencement of the *eschaton* to be near,
but not too near.[27] And furthermore, Kümmel refers especially to
the "urgent imminence of the end" expressed more than once in
Jesus' teaching; thus in the exhortations to be watchful (Mark 13:34-
36; Luke 12:36-38; Matt. 24:42; 45-51; Luke 18:8: "I tell you that
God will avenge them speedily," *en tachei*).[28]

It will have to be admitted that in the pronouncements in which
he tied the coming of the kingdom to a definite date—thus Kümmel
—Jesus was mistaken (there are *three* such passages in all, viz., Matt.
10:23; Mark 9:1; 13:30). But this fact is of no special importance
in Jesus' preaching. By the side of these three there are other texts
that call the time of the end urgent although unknown, or they say
emphatically that it must remain unknown (Mark 13:32). This is

a certain discrepancy that cannot be solved and is unimportant because the question about the time of the end was not in any way central for Jesus.[29] We must detach the *Nah-erwartung,* as a contemporary conception, from Jesus' eschatological preaching; the expectation *of the future,* however, is essential, because only in this can the historical character of the divine work of fulfillment be maintained. For it is not the *Nah-erwartung,* but the presence of the fulfillment in Christ that is the guarantee that the great consummation is sure to come.[30]

A slightly different conception is found in the commentaries by Schniewind. He, too, starts from the principal presence of the kingdom of heaven preached by Jesus. But there is no denying, says Schniewind, that according to Jesus' expectation the first generation of disciples would live to see the last day. Schniewind doubts whether this can be called an "illusion." When Jesus speaks like this, he does so on the basis of the absolute certainty of the new world. *We* speak of "eternity" in the language of our philosophico-mystical manner of thought. Jesus and the early Christians spoke of "the coming aeon."[31] Here it seems that Schniewind approaches the "supertemporal" (*überzeitliche*) interpretation. Elsewhere (Matt. 10:23), he speaks in a similar way of "a changed awareness of time," from the certainty that with Jesus' words and works the coming kingdom has already begun. Whether this is to be interpreted as a case of pure self-deceit depends upon the way one takes an eternity into account.[32]

A remarkable solution is offered by Michaelis. According to him, Jesus never tires of emphasizing the nearness of the last day, especially in the parables concerning vigilance.[33] In other passages, especially in the synoptic apocalypse, the statements about the signs, the destruction of Jerusalem, etc., show that the last day is yet at a comparatively great distance; but there is nowhere an answer to the question as to when this will be.[34] According to Michaelis, this also applies to Mark 13:30. For there is no certainty about what is meant by the phrase "this generation," nor is the meaning of the expression "all these things" at all certain.[35] Moreover, with respect to Mark 9:1, it is possible to ask many questions about its meaning. And yet, this is the only place enabling us to infer a comparatively accurate date for the last day.[36]

But the difficulty here is that this statement was not fulfilled. What must one say about it? Michaelis refers to Mark 13:32, "But of that day and that hour knoweth no man, no, not the angels which are in heaven, neither the Son, but the Father." This is the restriction to be observed by us also when reading Mark 13:30 and 9:1. During the time before his resurrection, Jesus was only able to speak of the term of his second coming on the basis of his "provisional knowledge." This is what is indicated in Mark 13:32. The question might be asked, why did not Jesus entirely refrain from making a pronouncement like that of Mark 9:1? But we do not know the occasion nor the motives that induced him to make such a pronouncement.[37]

Although reduced in part to a minimal comparison, all these conceptions are based on the assumption that at least in some of Jesus' pronouncements there is a certain time fixed for the *parousia* of the Son of Man and for the coming of the kingdom. In a temporal sense, this time specification has proved to be a failure, and to this extent, at any rate, this fact is a confirmation of Schweitzer's basic thesis. They maintain, in addition, however, that neither this specifying of the term of the great future, nor the expectation of the *near* end of things forms the basic truth of the gospel, but that this truth is much rather vested in the fact that in the person of Jesus as the Christ the fulfillment has already commenced and the consummation of the kingdom of heaven has already begun.

b. The conceptions mentioned under b) will be discussed in more detail when we deal with the so-called pronouncements on the temporal terminus (cf. § 48 below). In the present context, we will permit to suffice the quotation of Karl Barth who, commenting upon Jesus' appearance to his disciples after his resurrection and the words he then spoke (Matt. 28:16-20), writes as follows, "It became apparent that the petition 'Thy kingdom come' in the Lord's Prayer had not been in vain; that 'this generation,' i.e., the then living generation would certainly not pass 'till all these things be done,' as Jesus said according to Mark 13:30. It became clear that it was true that some of those that stood about Jesus 'should not taste of death till they had seen the kingdom of God come with power' (Mark 9:1). It became clear that the disciples would not have gone over the cities of Israel till the Son of Man came (Matt. 10:23). Now he had come, now 'everything' had happened."[38]

Here the problem of the *Nah-erwartung* has been entirely eliminated. That which Jesus preached as being near at hand was actually fulfilled by, and after, his resurrection.

Against the background of this struggle concerning the eschatology of which we have only been able to mention some principal elements, we will now try to discuss the complicated text-material under a few summarizing viewpoints.

44. Resurrection and Parousia

On the basis of all that has been established in the previous chapters of this book concerning the general meaning of Jesus' preaching of the kingdom of heaven, we can only reject as an absolute misrepresentation of the gospel the radical view which considers as original, and as Jesus' own view, only those passages in the synoptic tradition that are in accordance with the expectation of the immediate nearness of the end of the world. The present representatives of this interpretation subject the gospel to the well-known method of form criticism which has become influential through the important work of Bultmann.[39] This method first requires the investigation to establish the authenticity of every saying, parable, etc., to which reference has to be made, before expressing an opinion on the purport of Jesus' preaching. To our mind, there can be no doubt that the criticism thus applied to the gospel wrongly creates the impression that it is working with a criterion which is solely derived from the *form* of the data of the tradition. For the decision about what is to be considered as the original or the secondary form of the tradition respectively is, however, chiefly made on the basis of the *content* of the tradition. That is why the real point in question is not the debate about the originality of the form of many parts of the tradition that has been given to us. But the real issue lies in the answer to the question as to whether or not upon sound *factual* grounds their contents can be looked upon as unworthy of belief. And from this standpoint, it must be called an absolutely arbitrary prejudice if in an *a priori* way those parts of the gospel should be denied to Jesus that are not in accordance with the expectation of the exclusive futurity and imminence of the kingdom of God. For all that has been given to us in the gospels about Jesus' preaching—and we do not possess any other criterion of its "authenticity"!—is based on the certainty of the fulfillment inaugurated by Jesus, no less than on that of the future kingdom of God. In this case the knife of "form criticism's criterion" can only operate on the basis of subjective presuppositions and, in our opinion, it can therefore only be destructive. For the motif of the fulfillment is not present simply in a few scattered pronouncements that can be removed from the "body" of the gospel without any harm being done. But it is firmly grounded in what is the core and the center of the entire gospel, viz., that Jesus is the Christ and has as such been sent into the world by the Father as the fulfiller of time, of the Scriptures, of the law.

That is why it is impossible to eliminate from the gospel of the kingdom, as a *vaticinia ex eventu*, Jesus' predictions about his passion and death as not in accordance with his *Nah-erwartung*. For these prophecies more than simply represent a certain peripheral area far removed from the heart of Jesus' preaching; rather, they are indissolubly bound up with this central nucleus. The whole of Jesus' self-revelation is dominated by the great mission, the divine "must" that he has to perform. And its contents are from the outset determined by the motif of atonement and suffering, as well as by that of the authority of the Son of Man mentioned in Daniel 7. That is why that which Jesus preaches about the future of the kingdom must also be viewed in connection with his prophecies concerning his passion, death and resurrection. And the entire conception of the *Nah-erwartung* must also be confronted with these pronouncements.

This naturally leads us to those views which—in contradistinction to the radical-sceptical criticism of the tradition—tries to understand Jesus' pronouncements about his approaching sufferings and death as an integral part of his *Nah-erwar-tung*, of which Schweitzer's is no doubt the most characteristic. This attempt, however, has given such a fantastic interpretation of the gospel, and has occasioned such a reconstruction of "the life of Jesus" that, in spite of its own intentions, it has intensified rather than lessened the scepticism of the advocates of the *Nah-erwartung* with respect to the reliability of the tradition. This judgment at once applies to what may be called the foundation of Schweitzer's entire consistently eschatological experiment, viz., his appeal to Matthew 10:23, "But when they persecute you in this city, flee ye into another; for verily I say unto you, ye shall not have gone over the cities of Israel, till the Son of Man be come." No doubt the exegesis of this text is not simple. But whatever its meaning may be, it cannot at all be the foundation of the *Nah-erwartung* in the sense of the consistent eschatology. For it is beyond any possible doubt that this saying does *not* refer to the time of the sending forth of the disciples during Jesus' life, but to a far more distant future.

As a matter of fact, this also applies to the whole context of this place in the gospel and not merely to verse 23. To begin with verse 16, there events are mentioned in Jesus' speech in Matthew 10 which, already because of local-historical considerations, could not possibly take place at the time of the sending forth of the disciples, i.e., such as their being led before kings and governors, etc.[40] Besides, if Jesus actually expected these vicissitudes as foretold in verse 16ff to happen at this time, it cannot be understood why neither the disciples on their return, nor Jesus himself made any allusion to this "unfulfilled *parousia*." This entire conception of Jesus having already expected the coming of the Son of Man before his death is so fantastic that it is simply surprising to find, e.g., Werner still maintaining it.[41]

To our mind, matters are no better with respect to Schweitzer's second fundamental thesis; namely, that when the coming of the kingdom had failed during the missionary tour of the disciples, Jesus wanted to "force" this coming by means of his voluntary substitutionary suffering and death.

For—apart from the fact that there is no single solid basis to be found in the gospel for such "forcing"[42]—there can be no doubt that in all kinds of pronouncements Jesus spoke explicitly about the time *after* his death.   Thus, before all, in the so-called "synoptic apocalypse," but also elsewhere in his prophecies about the destruction of Jerusalem and the desolation of the temple (Matt. 23:38 and parallels; Luke 23:28ff); and also— to mention only one more case—in the well-known saying about the children of the bridechamber (the disciples) who would one day fast when the bridegroom (Jesus himself) should be taken away from them (Mark 2:18ff and parallels).   In order to be able to find a place in his consistently eschatological interpretation for the pronouncements about Jesus' imminent passion and death, Schweitzer is compelled to declare as secondary all those words that refer to the time after the passion and death.   But this also makes clear how unsatisfactory his grand experiment really is.   On a very important and decisive point, he has to cut the Gordian knot he has promised to untie.

This does not detract from the fact that in more than one respect Schweitzer's hypothesis has had an inspiring influence, and that he has pointed out particular phenomena in the tradition that had often remained unnoticed.   This holds especially for the circumstance to which Dodd and Jeremias appeal, no doubt influenced by Schweitzer.   It is the fact that in Jesus' words about the future there is hardly ever any *temporal* distinction made between his death (and resurrection) and his *parousia* as the Son of Man.

No doubt, we must reject what they infer from this, viz., that according to a particular trend in the tradition, the resurrection on the "third" day is identified with the *parousia* and is supposed to run "parallel" with another tendency according to which the *parousia* would come in the much more distant future.   For if, for the moment, we restrict ourselves to the phenomenon pointed out by Dodd and Jeremias, it is quite impossible to infer from it that, according to a particular trend in the tradition, the resurrection and the *parousia* coalesce. In itself, it may with equal right be used to prove the opposite thesis. For if Jesus' prediction of his resurrection "on the third day" is only another name for his *parousia*, it is surprising that it is never this *parousia* but always the resurrection which only is mentioned in connection with Jesus' death; and, conversely, that in the pronouncements about the events of the great final period, these are always described as the *parousia* of the Son of Man and never as the resurrection on the third day.[43]

If the conclusion arrived at by Dodd and Jeremias cannot be accepted, the phenomenon they have pointed out should not be overlooked by us when taking a general view of Jesus' expectation of the future. They noticed that Jesus repeatedly spoke of his approaching death and resurrection and of his *parousia*, but that in his prophecies his resurrection and *parousia* are nowhere united in one context. The result is that, especially in his eschatological discourses, the new interim inaugurated by his resurrection does not seem to be considered as such. On the other hand, in the prophecies about Jesus' death and resurrection, the perspective view into the future following it is in many cases absent. It may therefore be said that in Jesus' prophecies about the future, we are not given a clear, perspective description of the period starting with the resurrection and concluding with the *parousia*.

This phenomenon has also been noticed by Bultmann who considers as a later product both Jesus' announcement of himself as the Son of Man and the prophecies about his death and resurrection. His explanation is that one series of prophecies (viz., that about Jesus' passion, death and resurrection) represent the later Hellenistic type of theology of the church, while the prophecies about the *parousia* represent the older Palestinian type, and that their combination in the gospels is of a later date.[44] This hypothesis is unacceptable to us for the reason that Jesus' prophecies of his passion and death are far from representing a Hellenistic type, but are entirely oriented to the Old Testament (the prophecy of the Servant of the Lord), as we have established in great detail above.[45] According to our conviction, the characteristic feature in Jesus' self-revelation was the very fact that he identified himself with the Son of Man of Daniel 7, as well as with the Servant of the Lord in Isaiah.

This is no denial of the occurrence of *two* different figures, nor of the fact that the prophecies which Jesus applied to himself, from the outset display *two* distinct kinds of type. In the eschatological prophecies about the Son of Man, the motif of the passion, death and resurrection is absent. And conversely, what is said about the passion, death and exaltation of the Servant of the Lord in Isaiah 53 is of a different nature than the divine transfer of power to the Son of Man. Jesus connected these two figures in the paradoxical, mysterious words that the Son of Man (Dan. 7) must "be rejected," "suffer a great deal," "be killed" (Isaiah 53) and rise from the dead after three days. This was the new, the "revolutionary" element in his messianic self-revelation. He far transcended the national messianic ideal (Matt. 22:41-46),[46] and on the other hand realized that the way of Messiah went through suffering and death; for, "The Son of Man came not to be ministered unto but to minister, and to give his life a ransom for many" (Matt. 20:28).

This does not, however, mean that this combination in Jesus' self-revelation about the Son of Man and the Servant of the Lord is immediately transparent and that its factual and temporal connections can accurately be disclosed. Much rather, a veil lies over Jesus' entire messianic self-announcement, not only to the eyes of "outsiders" to whom "it was not given to know the mystery of the kingdom of God" (Mark 4:11), but also to the eyes of the disciples. The latter statement applies especially to what we may call the combination of Daniel 7 and Isaiah 53. When the disciples had professed Jesus' messianic glory through the mouth of Peter, the announcement of his passion is unintelligible to them (Matt. 16:21ff; 17:23; Mark 9:32; Luke 18:34). This lack of discernment by the disciples (Luke 24:25) was not only connected with Jesus' approaching passion and death, but no less with his resurrection. In Mark 9:10,11 we read that, when Jesus announced his resurrection, the disciples "questioned one with another what the rising from the dead should mean." This cannot mean that they had never heard of the general resurrection of the dead (cf. Mark 12:18-27), but it means that they did not understand what this "rising from the dead of the Son of Man" could mean.[47] And then they asked him whether Elijah must not "first" come (i.e., before this resurrection). They seem thus to begin with the idea that this "resurrection" could hardly mean anything else than that which was to happen at the consummation of all things, i.e., the last and great resurrection, because, in the Jewish expectation of the future, Elijah was connected with the coming of the Messiah. They had, consequently, no insight into the relation between Christ's resurrection and the *parousia*. And this not only appears in Mark 9:9,10; Matthew 17:9,10, but is also evident in their complete surprise at the *fact* of Jesus' rising from the dead. All this proves that the combination of the death and resurrection of the Servant of the Lord with the *parousia* of the Son of Man had not been made in the prophecies, so that it had neither been incorporated into the Jewish expectation of the future, nor did even Jesus' own disciples understand and accept it until after his rising from the dead. This lack of insight is not only attributed in the gospel to the subjective disposition of the disciples which made them into "fools and slow of heart to believe all that the prophets have spoken" (Luke 24:25); but it is also apparently due to the character of Jesus' self-revelation before his exaltation.[48] When Jesus acquaints his disciples with his approaching passion, death and resurrection; it not only appears that they do not understand its meaning, but also that they *are afraid* to ask him (Mark 9:32). There remains a veil lying over his death, and this veil must apparently be kept there;[49] cf. also Luke 9:45: "But they understood not this saying, and it was hid from them, that[50] they perceived it not: and they feared to ask him of that saying"[51] (cf. also Luke 18:34). All these things are an indication that, from Jesus as well, they were denied the full knowledge of his future (cf. John 16:12). Not before the resurrection did he "open their understanding" (Luke 24:45).[52]

These things contain important indications of what we are here discussing. From the outset there is indeed question of something like two "trends" in Jesus' prophecies about the future concerning himself. One of them ends in his death and resurrection, the other in his *parousia*. These two trends each have an origin of their own and remain parallel in many cases. But we should not speak of an antinomy, nor should we think that resurrection and *parousia* are two words for the same thing. Much rather, the combination of Christ's glory as the Son of Man along with his passion and death remains hidden before his rising from the tomb, and the disciples, at any rate, do not understand how the one trend (that of Jesus' self-revelation according to Isaiah 53) and the other (that of Daniel 7) were to agree with each other. The great drama of his passion and death, together with his resurrection, was the unexpected and incomprehensible intermezzo between the present and the great future. It is true that all of Jesus' announcements of his passion and death are accompanied by those about his resurrection on the third day. But the meaning of the latter remained hidden from the disciples, neither solving nor unravelling the mystery for them. It is true that we also possess the saying in which Jesus compares himself with Jonah, i.e., just as Jonah had been in the sea-monster's belly for three days and nights, so the Son of Man would be in the heart of the earth for three days and three nights (Matt. 12:40, cf. Matt. 16:4; Luke 11:29). But these words have the character of a riddle and could not explain to the disciples what would happen. Finally, we must refer to the words that Jesus spoke on the way to Gethsemane and to which the angel at the tomb was later to appeal: "But after I am risen again, I will go before you into Galilee" (Matt. 26:32, and parallels; cf. Matt. 28:7, and parallels). But these words—the only words that point to the resurrection as the starting-point of the subsequent history—were spoken immediately before his death. In summary, it must be stated that, insofar as we are able to judge from the record, it was in many ways dark to the minds of the disciples what place the resurrection was to occupy in the epoch previous to the *parousia*; and that Jesus, moreover, either did not give them a clear insight into it, or could not do so. The darkness caused in their thoughts by his approaching death deprived them of the light of the future following it. And this cannot be attributed alone to their lack of discernment. Jesus' death, which pressed him into the horror of utter abandonment (Matt. 26:37ff, and parallels; 27:46), was a satanic sifting of the disciples (Luke 22:31), while it was yet ahead of them and as they ultimately experienced it. It was an experience that filled their horizon entirely, a scattering of them like sheep that have lost their shepherd (Matt. 26:31), a taking away of the bridegroom (Matt. 9:15), and so, a *skandalon*, an offense to their faith and hope which none of them was able to overcome (Matt. 26:31), and from which they would be relieved only after the resurrection.

It is in accordance with all this that, provisionally, they were almost or entirely without the new orientation-point, which for the coming time would be given in the resurrection of Christ.

Now, however, two things are clear (and it is of the utmost importance for an insight into the total structure of Jesus' self-revelation and preaching to focus our attention on these points); in the first place, Jesus' death and resurrection and his subsequent self-revelation to his disciples do not cause an entirely new turn in his previous preaching. For they are not merely in agreement with some isolated and unintelligible predictions of his resurrection; but much rather, form *the organic conclusion of the great motif of the preliminary character of the fulfillment inaugurated by Christ's coming.* This is the climax of the "line" that John the Baptist could not distinguish, and which runs through Matthew 13; 16:18; 20:28; 26:28—to mention only these clearly marked "signposts"—(the kingdom will come like a seed, the Son of Man is like a Sower, the preaching is still in search of its intensive and extensive effects, the people of God must still be gathered, the ransom paid, the blood of the covenant shed for the salvation of "the many"). The fulfillment inaugurated with Jesus' coming, which is not yet the consummation of all things; this provisional, mysterious, although divine, dynamic, messianic fulfillment leads to the cross and to the resurrection. In them the mystery of the kingdom is most impenetrably veiled as well as most gloriously revealed. Now at last that which had been whispered into the ears can be preached from the house tops.

Consequently, the perspective given in Matthew 28:16-20 offers a new orientation point only insofar as it lifts the veil cast over the future by Jesus' death. But it must not be considered as a "theology of the resurrection" which arose outside of the boundaries of Jesus' preaching. All that Christ's resurrection brings to light is based on the new presuppositions from which the whole of his preaching of the kingdom begins, in contradistinction to the expectation of his contemporaries. And it is these presuppositions which must be fully taken into account when we discuss the question of the earthly perspective of the future in Jesus' preaching. No doubt this fact is not explicitly mentioned before the resurrection. But it is implicit in all that has been said in the preceding pages about the provisional character of what has come in Christ, which for this reason makes necessary the continuation of time for the world. This all-dominating basic motif (for it is based on Jesus' true and present messiahship) of the gospel implies that the great turning-point of history lies already in the coming, and especially in the death and resurrection of Christ; and not as late as or only in the *parousia* of the Son of Man. This is why the interim starting with the resurrection and extending to the *parousia* is not only oriented to the future but also to what has already happened. It is the fulfilled present of the provisional fulfillment, i.e., it is not only the time of waiting, the unfulfilled time, but also the time of the fulfillment, the time of grace for the gathering together of the church as the gospel of the fulfillment is preached and the "many" are given a share in the fruits of Christ's passion and death. It is true that we have not been given a clear indication of the duration of this time of fulfillment. But in the central importance of Jesus' suffering and death for the preaching of the gospel, and in the gathering together of the New Testament church; it is clearly implied that the time of fulfillment is not at an end with the death of Christ, but has its starting-point and pre-suppositions in this event. Cullmann therefore rightly argues that in the synoptic gospels the center of time no longer lies in the future (viz., in the *parousia* as the commencement of the new aeon) as it does in Judaism, but in the past, viz., in Christ's coming and action.[53] That is why the question about the *parousia* is no longer the only one, and the preaching of the gospel of the kingdom is not primarily oriented to the future, but to that which has already happened in Jesus Christ, especially in his death and resurrection as the fulfill-ment of time, of the law, and of the prophecies. All of this is *the first* great revelation given by the resurrection concerning the disclosure of the mystery in the whole of Jesus' previous preaching.

But *the second* revelation, which may be said to be "equal to the first" is that in Jesus' death and resurrection the "second line" in his prophecies about the future (relating to his *parousia*) intersects the "first" (which seems to be restricted to the resurrection alone). The resurrection discloses what was hidden in many respects in the time before it; namely, that *there is an intimate and indissoluble coherence between Jesus' exaltation as the suffering Servant of the Lord and his glory as the Son of Man invested with all power and authority in heaven and on earth.*

This coherence is not only manifest in a passage like Acts 2:36 which is often quoted because it explicitly states that God has placed Jesus on his right hand as a result of the resurrection and exaltation and has thus made *Lord and Christ*. But the same thing, viz., that for Christ, too, the resurrection meant his investiture with power in accordance with Daniel 7, is even more clearly expressed in the resurrection statement, "All power is given unto me in heaven and in earth." This is a clear reference to the prophecy in Daniel 7:14, not only as to the fact but in the words themselves. The resurrection is not only the exaltation of the Servant of the Lord who had to suffer a great deal and be rejected, but it also reveals that the power of the Son of Man is based completely upon the self-surrender of the Servant of the Lord. This already foreshadows the great future, the "coming in the clouds." For, in Jesus' words at the resurrection, there is already an echo of the harmony between heaven and earth for which he had taught his disciples to pray (Matt. 6:10). It is true that already during his earthly life the power of the Son of Man was placed at Jesus' disposal (Matt. 9:6, etc). But the phrase, "I have been given" (aorist: *edothē!*), indicates the change that had come about since his earthly mode of existence as the Messiah. His status and glory are now in accordance with what is said in Daniel 7 about the Son of Man to whom, also, "there was *given* dominion, and glory, and a kingdom," when he came to the Ancient of days with the clouds of heaven.[54]

And further, we must add to this the fact that at his death and after his rising from the dead came the signs of the catastrophe of the world and of the palingenesis attendant upon the *parousia* of the Son of Man. Judgment is visited upon the temple ("the veil of the temple was rent"), the eschatological movement of the world is manifested ("the earth quaked and the rocks rent") and the rising of the dead is seen ("many bodies of the saints which slept arose," Matt. 27:51-53, cf. also vs. 45, "there was darkness over all the land").[55] All these events clearly point to the connection between the resurrection and the coming *parousia* of the Son of Man. Here, also, the resurrection reveals the connection between the different "lines" in Jesus' self-revelation and his prophecy of the future. In the prophecies before Jesus' death, his *parousia* is distinguished from the resurrection of the suffering and dying Servant of the Lord; but now, after the resurrection, it is seen to be impossible apart from this resurrection in which it is already provisionally realized.

45. *The Great Future as Orientation-point*

It has now become clear that, basically, Jesus' prophecies about his resurrection and *parousia* form a unity. His announcement of the *parousia* of the Son of Man is even provisionally fulfilled in his resurrection. But this must not detract from the fact that in Jesus' eschatological speeches all the attention is directed to the ultimate and definitive coming of the kingdom of heaven. While at the beginning of his preaching all emphasis is laid upon the presence of the fulfillment, as is seen in connection with his miracles; at the end of the synoptic kerygma everything is again focused upon the future. The coming of the kingdom is then referred to in such an absolutely future sense as if it *had not* yet come, and the *parousia* of the Son of Man—the word *parousia* means arrival and not *second* coming!—is spoken of as if he were only a person of the future. This "line" reaches its climax in the great eschatological discourses at the close of the gospel, in the so-called synoptic apocalypse, and in the corresponding parables about the future. We should fail to do justice to the unity of the gospel that has been given to us if, in our discussion of these eschatological and apocalyptic pronouncements, we lost sight of the great motif of fulfillment which occupies such a dominant position in Jesus' preaching. And, in unbreakable coherence with this, we have to view the time of the world previous to the *parousia* in the light of the resurrection, and consequent to it, as the new time of the world, viz., that of the fulfillment. But this does not detract from the truth that the great orientation-point given us in Jesus' speeches about the coming epoch is before all else to be found in the as yet unfulfilled *parousia* of the Son of Man.

In the great context of the future of the kingdom as preached by Jesus, this is not surprising. The great presupposition of Jesus' initial proclamation of the coming of the kingdom was that its fulfillment had only begun and therefore bore a provisional character. The same thing holds for the new aeon that began with Jesus' resurrection. It is still "the time before"; the demons will be cast into the abyss. Of the great palingenesis in which the dead will rise from their graves and the world will be renewed, there are only *signs* and *pledges* to be seen. There is, however, progress noticeable here, for *after* the resurrection the gospel does away with its veiling and reserve with which it was preached before that event, so that now it fully comes to the fore as the *gospel of the fulfillment* founded in Jesus' sacrifice on the Cross (cf. Matt. 17:9), and it is not merely preached to Israel but to the whole world. Moreover, John the Baptist's prophecy that he who was to come would baptize not only with water, but with the Holy Spirit, is now provisionally realized (Acts 1:5). Nevertheless, the kingdom even now yet comes in the same way as the gospel which can only be accepted through faith (Mark 16:16). And the consummation to be brought by the kingdom does not bear the character of a historical development from a lower to a higher stage, or from less to more, but only that of the yet awaited powerful action of the Son of Man in his strength.

Nor is it in conflict with the great motif of fulfillment when Jesus repeatedly sets the life and the work of his disciples (and in them that of his church) in the light of the great antithesis left in the world in spite of the coming of the kingdom, and which is even intensified by this coming. Especially in the second part of his speech at the time of the sending forth of the disciples in Matthew 10 and in the speeches on the future (Matt. 24:9,13; Mark 13:9-13; Luke 12:11,12; 14:26; 21:12-17,19), but also, whenever he speaks of their position as his disciples, is this position and task described as dangerous and threatened. Already in the beatitudes of the Sermon on the Mount, he says that they will be reviled and persecuted like the prophets before them (Matt. 5:11,12). And this prophecy is found all through the gospel. False prophets in sheep's clothing, but who are ravening wolves inwardly, will come to them (Matt. 7:11ff). They are sent forth as sheep in the midst of wolves; they must beware of men for they will be delivered up to the councils, and they will be hated of all men for Jesus' sake. The same thing that happened to their master will happen to them, for the disciple is not above his master, nor the servant above his lord (cf. Matt. 10:16-25). That is why they must be prepared to sacrifice everything, even their dearest relations, in order to take up their cross (Matt. 10:37ff; 16:24ff; 19:29ff). They will be delivered up to be afflicted (Matt. 24:9), they will be beaten in judicial courts and synagogues and be brought before rulers and kings (Mark 13:9ff), and even be killed for the sake of the name of Jesus Christ (Matt. 24:9). Nowhere are the disciples or the coming church given the role of conquerors or rulers of the world. It is true that for their self-sacrifice and suffering they are promised temporal rewards, viz., the love and sympathy of those who are at one with them, but this is an accompaniment of the persecutions (Mark 10:29,30). It is also evident that in their obedience to, and also in their preaching of, Jesus' commandments, there is a conserving and beneficial power for temporal life (Matt. 5:13; Luke 14:34,35; Mark 9:50); and with this prospect they may preach the gospel to the nations (Matt. 28:18). But they are not given any promises of Christianizing the whole world nor are there any theocratic perspectives disclosed. Much rather, the emphasis lies on the necessity of endurance in affliction (Matt. 10:22; 24:13; Mark 13:13; Luke 21:19); perseverance in prayer in spite of apparent lack of redress (Luke 18:1-8); vigilance (Matt. 24:44; 25:13); faithfulness and sobriety (Luke 21:34ff).

In close connection with this, the life and destiny of the disciples and of the church is again and again set in the eschatological light. The coming of the Son of Man is the background ruling the whole of their struggle and difficulty. It is their consolation in times of persecution (Matt. 10:23), the secret of their constant prayers (Luke 18:1,8), the motive of their perseverance (Matt. 10:22); the incentive to faithfulness and vigilance (Luke 21:36).

Undoubtedly, all this does not cancel the task of the disciples described so clearly elsewhere. Moreover, the norm according to which they are to live remains the same. No "ethics of the interim," or "exceptional legislation" forbids them to be faithful to life, to the earth, to culture. It is unalterably "the law and the prophets" that Jesus holds up to his disciples as their guide, i.e., the law of God the Creator and Preserver of the world, which he has given for the maintenance and the development of life. In all this, the gospel is not only free from the tendency to depreciate life as the consistent eschatology supposed, but rather it accepts life for the time that God gives us to enjoy it. In a similar way it denotes the earth as the territory of God's coming revelation. However, everything here is subjected to the great proviso of the provisional and temporal character of this world, and the disciples are taught that the coming of the Son of Man is the real future event to which they are to direct their steps and on which they are to build their hope and their desire.

It is remarkable that this repeated reference to the coming of the Son of Man, especially in the last speeches, but also before them, is repeatedly represented as something of positive, immediate and actual importance. There is nowhere any hint that this future perspective might encompass several centuries. Those who listen to Jesus' words are, on the contrary, comforted with the assurance that God "is hastening" to do them justice (Luke 18:7), and they are warned against any weakening of their vigilance (Matt. 25:1ff). This immediate connection of the great future with the present is the problem of the synoptic eschatology, especially if we wish to preserve the unity of the gospel and to do full justice to the motif of fulfillment developed in the previous chapters of this study. It is true that Cullmann, Kümmel, Liechtenhan and others[56] have expressed as their opinion that, in view of the clear pronouncements in the gospel of *fulfillment,* this lack of "space" in the eschatological future perspective must not be thought of as important. But we are confronted with the fact that this direct temporal connection between the "present" of the gospel and the *parousia* of the Son of Man not only occurs in a few isolated pronouncements, but seems repeatedly to be the presupposition of all of Jesus' words on the future; a fact which in our opinion the authors mentioned do not sufficiently take into account. To gain a proper insight into the problems arising here, it will be necessary for us to examine closely not simply a few salient sayings, but rather, the entire picture Jesus gives in his detailed and explicit description of the future, both of the *parousia* of the Son of Man and of the signs and apocalyptic phenomena prior to it.

46. The "Discerning of the Time"

All kinds of questions arise with respect to the unity and coherence of Jesus' eschatological pronouncements. Some exegetes are of the opinion that, especially with regard to the signs to be expected prior to the coming of the kingdom and the *parousia* of the Son of Man, there is clearly a discrepancy to be discovered in the gospel. It is alleged that in some parts of the gospel, the idea of signs from which the approach of the end might be inferred is entirely rejected, and the *parousia* is described as a perfectly unexpected event taking humanity by surprise. In support of this view these authors refer to the description of the day of the Son of Man by Jesus and his warnings against the false alarm of those who say, "lo here!," or, "lo there!" (Luke 17:21-23). In opposition to this "eschatology of signs," Jesus is here supposed to have emphasized the suddenness of the *parousia* which will resemble the coming of the flood and the devastation of Sodom when people ate and drank, etc., without realizing the impending catastrophe. In this description of the *parousia*—they say—there is no room left for detailed "signs" or prior warning events, and it is entirely in conflict with all kinds of apocalyptic unheavals (as mentioned, e.g., in Mark 13)[57] inaugurating the end and of which it can safely be said—thus one exegete[58]—that they no longer leave people any opportunity to eat and drink. On the basis of this, many writers are inclined to deny that this more or less elaborate "synoptic apocalypse" which is especially found in Mark 13 (Matt. 24; Luke 21) owes its existence to Jesus. They restrict themselves to those passages which speak of the end without any further apocalyptic setting.

We have yet to deal with the objections raised against the "authenticity" of Mark 13. But in this context we would point out that the pronouncements in Luke 17:22ff (on the lightning-like coming of the *parousia* and the unconcern of people prior to it) also occur in Matthew 24:26-28, 37-41. Consequently, they are not thought by the evangelist to be in conflict with the occurrence of signs and of the events previous to the *parousia* mentioned in the same chapter. Yet it is without doubt important to examine more closely Jesus' rejection of the "lo here!" and "lo there!" as well as his comparison of the *parousia* with the appearance of lightning. The issue is especially the pronouncement in Luke 17:20,21, where in answer to the question asked by the Pharisees as to *when* the kingdom of God would come, Jesus says, "The kingdom of God cometh not with observation: neither shall they say, lo here! or, lo there! for behold, the kingdom of God is within you." And then follows the description of the lightning-like manner in which the day of the Son of Man will come (vss. 22-37).

Here everything depends upon what is meant by "cometh not with observation," which we would rather translate, "is not accompanied by observations."[59] Some writers think that Jesus is here speaking in a general way of the invisibility and imperceptibility of the kingdom,[60] as it had already come in the beginning with his appearance, words and works. The objection against this view is, in the first place, that already as far as the present is concerned, it is not in accordance with Jesus' usual preaching if the coming of the kingdom is denied any "visibility" (cf. Matt. 12:28ff; 13:16ff, etc.). And moreover—what is no less significant—the "observations" meant here do not in a general sense refer to sensory perceptibility or visibility, but to a very particular kind of observation. The word used here is also used of watching the stars, so that here it denotes the anxious watching and searching of every phenomenon that might be an indication of the coming of the kingdom. In our opinion, the words saying that the kingdom "does not come with (or in the way of) close observation" must be taken to mean that such observation will not be necessary in order to notice the coming of the kingdom.[61]   This exegesis is entirely in agreement with the following words, "neither shall they say, Lo here! or, lo there!"   These words are repeated in the sequel (vs. 23) and there, as elsewhere (Mark 13:21; Matt. 24:23), they are concerned with premature and false alarms as if the day of the Son of Man had already come.   Jesus here refers to the messianic movements and rumors that arose again and again among the Jewish people.   They originated in a nationalistic ideal of the Messiah and often made it difficult for its adherents to know what to think with respect to this ideal. This explains the question of the Pharisees about the time "when."   When Jesus answers them by saying that the coming of the kingdom and of the Messiah "is not accompanied by observations," he does not mean that we should not "heed" the signs of the times, but he rejects the idea—entertained by the adherents of the nationalistic expectation of the Messiah—that the coming of the kingdom *itself* is something that can only be detected by the well-trained eyes of the "observer."[62]   Its appearance will be so (overpowering) that nobody will be in need of any indication nor will have any doubt at all.[63]

Strictly speaking, this exegesis depends upon the way in which the following highly controversial[64] words are explained: "for, behold, the kingdom of God is within you," or "among you" (*entos humoon*).   In themselves, these words might very well be taken to refer to Jesus' self-consciousness, and be interpreted thus, "The kingdom is already present among you. Any one who has eyes to see no longer needs to be in doubt." Although this interpretation is quite plausible within the scope of Jesus' preaching, there is one important objection against it. For what follows immediately in the context of the gospel is concerned with the eschatological situation for which the evangelist apparently found his point of contact in verses 20 and 21. This argument is all the more convincing since in the following verses the eschatological coming of the Son of Man is announced with the rejection of the same error (of "lo here! lo, there!"). In this connection, therefore, it is improbable that in verses 20 and 21 Jesus should have wanted to divert attention from the eschatological future and direct it to the already "fulfilled" present. This conclusion is also borne out by the future tense in verse 21 ("neither *shall* they say"). That is why in our opinion the words, "For, behold, the kingdom of God is among you," certainly refer to the eschatological coming of the kingdom. As appears from the word "for," they explain why they *shall* not say, "Lo here!, or, lo there!" For when the kingdom comes *it is in your midst,* i.e., it will no longer need any indication, but will fill your whole horizon. Moreover, verse 24 speaks in the image of lightning with respect to the coming of the Son of Man. Very often the word "suddenly" is added to this exegesis,[65] but this word is not found in the text, and it shifts the point of this pronouncement to something else. For the issue is not the suddenness of the coming of the kingdom but its unmistakable and overpowering character,[66] so that we may paraphrase the whole of the passage as follows: "The kingdom will not come in such a way that only the expert observers can discern it; nor will any one need to say, Lo here! or, lo there!; but behold, when it appears it will be among you as the great work of God's power!"[67]

In this conception of Luke 17:20,21, it is clear that there is no question at all of a rejection of "signs," or of any prohibition to watch for them. It is, therefore, unnecessary to point out any contradiction in the gospel when in other passages

Jesus clearly speaks of "signs of the times" and of events indicating the advent of the *parousia*. Nor is this in itself in conflict with the following sayings which speak of the lightning-like coming of the *parousia*. For this image denotes the all-encompassing and unmistakable character of the *parousia*, and not its suddenness. And the fact that at that time there will be many who, as in Noah's day, live without any awareness of the coming catastrophe is not proof that, according to such a trend of thought, there will be no reason for uneasiness. It much rather proves that such will fling every warning to the winds and have no eye for the gravity of the situation in which they are.

Therefore, it is much rather their neglecting to observe the signs of the times for which Jesus in very sharp terms blames the people and their leaders (Luke 12:49-56; Matt. 16:2-3).[68] They are clever enough to draw conclusions from natural phenomena with regard to the weather, but they do not discern "this time" (*ton kairon touton*), nor do they "discern" (*dokimazein*) "the signs of the times" (*ta semeia toon kairoon*). The special character of "the time" or "the times" (*kairos*) is the fact that salvation has come with Christ and in him the last judgment is to be expected.[69] Therefore, special attention should be paid to what is coming and to the signs of the times. What these signs are is not clearly stated. Apparently what is mean is that all that has been revealed in (and by) Jesus' action, and became manifest as signs of the end (cf. also Matt. 12:38-42). For Jesus has come to send fire on the earth (Luke 12:49ff), he brings division, tension, separation, even among the most intimate relations. And this constitutes the character of the times as a time of judgment, in accordance with the prophecy to which Jesus here refers (Micah 7:6), the announcement of God's coming.[70] All this does not mean that, after the Jewish fashion, Jesus gives indications for *the calculation of the date* of the great future. But it does mean that he has commanded us very emphatically to watch the approach of the great day. And this is also the main purport of his great eschatological speech in Mark 13.

47. The Eschatological Speech of Mark 13

a) The authenticity of Mark 13 (and parallel places)

The "signs" appearing with Jesus' coming and those that are still to be expected point to the character of the time as one of "crisis." There is a much more elaborate description of them in the apocalyptical picture of the future found in the great speech of Mark 13. This speech is recorded in the synoptic gospels[71] on the occasion of the disciples' admiration of the beauty of the temple. Jesus replies by saying that there would not be left one stone upon another that would not be thrown down. When they were later seated on the Mount of Olives where they had a view of the temple, his disciples (according to Mark, some of them privately) asked him when these things would be and what would be the sign when all these things should be fulfilled. There is some difference in the account. Mark says, "Tell us, when shall these things be? and what shall be the sign when all these things shall be fulfilled?" (13:4). In Luke 21:7, this question is asked in almost the same words. But Matthew has, "Tell us, when shall these things be? and what shall be the sign of thy coming, and of the end of the world?" (24:3). Mark's and Luke's versions suggest at once that the disciples looked upon the destruction of Jerusalem and the great eschatological event of the *parousia* of the Son of Man as contemporaneous.[72] Hence their inquiry after "the sign" and their mention of "all these things" and of "being fulfilled."[73] Matthew expresses this explicitly. The question about "the sign" also implies that in their opinion the messianic *parousia* and its inauguration of the end of the world would be preceded by a period of great disasters in which even the temple would fall to ruin.[74]

Jesus answers this question with an elaborate prophecy of the future in which he first describes the distress preceding the coming of the Son of Man and then the *parousia* proper.

Most critical scholars deny that this speech was made by Jesus. According to Ed. Meyer,[75] the whole of it has nothing to do with the historical Jesus. Klostermann agrees with this judgment.⁷⁶ The speech is usually considered to be an adaptation of Judaistic apocalyptical material by the church.⁷⁷ The chief arguments for the rejection of this speech as one made by Jesus in the situation depicted in Mark 13:1-3 are the following. First, in verse 14 the *readers* are addressed, which fact clearly points to the use of a written (apocalyptical) source. Second, that which unfolds in the speech does not fit in with the situation described in verses 1-3. For here there is mention of the destruction of the temple, but the speech mentions as a sign of the end the sacrilegious violation of the temple. And finally, the speech is supposed to be incoherent and internally contradictory. It discusses the questions of the time and the signs of the end in a way that is in conflict with verse 28 where it is asserted with great force that the end of the world is unknown. It mixes Jewish and Christian elements. Its alternating use of the second and third persons is also considered to be evidence of its being composed of material derived from different origins.⁷⁸

These arguments, however, are untenable and cannot be adduced to deny the factual contents of this speech to Jesus.

As to verse 14—this is an argument which is repeated again and again⁷⁹—it is not at all necessary to explain the "reading" mentioned here (*ho anaginoosko noeito*) as a remark made by the evangelist or by the author of the written *Vorlage* (source) used here, rather than as the explicit indication given by Christ to pay attention to the prophecy of Daniel quoted here. It is true that Daniel is not explicitly mentioned, but it cannot be denied that, with an eye on Daniel's prophecy exclusively, Jesus is able to speak of "the abomination of desolation" without any further explanation. This is why Matthew mentions Daniel by name and the exhortation there to pay attention to what one reads (in Daniel) can hardly, without arbitrariness, be taken to refer to anything else than to Daniel's book.⁸⁰ We shall have to understand Mark 13:14 in the same way.⁸¹ And even if, with other authors, one should think that it is the evangelist speaking here, these few words could still be viewed as a signal to the reader to pay attention to these words of Jesus' so that it is not necessary to infer such conclusions from them as those mentioned above.[82]

As to the discrepancy which is supposed to exist between the introduction and the speech proper, we have already pointed out in the above that the question asked by the disciples in verse 3 is concerned not only with the devastation of the temple but also with the eschatological events of the end. And although in the speech proper the destruction of the temple is not again spoken of, it is certainly implicitly included—especially after Mark 13:14ff—in the great catastrophic events of the end. There is, therefore, no reason to say that Jesus' speech is no answer to the question of the disciples.

Things are not any different, to our mind, in the case of the objections raised against the factual contents of Jesus' speech. Although we shall have to take into account the possibility that the evangelist has influenced the form in which it has been given to us, it is not possible to see how its contents can on good grounds be denied to Jesus. This is partially admitted by those who make a reservation with respect to the apocalyptic passages in the narrow sense of the word, because there also occur in this speech all kinds of things that are entirely in accordance with what Jesus says elsewhere in the gospel. Thus, e.g., we find the warning against false leaders (Mark 13:6, and parallels), the prophecy of suffering and persecution (13:9,11,13,21-23, and parallels), and the watchfulness he demands in view of this. These same thoughts also occur in other sayings, at least as to their contents; thus, e.g., Matthew 5:11; 10:28,38; Mark 10:35ff; 8:34, in which Jesus also mentions the future sufferings of his disciples; and Matthew 7:15 and Luke 17:23, in which he warns his disciples against the danger of their being deceived. And the same thing holds for the prophecy of the devastation of the temple. It has more than once rightly been observed that this is not a *vaticinium ex eventu*, because then the destruction by fire would have been mentioned, whereas now only the razing of the temple is spoken of.[83] But in another context, also, Jesus spoke of the destruction of the temple (Matt. 23:38, cf. Mark 14:57,58; John 2:19; Mark 15:29). Even Ed. Meyer, who denies that Jesus made this apocalyptical speech, admits that Jesus' prophecy that not a single stone would be left lying on the other, "did not need any further elaboration," and he refers to Micah and

Jeremiah who had also preached of the devastation of the temple long before it occurred.[84]

The real objections against the authenticity of Mark 13 are levelled at those pronouncements which describe the final period, e.g., Mark 13:7-8, and parallels (the commotion among the nations, the cosmic events); 13:12 and parallels (the mutual enmity among men); 13:14-20 and parallels (the great affliction); 13:24,27, and parallels (the coming of the Son of Man). These pronouncements are supposed to have no parallel in the further account of Jesus' words. Moreover, they are held to be completely in conflict with those words according to which the day of the Son of Man cannot be known but will suddenly surprise those who are not watchful and sober, as is expressed by the parable on watchfulness occurring in the same context. That is why these words are considered as secondary Jewish-Christian tradition material.[85]

In opposition to such criticism, however, it must be maintained in the first place that within the scope of Mark 13 there is no contradiction between the so-called apocalyptic description of the end and the call to watchfulness, because nobody knows the day or the hour. The meaning is simply that, in spite of all the signs of the approaching end, people will continue to live in a false peace of mind and in an unwillingness to be converted (cf. also Rev. 9:20,21); and that they will refuse to take into account the coming of the Son of Man. Moreover, the ignorance of the day and the hour is no argument against the authenticity of the apocalyptic description of the signs as such, as we shall see later,[86] because such ignorance relates to the exact point of time. As to this apocalyptic description in itself, we cannot look upon it as a product of the late Jewish expectation of the future; but much rather, must see it in the light of the Old Testament revelation with which the whole of Jesus' teaching was continually in agreement. Of course, we do not deny that the later Jewish apocalyptic literature contains that which might be reasonably related to Jesus' expectation of the future.   Insofar as the former was connected with the Old Testament, there were all kinds of data in it to which Jesus could refer.[87]   But it is very doubtful whether or not such a connection can be made on sufficient grounds.   It is only necessary to become acquainted with the general nature and the tendency of these writings in order to discover the tremendous difference between the Jewish apocalyptic and Jesus' speech in Mark 13 (and parallels).   The whole of the bizarre, elaborate picture, as well as the complicated speculations with respect to the date of the end was alien to Jesus' preaching.   On the other hand, it is difficult to point out any one trait which he borrowed from the later Jewish apocalyptic rather than from the Old Testament.   The very parts which are denied to Jesus as due to the Jewish apocalyptic are full of allusions to the Old Testament prophets and quotations from them.   That nation shall rise against nation (Mark 13:8) is also said in Isaiah 19:2; famines, cosmic catastrophes at the end of time are not only mentioned in the apocalyptic books of *Enoch* and *Ezra,* but also in passages like Isaiah 8:21ff; 13:13; 24:17; Ezekiel 5:12ff; Joel 2:30,31, and others.[88]   It seems that the expression "the beginning of sorrows" (*archē oodinoon*—Mark 13:8) is the *terminus technicus* with the rabbis, at least in the singular form; but this, too, is connected with Old Testament usage (cf. Is. 26:17; 66:8; Jer. 22:23, etc.).[89]   Similarly, the detail about the mutual enmity among people who ought to be closest to each other (Mark 13:12 and parallels) is worded in a way that goes back to the prophecy of Micah 7:6; and the phrase about the "abomination of desolation" (Mark 13:14 and parallels) is derived from Daniel[90]; while the flight of the Judeans to the mountains can be found with even less certainty in Jewish literature than in the Old Testament.[91]

The words describing the "great affliction," as in Mark 13:19 (and parallels), "such as was not from the beginning of the creation which God created unto this time" are not only found in the apocryphal book, *The Assumption of Moses,* 8:1, but also in a slightly modified form in Daniel 12:1 (the Septuagint). For the idea of the "shortening" of those days of affliction, there is no clear parallel either in the Old Testament[92] or in Jewish literature.[93] And finally, the description of the *parousia* proper in Mark 13:24-27 (and parallels) is full of traits and expressions of a traditional character, but it is always the Old Testament to which they can be traced back. This is the case with the prophecy that the sun shall be darkened and the moon shall not give her light; and that the stars of heaven shall fall (cf. Is. 13:10; 24:23; Ezek. 32:7; Joel 2:10,31; 3:15). The distress of the nations foretold in Luke 21:25—"with perplexity; the sea and the waves roaring"—is probably an allusion to Psalm 65:8. Moreover, the phrase "the powers that are in heaven" (Mark 13:25, and parallels), is a very clear borrowing from Isaiah 34:4. And finally, the coming of the Son of Man in the clouds (Mark 13:26, and parallels), is clearly a reflex of Daniel 7:13,14.

It would be possible to mention other details. But from what has been mentioned, it is obvious that Jesus' prophetic-apocalyptic preaching does not go back to the late Judaistic apocalyptic, but much rather, to the Old Testament prophets.[94] And in this light there is no basis for the statement that there are here "entirely isolated elements of the tradition" which cannot belong to the oldest tradition about Jesus due to "conclusions derived from the history of tradition as well as from objective critical considerations"; but represent a Jewish-Christian tradition which Mark used for the composition of his speech without these texts being in agreement with all the other traditions about Jesus.[95] On the contrary, it must be said that these descriptions of the events of the final period which go back naturally to the Old Testament had a profound influence on Jesus' teaching and on his apocalyptic prophecies. In addition, it is impossible to deny the immense difference between the late Jewish apocalyptic and Jesus' prophecy of the future, so that from this standpoint it becomes evident how flimsy the arguments are for denying these prophecies to Jesus and explaining them as Jewish-Christian tradition material.

And lastly, as to the argument that these descriptions are supposed to be lacking in the rest of Jesus' teaching; it must in the first place be pointed out that in his teaching, Jesus' first task was not to emphasize to his disciples that the kingdom of heaven was something of the future, but much rather, that it was present. It is, therefore, not at all surprising that the manner of this great future is purposely not often discussed separately. But, secondly, there is an important reservation to be made with respect to the statement that these apocalyptic ideas are not found anywhere else in Jesus' preaching. Rather, they are the great presupposition of all that Jesus in his preaching reveals about the future. Recall the place in Jesus' preaching which is occupied by the prophecy of Daniel 7 about the Son of Man. By this Jesus in principle set his own coming in the light of the prophetic apocalyptic expectation of the future. Already on this basis there is no reason to deny to him some other, rather accessory, traits of this expectation. Moreover, we find that, fundamentally on the same level with what is said about the future of the kingdom and what precedes it in the speech of Mark 13, are the texts on the last judgment, the great wedding feast in the coming aeon, the rejection of the godless, the utter darkness (Matt. 7:21ff; 8:11ff; 11:20; 12:41ff); the sending forth of the angels to the world-harvest (13:41ff; 49ff); the coming of the Son of Man in his glory (Matt. 16:27ff); the necessity of afflictions and temptations (Matt. 10:24ff; 16:24ff; 18:7); the rule of the disciples over the twelve tribes of Israel in the regeneration (Matt. 19:28, cf. 20:23); the resurrection (Matt. 22:23-33); the fall of Jerusalem (Matt. 23:37ff, cf. also Luke 13:1ff); the announcement of the "woe" to the women of Jerusalem (Luke 23:29). There is only one difference, viz., that what is found elsewhere in isolated texts, as it were scattered about and incidental, occurs here in one context purposely focused on what will precede the coming of the kingdom. That is why the separation and exclusion of these thoughts from Jesus' teaching is an infringement upon the supernatural and cosmic character of the future of the kingdom of heaven, as announced by Jesus.

Our conclusion with reference to Mark 13:1-27, therefore, can only be that it is organically connected with all that Jesus has elsewhere prophesied about the great future, and that every attempt to deny to Jesus the factual contents of this speech is unwarranted and should be rejected. For the knowledge of what Jesus has foretold about the future of the kingdom of heaven, we may no less safely rely on Mark 13 (and parallels) than on what has been given to us in the rest of Jesus' teaching.

b. *The Beginning of Sorrows*

A closer study of the so-called synoptic gospels to form a clearer picture of the character and the duration of the future foretold there will reveal three different phases. The first of them is "the beginning of sorrows," the second is about the great tribulation, and the third is the *parousia* of the Son of Man. The first phase is described in Mark 13:5-8; Matthew 24:4-8; Luke 21:8-11. In all three gospels they are accompanied by a warning about the fate of believers at that time and about the way they should behave in it (Mark 13:9-13; Matt. 24:9-14; Luke 21:12-19). In this first part the chief emphasis lies on the warning to the disciples not to let themselves be led astray. They must *not* think *too soon* that the end has come, or even that it is immediately at hand (cf. Luke 21:9, "be not terrified: for these things must first come to pass; but the end is not by and by"). It is true that many will proclaim themselves to be the Christ. This no doubt refers to the action of the pretenders to the messiahship among the Jewish nation. Josephus mentions quite a series of messiahs that came to the fore shortly before and after Jesus. And the Jewish revolt of A.D. 70 seems to have been strongly influenced by the expectation that the *parousia* of the Messiah was at hand. In the Jewish revolt of 132-135 Bar-Cochba claimed to be the Messiah.[96] The same warning that we find in an altered form in Luke 17:23 (cf. above), is repeated further on in the speech (Mark 13:21-23; Matt. 24:23-26). It shows how dangerous this false expectation was in the eyes of Jesus. In his days the minds of the people were filled with such ideas. He counteracts the power of this temptation by the demand for caution. When they hear of wars or rumors of war, and of the rise of one nation against another, and of (great) earthquakes and famines, pestilences in various places occurring at this time, terrifying things and great signs from heaven, they must not be disconcerted. For these things[97] "must" happen, but they do not yet mean the end, nor do they prove that the end will be within a short time (Luke!). They are only the beginning of sorrows. And to this Jesus adds his prophecy about the persecution the disciples will have to endure at the hands of men, the absolute lack of love that will be even within the most intimate relationships; many who at first seemed to be friends and believers will become traitors and enemies.

In this context Mark speaks of the preaching of the gospel to all nations which is to take place "first." Some authors consider it beyond dispute that these words cannot be ascribed to a tradition that goes back to Jesus himself. This view is partially based upon the *factual* objection that Jesus himself did not think of preaching the gospel to the Gentiles.[98] To this is added the *formal* argument that regards the saying of Mark 13:10 as falling outside of the contents proper and having been inserted into it, as it were, "between brackets."[99] Comparison between the synoptics actually shows that within them the composition of this speech displays rather considerable variations so that we should not ignore the influence of the evangelists on the structure of the whole. This also holds for Mark 13:10 which appears clearly from the fact that the same pronouncement occurs in Matthew in a somewhat different context. And yet this saying is *not* a *corpus alienum* within an entirely different complex of thought, but is quite in accordance with its general tendency. For Jesus foretells to his disciples that they will have to suffer affliction, be delivered up to councils, be beaten in the synagogues, be brought before rulers and kings. Even if it were thought that all these things would happen within the Jewish community or the Jewish country, notwithstanding the mention of the "Gentiles" to whom the disciples must be witnesses for Christ (Matt. 10:18); the great presupposition must then be, anyway, that they will have to go through this as ministers of the gospel. In Matthew 24:9 it says that they will be hated of "all nations," and both Matthew 24:31 and Mark 13:27 speak of the "gathering together of the elect from the four winds from the uttermost part of the earth to the uttermost part of heaven." It is, consequently, impossible to maintain that in Matthew or Mark—in view of the meaning of Mark 13:27, and Matthew 24:31 which will be discussed presently in more detail[100]—the prediction of the mission among the Gentiles is a foreign element in the context of the synoptic apocalypse. There is, hence, no difficulty whatever in applying to this passage the conclusion of the announcement of the sorrows, namely, that the disciples will experience the help of God (Luke 21:18), and that they will be saved if they persevere and bear all that they will have to endure for Jesus' sake.

Although the chronological connection between the events (wars, etc.) mentioned first and the vicissitudes of the disciples is not quite clear, both series of events may be regarded as partially overlapping. Mark mentions them one after another without indicating the time. Matthew has the word *"then"* (vs. 9, *tote*), "at that time." Luke, however, says that the persecutions will take place "before all these things," viz., before the rise of one nation against the other, etc. Perhaps we may explain the latter indication in such a way as that the persecution of the believers will already have begun before the events mentioned have reached their climax in the last great tribulation.[101] At any rate, the two series of events represent the period of the "beginning of sorrows" preceding the final drama, and of which Jesus says that they (for the time being) are not the end itself. So this is a clear indication that one should not be too hasty in drawing conclusions, quite apart from the mention of the preaching of the gospel among all nations.

But on the basis of these passages, there is little to be

said about the duration of this future perspective. Greijdanus has remarked that, in the disciples, Jesus here addresses all believers in the course of the centuries till the end of the age, and that there is therefore no need for us to look for false messiahs before 70 A.D. The same thing applies, in his opinion, to the terrifying phenomena mentioned in Luke 21:11. Jesus—thus Greijdanus—surveys the centuries and here also includes that which will be at the end of the world.[102]

In our opinion, the above-named texts do not warrant our speaking of the disclosure of a future perspective which embraces centuries. Neither do they mean a "beginning of sorrows" repeatedly revealed over a long series of centuries in always new, powerful empires, signs, false Christs. Doubtless, the disciples are warned not to expect the end immediately because there are still so many events that must first happen. But it is impossible to infer from them even approximately the "length" of the perspective, whether it will extend over "years" or over "centuries." This also holds for the pronouncement in Mark 13:10 (the preaching of the gospel to all nations). There is no doubt that this pronouncement is intended to emphasize to the disciples the fact that the end cannot come until the gospel has been preached to all nations. And it will not do to restrict the purport of these words in such a general way that they only indicate the Gentiles as the recipients of the gospel, so that the question about the time might thus be eliminated.[103] Much rather, the category of time is purposely expressed by the words "first" (Mark) and "then shall the end come" (Matthew). This is why we must reject the suggestion that the word "first" means "in the first place," "in particular," meaning in this context that the disciples should remember, above all else, that they must preach the gospel to the Gentiles when they are tried before the councils.[104] This exegesis seems too much inspired by the wish to eliminate the category of time clearly present in this context. These words refer to the preaching of the gospel to all nations and is, therefore, entirely in agreement with Matthew 26:13 (and parallels) where Jesus speaks of "the whole world," and with the great commission of Matthew 28:18-20, which also speaks of "all nations" (cf. also Luke 24:47; Mark 16:15,20).

All this, however, does not mean that it is possible to form any conclusions from this commission given to the disciples as to the *duration* of the period before the *parousia* of the Son of Man. It is certain that the reckoning concerns many *years*. But it is very doubtful whether we can go any further and say that here a perspective extending over centuries is opened to the hearers. Moreover, the words "in all the world" and "all nations" do not imply an extensive-geographical and ethnological import, but are an intensive-summarizing indication as, for instance, Matthew 24:9 says that the disciples will have to endure the hatred of "all nations"; and within thirty years after this, Paul in writing to the Colossians says that the gospel is "bringing forth fruit in all the world" (Col. 1:6). No doubt we may say that, in the light of the fulfillment, Jesus' words were to prove of far-reaching significance—even in a geographical and temporal sense. But this is something different than the assertion that they would open a perspective embracing many centuries. We must, rather, say that the fact (of the preaching of the gospel to all nations) is stated here with great force; but that its temporal implications could not be ascertained or even approximately and in *a priori* fashion surmised by the disciples or the later church, so that they were, therefore, not revealed by Jesus (cf. also Acts. 1:6ff).

c. *The "Abomination of Desolation" and the Great Tribulation*

All this is even more convincing when we take account of the description of the "abomination of desolation," and the great tribulation mentioned in the synoptic apocalypse. Obviously this part (Mark 13:14-20; Matt. 24:15-22, cf. Luke 21:20-24), is no longer a part of the "beginning of sorrows." Here it is very important to know what is meant by this "abomination of desolation."

Various exegetes are of the opinion that here, and in the case of the "flight from Judea," we must not think of the desecration and devastation of the temple and of the flight of the Christian church from Jerusalem which attended it. Schniewind, e.g., says that this interpretation is not compatible with the simultaneity of this flight with the end of the world mentioned in this context. He holds that by the "abomination of desolation" the Antichrist is meant, and that flight is a permanent motif in the expectation of the last things and should not lead us to think of some historical event.[105] Lohmeyer, too, is of this opinion. He, too, is reminded of the Antichrist by the expression "the abomination of desolation," and from this he infers that it is impossible to find a chronological datum in this pronouncement.[106]

Other exegetes also incline towards detaching from identifiable historical events what is here said of the abomination of desolation. Thus also Schlatter, e.g., who says that Jesus' prediction does not represent a conception of prophecy according to which the prophet participates in divine omniscience. It is, therefore, not at all certain that the words in Daniel suggested to Jesus anything but the profanation of the temple which causes its desolation. The way in which this would happen is not further indicated. From Matthew 24:16ff, however, it appears that this profanation will be accompanied by the judgment on the Jews and by the duty of the disciples to flee and to detach themselves from the national bond. From the events it is impossible to infer a date in this conception of the prophecy, for there is no date known in the history of the Jewish war which corresponds with the moment described in the text when the Christians had to take flight. And, moreover, such a fact cannot with any certainty be pointed out in the history of the Jewish nation.[107]

Zahn is even more emphatic. He writes that if the readers of the gospels had paid attention to Jesus' exhortation, "Let him that reads understand," they would never have concluded that the quotation from Daniel predicted the devastation of Jerusalem. The text in Daniel has nothing to do with the destruction of Jerusalem, according to Zahn, but only with the abrogation of the lawful cultus and the desecration of the temple by a ruler of the world who is hostile to God (Daniel 11:30-39). The scene is laid in

Jerusalem. This manifestation of wickedness and godlessness which unchains the last tribulation against the church will begin from the holy place and be accompanied by the appearance of false Messiahs. When the Son of Man comes, he will immediately be seen everywhere on earth, but his appearance will also demand a definite locality. And although this locality is not geographically defined, the last judgment will strike like lightning where hostility to God and the church has reached that climax mentioned in Matthew 24:15 and there, too, will be the Judge.[108] As appears from his reference to 2 Thessalonians 2:8, Zahn, like Schniewind and others, thus thinks here of the Antichrist, although he does not find the latter explicitly indicated in Matthew.

According to Zahn, the corresponding passage in the speech on the future found in Luke 21:20-24 must be interpreted in an entirely different manner. Though in many respects this passage uses the same words as Matthew and Mark in the description of the flight of those who are in Judea, its prophetic content is so much different, according to Zahn, that a comparison of the details would only be confusing. For in Matthew and Mark, Jesus does not speak of the destruction of Jerusalem, whereas in Luke he does. For Luke 21:29 explicitly says, "And when ye shall see Jerusalem compassed with armies, then know that the desolation thereof is nigh." The distress mentioned in Luke 21:23, therefore, only concerns what happened in the Jewish land (*epitēsgēs*), during the fall of Jerusalem. The great final period, of which verse 25 enumerates the signs, is separated from the fall of Jerusalem by "the times of the Gentiles" that must first be fulfilled (vs. 24). The indication "until the times of the Gentiles be fulfilled" is not an accessory decoration in the margin of the description of the judgment on Jerusalem, but a clear indication of the end of the course of world history.[109]

Another explanation is given by Lagrange. According to him, "the abomination of desolation" in Mark and Matthew is also applicable to the fall of Jerusalem. But he does *not* think that the great tribulation in Mark and Matthew refers to the events during the devastation of Jerusalem and what precedes it, but he thinks of the great calamities preceding Christ's second coming, mentioned by Mark 13:24ff and Matthew 24:29ff.[110] However, he explains Luke in the same way as Zahn does. Here the distress and the affliction (*anagkē*, 21:23), are taken to refer to the fall of Jerusalem. The eschatological events begin only *after* "the times of the Gentiles" (vs. 25).[111]

In our opinion, it cannot be denied that the "abomination of desolation" mentioned in Mark and Matthew does not explicitly refer (as it does in Luke) to the destruction of Jerusalem. Strictly speaking, Jesus here speaks only of the desecration of the holy place (this is also the meaning of the veiled expression in Mark (standing) *"where it ought not"* (Mark 13:14). Moreover, the word "abomination" lies entirely within the religious sphere. In the Old Testament, the corresponding word denotes an idol, an idolatrous image or object (cf. I Kings 11:5,7; II Kings 23:13,24; Isaiah 66:3, and other places). The qualification "devastating" denotes the effect of this desolation. It implies the profanation, the desolation of the place where it is standing. This need not in itself mean a violent pulling down of the temple; the term may also be meant in a moral or a religious sense. On the other hand, Zahn's observation that nobody who really "pays attention" to what he reads in Daniel's prophecy would be given to think that the quotation from Daniel refers to the destruction of Jerusalem, is not, in our opinion, to the point. For although Daniel 11:31 (and 12:11) does not explicitly speak of the fall of Jerusalem; there, too, the occurrence of the terrible abomination is preceded by the coming of the military forces (of the Gentiles). The spiritual pollution is attended by the manifestation of military power.

To this announcement of the abomination of desolation must be added the warning that those who are in Judea must flee to the mountains. This local indication and this warning to take flight fit in best with the explanation that here a special kind of hostility will especially be manifested in the center of Jewish life where Jerusalem is situated. This cannot be satisfactorily explained by those who think only of the coming of the Antichrist and not of a definite historical event. Moreover, the details added to the description about the women "that are with child and those that give suck in those days," about the sabbath, and the winter, to our mind refer primarily to a different scope of events than those that are characteristic of the Antichrist.[112]   Instead of the expression "abomination of desolation" Luke has a clear description of the siege of Jerusalem by hostile armies.   Admittedly, as Zahn says, a comparison of the details of the picture of the future in Mark and Matthew, on the one hand, and that in Luke, on the other, is confusing because Luke exhibits a certain amount of independence.[113]   But in our opinion, it would be going too far to ignore the fact that here Luke's description is given in closest connection with Mark and Matthew.   To compare:

Mark 13:14 ff (Matt. 24:15ff)	*Luke 21:20ff*
But *when ye shall see* the abomination of desolation, spoken of by Daniel the prophet, standing where it ought not, (let him that readeth understand,) *then let them that be in Judaea flee to the mountains.*	And *when ye shall see* Jerusalem compassed with armies, then know that the desolation thereof is nigh. *then let them which are in Judaea flee to the mountains.*

In our opinion, the literal identity of the beginning of these texts, "when ye shall see," and the verbal agreement between them in the exhortation to take flight and escape from Judaea to the mountains, prove that Luke does not refer to any other event here than to what Mark and Matthew call "the abomination of desolation."   Apparently Luke wanted to interpret Mark and Matthew for his readers.   Only if we are prepared to assume a divergence between the synoptics with respect to the events that necessitate this flight, can we detach Luke's version from that of Mark and Matthew.   But in our opinion, Luke contains a strong support for the conception that, at least in the first instance, Mark and Matthew also speak of a hostile threat to the city and temple and not simply of the action of *the* Antichrist.   To our mind, the so-called "historical" exegesis of the abomination of desolation cannot be eliminated here.

Besides, the view that here only the activity of the Antichrist is meant, must take account of important objections. Strictly speaking it would only be the masculine form of the participle "standing" (*hestēkota*) in Mark which would denote the Antichrist. Then, Matthew already would no longer have understood this. Moreover, except for this, there is nothing in the phrase "abomination of desolation" that suggests a single prominent person. Much rather, what immediately follows about this "tribulation" speaks of pseudo-christs and pseudo-prophets (plural!—Mark 13:22; Matt. 24:24). This excludes the conception that the whole description in Mark is determined by the person of the Antichrist. It cannot be based on the masculine form of the participle used here, however striking this use may be.

This does not detract from the fact that the way in which Matthew and Mark speak of the cause of the coming tribulation is much less concrete and much more concerned with the desecration of the holy of holies than is Luke who, *expressis verbis,* but also exclusively, speaks of the siege of Jerusalem. We cannot, therefore, suffice by saying that, when Mark and Matthew foretell the fall of Jerusalem by mentioning the "abomination of desolation," this prophecy found its fulfillment in that event alone. It is true that the historical and local color (Judaea, winter, sabbath, women, etc.) in the picture of the terrifying events of the coming abomination suggests a catastrophic affliction to be expected in Judaea and one that will be disastrous to the Jewish nation. This is the justification for Luke's description of the siege of Jerusalem by hostile armies. Yet we must emphatically maintain that what is said in Mark and Matthew about these events was not at all realized completely in the fall of Jerusalem. For it is questionable whether the description of "the abomination of desolation" can be considered as exhaustively fulfilled by the destruction of the temple in A.D. 70. The phrase itself, rather, suggests a more deliberate and consciously anti-religious action in which the enmity to the God of revelation reaches its climax and its concrete embodiment.   As is generally admitted, there is no definite instance to be found of such a blasphemous and idolatrous desecration of the holy of holies in the events around the year 70 A.D.   This is the reason why the prophecy about the abomination of desolation has sometimes been applied to Caligula's intention to have his statue placed in the temple of Jerusalem in A.D. 40.[114]   But this opinion is entirely to be rejected, because it changes this prophecy into an allusion to an alleged incident in the time after Jesus' death, which had no effect upon the temple itself, and which has no support whatever in the context.   This is not to deny that the events about the year 70 are in a general way the partial fulfillment of the prophecy, as far as the destruction of the temple is concerned; but not because of some blasphemous desecration of the temple, as far as we know at least.

It is even more striking that, both in Mark and Matthew, the tribulation with respect to this abomination is clearly connected with the last days.   The following description of the signs in heaven (cf. Matt. 24:29, "*Immediately* after the tribulation of these days shall the sun be darkened, and the moon shall not give her light, and the stars shall fall from heaven") bears a clearly apocalyptic character.   It is true that Lagrange has tried to separate the prophecy of the "abomination of desolation" from that of the great tribulation by applying the former exclusively to the fall of Jerusalem and the latter to the coming of the Son of Man.   But this effort must be considered a failure.   For the announcement of the great tribulation is causally connected with what the fugitives from Judaea will have to suffer because of the events associated with the "abomination of desolation" ("*For* in those days shall be affliction such as was not," Mark 13:18,19, etc.).   In our opinion, it is impossible to say, upon any real basis, that Mark 13:19 and Matthew 24:21 are the beginning of something new in the text.[115]

All this makes it impossible to consider the destruction of the city and temple in the year 70 A.D. as the complete

fulfillment of the prophecy about the "abomination of desolation." In reality, such a view of the prophecy is only an
exegetical conclusion in the light of the fulfillment. It finds
only slight support in Mark and Matthew themselves (cf.
above). And as to Luke, he provides proof, it is true, that the
siege of Jerusalem by hostile armies—which in our opinion
can only refer to the Roman siege of the town—is also intended
by the prophecy in Matthew and Mark. But this is not all.
For Luke makes a distinction in what is a unity in Matthew
and Mark. For one thing, Luke does not mention the "abomination of desolation" but speaks of the siege of Jerusalem. And
in Luke the tribulation does not have the eschatological coloring that it has in Matthew and Mark. He does not speak of
the *thlipsis* (the word in Daniel 12), but of *anagkē*. Nor is the
further definition of this distress in Luke given in the words
used in Daniel. Luke clearly restricts the affliction to what
happens at the siege of Jerusalem and after. "There shall be
great distress in the land, and wrath upon this people. And
they shall fall by the edge of the sword, and shall be led away
captive into all nations; and Jerusalem shall be trodden down
of the Gentiles, until the times of the Gentiles be fulfilled"
(Luke 21:23,24). There is here no mention of the eschatological trait about the "shortening of these days" as is true in
Matthew and Mark; nor is there the immediate temporal connection between the distress and the cosmical-eschatological
signs in the heavens. Between them lie "the times of the
Gentiles" which, in Luke at any rate, prevent us from embracing the tribulation and the *parousia* of the Son of Man in one
glance, as is done by Matthew and Mark. Luke thus limits
the perspective to the destruction of Jerusalem and makes a
clear distinction between the fall of Jerusalem and the coming
of the Son of Man. Only in the 25th verse does he open the
eschatological perspective. Then he no longer speaks of "the
land" (vs. 23) but of the inhabited world (vs. 26). In Matthew
and Mark all this is a great deal more diffuse. They do not
give a distinct announcement of the siege and fall of Jerusalem,

but a more direct connection with the eschatological events of the final period. There is only one way in which we may explain this, and that is in the coalescence of two motifs in Matthew and Mark; that is to say, the motif of the destruction of the temple and the national distress of the Jewish nation, *and* the motif of the eschatological viewpoint repeatedly breaking through all bounds. These two can only be distinguished *a posteriori*, i.e., in the light of their fulfillment. The question as to whether or not Luke's greater distinctness about these things is to be explained in a similar way (viz., from the point of view of the fulfillment) must be left undecided. In any case, he contracts the perspective, on the one hand, and expands it on the other.

The question may arise whether in Matthew and Mark the whole of the future perspective is restricted to the Jewish land. The eschatological and particularistic elements (temple, Judaea) are indeed closely and indissolubly connected. But there are also universalistic traits. The signs in heaven can no longer be conceived of as only within the boundaries of the Jewish land. And when the sign of the Son of Man is seen[116] "then shall all the tribes of the earth mourn," and "he shall send his angels with a great sound of a trumpet and they shall gather together his elect from the four winds" (Matt. 24:30ff). The eschatology, as such, is universalistic. But in Matthew and Mark it is described and viewed from the particularistic standpoint. Only at the extreme end does the particular merge with the universal.

In our opinion, this coalescence constitutes the whole of the problem of the synoptic apocalypse. The great future is described from the point of view of Judaea and Jerusalem, at least by Matthew and Mark; but it implies a universal dynamic that cannot be understood within these limits. That is why it will not do to say that Jesus' prophecies have a strongly particularistic coloring and limitation. In a certain respect this is undeniably true. But they are related to a much wider spatial and temporal area than the one within which the prophecy primarily applies; as may be seen, not only in the light of the fulfillment, but also by virtue of their own intrinsic contents. That is why the abomination of desolation cannot be restricted to the temple, but has a much wider meaning that bears upon the action of the Antichrist, although the latter person is not spoken of. And that is why the flight from Judaea is basically an eschatological distress not simply concerning the Jews, although they only are mentioned.

No doubt it is possible to say that Jesus' prophecy follows certain categories which form an obstacle to a far and clear view of the future. But it must immediately be added that this phenomenon is entirely *in accordance with the nature of prophecy*. For the prophets do not speak from the standpoint of divine omniscience—this we must concede to Schlatter—and do not have all the details of the future at their disposal; but they bear witness to the certainty of God's coming, without distinguishing all its phases. This has been rightly called the *comprehensive character* of prophecy. This term denotes the frequent phenomenon that various future events (e.g., the messianic salvation and the end of a particular national crisis or distress), which in their fulfillment lie centuries apart from each other, are placed side by side, or one immediately after another, in the prophetic picture of the future. This shows the limitation of prophecy with regard to the view of the future. Very often there is no perspective. But on the other hand, this reveals the real coherence and unity of the various stages of the divine work.[117]   In our opinion, this conception is the nearest approach to the character of the synoptic apocalypse in Matthew and Mark. On the one hand, it shows the limited and vague character of the picture of the future given in them and, on the other, it does justice to the implicitly wider meaning (which is perhaps hidden from the writer) of the prophecy which transcends the literal sense of the words. In our summary of the character of Jesus' prophecies of the future, we will again return to this point (cf. §51).

48. *The So-called Time-Limit Pronouncements*

Finally, it is necessary to discuss separately those pronouncements to which an appeal is made for the view that
Jesus announced the great future as an event that his disciples
and his contemporaries would yet live to see. Two such sayings
occur in a typically eschatological context, viz., Mark 13:30
(and parallels) and Matthew 10:23, while one has come down
to us in connection with Jesus' first announcement of his passion,
viz., Mark 9:1 (and parallels).

We shall start with the relevant pronouncement in the
synoptic apocalypse (Mark 13:30; Matt. 24:34; Luke 21:32).
In all three evangelists, this passage is preceded by the "parable
of the fig-tree." Just as the disciples can see that summer is
near when the fig-tree's branches grow soft and the leaves
begin to sprout, they should also know that "it is near, even at
the doors" (Luke has, "that the kingdom of God is nigh at
hand") when they see "all this" happen (thus Mark and Matthew; Luke has only "these things"). It is clear that the
expressions "all this" and "these things" refer to the events
preceding the *parousia* of the Son of Man and the coming of
the kingdom in its glory as described by all three evangelists
(cf. also Luke 21:28). These events are thus once more clearly
evaluated and indicated as signs enabling us to recognize
the end.

Already these words, at least, seem to presuppose the
possibility that Jesus' audience would yet live to see the whole
complex of the events announced by him. But we cannot go
any further. The phrase "when ye see these things come to
pass" (*hotan idēte*), cannot be adduced as evidence that they
would actually see it. It denotes a possibility, but not a
reality.

But what about the pronouncement in all three gospels
saying, "Verily I say unto you that this generation shall not
pass till all these things be done" (Luke has only: "these
things")?

We have already mentioned the view of those who explain

"generation" literally as "generation" and "all these things" as the signs and the coming of the Son of Man. Then they draw the conclusion that Jesus was mistaken in the future perspective.[118]

However, there are other interpretations given which either understand by "this generation" something other than Jesus' contemporaries, or restrict the phrase "all these things" to only a part of the events foretold by Jesus (viz., to that part which the generation of that time actually witnessed).

The former opinion was already held by Jerome, who understood by "this generation" the human race or the Jews especially.[119] Some have thought of the generation of believers.[120] Among recent exegetes, Schniewind, e.g., wishes to take account of the possibility that by "this generation" Jesus did not mean his contemporaries but the people of Israel. Then Jesus is supposed to mean that the judgment will not come upon Israel any sooner than it comes upon the other nations. This implies that there will remain a possibility for Israel to be converted. This would open an expectation which is further developed in Romans 11.[121]

The second view mentioned by us rejects this extension of the concept "this generation." It is thought to mean exclusively the generation living at the time when these words were said.[122] The phrase "all (these) things," however, is then given a limiting interpretation. Thus Greijdanus, e.g., writes that this "all" is of course not unlimited; it is not all that must happen to the world according to the divine counsel, it is not the whole of the history of the world, but that which our Lord announces with respect to the generation that he mentions here, that which is especially concerned with that generation, so in particular that which he has indicated and foretold in verses 20-24, namely, all the distress that was to come to the Jewish people of that time and that would destroy and annihilate them.[123] In view of this opinion, this "of course" in Greijdanus apparently means, "because this pronouncement would otherwise not have been realized." So this is an *explicatio ex eventu*.

In our opinion, the latter view which is also advanced, e.g., by Plummer, Zahn, Wohlenberg, and Lagrange, although with some slight variation, does not do full justice to the clear words of the text. There may be some doubt as to whether the phrase "all (these) things" denotes the whole of the signs, as well as the *parousia* of the Son of Man. The expression in the 33rd verse of Matthew 24, "when ye shall see all these things, *know that it is near, even at the doors,*" would seem to favor the view that "all these things" refers to the signs. On the other hand, that which follows after Matthew 24:34, as well as that after the parallel text in Mark 13:30, clearly refers to the *parousia* also, "But of that day and of that hour knoweth no man," etc. Therefore, in our opinion, the rigorous restriction of the words "all (these) things" to the signs alone, with the exclusion of the *parousia* proper, is not justified. Here Jesus surveys the whole of the events announced by him. But even if "these things" should be taken exclusively to refer to that which precedes the coming of the Son of Man, there is no reason to be found in the text for making a further restriction in those events, and fixing the limit to the destruction of Jerusalem, or to that which became manifest in the first century affliction and persecution. We have already seen that in Mark and Matthew the desecration of the temple and the great eschatological final distress cannot be detached from each other. It would, therefore, be arbitrary to go back to Mark 13:4 for the explanation of Mark 13:30 as is done, e.g., by Lagrange and Wohlenberg. For then it becomes necessary to set apart what coalesces in the text. And in Luke things are not at all different. He more clearly distinguishes between the destruction of Jerusalem and the eschatological signs after "the times of the Gentiles" (21:25). But to our mind, it is perfectly arbitrary to refuse to take these signs into account in verses 31 and 32. The text explicitly says *"these things"* and *"all,"* both clearly referring to all that has gone before. Consequently, whatever difficulties these passages may offer, it is not permissible, we think, to get rid of them by making arbitrary restrictions in the meaning of the text.

The question, however, that remains is, what is meant by "this generation"? That it contains an indication of the continued existence of the Jewish people—as Schniewind holds to be plausible—until Jesus' second coming, and that it would also imply a certain expectation of salvation, seems to us to be far-fetched. We are unable to read such a special meaning in the text. In any case, if so, it has been expressed in a very obscure and incidental manner. In our opinion, there are only two explanations possible. The first is that here Jesus speaks of his contemporaries, and therefore, says that the then living generation would *witness all that* he had foretold of the future.

In this view—held to be unavoidable by those exegetes also who reject entirely the exclusive eschatology[124]—there are authors who speak of a *Perspektivenirrtum* (an error of perspective) which must be explained psychologically. In a higher sense it would not be an error if, with the evangelists, Jesus' pronouncement is applied to his death as the moment of fulfillment. But in our opinion, this explanation neither represents the meaning of the text, nor that of the evangelists. Others speak of an error which, however, was insignificant in Jesus' preaching but would be hard to reconcile fully with other texts which indicate, that the terminal date of the *parousia* is unknown.[125] In our opinion, it is necessary to take account of the comprehensive character of prophecy if "this generation" is taken to mean a temporal indication. Then "all these things" is to be conceived of as the unity of the divine work of the future to which the prophetic Spirit bears witness, without the distinction of the different times, in which it will be realized becoming clear to the subjective prophetic consciousness.[126] In our discussion of Matthew 10:23 and Mark 9:1 (and parallels), we shall again return to this point.

A fuller study and closer examination of this passage may, however, favor a different view. The great question is, does Jesus mention a particular *terminal date,* or does he only speak of the *certainty* of the things he has foretold? The supposition that he means a certain terminal date here remains striking in connection with the fact that a moment later he says, "but of that day and of that hour knoweth no man." Although we need not speak of a discrepancy (as Kümmel does) because we might explain the text by saying, "but of the date and the exact point of time no man knows"; the force of this pronouncement would be considerably weakened by this restriction of the fulfillment to the contemporary generation. In addition, the intervening verse, "heaven and earth shall pass away, but my words shall not pass away," would hardly fit in between these two verses that both speak of the time of the fulfillment. This is why, in our opinion, there is a great deal to be said in support of the conception that Mark 13:30 (and parallels) is a pronouncement upon the certainty of the fulfillment, without any further limitation of the time. In this case, we must not attribute a temporal meaning to the words "this generation," but must conceive of it in the unfavorable sense in which it occurs also elsewhere, viz., the people of this particular disposition and frame of mind who are averse to Jesus and his words.[127]

Then the meaning of this verse is clear, and the following verse which speaks of the passing away of heaven and earth fits in with it very naturally. Jesus bears witness that those who now turn away from him in unbelief and wickedness and who do not believe his words, will not be able to escape the judgments announced by him but will know them from experience. "Pass away" here means "become part of the past so that its significance is gone and no longer need be taken into account." This sense is clear from the following verse in which it is used twice. Hence, in this passage Jesus does not speak of this generation in order to denote the time of the future eschatological events, but to give assurance that all who now yet reject his words will inescapably be involved in their fulfillment. The words are not intended to denote a particular age or generation, but an objectionable mentality. Consequently, in our exegesis, this verse does not offer any support or starting-point for the determination of a time limit. And in this interpretation, the following verse fits in beautifully, "Heaven and earth shall pass away, but my words shall not pass away."

If one wishes a factual parallel to this pronouncement in Mark 13:30 as explained in this way, it is found in the conclusion of Jesus' lament over Jerusalem, "For I say unto you, ye shall not see me henceforth, till ye shall say, Blessed is he that cometh in the name of the Lord" (Matt. 23:39, cf. Luke 13:35); and also Jesus' words to the Sanhedrin, " . . . I say unto you, Hereafter shall ye see the Son of Man sitting on the right hand of power, and coming in the clouds of heaven" (Matt. 26:64; Mark 14:62; in Luke the words "shall ye see" are lacking). These words are also to be conceived, in our opinion, as the announcement of judgment against the Jewish people and its leaders without inferring from it that the latter would witness the *parousia* of the Son of Man before their deaths.

In the second place, we must discuss Jesus' well-known words at the end of his pronouncements on the persecution and sufferings of his disciples, "Verily I say unto you, that there be some of them that stand here, which shall not taste of death, till they have seen the kingdom of God come with power" (Mark 9:1). Matthew has, "till they see the Son of Man coming in his kingdom" (i.e., kingly dominion, *en basileia autou*, 16:28); Luke simply says, "till they see the kingdom of God" (9:27).

The meaning of the first part, unlike Mark 13:30 (and parallels), can hardly give rise to any serious difference of opinion. It states that a restricted number of those whom Jesus was addressing would not die before the things mentioned in the second part had been fulfilled. We might ask why Jesus speaks of "some" and not of "all." This may be due to the fact that the things announced in the second part would occur only after most of them had already died; or to the fact that but few of those living would be permitted to witness the events. Thus we are confronted with the question about the meaning of the second part. In this case, too, there are exegetes who want to restrict the meaning of the "coming of the kingdom of God with power," or of "the Son of Man in his kingdom" (i.e., kingly dignity), to one or more particular events of which Jesus' contemporaries were yet the witnesses.

Thus, e.g., Plummer writes that from the first part of Luke 9:27, it follows that the seeing of the kingdom is meant as a special privilege for some people in contradistinction to what all the members of the audience were to experience. This is why, in his opinion, we must think here of the transfiguration on the Mount, which only a few witnessed, or of the destruction of Jerusalem which only a few of those present were to live to see. According to Plummer, a *direct* reference to the *parousia* is excluded by the fact that none of the audience would witness it.[128]

Also among recent authors, there are those who do not want to explain the second part as concerned with the final advent of the kingdom. Consequently, they differ about the exact meaning of the text. Greijdanus writes that the event foretold in Luke 9:27 "was to become manifest already within a few decades," as appears from the words, "there be some of them that stand here, which shall not taste of death." "Then this coming of God's dominion cannot refer to our Lord's resurrection, nor to the gift of the Holy Spirit which were to be realized within the year. . . . Nor can it refer to our Lord's coming in judgment which is yet even now in abeyance. . . . Nor can the powerful spread of the gospel be meant, for this already came about within comparatively few years. . . . We shall have to think of the destruction of Jerusalem. . . . In it God revealed his kingly dominion in his judgment, a precursor of his judgment on the last day."[129]

Others again consider it possible that by the coming of the kingdom with power (Mark 9:1), Jesus means the preaching of the gospel and the miracles that accompanied the founding of the church,[130] often also including the gift of the Holy Spirit,[131] or the resurrection.[132] There are others who explain the coming of the Son of Man (*en tēi basileiai autou*), or the seeing of God's *basilⱬia* come with power, as the coming of Christ in his church.[133] Others again combine the different conceptions and interpret Mark 9:1 (and parallels) as a prophecy of Pentecost, as well as of the destruction of Jerusalem, the spread of the gospel, and the conversion of the Gentiles.[134]

In our opinion, the explanations mentioned show how very

carefully we should guard against interpreting the meaning of one evangelist differently than that of the other, and against the domination of our personal view of the parts of the text. According to Lohmeyer, Luke must be explained in a non-eschatological sense, in contradistinction to Matthew and Mark. According to Zahn, this is the case with Mark in contradistinction to Matthew and Luke. Lagrange says that Matthew speaks of the church, which cannot be said of Mark and Luke. According to Grosheide, it is precisely in Mark and Luke that such an interpretation is the obvious one, in contradistinction to Matthew.

To our mind, it will be impossible to eliminate without arbitrariness the eschatological coming of the kingdom and of the Son of Man in the explanation of any of the three parallel texts. We consider the restriction of the pronouncements made here to the revelation of the Son of Man and of the kingdom of the period before the *parousia* as an impermissible violation of the unmistakable meaning of the text in this connection. In all three gospels, the description of the *parousia* immediately precedes this passage. That is why this pronouncement cannot be separated from the *parousia*. The indication of the latter is conspicuously in the foreground. Moreover, the meaning of the words as such prove this, we think, especially in Matthew and Mark. Matthew says, "till they see the Son of Man coming in his kingly dignity." There is no passage in the whole of the synoptic tradition in which this phrase has the specified meaning of the exaltation of the Son of Man before (and apart from) the *parousia*. That is why in Matthew 16:28 the *parousia* cannot be left out of consideration. Lagrange's suggestion that *en basileiai autou* is an indication of the church is to be rejected. For one thing, "church" and "kingdom" do not coalesce anywhere in the synoptic gospels.[135] And then, *en basileiai autou* cannot here be interpreted in a spatial sense, but denotes the kingly dignity of the Son of Man, as all non-Roman Catholic exegetes admit. The same thing holds for Mark 9:1 in regards to this matter as well. In our opinion, the "coming of the kingdom of God with power" explicitly refers to the manifestation of the glory of the kingdom from which it is again impossible to detach the final coming of the kingdom. And the view that the words *en dunamei* denote a particular phase in the development of the coming divine kingdom, as Zahn says, is quite unintelligible to us. This view would make it necessary for us to assume that, in contradistinction to Jesus' previous activity on earth, the kingdom was to manifest itself with power only in the coming period, and before its ultimate coming, which is contrary to the whole of the testimony of the Scriptures concerning the revelation of God's power exactly during Jesus' earthly life. We cannot, therefore, detach this *en dunamei* from the manifestation of power that will be seen at the end and especially in the *parousia* of the Son of Man. And as regards Luke, his text simply says, "till they see the kingdom of God." In itself, this statement might only refer to the coming of the kingdom before the end. But the context clearly implies (cf. Luke 9:26) the eschatological events. Besides, the single indication of "the kingdom of God" proves that more is here intended than the revelation of the kingdom before the *parousia*. For those whom Jesus addressed had already seen the kingdom in Jesus' coming and work (cf., e.g., Luke 8:10; 10:23,24). The promise that they should see the kingdom of God, therefore, cannot be isolated from its ultimate revelation.

To our mind, there is no other conclusion possible for all three gospels than that Jesus speaks from the standpoint of prophecy, i.e., in a comprehensive, undifferentiating sense.[136] For if in the exegesis of these texts it is impermissible to eliminate the *parousia*, it is equally untenable to say that Jesus' prophecies had no other perspective than that of his *parousia*. Between the time of his speech and the *parousia*, there is the great fact of the resurrection. Of the latter he had also spoken *expressis verbis* in the first announcement of his passion, of which the pronouncement under discussion is the conclusion. It is true that, at least to the minds of the disciples, the relation between the resurrection and *parousia* was in many ways obscure (cf. above §44); and that so long as the meaning of his passion, death and resurrection was hidden from them, they were not further enlightened about all this. But on the other hand, it is an established fact that Jesus made a clear and factual-temporal distinction between his resurrection and his *parousia*. That is why in the general announcement of Jesus' future glory (as mentioned in particular by Matthew), and in the corresponding objectively identical announcement of the coming of the kingdom with power (Mark, Luke), we cannot eliminate his resurrection any more than his *parousia*. For in his resurrection, also, "the Son of Man comes in his kingly dignity" (cf. Matt. 28:18). And that is why we shall also have to consider the all-embracing significance of Christ's exaltation in Matthew 16:28 (and parallels).[137] It can only be said that in the pronouncement as such this perspective is absent, and that it would not be understood, even in the clear light of the fulfillment, by those from whom the meaning of Jesus' passion and death was hidden. But this is connected with the whole character of Jesus' self-revelation before his resurrection.[138]

Finally, Matthew 10:23 yet remains for us to discuss. We have already seen the impossibility of making this text the corner-stone of the construction of the consistent eschatology in Schweitzer's sense and in that of Werner and Buri. The question is, how must we understand this mysterious pronouncement within the scope of the whole of Jesus' prophecy of the future?

In addition to the explanations mentioned before which speak of an error in the future perspective, there are different views of the words, "Ye shall not have gone over the cities of Israel" (*ou mē telesēte*). Some authors think that here reference is made to the finishing of the missionary task. For the pronouncement is derived from Jesus' speech on sending forth the disciples (in Matt. 10). At the same time, the purport of this speech is not restricted to the sending forth, of which Matthew 10:1 speaks, but is extended to a much more remote future. Thus, e.g., Grosheide is of the opinion that the words, "till the Son of Man be come," refer to the *parousia*. According to him, however, this is concerned with the continuous missionary commandment to the disciples as the representatives of the church. This task extends to Christ's second coming. Moreover, the expression "the cities of Israel" must be taken in a wider sense than its strictly literal meaning, and must be conceived of as intending the various places inhabited by men who are in contact with Christianity but estranged from God.[139] This is a figurative or symbolical conception of the words "the cities of Israel." Something similar is found in Lagrange. Although he prefers to think of the flight of the disciples, not in the mission but in the tribulation, and takes the coming of the Son of Man to mean a great catastrophe, such as, e.g., the fall of Jerusalem; he does not entirely reject the conception by which this passage denotes the *parousia*. If the latter is meant, the "cities of Israel" will probably refer to the Jews in the diaspora.[140]

Schniewind, too, thinks of Matthew 10:23 in terms of the mission. The failure "to finish with the cities of Israel," he takes to mean the mission among the Israelites; and he explains the whole of the pronouncement (in accordance with his view of Mark 13:30 and parallels) in such a way that when the Son of Man appears in glory, the mission to Israel will not yet have been completed. Although they have rejected the salvation of the Lord, the Word of God continues to be preached to them till the end. He relates this view to the expectation that he finds in Romans 11 and Matthew 23:39 that Israel will then first recognize at the *parousia* him whom it has rejected, and then will turn to Christ.[141]

But others think that Matthew 10:23 does not offer such a wide eschatological perspective. We have already mentioned Lagrange who, when he reads the words about the "coming of the Son of Man," thinks of the divine judgment manifest in the fall of Jerusalem. And, to mention one more recent exegete, Stonehouse says that if Matthew 10:23 is explained in analogy with 16:28, it is not necessary to assume that Jesus was in error with respect to his *parousia*. For, in his opinion, we should think of the "supernatural activity of the risen Lord in the founding of his church" when we read about the "coming of the Son of Man."[142]

There can be no doubt that the words, "Ye shall not have

gone over the cities of Israel," do not denote the *mission* but the *flight* of the disciples. This is clear from the beginning of this verse, "When they persecute you in this city, flee ye into another." It is true that the entire future of the disciples is viewed in the light of their vocation as apostles, but in verses 21 and following, everything is dominated by the picture of persecution and affliction. In our opinion, therefore, there can be no question here of a hidden indication of future salvation for the Jews, nor of a reference to the missionary field in the Diaspora or in un-Christianized areas.

For the rest, we agree with those exegetes who understand by "the coming of the Son of Man" that the *parousia* is meant. Already in an earlier context we have tried to show that the missionary speech in Matthew 10, at least from the 16th verse onwards, displays a much wider perspective than that of the first missionary journey that the disciples made during Jesus' life on earth. In Matthew 10, the description of the experiences of the disciples during their first journey passes into that of their future fate as disciples of Christ after he has left the earth. Gradually, the speech assumes the character of what the synoptic apocalypse says about the vicissitudes of the disciples in the coming tribulation foretold by Jesus. Some of the pronouncements in Matthew 10 are even verbally identical, and many others are factually identical with those in Mark 13 and Luke 21 (cf. Matt. 10:17-21 with Mark 13:9-13 and Luke 21:12-17). We even find again in Matthew 24 what is said in Matthew 10 (cf. 10:17,22 with 24:9,13). In connection with this, it seems unwarranted to think of anything else than the *parousia* when Matthew 10:23 speaks of the coming of the Son of Man. For the resurrection here is no longer to be viewed as approaching, but occurs before the tribulation announced to the disciples. To think that here the supernatural power and help of the exalted Lord are spoken of is to offer a very unusual explanation of the synoptic "coming of the Son of Man." It will not be permissible in this case to argue from a particular conception of what is "possible" in the light of the realization, but here the words must be given their most obvious sense. And when such is done, we cannot see how the reference to the *parousia* can be eliminated.[143]   What is then to be understood, however, by the flight over the cities of Israel which the disciples will not be able to complete before the coming of the Son of Man?   In our opinion, these words can only be explained in the way mentioned above in which the coalescence of the particularistic and the eschatological motifs in Mark and Matthew have been set in the light. Similar to the explanation given there of the flight from Judaea into the mountains as being in close connection with the final distress, the cosmic catastrophes, and the end of all things; we find here a picture of the persecution of believers in the time previous to the *parousia* described within the boundaries of the Jewish country.

49. The Meaning of the "Parousia-Parables"

In addition to what in the synoptic apocalypse and the related parts of Jesus' preaching bears directly on the *parousia* of the Son of Man and the events before it, there are in the gospel a number of pronouncements, especially parables, in which Jesus applies this "eschatology," as it were, to the life of the disciples.   These parables are partly a continuation of the apocalypse (especially in Matthew) and are partly found apart from the latter (thus especially in Luke).   For our subject, they are no less important than the direct eschatological pronouncements because they contain the practical reflex of Jesus' prophecies of the future on the life of his disciples.

As such, we mention, e.g., the parable of the unjust judge in Luke 18:1-8, in which Jesus teaches his disciples "always to pray and not to faint."   In this connection we are told that God will avenge his elect *speedily* (*en tachei*).   It is clear that these words refer to the coming of the Son of Man mentioned in the 8th verse and to the ultimate liberation revealed thereby.[144]   The question is, what is meant by the term "speedily"?

The parable shows that, on the one hand, we cannot apply the measure of our subjective-human sense of time, for the whole parable is intended to emphasize that we "ought always (*pantote*) to pray," and should never get tired nor neglectful (*eakakein*) therein. This exhortation presupposes that our prayers for the coming of the kingdom are not immediately answered but that the answer is delayed for a very long time. And this is confirmed by the whole allegory of the widow who has to call upon the judge repeatedly. For the judge would not avenge her "for a while" (*epi chronon*). The duration of the time is not mentioned but seems to have been rather long (cf. also verse 4, "afterward").[145] And though these words belong to the allegorical picture, the *tertium comparationis* is clearly discernible in the waiting (cf. also the words "which cry day and night unto him," vs. 7, cf. Rev. 6:9ff). All this must be taken into account in the explanation of the word "speedily" in verse 8. In the parable and its application, two things are contrasted with each other; the subjectivity, on the one hand, of him who prays and has difficult in persevering in his prayers because of the delay in the answer, and the pronouncement made by Jesus, on the other hand, in the form of an oratorical question to the effect that "God will speedily avenge his elect who cry day and night unto him." The tension between these two is implied in the words "cry day and night" and "avenge speedily," both of which occur in the same sentence. This "speedily" (*en tachei*) is comparable with the same words in Revelation 1:1; 22:6. There, too, the speed of God's action is spoken of, notwithstanding the fact that it is very clear there that the "things which must shortly come to pass" comprise a great deal. In like manner Luke 18:8 must be explained that in "avenging his elect" God uses *speed*; but when there is question of *speed* in *God's* action, we should always remember that such speed is subject to God's fulfilling his own counsel.[146] Although he who prays is comforted with God's speedy action, it does not follow that the redemption will be accomplished within a short time as measured by subjective-human standards.[147]   Such a subjective-human idea of duration is not found here.

Related to this parable are those that exhort us to be watchful and mindful of our responsibility in view of the coming of the "Lord," or of the "bridegroom," and other sayings which bear upon this; thus Mark 13:33-37 (the man taking a far journey); Matthew 24:42-51, cf. Luke 12:35-46 (the watchful and faithful servant); Matthew 25:1-13 (the parable of the ten virgins).

All these parables undoubtedly refer to the *parousia* of the Son of Man (cf. Matt. 24:42,44; Luke 12:40; Mark 13:35; Matt. 25:1).[148]

It might be asked whether these exhortations to the disciples to be faithful and vigilant, as well as to persevere in prayer, suggest that Jesus took account of the fact that the Son of Man might yet delay his coming for a very long time. In this sense we might explain expressions like the one used by the evil servant saying, "My lord delayeth his coming" (*chronizei*, Matt. 24:49; Luke 12:45); and the statement made in the parable of the ten virgins, "while the bridegroom tarried" (*chronizontos*, Matt. 25:5).   Very often it is assumed that such traits or words are due to the work of the later church express-ing its uneasiness about the delay of the *parousia*.[149]   Such an interpretation is very arbitrary, since all traits hinting at the long delay of the *parousia* fit in very naturally with the contents of the parables.   Moreover, those in the parables who argue this way saying, "my lord delayeth his coming," may be very much mistaken.   If this detail is to be explained allegorically, it would not mean that Jesus was preparing his audience for such a delay; but that he rejected any idea that, for the present at least, there is yet no need to reckon with the com-mencement of the great future.   Things are yet different with respect to the parable of the ten virgins.   Here *the delay of the bridegroom's coming* is an integral part of the narrative. Yet its application is also, "Watch therefore, for ye know neither the day nor the hour wherein the Son of Man cometh" (Matt. 25:13).   The whole of this parable seems to mean (although it is difficult to say what details in the allegorical picture must be considered as relevant to its meaning) that "although the Son of Man should yet delay his coming, we ought always to be watchful." Perhaps we may even go a little further and say that here the danger is pointed out which besets the church when the Son of Man delays his coming longer than had been thought.[150] And all this is closely connected with the church's ignorance of the moment of his coming.

This *ignorance with respect to the time* is the motif which comes to the fore again and again in the exhortations to the disciples to be watchful. It is very elaborate, e.g., in Mark 13:33-37 (the parable of the man taking a far journey), verse 33, "Take ye heed, watch and pray; for ye know not when the time is." And verse 35, "Watch ye therefore: for ye know not when the master of the house cometh, at even, or at midnight, or at the cock crowing, or in the morning: lest coming suddenly he find you sleeping" (cf. Luke 12:38). So we cannot say that in these parables Jesus "never tires of laying emphasis on the close proximity of the last day,"[151] nor that here "the urgent approach of the end" is pointed out.[152] In reality, Jesus points out the need for incessant vigilance and unflagging perseverance because of the fact that we *cannot* know the moment of his coming, which may be sooner or later than we had expected, and may even come suddenly (*exaiphēs*).

The same idea is expressed by the image of "the thief in the night" (Matt. 24:43; Luke 12:39). We cannot say of this parable, either, that it is intended to urge us to be watchful "in view of the imminent, and even fast approaching eschatological crisis."[153] For this very element is lacking in the parable. If it were known that a thief were coming, it would not be difficult to frustrate his plans. But (as a rule) we know nothing about it. The thief's chance lies in our ignorance of his plans. That is why we should always reckon with his coming. The point of the comparison is not that he is sure to come, or that he will come soon, but that nobody knows if or when he will come.[154]

The strongest pronouncement with regard to our ignorance

of the moment when the Son of Man will come is found in Mark's and Matthew's words, "But of that day and hour knoweth no man, no, not the angels in heaven, neither the Son, but the Father" (Matt. 24:36; Mark 13:32). The very fact that the Son is also included in the ignorance about the last day,[155] shows how close a secret the time of the second coming is. If the text said, "of that day knoweth nobody," it might mean that, in general, there is nothing to be said about the *parousia,* for the word "that day" denotes the day of the Lord, the day of judgment (cf. Matt. 7:22). The question at stake, however, is *the exact point of time* of that day, as also appears from the following words "and that hour." Some authors have made the remark that, strictly speaking, this basic tenet renders all eschatological prophecy useless, and consider it to be in conflict with the "signs," etc., mentioned in what precedes, which enable us to know when the great events are at hand.[156] But we may say that the pronouncement in Mark 13:32 and in Matthew 24:36 is of a relative character, seen also in view of the context in which it occurs. Within the limits of what has been said about the Lord's future, nobody knows anything about the point of time when this future is to begin. This is unknown, it "has been put by the Father in his own power" (Acts 1:7).

Up to now, the result of our investigation has been that no conclusions as to a time limit can be drawn from the often quoted sayings which refer to the immediate coming of the day of the Lord and the *parousia* of the Son of Man, saying whose real purpose is to urge the necessity of faithfulness and vigilance. It is our very ignorance of this event upon which the stress is laid. We should only take account of its *possible* nearness (cf. also Matt. 24:37ff). The fact that people will not be aware of the imminent catastrophe, just as in the days of Noah (*ouk egnoosan:* they knew not), proves their folly. Everybody should reckon with the unexpected coming of the *parousia.*

But this is not all. Strictly speaking these pronouncements about watchfulness might mean that, from the moment when they were made, the kingdom might come any day and the last judgment occur. Yet this conclusion would not be in accordance with the whole scope of Jesus' teaching. From other data, it appears that Jesus did not expect this day in the very near future, and that, therefore, his saying about vigilance should be considered in connection with this data.

Thus, the parable of the pounds in Luke 19:11-27 has certain details (the departure of the nobleman, his command to his servants) which are closely related to those of Mark 13:31ff, cf. above. With reference to the *time,* however, the tendency is slightly different. This is already seen in the introduction which says that Jesus told this parable . . . "because he was nigh to Jerusalem, and because they thought that the kingdom of God should immediately appear."[157] In answer to this, Jesus states that "the nobleman went into a far country to receive for himself a kingdom, and to return." The meaning is apparently that those who expected the kingdom to appear immediately, did not take account of an interim that would first occur. This interim is represented here by the nobleman's departure and by the task he gave to his servants, for they are to administer his goods during his absence. It is hardly possible to explain all this in any other way than as a reference to Jesus' departure from earth to heaven, and to the vocation of the disciples on earth. It presupposes the continuation of the world's time after Jesus' departure, and it lays special emphasis upon the vocation of believers during that interim.

In a similar way, the parable of the talents speaks of "a man travelling into a far country" (Matt. 25:14-30). Here we are told that "the lord of those servants" came back only "after a long time" (*meta polun chronon,* Matt. 25:19). It is difficult to believe that this detail has no significance with reference to the total meaning intended, in view of the clear application made between the lord's going away on a journey and Jesus' own departure. So here the coming of the Son of Man is referred to a more remote future than many people would suppose.[158] There is again a special emphasis upon the task entrusted to the disciples. The expectation of our Lord's coming does not entail any stagnation, or passivity in the life of a disciple; but rather, true, sanctified activity in the service of God.[159]

50. Fulfillment and Consummation

When we try to give a final survey of the data in the gospel referring to the future perspective in Jesus' teaching and prophecies concerning the kingdom of heaven, we are struck by the variety of motifs, the fragmentary character of the indications, and the differences in the standpoints from which the future may be viewed; and we become fully aware of the difficulty of uniting all these data into a meaningful whole. There is no teaching of an eschatology in the sense of a complete and systematical doctrine of the "last things." The future is, rather, introduced for the purpose of warning or comforting believers, and certainly also to teach and instruct them. The audience, however, should always be fully aware of its own involvement in the future, and in the audience all future believers are also addressed (cf., e.g., Mark 13:37). This characteristic of Jesus' pronouncements on the future stands out clearly when we survey in the following summary all that we have hitherto found.

a) Without allowing themselves to be deceived by the rumors of false messianic claims, the disciples should pay attention to the signs of the times which were manifest already at the coming of our Lord, and as they were announced by him ("discerning the times," the lesson of the fig-tree, the warning against the "lo here!, or lo there!").

b) The signs announced are first "the beginning of sorrows," and then will come "the abomination of desolation," accompanied and followed by the great tribulation and the cosmic catastrophes inaugurating the *parousia* of the Son of Man (Matt. 24; Mark 13).

c) This "abomination of desolation" is a judgment on the Jewish nation and the holy place, and is manifest in the encirclement of Jerusalem by hostile armies (Luke 21). At the same time, it represents the culmination of the evil principle of the world which is inimical to God, as also appears from the tribulation which accompanies it and the world-wide distress which results from it.

d) Some of those listening to Jesus will witness the coming manifestation of the power of the Son of Man before their death (Mark 9:1, and parallels). And both Jesus' followers and his enemies will experience the truth of the words he addresses to them (Mark 13:30 and parallels; Matt. 10:23), unto redemption, on the one hand, or judgment on the other.

e) Jesus' disciples ought not to faint in their prayers for the coming of the kingdom, for God will speedily fulfill his promise (the parable of the unjust judge).

f) Jesus' disciples should be watchful and should not think that the coming of the kingdom is still very far away, because no man knows when the kingdom will come. It will make its entry unexpectedly and suddenly (the parables on watchfulness; the motif of the "thief in the night").

g) Jesus' disciples should not forget their great task because of the expectation of the future. This task is to be performed during the interim between Jesus' departure and the *parousia* of the Son of Man. They should look upon their vocation in the light of the salvation already revealed and given by his coming into the world (the parable of the pounds; that of the talents).

Now, it is not difficult to elaborate upon these motifs in such a way that they become mutually incompatible. This is clearest in a comparison of what is said under *f* with what is found under *a-c*. The warnings to be watchful may in themselves be interpreted in such a way that it is at any moment possible for the Lord to come. On the other hand, it appears from the synoptic apocalypse that very great and far-reaching events are to happen before that day, and that the disciples still have a great task to perform with reference to the *ekklesia* (which they represent) in the world (cf. also under *g*).

Yet it should not be difficult to interpret these motifs in

connection with each other. All things considered, they are the different segments of the one circle whose central point is the certainty that God is busy completing his work of fulfillment. This one central truth constrains us to persevere patiently and to be watchful and faithful. It implies the believer's watching the signs of the times, because God is accomplishing the consummation according to a pre-determined plan. He has revealed this plan to his people. On the other hand, it implies the great task of the believers in this world. All these facets are to be considered in connection with each other. They are all determined, however, by the certainty and proximity of the coming of the Son of Man, and also serve to transpose the lives of believers into the actuality of the coming kingdom.

Finally, the question may be asked, in what way is this all-embracing standpoint of the consummation to be combined with what has already been observed about *the resurrection* (§44) and the view of fulfillment given in it? In our answer we would point to the following.

First, the evangelists, who have given us Jesus' eschatological speeches as a part of the whole of their gospel, wrote from the standpoint of the resurrection. What they have told us of Jesus' prophecies about the future, they wanted to be read exactly from the point of view of the resurrection and not at all apart from it. All that has been brought together in these leave-taking speeches of Jesus is, therefore, not a misrepresentation nor an ignoring of the new perspective of the future which was opened by Jesus' resurrection; but much rather, reaches beyond that to the last and definitive things that can be said about the coming epoch. But it should be read in connection with what has been said about the resurrection elsewhere in the same gospel. We should fully take account of the fact that Jesus' words have been transmitted to us in a particular context, viz., in that of the writings of the evangelists who collected and arranged these words into a literary whole. This is why we have to understand and judge the meaning of the words of this tradition solely from the totality of the gospels thus composed.

In the second place, we should do justice to what has been said above about the restrained and veiled way in which Jesus spoke about his death and resurrection before they were realized. We must bear this in mind when we try to explain Jesus' prophecies of the *parousia,* insofar as the new perspective of the future created by the resurrection is lacking in them.

In the third place, it follows from this that the pronouncements on the *parousia* can only be evaluated properly from the reality of the resurrection. Then it will appear that what was said of the future revelation and glory of the Son of Man in a comphehensive and summarizing way before the resurrection, was provisionally fulfilled in the resurrection; and that the future, previously represented as a unity, now is to be fulfilled in more than one phase. This means that we must consider the interim between Jesus' resurrection and the *parousia* of the Son of Man, both from the viewpoint of the present (the kingdom *has* come, together with the power given to Jesus in heaven and on earth), and that of the future (the awaited appearing of the Son of Man). The latter view is preponderant in the eschatological speeches and must not be eliminated because of the importance of Jesus' words about the resurrection. In our opinion, this danger is imminent when we explain the so-called time limit pronouncements as exclusively related to Jesus' resurrection and ascension, or when we restrict them to Pentecost or to the devastation of Jerusalem. The resurrection did not shift the actuality of the coming of the Son of Man from what "was to happen speedily" to what had already happened. For Jesus' parting words consider from the all-important viewpoint of the great future all that has happened and all that is yet to happen. This also applies to the continued preaching of the gospel, and to the nobleman who in going away to receive a kingdom, instructs his servants to administer his goods. It finds expression both in the so-called imminence and time limit pronouncements. The church

is the church of the future.   The sending forth of missionaries
to all nations is a stage in the divine work of the consummation.
All the gifts and powers of earthly life, all that is brought about
in it by virtue of the progress of the preaching of the gospel
Matt. 28:20), may only be accepted in the watchfulness and
faithfulness of servants who are waiting for their Lord.

But all this is also based on the fact that the fulfillment
has come, and that in principle the prophecy of Daniel 7 *has*
been fulfilled in Jesus Christ.   In our opinion, this consideration
is no less essential for the understanding of the gospel than
all that has been said about the interim as the time of expectation.   It is based on the fulfilling character of the whole of
Jesus' coming and work.   He did not come simply to proclaim
the actual significance of his *parousia,* and to impart the sense
of a prelude to the remainder of the world's time.   Very often
the non-eschatological character of Jesus' commandments has
been pointed out in this connection.   And this is a very important argument.   But it is not the only one, nor is it the
principal argument.   Nor need we appeal simply to Jesus' words
on the resurrection.   The principal argument is the *Christological character* of the time of salvation inaugurated by Jesus'
coming.   Thus the period between his coming into the world
and his *parousia* is principally something more and something
different in a qualitative sense than the period of waiting and
watching for the end.   This time is determined and qualified
for believers by the fact of the fulfillment which culminates
provisionally in the resurrection.

We shall have to do full justice to this elliptical character
of Jesus' preaching of the kingdom and of his self-revelation.
Any one who thinks that the *Nah-erwartung* is the most essential characteristic of the gospel will come into conflict, not only
with particular texts, but with the whole of the basic character
of Jesus' preaching.   For in this preaching, the element of
fulfillment is no less striking and essential than that of expectation.   That is why we are of the opinion that the question
about the extent of the future perspective in Jesus' preaching

is one of degree, and not one in which the whole of Jesus' preaching is at stake. This preaching is determined by the Christological character of *all* of Jesus' works and words. This is not saying that, if need be, the eschatological aspect could be dispensed with, or interpreted and sublimated in an idealistic way. For the future and the present are indissolubly connected in Jesus' preaching. The one is the necessary complement of the other. The prophecy about the future can only be rightly viewed from the standpoint of the Christological present, just as the character of the present implies the necessity and certainty of the future. "The second coming of Christ is demanded by his first coming; the former is implied in the latter and necessarily follows from it, carries it to its full effect and completion, and is, therefore, in the Old Testament prophesy comprised in one picture with the first coming."[160] But we cannot say, after the manner of the more or less "consistent" eschatology, that the *proximity* of the *parousia* explains the Christological present and the pronouncements on the present. Much rather, the "breaking through" of salvation, the fulfilling character of the present, from the outset also includes the future as a reality ensured and guaranteed in the present. So the character of the present as fulfillment must not be approached from the proximity of the future; but rather, the proximity of the coming kingdom must be approached from the reality of the present kingdom. This is the truth of the pronouncement that the proximity of the *parousia* is in a certain sense only another expression of its absolute certainty.

That is why it is not so much the proximity as the certainty of the *parousia* which dominates Jesus' eschatological pronouncements. This, e.g., is the purport of the parables on vigilance. We must always be prepared, for although the moment of the coming of the Son of Man may be unknown and uncertain, the *fact* that he will come is certain. This certainty is the basis of the exhortation to the disciples to persevere in prayer and faith, for "shall not God avenge his own elect, which cry day and night unto him?" And from the certainty that God hears their prayers follows the promise that he will do so speedily.

The same thing holds for what has been said of the signs of the times. They, too, do not primarily serve to reveal the proximity of the end, but the unmistakable fact that God is at work. In this sense the Pharisees and scribes asked of Jesus a sign from heaven, and in the same sense Jesus rebuked the crowds for not understanding "this time." Their great error was not that they refused to hear of the nearness of the kingdom—for when that had been announced, they flocked to John and Jesus in great numbers!—but that they lacked the discernment to see that the signs of the kingdom and even the kingdom itself were visible in Jesus' words and actions.

And as to the great eschatological speech in Mark 13 (and parallels), here Jesus also urges the necessity of soberness and calm in answer to the question about the time "when" asked by the disciples. The events that will frighten them—wars, revolutions, etc.—*"must"* happen. They are part of God's counsel and prove that the history of the world is in its final, its decisive stage. But they are not yet the end. They are only the beginning of sorrows.

The end is not near at hand and "at the door" until, not only the beginning of sorrows, but also the great signs are seen that will appear with the abomination of desolation. Then what has been said of the fig-tree when its branches get soft and the leaves appear will prove to be true, viz., that summer is approaching. The conclusion of the speech is, therefore, not that "the end is near"; but that the end will certainly come. Even those who are now deaf and blind to what is happening ("this generation") will experience it. For heaven and earth shall pass away, but my words shall not pass away. But of that day and that hour no man knows. . . . And the conclusion is, "since you do not know, be watchful" (Mark 13:28-37). There can, therefore, be no question of calculating the time of the end. Nor should the idea of the imminence of the event paralyze our activity. We should live simply in the certainty of its coming.

Jesus' pronouncements on the present and the future—this is our conclusion—are filled with a profound seriousness and are burdened with such an actual tension because they are all sustained by the certainty that God is busy fulfilling the promise and realizing the consummation. All this has its deepest foundation in the self-consciousness of the Son of Man in whom God brings the salvation, and in whose exaltation he will establish his kingdom with power.[161]

51. *Prophecy and History*

Finally, all that has been said up till now may also give us an insight into the phenomenon of the combination into one whole of various pictures of the future. Things that appear to be centuries apart in the fulfillment are sometimes comprehended by Jesus' prophecy in the same temporal frame and within the same local framework. This does not mean that the whole of Jesus' expectation of the future is timeless and lacks any temporal distinctions. The distinction between what is earlier and what is later is explicitly given (in the signs, in the precedence of the preaching of the gospel, etc.). But there is no perspective of time that embraces the centuries. The great tribulation of the world, the last persecution of the church, the abomination of desolation, the cosmic catastrophes, and finally, the *parousia* of the Son of Man, are connected with the judgment upon Israel, the coming events in Judaea, the persecution of the disciples in the Jewish land. The eschatological prospects, it is true, cannot be said to *remain* within the particularistic Jewish framework. They exceed this, to be sure. The ends of the earth, the nations of the world, the inhabited earth (Luke 21:26) also come repeatedly into sight, not only in the announcement of the last judgment, but also in the prophecy of salvation. All the peoples of the earth will first hear the gospel, the elect will be gathered together from the four corners of the earth, they will come from the east and the west and sit down with Abraham, Isaac and Jacob in the kingdom of heaven. But by the side of this, the towns of Israel, the Judaean plains and mountains are the setting for the eschatological scenes proper. This interwoven structure cannot be disentangled, either after the manner of the form criticism school by cutting up the whole of the synoptic picture of the future into a plurality of Jewish, Jewish-Christian, ecclesiastical elements (and perhaps also original parts that have come down to us from Jesus himself?), or by *arguing from the course of history* and giving to all kinds of pronouncements a special explanation not warranted by the text. Although the second method is based upon presuppositions that are more in accordance with the gospel than those of the first, we consider them both as arbitrary and as a disregard of the specific character and the peculiar complication of the eschatological picture of the future found in the synoptic gospels.

The only explanation that can do justice to this prophecy of the future is the one that fully takes account of its *prophetic* character. The attempt to give an exegesis in accordance with the standards of historiography is bound to come to the conclusion that this description not only lacks clarity and is diffuse, but also connects events and places not belonging together. Then the inevitable inference is that we must speak of a *Perspektivenirrtum*, i.e., an error in perspectives. Or, to avoid such an opinion, various pronouncements must be given a meaning that they do not have in themselves. Basically, we are then compelled to have recourse to expansions and restrictions, i.e., to *historizing corrections*. In both cases, it is not the text as such but the one-sidedly historical exegesis that compels us to accept the text only with these corrections.

Instead of applying such a historizing exegesis, we must try to gain an insight into the character of the prophetic way of foretelling the future. And it should not be forgotten that this is something different than a diary of future events. Prophecies are not based on a partial transference of the divine omniscience to man. Jesus explicitly states that even the Son does not share in the divine omniscience with respect to the time of the end. The function of prophecy is consequently not that of a detailed projection of the future, but is the urgent insistence on the certainty of the things to come. This explains why, at the end of the vista, the perspective is lacking. The prophet sees all kinds of events that will come and he sees in all of them the coming of God. But he cannot fix a date for the events, he cannot distinguish all the phases in God's coming. To him it is one great reality.

This limitation of the perspective, as regards the time of the events, is connected with the fact that the prophet paints the future in the colors and with the lines that he borrows from the world known to him, i.e., from his own environment. It is also true that the nations, the inhabited world, etc., occur in the eschatological picture. But this does not imply that the prophet has been equipped with geographical omniscience, that his view comprises continents in their qualities and differentiation, and that he is now able to give a universal geographical picture of the world. Just as the *time* of the future is ultimately contracted to one point, so the world-space is to him a totality and not an accurately differentiated magnitude. We see the prophets paint the future with the palette of their own experience and project the picture within their own geographical horizon. This appears in the Old Testament prophets in all kinds of ways. And in our opinion, this is also the explanation of Jesus' description of the future. He follows the Old Testament most closely, and not only is the temporal perspective lacking at the end, but the geographical horizon within which the eschatological events take place is also restricted in some places to the country of Judaea or to the cities of Israel. To our mind, this must not be explained *allegorically* (e.g., Israel is the de-christianized world), nor should we speak of errors. Here we are confronted with a peculiarity in the prophetic description of future events. It is better to speak here of poetic and figurative representations than of allegorical pictures.[162]

This conception of the prophetic way of foretelling the future should not be characterized as a *theological interpretation* which has been based on the course of history, but rests on the clear data of the gospel itself. More than once we have referred to Jesus' words at his resurrection and to the eschatological signs that took place at his death. They clearly point to the provisional fulfillment of the *parousia* of the Son of Man announced as a unity. But we may refer to another central passage in the gospel, viz., to Jesus' proclamation at the beginning, "The kingdom of heaven is at hand" (Matt. 3:2). The disciples were told to repeat it when they were sent forth into the cities of Israel (Matt. 10:7; Luke 10:9). It is clear that it is impermissible to apply the "proximity of the kingdom," mentioned here exclusively and without any reservation, to the ultimate and definitive coming of the kingdom—as, e.g., in the parable of the fig-tree (Matt. 24:32,33; Mark 13:28,29; Luke 21:29,31). For between this initial proclamation and the great *Eschaton* lies the whole of the tremendous reality of the kingdom *having* come. Yet it cannot be said that Jesus' initial proclamation of the proximity of the kingdom is exclusively related to its initial coming. Here, too, Jesus speaks of the kingdom as a *unity* and as *indivisible.* That which has come in him is *the* end of things. Here is already revealed the nature of this comprehensive manner of speech about the proximity of the kingdom. The kingdom is at hand. But this statement does not exclude the idea of a provisional fulfillment; not that the fulfillment thus pointed out is only an anticipation of the kingdom of God that has not yet been actually realized. The whole of Jesus' messianic self-revelation is a guarantee of the fulfillment in the most legitimate sense of the word. *The pronouncement on the proximity of the kingdom in which the "definitive" character is not distinguished from the "provisional," or at least has not been expressed, proves to be a temporal indication of a complicated reality which must be explained in a differentiated sense by the light of the fulfillment.*

When to a certain extent we have thus done justice to the prophetic description of the future, its summary of the future in one picture and also partly within the local framework of the Jewish land will be less strange to us. It will not do to make all kinds of corrections or to formulate a one-sidedly historical kind of criticism. The issue is the recognition of the specific character of the prophetic method of foretelling the future.

In conclusion, it is possible to think that the subjective expectations of the future by Jesus and his audience did not consider a prolonged delay of the end of all things. As far as Jesus himself is concerned, it will be necessary to take into account all that has been said above about the fulfillment of God's promise in his coming and work. And lastly, we should be aware of the fact of our Lord's incomprehensible self-consciousness that the drama of God's redemptive work and judgment encompassing the whole world and all time was being realized in him as the Christ and the Son of God. This awareness enabled him to speak about the future with such authority and certainty. But then, the undoubted urgency and the directness of Jesus' prophecy of the future cannot be judged according to our subjective human standards, but only from the standpoint of this messianic consciousness of authority, which should be evaluated by us only with reverence and awe. The problem of the proximity of the kingdom is basically a matter of a *Christological* order and determination, like the entire content of the gospel.

Notes to Chapter X

[1] Cf. also the *Introduction* above, and especially the historical survey of the older literature in F. Busch, *Zum Verständnis der synoptischen Eschatologie*, 1938, pp. 3ff.

[2] Thus, e.g., Bultmann, in his *Das Urchristentum im Rahmen der antiken Religionen*, published in 1949, p. 96.

[3] Cf. for the older literature, e.g., F. W. Grosheide, *De verwachting der toekomst van Jezus Christus*, 1907, pp. 7, 8; for the more recent literature, cf. also E. Masselink, *Eschatologische motieven in de nieuwe theologie*, 1946, pp. 39ff, 105ff.

[4] Cf. the newer commentaries, e.g., Klostermann on Matthew 10:23, *op. cit.*, p. 89; and on Mark 9:1, *op. cit.*, pp. 79, 85; and Mark 13:30, *op. cit.*, p. 138; Lohmeyer on Mark 9:1, *op. cit.*, p. 172, who, however, discovers another conception revealed in the parallel text in Luke 9:27 (viz., that by *basileia*—without the words "come in glory"—is to be understood the communion of many believers with God); W. C. Allen on Matthew 10:23; 16:28; *op. cit.*, pp. 107, 183; Gould on Mark 9:1; 13:30; *op. cit.*, pp. 159, 253; Manson on Matthew 10:23, *The Mission and Message of Jesus*, p. 474; Hauck on Mark 9:1 and 13:30, *op. cit.*, pp. 106, 160; Schlatter on Matthew 10:23; 16:28; *op. cit.*, pp. 342, 524.

[5] 2nd edition, 1913. Cf. on Wrede's construction and that of the radical sceptical trend agreeing with him, my *Zelfopenbaring en Zelfverberging*, 1946, pp. 10-17.

[6] In his well-known commentaries on the synoptic gospels.

[7] *Geschichte der synoptischen Tradition*,[2] 1931, pp. 129, 132.

[8] Cf. Busch, *op. cit.*, pp. 5ff.

[9] Bultmann, *Das Urchristentum*, pp. 96ff.

[10] Cf. *Geschichte der Leben-Jesu-Forschung*, pp. 390-433. In Schweitzer's steps, F. Buri, *Die Bedeutung der neutestamentlichen Eschatologie für die neuere protestantische Theologie*, 1934, pp. 21-29; the same, *Das Problem der ausgebliebenen Parusie*, *Vox Theologica*, April 1948, pp. 104-126; M. Werner, *Die Entstehung des Christlichen Dogma's*, 1941, pp. 61-79.

[11] Cf. also J. Jeremias, *Eine neue Schau der Zukunftaussagen Jesu, Theol. Blätter*, 1941, pp. 217-222, "*Die Dinge* (i.e., the interpretation of all Jesus' pronouncements on the future from this expectation of the kingdom as being imminent (*Naherwartung*)) *liegen seit A. Schweitzer's Forschungen in die Luft*" (These things, since A. Schweitzer's investigations, are still very much up in the air).

[12] Others have tried to prove that, not only in Jesus' preaching, but also in the conception of the oldest church the resurrection was equated with the *parousia*, cf., e.g., the discussion in H. W. Bartsch, *Parusieerwartung und Osterbotschaft*, *Evangel. Theologie*, 1947, 1948, pp. 115-126, by W. G. Kümmel, *Das Urchristentum*, *Theol. Rundschau*, 1950, pp. 21ff.

[13] C. H. Dodd, *The Parables of the Kingdom*, 194, p. 98. This interim is first supposed to have appeared in Acts 1:8.

[14] *Op. cit.*, p. 101.

[15] *Op. cit.*, p. 103.

[16] *Op. cit.*, pp. 105-110.

[17] J. Jeremias, *Eine neue Schau der Zukunftaussagen Jesu, Theol. Blätter*, 1941, pp. 217-222.

THE FUTURE OF THE KINGDOM OF HEAVEN 529

[18] Thus, e.g., Hauck, *Markus*, p. 194, agreeing with Weiss.

[19] Cf. E. Lohmeyer, *Das Evangelium des Markus*, 1937, p. 356, cf. p. 312. In more detail, his *Galiläa und Jerusalem*, 1936 pp. 10ff. Cf. also N. B. Stonehouse *The Witness of Matthew and Mark to Christ* 1944, pp. 39, 114ff, 170ff; and H. Holtrop, *De verschijningen onzes Heeren te Jeruzalem en in Galilea*, 1947, pp. 161ff.

[20] Thus Michaelis in his *Täufer, Jesus, Urgemeinde*, 1928.

[21] *Christus und die Zeit*, pp. 75, 76, 130, 131; cf. *Le retour du Christ*, pp. 25ff.

[22] *Verheiszung und Erfüllung*, pp. 14ff.

[23] *Op. cit.*, pp. 35ff.

[24] *Op. cit.*, pp. 33ff.

[25] *Op. cit.*, p. 11.

[26] *Op. cit.*, p. 20.

[27] *Op. cit.*, p. 24.

[28] *Op. cit.*, pp. 29-33.

[29] *Op. cit.*, p. 92.

[30] *Op. cit.*, p. 95. In this sense R. Liechtenhan also, *Die urchristliche Mission*, 1946, p. 14.

[31] *Markus*, p. 115. In the same sense, apparently, also Rengstorf, *Lukas*, p. 108, although less clearly.

[32] *Matthäus*, p. 127.

[33] W. Michaelis, *Der Herr verzieht nicht die Verheiszung*, 1942, pp. 5ff.

[34] *Op. cit.*, pp. 18ff.

[35] *Op. cit.*, pp. 30ff.

[36] *Op. cit.*, p. 45.

[37] *Op. cit.*, pp. 46ff.

[38] *Auslegung von Matthäus*, 28, 16-20, 1945, pp. 5, 6, cf. also p. 11.

[39] *Die Geschichte der synoptischen Tradition,*[2] 1931.

[40] Cf. the arguments in my *Matth.*, I, p. 201. Cf. also Schlatter, *op. cit.*, p. 337, "*Hier wird nicht nur von dem gesprochen was durch ihre Aussendung in die galiläischen Dörfer von ihnen gefordert wird, sondern diese gibt den Anlasz, um die ganze apostolische Wirksamkeit bis zur Parusie hinaus zu beschreiben*" ("This not only refers to what is required of them as they are sent forth into the Galilaean villages, but this is an occasion for the description of the entire apostolic activity until the *parousia*."); Zahn, *op. cit.*, p. 402; Grosheide, *op. cit.*, p. 125; cf. also Schniewind's refutation, *Matth.*, p. 127.

[41] Werner's chief argument is that if this speech does not, as a whole, correspond with the situation at the sending forth of the disciples, it is not to be understood how it got into the gospel in this situation, *op. cit.*, pp. 71, 72. But from the historical standpoint of the evangelist this is clear enough. At the time of the writing, the affliction of the apostles had already come. His readers would not misunderstand; rather, they would understand all the better why the sayings on the sending forth of the disciples and the prophecy of the coming distress blended with one another, because apostolate and persecution belong together, cf. my *Matth.*, I, p. 202.

[42] Cf. my *Zelfopenbaring en Zelfverberging*, pp. 84, 85.

[43] Jeremias' appeal to "I will destroy this temple within three days," cannot make plausible his identification of the resurrection and the *parousia*. For in the synoptic tradition, this pronouncement is mentioned as a "false testimony" on the part of Jesus' accusers before the Sanhedrin, while the explanation of it in John 2:21 explicitly mentions "the temple of his body." At any rate, these

words are not so transparent in themselves that they can be used to prove the thesis that "the third day" was originally meant as "the day of the Son of Man."

Nor can Lohmeyer's exegesis (and that of Hauck and others) of Mark 14:28; 16:7 contribute anything in favor of this view. There is no reason not to conceive of Mark 14:28 as an indication of the time after the resurrection, according to the current explanation; it is an indication that was perhaps not understood by the disciples, but in itself it was perfectly clear. That Jesus' "going into Galilaea" and the disciples' seeing him should allude to the *parousia* that would then take place, cannot be inferred from any of the data. Much rather, this passage proves that, for Jesus, resurrection and *parousia* did not coalesce but that he had important tasks to give to his disciples *after* his resurrection and *before* his *parousia*, cf. also Kümmel, *op. cit.*, pp. 43, 44; N. B. Stonehouse, *The Witness of Matthew and Mark to Christ*, 1944, pp. 114ff; 170ff; H. Holtrop, *De verschijningen onzes Heeren te Jeruzalem en in Galilea*, 1947, pp. 161ff.

[44] R. Bultmann, *Die Frage nach der Echtheit von Mt. 16,17-19*, in: *Theol. Blätter*, 1941, p. 279.

[45] Cf. above, § 22.

[46] Cf. above, § 6.

[47] Cf. also M. J. Lagrange. *Evangile selon St. Marc*,[6] 1942, p. 234.

[48] Cf. also my *Zelfopenbaring en Zelfverberging*, 1946, pp. 42, 86.

[49] Cf. also Lagrange, *op. cit.*, p. 244, "*Il semble donc que Jésus s'est tenu à une prédiction générale . . . sans leur expliquer les raisons de la passion, etc. L'intelligence de tout cela ne devait leur être donnée que plus tard.*" ("It seems, therefore, that Jesus has been content to make a general prediction . . . without explaining to them the reasons of the passion, etc. Only later were they to understand all this").

[50] *Hina*. Greijdanus writes, "We may take *hina* in a consecutive sense, 'so that'; but also in a final sense, 'in order that'; and then translate it by the word 'that.' For here should also be seen a divine arrangement and intention. They could not yet bear the full truth. . . . This first came later," *Lucas*, I, p. 439.

[51] Cf. Greijdanus, "The Lord displayed his majesty, . . . which also made a deep impression on his disciples and deprived them of the courage to ask him the meaning of this statement," *op. cit.*

[52] Cf. Michaelis, also, on the provisional character, before the resurrection, of Christ's pronouncements on the future, *Der Herr verzieht nicht die Verheiszung*, 1942, p. 29.

[53] *Christus und die Zeit*, p. 71, cf. also pp. 126ff; *Le retour du Christ*, pp. 25ff; cf. also his article: *Das wahre durch die ausgebliebene Parusie gestellte neutestamentliche Problem* (against Buri), in: *Theologische Zeitschrift*, 1947, pp. 177ff; Kümmel also, *op. cit.*, p. 95.

[54] Cf. Schniewind, *Matth.*, p. 271; Barth, *Auslegung von Matthäus 28,16-20*, p. 13; O. Michel, *Menschensohn und Völkerwelt*, in: *Evang. Missions Zeitschrift*, 1941, pp. 257ff.

[55] The advocates of the "consistent eschatology" explain this account as follows; when, in conflict with the original Christian basic dogma of the eschatological meaning of Jesus' death and resurrection, the events for the ushering in of the new aeon did not occur; the original Christian church's *Nah-erwartung* postulated that at Jesus' death similar signs had occurred in

which the approaching end was at any rate clearly announced; cf. Werner, *op. cit.*, p. 90; also Buri, *Die Bedeutung der neutest. Theologie*, p. 26, who calls these signs *"die einzigen Ueberbleibsel der erwarteten kosmischen End-katastrophe!"* ("the only remnants of the awaited final cosmic catastrophe"). What is fatal to this exegesis is the fact that nowhere in the gospel is there any indication that with Jesus' death is there such an expectation of the commencement of the cosmic final catastrophe.

[56] Cf. above, § 43.

[57] Cf., e.g., H. A. Guy, *The New Testament Doctrine of the "Last Things,"* 1948, p. 59, with an appeal to T. W. Manson.

[58] Cf. Dodd, *The Parables of the Kingdom*, pp. 83, 84.

[59] *Meta paratēreseoos.*

[60] Cf., e.g., Greijdanus, *Lukas*, II, p. 830.

[61] Cf. for *paratērein*, also Luke 6:7; 14:1; 20:20, etc.

[62] That is why in my opinion the translation of the Netherlands Bible Society: *"Het koninkrijk Gods komt niet zo'o dat het te berekenen is"* ("The kingdom of God does not come in such a way that it can be calculated") (as also: Kümmel, *op. cit.*, p. 17, and many others) does not really hit the mark.

[63] Greijdanus, *op. cit.*, II, p. 829.

[64] In addition to the commentaries see, e.g., W. G. Kümmel, *Die Eschatologie der Evangelien*, 1936, p. 13, and *Verheissung und Erfüllung*, p. 19.

[65] Thus, e.g., Bultmann, *Jesus*, p. 39, *"mit einen Schlage"* ("with a stroke"). Cf. Kümmel, *Die Eschatologie der Evangelien*, 1936, p. 11; and *Verheissung und Erfüllung*, p. 19.

[66] Thus also Strack-Billerbeck, *op. cit.*, I, p. 954 (on Matt. 24:27, *"Der Vergleichungspunkt ist hier nicht die Plötzlichkeit der Ankunft des Messias, sondern die bei seinem Kommen jedermann unwiderstehlich sich aufdrängende Sichtbarkeit seiner richterlichen Machtfülle."* ("The point of comparison here is not the suddenness of the coming of the Messiah, but the visibility of the fullness of his judicial power irresistibly urging itself on everybody"). He adds—and this is also important for the purport of Luke 17:20,21—*"Diese Vorstellung ist in der altjüdischen Literatur selten. Meist musz der Messias die Israelieten erst mühsam überreden, dasz sie ihn als ihren König und Erlöser anerkennen. Nach einer andren Tradition soll es zu den Obliegenheiten des Elias gehören, den bis dahin unbekannten Messias seinem Volke bekannt-zugeben."* ("This view is rare in the old-Jewish literature. Mostly, the Messiah must persuade the Israelites to acknowledge him as their king and redeemer. According to another tradition, it will be one of the duties of Elijah to make the previously unknown Messiah known to his people").

[67] In this translation and exegesis, *entos humoon* is emphatic, (as is also true in the interpretation we have rejected). It is true that others reject this translation because they think that *entos* means "within." They conceive of the kingdom as something internal, spiritual, that is present within hearts, cf., e.g., P. Feine, *Theologie des N.T.,*[7] 1936, p. 79; and Dodd, *op. cit.*, pp. 83, 84. This is also Luther's translation. Apart from the fact that this translation takes us away from the eschatological situation (cf. above), it is to be considered as very unlikely in view of the fact that Jesus is speaking here to the Pharisees; see, moreover, Greijdanus, *op. cit. Entos* cannot be related to an inner state of mind, but is used in the sense of "among you, in your midst." The use of *entos* (which hardly ever occurs in the N. Testament) instead of *en*, makes for emphasis and has an intensifying function with reference to what is intended

here: *in your very midst*, cf. also A. Sledd in *The Expository Times*, 1939, pp. 233ff.

⁶⁸ It has not been established whether or not these words in Matthew are original.

⁶⁹ Cf., e.g., Grundmann, *TWB*, II, pp. 259.

⁷⁰ The dissensions among friends, and in general the disturbances among men repeatedly occur in the Jewish apocalypses also, as signs of the end; cf. Strack-Billerbeck, *op. cit.*, IV, 2, pp. 978ff.

⁷¹ For this speech and for the history of the criticism of Jesus' prophetic eschatological pronouncements, compare F. Busch's monograph, *Zum Verständnis der synoptischen Eschatologie; Markus 13 neu untersucht*, 1938.

⁷² Cf. Greijdanus, *Lukas*, II, pp. 982, 983; cf. also Kümmel, *Verheissung*, pp. 39ff.

⁷³ Cf. Hauck, *op. cit.*, p. 154, "*sunteleisthai panta, ist dabei fast terminus technicus*," (" . . . etc. is practically a *terminus technicus* here").

⁷⁴ Cf. Strack-Billerbeck, *op. cit.*, I, p. 949.

⁷⁵ Ed. Meyer, *Ursprung und Anfänge des Christentums*, I, p. 129.

⁷⁶ *Markusev.*, p. 131.

⁷⁷ Thus, e.g., Bultmann, *Gesch. d. syn. Trad.*,² p. 129, and many others. Some think of a Jewish apocalyptic source; others, rather, look upon the speech in Mark 13 as a collection of separate sayings or as groups of sayings derived from different sources; thus, e.g., Kümmel, *op. cit.*, p. 58, and Lohmeyer, *op. cit.*, pp. 270ff. For older literature cf., e.g., R. H. Charles, *A Critical History of the Doctrine of a Future Life*,² 1913, pp. 278, 284

⁷⁸ Cf., e.g., Klostermann, *op. cit.*

⁷⁹ Also, e.g., in Kümmel, *op. cit.*, p. 61; who, however, holds a more conservative view than Klostermann and Bultmann.

⁸⁰ Cf. also Grosheide on Matthew, *op. cit.*, p. 288, and Schniewind, *op. cit.*, p. 235.

⁸¹ Elsewhere, *anaginooskein* is used for the reading of the Old Testament without any mention of a particular scriptural text; cf. Mark 2:25.

⁸² Thus, e.g., Schniewind explains Mark 13:14, *op. cit.*, p. 163; Lagrange, *op. cit.*, p. 341; Van Leeuwen, *op. cit.*, p. 237.

⁸³ Cf. Schniewind, *Markus*, p. 158; Kümmel, *op. cit.*, p. 59.

⁸⁴ *Ursprung und Anfänge*, I, p. 125; cf. the literature cited by Kümmel, *op. cit.*, p. 60.

⁸⁵ Thus also Kümmel, *op. cit.*, pp. 61, 62; cf. the details in R. H. Charles, *op. cit.*, p. 379.

⁸⁶ See below on the parables about vigilance, § 49.

⁸⁷ Cf. on this, e.g., W. O. E. Oesterley, *The Doctrine of the Last Things, Jewish and Christian*, 1903, pp. 169ff; R. H. Charles, *op. cit.*, pp. 307ff.

⁸⁸ Cf. also Lohmeyer, *op. cit.*, p. 271; and Schniewind, *Markus*, p. 159.

⁸⁹ Cf. Strack-Billerbeck, *op. cit.*, I, p. 950.

⁹⁰ Cf. on this my *Matth.*, II, pp. 149ff.

⁹¹ Huck-Lietzmann, *Synopse der drei ersten Evangelien*,⁹ 1936, refer to Ezekiel 7:16.

⁹² Lohmeyer thinks that this idea is derived from Daniel 9:24, *op. cit.*, p. 277; but this connection seems to be rather loose when the reference is more closely examined.

⁹³ The passages quoted by Strack-Billerbeck from the Jewish eschatology

can hardly be the background to the shortening mentioned in the synoptic apocalypse, *op cit.*, I, p. 953.

[94] For this proof cf. the elaborate discussion in F. Busch, *Zum Verständnis der synoptischen Eschatologie*, 1938, pp. 63-120. He arrives at the conclusion that Mark 13 is closely related to the Old Testament tradition in all its parts, both as to the manner of expression and as to the matter dealt with. Mark 13 is, therefore, not an "alien body" in the synoptic eschatology but rather a key to it. This correspondence—thus Busch—is accompanied by the explicit rejection of Judaism. The way from the Old Testament to the New, also in regard to things eschatological, does not lead in a straight line through Judaism; but there is, rather, a separation between the Old Testament and Jewish literature, with Jesus following the Old Testament, *op. cit.*, p. 117.

[95] Cf. Kümmel, *op. cit.*, pp. 61, 62.

[96] E. Schürer, *Gesch. d. jüdischen Volkes*, I,[3, 4] 1901, pp. 660ff; 685; II,[4] 1907, p. 604.

[97] Greijdanus reminds us of "all kinds of strange phenomena seen in the sky before the destruction of Jerusalem, such as war-chariots and armed phalanxes," according to Josephus, *Bell. Jud.*, VI, 5, 3, *op. cit.*, II, p. 987; cf. also Eusebius, *Hist. Eccl.*, III, 8.

[98] Cf. above, § 38.

[99] Klostermann, *Markusev.*, p. 134; cf. also, e.g., Kümmel, *Verheissung und Erfüllung*, p. 48; Hauck, *Markus*, p. 155.

[100] Cf. Sub. C. and § 51.

[101] Cf. also Greijdanus on this *pro toutoon pantoon*, *op. cit.*, II, pp. 987ff.

[102] *Op. cit.*, II, pp. 983, 984, 987.

[103] Thus Michaelis, *Der Herr verzieht nicht die Verheissung*, p. 20, following F. Busch, *Zum Verständnis der synoptischen Eschatologie*, 1938, pp. 87ff.

[104] Michaelis, *op. cit.*, p. 21.

[105] *Markus*, p. 163. Schniewind is more reserved in his commentary on Matthew. He says that Matthew restricts himself to a reference to Daniel, whose words only suggest a horrible profanation of the holy place. The difference between Matthew and Mark is that Mark speaks of the "desolating abomination" (*to bdelugma tēs erēmooseoos*) as a masculine word (*hestēkota hopou ou dei*). This is supposed to denote a person, viz. the Antichrist. Matthew, on the other hand, has a neuter gender (*hestos*). Schniewind also admits that the meaning of the whole of the words in all three gospels is intended for Judaea. Yet they have a peculiar ring to him so that the details of the siege of Jerusalem are not recognizable. Hence, this is also taken to signify a close connection between this distress and the second coming of Christ, *Matth.*, p. 235, 236.

[106] *Op. cit.*, p. 276; cf. also Klostermann on Mark 13:14, *op. cit.*, p. 135.

[107] *Der Evangelist Matthäus*,[2] 1933, pp. 702-707.

[108] Th. Zahn, *Das Ev. d. Matth.*,[4] 1922, pp. 666-670. The same explanation is found in G. Wohlenberg, *Das Ev. d. Markus*,[3] 1930, pp. 333-336, who explains the masculine form in Mark, *hestēkota*, as denoting that the "abomination of desolation" is not merely an idol but a profanation proceeding from a masculine person who, as an idol opposing God, will demand that people worship him. Cf. 2 Thessalonians 2:3ff; p. 334.

[109] *Das Ev. d. Luk.*,[3, 4] 1920, pp. 651-655. Greijdanus explains the picture of the future in Luke in the same sense, *op. cit.*, II, pp. 996ff.

[110] *Evangile selon S. Matthieu,*[5] 1941, pp. 462, 463, 466, 467; *Evangile selon S. Marc.,*[6] 1942, pp. 340-343.

[111] *Evangile selon S. Luc.,*[5] 1941, pp. 527, 528.

[112] Lohmeyer realizes this difficulty. He says that the words "who are in Judaea" are not clear (*"unklar"*). He supposes that the original sentence was, "Then flee into the mountains!" In our opinion this is an entirely arbitrary change. And even at that, it remains a strange idea that staying in the moun-tains will offer protection against the Antichrist, which is also in Lohmeyer's opinion, *op. cit.,* p. 276.

[113] *Das Ev. d. Luc.,* p. 652.

[114] Thus, e.g., Torrey, cf. Lagrange, *Marc.,* p. LIIff, 340. Klostermann, too, is of the opinion that *"die Mc. zugrunde liegende ältere Weissagung"* ("the older prophecy lying at the base of Mark") referred to this, *Das Marcusev.,* p. 135.

[115] Lagrange recognizes the importance of the argument derived from *gar.* He says, *"C'est précisément la difficulté de tout le discours"* ("This is exactly *the* difficulty of the whole discourse"). He thinks, however, that here we are concerned with a soldering (*"Soudure"*) rather than with an organic bond (*"lien organique"*), which would induce us to accept only one theme, *Matthieu,* p. 462. But this distinction cannot without arbitrariness deprive the causal meaning of the word *gar* of its force in this context.

[116] Cf. my *Matth.,* II, p. 154.

[117] Cf., e.g., J. Ridderbos, *Over de uitlegging der Heilige Schrift,* in: *Bijbels Handboek,* I, 1935, pp. 401ff and the literature quoted there. J. van Dodewaard, *De gruwel der verwoesting* (Matth. 24,15—Mc. 13,14) *Studia Catholica,* 1944, p. 130, also appeals to this. And in the same spirit cf. F. W. Grosheide, *Hermeneutik,* 1929, p. 205, on the exegesis of Matthew 24. He also rejects the exegesis combated by us which relates one verse or one expression to the fall of Jerusalem and the other to the second coming of Christ; "Such a procedure seems to be impermissible because it destroys the unity of the prophecy in every respect. But on analogy of what happens in the Old Tes-tament predictions, we shall sometimes have to explain some parts of a prophecy, which one may take as referring in its entirety to the end of all things, as nevertheless relating in some respects to the destruction of Jerusalem," *op. cit.*

[118] Cf. above, § 43, sub 3.

[119] *"Genus hominum . . . aut specialiter Judaeorum,"* in Klostermann, *Das Markusev.,* p. 138.

[120] Thus Theophylact, *"toon pistoon,"* Klostermann, *op. cit.*

[121] *Markus,* p. 167. The context in Matthew is supposed to point even more emphatically in this direction than Mark. Schniewind refers to places like Matthew 23:36; 10:23, and others; *Matthäus,* p. 239.

[122] Thus, e.g., A. Plummer, *op. cit.,* p. 485 and Zahn, *Das Ev. d. Luc.,* p. 659. Greijdanus agrees with them, *op. cit.,* II, p. 1003.

[123] *Op. cit.,* II, p. 1004. Plummer thinks that here (in Luke) the destruction of Jerusalem is meant as a type of the end of the world, *op. cit.,* p. 485. Lagrange is also of the opinion that *tauta panta* in Mark 13:30 may very well be applied to the destruction of the temple and not to the end of all things, because in this (destruction of the temple) lay the occasion for the whole of the speech, vs. 4, *op. cit.,* p. 348. He considers as an evasion (*"echappatoire"*) any explanation of the words "this generation" that is different than "con-

temporaries." Zahn also considers "all these things" to be applicable to all the signs and judgments announcing the end that Jesus' contemporaries witnessed; *Das Ev. d. Luc.,* p. 659, where he explains *panta* as, *"die in vs.* 31 *erwähnten Ereignisse in ihrer Gesamtheit"* ("the events mentioned in vs. 31 as a whole"). But he does not include all that immediately precedes the *parousia,* and restricts his exegesis to the events described as far as vs. 19, inclusive of the destruction of Jerusalem. Wohlenberg's explanation also comes to the same thing with reference to Mark 13:29,30; *op. cit.,* pp. 337, 338. Calvin's view is slightly different. He admits that Christ uses a general indication (all these things) but he is apparently of the opinion that it denotes *species.* All that will be seen in the course of time by way of judgments and afflictions will already have been experienced by the first generation. *"Sensus est igitur, Prophetiam hanc non esse de malis longinquis, quae multis post saeculis visura sit posteritas, sed quae iam impendent, et quidem una simul congerie, ut praesens aetas nullius partis expers futura sit. Itaque Dominus omnes malorem species in unam aetatem congerens, minime ab iisdem posteros eximit, sed tantum discipulos ad omnia constanter ferenda paratos esse iubet";* ed. Tholuck, II, 1833, p. 280. Finally, Lagrange's view is also found in Josef Schmid, *Das Evangelium nach Markus* (in *Das Neue Testament,* hrsgeg. von Alfred Wikenhauser und Otto Kusz, 2, Band), 1938, p. 159.

[124] Thus Cullmann, § 43, sub 3.

[125] Thus Kümmel, § 43, sub 3.

[126] Cf. also my *Matth.,* II, pp. 158, 159.

[127] Lexicographically, it is easily proved that this is the usual meaning of the expression "this generation." Even if we pass by the texts in which Jesus emphatically speaks of "this wicked generation" (Matt. 12:45; Luke 11:29), or "faithless and perverse generation" (Matt. 17:17; Luke 9:41), or of "this adulterous and sinful generation" (Mark 8:38), or of "O, faithless generation" (Mark 9:19); it is clear that by this term "generation" Jesus always denotes a particular, unfavorable disposition of the heart, and that often the temporal meaning of *genea* recedes into the background or is ignored (cf. Matt. 11:16, "But whereunto shall I liken this generation?"); (12:41—Luke 11:32, "The men of Nineveh shall rise in judgment with this generation"); (Mark 8:12, "Why doth this generation seek after a sign? Verily I say unto you, there shall no sign be given unto this generation"); (Luke 17:25, "But first must he suffer many things, and be rejected of this generation"). It is true that there are other places where the temporal meaning seems to have more importance (e.g., Matt. 23:36, "All these things shall come upon this generation"; or, "It shall be required of this generation," Luke 11:51, cf. vs. 50); but here, too, the qualifying sense remains unmistakable. Büchsel writes, *"Dieses Geschlecht ist zunächst zeitlich zu verstehen, es enthält aber immer eine verurteilende Nebenbedeutung."* ("'This generation' is primarily meant in a temporal sense, but in a secondary sense it always implies an unfavorable connotation"), *TWB,* I, p. 661, the article on *"genea."* He might have added that the secondary connotation sometimes suppresses the original sense (cf. above, e.g., Mark 8:12!) Büchsel rightly adds, *"In der Rolle, die genea in den Worten Jesu spielt, zeigt sich das Umfassende seiner Absicht—sie ist auf das Volksganze, nicht auf Einzelne gerichtet—und seine Schätzung der Gemeinschaft in der Sünde"* ("The part played by the word *genea* among the words of Jesus shows the comprehensive character of his intention—it is directed to the whole of the people, not to individuals—and his evaluation of the community

in sin"), *op. cit.* The fact that Jesus' use of the word "generation" is determined especially by this unfavorable meaning and not by its temporal sense, appears very clearly from the circumstance that his usage is undeniably founded upon the Old Testament in which "generation" or "this generation" also occur in *malam partem,* cf. Ps. 12:8; 95:10; Deut. 32:5; (Matt. 17:17); cf. also Gesenius-Buhl, *Hebr. und Aram. Handwörterbuch über das A.T.,* the article on *"dor."*

[128] *Op. cit.,* p. 250. Plummer mentions seven different interpretations and their advocates: 1. the transfiguration on the Mount (most of the church fathers); 2. the resurrection and ascension (Calvin, Beza, etc.); 3. Pentecost and the signs after it (Godet); 4. the spread of Christianity (Nösgen); 5. the inner development of the gospel (Erasmus); 6. the destruction of Jerusalem (Wetstein, Alford, etc.); 7. the second coming of the kingdom (Weiss, Holtzmann, etc.), *op. cit.,* p. 249.

[129] *Op. cit.,* I, pp. 424, 425. H. D. A. Major also thinks this explanation possible, *The Mission and Message of Jesus,* 1946, p. 113; as also Lagrange on Mark 9:1, *op. cit.,* p. 227.

[130] Lagrange, *op. cit.*

[131] Cf. Wohlenberg on Mark 9:1, *op. cit.,* pp. 240, 241; and Grosheide on Matthew 9:27, "Jesus speaks of the manifestation of power that will issue forth from him, and that began at Pentecost," *op. cit.,* p. 207. Also N. B. Stonehouse, *The Witness of Matthew and Mark to Christ,* 1944, p. 240.

[132] Calvin is of opinion that Mark 9:1 (and parallels) is to be understood in the sense of the manifestation of Christ's heavenly glory, which began at his resurrection and was thereafter even more fully revealed in the sending of the Spirit and the working of miracles; ed. *Tholuck,* II, 1833, p. 115.

[133] Thus M. J. Lagrange on Matthew 16:28, because the coming of the Son of Man is mentioned here *en tēi basileiai autou.* He writes, *"Le royaume du fils de l'homme, par opposition au royaume du Père, c'est précisément l'Eglise, comme le marque bien la parabole de l'ivraie"* (13:24) ("The kingdom of the Son of Man, in contradistinction to the kingdom of the Father, is exactly the church, as appears clearly from the parable of the tares"), *S. marc.,* p. 227; cf. *S. Matthieu,* p. 333. Lohmeyer thinks such an explanation possible with respect to Luke 9:27, *"Lukas scheint die zeitliche Schwierigkeit zu fühlen; er läszt die drei Worte 'gekommen in Herrlichkeit' fort und gibt es damit frei, unter der basileia tou theou auch an die Gottesgemeinschaft vieler Gläubiger zu denken"* ("It seems that Luke realizes the temporal difficulty; he leaves the three words "come in glory" out, and thus makes it also possible to interpret the *basileia tou theou* as the communion of many believers with God"). *Markus,* p. 172. And finally, Grosheide takes *bdsileia* in Mark 9:1 to refer to the spiritual kingdom preached by Jesus to which all believers belong, *De Verwachting der Toekomst van Jezus Christus,* 1907, p. 97. It is true that there are difficulties in Matthew 16:28, but this less transparent text should be explained in the light of those that are clearer, p. 98. Cf. also his *Matth.,* pp. 206, 207.

[134] J. A. C. van Leeuwen, *op. cit.,* p. 154. Zahn's view is very remarkable. He takes Matthew 16:28 and Luke 9:27 to refer to the *parousia.* With regard to Mark 9:1, he considers another opinion to be possible. He says that the addition of *elēluthuian en dunamei* is a further definition, in a formal sense, of the coming of the kingdom. Thus Mark has *"eine, nicht leicht im voraus zu bestimmende Phase in der allmählichen Entwicklung der herankommenden*

Gottesherrschaft an die Stelle ihrer endgiltigen Verwirklichung gesetzt" ("Mark has replaced the final realization of the coming divine dominion by a phase in its gradual development which cannot be easily defined in advance"). *D. Ev. d. Luc.,* p. 381.

[135] Cf. § 36.

[136] Cf. above, p. 476. Zahn also ultimately arrives at this conception. In *D. Evang. d. Matth.* he writes, (p. 675), *"Jesus hat also das eine und andere Mal (10,23; 16,28) das Wort von seinem Kommen so gebraucht, dasz er die vorbereitenden Anfänge des Endes (24,8:32ff; Luc. 21,28:31) nach Art der prophetischen Rede mit dem Hauptpunkt der Endereignisse, seiner Parusie, zusammenfaszt. Daher könnten die Jünger so fragen, wie 24, 3 berichtet ist. Zu sagen dasz Jesus hierin sich geirrt und falsch geweissagt habe, erscheint angesichts der ausführlicheren und daher die einzelnen Momente des Zukunftbildes schärfer sonderden Weissagungen Jesu ebenso töricht, wie wenn iemand den Täufer einen falschen Propheten nennen wollte, weil das Himmelreich, dessen Nähe er predigte, nicht sofort so allseitig, wie er seinen Kommen vorstellte und schilderte, verwirklicht worden ist"* ("Consequently, Jesus has used this word of his coming (Matt. 10:23,16:28) in such a way that, according to the character of the prophecy, he summarizes the chief point of the final events, i.e., his *parousia*, with its preparatory beginnings. Hence, the question asked by the disciples as recorded in 24:3. To say that Jesus was mistaken in this and made a false prophecy seems as foolish, in the light of Jesus' more elaborate predictions which distinguish the individual moments of the picture of the future more sharply, as calling the Baptist a false prophet because the kingdom of heaven whose nearness he proclaimed was not so immediately and completely realized as he had described"). It is clear enough, for the rest, that we cannot identify Jesus' prophetic insight into the future with the expectations of the disciples nor with the Baptist's outlook, and neither does Zahn mean to do so.

[137] Greijdanus' view (cf. Plummer) that at the moment when Jesus said these words the resurrection was too near for the words "some of those that stand here will not taste death" to be applicable to it, is in our opinion untenable; especially if it be borne in mind that these words need not presuppose that the majority of the audience would have died by the time this pronouncement was realized. These words may as well denote that the seeing the Son of Man in his kingly glory was to be *the* great event in the lives of those who were to witness it.

[138] Cf. also my *Matth.,* II, pp. 22, 23; and my *Zelfopenbaring en Zelfverberging,* 1946, pp. 86, 87.

[139] *De Verwachting der toekomst,* pp. 92, 93; cf. also his commentary, p. 127.

[140] *Op cit.,* pp. 204, 205.

[141] *Op. cit.,* pp. 127, 128.

[142] N. B. Stonehouse, *The Witness of Matthew and Mark to Christ,* 1944, p. 240. In support of his view, he appeals to the fact that any allusion to the clouds of heaven, the presence of angels, etc., is lacking. A similar view is found in Calvin. According to him, Christ here promises his apostles, who faced such a tremendous task, that he would show them his kingdom by the power of his Spirit, ed. *Tholuck,* I, 1883, p. 246.

[143] Cf. also the conclusive argumentation of Grosheide, *De Verwachting,* pp. 91ff.

[144] Cf., e.g., Greijdanus, *Lukas,* II, pp. 843, 849ff; Kümmel, *op. cit.,* p. 33.

[145] Perhaps this is also clearly stated in verse 7. Greijdanus translates, "Will God not certainly avenge his elect . . . although with respect to them he waits a long time?" (*kai makrothumei ep' autois*), op. cit., II, pp. 848ff; cf. also Rengstorf, "*auch wenn er über ihnen langmütig bleibt?*" ("even when he remains long-suffering with respect to them"); *op. cit.*, p. 185 (in agreement with Schlatter). This translation, however, is not certain, as Rengstorf also admits; cf. also Klostermann, *op. cit.*, pp. 178, 179; and Plummer, *op. cit.*, p. 414. Yet there is the question here of the fact that God does not act at once, but delays his action. And the words *ep' autois* cannot refer to enemies, but must mean the elect. Then, however, *makrothumei* cannot depend on *ou mē*. For then the first question would have to be answered with "yes" and the second with "no." Greijdanus's and Rengstorf's translations, hence, seem to render the true sense, cf. also Plummer, *op. cit.* Then this text emphatically denotes the divine waiting. But in view of the obscurity of the text, we must not stress this too much.

[146] Cf. also Greijdanus, *op. cit.*, II, p. 850. "He delays because there is so much yet to happen. But in all his work God acts quickly."

[147] Cf. Plummer, . . . "however long the answer to prayer may *seem* to be delayed" . . . and Rengstorf, "*Darum mahnt Jesus auch besonders zur Geduld*" ("That is why Jesus exhorts (his disciples) to have patience"), *op. cit.*, p. 186.

[148] Dodd, it is true, thinks that these parables, which have been handed down by the evangelists, have been recast and applied to the situation after Jesus' death; but that originally, they referred to the situation during Jesus' activity on earth, viz., to the crisis that began with Jesus' appearance, and which would come to its climax in Jesus' passion. He compares the sayings on vigilance with Jesus' warning in Gethsemane ("watch and pray that ye enter not into temptation"), *The Parables*, pp. 154-174; but this conception is based on the supposition that Jesus expected the *parousia* of the Son of Man to be simultaneous with his death and resurrection; cf. above, § 43.

[149] Cf., e.g., Klostermann, *op. cit.*, p. 199.

[150] Cf. my *Matth.*, II, p. 164.

[151] Michaelis, *Der Herr verzieht nicht die Verheissung*, p. 5.

[152] Kümmel, *op. cit.*, p. 29.

[153] Jeremias, *Theol. Bl.*, 1941, p. 221.

[154] "*Das Bild vom Dieb . . . steht der jüdischen Ueberlieferung völlig entgegen. Dort wird erwartet, dasz man die Tage des Messias vorher errechnen kann*" ("The image of the thief . . . is completely contrary to the Jewish tradition. There it was expected that the day of the Messiah could be calculated beforehand"); Schniewind, *Matth.*, p. 240.

[155] This is also an important argument in favor of the authenticity of these words, cf. Kümmel, *op. cit.*, pp. 22, 23. Cf., e.g., Klostermann, *Markusev.*, pp. 138, 139, on the difficulties of old exegetes with respect to these words.

[156] Cf. in Lohmeyer, *Markus*, p. 283.

[157] Here, too, radical criticism denies the historicity of this connection and, therefore, the originality of the meaning imparted to the parable by this connection; cf., e.g., Bultmann, *Gesch. d. syn. Trad.*,[2] pp. 208, 360, "*Sehr deutlich ist auch Lk. 19,11 eine von Lk für die Parabel von den anvertrauten Geldern konstruierte Einleitung, die Angabe einer Situation, aus der nach seiner Meinung die Parabel verstanden werden soll, die er aber aus seinem Verständnis erschlossen hat,*" p. 208 ("Luke 19:11 is very clearly an introduction construed by Luke for the parable of the entrusted funds, and denotes a situation

that in his opinion explains the parable, but which he has disclosed from his own understanding"). But proofs of this assertion cannot be given. That Luke reasons from a particular interpretation of the parable is certain. But how can Bultmann, apart from his own arbitrary presuppositions, prove that this interpretation is not applicable to the historical situation depicted by Luke?

[158] Cf. also Klostermann, according to whom in this case we have only to do with the view of the evangelist, op. cit., p. 203.

[159] Cf. also my Matth., II, p. 172.

[160] H. Bavinck, Gereformeerde Dogmatiek, IV,[4] 1930, p. 667.

[161] In the same sense P. A. Verhoef also writes about the prophetic "soon" of the O.T., "On the other hand, it must be admitted that the great future is, in a general sense, at hand. Viewed from the subjective point of view, the coming of the completed divine dominion has been delayed longer than had been expected. . . . But this is not all. The coming of the "day of the Lord" is a continuous, immanent, dynamic reality. Seen objectively, it is *present* and *at hand!* It is present in the temporal judgments or evidences of his grace with which the Lord God visits the humanity of every period. But it is also at hand insofar as every temporal judgment or proof of divine salvation precedes, as its herald, the full manifestation of the great "day." Thus the prophets saw the coming of this day, and thus they spoke a language that infinitely transcends the rationalistic theories of many scholars of our day." *Die vraagstuk van die onvervulde voorsegginge,* 1950, pp. 312, 313.

[162] Cf. on this also Verhoef, op. cit., pp. 31ff; 307ff.

INDEX OF SUBJECTS
(Consult also the other indices and the Table of Contents)

INDEX OF AUTHORS

INDEX OF SCRIPTURE REFERENCES

546